PRINCIPLES OF REAL ESTATE PRACTICE IN FLORIDA

2ND EDITION

PERFORMANCE
PROGRAMS
COMPANY

STEPHEN METTLING
DAVID CUSIC
JANE SOMERS

Material in this book is not intended to represent legal advice and should not be so construed. Readers should consult legal counsel for advice regarding points of law.

© 2022 by Performance Programs Company
6810 190th Street East, Bradenton, FL 34211
info@performanceprogramscompany.com
www.performanceprogramscompany.com

ISBN: 978-1955919227

Table of Contents

PREFACE

About the text

Principles of Real Estate Practice in Florida is a modern learning tool for the student preparing to enter the real estate business in Florida as a licensed professional. It contains the essentials of real estate law, principles, and practices taught in Florida real estate schools and colleges, including all those fundamentals that real estate educators, practicing professionals, testing services, and licensing officials agree are necessary for basic competence. **Principles of Real Estate Practice in Florida** covers the prelicense requirements mandated by Florida license law.

Principles of Real Estate Practice is tailored to the needs of the prelicense student. It is designed to

- make it easy for students to learn the material
- prepare students for numerous career applications
- stress practical, rather than theoretical, skills and knowledge.

Inside the cover

Each section begins with an overview of the main heads covered in the section. As each of these heads is expanded, the subheads are displayed in the margin. Key terms are printed in bold type the first time they are used and defined. The sections conclude with a study aid called the "Snapshot Review," which compresses the main points of the section into one or two pages. After the last section are tests for all the sections. The answer key following the tests refers to the page in the text that explains the correct answer. The book is also provided with a special section on real estate math, a practice exam reflecting the content of the Florida licensing examination, and two glossaries of real estate terminology. A table listing important dates, deadlines, and timeframes for Florida licensees follows the glossaries.

About the authors

For over forty years, Stephen Mettling and David Cusic have operated one of the nation's most successful custom training organizations specializing in real estate program development. Mr. Mettling has also served as vice president and author for a major real estate training and publishing organization. Under various capacities, he has managed the acquisition, development, and sale of national real estate textbooks and publications, as well as directed the country's largest affiliated group of real estate schools.

Mr. Cusic, an author and educator with international real estate training experience, has been engaged in vocation-oriented education since 1966. Specializing in real estate training since 1983, he has developed numerous real estate training programs for corporate and institutional clients around the country.

Jane Somers has been a writer and educator for over thirty years. She has directed the academic programs for a multi-campus college and has in recent years become an accomplished developer of online and classroom real estate curricula for a major real estate licensing organization, specializing in licensing laws. Ms. Somers is also active in condominium association management and has served as president of a condominium owners' association for ten years.

About the consulting editor

Cheryl Davis is a real estate author and instructor. She co-owns Cross Streets Academy, Inc. and is a broker with JoAnn P. Davis Realty, Inc. She has written curriculum for her own school and created classes for Florida Realtors and the Department of Education in Florida, New Jersey, Pennsylvania, and Louisiana. Ms. Davis is also a disability advocate focusing on housing and employment for individuals with disabilities. Ms. Davis currently serves as a Director for the Real Estate Educators Association.

1 The Real Estate Business

Introduction to the Real Estate Business
Real Estate Brokerage
Development and Construction
The Role of Government
Professional Organizations

Learning Objectives

- Describe the central activities of real estate brokerage
- Distinguish among the five major sales specialties
- Identify the role of property managers
- Describe activities that require appraiser services and distinguish among CMA, BPO, and appraisal
- Summarize the mortgage process and the role of mortgage loan originator
- Explain the three phases of development and construction
- Distinguish among the three categories of residential construction

Key Terms

absentee owner
appraisal
appraiser
broker price opinion (BPO)
business broker
business opportunity
community association manager (CAM)
comparative market analysis (CMA)
dedication

farm area (target marketing)
follow-up
Multiple Listing Service (MLS)
property management
property manager
real estate brokerage
subdivision plat map
Uniform Standards of Professional Appraisal
    Practice (USPAP)

INTRODUCTION TO THE REAL ESTATE BUSINESS

Real estate activities
Professional specialties
Property type specialization
Why hire a real estate professional

In its broadest sense, the real estate industry is the largest single industry in the American economy. Within it one might include the construction industry, itself often considered our country's largest business. In addition, the real estate industry may be said to include the creation, management, and demolition of every residence and business facility in the nation: offices, warehouses, factories, stores, and special purpose buildings such as hospitals and government facilities. The real estate business would include as well the managing of all the undeveloped land in the country: national parks, forests, and the vast quantity of unused federal property.

Real estate professionals are individuals and business organizations whose *sole enterprise is performing a real estate-related service or function.* A wide range of professions is available to persons wishing to enter the real estate business.

Real estate activities

Real estate professionals perform the following property-related functions:

- creation and improvement
- management and maintenance
- demolition
- investment ownership
- regulation
- transfer

Creation and improvement. Creating real properties from raw land involves capital formation, financing, construction contracting, and regulatory approvals. The key parties involved in this aspect of the business are generally the developer, the landowner, and the mortgage lender. Also involved are market analysts, architects, engineers, space planners, interior designers, and construction subcontractors.

Experts who manage the legal aspects of the development project include real estate attorneys, title companies, surveyors, property insurance companies, and government regulatory officials. The brokerage community, with the assistance of professional appraisers, usually handles the ownership and leasing transactions that occur over the many phases of development.

Management and maintenance. All real estate, whether raw land or improved property, must be managed and maintained. The two principal types of managers are property managers and asset managers. Property managers and their staff oversee specific properties on behalf of the owners, making sure the condition of the property and its financial performance meet specific standards.

Community association managers (CAMs) manage such residential properties as mobile home parks, planned unit developments (PUDs), cooperatives, time-shares, condominiums, and homeowners' associations.

Asset managers oversee groups of properties, or portfolios. Their role is to achieve the investment objectives of the owners as opposed to managing day-to-day operations.

The scope of management work is detailed in a management agreement.

Maintenance personnel include engineers, systems technicians, janitorial staff, and other employees needed to maintain the property's condition.

Demolition. Demolition experts in conjunction with excavation and debris removal experts serve to remove properties that are no longer economically viable from the market.

Investment ownership. A specialized niche in the real estate business is the real estate investor who risks capital in order to buy, hold, and sell real properties. In contrast to property owners whose primary interest is in some other business, the real estate investor focuses on identifying and exploiting real estate investment opportunities for profit. The real estate investor provides capital and liquidity to the real estate market.

Regulation. All real estate is to some degree regulated by government. The principal areas of regulation are usage, taxation, and housing administration. Professional regulatory functions include public planners, zoning administrators, building inspectors, assessors, and administrators of specific federal statutes such as Federal Fair Housing Laws.

Transfer. Rights and interests in real estate can be bought, sold, assigned, leased, exchanged, inherited, or otherwise transferred from one owner to another. Real estate brokers and the brokers' associates are generally centrally involved in such transfers. Other professional participants are mortgage brokers, mortgage bankers, appraisers, insurers, and title companies.

Professional specialties

In summary, the six primary functional areas are populated by professionals with the following specialties.

Professions in Real Estate

Creating	developers	market analysts
	public and private planners	surveyors
	architects	engineers
	building contractors	public and private inspectors
	space planners	mortgage brokers
	mortgage lenders and bankers	securities companies
	title and escrow companies	attorneys
	insurers	appraisers
	real estate brokers and agents	
Managing & Maintaining	property managers	asset managers
	maintenance engineers	maintenance
	technicians corporate managers	
Destroying	demolition contractors	excavators
Holding	investors	corporate managers
Regulating	assessors	public planners
	zoning administrators	building inspectors
Transferring	brokers and agents	appraisers
	lenders and bankers	mortgage brokers
	title and escrow companies	attorneys
	insurers	surveyors

Property type specialization

In addition to specializing by function, many professionals also specialize in the type of property they work with. According to the purpose of ownership, properties are classified as residential, commercial, or investment properties.

Residential property refers to property that is owned and used for habitation. Such properties may be further classified in terms of how many families they are designed to house, whether they are attached to other units or detached, and so forth.

Commercial property generally refers to retail and office properties, but may also include industrial real estate. The term "commercial" relates to the fact that the property can potentially generate income from a business's usage.

Investment property refers to any property that is held by its owners for investment purposes. All classifications of property may be investment properties. Generally, however, the term does not refer to owner-occupied residences, even though such properties constitute an investment. Apartments, condominiums, cooperatives, and single-family homes may be considered as investment property if non-occupants own the property for investment purposes. These properties are also referred to as residential income properties.

According to use, the following classifications of real properties are commonly accepted.

Classifications of Real Estate by Use

residential	industrial
residential income	farm and ranch
office	special purpose
retail	land

These categories often have overlapping uses. A bank, for example, may have retail as well as office operations. An industrial distribution facility may include extensive office space. A retail center may contain offices.

Special purpose properties include publicly or privately owned recreational facilities, government buildings, churches and schools.

Why hire a real estate professional

There are many reasons a member of the public hires a real estate professional. The real estate professional offers expert information on the real estate market, specifically in the areas of:

▶ property transfer

The real estate professional knows how to transfer real property and who needs to be involved in transferring the property legally.

▶ market conditions

The real estate professional understands the current economic market conditions and the current local real estate market.

▶ how to market real estate

The real estate professional understands the best way to advertise and/or promote a specific piece of real property depending on the audience that may buy the property.

REAL ESTATE BROKERAGE

Forms of specialization
Additional areas of specialization
Skills and knowledge

Most newly licensed practitioners choose to begin their real estate careers in residential brokerage.

Primary real estate brokerage activities involve performance of one or more of the following tasks:

- locating a buyer for a seller
- locating a seller for a buyer
- locating a tenant for a landlord
- locating a landlord for a tenant

A seller, buyer, landlord or tenant hires a broker to procure the opposite party to the sale or lease transaction. To help get the job done, the broker hires licensed agents as assistants. The brokerage company, in its simplest form, consists of a broker and the broker's agents, who together work to locate buyers, sellers, tenants and landlords for the broker's clients.

Forms of specialization

In the modern brokerage environment, brokers and agents specialize along the following lines:

- property type
- geographical area
- type of transaction
- type of client
- type of relationship

One's choice of specialization is influenced by competitive factors in the market and by perceived opportunities.

Property type. Since different properties have different features and potential buyers, brokers commonly choose to specialize in a property type. Thus there are:

- residential agents
- commercial agents (office, retail)
- industrial agents
- land agents

Geographical area. Brokers and agents must maintain current, accurate data on properties. It is not possible to keep track of every property in larger markets. Therefore, one must create an area of geographical specialization. One's area may be defined by natural barriers; by streets and highways; or by a certain set of subdivisions.

Type of transaction. The principal types of transaction are sales, leases and subleases, exchanges, and options.

Each form of transaction involves particular legal documents and considerations. As a result, many agents, particularly commercial agents, specialize in a type of transaction. For example, in an urban commercial property market, agents generally specialize in either leases or sales.

Type of client. Brokers increasingly represent buyers and tenants as well as sellers and landlords. Since conflicts of interest may be involved, many brokers restrict their business to representing either buyers and tenants or sellers and landlords exclusively.

Some brokers and agents also specialize according to the type of business their clients are in or their motivations for the transaction. Thus one finds brokers who focus exclusively on hospitals, or fast food chains, or executive relocations.

Type of relationship. In recent years, many brokers have specialized in providing advisory services to clients instead of the traditional transaction-based, commission-compensated services. In the advisory relationship, the broker works on identified real estate tasks or projects in exchange for a fee, salary, or retainer. The fee advisor may or may not focus on completing a transaction.
Some of the individual brokerage services that one might perform for a pre-set fee are:

- comparative price analysis
- database search
- prospect screening
- site analysis

Additional areas of Specialization

In addition to residential real estate brokerage, there are other areas of specialization a real estate agent may engage in. These include property management, appraising, financing, and counseling.

Property management. This is a rapidly growing area of real estate due to the growth in "absentee ownership." Here, the property manager serves as the owner's agent in controlling the property. Such oversight allows the owner to minimize involvement in the innumerable tasks involved in sustaining income properties.

Property managers work via an employment contract known as a management agreement. It lays out all the duties the property manager must perform on behalf of the property owner. The management agreement also stipulates how and when the property manager gets compensated.

Appraising. Appraising is a process of estimating the value of real estate. Certified appraisers are licensed and registered by the Florida Real Estate Appraisal Board.

Florida real estate agents are legally authorized per F.S. 475 to appraise property in Florida. However, they must be careful not to represent themselves as an appraiser or their valuation report as a certified appraisal.

If a real estate agent performs an appraisal, it must follow the laws and guidelines of the Uniform Standards of Professional Appraisal Practices (USPAP). The law also states that a real estate agent may not appraise a property that involves federally-related transactions.

Instead of appraisals, most real estate agents complete a Comparative Market Analysis (CMA) or a Broker's Price Opinion (BPO) to determine the approximate value of a piece of property. Both methods are exempt from following the Federal USPAP rules and regulations. These topics will be covered in greater detail in Chapter 16.

Financing. Financing is the business of providing funds for real estate transactions. The source of funding for most real estate transactions is the mortgage loan. Overall, it is vital for real estate agents to understand financing and be able to solve elementary financing problems.

Real estate agents do not need to be experts in the field of financing. Loan Mortgage Originators and Mortgage Brokers are licensed to make more sophisticated recommendations and assist the buyer in procuring the funding they need.

Counseling. Counseling is a very specialized and advanced area of real estate practice. Counselors must know every facet of the real estate business, including property transfers, permitting, subdividing, zoning, and construction. They are hired on a set fee basis because it would be a conflict of interest for them to be paid based on the value of the project.

Skills and knowledge

Professionals in the brokerage business must have a broad range of real estate knowledge and skills. Agents must develop a thorough awareness of their local market and the properties within it. In addition, agents must develop a proficiency with the economics of real estate: prices, financing, closing costs, and so forth. Equally important are "people" skills: communicating with clients and responding to their needs.

Required Skills and Knowledge in Real Estate Brokerage

Knowledge	Skills
local market conditions	financial qualification
local properties	market analysis
real estate principles	marketing practices
real estate law	ethical practices
value estimation	liability management
real estate financing	data management
investment principles	selling
license laws	time management
related math	communication
calculations	writing
closing procedures	basic computer operation

DEVELOPMENT AND CONSTRUCTION

Land acquisition
Subdividing and development
Construction

Development and construction involve a complex process consisting of many stages requiring the participation of numerous parties and entailing many financial risks. The physical process consists of a sequence of events from land acquisition through subdividing, land preparation, construction, leasing, and sale,

Land acquisition

Before land is located for a development, the developer undertakes a strategic analysis of what uses the area requires, the market demographics, potential trade areas and locational features for users, whether the use is to be commercial or residential, competitive projects in the region, supply and demand, and financing options. Careful study of the features of the potential site and a highest and best use and feasibility analysis go into creation of a master development plan.

An estimate of land and development costs representing the developer's outlays, including site preparation, engineering and design, commissions, construction, permits, financing and other items will guide how much the developer can pay for the land. These costs will vary depending on whether the developer intends to proceed with the entire development to finished product or will re-sell the land at an earlier stage of the process to another developer or builder.

Subdividing and development

A division of land into two or more lots, units, parcels or interests may or may not include a plan for streets and utilities. Subdivision is regulated by state and municipal laws concerning zoning, permissible uses, construction standards, and environmental constraints, among other things. One essential step is the creation and recording of a subdivision plat map. This map lays out the proposed building sites, streets, and public utilities. Also, improvements that will not be sold to individuals, such as parks, streets, sidewalks, and curbs, are typically donated to the local municipality or county by means of a recorded dedication. This dedication ensures that the local government will be responsible for maintaining those improvements.

Construction

Residential construction falls into three general categories.

Spec homes. Speculative or spec homes are those that are built without a prior commitment from a homebuyer.

Custom homes. When there is a contract with a buyer for a particular home before there is any construction, the builder constructs a custom home, usually according to a plan presented by the buyer or an architect.

Tract homes. Here the builder offers a choice of floor plans and designs, often represented by one or more model homes, for the buyer to choose along with a particular lot.

THE ROLE OF GOVERNMENT

Regulation of business practices
Real estate license laws

Regulation of business practices

The real estate industry is regulated by every level of government. Federal and state statutes, as well as a large body of court decisions, generally referred to as common law, circumscribe how real estate can be developed, managed, and transferred.

Among the laws most relevant to agents and brokers are those relating to:

> ▶ agency
> ▶ contracts
> ▶ disclosure
> ▶ environmental impact
> ▶ fair housing

In addition to federal, state, and local laws and regulations, the real estate industry is, to a degree, self-regulated by the codes of ethical conduct propounded by the industry's many trade organizations. For example, the National Association of Realtors® Code of Ethics not only reflects the law but sets an even higher standard of performance for member brokers and agents.

It is imperative for new practitioners to understand and abide by the many laws which regulate the industry.

Real estate license laws

State real estate license laws comprise the primary body of laws and regulations governing real estate brokerage practice. License laws in each state specify who must obtain a license to practice real estate and set the requirements for obtaining and maintaining the license. License laws also define critical aspects of real estate brokerage, including

- procedures for handling escrow deposits and fees
- procedures for advertising
- guidelines for dealing with clients and customers

State license laws are administered in each state by a **real estate commission**. The commission is charged with administering and enforcing license laws. In addition, the commission may pass regulations that further refine or clarify state statutes.

PROFESSIONAL ORGANIZATIONS

There are trade organizations within the real estate industry that support and promote virtually every form of business specialization. Benefits of membership include training programs, professional designations, and communication channels for keeping abreast of events and laws. Trade organization membership also generally enhances one's business image in the eyes of clients and the public at large.

Some of the major trade organizations, institutes and related professional designations are listed below.

Real Estate Trade Organizations and Designations

American Society of Appraisers
www.appraisers.org

American Society of Home Inspectors
www.ashi.com

Building Owners and Managers Association
www.boma.org

CCIM Institute
www.ccim.com

    Certified Commercial-Investment Member (CCIM)

Corenet Global
www.corenetglobal.org

    Master of Corporate Real Estate (MCR)

Counselors of Real Estate
www.cre.org

    Counselor of Real Estate (CRE)

Institute of Real Estate Management
www.irem.org

    Certified Property Manager (CPM)

International Association of Assessing Officers
www.iaao.org

International Council of Shopping Centers
www.icsc.org

Mortgage Bankers Association of America
www.mbaa.org

    Certified Mortgage Banker (CMB)

National Association of Exclusive Buyer's Agents
www.naeba.org

National Association of Home Builders
www.nahb.org

NAIOP Commercial Real Estate Development Association
www.naiop.org

National Association of Real Estate Brokers
www.nareb.com

National Association of Realtors
www.nar.realtor

    Graduate, Realtors Institute (GRI)
    Certified International Property Specialist (CIPS)

Real Estate Educators Association
www.reea.org

Realtors Land Institute
www.rliland.com

    Accredited Land Consultant (ALC)

Society of Industrial and Office Realtors

www.sior.com

The Appraisal Institute
www.appraisalinstitute.org

    Member, Appraisal Institute (MAI)
    Senior Residential Appraiser (SRA)

Women's Council of Realtors
www.wcr.org

Performance Management Network (PMN)

1 Course Overview: The Real Estate Business Snapshot Review

INTRODUCTION TO THE REAL ESTATE BUSINESS

Real estate activities
- create, improve, manage, maintain, demolish, own, regulate, and transfer real properties

Property type specialization
- residential; residential income; office; retail; industrial; farm and ranch; special purpose; land

Additional areas of specialization
- property management; appraising; financing counseling

REAL ESTATE BROKERAGE
- procure a buyer or tenant for an owner or landlord, or vice versa

Forms of specialization
- by property type; geographical area; type of transaction; type of client; by form of business organization; or by form of client relationship

Additional areas of Specialization
- property management; appraising; financing; counseling

Skills and knowledge
- market conditions; law; financing; marketing; ethics; selling; communications; computer basics; and other skills

DEVELOPMENT AND CONSTRUCTION

Land acquisition
- components of acquiring land for development: strategic planning, market analysis, locational features, demographics, intended use, highest and best use, financing, competition, supply and demand, feasibility, costs of site preparation, engineering, design, construction, permits to determine affordable price

Subdividing and development
- state and municipal regulation: zoning, uses, construction standards, environment, recording of plat map, dedication of non-private areas

Construction
- three types of residential construction: spec home, custom homes, tract homes

THE ROLE OF GOVERNMENT

Regulation of business practices
- all facets of the industry are regulated by federal, state, and local laws; agents must understand relevant laws and adapt business practices accordingly

Real estate license laws
- the primary body of laws and regulations governing the licensure and conduct of real estate brokers and agents
- license laws are administered and enforced under the jurisdiction of the state

PROFESSIONAL ORGANIZATIONS
- promote interests of practitioners and enhance their professional standing real estate commission

SECTION ONE: Course Overview: The Real Estate Business

Section Quiz

1. Property management is a growing area of real estate. This growth is mainly due to the increase in

    a. absentee ownership.
    b. an increase in property sales.
    c. a decrease in financing available to buy property.
    d. no known reason.

2. People in the real estate business who primarily focus on creating new properties are

    a. brokers.
    b. developers.
    c. zoning administrators.
    d. excavators.

3. The term "commercial property" generally refers to

    a. non-owner-occupied properties.
    b. retail, office and industrial properties.
    c. multi-tenant properties.
    d. retail properties.

4. Which of the following professionals involved in the real estate business are most concerned about procuring buyers and sellers for clients?

    a. Brokers and agents
    b. Property managers
    c. Corporate real estate managers
    d. Appraisers

5. Which of the following ways of specializing is common in the real estate brokerage business?

    a. By type of house
    b. By geography
    c. By financial background of client
    d. By type of mortgage

6. What is an appraisal?

    a. A report completed by a real estate broker giving information about a piece of property.
    b. Contains information such as a title report and survey
    c. It is an opinion of a property's value.
    d. Not allowed to be completed by a real estate agent.

7. The level of government which is most active in regulating real estate licensees is the

    a. federal government.
    b. state government.
    c. county government.
    d. municipal government where the person resides.

2 Real Estate License Law and Qualifications for Licensure

History and Purposes of Real Estate License Laws
License Categories
General Licensure Provisions
Application Requirements
Sales Associate License Requirements
Broker License Requirements
Nonresident License Requirements
License Information; Registration
License Renewal Education

Learning Objectives

- Identify the qualifications for a sales associate's license
- Describe the application requirements for licensure including nonresident application requirements
- Explain the importance of responding accurately and completely to the background information questions on the licensure application
- Illustrate the background check procedure conducted by the DBPR
- Describe the education requirement for pre- and post-license education and continuing education
- Distinguish among the various license categories
- Identify services of real estate where licensure is required
- Recognize actions that constitute unlicensed activity
- Recognize exemptions from real estate licensure
- Distinguish between registration and licensure
- Explain mutual recognition agreements

Key Terms

adjudication withheld
broker
broker associate
compensation
expungement
Florida resident
license/registration

mutual recognition agreement
nolo contendere/ no contest
owner-developer
prima facie evidence
real estate services
reciprocity
sales associate
sealed

HISTORY AND PURPOSES OF
REAL ESTATE LICENSE LAWS

History of Florida's real estate license law
Purpose of regulation
Important Florida real estate statutes and rules

History of Florida's real estate license law

In the early 1900s, the Florida Legislature determined it was necessary to protect public welfare by regulating the real estate industry. As a result, Florida put into place laws and authorities to regulate the licensing and practices of real estate brokers, sales associates, and schools in the state.

In 1923, the Legislature passed Chapter 475 and added it to the Florida Statutes as the first real estate license law.

Department of Business and Professional Regulation (DBPR). The DBPR was created and structured by Title IV, Section 20.165 of the Florida Statutes and is governed by Chapter 120, F.S.

Division of Real Estate (DRE). As a division of the DBPR, the Division of Real Estate provides all the services necessary to administer Chapter 475. The DRE establishes both the Florida Real Estate Appraisal Board and the Florida Real Estate Commission.

Florida Real Estate Commission (FREC). To further administer the license law and regulate real estate professionals, the Florida Legislature established the FREC in 1925 under Chapter 475 and gave it the authority to establish rules necessary to perform its duties.

The above organizations are covered in detail in a later section.

Purpose of regulation

When the Florida Legislature determined that the public needed protection when engaging in real estate transactions, it put several regulations, laws, and rules into place for that purpose. The purpose of all Florida real estate regulations is **consumer protection**.

Caveat emptor. Caveat emptor means "buyer beware" and signifies that buyers purchase properties at their own risk regarding the condition of the property. Florida subscribed to caveat emptor until 1985, when a buyer sued a seller for not disclosing the property's defective roof. Under caveat emptor, the buyer would have been out of luck. However, the Florida Supreme Court ruled in favor of the buyer, thereby reversing Florida's use of caveat emptor.

This ruling showed the need for further regulation in real estate sales and established that a seller has a duty to disclose known defects. As indicated in Chapter 455, Section 201 of Florida statutes, this ruling and subsequent rulings laid out that a seller must disclose defects if all four of the following elements are present:

- the seller has knowledge of a defect in the property
- the defect materially affects the value of the property
- the defect is not readily observable and is not known to the buyer
- the buyer establishes that the seller failed to disclose the defect

With caveat emptor, if the buyer asked, the seller was required to answer honestly. However, if the buyer didn't ask, then the seller had no obligation to disclose. With this change of regulation, sellers are now required to disclose defects in the property whether or not the buyer asks.

Important Florida real estate statutes and rules

As mentioned earlier, the Florida legislature saw a need to protect consumers during real estate transactions from unethical and illegal practices such as fraud. Legislators also did not want to make it unreasonably difficult for an individual to enter into the real estate profession. Consequently, they established specific laws to meet these needs. The statutes are updated annually to create, amend, transfer, or repeal statutory material.

Chapter 20 of the Florida code covers the organizational structure of the Executive Branch of the state government. It is the statute that created the Department of Business and Professional Regulation and established the Divisions within the DBPR, such as the Division of Real Estate. This statute also established the organizational structure of the DBPR.

Chapter 475 is divided into four parts and provides regulations for brokers, sales associates, appraisers, and schools. Part I created the FREC and includes its organization, powers, and duties. It also covers regulations for licensure and brokerage practices, including violations and penalties.

Part II provides regulations for appraisers. Part III is known as the Commercial Real Estate Sales Commission Lien Act and provides regulations for a broker's lien for unpaid sales commission. Part IV is known as the Commercial Real Estate Leasing Commission Lien Act and provides regulations for a broker's lien for unpaid commission earned by a lease of commercial real estate.

Chapter 455, or the Business and Professional Regulation: General Provisions, is the law used by the DBPR in regulating the professions under the Department's auspices. It outlines the legislative intent in regulating these professions and includes restrictions on deterring qualified individuals from entering any of the chosen professions. It specifically holds that non-U.S. citizens may not be disqualified from practicing any of the professions regulated by the DBPR and covers the required qualifications to do so.

Chapter 455 also includes the powers and duties of the DBPR and the organizational and operational requirements of the boards under the DBPR. This chapter covers general licensing provisions; education requirements; licensure examinations and testing services; disciplinary grounds, actions, procedures, and penalties; and legal and investigative services. Section 455.02 provides guidelines for licensure of members of the armed forces and their spouses.

Chapter 120 is known as the Administrative Procedure Act and provides procedures for government agencies to exercise their specified authority, including rulemaking authority, procedures, requirements, and challenges. It also covers licensing requirements, along with disciplinary procedures and enforcement. Exemptions and exceptions from this Act are also included.

Chapter 61J2 contains the Florida Real Estate Commission's (FREC) rules. These rules cover licensure and education requirements, non-resident licensure, brokerage operation and business practices, trust fund handling, and disciplinary matters and procedures.

Other state statutes regulate taxation and collections, construction standards, lien foreclosures, and tax breaks for undeveloped land used for agricultural purposes (Florida Greenbelt Law of 1959). The Online Sunshine website provides access to these and other applicable Florida statutes.

LICENSE CATEGORIES

Broker
Sales associate
Broker associate

Florida offers real estate licenses that fall into one of three categories: broker, sales associate, and broker associate. A broker associate and a sales associate may be licensed as an individual or as a professional corporation, limited liability company, or professional limited liability company, if the individual has obtained authorization to do so from the Department of State. A broker associate and sales associate may not be licensed as a general partner, member, manager, officer, or director of a brokerage firm.

Broker   A broker is someone who is licensed to perform real estate services for another person for compensation or the expectation of compensation. Compensation can be monetary or anything else of value.

Real estate services include the sale, exchange, purchase, rental, appraisal, auction, advertising of real property, business enterprises, or business opportunities or the offer to perform any of these services. Services also include procuring sellers, buyers, lessors, or lessees.

Although a broker may "appraise" property, such appraising does not equate to appraisal services that must be performed by a registered or licensed appraiser.

The broker category of licensure also includes any individual who is a general partner, officer, or director of a partnership or corporation that acts as a broker.

Sales associate   A sales associate is someone who performs the same real estate services as a broker but who works under the direction, control, and management of a specified broker or owner-developer. A sales associate must meet additional licensure requirements to become a broker or broker associate.

Broker associate   A broker associate is someone who has obtained a broker license but performs real estate services as a sales associate under the direction, control, and management of a specified broker.

GENERAL LICENSURE PROVISIONS

General qualifications
Required disclosures
Reasons for denial

General qualifications   To qualify for a real estate license in Florida, an individual must be at least 18 years old; hold a high school diploma or its equivalent; and be honest, truthful, trustworthy, and of good character. He or she must have a good reputation for fair dealing and be competent to handle real estate transactions. Being a U.S. citizen or a Florida resident is not a requirement for licensure as long as the individual meets all other requirements of licensure. However, applicants must have a Social Security number. A Social Security number or equivalent is not required for tax purposes but to ensure that the applicant is not behind on spousal or child support.

Required disclosures   An applicant must disclose any alias or also-known-as (aka) name. The applicant must also disclose whether he or she

- ▸ is under investigation for any crime or violation
- ▸ has been convicted or entered a plea of nolo contendere, no contest, or guilty for any crime
- ▸ has been denied licensure or registration for a regulated profession
- ▸ has been disciplined or is pending discipline in any jurisdiction
- ▸ has surrendered a license or had a license suspended or revoked
- ▸ has been guilty of any conduct that would be grounds for license suspension or revocation. (F.S. 475)

Reasons for denial   An applicant may not qualify for licensure if he or she has been denied a license, had a license revoked or suspended, or has committed offenses that would be grounds for license revocation or suspension. In such cases, when considerable time has passed since the offense or if the applicant has since demonstrated conduct good enough to assure he or she is of no danger to the public, the FREC may determine that he or she is then qualified to apply for licensure.

The applicant may also be denied licensure if the applicant acted as a licensee in performing real estate activities or presented him- or herself as a licensee within one year prior to applying for a license.

Applicants may not be denied licensure based on conviction of a crime that occurred five or more years prior to submission of the application unless the crime was related to the practice of real estate or related to the absence of good moral character.

APPLICATION REQUIREMENTS

Fees
Application form
Background checks
Application omissions
Application approval
Appealing denials
Application validity period
Nonresident applications
Course requirements
Education exemptions

Fees   The FREC charges fees for:

- ▸ licensure application
- ▸ examination
- ▸ reexamination
- ▸ licensing
- ▸ license renewal
- ▸ license reinstatement
- ▸ unlicensed activity
- ▸ the Real Estate Recovery Fund

License examination fees and fingerprint processing fees are paid directly to the testing vendor. If for any reason the application for licensure is not completely processed, the application fee may be refunded.

There are maximum limits set for each fee based on the estimate of funds the Commission needs for operations. In case of an excess in the funds collected, the Department may waive license renewal fees for up to 2 years. If the funds run low, the fee amount can be increased or the FREC can charge a one-time fee from each active and inactive licensee to remove the deficit.

Waivers. Florida waives the initial licensing fee for the following individuals:

▶   *A member of the U.S. armed forces* who served on active duty, a spouse who was married to a member while on active duty, and a surviving spouse of a member who died while on active duty

▶   *A low-income person* whose pretax household income is at or below a specified percentage of the federal poverty guidelines based on the family's household size and proven by enrollment in a public assistance program

These individuals must pay the application fee, unlicensed activity fee, the Real Estate Recovery Fund fee, examination fee, and the fingerprint processing fee.

Florida also waives the initial licensing fee, the initial application fee, and the initial unlicensed activity fee for

▶   *A military veteran or the veteran's spouse* if he or she applies for licensure within 60 months after the veteran has been honorably discharged from active duty in any branch of the U.S. armed forces.

These individuals must pay the examination fee, the fingerprint processing fee, and the Real Estate Recovery Fund fee.

Application form   Applicants for a Florida real estate license must submit the designated DBPR application form as provided on the DBPR's website. The application must include the applicant's social security number and name as it appears on the applicant's social security card.

The applicant must also submit any additional documentation required by the Department, including documentation on the applicant's education, work history, criminal history, discipline, fingerprints, and so on.

Background checks   Applicants for a real estate license in Florida must submit to a background check and provide their fingerprints to the DBPR.

Fingerprints. Applicants may use any approved Level 2 FDLE fingerprinting Livescan vendor to submit their fingerprints. When submitting fingerprints, the applicant must also submit the Originating Agency Identification (ORI) number (which can be found on the www.myfloridalicense.com website).

Background check. On receiving the applicant's fingerprints, the Department will forward them to the Florida Department of Law Enforcement and the FBI for use in conducting a criminal history check on the applicant. Both agencies will send their background reports to the DBPR, usually within 3-5 days. To allow for adequate processing time, applicants should submit their fingerprints at least 5 days prior to submitting the license application. The DBPR will use these reports to determine if the applicant is qualified for examination and licensure based on the presence or lack of a criminal history.

Criminal history. If the background report indicates a criminal history, it is best if the applicant has already provided all associated information to the Department along with the application. This is accomplished by answering all application background questions completely and honestly and including documentation that provides details of any investigations, convictions, guilty pleas, or nolo contendere pleas with dates, findings, and penalties.

If the penalties have already been satisfied, the applicant should include documentation proving the satisfaction for each conviction.

Any applicant currently on probation as a result of a conviction should also include an official letter from the probation officer regarding the status of the current probation. The applicant may also want to include at least three character references with the application and other documentation. One reference letter may be from a family member, but all others must be from other people who know the applicant and can attest to his or her character.

Summary of applicants. If an applicant's background check indicates a criminal history, the application is placed on a Summary of Applicants list and submitted to the FREC for review in its monthly meeting. During the review, the FREC will determine if the applicant is approvable for examination and licensure or if the application requires additional consideration and information.

Additional information on digital fingerprinting and the approved vendors can be found on the DBPR's website at www.myfloridalicense.com. An applicant may order a criminal background report on him or herself on the Florida Department of Law Enforcement's website at www.fdle.state.fl.us.

Application omissions

If an applicant makes an error or omits pertinent information on the application, the licensing department must notify the applicant within 30 days of receiving the application. The notice is to include any additional information needed and a time period for the applicant is to make the corrections and submit additional information. If the department does not send the notice within 30 days, they may not deny the application for the uncorrected errors and omissions.

Application approval

The Department must approve or deny a license application within 90 days of receiving it. If the Department fails to meet that deadline, the application is considered approved by default. Applicants who are approved by default are to notify the Department in writing of their intent to rely on the default approval. If the Commission denies the application, it must notify the applicant in writing of the denial and reasons for denial. The notice must inform the applicant of his or her appeal rights.

Appealing denials

If an application has been denied, the applicant will receive a Notice of Intent to Deny. He or she then has the right to choose to:

▶ accept the denial and forfeit the opportunity to become licensed
▶ petition for an informal hearing before the FREC to present argument against the reasons for denial
▶ petition for a formal hearing before an administrative law judge to review the denial order

An applicant who chooses to request a hearing on the denial must file a petition with the DRE within 21 days of receiving the denial notice.

Application validity period

Initial application. The initial license application remains valid for two years after the date it was received by the DBPR.

Exam eligible. The applicant has two years after completing the prelicense course work to pass the licensure examination. If the applicant fails to pass the examination within those two years, the completed course work becomes invalid.

Nonresident applications

See "Nonresident license requirements" section below.

Course requirements

The FREC requires applicants for licensure to complete prelicense real estate educational courses. These can be taken at an accredited college or university, a career center, or registered real estate school.

Each classroom hour is equal to 50 minutes with each license type requiring a specific number of classroom hours (see requirements sections below). Missing more than 8 classroom hours during the course is an automatic failure. If a student misses more than 8 hours due to student or family illness, he or she may attend make-up classes within 30 days of the scheduled end-of-course examination date. Classes taken after the 30 days need Commission approval. Make-up classes must cover the same material as the classes missed.

After completing the coursework, the applicant must pass an end-of-course examination with a score of 70% or higher. A student who fails the examination may retake a different form of the examination 30 days after failing. The student may retake the examination only one time during the year after failing. If the student does not pass the end-of-course examination within the year, the student must repeat the prelicense courses.

When the student completes the coursework and passes the end-of-course examination, the school must provide the student with a certificate of course completion and notify the FREC of all students who completed the course.

The FREC is required to approve distance learning courses through Internet streaming or other means of video conferencing as an option to classroom hours. Students taking distance learning courses must pass a timed course examination.

The prelicense courses must also be made available by correspondence or other suitable means for students whose hardships prevent them from attending the classroom courses and from having access to distance learning courses.

Students with a 4-year degree or higher are exempt from post-licensing requirements for both Sales Associates and brokers. They will immediately start 14-hour continuing education requirements.

A prelicense student may demonstrate FREC-approved minimal competencies that show the student is qualified for licensure as a substitute for taking specific classroom hours.

Education exemptions

Persons seeking licensure who are exempt from the requirement to complete prelicense education include the following.

- An active attorney in good standing with the Florida Bar who is qualified under real estate license law may obtain a real estate sales associate license without completing prelicense education courses. However, attorneys must pass the licensure examination.
- Anyone who has earned a 4-year degree or higher in real estate from a school of higher education may obtain a real estate license without completing prelicense education courses. However, individuals with this degree must pass the licensure examination.
- A nonresident licensed in a state that has a mutual recognition agreement with Florida may obtain a real estate license without completing prelicense education courses. However, these nonresidents must pass a 40-question licensure examination.

SALES ASSOCIATE LICENSE REQUIREMENTS

General license requirements
Prelicense course
State license examination

General license requirements

To qualify for a Florida sales associate license, the applicant must

- have a Social Security number
- receive approval of the license application
- pay all required fees

> ▸ meet all general licensure provisions including age, education, character, competency, submission of associated background history and fingerprints, as discussed in a previous section.

Prelicense course

Applicants for a sales associate license must complete 63 classroom hours of an FREC-approved prelicense course, referred to as Course I, to be taken at an accredited college, career center, or registered real estate school. The course includes the fundamentals of real estate principles and practices, real estate law and license law, and associated mathematics. The required hours consist of 60 hours of instruction, either in the classroom or through distance learning, and three hours allowed for the end-of-course examination.

State license examination

After completing the prelicense coursework and passing the end-of-course examination, an applicant has 2 years to take and pass the state licensure examination. If the applicant waits longer than the 2 years, he or she must retake the prelicense course to be eligible to take the licensure examination.

Applicants must schedule the exam directly with the testing vendor and pay the exam fee at that time. Prior to taking the exam, the applicant must present the prelicense course completion certificate and two forms of identification, one of which is to be government-issued and include a photo.

The examination is given on a computer-based system that allows students to answer questions or skip questions and go back to them later. It also provides a summary of how many questions have been answered, how many were skipped, and how much time is remaining on the test. The exam is available in English and in Spanish. Non-electronic foreign language translation dictionaries are allowed in the exam room but must be approved by the test administrator. No other reference materials are allowed in the examination room during the test.

The state examination includes 100 multiple-choice questions and may include pilot questions that are not included in the final test score. The applicant must pass the test with a score of 75% or higher. If the applicant is a Florida nonresident from a Mutual Recognition State, he or she must take the designated Laws and Rules 40-question examination and pass with a score of 30 out of 40 points (75%).

Both the school final exam and the state exam are the same basic format, with 45% of the questions based on Florida Real Estate Law, 45% of the questions on Real Estate Principles and Practices, and 10% of the questions based on real estate math.

Failing the examination. If an applicant fails the examination, he or she will be given a photo-bearing exam report that will provide them with their score on the exam and a breakdown of what they missed. The report will also provide instructions on reviewing what they missed on their examination.

The request to review the exam must be made within 21 days of taking the exam and may be performed only for the applicant's most recent exam. The applicant must pay a fee for the review and is given half of the exam administration time for the review. The applicant may not take notes during the review.

The applicant may challenge any incorrect answers and have the question reviewed by a Florida Administrative Law judge

Whether or not the applicant challenges the results of the failed exam, he or she may pay a fee and retake the exam as many times as necessary within 2 years. There is no waiting period to retake the examination.

License issuance. An applicant who passes the examination will be given a photo-bearing exam report indicating the applicant passed the examination. The applicant's score will be provided to the DBPR, who will issue a sales associate license number and provide instructions for printing the license.

The license is issued in an inactive status. To activate the license, the sales associate must establish an association with a broker and then either activate his or her own license by printing the DBPR RE 11 Sales Associate or Broker Sales Associate – Become Active form and having the broker sign it or by having the broker add the sales associate to the broker's online account.

The sales associate must be licensed, associated with a broker or owner/developer, and activated prior to performing any real estate services which require a license.

The RE 11 form can be found online at http://www.myfloridalicense.com/dbpr/re/documents/DBPR_RE_11_Change_of_Status_Associates.pdf.

BROKER LICENSE REQUIREMENTS

General license requirements
Experience requirement
Prelicense course
State license examination

General license requirements

Just as with a sales associate license, an applicant for a Florida broker license must meet certain general licensure requirements. To qualify for a broker license, the applicant must

> ▸ have a Social Security number
> ▸ submit and receive approval of the DBPR RE-2 license application
> ▸ pay all required fees

> ▸ meet all general licensure provisions including age, education, character, competency, submission of all associated background history and fingerprints, as discussed in a previous section

An applicant who has been licensed as a sales associate in Florida during the preceding 5 years must complete the sales associate post license education requirements, as discussed in an upcoming section, prior to applying for the broker license. This post license education requirement does not apply to applicants who hold an out-of-state sales associate license.

Experience requirement

In addition to meeting the general licensure requirements, the applicant must have held an active real estate sales associate license for at least 2 years during the 5 years prior to applying for a broker license. The applicant must also have

> ▸ worked under one or more real estate brokers who are licensed in Florida or any other U.S. state, territory, or jurisdiction or in any foreign national jurisdiction. Time under an owner/developer does not count toward the experience requirement.
> ▸ performed real estate services as a salaried employee of a governmental agency, or
> ▸ been licensed in any other U.S. state, territory, or jurisdiction or in any foreign national jurisdiction

Applicants who have gained their required experience from a jurisdiction outside of Florida need to submit a current certification of real estate license history from the licensing agency of that jurisdiction. The certificate must not be more than 30 days old and should be attached to the broker license application.

Prelicense course

A licensed sales associate who is applying for a broker license must complete the required prelicense Course II. The course includes 69 classroom hours and 3 end-of-course examination hours. The course covers the fundamentals of real estate appraising, investment, financing, and brokerage and management operations.

Just as with the sales associate prelicense coursework, each classroom hour is 50 minutes of live instruction in the classroom or of live streaming or video conferencing. The course may be taken at an accredited college, technical center, or registered real estate school or through interactive distance learning. A student who demonstrates hardship may qualify to take the course through correspondence. The student must not miss more than 8 hours of classroom instruction.

The broker end-of-course exam includes 95 multiple choice questions, 90 of which are worth 1 point each and 5 of which may cover closing statements or escrow accounts and are worth 2 points each. The student must pass the exam with a score of 70% or higher to complete the course. Students who fail the exam may retake it once.

State license examination

After successfully completing the broker prelicense coursework and passing the end-of-course exam, the applicant must take and pass the state licensure examination within 2 years of completing the course. If the applicant waits longer than the 2 years, he or she must retake the prelicense course to be eligible to take the licensure examination.

The exam for brokers is based on knowledge, understanding, and application of real estate law and real estate principles and practices and includes appraising, finance, investment, brokerage management, and real estate mathematics. The exam is divided into 45 points based on law, 40 points on principles and practices, and 15 points on real estate mathematics. The student must pass the exam with a score of 75% or higher.

The processes for qualifying for, taking, passing, failing, and retaking the exam are the same as for the sales associate state exam. After passing the state exam, the student must print his or her license. Because the license is issued as inactive, the individual must submit a completed DBPR RE 13 Broker Transactions form to activate the license prior to operating as a broker.

An individual who passes the broker's exam but chooses to continue to work under a broker may register as a broker associate and work under an active Florida Broker.

NONRESIDENT LICENSE REQUIREMENTS

Florida resident defined
Nonresident application requirements
Mutual recognition
The Occupational Opportunity Act

Florida resident defined

Florida statutes define a resident as

1) a person who has resided in Florida, continuously for a period of 4 calendar months or more, within the preceding one year; or

2) a person who presently resides in Florida with the intention to reside continuously in Florida for a period of 4 months or more, commencing on the date that the person began the current period of residence in Florida.

Nonresident application requirements

Nonresident applicants need not hold a license in their state of residency to become Florida-licensed. To apply for licensure in Florida, an applicant must submit the appropriate DBPR application form for a sales associate or broker license along with the required fee, fingerprints, and any required supporting documentation, including a certification of license history issued by the state from which the applicant is claiming mutual recognition.

Mutual recognition

Mutual recognition agreements allow Florida to recognize and accept the prelicense education and experience obtained in the other state as a substitute for the requirements in the state where the nonresident is applying for a license.

The nonresident applicant must pass a written examination on general real estate law and codes with emphasis on Chapters 455 and 475 and Chapter 61J2. The Laws and Rules examination contains 40 questions and requires the applicant to correctly answer at least 30 of those questions. Only after passing the examination will the applicant be issued a Florida license. The nonresident licensee is then responsible for completing all post-license and continuing education that is required of a Florida licensee.

Florida licensees may seek licensure in any state that has a mutual recognition agreement with Florida, keeping in mind that each state may have different requirements for nonresident licensure. To apply for a nonresident license, the Florida licensee should contact the other state's real estate commission.

Mutual recognition vs. reciprocity. A *mutual recognition agreement* is contracted between two states and sets forth that the states will recognize and accept each other's real estate prelicense education requirements.

Reciprocity is an agreement between states to allow licensees of one state to obtain a license in the other state without completing the full licensing requirements of the other state. While each reciprocal state has its own specific requirements, most do not require the nonresident licensee to pass an examination for licensure in the reciprocal state.

Florida currently holds mutual recognition agreements with several states but does not have reciprocity agreements with any states.

The Occupational Opportunity Act

Although Florida does not have reciprocity agreements with other states, the Occupational Opportunity Act (FL House Bill 615, as amended in Chapter 2017-135) mandates that Florida provide reciprocal licensure for military members, their spouses, their surviving spouses, and low-income individuals. The Act covers all professions regulated by the DBPR, including real estate. The purpose of the Act is to make transfers to Florida easier for military members and spouses who hold licenses in the same profession in another state.

To qualify under the Act, military members must either be currently on active duty or have been honorably discharged. Surviving spouses qualify if the military member was on active duty at the time of death. Proof of the member's active duty must be submitted at the time of application. Applicants must be licensed in good standing in another state and must submit fingerprints for a background check at the time of application.

The Act waives initial license fees, but the applicant must pay fingerprint fees. The Act also waives requirements for prelicense education and examination, but the licensee must meet all renewal education and fee requirements. Reciprocity is available for up to 2 years after discharge from active duty to those who qualify under the Act.

LICENSE INFORMATION; REGISTRATION

License information
Registration

License information

Identity, contact information, license type and number, dates. Real estate licenses issued in Florida include the licensee's name and address, type of license, license issue and expiration dates, and the license number. The license number includes a two-letter prefix that indicates the type of license: BK for broker, SL for sales associate, BL for broker associate, BO for branch office, CQ for corporation or limited liability company, or PR for partnership and limited liability partnership.

Prima facia evidence of currency and validity. The license serves as prima facia evidence that the individual holds a current, valid license.

Prima facia evidence is defined as evidence that, at first view, is good and sufficient on its face to establish a given fact or to prove a case. Unless the evidence is contradicted, it proves a case or, as in the case of licensure, proves the license is valid.

As discussed throughout this section, real estate licensure is obtained by meeting all state requirements, including completing education and examination requirements, submitting to background history checks, paying applicable fees, meeting general age and character requirements, and so on.

When the individual or entity has met the requirements, the state will issue the license that allows the licensee to perform real estate services for compensation. The license must be timely renewed to allow for continued performance of real estate activities.

Registration

Every person or entity who is licensed is required to register with the FREC, pay a registration fee, and submit all required information: name and address of the licensee, name and business address of the sales associate licensee's employing broker, license status of the sales associate and his or her employing broker, and whether or not the licensee is an officer, director, or partner of a real estate brokerage. Registrations must be renewed when the license is renewed.

Florida sales associates and broker associates are required to register under the employing broker and can only register under one broker at a time.

Partnerships, limited liability partnerships, limited liability companies, and corporations that act as brokers must register. Partnerships are required to license and register at least one partner as an active broker. Real estate brokerage corporations must license and register their officers and directors. Brokers must also register all branch offices.

If a licensee changes names or trade names, the license must be reissued in the new name and re-registered. Trade names are to be shown on both the license and the registration.

Licensees and companies are registered when they provide the appropriate completed form to DBPR, giving their name, address, and other information. Persons do not have licensure until they have completed all the education and testing requirements. At that time, they will receive their license.

LICENSE RENEWAL EDUCATION

Post license requirement
Continuing education
Reactivation education

**Post license
requirement**

Course completion. All *sales associate* licensees are required to complete a post-licensing course before the first license renewal, even if the license is inactive. The course is 45 classroom hours and includes an end-of-course examination. The course emphasizes development of skills for licensees to operate effectively and to increase public protection. Any sales associate licensee who applies for broker licensure must have completed all sales associate post-license requirements.

All *broker* licensees are required to complete post-license education which includes either one 60-hour course or two 30-hour courses and the related exams. All post-license requirements must be met prior to their first broker license renewal date.

The course is to be taken at an accredited college, technical center, registered real estate school, FREC-approved sponsor, or through a distance learning program. A licensee who is absent from more than 10% of the classroom hours will not be given credit for completing the course. The licensee must pass the end-of-course exam with a 75% or higher score.

Exam failure. On failing the course exam, a licensee may retake the exam after failing. However, the licensee may retake the exam only one time during the year after failing. A licensee who does not pass the exam within that year must then repeat the post-license course. If the licensee does not complete the post-license course and pass the exam prior to the first license renewal date, his or her license will be deemed null and void.

To re-qualify for licensure, the individual must retake the entire prelicense course, pass that end-of-course exam, and again pass the state licensure exam. However, a broker who does not meet the broker post-license requirements may be issued a sales associate license by completing a 14-hour continuing education course within 6 months of the expiration of the broker license.

Exemption. Licensees who hold a four-year degree in real estate from an accredited institute of higher learning are exempt from post-license education requirements.

Hardship cases. The FREC may allow a six-month extension past the first license renewal date for a licensee to complete post-license requirements if the licensee cannot meet the education completion deadline due to a personal hardship. The FREC administrative code qualifies the following as hardships:

> ▶ the long-term illness of the licensee or a close relative or person for whom the licensee has care-giving responsibilities
> ▶ the lack of reasonable availability of the required course
> ▶ the licensee's economic or technological hardship that substantially interferes with the ability to complete education requirements
> ▶ the licensee's economic inability to meet reasonable basic living expenses

To obtain the time extension, the licensee must submit a written request to the Commission explaining the basis for the alleged hardship and submit any documentation the Commission requires as support and/or proof.

Licensees may also claim a hardship to be allowed to complete post-license education through correspondence if they cannot attend the classroom course or do not have access to distance learning courses.

Continuing education

Course completion. Florida real estate licenses are issued for 2-year periods, requiring renewal every 2 years. During the initial licensing period, licensees are required to complete post-licensing education based on the type of license held. During that same initial period, licensees are not required to complete continuing education, but continuing education is required for every 2-year licensing period thereafter.

During each licensing period, active and inactive sales associates and brokers are required to complete 14 continuing education hours, including at least 3 hours of Core Law education , 3 hours of Business Ethics and 8 hours of specialty education.

Continuing education courses may be taken in the classroom, through distance learning, or by correspondence (if the licensee qualifies for a hardship). The licensee must attend at least 90% of each of the classroom hours to receive the notice of completion. The DBPR may deny license renewal for any licensee who fails to complete continuing education requirements. Failure to provide proof of continuing education or providing false proof are grounds for disciplinary action

Course credits. Because Core Law covers Florida real estate license law, Commission rules, and agency law and provides an introduction to other state laws, federal laws, and taxes affecting real estate, it is advisable for the licensee to take a 3-hour Core Law course every year to stay up to date on the laws and rules.

Any licensee who does take the course each year will be awarded 3 hours of Core Law education and 3 hours of specialty education. Licensees whose licenses expire after September 30, 2018, are also required to take a 3-hour Business Ethics course every license period. Licensees who take the Business Ethics course each year will be awarded 3 hours of Business Ethics education and 3 hours of specialty education. The remaining hours required towards the total 14 hours may be taken in specialty education courses, also known as electives.

One time during each license period, the licensee may be awarded 3 classroom hours for attending an FREC legal agenda session. To receive the credit, the licensee needs to notify the Division of Real Estate of the intent to attend the session. No credit will be awarded if the licensee attends the session as a party to a disciplinary action.

The courses must be completed by either March 31 or September 30 based on the license expiration date. A 6-month extension past the renewal date may be available if the licensee cannot meet the education completion deadline due to a personal hardship.

Exemption. These continuing education requirements do not apply to attorneys in good standing with the Florida Bar.

Reactivation education

A licensee who has been on involuntary inactive status for 12 to 24 months may complete an FREC-prescribed 28-hour education course towards reactivating the license. The course covers material from the sales associate prelicense course. The course may be taken in the classroom, through distance learning, or by correspondence if the licensee qualifies for a hardship. Completion of the course does not entitle the licensee to reactivate the license until he or she has met all other requirements.

The licensee must also pass the end-of-course exam with a score of 70% or higher. Licensees must attend a minimum of 90% of the instruction hours to be eligible to take the exam. Licensees who fail the exam may retake it one time within a year of failure. If the licensee fails the retake exam, he or she must retake the reactivation course and the end-of-course exam.

Licensees who meet the qualifications of a hardship may request a 6-month extension after license expiration by submitting the hardship basis to the FREC.

ACTIVITIES REQUIRING LICENSURE & EXEMPTIONS

**Individuals required to be licensed
Individuals exempt from licensure**

Individuals required to be licensed

Individuals who perform real estate services for compensation or the expectation of compensation must be licensed as real estate sales associates or brokers. As noted earlier, real estate services that require licensure include the sale, exchange, purchase, rental, appraisal, auction, and advertising of real property, business enterprises, and business opportunities, and the offer to perform any of these services. Services include procuring sellers, buyers, lessors, and lessees.

Individuals exempt from licensure

The following individuals are not required to hold a Florida real estate license:

- owners who sell, exchange, or lease their own properties
- corporations, partnerships, trusts, joint ventures, or other entities or officers, partners, or directors of entities that sell, exchange, or lease their own properties, unless an agent, employee, or independent contractor is employed and paid by the entity on a transactional basis to sell, exchange, or lease property; however, partners must be licensed if their percent of sale profits are higher than their individual percent of ownership in the business
- any person acting as an attorney in fact who is authorized to act in another person's place to execute contracts or conveyances
- any attorney at law performing his or her duties without being compensated for performing real estate services
- any certified public accountant performing his or her duties
- any personal representative, receiver, trustee, or general or special magistrate appointed by a will or court order
- any trustee acting under a deed of trust or trust agreement
- any salaried employee of an apartment community who works in an onsite rental office to lease apartments for any time period and who is not paid on a transactional basis
- any apartment community tenant who receives a referral fee of $50 or less for referring a new tenant to the community
- any salaried manager of a condominium or cooperative apartment complex who handles individual unit rentals for periods of 1 year or less, not paid per transaction
- any owner occupant of a timeshare period selling the period
- any licensed or certified appraiser performing appraisal duties
- any person or entity who is paid to rent or advertise for rent transient lodgings, such as hotels or motels

- any dealer registered under the securities and exchange act who sells, buys, exchanges, or rents business enterprises to accredited investors
- any employee of a real estate developer who is paid a salary but not paid on a transactional basis
- any individual who rents lots in mobile home parks or recreational travel parks
- any individual who sells cemetery plots

2 Real Estate License Law and Qualifications for Licensure
Snapshot Review

**HISTORY AND
PURPOSES OF REAL
ESTATE LICENSE LAWS**

**History of Florida's real
estate license law**
- Chapter 475 passed in 1923 as first FL real estate law
- FREC created in 1925

**Purpose of
regulation**
- protect consumers
- caveat emptor overturned in 1985; sellers must disclose property defects even if not asked

**Important FL real estate
statutes and rules**
- several enacted to protect consumers and to allow qualified individuals to enter real estate profession

LICENSE CATEGORIES

Broker
- licensed to perform real estate services for compensation
- real estate services: sale, exchange, purchase, rental, appraisal, auction, advertising; procuring sellers, buyers, lessors, or lessees

Sales associate
- licensed to perform real estate services under direction of broker

Broker associate
- same license as broker but works under direction of broker

**GENERAL LICENSURE
PROVISIONS**

General qualifications
- 18 years old, high school education, good character, competence, Social Security number; US citizenship not necessary

Required disclosures
- disciplinary or criminal history
- aliases

Reasons for denial
- previous license discipline; performed real estate activities without a license

**APPLICATION
REQUIREMENTS**

Fees
- several fees charged; some waived for military members and veterans, spouses, and surviving spouses

Application form
- must use DBPR form, submit additional documentation

Background checks
- submit to background check, provide fingerprints; provide information about criminal history

Omissions
- applicant to be notified within 30 days of errors and omissions on application

Application approval
- DBPR to approve or deny application within 90 days of receipt; applicant has right to appeal denial

Appealing denials
- accept denial; petition for informal or formal hearing to challenge denial

Application validity
- application valid for 2 years; prelicense course valid for 2 years for licensure exam

Nonresident applications	•	detailed later
Course requirements	•	applicant to complete courses with 8 or fewer misses, to pass end-of-course exam with 70% score or retake once in a year
	•	courses to be taken at school, distance learning, correspondence if hardship
	•	4-year degree substitutes for prelicense course
Education exemptions	•	exempt: attorneys; those with 4-year real estate degrees; those with mutual recognition agreement
Public records	•	made or received in accordance with law or ordinance in official transaction

SALES ASSOCIATE LICENSE REQUIREMENTS

General requirements	•	SS number, application approval, fees paid, meet age, education, character, competency, background requirements
Prelicense course	•	60-hour course, 3-hour exam with 70% pass score
State license examination	•	within 2 years of course completion; pass with 75% score; print and activate license
	•	retake failed exam unlimited times; may review incorrect answers
	•	license issued in inactive status; licensee must associate with broker before performing services

BROKER LICENSE REQUIREMENTS

General requirements	•	SS number, application approval, fees paid, meet age, education, character, competency, background requirements; complete sales associate post license education
Experience requirement	•	active sales associate license for 2 years within past 5 years; worked under broker
Prelicense course	•	69-hour course and 3-hour exam with 70% pass score
State license examination	•	within 2 years of course completion; pass with 75% score; print and activate license
	•	retake failed exam unlimited times; may review incorrect answers
	•	issued as inactive; activate by filing form

NONRESIDENT LICENSE REQUIREMENTS

Florida resident defined	•	reside in FL for 4 months or intend to continue to reside for 4 months
Nonresident application requirements	•	hold license in resident state; submit certificate of license history; meet FL application requirements
Mutual recognition	•	agreement of FL and another state to recognize other state's prelicense education and require laws and rules exam
	•	reciprocity allows one state's licensees to obtain another state's license without meeting all requirements; FL has no reciprocity with other states

Occupational Opportunity Act

- reciprocal license for military, spouses, surviving spouses, low income licensed in another state; prelicense course and exam waived

LICENSE INFORMATION; REGISTRATION

License information

- identity, contact, license type, number, dates
- license serves as prima facia evidence of valid licensure
- license issued after applicant meets all requirements

Registration

- all licensees to register with FREC; sales & broker associates to register under broker

LICENSE RENEWAL EDUCATION

Post licensure requirement

- sales associates – 45-hour course and end-of-course exam with 75% pass score
- brokers – 60-hour course and end-of-course exam with 75% pass score

Continuing education

- 14 hours every 2-year license period to include 3 hours of Core Law & 3 hours of Business Ethics

Reactivation education

- involuntary inactive status for 12-24 months can reactivate with 28-hour course and exam with 70% pass score

ACTIVITIES REQUIRING LICENSURE; EXEMPTIONS

Individuals required to be licensed

- anyone who performs real estate services for compensation

Individuals exempt from licensure

- owners selling own property; attorney in fact or at law; CPA, trustee; certain paid employees; timeshare owner occupant; transient lodging employee, cemetery sales

SECTION TWO: Real Estate License Law and Qualifications for Licensure

Section Quiz

1. Which of the following occurred in 1923 to protect public welfare regarding real estate transactions?

   a. The Florida Real Estate Commission was established.
   b. The Department of Business and Professional Regulation established the Division of Real Estate.
   c. The Florida Legislature passed F. S. Chapter 475 as the first real estate license law.
   d. The Florida Real Estate Commission established the first license law.

2. A property seller must disclose defects in the property

   a. even if the seller has no knowledge of the defects.
   b. only if a property inspector uncovers a defect.
   c. if the defect materially affects the value of the property.
   d. as required under caveat emptor.

3. Which Florida statute is known as the Administrative Procedure Act and provides procedures for government agencies to exercise their specified authority, including rule making?

   a. Chapter 120
   b. Chapter 61J2
   c. Chapter 455
   d. Chapter 20

4. Which of the following is a general requirement to obtain real estate licensure in Florida?

   a. Must be at least 21 years old
   b. Must disclose any criminal history
   c. Must be a U.S. citizen
   d. Must have a 4-year college degree

5. Which of the following fees may be waived for a member of the U.S. armed forces?

   a. Real Estate Recovery Fund fee
   b. Application fee
   c. Fingerprint processing fee
   d. Initial licensing fee

6. Which of the following statements is true?

   a. An applicant with an expunged criminal conviction does not need to disclose that conviction.
   b. An applicant who is currently on probation for a criminal conviction will not be placed on the Summary of Applicants list.
   c. An applicant's fingerprints are sent to the FBI for a criminal background check.
   d. If an applicant has a criminal history, he or she will automatically be denied licensure.

7. An applicant must be approved or denied within _____ days of application receipt.

   a. 90
   b. 60
   c. 45
   d. 30

8. Under what circumstances may pre-license class hours be made up?

   a. Only with Commission approval
   b. If any student misses more than 8 classroom hours
   c. If a student misses more than 8 hours due to an economic hardship
   d. If a student misses more than 8 hours due to illness

9. Attorneys in good standing with the Florida Bar

   a. must complete pre-license education and pass the state exam.
   b. must complete pre-license education but are exempt from the state exam.
   c. are exempt from pre-license education but must take the state exam.
   d. must complete pre-license education and pass the end-of-course exam.

10. Sales associate applicants must

   a. complete 72 hours of pre-license education.
   b. pass the end-of-course exam with a score of 70% or higher.
   c. pass the state license exam with a score of 75% or higher.
   d. pass the state license exam on the first

attempt.

11. Which of the following statements is false?

    a. Applicants who fail the state license exam
       may retake it only once within a year of
       failing it.
    b. Applicants who fail the state license exam
       may retake it as many times as necessary to
       pass it within 2 years of failing it.
    c. Applicants who pass the state license exam are
       issued a license in inactive status.
    d. Sales associate applicants who pass the state
       exam must become associated with a specific
       broker.

12. Which of the following is a requirement for
    a broker license but not a requirement for a
    sales associate license?

    a. Prelicense coursework
    b. Post-license coursework
    c. 4-year college degree
    d. 2-year experience requirement

13. A broker pre-license course includes

    a. the fundamentals of real estate appraising.
    b. 75 classroom hours.
    c. 73 classroom hours.
    d. 60-minute classroom hours.

14. A Florida resident is someone who

    a. plans to move to Florida within the next year.
    b. was born in Florida regardless of where the
       person now resides.
    c. has resided in Florida continuously for 4 or
       more months within the previous year.
    d. owns property in Florida whether or not the
       person lives on the property.

15. Florida provides reciprocity licensure for

    a. nonresidents from states with whom Florida
       has a reciprocity agreement.
    b. active duty military personnel who are
       licensed in another state.
    c. any low-income individuals from another
       state.
    d. non U.S. citizens.

16. Who must register with the FREC?

    a. Corporations who wish to become licensed
    b. Only sales associates
    c. Only brokers
    d. Every licensed person or entity

17. Brokers must complete _____ hours of post-
    license education.

    a. 60
    b. 45
    c. 30
    d. 0

18. When must post-license education be
    completed?

    a. During each license period after the initial
       renewal
    b. During the first license period prior to license
       expiration
    c. Prior to the license expiration date of every
       license period
    d. Within 1 year of initial licensure

19. If a licensee completes 3 hours of Core Law
    education each year during a license period,
    how many additional continuing education
    hours must be completed for that period?

    a. 14 hours
    b. 11 hours
    c. 8 hours
    d. 6 hours

20. Which of the following is NOT a
    requirement of reactivating an involuntary
    inactive license?

    a. Completing a 28-hour education course
    b. Passing an end-of-course exam with a 70%
       score
    c. Having a hardship
    d. Attending at least 90% of the instructional
       hours

3 Real Estate License Law and Commission Rules

Department of Business and Professional Regulation
Division of Real Estate
The Florida Real Estate Commission
License Renewal and Status
Multiple and Group Licenses

Learning Objectives

- Describe the composition, appointment and member qualifications of the Florida Real Estate Commission
- Define the powers and duties of the Commission
- Describe the scope and function of the DBPR and the DRE
- Explain the different licensure statuses
- Distinguish between active and inactive license status
- Describe the regulations regarding involuntarily inactive status
- Distinguish between multiple and group licenses

Key Terms

active/inactive
canceled
cease to be in force
current mailing address
current status
group license
involuntarily inactive

license authority voided
multiple licenses
null and void
probation
promulgates
voluntarily inactive

DEPARTMENT OF BUSINESS AND PROFESSIONAL REGULATION

Organizational structure
Definitions
Legislative intent
Department powers and duties
Licensing examinations

Organizational structure

The Department of Business and Professional Regulation (DBPR; Department) is the Florida State agency responsible for licensing and regulating businesses and professionals, including real estate licensees. The DBPR's mission is to license efficiently and regulate fairly.

The DBPR was created and structured by Florida Statutes and is governed by Chapter 120, F.S. as part of the government's executive branch. The head of the Department is the Secretary of Business and Professional Regulation, who is appointed by the governor and confirmed by the state senate. The Department's main office is in Tallahassee, Florida.

The Department consists of separate divisions for each of several professions under its administration, including the Division of Real Estate (discussed in an upcoming section). Other divisions relevant to real estate include the following:

> ▶ **Division of Professions** – regulates education courses and license examinations
>
> This division is tasked with providing, contracting, and approving services for all examinations, including development, administration, scoring, reporting, and evaluation.

> ▶ **Division of Service Operations** – processes license applications and related fees, issues licenses and renewal notifications, and responds to licensee and public inquiries
>
> The director of this division is appointed by the Secretary of the DBPR.

> ▶ **Division of Florida Condominiums, Timeshares, and Mobile Homes** – provides oversight of the Florida residential communities, specifically condominiums, cooperatives, timeshares, and mobile home parks
>
> This division provides education, resolution of complaints, mediation, arbitration, and developer disclosure for Florida residents of these types of dwellings. It also handles homeowner association election disputes and board member recalls.

Definitions

Board – any board, commission, or other entity created by statute within the DBPR that is authorized to exercise regulatory or rulemaking functions, such as the Florida Real Estate Commission.

Consumer member – a person appointed to serve on a specific board who is not, and never has been, a member or practitioner of the specific profession regulated by the board.

Involuntarily inactive status – the licensure status that results when a license is not renewed at the end of the license period.

Voluntarily inactive status – the licensure status that results when a licensee applies to the DBPR to be placed on inactive status and has paid the related fee.

Profession – any activity, occupation, or vocation that is regulated by the DBPR through the Divisions of Professions or Real Estate.

Legislative intent

The legislative intent in establishing the DBPR and related statutes is twofold. First, the legislature wanted to protect the public from unregulated business practices. The legislature also did not want to place unreasonable restrictions on qualified individuals who sought to practice one of the regulated professions. In striving to balance those two goals, the Florida Legislature and the DBPR have identified three situations that require regulations to be applied (as listed in Chapter 455.201).

- ▶ when the profession's unregulated practice could harm or endanger the health, safety, and welfare of the public, and when the potential for such harm is recognizable and clearly outweighs any anticompetitive impact which may result from regulation
- ▶ when the public is not effectively protected by other means, including, but not limited to, other state statutes, local ordinances, or federal legislation
- ▶ when less restrictive means of regulation are not available

The legislature's intent in establishing these regulations prohibited the DBPR from creating unreasonably restrictive standards for professional licensure and prohibited the DBPR or any board or commission from creating an economic condition that would unreasonably restrict competition or job creation or retention.

Department powers and duties

The DBPR's duties and powers include the following:

- ▶ adopt rules for license renewals
- ▶ select investigators who meet established criteria
- ▶ investigate consumer complaints, including issuing subpoenas
- ▶ issue cease and desist orders to individuals practicing without a license
- ▶ issue citations to licensees
- ▶ under court order, suspend or deny licensure for anyone out of compliance with a support order or other legal order; issue or reinstate licensure when the order has been satisfied
- ▶ require all proceedings regarding licensing or discipline to be electronically recorded
- ▶ approve licensure applications that meet established requirements

Licensing examinations

Under the DBPR and with the advice of the FREC, the Division of Professions has the duty to set up services for developing, preparing, administering, scoring and reporting, and evaluating all examinations. The DBPR also works with the Divisions of Professions, Service Operations, and Real Estate to ensure all examinations sufficiently and reliably measure an applicant's ability to successfully practice the profession for which the applicant is being tested.

The Department also provides the procedures for an applicant to review incorrectly answered questions on a failed exam. The review is completed at the applicant's expense.

Records of each applicant's exam are to be maintained for at least 2 years. While exam scores are to be confidential, applicants may waive the confidentiality in writing.

DIVISION OF REAL ESTATE

Organizational structure
Duties

Organizational structure

The Division of Real Estate (DRE) is one division within the Department of Business and Professional Regulation. The DRE is headed by a director who is appointed by the Secretary of the DBPR and approved by a majority of the FREC. The DRE's staff is employed to support functions of the FREC. Funding for the DRE's real estate regulation comes from fees and assessments collected by the FREC. Florida law mandates that the DRE's offices are to be located in Orlando, Florida.

Both the Florida Real Estate Appraisal Board and the Florida Real Estate Commission were established within the DRE.

Duties

The DRE carries out the decisions and policies of the FREC. It is responsible for examining, licensing, and regulating individual licensees, corporations, and schools in Florida. Its duties also include recordkeeping, legal and investigative services, and other services in Chapter 455 which are related to Florida's real estate license law.

FLORIDA REAL ESTATE COMMISSION

Purpose of regulation
Rules governing internal organization and operation
General structure
Duties and powers

Purpose of regulation

As with all real estate laws and statutes, the purpose of the FREC's rules is to protect the public from fraud and incompetent practices. The DRE provides administrative support to the Commission in providing this protection.

Rules governing internal organization and operation

Chapter 61J2-20 of the FREC administrative codes lays out the rules that govern the organization and operation structure of the Commission.

- A probable cause panel must be established to determine if probable cause exists to charge a licensee with a license law or FREC rules violation. The panel must include one current member of the Commission and can include one former member.
- Any member of the Commission who misses three consecutive meetings or 50 percent or more of the meetings, all without advance notice, within 1 year will be removed from the Commission. That member's position will be considered vacant.
- The main office of the Commission is to be in Orlando, Florida.
- The DBPR is the designated reporter for all rendered orders of the Commission and maintains those orders in Tallahassee, Florida.
- Members of the public may notify the Commission in writing of their wish to be heard on a specific subject and then be provided 3 minutes to speak at an official Commission meeting.

General structure

Composition and qualifications of members. The Commission is made up of seven members who are appointed by the Governor and confirmed by the Senate. Of these seven members,

- four must be licensed brokers who have held active licenses for the preceding 5 years
- one must be a licensed broker or sales associate who has held an active license for the preceding 2 years
- two must not be, nor ever have been, licensed brokers or sales associates.

At least one of the members must be 60 years or older. Of the seven members, one is elected annually from the membership to serve as chairperson and a second to serve as vice-chairperson.

All members are appointed for 4-year staggered terms, with not more than two members' terms expiring on the same year. A new member may be appointed to fill a vacancy created during an unexpired term. While there is no limit on the total number of years a member may serve, he or she may serve the remaining portion of a previous member's unexpired term and then not more than two consecutive terms of his or her own. Members also may not hold any other public office while serving on the FREC.

Legal counsel. If the Commission obtains approval from the Attorney General, it may hire an independent attorney to provide legal advice on a specific matter. An attorney working for the commission is not allowed to prosecute a specific matter and also provide legal services to the commission regarding the same matter.

Meetings and minutes. The FREC meets monthly with each meeting typically lasting for 2 days and each Commissioner being paid a per diem rate rather than a salary and reimbursement for out-of-pocket business expenses. There must be one annual meeting wherein the members elect a chairperson and vice-chairperson. Meetings are held at the DRE's main offices in Orlando. A four-member quorum must be present.

Duties and powers

Specific areas of responsibility. The FREC has the power and duty to enforce the license law. In doing so, it is authorized to

- establish rules and regulations to execute the provisions of law
- decide questions of practice that come up during Commission proceedings
- investigate complaints against licensees
- certify or refuse to certify applicants as qualified for licensure
- issue, deny, suspend, or revoke real estate licenses
- keep records

Fees. The commission has the authority to establish fees which an applicant or licensee is to pay for application, examination, reexamination, initial licensing and license renewal, certification and recertification, reinstatement, record making, and recordkeeping.

By the end of September each year, the Commission is to perform a review to ensure that the fees collected are adequate to cover all anticipated costs and to maintain a reasonable cash balance. If the fees will not be adequate to cover the costs and cash balance, the Commission may increase the appropriate fees or assess a one-time fee to cover the deficiency. If the collected fees will be more than required for a cash balance, the Commission may decrease the appropriate fees.

Rulemaking. The Commission has the authority to pass rules to enable it to perform its duties. Such rules make up Chapter 61J2 of the Florida Administrative Code. The Commission has adopted and uses a seal to authenticate its proceedings. Printed or written copies under the seal of the Commission are considered prima facie evidence of their existence and substance, and the courts are mandated to recognize the rules.

Because FREC does not make laws but instead makes rules to ensure the laws are followed, FREC is considered to be quasi-legislative.

Education. The Commission has a duty to prescribe or approve real estate education courses for applicants, licensees, and instructors concerning the ethical, legal, and business principles that should govern their conduct.
This duty includes courses for prelicense, post-license, and continuing education requirements.

To encourage this education, the Commission may publish and sell educational materials to applicants, licensees, and members of the public. The Commission also has a duty to regulate proprietary real estate schools and non-credit courses offered by institutes of higher education and technical centers.

Discipline. The Commission has the authority to deny an application for licensure or renewal, to place a licensee on probation, to suspend or revoke a license, to administer fines, and to issue reprimands if it determines the applicant or licensee has

- been guilty of fraud or dishonesty
- violated a legal or contractual duty
- failed to account for or deliver someone else's personal property
- been guilty of any real estate-related crime or a crime involving moral turpitude
- had a license suspended, revoked, or acted against or had an application for licensure denied in any jurisdiction
- in any way violated any Florida license law

The Commission is required to report any known criminal violations of license law to the State Attorney. It must also notify the Division of Florida Condominiums, Timeshares, and Mobile Homes of any disciplinary action taken against an associated licensee.

Since FREC has the authority to act as judge and jury for violation of F.S. 475, it is considered to be quasi-judicial.

In summary, FREC's duties are executive, quasi-legislative, and quasi-judicial.

LICENSE RENEWAL & STATUSES

License renewal
License statuses

License renewal

Issue and expiration. Licenses are issued for 2-year licensure periods, at the end of which the license needs to be renewed to prevent it from expiring. All licenses expire on, and must be renewed by, either March 31 or September 30, depending on the date of issue. Consequently, the initial licensure period will be no less than 18 and no greater than 24 months. To calculate when the initial license expires, add 2 years to the last expiration date-- March 31st or September 30th -- before the date of issue, and add 2 years.

For example, if John's sales associate license was initially issued on February 28, 2019, a 2-year license period would mean his license would expire at midnight on February 27, 2021. However, since all licenses expire on March 31 or September 30, John's license would expire on September 30, 2020, providing John with 19 months of initial licensure, thereby complying with the 18 to 24-month requirement. Once John renews his license the first time, each license period after that will be 24 months (2 years), with John's license expiring on September 30 each time.

Postlicense education. The licensee must complete the required post-license course prior to renewing his or her initial license. After the initial license period, the licensee must complete continuing education each license period prior to renewing the license.

License renewal and status. The DBPR sends a license renewal notice to the licensee at least 90 days before the license expiration date. The notice is sent to both active and inactive licensees at the last known address or e-mail address.

The licensee then must submit a completed renewal application, renewal fee, and proof of completing either the post-license or the continuing education courses. The licensee is to indicate whether he or she wants to renew in active or inactive status (discussed in an upcoming section). Once the licensee has met all renewal requirements, the DBPR will issue a renewed license with the appropriate expiration date.

If the licensee does not renew by the expiration date, the license automatically becomes involuntarily inactive and may only be renewed when applicable requirements are met (discussed in an upcoming section). The license is deemed delinquent for the following license period. The licensee is not allowed to practice real estate while on inactive status. If the licensee was on active status at the license expiration date, he or she may renew the license within 24 months by meeting renewal requirements and paying a late fee. If the licensee fails to renew within that time period, the license is rendered void.

Members of armed forces. Active duty members of the U.S. armed forces who are in good standing with the FREC are exempt from license renewal requirements. This exemption is extended to 2 years after the member is discharged from active duty. However, if the member is engaged in real estate for profit in the private sector within Florida while on active duty and for 2 years after discharge from active duty, he or she must meet all renewal requirements but is exempt from paying the renewal fee.

The military member's spouse or the surviving spouse of a member who died while on active duty is also exempt from license renewal requirements if the member's active duty is outside of Florida. The spouse must be in good standing with the FREC and not be practicing in the private sector for profit. This exemption is in effect while the member is on active duty and for 6 months after the member's discharge.

License status

Active status. Sales associate or broker licenses are initially issued on inactive status. Since licensees are allowed to practice real estate only if their licenses are on active status, they must activate their licenses before they offer or provide real estate services. Their licenses must also be on active status before the licensee can accept commission or other fees for a real estate service.

A sales associate can activate the license by registering under an employing broker or by having the employing broker activate the license through the broker's online account. Anyone who practices without an active status license is violating license law and may be disciplined. At any time after a license is issued, the licensee may decide to place the active license on inactive status. During the license renewal process, the licensee may choose to renew in either active or inactive status. Again, while on inactive status, the licensee may not practice real estate activities.

Voluntary inactive status. There are multiple ways a license may become voluntarily inactive: the licensee does not activate the license when it is initially issued; the licensee chooses to renew an active license on inactive status; or a licensee requests the DBPR place the license on inactive status. Most often, licensees choose voluntary inactive status because they have decided not to practice real estate for a period of time.

When a license is in voluntary inactive status, the licensee may reactivate the license at any time by applying to the DBPR, paying a reactivation fee, and meeting all post-license or continuing education requirements.

Just as with active licenses, voluntarily inactive licenses must be renewed every two years to remain valid. The inactive licensee needs to apply for renewal on inactive status, complete 14 hours of continuing education for each 2- year period the license was inactive, and pay the renewal fee.

Involuntary inactive status. If the licensee does not renew the active or voluntarily inactive license by the expiration date, the license status automatically becomes involuntarily inactive. The license is also deemed delinquent.

The DBPR will send a notice of involuntary inactive status at least 90 days prior to the license expiration date. If a broker's license is suspended or revoked, all sales associates and broker associates registered under that broker will automatically become involuntarily inactive. Their licenses will remain in that status until the broker is again reinstated or until they register under a new broker.

If these licensees decide not to practice real estate, they may change their licenses' involuntarily inactive status to voluntarily inactive through their online DBPR account.

Once in involuntarily inactive status for nonrenewal, the license can be renewed if the licensee applies to the DBPR, pays the renewal fee for each year the license was involuntarily inactive plus any associated late fees, and completes the required continuing education based on the time frame of inactive status.

The licensee can renew as either active or voluntarily inactive but must do so within 2 years of becoming involuntarily inactive. If the licensee fails to renew during the 2 years, the license automatically expires and becomes null and void.

Null and void license status. A license may become null and void under any of the following conditions.

> ▶ The sales associate does not complete post-license education prior to the renewal date for the initial licensure period. To reengage in real estate activities, the individual must requalify for licensure by retaking the prelicensure education and exams and passing the state examination.

> ▶ A licensee on involuntary inactive status does not renew the license within 2 years of becoming involuntarily inactive. The FREC may reinstate this license if the individual applies to the Commission within 6 months of becoming null and void, shows proof of a physical or financial hardship, completes continuing education, and pays all required fees.

> If the licensee receives the hardship extension, the license will remain null and void until the individual submits a reinstatement application, related fees, and proof of reactivation education completion.

> ▶ A license is revoked for disciplinary reasons. Revoked licenses may never be reinstated, and the individual may never reapply for licensure.

> ▶ A licensee relinquishes the license unrelated to any disciplinary actions or investigations. The licensee must notify the DBPR of the intent to relinquish the license.

Null and void licenses are those that no longer exist unless they are reactivated under the above allowable conditions.

Reporting address changes. A broker must notify the Commission within 10 days of any business address change. Until the Commission is notified of the address change, the broker's license ceases to be in force. While the license is in that status, the broker may not engage in real estate activities.

The notice of change of address must include the names of any associates who are no longer employed by the broker. The notice will also serve as change of address notification for associates still employed by the broker. These licensees can notify the Commission of the changes on a Commission-provided form or through their online portal.

All licensees must notify the DBPR in writing of their *current residential mailing addresses and current email address.* They must notify the Department within 10 days of any changes of residential mailing addresses. Failure to do so can result in a disciplinary fine.

Any Florida resident licensee who becomes a nonresident by moving out of the state is required to notify the Commission within 60 days of the change of residency. If the licensee wishes to continue practicing in Florida, he or she must comply with all nonresident requirements. Failure to notify the Commission and comply with the requirements is a violation of license law and can result in disciplinary penalties.

MULTIPLE AND GROUP LICENSES

Multiple licenses. Brokers are required to hold a separate individual license for each entity or business they serve. A broker who serves multiple entities needs multiple licenses. The broker must show that the multiple licenses are necessary to conduct the brokerage business and that the licenses will not be harmful or prejudicial to anyone. Each license must be renewed separately.

The Commission may deny a multiple license for the same reasons it can deny individual licenses. Any discipline against the broker's primary license will apply equally to his or her multiple licenses. Multiple licenses are not transferable to new relationships unless the broker ends all current relationships at the same time and then moves only one license to a new relationship.

Sales associates and broker associates are not eligible for multiple licenses because they are only allowed to work for one broker or brokerage at a time.

Group licenses. Property owner/developers are exempt from licensure. Consequently, they employ licensed sales associates or broker associates to sell their properties. Sometimes, an owner/developer owns properties through multiple business entities with different names. When those entities are connected (for example, subsidiaries) so that they are owned or controlled by one individual or group of individuals, any licensee employed by the owner/developer may obtain a group license to be eligible to sell for all of the entities.

Remember that a sales associate or broker associate may only be employed by one broker or owner/developer at a time. The group license allows the licensee to be employed by the one owner/developer but still sell properties for multiple entities as long as they are all owned or controlled by the employing owner/developer.

3 Real Estate License Law and Commission Rules Snapshot Review

DEPARTMENT OF BUSINESS AND PROFESSIONAL REGULATION

Organizational structure
- structured by F.S. Title IV, Section 20 and governed by F.S. Chapter 120
- headed by Secretary of BPR with main office in Tallahassee
- consists of several divisions, including those related to real estate

Legislative intent
- protect public and not allow unreasonable restrictions on those seeking to practice
- regulations necessary when unregulated practice could harm public; when other means do not protect public; when less restrictive regulations do not exist

Powers & duties
- establish licensure rules; investigate complaints; impose penalties; approve licensure

Licensing examinations
- exam prep and services set up by Division of Professions under DBPR, assuring that exams measure applicant's ability to practice
- provides exam review procedures
- exams scores are confidential and kept for 2 years

DIVISION OF REAL ESTATE

Organizational structure
- director appointed by DBPR Secretary; approved by FREC; staff to support FREC; offices in Orlando; funded by FREC fees and assessments; established FREC

Duties
- carry out FREC policies; exams, licenses, regulates licensees; records; investigations

FREC

Purpose of regulation
- protect public from fraud and incompetent practices

Rules
- establish probable cause panel; remove FREC members for excessive absences; office in Orlando; DBPR reporter for FREC orders; provide public speaking time at meetings

General structure
- 4 licensed brokers for past 5 years; 1 licensed broker or sales associate for past 2 years; 2 members of public never licensed; all appointed by governor, confirmed by senate
- 1 to be 60 years or older; members elect chairperson and vice-chairperson; 4-year terms
- may hire attorney as approved by Attorney General
- monthly meetings with one annual meeting; quorum required; members paid per diem

Duties & powers
- enforce license law; investigate complaints; issue, deny, suspend, or revoke licenses; decide questions of practice; keep records
- establish fees; create rules; prescribe education courses; discipline licensees or applicants

LICENSE RENEWALS, STATUSES, TYPES

License renewal

- renew for 2-year periods; initial period 18-24 months; renew March 31 or September 30; complete post-license or continuing education; involuntary inactive status for nonrenewal
- renewal provisions or fees waived for military members and spouses of out-of-state members or deceased members

License status

- active required for practicing
- voluntary inactive when initial license not activated, when licensee chooses status at renewal, when licensee requests; reactivate by applying, paying fee, completing CE; renew every 2 years
- involuntary inactive for nonrenewal; reactivate by applying, paying fee, completing CE, all within 2 years of involuntary inactive status
- null and void for not completing post-license course, for not renewing involuntary inactive license within 2 years, for revoked license, for voluntary license relinquish
- ceases to be in force when business address changes; must report within 10 days
- licensee to notify DBPR of current mailing address or change of address within 10 days
- FL resident licensee becoming nonresident to notify FREC within 60 days

Multiple and group licenses

- multiple - brokers who serve multiple business entities need a license for each entity; sales associates and broker associates not eligible for multiple licenses
- group - for sales associates or broker associates working for owner/developer who owns properties through multiple business entities that are connected and controlled by owner

SECTION THREE: Real Estate License Law and Commission Rules

Section Quiz

1. The DBPR is governed by

   a. F.S. Title IV, Section 20.
   b. F.S. Chapter 455.
   c. F.S. Chapter 120.
   d. F.S. Chapter 475.

2. The legislative intent in establishing the DBPR and its related statutes was to

   a. restrict competition in the real estate profession.
   b. create restrictive standards for professional licensure.
   c. place restrictions on qualified individuals who wanted to practice the real estate profession.
   d. protect the public from unregulated business practices.

3. Which of the following does NOT investigate complaints against licensees?

   a. Florida Real Estate Commission
   b. Division of Real Estate
   c. Division of Professions
   d. Department of Business and Professional Regulation

4. Records of each applicant's examination are to be kept

   a. for 2 years.
   b. until the applicant passes the exam.
   c. until the licensee's first license renewal.
   d. for 7 years.

5. The function of the Division of Real Estate is to

   a. collect fees and assessments from licensure applicants.
   b. support the Florida Real Estate Commission.
   c. provide services for all examinations.
   d. oversee license renewal procedures.

6. The probable cause panel

   a. imposes penalties on licensees who have violated license law.
   b. determines if an applicant qualifies for licensure.
   c. must include one current member of the FREC.
   d. must not include former members of the FREC.

7. The FREC includes

   a. five members who hold real estate licenses.
   b. four members of the general public who have never been licensed brokers.
   c. seven members who have held broker licenses for the previous 5 years.
   d. two members who have held sales associate licenses for the preceding 2 years.

8. Which of the following statements is true?

   a. At least one member of the FREC must be at least 65 years old.
   b. The governor appoints the FREC chairperson and vice-chairperson annually.
   c. Members of the FREC must not serve more than two consecutive terms.
   d. All FREC members serve 2-year staggered terms.

9. If the fees to be collected by the FREC will be more than required for a cash balance, the FREC may

   a. refund the difference to the individuals who paid the fees.
   b. place the excess funds into an account for economically challenged licensees and applicants.
   c. cease collecting fees for the following 2 years.
   d. decrease the amount of appropriate fees to be collected.

10. If a licensee criminally violates license law, the FREC is required to

    a. report the violation to the State Attorney.
    b. notify the Attorney General of the violation.
    c. place the licensee on probation.
    d. impose a civil fine on the licensee.

11. All licenses expire

    a. on April 30 or October 31.
    b. on March 31 or September 30.
    c. 2 years after the date of license issuance.
    d. on January 1 every 2 years.

12. Sally's first sales associate license was issued on March 15, 2019. When will her license expire?

    a. September 30, 2021
    b. March 15, 2021
    c. September 30, 2020
    d. March 31, 2021

13. Sally's first sales associate license was issued on March 15, 2019. What happens if Sally does not complete her post-license education before her license expiration date?

    a. Sally has 2 additional years to complete the education and renew her license.
    b. She will be charged a late renewal fee.
    c. Her license will become involuntarily inactive until she completes the post-license education.
    d. Sally's license will become null and void.

14. Sally is a member of the U.S. Navy. What must she do to renew her real estate license?

    a. Complete continuing education and apply for renewal
    b. Apply for renewal and pay the renewal fee
    c. Complete continuing education, apply for renewal, and pay the renewal fee
    d. Sally is exempt from renewal requirements.

15. If a licensee does not renew an active license by the expiration date, what happens?

    a. The license becomes voluntarily inactive.
    b. The license becomes null and void.
    c. The license becomes involuntarily inactive.
    d. Nothing, the licensee is automatically given 2 years to renew the license.

16. If a licensee commits a criminal violation of license law, the FREC must

    a. criminally prosecute the licensee.
    b. immediately revoke the licensee's license.
    c. report the violation to the State Attorney.
    d. notify the police.

4 Authorized Relationships, Duties, And Disclosure

Essentials of Real Estate Agency
Fiduciary Duties
Brokerage Relationship Disclosure Act

Learning Objectives

- Describe which provisions of the Brokerage Relationship Disclosure Act apply only to residential real estate sales and list types of real estate activities that are exempt from the disclosure requirements
- Define residential transaction
- Distinguish among nonrepresentation, single agent and transaction broker
- List and describe the duties owed in the various authorized relationships
- Compare and contrast the fiduciary duties owed in a single agent relationship and the duties owed in a transaction broker relationship
- Describe the disclosure procedures for the various authorized relationships
- Describe the required content and format of the various disclosure forms
- Explain the procedure for the transition from a single agent to a transaction broker
- Describe the disclosure requirements for non-residential transactions where the buyer and seller have assets of $1 million or more
- List the events that will cause an authorized relationship to be terminated

Key Terms

agent
caveat emptor
consent to transition
customer
designated sales associate
dual agent
fiduciary
general agent
limited representation

nonrepresentation
principal
residential sale
single agent
special agent
subagency
transaction broker

ESSENTIALS OF REAL ESTATE AGENCY

Historical perspective
Basic roles
Types of agency
Creating an agency relationship
Terminating an agency relationship

Historical perspective

The most primary of relationships in real estate brokerage is that between broker and client, the relationship known in law as the **agency relationship**. The laws controlling agency grow out of two types of law: common law and statutory law. Common law is based on customary usage and the decrees and judgments of courts. Statutory law is the law written by legislatures. A body of law, generally called the **law of agency,** defines and regulates the legal roles of this relationship. The parties to the relationship are the **principal** (a client), the **agent** (a broker), and the **customer** (a third party).

The laws of agency are distinct from laws of contracts, although the two groups of laws interact with each other. For example, the listing agreement -- a contract -establishes an agency relationship. Thus the relationship is subject to contract law. However, agency law dictates how the relationship will achieve its purposes, regardless of what the listing contract states.

The essence of the agency relationship is *trust, confidence, and mutual good faith*. The principal trusts the agent to exercise the utmost skill and care in fulfilling the authorized activity, and to promote the principal's best interests. The agent undertakes to strive in good faith to achieve the desired objective, and to fulfill the fiduciary duties.

It is important to understand that the agency relationship does *not* require compensation or any form of consideration. Nor does compensation define an agency relationship: a party other than the principal may compensate the agent.

Basic roles

In an agency relationship, a principal hires an agent as a *fiduciary* to perform a desired service on the principal's behalf. As a fiduciary, the agent has a legal obligation to fulfill specific *fiduciary duties* throughout the term of the relationship.

The **principal,** or **client**, is the party who hires the agent. The agent works *for* the client. The principal may be a seller, a buyer, a landlord, or a tenant.

The **agent** is the fiduciary of the principal, hired to perform the authorized work and bound to fulfill fiduciary duties. In real estate brokerage the agent *must* be a licensed broker.

The **customer** or **prospect** is a third party in the transaction whom the agent does not represent. The agent works *with* a customer in fulfilling the client's objectives. A seller, buyer, landlord, or tenant may be a customer. A third party who is a potential customer is a **prospect**. Another example of a nonrepresentative relationship is working with a For Sale By Owner (FSBO) prospect.

Types of agency

According to the level of authority delegated to the agent, there are three types of agency: *universal, general, and special.*

Universal agency. In a universal agency relationship, the principal empowers the agent to perform any and all actions that may be legally delegated to an agency representative. The instrument of authorization is the power of attorney.

General agency. In a general agency, the principal delegates to the agent ongoing tasks and duties within a particular business or enterprise. Such delegation may include the authority to enter into contracts.

Special, or limited, agency. Under a special agency agreement, the principal delegates authority to conduct a specific activity, after which the agency relationship terminates. In most cases, the special agent *may not* bind the principal to a contract. An example of a special agency is the relationship between the sales associate and the buyer or seller the associate represents.

In most instances, real estate brokerage is based on a special agency. The principal hires a licensed broker to procure a ready, willing, and able buyer or seller. When the objective is achieved, the relationship terminates, although certain fiduciary duties survive the relationship.

Creating an agency relationship

An agency relationship may arise from an express oral or written agreement between the principal and the agent, or from the actions of the parties by implication.

Written or oral listing agreement. The most common way of creating an agency relationship is by listing agreement, which may be oral or written. The agreement sets forth the various authorizations and duties, as well as requirements for compensation. A listing agreement establishes an agency for a specified transaction and has a stated expiration.

Implied agency. An agency relationship can arise by implication, intentionally or unintentionally. Implication means that the parties act *as if* there were an agreement. For example, if an agent promises a buyer to do everything possible to find a property at the lowest possible price, and the buyer accepts the proposition, there may be an implied agency relationship even though there is no specific agreement. Even if the agent does not wish to establish an agency relationship, the agent's actions may be construed to imply a relationship. Whether intended or accidental, the creation of implied agency obligates the agent to fiduciary duties and professional standards of care. If these are not fulfilled, the agent may be held liable

Terminating an agency relationship

Full performance of all obligations by the parties terminates an agency relationship. In addition, the parties may terminate the relationship at any time by *mutual agreement.* Thirdly, the agency relationship automatically terminates on the *expiration* date, whether the obligations were performed or not.

Involuntary termination. An agency relationship may terminate contrary to the wishes of the parties by reason of:

> ▸ death or incapacity of either party
> ▸ abandonment by the agent
> ▸ condemnation or destruction of the property
> ▸ renunciation
> ▸ breach
> ▸ bankruptcy
> ▸ revocation of the agent's license

Involuntary termination of the relationship may create legal and financial liability for a party who defaults or cancels. For example, a client may renounce an agreement but then be held liable for the agent's expenses or commission.

FIDUCIARY DUTIES

Fiduciary duties to the client
Agent's duties to the customer
Principal's general duties

The agency relationship imposes fiduciary duties on the client and agent, but particularly on the agent. An agent must also observe certain standards of conduct in dealing with customers and other outside parties.

Fiduciary duties to the client

Skill, care, and diligence. The agent is hired to do a job, and is therefore expected to do it with diligence and reasonable competence. Competence is generally defined as a level of real estate marketing skills and knowledge comparable to those of other practitioners in the area.

The notion of care extends to observing the limited scope of authority granted to the agent. A conventional listing agreement does not authorize an agent to obligate the client to contracts, and it does not allow the agent to conceal offers to buy, sell, or lease coming from a customer or another agent. Further, since a client relies on a broker's representations, a broker must exercise care not to offer advice outside of his or her field of expertise. Violations of this standard may expose the agent to liability for the unlicensed practice of a profession such as law, engineering, or accounting.

Fiduciary Duties

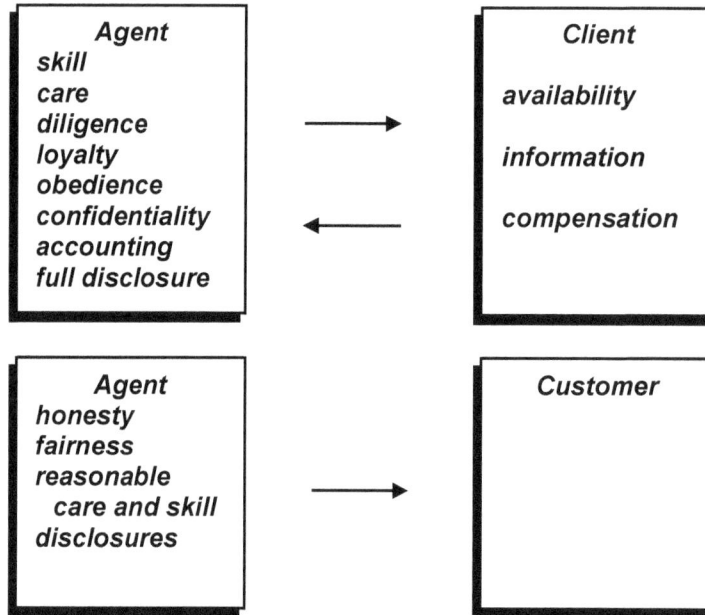

Agent *skill* *care* *diligence* *loyalty* *obedience* *confidentiality* *accounting* *full disclosure*	**Client** *availability* *information* *compensation*
Agent *honesty* *fairness* *reasonable* *care and skill* *disclosures*	**Customer**

Loyalty. The duty of loyalty requires the agent to place the interests of the client above those of all others, particularly the agent's own. This standard is particularly relevant whenever an agent discusses transaction terms with a prospect.

Obedience. An agent must comply with the client's directions and instructions, *provided they are legal.* An agent who cannot obey a legal directive, for whatever reason, must withdraw from the relationship. If the directive is illegal, the agent must also immediately withdraw.

Confidentiality. An agent must hold in confidence any personal or business information received from the client during the term of employment. An agent may not disclose any information that would harm the client's interests or bargaining position, or anything else the client wishes to keep secret.

The confidentiality standard is one of the duties that extends *beyond the termination of the listing*: at *no time* in the future may the agent disclose confidential information.

An agent must exercise care in fulfilling this duty: if confidentiality conflicts with the agent's legal requirements to disclose material facts, the agent must inform the client of this obligation and make the required disclosures. If such a conflict cannot be resolved, the agent must withdraw from the relationship.

Accounting. An agent must safeguard and account for all monies, documents, and other property received from a client or customer. Florida license law regulates the broker's accounting obligations and escrow practices.

Full disclosure. An agent has the duty to inform the client of all material facts, reports, and rumors that might affect the client's interests in the property transaction.

In recent years, the disclosure standard has been raised to require an agent to disclose items that a practicing agent *should know,* whether the agent actually had the knowledge or not, and regardless of whether the disclosure furthers or impedes the progress of the transaction.

The most obvious example of a "should have known" disclosure is a property defect, such as an inoperative central air conditioner, that the agent failed to notice. If the air conditioner becomes a problem, the agent may be held liable for failing to disclose a material fact if a court rules that the typical agent in that area would detect and recognize a faulty air conditioner.

There is no obligation to obtain or disclose information related to a customer's race, creed, color, religion, sex or national origin: anti-discrimination laws hold such information to be immaterial to the transaction.

Florida law requires a seller to make a written disclosure about property condition to a prospective buyer.

Disclosure of Material Facts

Critical material facts for disclosure include:

- the agent's opinion of the property's condition

- information about the buyer's motivations and financial qualifications

- discussions between agent and buyer regarding the possibility of the agent's representing the buyer in another transaction.

- adverse material facts, including property condition, title defects, environmental hazards, and property defects

**Agent's duties
to the customer**

The traditional notion of *caveat emptor*-- let the buyer beware-- no longer applies unequivocally to real estate transactions. Agents *do* have certain obligations to customers, even though they do not represent them. In general, they owe a third party:

▸ honesty and fair dealing
▸ reasonable care and skill
▸ proper disclosure

An agent has a duty to deal fairly and honestly with a customer. Thus, an agent may not deceive, defraud, or otherwise take advantage of a customer.

"Reasonable care and skill" means that an agent will be held to the standards of knowledge, expertise, and ethics that are commonly maintained by other agents in the area.

Proper disclosure primarily concerns disclosure of agency, property condition, and environmental hazards.

An agent who fails to live up to prevailing standards may be held liable for negligence, fraud, or violation of state real estate license laws and regulations. Agents should be particularly careful about misrepresenting and offering inappropriate expert advice when working with customers.

Intentional misrepresentation. An agent may intentionally or unintentionally defraud a buyer by misrepresenting or concealing facts. While it is acceptable to promote the features of a property to a buyer or the virtues of a buyer to a seller, it is a fine line that divides promotion from misrepresentation. Silent misrepresentation, which is intentionally failing to reveal a material fact, is just as fraudulent as a false statement.

Negligent misrepresentation. An agent can be held liable for failure to disclose facts the agent was not aware of if it can be demonstrated that the agent *should have known* such facts. For example, if it is a common standard that agents inspect property, then an agent can be held liable for failing to disclose a leaky roof that was not inspected.

Misrepresentation of expertise. An agent should not act or speak outside the agent's area of expertise. A customer may rely on anything an agent says, and the agent will be held accountable. For example, an agent represents that a property will appreciate. The buyer interprets this as expert investment advice and buys the property. If the property does not appreciate, the buyer may hold the agent liable.

**Principal's
general duties**

The obligations of a principal in an agency relationship concern the following:

Availability. In a special agency, the power and decision-making authority of the agent are limited. Therefore, the principal must be available for consultation, direction, and decision-making. Otherwise the agent cannot complete the job.

Information. The principal must provide the agent with a sufficient amount of information to complete the desired activity. This may include property data, financial data, and the client's timing requirements.

Compensation. If an agreement includes a provision for compensating the agent and the agent performs in accordance with the agreement, the client is obligated to compensate the agent. As indicated earlier, however, the agency relationship does not necessarily include compensation.

BROKERAGE RELATIONSHIP DISCLOSURE ACT

Residential transactions
Disclosure notices
Nonrepresentation relationships
Single agency relationships
Transaction broker relationships
Transitioning to transaction broker
Designated sales associate
Documentation

Residential transactions

Under the Brokerage Relationship Disclosure Act, all real estate transactions impose certain duties and obligations on licensees. Written disclosures, however, are required only when a brokerage is acting as a single agent or in a no-brokerage relationship in a residential sale transaction.

Residential sale transactions are those involving

- improved residential properties with four or fewer dwelling units
- unimproved residential properties zoned for four or fewer residential units
- agricultural properties of ten acres or less

The requirement for agency disclosures to be written thus excludes

- non-residential transactions
- rental or leasing transactions and sales of business opportunities unless they include an option to purchase a property with four or fewer residential units
- auctions
- appraisals

No written disclosure is needed when the brokerage is acting as a transaction broker, as this relationship is the default presumed under Florida law.

Disclosure notices

The mandated disclosures do not include language about whom the agent represents or about the choices of representation the clients or customers have; they simply disclose the duties. However, there are separate disclosures for each relationship which do include the type of representation.

Other disclosure notices include "No Brokerage Relationship Notice" and "Consent to Transition to Transaction Broker." This second disclosure includes the duties owed by the transaction broker to the customer.

The authorized relationships, duties, and disclosure notices are described below.

Under Florida's Brokerage Relationship Disclosure Act, licensees may establish a relationship with a buyer or seller as either a transaction broker or as a single agent. The licensee may also assist a buyer or seller with no brokerage relationship, known as nonrepresentation. The licensee may not establish a dual agency relationship with both a buyer and a seller in the same transaction. The relationship established must be disclosed in writing to the involved party(ies). The licensee may transition from one type of relationship to the other type with the consent of the buyer and/or seller and with the disclosure of the duties owed to the client or customer under the new relationship.

The customer is not required to enter into any brokerage relationship with a licensee.

Nonrepresentation relationships

A licensee may enter into a listing agreement with a seller and be paid a commission or other compensation while having no brokerage relationship with buyer or seller. In this situation, the licensee owes no loyalty or other fiduciary duties to either party but still owes certain duties to the party or parties as customers. Those duties must be disclosed in writing before the licensee shows a property. F.S. Chapter 475.278(4)(c) mandates the following form and language for the disclosure:

NO BROKERAGE RELATIONSHIP NOTICE

FLORIDA LAW REQUIRES THAT REAL ESTATE LICENSEES WHO HAVE NO BROKERAGE RELATIONSHIP WITH A POTENTIAL SELLER OR BUYER DISCLOSE THEIR DUTIES TO SELLERS AND BUYERS.

As a real estate licensee who has no brokerage relationship with you, (insert name of Real Estate Entity and its Associates) owe to you the following duties:

1. *Dealing honestly and fairly.*
2. *Disclosing all known facts that materially affect the value of the residential property that are not readily observable to the buyer.*
3. *Accounting for all funds entrusted to the licensee.*

Single agency relationships

A buyer or seller who is looking for additional duties and a different level of assistance needs to enter into an agency relationship with the broker.

The agent represents one party in a transaction. The client may be either seller or buyer.

Seller agency. In the traditional situation, a seller or landlord is the agent's client. A buyer or tenant is the customer.

Buyer agency. Recently, it has become common for an agent to represent a buyer or tenant. In this relationship, the property buyer or tenant is the client and the property owner is the customer.

Dual agency. An agency relationship is established with a brokerage firm and not with any one agent within the firm. Therefore, a dual agency would exist if one agent within the firm represented the seller while another agent in the same firm represented the buyer. *Dual agency as a form of representation is prohibited in Florida whether it is disclosed or nondisclosed.*

Subagency. In a subagency, a broker associate or sales associate works as the agent of a broker who is the agent of a buyer or seller. In effect, the associate, as agent of the broker, is the subagent of the client. The subagent owes the same duties to the broker's client as the broker does.

The disclosure required for single agency is as follows. The disclosure must be made at the time of, entering into a listing agreement or an agreement for representation or before showing the property, whichever occurs first.

SINGLE AGENT NOTICE

FLORIDA LAW REQUIRES THAT REAL ESTATE LICENSEES OPERATING AS SINGLE AGENTS DISCLOSE TO BUYERS AND SELLERS THEIR DUTIES.

1. *As a single agent, (insert name of Real Estate Entity and its Associates) owe to you the following duties:*
2. *Dealing honestly and fairly;*
3. *Loyalty;*
4. *Confidentiality;*
5. *Obedience;*
6. *Full disclosure;*
7. *Accounting for all funds;*
8. *Skill, care, and diligence in the transaction;*
9. *Presenting all offers and counteroffers in a timely manner, unless a party has previously directed the licensee otherwise in writing; and*
10. *Disclosing all known facts that materially affect the value of residential real property and are not readily observable.*

Transaction broker relationships

Florida prohibits both parties to a transaction from being represented by the same brokerage in a dual agency relationship. Instead, the transaction broker relationship was created to allow a single brokerage to provide limited representation and duties to both the seller and the buyer in the same transaction. Limited representation means neither party is responsible for the licensee's actions.

In a transaction broker relationship, the broker does not represent either party in a fiduciary capacity or as a single agent. Neither party has the right of the licensee's undivided loyalty. Further, because the broker is not representing either one of the parties as a client, then all parties to the transaction are considered customers.

The transaction broker relationship is between the brokerage and the client. Consequently, one licensee within the brokerage may represent both the seller and the buyer, or one licensee may represent the seller while another licensee within the same brokerage represents the buyer. All licensees in the firm are providing the same limited representation to both parties. Neither the seller nor the buyer may be represented to the detriment of the other party.

Florida law makes the presumption that all licensees are operating as transaction brokers unless the broker and the customer have entered into a written single agent or nonrepresentation agreement. Consequently, transaction brokers are not required to provide customers with a transaction broker relationship notice or disclosure.

Duties of a transaction broker. As with any Florida agency relationship, the broker must disclose the duties owed to both parties.

- dealing honestly and fairly
- accounting for all funds
- using skill, care, and diligence in the transaction
- disclosing all known material facts that are not readily observable and that affect the property's value
- presenting all offers and counteroffers in a timely manner unless directed otherwise
- providing limited confidentiality unless either party waives in writing
- performing any additional duties agreed upon by both parties

The duty of limited confidentiality prevents the broker or licensee from disclosing any of the following information:

- the seller will accept a price less than the asking or listed price
- the buyer will pay a price greater than the price submitted in a written offer
- the motivation of any party for selling or buying property

> ▸ a seller or buyer will agree to financing terms other than those offered
>
> ▸ any other information requested by a party to remain confidential

Duties not imposed on the transaction broker. Since there are no fiduciary duties binding the transaction broker, the broker is held to standards for dealing with customers as opposed to clients. These include honesty, fair dealing, and reasonable care. The transaction broker is under no obligation to inspect the property for the benefit of a party or verify the accuracy of statements made by a party.

Transitioning to transaction broker

Timing. A single agency relationship may transition to a transaction broker relationship at any time the agent and principal wish to do so. With the transition, the licensee will now be providing limited representation and can assist both the buyer and the seller with no dedicated loyalty. The licensee must not represent one party to the detriment of the other party.

Procedure. The licensee must obtain the principal's written consent to the single agency before or at the time of entering into a listing agreement, entering into an agreement for representation, or showing a property, whichever occurs first. Consent **to change the relationship from single agent to transaction representation must be obtained before the change occurs.**

Format. When the disclosure of relationship change is part of other documents, it must be the same type size or larger and be placed conspicuously with the first sentence in uppercase and bold type. It must include its own initials or signature line directly under the disclosure language. The disclosure must also include the duties the licensee owes to the principal. The consent to transition form below can also be found in F.S. Chapter 475.278.

CONSENT TO TRANSITION TO TRANSACTION BROKER

FLORIDA LAW ALLOWS REAL ESTATE LICENSEES WHO REPRESENT A BUYER OR SELLER AS A SINGLE AGENT TO CHANGE FROM A SINGLE AGENT RELATIONSHIP TO A TRANSACTION BROKERAGE RELATIONSHIP IN ORDER FOR THE LICENSEE TO ASSIST BOTH PARTIES IN A REAL ESTATE TRANSACTION BY PROVIDING A LIMITED FORM OF REPRESENTATION TO BOTH THE BUYER AND THE SELLER. THIS CHANGE IN RELATIONSHIP CANNOT OCCUR WITHOUT YOUR PRIOR WRITTEN CONSENT.

As a transaction broker, (insert name of Real Estate Firm and its Associates) , provides to you a limited form of representation that includes the following duties:

1. *Dealing honestly and fairly;*
2. *Accounting for all funds;*
3. *Using skill, care, and diligence in the transaction;*
4. *Disclosing all known facts that materially affect the value of residential real property and are not readily observable to the buyer;*
5. *Presenting all offers and counteroffers in a timely manner, unless a party has previously directed the licensee otherwise in writing;*
6. *Limited confidentiality, unless waived in writing by a party. This limited confidentiality will prevent disclosure that the seller will accept a price less than the asking or listed price, that the buyer will pay a price greater than the price submitted in a written offer, of the motivation of any party for selling or buying property, that a seller or buyer will agree to financing terms other than those offered, or of any other information requested by a party to remain confidential; and*
7. *Any additional duties that are entered into by this or by separate written agreement.*

Limited representation means that a buyer or seller is not responsible for the acts of the licensee. Additionally, parties are giving up their rights to the undivided loyalty of the licensee. This aspect of limited representation allows a licensee to facilitate a real estate transaction by assisting both the buyer and the seller, but a licensee will not work to represent one party to the detriment of the other party when acting as a transaction broker to both parties.

I agree that my agent may assume the role and duties of a transaction broker. [must be initialed or signed]

Designated sales associate

Non-residential transaction limitations. When a broker is dealing with a non-residential transaction where the buyer and seller have assets of $1 million or more, the customers may request that the broker designate sales associates to act as single agents for each customer in the same transaction. In other words, the broker may designate one sales associate to the buyer and another sales associate to the seller. Each of these sales associates has the same duties to the customer as a single agent does, including disclosures.

Disclosure requirements. While brokers who deal in residential sale transactions must comply with mandated disclosure requirements, those who deal in non-residential transactions do not have the same mandated disclosure requirements. The broker does not have to disclose duties to the customers, but the designated sales associates must disclose their single agent duties.

Additionally, the buyer and the seller must each sign disclosures stating that their assets meet the $1 million requirement and that they are requesting designated sales associates. The disclosure must include the following language:

> FLORIDA LAW PROHIBITS A DESIGNATED SALES ASSOCIATE FROM DISCLOSING, EXCEPT TO THE BROKER OR PERSONS SPECIFIED BY THE BROKER, INFORMATION MADE CONFIDENTIAL BY REQUEST OR AT THE INSTRUCTION OF THE CUSTOMER THE DESIGNATED SALES ASSOCIATE IS REPRESENTING. HOWEVER, FLORIDA LAW ALLOWS A DESIGNATED SALES ASSOCIATE TO DISCLOSE INFORMATION ALLOWED TO BE DISCLOSED OR REQUIRED TO BE DISCLOSED BY LAW AND ALSO ALLOWS A DESIGNATED SALES ASSOCIATE TO DISCLOSE TO HIS OR HER BROKER, OR PERSONS SPECIFIED BY THE BROKER, CONFIDENTIAL INFORMATION OF A CUSTOMER FOR THE PURPOSE OF SEEKING ADVICE OR ASSISTANCE FOR THE BENEFIT OF THE CUSTOMER IN REGARD TO A TRANSACTION. FLORIDA LAW REQUIRES THAT THE BROKER MUST HOLD THIS INFORMATION CONFIDENTIAL AND MAY NOT USE SUCH INFORMATION TO THE DETRIMENT OF THE OTHER PARTY.

Single agent duties. As a designated single agent, the sales associate has the following duties to buyers and sellers:

1. dealing honestly and fairly
2. loyalty
3. confidentiality
4. obedience
5. full disclosure
6. accounting for all funds
7. skill, care, and diligence in the transaction
8. presenting all offers and counteroffers in a timely manner, unless a party has previously directed the licensee otherwise in writing
9. disclosing all known facts that materially affect the value of residential real property and are not readily observable

Documentation

Brokers are required to keep their business records for at least 5 years from the date of agreement execution. Disclosure documents related to transactions that resulted in a written contract to sell or purchase must be retained for 5 years.

Any document that has been the subject of or served as evidence in any civil action or appellate proceeding must be retained for at least 2 years after the conclusion of the action or proceeding, but no less than the required 5 years.

Even records related to transactions that did not close should be retained for 5 years.

4 Authorized Relationships, Duties, and Disclosure Snapshot Review

ESSENTIALS OF REAL ESTATE AGENCY

Historical perspective
- agency law grows out of common law and statutory law
- essence of agency relationship: trust, confidence, mutual good faith

Basic roles
- principal, or client, hires agent (broker) to find a ready, willing, and able customer (buyer, seller, tenant); client-agent fiduciary foundations: trust, confidence, good faith

Types of agency
- universal: represent in business and personal matters; can contract for principal
- general: represent in business matters; agent can contract for principal
- special: represent in single business transaction; normally agent cannot contract for principal; the brokerage relationship is usually special agency

Creating an agency relationship
- created by express written or oral agreement or as an implied agreement by actions of either party

Terminating an agency relationship
- causes: fulfillment; expiration; mutual agreement; incapacity; abandonment; or destruction of property; renunciation; breach; bankruptcy; revocation of license

FIDUCIARY DUTIES

Fiduciary duties to the client
- skill, care, diligence; loyalty; obedience; confidentiality; disclosure; accounting

Agent's duties to the customer
- honesty and fair dealing; exercise of reasonable care and skill; proper disclosures; danger areas: misrepresentation; advising beyond expertise

Principal's general duties
- availability; provide information; compensation

Breach of duty
- liabilities: loss of listing, compensation, license; suit for damages

BROKERAGE RELATIONSHIP DISCLOSURE ACT

Transaction types
- written disclosure required for single agent or no-brokerage relationship in residential sale transaction
- residential sale: property with four or fewer dwelling units or zoned for four or fewer dwelling units

Disclosure notices
- duties, not representation choices
- separate forms for each representation type
- FL Brokerage Relationship Disclosure Act allows transaction broker, single agent, and nonrepresentation
- must disclose duties of each relationship

Nonrepresentation relationships
- no brokerage relationship with buyer or seller; still owe some duties

Single agency relationships	• seller agency; buyer agency; no dual agency in Florida
	• broker's associates are agents of the broker, subagents of the broker's client; owe same duties to client as broker
Transaction broker relationships	• allows broker to represent both buyer and seller in same transaction; no fiduciary duties but limited duties still owed and must be disclosed
	• relationship presumed unless another agency agreement is signed
	• limited confidentiality – no disclosure that seller will lower price, buyer will raise offer, either will agree to other financing terms, either party's motivation, other information requested to remain confidential
Transitioning to transaction broker	• can transition from single agent to transaction broker with principal's written consent at any time
	• disclosure requirements apply to residential and agricultural properties with exemptions
	• disclosure provided prior to agreement execution or property showing; to meet type requirements and include signature line and duties
Designated sales associate	• nonresidential buyer and seller need assets in excess of $1 million; broker to designate separate sales associates to each as single agent
	• standard disclosure requirements apply plus written assets disclosure and request for designated sales associates to follow required language
	• must offer standard single agent duties
Documentation	• all records to be kept for 5 years, including disclosures related to written contracts; records related to legal proceedings to be kept for 2 years within the 5 or in addition to the 5 years

SECTION FOUR: Authorized Relationships, Duties, and Disclosure

Section Quiz

1. The essence of the agency relationship between an agent and a principal can best be described as a relationship of

   a. mutual consent, consideration, and acceptance.
   b. diligence, results, and compensation.
   c. service, dignity, and respect.
   d. trust, confidence, and good faith.

2. In an agency relationship, the principal is required to

   a. promote the agent's best interests.
   b. accept the advice of the agent.
   c. provide sufficient information for the agent to complete the agent's tasks.
   d. maintain confidentiality.

3. A principal empowers an agent to conduct the ongoing activities of one of her business enterprises. This is an example of

   a. limited agency.
   b. general agency.
   c. universal agency.
   d. special agency.

4. A property seller empowers an agent to market and sell a property on his behalf. This is an example of

   a. general agency.
   b. special agency.
   c. universal agency.
   d. no agency.

5. Implied agency arises when

   a. an agent accepts an oral listing.
   b. a principal accepts an oral listing.
   c. a party creates an agency relationship outside of an express agreement.
   d. a principal agrees to all terms of a written listing agreement, whether express or implied.

6. An agency relationship may be involuntarily terminated for which of the following reasons?

   a. Death or incapacity of the agent
   b. Mutual consent
   c. Full performance
   d. Renewal of the agent's license

7. A principal discloses that she would sell a property for $375,000. During the listing period, the house is marketed for $425,000. No offers come in, and the listing expires. Two weeks later, the agent grumbles to a customer that the seller would have sold for less than the listed price. Which of the following is true?

   a. The agent has violated the duty of confidentiality.
   b. The agent has fulfilled all fiduciary duties, including confidentiality, since the listing had expired.
   c. The agent is violating the duties owed this customer.
   d. The agent has created a dual agency situation with the customer.

8. A principal instructs an agent to market a property only to families on the north side of town. The agent refuses to comply. In this case,

   a. the agent has violated fiduciary duty.
   b. the agent has not violated fiduciary duty.
   c. the agent is liable for breaching the listing terms.
   d. the agent should obey the instruction to salvage the listing.

9. An owner's agent is showing a buyer an apartment building. The buyer notices water stains on the ceiling, and informs the agent. The agent's best course of action is to

   a. immediately contract to paint the ceiling.
   b. immediately contract to repair the roof.
   c. suggest the buyer make a lower-price offer.
   d. inform the seller.

10. An agent owes customers several duties. These may be best described as

    a. fairness, care, and honesty.
    b. obedience, confidentiality, and accounting.
    c. diligence, care, and loyalty.
    d. honesty, diligence, and skill.

11. An agent fails to discover flood marks on the walls in the basement of a property. The agent sells the property, and the buyer later sues the agent for failing to mention the problem. In this case, the agent

    a. may be guilty of intentional misrepresentation.
    b. has an exposure to a charge of negligent misrepresentation.
    c. has little exposure, since the problem was not mentioned on the signed disclosure form.
    d. is not vulnerable, since the problem was not discovered.

12. An agent informs a buyer that a clause in a contract is standard language. After explaining the clause, the agent assures the buyer that the clause does not mean anything significant. If something goes wrong with the transaction, the agent could be liable for

    a. violating duties owed a customer.
    b. misinterpreting the clause.
    c. intentional misrepresentation.
    d. practicing law without a license.

13. An outside broker locates a seller for a buyer representative's client. In this instance, the outside broker is acting as

    a. a single agent.
    b. a dual agent.
    c. a subagent.
    d. a secret agent.

14. Agent Bob, who works for Broker Bill, obtains an owner listing to lease a building. Bill's other agent, Sue, locates a tenant for Bob's listing. This situation is illegal in Florida unless

    a. Bob and Sue are implied agents.
    b. Bob and Sue are acting as transaction brokers.
    c. Bob and Sue are single agents.
    d. Sue is Bob's subagent.

15. A licensee acting as a transaction broker

    a. may not represent any party's interests to the detriment of the other party in the transaction.
    b. may not disclose material facts to any party in the transaction.
    c. must be obedient and loyal to both parties.
    d. must require that the principals share equally in paying the commission.

16. When may a licensee acting as a single agent transition to a transaction brokerage relationship with a principal?

    a. Only before an offer has been presented
    b. Only at the time of signing a listing agreement
    c. Whenever the licensee and principal agree to do so
    d. At no time; a single agent may not become a transaction broker..

17. What is a designated sales associate?

    a. A sales associate designated by a broker to represent one party in a transaction while another associate of the broker is designated to represent the other party
    b. A sales associate designated by a broker to manage a branch office for the broker.
    c. A sales associate who is a signatory on a broker's escrow account.
    d. An unlicensed person designated by a broker to perform a specific licensed task on a temporary basis.

18. For how long must a broker retain documents and records relating to a transaction?

    a. One year
    b. Three years
    c. Five years
    d. Permanently

19. A single agency disclosure must be made

    a. immediately prior to initial contact with a principal.
    b. at the time of signing a listing or representation agreement or before showing a property.
    c. immediately prior to substantive contact with any party.
    d. immediately following any offer executed by a buyer.

20. A licensee has a nonrepresentation relationship with a transaction principal. What fiduciary duties does the licensee owe to that person?

    a. None
    b. Confidentiality only
    c. Loyalty and confidentiality.
    d. Skill and care

21. Which type of brokerage relationship is illegal in Florida?

    a. Single agency
    b. Transaction broker
    c. Dual agency
    d. Nonrepresentation

22. Which duty is required in a nonrepresentation relationship?

    a. Disclosing facts that materially affect the property's value
    b. Using skill, care, and diligence in the transaction
    c. Limited confidentiality unless waived in writing
    d. Presenting all offers and counteroffers in a timely manner

23. Designated sales associates are used when

    a. the brokerage wants to represent both the residential buyer and the residential seller.
    b. the nonresidential buyer and seller have assets of $1 million or more.
    c. any client requests the designation.
    d. the broker is handling any nonresidential sale.

24. Which of the following statements is true?

   a. Transaction brokers owe fiduciary duties to their clients.
   b. The duty of limited confidentiality prevents the transaction broker from disclosing known material facts.
   c. Transaction brokers have no duty of undivided loyalty.
   d. Transaction brokers and single agents owe the same duties to their clients.

25. Brokerage relationship disclosure records must be retained

   a. until the transaction closes.
   b. for 2 years.
   c. for 5 years.
   d. only if related to a legal proceeding.

5 Real Estate Brokerage Activities and Procedures

Brokerage Offices
Guidelines for Advertising
Handling Deposits
Representing Licensee Expertise
Commissions
Change of Employer or Address
Business Entity Licensing & Registration
Trade Names
Ethical Practices

Learning Objectives

- Identify the requirements for real estate brokerage office(s) and the types of business entities that may register
- Explain what determines whether a temporary shelter must be registered as a branch office
- List the requirements related to sign regulation
- List the requirements related to the regulation of advertising by real estate brokers
- Explain the term *immediately* as it applies to earnest money deposits
- Describe the four settlement procedures available to a broker who has received conflicting demands or who has a good-faith doubt as to who is entitled to disputed funds
- Describe the obligations placed on a sales associate who changes employers and/or address
- Describe the regulations regarding lien rights for unpaid sales commission
- Contrast the features and requirements of the various types of business organizations

Key Terms

arbitration
blind advertisement
commingle
conflicting demands
conversion
corporation (INC)
deposit
earnest money
escrow account
escrow disbursement order (EDO)
failure to account and deliver
general partnership
good-faith doubt
interpleader

kickback
limited liability company (LLC)
limited liability partnership (LLP)
limited partnership
litigation
mediation
ostensible partnership
personal assistant
point of contact information
professional association (PA)
sole proprietorship
team advertising
trade name

BROKERAGE OFFICES

Office requirements
Branch offices
Entrance sign requirements
Temporary shelters
Sales associate officing

Office requirements

Florida statute mandates that each active broker maintain an office that is located in a building of "stationary construction." The law further mandates that only brokers can own and maintain an office. Sales associates and broker associates may not have their own offices.

Brokers' offices must be registered with the Department of Business and Professional Regulation (DBPR). The office must include at least one enclosed room and have space to conduct private transactions. Additionally, the broker is required to keep any real estate files and records (physical or electronic) in the office so they are immediately available for inspection by the FREC or other governing authority.

A broker may have an office that is located outside the state of Florida if the broker agrees in writing to cooperate with any investigation conducted in accordance with Florida statutes and rules. The broker must also register the out-of-state office with the DBPR.

If local zoning allows, the broker may set up the office in a residential location, such as the broker's home, as long as all office requirements are met, including display of the broker's sign.

According to law, a brokerage office is considered public accommodation and a commercial facility. Consequently, the office must comply with federal and state laws regarding accessibility for the physically or mentally disabled. The office will need clearly marked handicapped parking spaces and wheelchair accessible ramps and doorways. These requirements also apply to residential offices.

Branch offices

If a broker conducts business at a location other than the main office, the broker may be required to register the additional office as a branch office and pay the required registration fee for each such office. All branch offices must be registered.

Additionally, if the broker or brokerage's name or advertising is displayed on an office other than the main office in such a way as to lead the public to believe the office is owned or operated by that same broker, then that office must be registered as a branch office.

If a broker decides to close a branch office and open a new branch office at a different location, the broker must register the new office and pay the registration fee for that office. The registration for the closed branch office may not be transferred to the new branch office. If the broker decides to re-open the closed branch office within that office's license period, no additional fee will be required.

Entrance sign requirements

Every office, whether main or branch, is required to display a sign at the entrance which can be seen and read easily by anyone entering the office. The sign can be on the exterior or interior entrance of the office. Florida law requires the sign to contain the broker's name and any trade name. If the brokerage is a partnership or corporation, the sign must contain the partnership or corporation's name or trade name as well as at least one of the brokers. The words "Licensed Real Estate Broker" or "Lic. Real Estate Broker" must be included on the entrance sign of any real estate brokerage or business entity.

> Sunshine State Realty, LLC
> John Kennedy
> Licensed Real Estate Broker

The law does not require that sales or broker associates' names be included on entrance signs. If the broker chooses to include them, the names must be below the broker's name with space between the broker's name and the associates' names. The associates' names must also include "Sales Associate" or "Broker Associate," as appropriate.

> Sunshine State Realty, LLC
> John Kennedy
> Lic. Real Estate Broker
>
> Sally Kenney, Broker's Associate

Temporary shelters

Brokers sometimes set up a temporary shelter on a subdivision being sold by a broker to protect associates and customers. If the shelter is to be deemed temporary, associates may not be permanently assigned there and transactions may not be closed there. In that case, the shelter need not be registered as a branch office. However, the permanence, use, and type of activities that are conducted at the shelter will determine whether or not it must be registered. If, for example, transaction closings take place within the shelter, then it must be considered a branch office and be registered as one.

Sales associate officing

At initial licensure, a sales associate must be registered with an employing broker. The sales associate must work under the direction, control, and management of the specified broker or an owner-developer. The associate must work out of an office maintained by that same broker. The sales associate may be registered under only one broker at a time and may not operate as a broker or operate for any other broker who is not the associate's registered employing broker.

GUIDELINES FOR ADVERTISING

Prohibitions
Wording of advertisements
Internet advertising
Telephone solicitation laws
Florida telemarketing laws

Prohibitions

False or misleading advertising. Florida law prohibits licensees from placing or causing to be placed any advertisement for property or services that is fraudulent, false, deceptive, misleading, or exaggerated. This includes written ads as well as ads on television or radio that are used to induce the sale, purchase, or rental of real property.

Penalties. False, deceptive, fraudulent, or misleading advertising can result in administrative fines and license suspension.

Blind advertising. Florida law requires that all advertisements include the brokerage's licensed name so any reasonable person would know the ad is from a real estate licensee. The broker's nickname may be included in the advertising as long as his or her legal registered name is also included. The broker's personal name may also be included in the ad as long as the broker's last name as it is registered with the DBPR is included. Ads that do not include the brokerage's name are considered blind advertising and are prohibited.

Sales associates advertising or conducting business in own name. Brokerage services include advertising. Consequently, anyone placing advertisements must be a broker. Sales associates may create or place advertisements only under the supervision and in the name of their employing broker. Sales associates may not advertise in their own names. Any form of advertising created by a sales associate must include the brokerage's licensed name.

Sales associates and broker's associates may sell their own property under their own name with the permission of their broker. If selling under their own name and phone number, they do not need to display the brokerage name in the advertisement. However, the associates must disclose to anyone whom they are going to show the property that they are licensed real estate agents.

Team advertising. Teams within a brokerage firm may advertise only under the supervision of the broker and in the name of the brokerage firm. Certain words, namely "brokerage," "realty," and the like, are not allowed as potentially creating confusion for the public. The name of the team must be in a font that is no larger than that used for the name or logo of the registered broker. The team name must also be adjacent to the name of the brokerage. For example, the name of the team cannot be at the top of the page and the brokerage name at the bottom of the page. They must both be either at the top of the page or at the bottom of the page.

Wording of advertisements

In addition to including the brokerage's name, real estate advertisements must be worded so that any reasonable person knows that the advertiser is a real estate licensee. They may not be worded in a way that makes the public believe the ad is from someone other than a real estate licensee.

.

Advertisements must be worded to make it clear to responding buyers or renters who it is they are calling when they answer the ad. Consider the following sets of ad copy:

> "Three bedroom, 2 bath ranch style home in good neighborhood. $350,000. Contact John Kennedy Sunshine State Realty (816) 259-7802."

Here, it is not clear who the buyer would be contacting -- John Kennedy or Sunshine State Realty. Consider a clearer version:

> "3 bedroom, 2 bath. Ranch style home in good neighborhood. $350,000. Sunshine State Realty. Contact John Kennedy, cell (816) 259-7802."

In this ad, it is clear that John Kennedy is associated with Sunshine State real estate company and that when the number is called, John Kennedy will be answering the phone.

Internet advertising

Just as with any other form of advertising, the brokerage's name must appear within an internet advertisement. Florida administrative rule requires the name to be placed adjacent to, immediately above, or immediately below the point of contact information. Again, this prevents blind advertising and any related penalties.

Point of contact information. Information on how to contact the brokerage firm or the individual licensee is referred to as "point of contact information." Such contact information includes mailing address, physical street address, e-mail address, telephone number, and facsimile (fax) telephone number.

Telephone solicitation laws

Telephone Consumer Protection Act. The TCPA (Telephone Consumer Protection Act) addresses the regulation of unsolicited telemarketing phone calls. Rules include the following:

- ▸ Telephone solicitors are banned from using an artificial or a pre-recorded voice to a residential line without prior express consent.

- ▸ Robocalls (prerecorded calls) from telemarketers or debt collectors without prior express consumer consent are banned.

- ▸ Solicitors are banned from using a fax or computer to fax unsolicited advertisements.

- ▸ Solicitors are banned from using an auto dialer to send text messages to cell phones without prior express consumer consent.

- ▸ Calls after 9 p.m. and before 8 a.m. in the consumer's time zone are banned.

- ▸ telephone solicitors must identify themselves, on whose behalf they are calling, and how they can be contacted

- ▸ telemarketers must comply with any do-not-call request made during the solicitation call

- ▸ consumers can place their home and wireless phone numbers on a national Do-Not-Call list which is maintained by the Federal Trade Commission and which prohibits future solicitations from telemarketers.

- ▸ Information on the national registry can be found online at https://www.consumer.ftc.gov/articles/0108-national-do-not-call-registry or https://www.donotcall.gov/.

- ▸ Robocalls must provide an automated opt-out function during the call.

- ▸ Consumers may sue companies that violate the law on a per-call basis.

Exemptions from the Act.

- ▸ Debt collection calls with express consent (not written) and without any advertisements.

- ▸ Calls from nonprofit organizations, political organizations, and healthcare organizations.

- ▸ Certain exigent circumstances calls, such as fraud or cyber breach warnings.

- ▸ Federal debt collectors up to three times per month.

- ▸ A real estate licensee who has an actual buyer for an advertised "for sale by owner" property only to negotiate a sale or to arrange a showing for a current customer.

- ▸ A real estate licensee with an established business relationship with a customer even if the customer's number is on the national do not call list. Here, one may call for up to 18 months after the relationship began.

▶ A real estate licensee who has accepted a business inquiry or application from a customer within the last 3 months.

CAN-SPAM Act. The CAN-SPAM Act (Controlling the Assault of Non-Solicited Pornography and Marketing Act of 2003) supplements the Telephone Consumer Protection Act (TCPA) by covering solicitations through email. It

▶ bans sending unwanted email 'commercial messages' to wireless devices
▶ requires express prior authorization
▶ requires giving an 'opt out' choice to terminate the sender's messages

Junk Fax Prevention Act. Both the Junk Fax Prevention Act and the Federal Communications Commission (FCC) cover the use of faxing as a means for solicitations. Faxing unsolicited advertisements to residential or business fax machines is prohibited unless the consumer's prior express consent. Both solicited and unsolicited faxes must include the following:

▶ the date and time the fax was sent
▶ the sending company's registered name
▶ the sending company's telephone number or the sending fax machine's telephone number
▶ an opt-out option on unsolicited faxes

Florida telemarketing laws

Florida state telemarketing laws apply to businesses located within Florida and those outside the state who call Florida residents. The laws include the Florida Telemarketing Act and the Florida Telephonic Sales law. They are administered by the Florida Department of Agriculture and Consumer Affairs (FDACS) and the Attorney General who investigate and assess penalties against violators. Penalties for violations are based on each call. The maximum fine is $10,000 per call. The laws include the following:

▶ Telephone solicitors must obtain a license from the Florida Division of Consumer Services before operating in Florida.

▶ Solicitors must restrict their calls to 8 a.m. to 9 p.m.

▶ Solicitors may not block caller ID.

▶ Solicitors may not accept only credit card payments.

▶ The solicitor has 30 seconds to state his or her true name, the name of the company the telemarketer represents, and the goods or services being sold.

▶ Solicitors must tell consumers about their right to cancel any agreement to purchase the goods or services being offered.

Florida has its own do not call list that prohibits telemarketers from calling residential phones, cell phones, or paging devices. The FDACS is required to merge all Florida listings within the national do-not-call list with the Florida do-not-call list. Additional information and the registry can be found online at https://www.fdacs.gov/Consumer-Resources/Florida-Do-Not-Call.

Exemptions from the Florida laws. The following are exempted from Florida's telemarketing laws in some cases:

- ▶ licensed insurance professionals
- ▶ nonprofit and religious organizations
- ▶ political organizations
- ▶ certain newspapers
- ▶ certain banks

Real estate licensees are also exempt when they are calling a property seller in response to a yard sign or other advertisement placed by the seller. However, a licensee is not exempt if the seller is a "for sale by owner" advertiser who has placed his or her telephone number on the national do-not-call list.

Brokers are required to develop written procedures for solicitation calling policies. They must obtain the do-not-call lists and train their employees and independent contractors on using and maintaining the lists. The lists should be reviewed periodically for new additions so the licensees can remove those additions from their own solicitation call lists. Reviewing the national list is critical since federal law does not exempt real estate licensees. If a number is on the national list, whether or not it is on the state list, real estate licensees must not call that number.

HANDLING DEPOSITS

Escrow account deposit requirements
Management of escrow accounts

Escrow account deposit requirements

Definition of escrow account. An escrow account, also known as a trust account, is an account in a bank, credit union, or savings and loan association within Florida that is established to hold funds until the time comes to disburse them for a particular purpose. The account is held by a third party to a transaction and holds money, such as earnest money from a property buyer, until the property ownership is transferred at closing. Title companies with trust powers and attorneys may also be used to hold funds in escrow.

Escrow accounts may be used to hold rental property deposits and rent payments; however, while not required, sales funds and rental funds should be kept in separate escrow accounts. The funds deposited into the escrow account include cash, checks, money orders, drafts, personal property, or item of value.

Florida law mandates that the account is to hold only third-party funds with no licensee personal funds commingled. However, the law also allows the broker to deposit personal or brokerage funds into each escrow account to be used for account maintenance fees. Thus, the broker may deposit $1,000 into each sales escrow account and $5,000 into each property management escrow account.

Escrow deposit money is to be kept in the broker's escrow account until the transaction has closed or one of the proper settlement procedures has been undertaken. (See following **Settlement procedures** section)

If a broker uses trust funds in the account for any personal reason, the activity constitutes illegal *conversion*. One of the duties owed to any client or customer is to account for all funds. Acceptable trust fund management requires that the client or customer be kept informed of where the money is at all times.

Sales associate funds delivery requirements. If a property buyer gives earnest money or any other deposit to a sales associate in relation to a real estate transaction, the sales associate is required to turn the money over to his or her employing broker no later than the end of the next business day, not counting Saturdays, Sundays, or legal holidays. The same timing is required for rental deposits.

For example, Buyer Susan gives Sales Associate John an earnest money check on Monday morning. John must turn the check over to Broker Justin by the end of the day on Tuesday. Let's say that Tuesday is a legal holiday. That means John needs to turn the check over to Justin by the end of the day on Wednesday.

Definition of "immediately" for a broker. Florida administrative rules state that brokers who receive any form of funds from their sales associates related to a real estate transaction must immediately deposit those funds into an escrow account. The rule defines "immediately" as no later than the end of the third business day following receipt of the item to be deposited, with Saturdays, Sundays, and legal holidays not considered business days. The three business days begin when the sales associate receives the funds, not when the broker receives them from the sales associate.

Here's how this works: If the funds are received on Monday, Tuesday is the first business day "following receipt of the item to be deposited." Wednesday is the second business day following receipt of the deposit; and Thursday is the third business day, the end of which is the deadline for depositing the funds into the escrow account.

So, given the previous example, if associate John receives the earnest money check from Susan on Monday and turns it over to broker Justin on Tuesday, Justin must deposit the check into his escrow account no later than the end of the day on Thursday. If Tuesday is a holiday and John turns the check over to Justin on Wednesday, Justin has to deposit the funds into his escrow account by the end of the day on Friday.

Requirements if deposited with title company or attorney. Funds related to a real estate transaction may be deposited or placed in escrow with a title company or an attorney. When this happens, the name, address, and telephone number of the company or attorney must be noted on the sales contract by the licensee who prepared the contract. All deposit requirements for the broker's escrow account also apply to deposits made with a title company or attorney.

When funds are due for deposit, the licensee's broker has 10 business days to request in writing that the title company or attorney provide written verification that the funds were received and deposited. Then, within 10 business days of that request, the broker must provide the seller's broker either a copy of the written verification that the funds were received and deposited or a written notice that the broker did not receive verification of the funds and deposit. This verification is not necessary if the title company or attorney was nominated in writing by the seller or the seller's agent. If the seller is not represented by a broker, the buyer's broker is to notify the seller directly.

If the funds have been placed in escrow with a title company or attorney, there is no Florida statute regulating those accounts. Consequently, the FREC will not step in to resolve any conflict over disbursement of the funds if the transaction does not close. To settle the dispute, the parties will need to rely on the appropriate court and bear the expense of doing so.

Management of escrow accounts

Escrow account signatory. Florida administrative rules require the broker to be the signatory on all escrow accounts. If there is more than one broker licensee within the brokerage, then any one of those licensees may be the designated signatory.

Escrow account maintenance. The broker is responsible for reconciling the accounts each month and for ensuring the accounts comply with Florida laws. The broker also must make a monthly written statement that compares the broker's total liability with the bank balances of all escrow accounts.

The statement needs to include the date the account reconciliation was completed, the date used to reconcile the balances, the name of the bank and the account, the account number, account balance and date, any deposits in transit, outstanding checks, and an itemized list of the broker's trust liability.

The broker must keep records of all deposits, the source of the funds, and each account and provide those records and transaction-related agreements to the DBPR when requested. The records must be kept for at least 5 years.

Requirements for interest distribution. The broker may hold escrow funds in an insured interest-bearing account in a banking facility located within Florida. All parties associated with the particular transaction must agree in writing to use an interest-bearing account. They must also agree to whom and when the interest will be disbursed.

Requirements for conflicting demands for escrow funds. When a real estate transaction does not close, the earnest money and any other related funds must be disbursed to the appropriate party. If the parties to the transaction do not agree on who should receive the funds and both parties make demands for the funds, the broker must notify the FREC of the conflict within 15 business days of the last demand received for the funds. The broker should use the Notice of Escrow Dispute/Good Faith Doubt form found online at

http://www.myfloridalicense.com/dbpr/re/documents/EDO_Notice.pdf.

The broker must also proceed with a settlement procedure (see below) within 30 business days after the last demand and notify the FREC of the procedure being used to resolve the conflict. The notification timing requirements for both the conflict and the settlement procedure start on the same day.

For example, if the broker received the last demand for escrow funds on June 1, the 15 business days for notifying the FREC of the conflict begins on June 1; and the 30 business days for notifying the FREC of the settlement procedure also starts on July 1.

Good-faith doubt procedure and situations. The term "good faith" is used to describe a sincere or honest motive without any malice or intent to defraud someone else. People enter into contracts, such as real estate sales contracts, with a presumption of good faith that the parties will be honest and fair and not negatively impact the other party's right to benefit from the contract. When one party appears not to be behaving in good faith, the behavior creates doubt in that party's good faith. If that doubt is sincere and honest, it is referred to as good-faith doubt.

If a broker has good-faith doubt as to who is entitled to the funds held in the broker's escrow account, he or she should first look to the sales contract for the escrow instructions. If the contract does not clear up the doubt, the broker must notify the FREC within 15 business days after having such doubt, using the Notice of Escrow Dispute/Good Faith Doubt form. The broker may have a good-faith doubt based on any of many situations.

For example, one party indicates he does not plan to comply with the closing schedule and terms but does not provide the broker with instructions for disbursement of the trust funds or provides instructions that do not match those in the sales contract.

Another example would be that the transaction does close, and the parties provide different instructions for the disbursement of the funds.

Yet another situation leading to good-faith doubt for the broker would be if the transaction fails to close and one party does not respond to the broker's request for disbursement instructions, thus requiring the broker to send notice to that party that the funds will be released to the other party if he or she does not respond by a given date.

Once the broker develops good-faith doubt, he or she must then proceed with a settlement procedure (see below) within 30 business days after having such doubt. The determination of good faith doubt is based upon the facts of each case brought before the FREC.

Settlement procedures. When the need arises to settle an escrow conflict or a good-faith doubt, the broker may use any of four settlement procedures:

> *mediation* – an informal conflict settlement procedure that is conducted by a qualified third party
>
> The intention is to bring the parties together and with the guidance of the mediator have the parties come to a mutually agreeable resolution. Mediation may be used to settle the conflict if all of the associated parties give written consent. Once an agreement is reached, it is put into writing and signed by both parties. It then becomes a binding contract.
>
> If the parties do not all consent to mediation or if the conflict is not settled in mediation within 90 days of the last demand, the broker must employ one of the other settlement procedures. All statements made during mediation are confidential and may not be used in any other proceeding.

> *arbitration* – a process conducted by one or more (usually three) third party arbitrators acting as judges
>
> Typically, each side chooses one arbitrator, and then those two select a third. The arbitrators hear evidence, make decisions, and give written opinions. The arbitrators' decisions are binding. The conflicting parties must agree in writing to go to arbitration and must agree to comply with the arbitrators' final decision.

> *litigation* – a legal procedure either party may use if parties do not agree to mediation or arbitration
>
> In this case, one party would file a lawsuit for the conflict to be heard in court to reach a resolution. However, because mediation is so successful and cost effective, Florida courts require most lawsuits to be mediated before a court will hear the case. Litigation can involve either of the following procedures:
>
> > ▪ *interpleader action* – a means for the broker holding the escrow funds to be removed from the dispute over the disbursement of the funds

The funds are placed in the court depository, and it is left up to the court to determine who is to receive the funds. This also removes the broker from any potential liability as a result of the final disbursement. Contracts often include provisions for the interpleader action costs to be paid with the escrow funds or for the loser of the case to pay the other party's attorney fees.

- *declaratory judgment* – requested when the broker claims part of the escrow funds

  The broker would file for a declaratory relief or judgment to have the appropriate trial court decide each party's rights to the escrow funds.

▸ *Escrow Disbursement Order (EDO)* – a determination made by the FREC as to who is entitled to the escrow funds

  If the funds are held by the broker, he or she can request the FREC issue an EDO. If the EDO is denied, then the broker must employ one of the other settlement procedures and notify the FREC of which procedure will be used. If the funds are held by an attorney or title company, the FREC will not issue an EDO.

  Even though the broker is employing one of the settlement procedures, either party may still choose to file a civil lawsuit to settle the matter. If the broker has requested an EDO but the parties settle the matter by another means before the EDO is issued, the broker must notify the FREC of the settlement within 10 business days.

If the broker follows the notice and settlement procedures under the required timeframes and follows the resulting order or judgment, no administrative complaint may be filed against the broker for failure to account for, deliver, or maintain the escrowed property.

Notice and settlement procedure exceptions. Not all situations regarding disbursement of escrow funds require the broker to give notice or employ any of the settlement procedures. Florida statute and administrative rule allow three specific exceptions:

▸ If the buyer of a residential condominium gives the broker a written sales contract cancellation notice in accordance with Florida Condominium law, the broker may release the escrowed funds to the buyer without notifying the FREC or employing any of the settlement procedures.

▸ If a real property good-faith buyer fails to meet the financing provisions within the sales contract, the broker may release the escrowed funds to the buyer without notifying the FREC or employing any of the settlement procedures.

▸ If a broker receives an earnest money deposit as a result of a Department of Housing and Urban Development (HUD) residential sales contract for the sale of a HUD-owned property, the broker is not required to follow the notice or settlement procedures. Rather, the broker must follow HUD's Agreement to Abide, Broker Participation Requirements and the HUD Act of 1968 (24 C.F.R. s. 291.135) as they pertain to the proper disbursement of earnest money deposits.

REPRESENTING LICENSEE EXPERTISE

Offering an opinion of title
Offering a representation of value
Misrepresentation of value
Unauthorized practice of law

Offering an opinion of title

In Florida, real estate licensees are seen as experts in the field of real estate. Consequently, their clients rely on them to provide expert opinions. However, there are some opinions that licensees are not qualified or permitted to provide. For example, an opinion of title is to be provided by an attorney and not by a real estate licensee. The attorney will use the abstract of title to give an opinion of the condition and marketability of the property's title. It is indeed an opinion and not a guarantee or proof of a clear title.

Under Florida law, no one with a real estate license is allowed to give any opinion on the title to real estate. Instead, a Florida licensee is required to advise the property buyer to consult with an attorney or a title company for an opinion of title and/or to purchase title insurance. Licensees may obtain the opinion from an attorney and then provide information on the title to the buyer.

If a real estate agent gives an opinion of title, this can be considered as the practice of law. The agent can then be charged with a third-degree felony for practicing law without a license.

Offering a representation of value

There are several ways to derive an opinion of a property's value. Real estate licensees are qualified and permitted to perform comparative market analyses, broker price opinions, and opinions of value and then provide the resulting information to their buyers and sellers. They may not represent any of these methods as an appraisal, which is performed only by a licensed or certified appraiser.

Opinions of value ae not subject to regulation nor required to follow any specific professional standards. As a result, licensees who are motivated to obtain a listing may be led to distort the estimated value or price of the property. However, licensees must comply with their duty of honest and fair dealings with their customers and represent the value as accurately as possible with no exaggerations or misrepresentations.

Misrepresentation of value

Again, licensees have a duty to deal honestly and fairly with their customers and clients. They are required to disclose all known facts that materially affect the value of property even when the facts are not readily observable. Omitting a material fact may result in the value of the property being misrepresented. Other ways the value may be misrepresented include the following:

▸ listing a lower value for the property so as to obtain a quick sale
▸ overvaluing the property resulting in the buyer paying too much
▸ misrepresenting the comparable properties to induce a buyer to offer higher than is justified
▸ misrepresenting the square footage of the property

Misrepresenting the property's value can constitute fraud, breach of contract, or breach of trust and can result in lawsuits and disciplinary action against the licensee. When a buyer or seller is harmed because of the misrepresentation of value, his or her only real remedy is to file a lawsuit to either rescind the transaction or to seek financial recovery of damages.

The injured party can sue the other party, the licensee, and the brokerage that employs the licensee. Even if the misrepresentation was a mistake, Florida law allows the offending party(ies) to be held liable for negligent misrepresentation.

Unauthorized practice of law

The Supreme Court of Florida established the Unlicensed Practice of Law (UPL) program to protect the public against harm caused by individuals practicing law without a law degree and license. The Florida Bar will investigate and take legal action against anyone practicing law without a license to do so. The unlicensed practice of law is a third-degree felony in Florida, punishable by up to 5 years of probation, up to 5 years in prison, up to $5,000 in fines, and restitution paid to the victim(s).

Practicing law in Florida involves giving advice that requires the legal knowledge of someone who is licensed to practice law. Real estate law is complex, making it easy for innocent people to get hurt by licensees who give advice when they are not educated and licensed to do so.

While licensees need to be familiar with real estate laws, at no time is the licensee allowed to give legal advice. It is common for clients to ask licensees legal questions, but answering those questions could result in the licensee being held liable if the answers are incorrect.

Further, when completing contracts, such as a purchase contract, licensees must not make additions or modifications to the contract itself. To do so is considered the unlicensed practice of law.

COMMISSIONS

Prohibitions
Kickbacks
Procuring cause

Prohibitions

Price fixing. When two or more brokers get together and agree to charge the same set commission percentage or fee for their services, this is called price fixing. Price fixing is against the law and leads to monopolies wherein competition is restricted. Antitrust laws encourage and protect competition and can impose criminal penalties on the price fixers. Each broker must establish his or her own commission rate separately from other brokers.

Sales associate contracting directly with principal. Sales associates work under the employment and supervision of a broker. They are prohibited from contracting directly with the principal or being paid directly by the principal. Any commission the sales associate receives must come directly from the employing broker based on the commission agreement the associate has with the broker and not directly from the principal.

Sales associate suing principal for commission. Because all contracts are between the principal and the broker, only the broker may sue a principal for unpaid commission. If the broker has been paid by the principal but does not pay the sales associate, the associate may sue the broker for the unpaid compensation but may not sue the principal directly.

Sharing a commission with an unlicensed person. Commissions are paid for services rendered in selling or purchasing property. Providing real estate services requires a real estate license. Therefore, only licensed real estate brokers and sales associates may provide such services. Consequently, sharing a commission with an unlicensed person is a violation of license law. The one exception allowed by the FREC is sharing the commission with a party to the transaction, such as the buyer or seller, as long as doing so is disclosed in writing to all parties to the transaction.

Paying an unlicensed person for performing real estate services. Again, providing real estate services requires a real estate license. Just as sharing a commission with an unlicensed person is prohibited, so is paying an unlicensed person to perform real estate services. Paying an unlicensed person for these services is a violation of license law.

Kickbacks

Conditions. Under the Real Estate Settlement Procedures Act (RESPA), it is illegal for a real estate licensee to accept a kickback or rebate from any business providing a service used to close a real estate transaction, such as a surveyor, appraiser, property inspector, title company, mortgage lender, etc. A kickback may take the form of favors, advertising, money, gifts, or other items of value given to the licensee or broker in return for sending clients to the particular service provider.

The licensee may utilize these service providers and pay them for services they actually perform. However, the licensee must not accept anything in return from the service provider for utilizing a particular provider.

The licensee also may not give or accept any portion, split, or percentage of any fee the service provider is paid for the service. Brokers may have affiliated business arrangements with certain service providers but must be careful that the arrangement does not include any illegal kickback or rebate.

However, under certain conditions, kickbacks are legal:

- all parties to the transaction must be fully informed of the kickback
- the kickback must not be prohibited by any other law, such as RESPA
- a referral or finder's fee (no more than $50) may be paid to a tenant in an apartment complex for introducing a prospective tenant to the property management company or the complex owner for the purpose of renting or leasing an apartment
- as mentioned above, sharing a commission with an unlicensed buyer or seller as a rebate is allowed as long as all parties to the transaction are informed in writing
- a broker licensed in Florida may pay a referral fee or share a commission with a broker licensed or registered in a foreign state as long as the foreign broker does not violate any Florida law

Procuring cause

The main item of performance for the client is payment of compensation, if the agreement calls for it. A broker's compensation is earned and payable when the broker has performed according to the agreement. The amount and structure of the compensation, potential disputes over who has earned compensation, and the client's liability for multiple commissions are other matters that a listing agreement should address.

Disputes often arise as to whether an agent is owed a commission. Many such disputes involve open listings where numerous agents are working to find customers for the principal, and none has a clear claim on a commission. In other cases, a client may claim to have found the customer alone and therefore to have no responsibility for paying a commission. There are also situations where cooperating brokers and subagents working under an exclusive listing dispute about which one(s) deserve a share of the listing broker's commission.

The concept that decides such disputes is that the party who was the "procuring cause" in finding the customer is entitled to the commission or commission share. The two principal determinants of procuring cause are:

- ▸ being first to find the customer
- ▸ being the one who induces the customer to complete the transaction

For example, Broker A and Broker B each have an open listing with a property owner. Broker A shows Joe the property on Monday. Broker B shows Joe the same property on Friday, and then Joe buys the property. Broker A will probably be deemed to be the procuring cause by virtue of having first introduced Joe to the property.

Procuring cause can be difficult to understand. It is the number one cause of disputes that come before local association professional standards and arbitration boards. Procuring cause is attributed to "the person who starts the chain of events that leads to the sale of the property." Such a party is deemed to have procuring cause. Usually, activities such as holding an open house or answering a call about a piece of property do not constitute procuring cause.

CHANGE OF EMPLOYER OR ADDRESS

FREC notification
Prohibitions during changeover
Change of address

FREC notification

If a sales associate or broker associate changes employing brokers, he or she must notify the FREC of the change within 10 days after the change. The licensee is required to use the FREC's Change of Status for Sales Associates or Broker Sales Associates (DBPR RE 11) form found online at

https://www.myfloridalicense.com/CheckListDetail.asp?SID=&xactCode=9001
&clientCode=2501&XACT_DEFN_ID=1065.

If the licensee chooses to use the printable form, it must be signed by the new employing broker and submitted to the FREC. Rather than using the printable form, the new employing broker can add the licensee to his or her own license through the broker's online account. The licensee's license ceases to be in force until a new license is issued under the new broker.

Sales associate broker change

Violation of the obligation of confidentiality. When a licensee changes employing brokers, he or she is still held to the duty of confidentiality to transaction principals and to the former employing broker. That duty does not end with the end of employment with a broker.

Duplication of records. When a licensee changes employing brokers, he or she may not duplicate records to take the copies to the new employing broker. Doing so is a breach of trust and violation of license law, even if the records were originated by the licensee.

Removal of records from previous broker's office. When a licensee changes employing brokers, he or she may not remove records from the former broker's office. Doing so constitutes theft and is punishable as such.

Change of address　Florida license law requires all licensees to submit their current mailing address to the FREC. If a licensee changes mailing addresses, he or she must notify the FREC within 10 days of the change. The licensee is required to use the Demographic Changes for Real Estate Individuals (DBPR RE 10) form found online at

http://www.myfloridalicense.com/dbpr/re/documents/DBPR_RE_10_Demographic_Changes_and_Dup_Lic_Individuals.pdf.

Broker change of business address. If a broker changes business address, the broker must notify the FREC within 10 days of the change. The broker must use the required form found online at

http://www.myfloridalicense.com/dbpr/re/documents/DBPR_RE_12_Company_Transactions.pdf

and include the names of all sales associates and broker associates who remain in the broker's employ and those who are no longer employed by the broker. The form serves to notify the FREC of the business address change for those remaining associates. The broker and sales associates' licenses cease to be in force until new licenses are issued for the new address.

BUSINESS ENTITY LICENSING & REGISTRATION

May register as brokerage
May not register as brokerage

May register as brokerage　**Sole proprietorship.** A business or brokerage that is owned by one individual is called a sole proprietorship. A licensed broker may form a sole proprietorship by filing with the Florida Department of State (FDOS) and registering with the DBPR. The sole broker is responsible for all business and employee activities.

General partnership. Two or more individuals may form a general partnership and share in the business activities, finances, and profits of the partnership. The partnership must be registered with the DBPR. At least one partner must be a licensed broker, and all partners who deal with the public to perform real estate services must hold valid and current broker licenses. Every active broker partner is responsible for making sure that each partner who must be registered and licensed is indeed registered and licensed.

If the only licensed broker dies or withdraws from the partnership, another licensed broker must be appointed within 14 days or the partnership's registration will be cancelled and all licenses within the partnership will be placed on involuntary inactive status. New brokerage business may not be performed during those 14 days until the new licensed broker is appointed. The FREC must be notified immediately of the death or removal of the licensed broker and what steps were taken to fill the vacancy.

Limited partnership. Limited partnerships are created by filing with the FDOS and must be registered with the DBPR. They must include at least one general partner, with all general partners required to register with the DBPR. At least one general partner must be a licensed broker. All general partners who deal with the public to perform real estate services also must be licensed brokers. The limited partnership must also include at least one limited partner who must invest cash or property but not services. Limited partners are not liable for the partnership's debts unless their names are part of the partnership's name or they participate in managing the business.

Ostensible partnerships are prohibited because they are not actually partnerships. Instead, they occur when two or more people deceive others by acting as though a business partnership really exists. For example, if two unassociated brokers work in the same office but do not have separate signs, they are giving the appearance of a business partnership when one does not exist.

For profit corporation. A corporation is created by one or more individuals who file articles of incorporation with the FDOS and who are the owners and stockholders of the corporation. Corporations may be domestic or foreign. Domestic corporations are incorporated in Florida and conduct business within Florida. Foreign corporations, on the other hand, are incorporated outside of Florida but conduct business within Florida. The corporation is managed by a board of directors elected by the owners/stockholders.

To become a real estate brokerage, the corporation must register with the DBPR as a brokerage entity by submitting a brokerage corporation application. The corporation is required to have at least one of the officers or directors licensed as an active broker. The corporation may have licensed, unlicensed, and inactive brokers serve as officers or directors, but all who provide real estate services to the public must be licensed active brokers. The corporation must also register all unlicensed officers and directors for identification purposes. The brokerage corporation application includes a section for this purpose.

If the brokerage does not have at least one registered licensed active broker, the corporation's registration will be automatically canceled until the license and registration are deemed in force.

Sales associates and broker associates may not be officers or directors within a corporation, but they may be shareholders.

Not for profit corporation. Florida not for profit corporations are created by filing a Florida Not for Profit Corporations application. The specific purpose of the corporation must be included, as well as whether or not the corporation will be seeking 501(c)(3) federal tax-exempt status. The corporation is required to file an annual report to maintain its active status. Failure to file the report will result in the corporation being administratively dissolved.

The corporation may have one or more classes of members or no members at all, but it must have at least three directors. Unlike for profit corporations, these corporations are prohibited from paying dividends or any part of their income or profit to the corporation's members, directors, or officers.

Limited liability company (LLC). LLCs are separate and distinct legal entities wherein the owners are not personally liable for the entity's debts and liabilities. It allows owners to separate their business dealings from their personal affairs. Like other business entities, an LLC must be filed with the FDOS.

An LLC can be taxed as a pass-through entity like a sole proprietorship or partnership or as a regular corporation. With the pass-through, the owners pay taxes only once on the profits, whereas a regular corporation's income is taxed twice – once on its net income and then again on the profit distribution to stockholders.

LLCs can be converted to corporations if the owners so choose.

Limited liability partnership (LLP). An LLP is a business entity that requires a written partnership agreement between the partners. Unlike limited partnerships, all partners in an LLP can participate in managing the business with no one partner having explicit control. New partners can be added and others removed according to the provisions of the partnership agreement. Liability is split among the partners in that each partner is liable for his or her own acts and those of the partner's employees, and no partner is responsible for the errors or acts of another partner. The partners are not liable for debts incurred by another partner.

The LLP is a pass-through entity wherein the partners receive untaxed profits and then pay their own income taxes. As with other entities, an LLP must be registered with the FDOS.

Sales associates and broker associates are prohibited from being officers, members, managers, or directors in a real estate brokerage corporation or a general partner in a brokerage limited or general partnership.

Broker associates or sales associates are licensed as individuals, but can be licensed as a professional corporation, limited liability company, or professional limited liability company if the licensee submits authorization from the Department of State to the FREC.

The new broker's name must be placed on the business through the Florida Department of State (FDOS). Because this process takes time, FREC now allows a temporary broker to be named and registered with DBPR within 14 days. This temporary broker may remain in place for 60 days. Within that timeframe, a new broker must be registered with the FDOS and DBPR.

May not register as brokerage

Corporation sole. A corporation sole is made up of one individual occupying one incorporated office and may consist of only one member at a time. This one member is typically a bishop or other church official. While the corporation sole is typically a church organization, it can also be a political organization.

The purpose of the entity is to ensure the continuity of ownership of property that has been dedicated to the benefit of a particular religious organization. The one member holds title to the property but does not personally own the property. If the one member dies or is removed, the property title is passed on to a successor and not to the previous member's heirs.

Corporation soles are not recognized in all states, and while the Supreme Court of Florida does recognize them, they cannot be registered as real estate brokers.

Joint venture. This business arrangement is formed when two or more individuals or entities join together to carry out a single business activity or a designated number of activities. The arrangement is not permanent and requires the participating individuals to have joint control and to share in the profits and losses. Under Florida law, each partner owes the duties of care and loyalty to the venture and the other partners.

In a real estate joint venture, each individual must be an active licensed broker. Consequently, the venture is not registered as an entity with the FDOS because there is no written arrangement and the licensed brokers are already registered.

Business trust. A business trust is typically set up when the assets and property of a business corporation are entrusted to an appointed trustee. The trustee then manages the operation and assets of the business for the benefit and profit of the beneficiaries.

A real estate business trust is used for transactions involving the trust's own property. Each individual invests in the entity so the trust can buy, develop, and/or sell property. The title to any property purchased is filed in the trustee's name, but the property does not belong to the trustee. All property and assets belong to the trust itself.

While every participant in the trust who performs real estate services must be licensed and registered, the trust itself does not register with the DBPR as a real estate broker.

Cooperative association. A cooperative association is a business organization that is formed, owned, and operated by its members for their mutual benefit. The association may buy or sell its own property, but it is not registered as a real estate broker. Each member is a shareholder who has equal ownership and equal control of the association, with each shareholder having one vote. Profits earned by the association are divided among the shareholders.

Unincorporated association. An unincorporated association is a group of people who form the association for a common non-business purpose and to create a legally binding relationship among themselves. The associations are easy to form and extremely flexible. They can, for example, be a small neighborhood group or a national organization.

Because they are unincorporated, they are not permitted to own property in their own name or to enter into contracts. Consequently, they may not register as a real estate broker.

TRADE NAMES

Brokers register their brokerages under the broker's legal name or the business's legal name. They may also register under a trade name, a fictitious name other than their own name that the broker would like to use for the brokerage. The trade name must appear on the broker's license and registration and must be unique from any other business or trade name.

The broker may only register under one trade name and must have a new license issued if he or she changes the trade name. The registered trade name must appear on all brokerage signage and advertising.

LLC registration and trade name usage. DBPR does allow sales associates and broker associates to register as limited liability companies (LLC) or as professional associations (PA) with the FDOS. It does not permit them to use a trade name or fictitious name. They must register under their real names and have only the real name show on the license. For example, John Kennedy, may form an LLC and be licensed as John Kennedy, LLC. This is the name he must operate under and which must appear on all official documents. All money must go into an account with this name.

It is recommended that sales associates and broker associates talk with a Certified Public Accountant (CPA) or lawyer to ensure they understand all of the consequences and requirements of this form of registration.

Display of names. FREC administrative rules prohibit licensees from using or displaying any name, insignia, or designation of a real estate association or organization unless they are authorized to do so.

ETHICAL PRACTICES

Codes of ethics
Disclosure
Fraud and negligence
Brokerage cooperation
Personal assistants

Codes of ethics

The real estate industry has developed a code of professional standards and ethics as a guideline in serving the real estate needs of consumers. This professional code has emerged from three primary sources:

▸ federal and state legislation
▸ state real estate licensing regulation
▸ industry self-regulation through trade associations and institutes

Federal legislation focuses primarily on anti-discrimination laws and fair-trade practices. State laws and licensing regulations focus on agency and disclosure requirements and regulating certain brokerage practices within the state jurisdiction. Real estate trade groups focus on professional standards of conduct in every facet of the business.

By observing professional ethics and standards, licensees will serve clients and customers better, foster a professional image in the community, and avoid regulatory sanctions and lawsuits.

Today's professional ethics are not only important for one's career; they are also legal imperatives. Unethical practice, such as misrepresentation of material facts, fraud, and culpable negligence, is prohibited and punishable in all aspects of real estate practice.

Disclosure

Proper disclosures are an integral part of ethical behavior. In compliance with applicable laws and to promote respect for the real estate profession, licensees should be careful to disclose

▸ that the agent is going to receive compensation from more than one party in a transaction
▸ property defects if they are reasonably apparent; however there is no duty to disclose a defect which it would require technical expertise to discover
▸ any interest the agent has in a listed property if the agent is representing a party concerning the property
▸ any profits made on a client's money
▸ the agent's identity in advertisements
▸ the agent's representation of both parties in a transaction
▸ the existence of accepted offers
▸ identity of broker and firm in advertising as required by state law

Fraud and negligence

Fraud. Fraud is a misrepresentation of a material fact used to induce someone to do something, like sign a contract. *Actual fraud* occurs when one person intentionally deceives another person by misrepresenting a material fact that induces the person to rely upon the fact. *Negative fraud* is intentionally failing to disclose a material fact.

For a cause of action for fraud to be initiated, the following elements must exist:

- The licensee must have misrepresented a material fact or must have failed to disclose the material fact.
- The licensee must have known or should have known that he or she was misrepresenting the fact or that he or she should have disclosed the fact.
- The buyer or other party to whom the licensee misrepresented the fact relied on what the licensee said.
- The buyer or other party to whom the licensee misrepresented the fact or failed to disclose the fact was damaged as a result of the misrepresentation or omission.

Culpable negligence. Culpable negligence occurs when a person, such as a real estate broker, does not perform his or her required duties and responsibilities as the broker knows he or she should. The failure to perform need not be intentional to be considered negligent. It is more of a disregard of the duties and consequences of not performing them. Remember, three critical duties of brokers are skill, care, and diligence. Failure to perform real estate activities with skill, care, and diligence may be ruled culpable negligence. In Florida, culpable negligence is not only unethical, but is also a second-degree misdemeanor.

Brokerage cooperation

Professional conduct excludes disparagement of competitors. Real estate professionals also

- forgo pursuit of unfair advantage
- arbitrate rather than litigate disputes
- respect the agency relationships of others
- conform to accepted standards of co-brokerage practices

Personal assistants

Sales associates are permitted to have personal assistants if they so choose. They should discuss this with their broker prior to hiring a personal assistant. The personal assistant may be a licensed or unlicensed person.

An unlicensed personal assistant may help an agent create advertisements, run errands, enter information into the computer, etc. FREC and Florida Realtors® have a list of the duties unlicensed assistants may perform listed on their respective websites. Unlicensed personal assistants may not be hired as independent contractors but must be treated as employees.

Either the broker or the licensee may pay the personal assistant. Whoever pays the assistant must withhold the required state and federal employment taxes. This party is also responsible for forwarding funds to the government according to federal employment law.

A **licensed** personal assistant is allowed to perform all real estate services on the licensee's behalf. If a personal assistant receives a salary or hourly pay, either the licensee or the broker may pay it. Any commission must be paid the broker. The personal assistant must be registered under the broker's name with DBPR.

5 Real Estate Brokerage Activities & Procedures
Snapshot Review

BROKERAGE OFFICES

Office requirements
- per Florida, each broker to have an office in building with stationary construction; office to be registered with DBPR; to include enclosed room and space for private meetings; records to be kept in office; only brokers may have offices; may have office outside of Florida or at broker's residence; must comply with ADA

Branch offices
- any office in addition to main office; must be registered; new offices to be registered

Entrance sign requirements
- sign to be displayed at office entrance; must contain broker's name and trade name with "Licensed Real Estate Broker" included; sales associates' names not required but must be below broker's name

Temporary shelters
- to protect associates and customers; cannot be permanent assignment; no transaction closings

Sales associate officing
- sales associates to be registered under a broker and work out of broker's office; registered under one broker at a time

GUIDELINES FOR ADVERTISING

Prohibitions
- false or misleading advertising; blind advertising; sales associate advertising or conducting business under own name
- licensees may sell their own property outside the brokerage; may advertise in own name with broker's permission; must disclose ownership and licensure
- team advertising to be done under employing broker's supervision and name
- must be clear the advertiser is a real estate licensee; team name must be next to firm name

Wording of advertisements
- must make clear the advertiser is a real estate licensee

Internet advertising
- broker's name to be included with point of contact information

Telephone solicitation laws
- Telephone Consumer Protection Act – no unsolicited calls, no robocalls, do not call compliance; opt-out option required; time of day restrictions
- exemptions include nonprofits, political organizations, federal debt collectors, real estate licensee with buyer for "for sale by owner", with established business relationship, with business inquiry within last 3 months
- CAN-SPAM Act – no unsolicited email with commercial message and without prior consent
- Junk Fax Prevention Act – no unsolicited faxes; all faxes to include date and time, company's name and phone number; unsolicited faxes to include opt-out option

Florida telemarketing laws
- Florida Telemarketing Act and Florida Telephonic Sales law – solicitors need license; time of day restrictions; no blocking caller ID; payments not limited to credit cards; caller has 30 seconds to identify him/herself; provide right to cancel info
- Florida do not call list to be merged with national list; exemptions include nonprofit, political, and religious organizations and licensed insurance professionals; also includes real estate licensees calling about yard sign placed by seller unless seller is on national do not call list

HANDLING DEPOSITS

Escrow account deposit requirements

- bank account used to hold funds belonging to third party until time to disburse; no comingling of broker funds with third party funds
- funds to be delivered to broker by end of next business day; broker to deposit funds immediately – by end of the third business day following receipt of funds
- attorney or title company escrow - same deposit requirements as for broker; licensee to note name, address, and phone on sales contract; broker to request proof of deposit within 10 business days of due date and provide seller proof within 10 business days of request

Management of escrow accounts

- broker to be signatory on escrow account; broker to reconcile account monthly and keep records; account may be interest bearing with parties agreeing on receiver of interest
- conflicting demands for escrow funds to be reported to FREC within 15 business days; broker to initiate settlement procedure within 30 business days; broker's good faith doubt results in notifying FREC and initiating settlement procedure
- settlement procedures include mediation, arbitration, litigation with interpleader action or declaratory judgment, escrow disbursement order; 3 exceptions to settlement procedures

REPRESENTING LICENSEE EXPERTISE

Opinion of title

- prohibited from offering opinion of title not written by attorney

Representation of value

- may offer value opinion derived from BPO or CMA; not to represent as appraisal

Misrepresentation of value

- constitutes fraud, breach of contract, or breach of trust, resulting in lawsuits and discipline

Unauthorized practice of law

- third degree felony punishable with probation, prison time, fines, and restitution

COMMISSIONS

Prohibitions

- price fixing, sales associate contracting directly with principal, sales associate suing principal for commission, sharing commission with unlicensed person, paying unlicensed person for performing real estate services

Kickbacks

- prohibited acceptance of favors, advertising, money, gifts, etc. for referring clients to certain businesses unless all parties are informed, no other law prohibits it, paying referral fee to tenant for prospective other tenant, sharing commission with foreign broker

Procuring cause

- broker's compensation is earned and payable when the broker has performed according to the agreement; two determinants: first to find customer, inducing customer to complete transaction; procuring cause attributable to party initiating a chain of events leading to a sale.

CHANGE OF EMPLOYER OR ADDRESS

FREC notification

- notify FREC within 10 days of change; license not in force until new license issued

Sales associate Broker change

- violating confidentiality, duplicating records, removing records from broker's office

| **Change of address** | • | notify FREC within 10 days of change; broker to include names of associates still employed and those who have left; licenses not in force until new license issued |

BUSINESS ENTITY LICENSING & REGISTRATION

May register as broker	•	sole proprietorship, general partnership, limited partnership, for profit corporation, not for profit corporation, LLC, LLP
	•	ostensible partnerships prohibited
May not register as broker	•	corporation sole, joint venture, business trust, cooperative association, unincorporated associations

TRADE NAMES	•	fictitious name used as business name; must be registered and appear on license, signage and advertising
	•	sales associates prohibited from using trade name
	•	licensee must be authorized to display name, insignia, or designation of an association

ETHICAL PRACTICES

| **Codes of ethics** | • | codes provide self-regulating standards of conduct covering all facets of the profession; serve clients, customers, and the public; avoid sanctions and liability; cover practices such as job performance, duties to clients and customers, disclosures, non-discrimination, professional relationships |

| **Disclosure** | • | disclosure: compensating parties; property defects; agent's interest in property; use of client funds; agent's identity in advertising |

| **Fraud & negligence** | • | fraud: actual fraud when misrepresentation of material fact is intentional; negative fraud when failure to disclose material fact is intentional |
| | • | culpable negligence: when duties are not performed as required, whether or not intentional |

| **Brokerage cooperation** | • | professional conduct: no unfair advantage; arbitrate disputes; respect relationships; follow accepted practices |

| **Personal assistants** | • | licensees may hire licensed or unlicensed assistants who may be paid by salary or, if licensed, by commission paid by broker; duties are administrative if unlicensed and must be in compliance with FREC regulations if licensed |

SECTION FIVE: Real Estate Brokerage Activities & Procedures

Section Quiz

1. Two real estate companies agree to conjoin their resources for the development and sale of an apartment complex, for which profits will be shared equally. This is an example of

   a. a cooperative association.
   b. a real estate investment trust.
   c. a limited partnership.
   d. a joint venture.

2. Real estate advertising is a regulated activity. One important restriction in placing ads is

   a. a broker may only place blind ads in approved publications.
   b. a broker must have all advertising approved by the proper state regulatory agency.
   c. the advertising must not be misleading.
   d. sales agents may only advertise in their own name.

3. The three principal brokerage firms in a market agree to charge clients the same commission rate, regardless of market conditions. This is an example of

   a. redlining.
   b. price fixing.
   c. allocation of markets.
   d. steering.

4. Which of the following is NOT a state mandated requirement for a broker's office?

   a. Located in a building with stationary construction
   b. Separate enclosed offices for each broker and associate
   c. Located within State of Florida
   d. Accessible to handicapped individuals

5. Which of the following statements is true?

   a. Only the broker's main office must be registered.
   b. Closed branch offices may not be reopened.
   c. Sales associates' names must be shown on all office signage.
   d. The registration for a closed branch office may not be transferred to a new branch office.

6. Advertising that does not include the broker's licensed name is

   a. appropriate for signage.
   b. considered fraud.
   c. considered blind advertising.
   d. appropriate for internet advertising.

7. If a sales associate accepts as earnest money payment from a property buyer, what must the associate do with the check?

   a. Cash it and wait for it to clear the bank before depositing the funds into an escrow account.
   b. Deposit the check into the brokerage's escrow account within 48 hours.
   c. Turn the check over to the employing broker by end of the next business day.
   d. Give the check to the employing broker by end of the third business day following receipt of the check.

8. Brokers are required to deposit third party funds immediately. How does Florida define "immediately"?

   a. The same day the broker received the funds
   b. No later than the end of the third business day following receipt of the funds
   c. No later than the end of the next business day following receipt of the funds
   d. Within 24 hours of receipt of the funds

9. If a broker chooses to use an interest-bearing account for escrow funds, he must

   a. obtain written agreement from all involved parties.
   b. disburse the interest in equal amounts to all involved parties each month.
   c. withdraw the interest from the escrow account monthly and deposit it into his business account.
   d. Brokers are not permitted to use interest-bearing escrow accounts.

10. If the parties to a transaction do not agree on the disbursement of escrow funds, the broker must notify the FREC

    a. within 15 business days of the last demand.
    b. within 30 business days of the last demand.
    c. by end of the next business day.
    d. no later than the end of the third business day following the last demand.

11. An escrow conflict resolution procedure that places the funds into a court's depository and removes the broker from the dispute is called

    a. arbitration.
    b. escrow disbursement order.
    c. interpleader action.
    d. mediation.

12. If a property buyer fails to meet the financing provisions of the sales contract, what may the broker do with the escrow funds?

    a. Notify the FREC within 10 days
    b. Began a settlement procedure within 30 days
    c. Release the escrow funds to the buyer without notifying the FREC
    d. Release the escrow funds to the seller within 15 business days

13. What can happen if a licensee pays hourly wages to a personal assistant?

    a. The licensee's license can be suspended or revoked.
    b. The licensee may face prison time.
    c. The broker may face criminal charges.
    d. This is legal.

14. Under what circumstances may a licensee offer an opinion of title?

    a. When the licensee develops the opinion of title with assistance from his employing broker
    b. When the licensee obtains the opinion of title from an attorney and passes the information on to the client
    c. When the licensee uses the abstract of title completed by the title company to develop the opinion of title
    d. When the client does not wish to consult an attorney

15. In Florida, the unlicensed practice of law is a

    a. misdemeanor of the third degree.
    b. first-degree felony.

    c. civil violation.
    d. third-degree felony.

16. Sarah is a sales associate who handled the sale of John's property. John paid the commission to Sarah's employing broker, Stan, but Stan never paid Sarah her share of the commission. What can Sarah do?

    a. Sue John for not paying Sarah directly.
    b. Sue Stan for not paying Sarah her share of the commission.
    c. Report Stan to the FREC for a license law violation.
    d. Nothing, sales associates are not permitted to sue.

17. If a licensee changes employing brokers, he or she must notify the FREC of the change

    a. immediately.
    b. within 30 days of the change.
    c. within 10 days after the change.
    d. There is no need to notify the FREC of an employing broker change.

18. Which of the following entities may register as a brokerage?

    a. Corporation sole
    b. Business trust
    c. Unincorporated association
    d. Limited partnership

19. Which of the following statements is true?

    a. Sales associates are not permitted to use a trade name.
    b. Trade names are not included on the broker's license.
    c. A broker need not have a new license issued if his trade name changes.
    d. Once registered, a broker is prohibited from changing trade names.

20. An unincorporated association

    a. may register as a real estate brokerage.
    b. is a legally binding relationship among its members.
    c. is complicated to form.
    d. may own property in its own name.

21. In a joint venture,

    a. the arrangement is permanent.
    b. a written agreement is required.
    c. participating members must have joint control.
    d. only the controlling partner owes the duty of care and loyalty.

22. An LLC is a

    a. limited legal corporation.
    b. limited liability company.
    c. legal liability company.
    d. limited liability corporation.

23. Which of the follow entities may file 501(c)(3) federal tax-exempt status?

    a. Limited liability partnership
    b. Ostensible partnership
    c. Sole proprietorship
    d. Not for profit corporation

24. Which type of business entity is prohibited?

    a. For profit corporation
    b. Limited partnership
    c. Ostensible partnership
    d. Corporation sole

25. Which of the following may not register as a brokerage?

    a. Cooperative association
    b. Limited liability partnership
    c. Not for profit corporation
    d. General partnership

26. If a licensee changes from one employing broker to another, the licensee

    a. still owes the duty of confidentiality to the former broker and principals.
    b. has no further duties to the former broker.
    c. owes the full range of duties to both brokers.
    d. can be placed on probation.

27. Licenses changing employing brokers are prohibited from

    a. listing the former broker's trade name on a resume.
    b. acting as a cooperating broker with the former broker.
    c. performing any licensed acts under the new broker for six months.
    d. removing records from the previous broker's office.

6 Violations of License Law, Penalties, and Procedures

Definitions
Disciplinary Procedure
Commission Meeting
Violations and Penalties
Real Estate Recovery Fund

Learning Objectives

- Explain the procedures involved in the reporting of violations, the investigation of complaints and the conduct of hearings
- Enumerate the causes for a license application to be denied
- Distinguish actions that would cause a license to be subject to suspension or revocation
- Identify individuals who would be eligible and the procedure to seek reimbursement from the Real Estate Recovery Fund
- Identify individuals who are not qualified to make a claim from the Real Estate Recovery Fund
- Describe the monetary limits imposed by law on the Real Estate Recovery Fund
- Distinguish among the various penalties that may be issued by a court of law

Key Terms

breach of trust
citation
complaint
concealment
culpable negligence
formal or administrative complaint
fraud
legally sufficient
misrepresentation
moral turpitude

notice of noncompliance
probable cause
recommended order
stipulation
subpoena
summary/emergency suspension order
voluntary relinquishment for permanent revocation

DEFINITIONS

Administrative complaint – an initial written summary of allegations of license law violation(s) filed against a licensee

Breach of trust – failure to carry out promises or obligations owed to another person whether intentional or negligent

Commingling – mixing funds which belong to one party with the funds of another party; depositing a licensee's personal or business funds into the same escrow account that holds clients' funds

Concealment – the failure to disclose material facts or information as required by law; an act that prevents or hinders discovery of facts that could potentially affect the decision to move forward with a contract

Conversion – one party's use, alteration, or destruction of another party's property or funds for the first party's own purposes; a licensee's personal use of a client or customer's funds

Culpable negligence – actions or lack of actions that negatively or harmfully affect others; failure to consider the potential results of one's actions

Formal complaint – an administrative complaint which lists all of the charges against a licensee and which is filed when the Probable Cause Panel determines that probable cause exists for prosecution by the DBPR

Formal hearing – a hearing chosen by an offender when there are disputed facts after probable cause has been determined to exist; held before an administrative law judge and allows the offender to present his or her side of the case

Fraud – the deliberate deception for the purpose of unfair or unlawful personal gain; use of a dishonest action to deprive another person of his or her money, property, or legal right

Good faith – a sincere belief, motive, or intention to deal honestly with others without malice or unfair advantage

Informal hearing – a hearing chosen by an offender when there are no disputed facts after probable cause has been determined to exist; held during a regular meeting of the FREC

Material fact – significant or essential information that may affect a property's value and/or a person's willingness to enter into a contract or transaction

Misrepresentation – one party providing a false or misleading statement that can affect another party's decision to enter into a contract or transaction

Moral turpitude – a type of act or behavior that is considered vile or depraved and goes against accepted moral standards and/or insults general morality; for example, murder, robbery, counterfeiting, and arson

Nolo contendere or **no contest** – a plea made by a defendant in a criminal case that accepts conviction without admitting guilt

Probable cause – a reasonable basis or concrete evidence to indicate that a crime may have been committed

Summary suspension – an emergency suspension order issued when the public is in immediate danger from the actions of a licensee

---

DISCIPLINARY PROCEDURE

The complaint
DBPR investigation
Probable-cause panel
Formal/administrative complaint
Stipulation
Voluntary relinquishment

The complaint

Any person who believes a licensee, applicant, or unlicensed person has violated Florida real estate license law may file a complaint with the Department of Business and Professional Regulation (DBPR). The complaint must be in writing, signed by the complainant, and legally sufficient. That is, the complaint must include ultimate facts that show a violation of Florida statutes and/or FREC administrative rules. The DBPR may require supporting documentation to determine legal sufficiency.

An administrative complaint alleging a violation by a broker, broker associate, or sales associate must be filed within 5 years after the violation occurred or after the violation was discovered or should have been discovered. If the complaint is filed with the DBPR or FREC against a sales associate, the associate's employing broker will be notified of the complaint in writing. However, the notice will not be sent until 10 days after probable cause has been found by the Probable Cause Panel or until the licensee waives his or her confidentiality privilege, whichever occurs first.

Investigate if warranted. If the DBPR determines the allegations would constitute a violation, the Department will initiate an investigation and send a copy of the complaint to the violating licensee or the licensee's attorney. The DBPR will also notify the complainant of whether probable cause was found and the status of the investigation and administrative proceedings. If the complaint is the result of a criminal act by the offender, the Department is not required to notify anyone of the investigation. Further, if those conducting the investigation agree in writing that notifications would adversely affect the investigation, notification may be withheld.

If the complaint is for a first-time minor violation, the DBPR may simply issue a notice of noncompliance to the offender. However, if the DBPR believes the public is in immediate danger from the actions of the offender, the Department's secretary may issue a summary suspension.

DBPR investigation   The Department of Business and Professional Regulation (DBPR) may investigate the following:

> ▶ an anonymous complaint, as long as the complaint is in writing and legally sufficient and if the alleged violation is substantial and the department believes the allegations are true

> ▶ a complaint from a confidential informant, as long as the complaint is in writing and legally sufficient and if the alleged violation is substantial and the department believes the allegations are true

> ▶ a complaint that the original complainant withdraws or tries to dissuade the DBPR from investigating or prosecuting

> ▶ the DBPR or FREC's own reasonable belief that a licensee or group of licensees has violated a Florida statute or rule

After the Department has initiated an investigation and notified the violating licensee or the licensee's attorney, the licensee has 20 days to submit a written response. The response is forwarded to the Probable Cause Panel for consideration.

When the Department completes the investigation, it will submit an investigative report to the Panel, complete with the investigative findings and recommendations for probable cause. However, if the Department determines a lack of sufficient evidence to support the allegations, it may submit a report to the Panel, dismiss the case, and notify the subject of the complaint.

Probable-cause panel   Based on the volume of cases to be handled, the FREC may provide multiple probable cause panels. Each panel will consist of at least two members who meet the following requirements:

> ▶ one or more may be former Commission members

> ▶ one must be a current Commission member

> ▶ one must be a former or current consumer Commission member

> ▶ one must be a former or current professional Commission member who holds an active valid real estate license

Members of the Panel serve varying terms or repetition of service as determined by the FREC.

The sole purpose of the Panel is to determine whether probable cause exists for any complaint investigated by the DBPR. The determination is made by a majority vote of Panel members. To make an informed determination, the Panel may request additional investigative information from the DBPR within 15 days of receiving a case's investigative report. The Panel must then make its determination of probable cause within 30 days of receiving a final investigative report. The Department's secretary may provide an extension to the 15 and 30-day timelines.

If the Panel finds there is no probable cause, it may dismiss the case with or without a Letter of Guidance suggesting what action the subject of the complaint should take. If the Panel does not determine probable cause or issue a letter of guidance within the 30 days, the DBPR will make a determination one way or the other within the next 10 days. If either the Panel or the DBPR finds probable cause, a formal complaint will be filed against the offender, and his or her employing broker and the complainant will be notified.

Probable cause proceedings are confidential and not open to the public. Nor are they open to FREC members who are not members of the Panel, because those members need to remain objective in case they are to participate in an informal hearing on the matter.

Formal/ administrative complaint

The filing of a formal complaint will result in the complaint being prosecuted by the DBPR. However, if the Department believes the Panel was faulty or careless in finding probable cause, the Department may decide not to prosecute.

The formal complaint will be sent to the offender either by regular mail, certified mail, or email. It is the responsibility of the licensee to ensure that the Department has a record of the licensee's current mailing address, email address, and place of practice. The formal complaint lists the charges and provides the offender with an Election of Rights, which is a choice of which way the offender wishes to respond. The offender may choose

- ▸ not to dispute the allegations of fact and to request an informal hearing
- ▸ to dispute the allegations of fact and to request a formal hearing, or
- ▸ not to dispute the allegations of fact and to waive the right to be heard

The offending licensee must submit his or her Election of Rights choice within 21 days from the date it was received and be given at least a 14-day notice of a hearing date. Failing to respond within the required timeframe results in the licensee waiving the right to choose. Consequently, the case will then be heard in an informal hearing before the FREC.

Stipulation

Rather than attend a hearing when the licensee does not dispute the facts, he or she may agree to meet with the Division of Real Estate to discuss an agreement that will end the case. The agreement, called a stipulation, will take into consideration the facts of the case and what, if any, penalties both parties can agree upon. The stipulation must be approved by the FREC before it becomes effective. If the FREC denies the terms of the stipulation, it can make recommendations for changes to the penalties that it feels are more appropriate for approval.

Voluntary relinquishment

Another decision the offending licensee may make to avoid going through a complaint hearing is a voluntarily relinquishment for permanent revocation of his or her license. Doing so will permanently revoke the license and prohibit the licensee from ever practicing real estate again. The relinquishment will take the place of any potential penalties that may have been deemed appropriate as a result of a hearing. The relinquishment must be approved by the FREC, who will notify the offender of their approval through a final order.

COMMISSION MEETING

Informal hearing
Formal hearing
FREC-issued final order
Judicial review

If neither a stipulation agreement nor a voluntary relinquishment for permanent revocation is agreeable to the offending licensee, then the complaint case must be heard in an informal or formal hearing.

Informal hearing

If the licensee chooses not to dispute the allegations presented in a formal complaint, he or she may request an informal hearing before the FREC. The meeting is held during a meeting of the FREC. The licensee may present his or her side of the case and have an attorney and/or witnesses attend on his or her behalf. Only those FREC members who did not serve on the Probable Cause Panel may attend the hearing.

After hearing the case, the Commission will determine the guilt or innocence of the licensee and impose the appropriate penalty, if any. The Commission will send formal notice to the licensee in the form of a final order. If any dispute arises during the informal hearing, the hearing is to be terminated and the case moved to a formal hearing.

Formal hearing

A formal hearing may be held in either of two situations: the offending licensee disputes allegations and requests a formal hearing, or disputes that arise during an informal hearing result in the case being heard in a formal hearing. The hearing is similar to how a case is tried in a civil or criminal court with each party presenting facts and witnesses.

As in an informal hearing, the licensee may have an attorney and/or witnesses on his or her behalf. If necessary, witnesses may be subpoenaed by the judge.

After the case is heard, the judge will issue a recommended order to the FREC and provide a copy to the licensee. The order will contain the judge's findings, conclusions, and recommended penalties, if any. Parties of record in the case may submit written exceptions to the judge's recommended order that clearly identify the legal basis for the exception.

FREC-issued final order

After receiving the recommended order from the formal hearing judge, the Commission will review all information from the informal and formal hearings as well as any stipulations, voluntary relinquishments, and exceptions to determine if guilt has been established and if discipline is warranted. The Commission may reject, modify, or accept the recommended order as the final order.

If penalties are deemed warranted, the Commission can impose fines, license suspension, or license revocation to permanently block the offender from practicing real estate in Florida. At any point in the complaint process that the offender's actions are considered dangerous to the public, the DBPR Secretary may issue a summary suspension of the offender's license.

After the Commission has reviewed the case and ruled on guilt or innocence and discipline, it will issue a final order within 90 days of receiving the recommended order. The final order will include a ruling on each exception previously submitted.

The Commission will then send a copy of the final order to all parties to the case and inform them of the process to appeal the ruling. A copy of the final order must also be sent to the DRE within 15 days after the order is filed with the clerk. The final order can be used as prima facie evidence in any resulting civil case related to the complaint and final ruling.

Judicial review   A licensee who disagrees with the final order may file an appeal with the DBPR and the District Court of Appeals within 30 days of receiving the order. The licensee may also file a stay of enforcement to stop the enforcement of the final order until the appeal is completed. When the stay request is filed, the court issues a writ of supersedeas which overrides the Commission's final order and allows the licensee to continue practicing real estate until completion of the appeal.

During the appeal, if the court finds that the Commission made a material error, the court will require corrective action by the Commission. However, with no finding of error by the FREC and no other legitimate grounds for modifying or dismissing the final order, the court must find in support of the FREC's final order. If the court finds in favor of the licensee, the licensee's rights must be restored. The court may award the licensee attorney and court fees.

VIOLATIONS AND PENALTIES

FREC authority
Violations and penalties
Penalties issued by court of law

FREC authority   The Commission has the authority to set guidelines for penalties to be imposed on a licensee who violates Florida's real estate laws, specifically Chapter 455 and Chapter 475, as well as the FREC Administrative Code. Because the Commission's jurisdiction is limited to the practice of real estate in Florida, it may only impose administrative penalties related to that practice. Criminal and civil penalties must come from the courts. Restitution to an injured party is a civil matter and, therefore, cannot be granted by the FREC.

The FREC is authorized to carry out the following actions:

▶ **deny a license application**

Grounds for application or licensure denial include errors on the application, failure to meet the application or licensure qualifications, failure to pay applicable fees, lack of required character, acts that would warrant suspension or revocation of a license, caught cheating on the licensure examination.

▶ **refuse to renew a license**

Grounds for refusing to renew an existing license are much the same as those for denying the license application

▶ **reprimand**

Similar to a notice of noncompliance, a letter of reprimand may be issued to a licensee who has violated real estate law or code.

▶ **issue notice of noncompliance**

As established by the Commission, violations of certain statutes and rules are considered minor violations

These laws are those that do not result in economic or physical harm or negatively affect the health, safety, or welfare of the public or create a threat of harm.

First-time violators of these laws can receive a notice of noncompliance that identifies the law violated and contains instructions on how and by when to correct the violation. The law gives these violators 14-days to correct the violation. Failure to correct the violation can result in the licensee receiving a citation or being further disciplined.

Administrative Code 61J2-24.003 contains the list of these statutes and rules and can be found online at

http://www.myfloridalicense.com/DBPR/servop/testing/documents/ Printable_LawBook.pdf

▶ **impose an administrative fine**

Fines range from $100 to $5,000 per violation for certain violations.

▶ **impose probation**

In addition to other disciplinary penalties, the Commission may place a licensee on probation. The Commission will designate the time period and conditions it deems appropriate.

Standard probationary conditions may include requiring the licensee to complete a prelicense or postlicense course, to successfully complete the state-administered examination, and/or to be periodically interviewed by a DBPR investigator.

Brokers on probation may have their licenses placed on a broker associate status or be required to file escrow account status reports with the Commission or with a DBPR investigator at prescribed intervals.

▶ **issue citations**

Citations are issued for specific violations that do not pose a substantial threat to the public health, safety, and welfare. DBPR investigators and FREC may issue a maximum citation of $500. Citations must be paid or disputed within 30 days. If disputed, the matter will be forwarded for a formal hearing before an administrative law judge.

▶ **suspend a license**

Based on disciplinary guidelines and associated penalties, a license may be suspended for law and code violations for up to 10 years.

▶ **revoke a license**

Based on disciplinary guidelines and associated penalties, this penalty is intended to permanently remove the violator from the practice of real estate; however, further language in the law states that the FREC may approve an application from a previously revoked licensee if *"because of lapse of time and subsequent good conduct and reputation, or other reason deemed sufficient, it appears to the commission that the interest of the public and investors will not likely be endangered."*

Regardless of this language in the law, the FREC maintains its policy not to license previously revoked licensees.

▶ **revoke without prejudice**

If the license was issued by mistake or inadvertence of the Commission, it can be revoked or canceled without prejudicing a later application by the same individual.

▶ **mediation**

Violations that are economic in nature and involve disputes are subject to being referred to mediation for resolution.

Such violations include: a broker's failure to maintain an office or entrance sign, failure to register a branch office, and failure to pay a licensee the amount of commission designated in a civil judgment.

Violations and penalties

Florida Administrative Code contains an exhaustive list of actions that constitute real estate law violations and the penalties for first and subsequent violations. The list may be found online at

http://www.myfloridalicense.com/DBPR/servop/testing/documents/Printable_LawBook.pdf.

The following are examples of violations and associated penalties from that list.

Violation	First Violation	Subsequent Violations
Fraud, misrepresentation, and dishonest dealing	administrative fine and 30-day suspension to revocation	administrative fine and 6-month suspension to revocation
False, deceptive or misleading advertising	administrative fine and 30 to 90-day suspension	administrative fine and 90-day suspension to revocation
Culpable negligence or breach of trust	administrative fine and 30-day suspension to revocation	administrative fine and 6-month suspension to revocation
Failure, as a broker, to deposit any money in an escrow account immediately upon receipt until disbursement is properly authorized;. as a sales associate, to place any money to be escrowed with his registered employer	administrative fine and 30-day suspension to revocation	administrative fine and suspension to revocation
Failure to report in writing to the Commission within 30 days after the licensee is convicted or found guilty of, or entered a plea of nolo contendere or guilty to, regardless of adjudication, a crime in any jurisdiction.	administrative fine and suspension to revocation	administrative fine and suspension to revocation

Collection, by a sales associate, of any money in connection with any real estate brokerage transaction except in the name of the employer	administrative fine and suspension to revocation	administrative fine and suspension to revocation
Rendering an opinion that the title to property sold is good or merchantable when not based on opinion of a licensed attorney	administrative fine and 30-day suspension to revocation	administrative fine and suspension to revocation

These penalties are typically imposed during an informal or formal hearing. The order of penalties for violations, ranging from lowest to highest, is reprimand, fine, probation, suspension, and revocation or denial. Any of these penalties may be combined.

The penalties are as listed unless aggravating or mitigating circumstances can be demonstrated during a hearing, in which case, the Commission may deviate from the penalty guidelines listed in the Administrative Code.

Additional violations and grounds for discipline are contained in Chapter 455.227 found online at http://www.flsenate.gov/Laws/Statutes/2019/Chapter455/All.

The following are examples of violations that may result in the issuance of a *citation*. The entire list is found in 61J2-24.002 F.A.C. online at http://www.myfloridalicense.com/DBPR/servop/testing/documents/Printable_La wBook.pdf.

Section 475.25(1)(q), F.S.	failed to give the appropriate disclosure or notice at the appropriate time under the provisions of Section 475.2755 or 475.278, F.S. (A citation may only be given for a first-time violation.)
Section 475.25(1)(r), F.S.	failed to include the required information in a listing agreement; failed to give a copy to a principal within 24 hours; contains a self-renewal clause
Section 475.4511(2), F.S.	advertised false, inaccurate, misleading, or exaggerated information
Rule 61J2-10.025, F.A.C.	advertised in a manner in which a reasonable person would not know one is dealing with a real estate licensee or brokerage; failed to include the registered name of the brokerage firm in the advertisement; failed to use the licensee's last name as registered with the Commission in an advertisement

Rule 61J2-10.038, F.A.C	failed to timely notify the DBPR of the current mailing address or any change in the current mailing address
Subsection 61J2-14.012(2), F.A.C.	failed to properly reconcile an escrow account when the account balances

Penalties issued by court of law

Civil penalties. Civil penalties are monetary punishment for violating a statute or administrative code and are imposed as restitution for wrongdoing. The penalty can be a fine, surcharge, or compensation imposed to enforce regulations and/or recover funds owed. Civil penalties are not the result of a private suit between two private parties. Those suits result in civil damages, not penalties. Civil penalties are imposed by the courts for such violations as writing bad checks, practicing real estate without a license, filing a false complaint against a licensee, failure to pay an imposed fine, etc.

Criminal penalties. Criminal penalties are a result of violations of local, state, or federal laws that prohibit certain conduct. The penalty may be a fine, an arrest, or jail/prison time. These penalties are imposed by criminal courts. Neither the FREC nor the DBPR has the authority to impose criminal penalties. However, the DBPR is required to refer criminal matters to the Florida Attorney General's office. Criminal offenses fall into separate classes:

> ▸ **misdemeanor of the first degree** results in a penalty of a fine up to $1,000 and/or up to 1 year in jail; offenses such as failing to provide accurate and current rental information for a fee are misdemeanors of the first degree

> ▸ **misdemeanor of the second degree** results in a penalty of a fine up to $500 and/or up to 60 days in jail; offenses such as false advertising, filing false statements to the FREC, or other violations of Chapter 475 F.S. are misdemeanors of the second degree

> ▸ **felony of the third degree** results in a penalty of a fine up to $5,000 and/or 5 years in jail; offenses such as stealing or copying the state licensure examination, making misleading statements on a licensure application, and practicing real estate without a valid license are felonies of the third degree

Any licensee who pleads guilty or *nolo contendere* or is found guilty of a misdemeanor or felony must notify the Commission within 30 days of the plea or conviction. Failure to report the plea or conviction may result in the licensee being disciplined.

Reporting licensees should use Florida's Criminal Self-Reporting Document which can be found online at

http://www.myfloridalicense.com/dbpr/pro/documents/Criminal%20Self%20Reporting_05.2019.pdf

REAL ESTATE RECOVERY FUND

Brokerage transactions
Persons unqualified to make claim
Payment for claims
Fund limit and fees

Brokerage transactions

The purpose of the Florida Real Estate Recovery Fund is to reimburse individuals or business entities for monetary damages caused by the actions of a real estate licensee in relation to a real estate transaction. Payments from the Fund will be approved by the FREC if

▸ the licensee held a current, valid, active real estate license at the time the act was committed

▸ the licensee was neither the seller, buyer, landlord, or tenant nor an officer, director, partner, nor member of a business entity which was the seller, buyer, landlord, or tenant in the transaction

▸ the licensee was acting solely as a real estate licensee in the transaction; and

▸ the act was a violation of Chapter 475 F.S

Furthermore, the damaged claimant will be eligible for monetary reimbursement from the Fund if

▸ the claimant has filed suit in a civil court and obtained a final judgment against the licensee for his or her actions during the course of a real estate transaction

▸ the claimant has notified the FREC of the licensee's actions

▸ the claim for recovery is made within 2 years of the date of the action or the date the action was discovered

▸ the claim for recovery is not made more than 4 years after the date of the alleged action was committed

▸ the claimant obtains a writ of execution on the judgment and executes an affidavit showing the claimant has made a concerted effort to find sufficient personal or real property belonging to the licensee that could be used to satisfy the judgment; and

▸ the claimant executes an affidavit showing the final judgment is not on appeal or an appeal has concluded

Additionally, a real estate licensee is eligible for monetary reimbursement from the Fund if the licensee:

▸ was the buyer, seller, landlord, or tenant in the transaction as a consumer and not as a licensee handling the transaction; and

▸ suffers monetary damages as a result of acts committed by the licensee/agent handling the transaction

Persons unqualified to make claim

An individual or business entity is not eligible to make a claim for payment from the Fund if

> ▶ the claimant is the spouse of the offending licensee or a personal representative of the spouse
>
> ▶ the claimant is a licensed broker or sales associate who performed as a single agent or transaction broker in the subject transaction
>
> ▶ the claim is based on a transaction in which the offending licensee owned or controlled the property in the subject transaction or in which the licensee was not acting as a broker or sales associate
>
> ▶ the claim is based on a transaction in which the offending broker or sales associate did not hold a current, valid license; and/or
>
> ▶ the judgment is against a real estate brokerage corporation, partnership, LLC, or LLP

Additionally, those seeking punitive damages in lieu of compensatory damages are not eligible for payment from the Fund.

Payment for claims

An injured party who meets all of the eligibility requirements may apply to the FREC for a reimbursement payment from the Fund. Florida statutes limit each payment to the lesser of the amount of the unsatisfied judgment or $50,000. Multiple claims for payments based on the same transaction are limited to a total of $50,000 regardless of the number of claims, claimants, or land parcels involved. Multiple claims against any one licensee are limited to a total of $150,000.

The license of a licensee whose actions have resulted in a reimbursement to a claimant is suspended from the date of the payment until the licensee has repaid with interest the total amount paid by the Fund.

Statutes limit the payments to compensatory or actual damages and do not pay treble damages, court costs, attorney fees, or interest unless the claimant is a licensee who is ordered by the court to pay monetary damages as a result of an escrow disbursement order (EDO) issued by the FREC. In that case, treble damages, court costs, attorney fees, and interest may be paid to the licensee. Again, the payment is limited to the amount of the judgment against the licensee or $50,000, whichever is less.

Fund limit and fees

The Florida Real Estate Recovery Fund is funded by fees charged to licensees. A $3.50 fee per year is charged for new and renewal broker licenses. A $1.50 fee per year is charged for new and renewal sales associate licenses. All moneys collected from disciplinary fines are also deposited into the Fund.

If the Fund's balance reaches $1 million, the special fee for new and renewal licenses stops being charged. Once the balance reaches $500,000 as a result of payments being made, the fees will again be charged.

6 Violations of License Law, Penalties, & Procedures
Snapshot Review

**DISCIPLINARY
PROCEDURE**

Complaint
- in writing, signed, and legally sufficient; filed within 5 years of violation; DBPR initiates investigation, may issue notice of noncompliance

DBPR Investigation
- investigates anonymous, confidential informant, withdrawn, and DBPR or FREC complaints

Probable-cause panel
- at least 2 FREC members who meet requirements; determines if probable cause exists; may dismiss case or issue letter of guidance when no probable cause
- probable cause found – formal complaint filed

Formal/administrative complaint
- prosecuted by DBPR; offender notified and given Election of Rights on how to proceed

Stipulation
- agreement to end case when licensee does not dispute accusation; approved by FREC

Voluntary relinquishment
- licensee agrees to permanently relinquish the license; approved by FREC

COMMISSION MEETING

Formal/informal hearing
- licensee does not dispute allegations; FREC holds hearing FREC determines guilt or innocence
- if dispute arises, case sent to formal hearing

Formal hearings
- heard by administrative law judge who is member of Florida Bar for 5 years; judge issues recommended order to FREC

FREC-issued final order
- FREC reviews recommended order and issues final order and penalties if warranted

Judicial review
- licensee can disagree with final order and request appeal; may also file stay of enforcement until appeal completed

VIOLATIONS & PENALTIES

FREC authority
- FREC has authority to deny license application; refuse license renewal; reprimand licensee; issue notice of noncompliance; impose fines, probation, and citations; suspend license; revoke license; revoke without prejudice; order mediation

Violations & penalties
- list of violations contained in F.A.C. 61J2-24.001 and Chapter 455.227; penalties imposed during hearings; aggravating or mitigating circumstances alter imposed penalty
- violations resulting in citation found in 61J2-24.002 F.A.C

Penalties by court of law
- civil – monetary only; criminal – misdemeanors and felonies

REAL ESTATE RECOVERY FUND

Brokerage transactions
- payments approved if licensee and claimant requirements met

Unqualified to make claim
- offending licensee's spouse; single agent or transaction broker; licensee owned property; no current license; no punitive damages

Payment for claims   •   limited to lesser of total judgment or $50,000 each claim; $150,000 total per licensee; licensee must repay Fund

Fund limits and fees   •   funded by fees charged for new and renewal licenses and by disciplinary fines

SECTION SIX: Violations of License Law, Penalties, & Procedures

Snapshot Review

1. An administrative complaint against a broker must be filed _____ after the violation occurred or after the violation was discovered.

   a. 2 years
   b. be end of business the next day
   c. no longer than 4 years
   d. within 5 years

2. Under what circumstances may the DBPR not notify the offending licensee of an investigation.

   a. If the offender is a danger to the public
   b. If the Probable Cause Panel finds probable cause
   c. If the offense is a criminal act
   d. If the offender is a broker who employs sales associates

3. When may the DBPR issue a notice of noncompliance to a licensee?

   a. When the complaint is for a first-time minor violation
   b. When the licensee disputes the allegations of a complaint
   c. When the complaint is for a misdemeanor in the first degree
   d. When the FREC directs the DBPR to issue the notice

4. When is a summary suspension issued?

   a. When there are multiple violations by the same licensee
   b. When the complaint is the result of the licensee committing a felony
   c. When the DBPR believes the licensee poses an immediate danger to the public
   d. When an investigation results in a finding of probable cause

5. When the DBPR initiates an investigation and notifies the offending licensee, the licensee may respond to the complaint within

   a. 24 hours.
   b. 10 days.
   c. 20 days.
   d. 30 days.

6. How many current Commission members must participate in a Probable Cause Panel?

   a. None
   b. 1
   c. 2
   d. 3 or more

7. The Probable Cause Panel must make its determination of probable cause within _____ days of receiving the final investigative report.

   a. 10
   b. 15
   c. 20
   d. 30

8. When is a Letter of Guidance issues?

   a. When the violation is a first-time minor violation
   b. When no probable cause is determined
   c. When the DBPR believes the offending licensee is a danger to the public
   d. When the DBPR completes its investigation

9. What happens next if probable cause is found for a complaint?

   a. A letter of guidance is issued.
   b. The complaint is turned over to the state's attorney.
   c. A formal complaint will be filed against the offender.
   d. The offending licensee is suspended.

10. Which right is provided to the offending licensee through the Election of Rights notice?

    a. Dispute the allegations and request an informal hearing
    b. Do not dispute the allegations and request a formal hearing
    c. Dispute the allegations but plea nolo contendere
    d. Do not dispute the allegations and waive the right to a hearing

11. A stipulation agreement must be approved by the

    a. FREC.
    b. DBPR.
    c. DRE.
    d. employing broker.

12. If an offending licensee chooses to voluntarily relinquish his license for permanent revocation, which penalties are included in that choice?

    a. Any imposed fines
    b. Restitution to the complainant
    c. Any penalties imposed by the FREC during its approval procedure
    d. None

13. If a real estate license is issued in error,

    a. the license may be revoked without prejudice.
    b. the licensee must retake the state examination.
    c. the license must be cancelled.
    d. the licensee can pay a fee to validate the license.

14. To be eligible for monetary reimbursement from the Florida Real Estate Recovery Fund, a claim must be filed within _____ of the date of the action.

    a. 1 year
    b. 2 years
    c. 3 years
    d. 5 years

15. Under no circumstances does the Recovery Fund pay _____ damages.

    a. compensatory
    b. actual
    c. punitive
    d. treble

16. Conversion is the act of

    a. mixing escrow funds with the broker's operating funds.
    b. appropriating client or customer deposits for use in the agency's business.
    c. converting an offer into a binding contract.
    d. converting escrow funds into equity funds in a property at the closing.

17. Commingling is the practice of

    a. blending escrow funds on a number of properties in one escrow account.
    b. mixing socially with prospects at open houses or other marketing functions.
    c. appropriating client or customer deposits for use in the agency's business.
    d. mixing escrow funds with the broker's operating funds.

7 Federal and State Laws Pertaining to Real Estate

Fair Housing Aims
Federal Fair Housing and Other Laws
Florida Fair Housing and Landlord-Tenant Laws

Learning Objectives

- Explain the significance of the Jones vs. Mayer court case
- List the real estate included under the different fair housing acts
- Recognize the groups protected under the 1968 Fair Housing Act
- List the property exempt from the 1968 Fair Housing Act and the protected classes
- List the two protected classed added to the 1988 Fair Housing Amendment
- Describe the types of discriminatory acts that are prohibited under the 1968 Fair Housing Act
- Describe the HUD process for handling a complaint under the 1968 Fair Housing Act
- Describe the objectives and major provisions of the Americans with Disabilities Act
- Describe the major provisions of the Florida Residential Landlord and Tenant Act
- Describe the major provisions of the Interstate Land Sales Disclosure Act

Key Terms

blockbusting	public accommodation
familial status	redlining
handicap status	steering
property report	subdivided land

FAIR HOUSING AIMS

Federal and state governments have enacted laws prohibiting discrimination in the national housing market. The aim of these **fair housing laws,** or **equal opportunity housing laws,** is to give all people in the country an equal opportunity to live wherever they wish, provided they can afford to do so, without impediments of discrimination in the purchase, sale, rental, or financing of property.

State Fair Housing Laws. While states have enacted fair housing laws that generally reflect the provisions of national law, each state may have slight modifications of national law. For that reason, it is incumbent upon Florida real estate students to learn the Florida laws and, in particular, note where these laws differ from national fair housing laws.

Fair Housing and Local Zoning. The Fair Housing Act prohibits a broad range of practices that discriminate against individuals on the basis of race, color, religion, sex, national origin, familial status, and disability. The Act does not pre-empt local zoning laws. However, the Act applies to municipalities and other local government entities and prohibits them from making zoning or land use decisions or implementing land use policies that exclude or otherwise discriminate against protected persons, including individuals with disabilities.

FEDERAL FAIR HOUSING AND OTHER LAWS

Civil Rights Act of 1866
Civil Rights Act of 1964
Civil Rights Act of 1968
Forms of illegal discrimination
Title VIII exemptions
Jones v. Mayer
Equal Opportunity in Housing poster
Fair Housing Amendments Act of 1988
Fair housing exemptions
Discrimination by the client
Violations and enforcement
Fair financing laws
Americans with Disabilities Act of 1990
Interstate Land Sale Full Disclosure Act

Civil Rights Act of 1866

The original fair housing statute, the Civil Rights Act of 1866, prohibits discrimination in housing *based on race*. The prohibition relates to selling, renting, inheriting, and conveying real estate. This law is still in effect and there are no exceptions to the law's prohibitions against discrimination.

Executive Order 11063. While the Civil Rights Act of 1866 prohibited discrimination, it was only marginally enforced. In 1962, the President issued Executive Order 11063 to *prevent discrimination in residential properties financed by FHA and VA loans*. The order facilitated enforcement of fair housing where federal funding was involved.

Civil Rights Act of 1964

The Civil Rights Act of 1964 addressed segregation in schools, public accommodations, and the workplace. Title II prohibited discrimination on the basis of race, color, religion, and national origin in places of public accommodation engaged in interstate commerce. Title III prohibited state and local governments from denying access to public facilities based on the same protected classes.

The Civil Rights Act of 1964 was amended in 1988 to include **handicapped status** and **familial status** as protected classes.

Civil Rights Act of 1968

Title VIII (Fair Housing Act). Title VIII of the Civil Rights Act of 1968, known today as the Fair Housing Act, prohibits discrimination in housing *based on race, color, religion, or national origin.* In 1988, **handicapped status** and **familial status** were added to the Fair Housing Act. The Office of Fair Housing and Equal Opportunity (FHEO) administers and enforces Title VIII under the supervision of the Department of Housing and Urban Development (HUD).

Forms of illegal discrimination

The Fair Housing Act specifically prohibits such activities in residential brokerage and financing as the following.

Discriminatory misrepresentation. An agent may not conceal available properties, represent that they are not for sale or rent, or change the sale terms for the purpose of discriminating. For example, an agent may not inform a minority buyer that the seller has recently decided not to carry back second mortgage financing when in fact the owner has made no such decision.

Discriminatory advertising. An agent may not advertise residential properties in such a way as to restrict their availability to any prospective buyer or tenant.

Providing unequal services. An agent may not alter the nature or quality of brokerage services to any party based on race, color, sex, national origin, or religion. For example, if it is customary for an agent to show a customer the latest MLS publication, the agent may not refuse to show it to any party. Similarly, if it is customary to show qualified buyers prospective properties immediately, an agent may not alter that practice for purposes of discrimination.

Steering. Steering is the practice of directly or indirectly channeling customers toward or away from homes and neighborhoods. Broadly interpreted, steering occurs if an agent describes an area in a subjective way for the purpose of encouraging or discouraging a buyer about the suitability of the area.

For example, an agent tells Buyer A that a neighborhood is extremely attractive, and that desirable families are moving in every week. The next day, the agent tells Buyer B that the same neighborhood is deteriorating, and that values are starting to fall. The agent has blatantly steered Buyer B *away* from the area and Buyer A *into* it.

Blockbusting. Blockbusting is the practice of inducing owners in an area to sell or rent to avoid an impending change in the ethnic or social makeup of the neighborhood that will cause values to go down.

For example, Agent Smith tells neighborhood owners that several minority families are moving in, and that they will be bringing their relatives next year. Smith informs homeowners that, in anticipation of a value decline, several families have already made plans to move.

Restricting / denying MLS participation. It is discriminatory to restrict participation in any multiple listing service based on one's race, religion, national origin, color, or sex.

Redlining. Redlining is the residential financing practice of refusing to make loans on properties in a certain neighborhood regardless of a mortgagor's qualifications. In effect, the lender draws a red line around an area on the map and denies all financing to applicants within the encircled area.

Title VIII exemptions   The Fair Housing Act allows for exemptions under a few specific circumstances. These are:

> ▸ a privately owned single-family home where no broker is used and no discriminatory advertising is used, with certain additional conditions
>
> ▸ rental of an apartment in a 1-4 unit building where the owner is also an occupant, provided the advertising is not discriminatory
>
> ▸ facilities owned by private clubs and leased non-commercially to members
>
> ▸ facilities owned by religious organizations and leased non-commercially to members, provided membership requirements are not discriminatory

Jones v. Mayer   In 1968, the Supreme Court ruled in *Jones v. Mayer* that all discrimination in selling or renting residential property based on race is prohibited under the provisions of the Civil Rights Act of 1866. Thus, while the Federal Fair Housing Act exempts certain kinds of discrimination, anyone who feels victimized by discrimination *based on race* may seek legal recourse under the 1866 law.

Equal Opportunity in Housing poster   In 1972, HUD instituted a requirement that brokers display a standard HUD poster. The poster affirms the broker's compliance with fair housing laws in selling, renting, advertising, and financing residential properties. Failure to display the poster may be construed as discrimination.

Fair Housing Amendments Act of 1988   Amendments to federal fair housing laws prohibit discrimination based on sex and discrimination against handicapped persons and families with children.

Fair housing exemptions   Federal fair housing laws do not prohibit age and family status discrimination under the following circumstances:

> ▸ in government-designated retirement housing
>
> ▸ in a retirement community if all residents are 62 years of age or older
>
> ▸ in a retirement community if 80 % of the dwellings have one person who is 55 years of age or older, provided there are amenities for elderly residents

> ▸ in residential dwellings of four units or less, and single family houses if sold or rented by owners who have no more than three houses

Discrimination by the client

Fair housing laws apply to home sellers as well as to agents, with the exception of the exemptions previously cited. If an agent goes along with a client's discriminatory act, the agent is equally liable for violation of fair housing laws. It is thus imperative to avoid complicity with client discrimination. Further, an agent should withdraw from any relationship where client discrimination occurs.

Examples of potential client discrimination are:

> ▸ refusing a full-price offer from a party
> ▸ removing the property from the market to sidestep a potential purchase by a party
> ▸ accepting an offer from one party that is lower than one from another party

Violations and enforcement

Persons who feel they have been discriminated against under federal fair housing laws may file a complaint with the Office of Fair Housing and Equal Opportunity (FHEO) within HUD, or they may file suit in a federal or state court.

Filing an FHEO complaint. Complaints alleging fair housing violations must be filed with the Office of Fair Housing and Equal Opportunity within one year of the violation. HUD then initiates an investigation in conjunction with federal or local enforcement authorities.

If HUD decides that the complaint merits further action, it will attempt to resolve the matter out of court in a process known as conciliation. If efforts to resolve the problem fail, the aggrieved party may file suit in state or federal court.

Filing suit. In addition to or instead of filing a complaint with HUD, a party may file suit in state or federal court within two years of the alleged violation.

Penalties. If discrimination is confirmed in court, the respondent may be enjoined to cease practicing his or her business. For example, a discriminating home builder may be restrained from selling available properties to buyers. Also, the plaintiff may be compensated for damages including humiliation, suffering, and pain. In addition, the injured party may seek equitable relief, including forcing the guilty party to complete a denied action such as selling or renting the property. Finally, the courts may impose civil penalties for first-time or repeat offenders.

Fair financing laws

Parallel anti-discrimination and consumer protection laws have been enacted in the mortgage financing field to promote equal opportunity in housing.

Equal Credit Opportunity Act (ECOA). Enacted in 1974, the Equal Credit Opportunity Act requires lenders to be fair and impartial in determining who qualifies for a loan. A lender may not discriminate on the basis of race, color, religion, national origin, sex, marital status, or age. The act also requires lenders to inform prospective borrowers who are being denied credit of the reasons for the denial.

Home Mortgage Disclosure Act. This statute requires lenders involved with federally guaranteed or insured loans to exercise impartiality and non-discrimination in the geographical distribution of their loan portfolio. In other words, the act is designed to prohibit redlining. It is enforced in part by requiring lenders to report to authorities where they have placed their loans.

Equal Opportunity in Housing Poster

U. S. Department of Housing and Urban Development

EQUAL HOUSING OPPORTUNITY

We Do Business in Accordance With the Federal Fair Housing Law

(The Fair Housing Amendments Act of 1988)

> ## It is illegal to Discriminate Against Any Person Because of Race, Color, Religion, Sex, Handicap, Familial Status, or National Origin

- In the sale or rental of housing or residential lots
- In advertising the sale or rental of housing
- In the financing of housing
- In the provision of real estate brokerage services
- In the appraisal of housing
- Blockbusting is also illegal

Anyone who feels he or she has been discriminated against may file a complaint of housing discrimination:
1-800-669-9777 (Toll Free)
1-800-927-9275 (TTY)
www.hud.gov/fairhousing

U.S. Department of Housing and Urban Development
Assistant Secretary for Fair Housing and Equal Opportunity
Washington, D.C. 20410

Previous editions are obsolete

form HUD-928.1 (6/2011)

Americans with Disabilities Act of 1990

Purpose. The Americans with Disabilities Act (ADA), which became law in 1990, is a civil rights law that prohibits discrimination against individuals with disabilities in all areas of public life, including employment, education, transportation, and facilities that are open to the general public. The purpose of the law is to make sure that people with disabilities have the same rights and opportunities as everyone else.

The Americans with Disabilities Act Amendments Act (ADAAA) became effective on January 1, 2009. Among other things, the ADAAA clarified that a disability is "a physical or mental impairment that substantially limits one or more major life activities." This definition applies to all titles of the ADA and covers private employers with 15 or more employees, state and local governments, employment agencies, labor unions, agents of the employer, joint management labor committees, and private entities considered places of public accommodation. Examples of the latter include hotels, restaurants, retail stores, doctor's offices, golf courses, private schools, day care centers, health clubs, sports stadiums, and movie theaters.

Components. The law consists of five parts.

> ▸ Title I (Employment) concerns equal employment opportunity. It is enforced by the U.S. Equal Employment Opportunity Commission.

> ▸ Title II (State and Local government) concerns nondiscrimination in state and local government services. It is enforced by the U.S. Department of Justice.

> ▸ Title III (Public Accommodations) concerns nondiscrimination in public accommodations and commercial facilities. It is enforced by the U.S. Department of Justice.

> ▸ Title IV (Telecommunications) concerns accommodations in telecommunications and public service messaging. It is enforced by the Federal Communications Commission.

> ▸ Title V (Miscellaneous) concerns a variety of general situations including how the ADA affects other laws, insurance providers, and lawyers.

Real estate practitioners are most likely to encounter Titles I and III and should acquire familiarity with these. In advising clients, licensees are well-advised to seek qualified legal counsel.

Requirements. The act requires landlords in certain circumstances to modify housing and facilities so that disabled persons can access them without hindrance.

The ADA also requires that disabled employees and members of the public be provided access that is equivalent to that provided to those who are not disabled.

> ▸ Employers with at least fifteen employees must follow nondiscriminatory employment and hiring practices.

> ▸ Reasonable accommodations must be made to enable disabled employees to perform essential functions of their jobs.

> ▸ Modifications to the physical components of a building may be necessary to provide the required access to tenants and their customers, such as widening doorways, changing door hardware, changing how doors open, installing ramps, lowering wall-mounted telephones and keypads, supplying Braille signage, and providing auditory signals.

> ▸ Existing barriers must be removed when the removal is "readily achievable," that is, when cost is not prohibitive. New construction and remodeling must meet a higher standard.

> ▸ If a building or facility does not meet requirements, the landlord must determine whether restructuring or retrofitting or some other kind of accommodation is most practical.

Penalties. Violations of ADA requirements can result in citations, business license restrictions, fines, and injunctions requiring remediation of the offending conditions. Business owners may also be held liable for personal injury damages to an injured plaintiff.

Interstate Land Sales Full Disclosure Act

The Interstate Land Sales Full Disclosure Act (ILSA) is a federal law passed by Congress in 1968. The purpose of the Act is to protect consumers from a developer's misrepresentation of material facts about a property being purchased sight unseen through means of interstate commerce or the mail.

The Act prohibits fraud and misrepresentation. It also requires specific provisions in purchase and lease agreements. One such provision is the buyer's right to cancel. Further, it requires the developer of a subdivision containing 100 or more lots to register the property by submitting a Statement of Record with HUD and to provide a property disclosure report to a buyer prior to the contract being signed. The Statement and the disclosure report include the state of the property's title, physical characteristics of the property, availability of roads and utilities, and current ownership information.

The Act specifically prohibits a developer or agent from using interstate commerce or mail to lease or sell any lot without meeting these requirements. Antifraud provisions applicable to subdivisions with 25 or more lots are included in the Act.

Once the buyer receives the report, he or she may cancel the contract any time before midnight on the seventh day after signing the contract. If the buyer does not receive the report prior to signing the contract, he or she may bring legal action within 2 years of contract signing to have the contract revoked.

If the subdivision contains fewer than 25 lots, it is exempt from provisions of the Act. If the land is already developed, it is exempt from the Act. Transactions that do not involve a developer or agent in the sale or lease of a lot in a subdivision are also exempt.

Other exemptions include cemetery lots, sales to builders, land being sold by any government agency, and land zoned for industrial or commercial development.

ILSA is administered by the Consumer Financial Protection Bureau and enforced by HUD. Violations of ILSA are subject to criminal penalties, civil damages and monetary penalties, and/or suspension of the developer's registration.

FLORIDA FAIR HOUSING AND LANDLORD-TENANT LAWS

Florida Fair Housing Act
Florida Americans with Disabilities Accessibility Implementation Act
Florida Residential Landlord and Tenant Act

Florida Fair Housing Act

As discussed earlier, the Fair Housing Act is a federal law that prohibits housing discrimination based on seven protected classes. In conjunction with that federal law, Florida Statute Title XLIV, Chapter 760, Section 20, known as the Florida Fair Housing Act, protects those same seven classes: race, color, religion, sex, national origin, disability, and familial status. Marital status, age, and occupation are not covered.

The following acts are discriminatory and prohibited by the Florida Fair Housing Act:

▶ A prospective tenant is told on the telephone that an apartment rents for a certain price and is currently available but then, when meeting the landlord face to face, is told the rental price is higher or the apartment is no longer available when it is still available.

▶ A condominium association refuses to provide handicapped parking for a person with a disability.

▶ A landlord enforces a no pets policy when the prospective tenant has a service dog.

▶ A homeowner refuses to sell property to a member of any of the protected classes.

▶ A real estate licensee encourages a buyer to purchase a particular house because it is located in a specific religious community.

▶ A landlord refuses to rent to a single woman who is pregnant.

In Florida, someone who believes he or she has been the victim of housing discrimination may file a complaint with the Florida Commission on Human Relations and/or HUD within 1 year of the alleged discrimination. Further, he or she may file a civil lawsuit within 2 years of the alleged discrimination. If the court finds in favor of the complainant, a fine up to $10,000 may be imposed on a first-time violator or up to $25,000 on a repeat violator within the previous 5 years.

Florida Americans with Disabilities Accessibility Implementation Act

The Florida **Americans with Disabilities Accessibility Implementation Act** was established to incorporate the accessibility requirements of the Americans with Disabilities Act (ADA) into Florida law. The statute adopts the ADA Standards for Accessible Design and incorporates the standards into the Florida Accessibility Code for Building Construction.

The Act also mandates that all new residential buildings, structures, and facilities in the state must provide at least one bathroom on grade level with a door opening of at least 29 inches and with wheelchair-accessible sinks and that any barriers at common or emergency doors must be removed.

The Act covers several other accessibility issues such as parking, building remodeling and conversions, grab-rail requirements in hotel and motel bathrooms, and accessibility to levels above the ground floor.

Florida Residential Landlord and Tenant Act

Overview. The Florida Residential Landlord and Tenant Act applies to the rental of a residential unit and provides regulations for all aspects of rental occupancies. It does not apply to rent-to-own contracts where required funds have been paid. Nor does it apply to transient occupancy in public lodging or occupancy in a cooperative unit or condominium unit.

Under the Act, unconscionable (unjust or one-sided) provisions within a rental agreement are not enforceable. If a rental agreement does not specify the duration of the tenancy, then the duration is determined to be the length of residency between rental payments. For example, if the rent payment is due each month, then the tenancy is for one month at a time.

Deposits and advance rents. Landlords may require a security deposit and advanced rent payments (typically the last month's rent). In Florida, there is no limit on the amount of deposit landlords can charge, but they must comply with the Act in how they handle deposits and advanced rent payments.

For payments other than the first month's rent, the landlord is required to comply with one of the following:

> ‣ hold the funds in a separate non-interest-bearing escrow or bank account within Florida for the benefit of the tenant, with no commingling with the landlord's own funds, no pledging the funds as security for a debt, and no using the funds until they are actually due to the landlord
>
> ‣ hold the funds in a separate interest-bearing escrow or bank account within Florida for the benefit of the tenant, with the landlord choosing to pay the tenant at least 75% of the annual interest rate payable on the account or 5% simple interest each year; again, with

no commingling with the landlord's own funds, no pledging the funds as security for a debt, and no using the funds until they are actually due to the landlord

▸ along with a Florida-licensed surety company, execute and post a surety bond with the circuit court clerk in the same county where the rental property is located for an amount equal to the total funds collected or $50,000, whichever is less; and pay the tenant 5% simple interest each year

Either in the lease agreement or within 30 days of receiving the security deposit and advance rent, the landlord is required to give the tenant written notice of the advance rent or security deposit.

If the landlord changes where the funds are being held after the notice is sent, he or she must notify the tenant in writing within 30 days of the change. The notice must

1) be given in person or mailed to the tenant
2) include the name and address of the bank where the funds are being held or state a surety bond has been posted
3) indicate if the tenant is entitled to interest, and
4) contain the following disclosure:

Your lease requires payment of certain deposits. The landlord may transfer advance rents to the landlord's account as they are due and without notice. When you move out, you must give the landlord your new address so that the landlord can send you notices regarding your deposit. The landlord must mail you notice, within 30 days after you move out, of the landlord's intent to impose a claim against the deposit. If you do not reply to the landlord stating your objection to the claim within 15 days after receipt of the landlord's notice, the landlord will collect the claim and must mail you the remaining deposit, if any.

If the landlord fails to timely mail you notice, the landlord must return the deposit but may later file a lawsuit against you for damages. If you fail to timely object to a claim, the landlord may collect from the deposit, but you may later file a lawsuit claiming a refund.

You should attempt to informally resolve any dispute before filing a lawsuit. Generally, the party in whose favor a judgment is rendered will be awarded costs and attorney fees payable by the losing party.

This disclosure is basic. Please refer to Part II of Chapter 83, Florida Statutes, to determine your legal rights and obligations.

This notification and disclosure requirement applies only to landlords of five or more dwelling units.

Landlord's obligation to maintain premises. Landlords are required to comply with building, housing, and health codes in maintaining the rental property. If none of these codes exist, the landlord is required to keep the premises in good repair and maintain systems such as plumbing and heating in working condition.

The Act specifically states that window screens must be installed and kept in good repair, pests must be exterminated, and garbage is to be removed with outside receptacles provided. The landlord must also install smoke detectors in single family or duplex rental homes.

The landlord may charge the tenant for garbage removal, water, fuel, or utilities if included in the lease. The landlord is not responsible for conditions caused by negligence or wrongful acts of the tenant, family members, or guests.

Tenant's obligations. The tenant is obligated to comply with applicable building, housing, and health codes. The tenant must keep the premises clean and sanitary, including removing garbage, cleaning plumbing fixtures, and operating the dwelling's systems in a reasonable manner. Tenants are also obligated to conduct themselves so as not to disturb neighbors and refrain from damaging or removing any part of the premises that belongs to the landlord.

Landlord's access to premises. The landlord is permitted by law to enter the rental unit from time to time for inspections, repairs, alterations, supplying services, or show the unit to prospective tenants or buyers. The landlord is required to give the tenant at least 12 hours' notice prior to entry for repairs and may only enter between 7:30 a.m. and 8:00 p.m. The landlord may enter the premises for any of the above reasons only with the tenant's consent, if the tenant unreasonably withholds consent, or in case of an emergency.

If the tenant's rent is current and the tenant notifies the landlord of an intended absence from the unit, the landlord may not enter the unit except with the tenant's permission or for an emergency.

Vacating premises. A tenant planning to vacate the rental premises must give the landlord a 7-day written notice that includes an address where the tenant can be reached.

When the lease terminates and the tenant vacates the premises, the landlord is required to return the security deposit and pay any earned interest within 15 days. However, if the landlord intends to impose a claim on the deposit, written notice of the intention and the reason for the claim must be sent to the tenant's last known mailing address by certified mail within 30 days of the tenant vacating the premises.

Failure to send the notice within 30 days will result in the landlord forfeiting the right to impose a claim on the deposit. The landlord is prohibited from seeking a setoff against the deposit but may file legal action for damages after the deposit is returned.

If the landlord imposes a claim on the deposit and complies with notice requirements, the landlord may deduct the amount of the claim from the total deposit and then return the balance to the tenant within 30 days of the intention notice. The tenant may file an objection to the claim within 15 days of receiving the intention notice. If the tenant does not meet the timeline for objection, he or she may still seek damages in a separate legal action.

Termination of rental agreements by the tenant. The tenant may terminate the rental agreement if the landlord fails to maintain the premises as required by law or fails to comply with the provisions in the rental agreement. To do so, the tenant needs to deliver a written 7-day notice to the landlord specifying the noncompliance and stating the intention to terminate. If the landlord does not correct the noncompliance within the 7 days, the tenant may terminate the rental agreement.

However, if the noncompliance issues are out of the landlord's control and the tenant does not want to terminate, the law allows the following:

▸ If the noncompliance issue makes the unit uninhabitable, the tenant may vacate and not be held liable for paying rent while the unit is uninhabitable.

▸ If the unit is habitable with the noncompliance issue and the tenant stays in the unit, the rent is to be reduced while the unit is out of compliance. The reduction is to be by an amount in proportion to the loss of rental value caused by the noncompliance.

Termination of rental agreements by the landlord. The landlord may terminate the rental agreement if the tenant fails to comply with tenant obligations or fails to comply with the provisions of the agreement. Just as when the tenant terminates the agreement, the landlord must deliver a written 7-day notice to the tenant specifying the noncompliance and stating the intention to terminate. If the tenant does not correct the noncompliance within the 7 days, the landlord may terminate the rental agreement.

However, if the tenant's noncompliance is such that the tenant should not be given an opportunity to correct it or if the noncompliance has previously been the subject of a written notice within the past 12 months, the landlord may terminate without giving the tenant time to correct the problem. To do so, the landlord is to deliver a written notice to the tenant that specifies the noncompliance and states the landlord's intent to terminate the agreement. The tenant has 7 days from the date of the notice to vacate the rental dwelling.

If the tenant's noncompliance is nonpayment of rent, the landlord must give the tenant written notice of the requirement to pay the rent or vacate the premises within 3 business days. If the tenant still does not pay the rent after the 3 days, the landlord may terminate the rental agreement. The notice must state the amount of rent that is overdue and is to be mailed, delivered, or left at the rental unit. If the tenant vacates the premises, the landlord must follow procedures for notifying the tenant of the return of all or part of the security deposit. If the tenant does not vacate the premises, the landlord will need to start an eviction.

Eviction procedure. A landlord who needs to remove a tenant from the rental unit must follow the procedure mandated by Florida statute.

▸ After serving the tenant notice to vacate the premises, the landlord must give the tenant 3 business days to vacate for not paying rent or 7 days to vacate for other noncompliance issues.

- ▸ If the tenant does not vacate in the allowed timeframe, the landlord, the landlord's attorney, or the landlord's agent must file a complaint in the local county court that describes the rental unit and the reason it needs to be recovered. A copy of the complaint is delivered to the tenant by the local sheriff's department.

- ▸ If the tenant files a response to the complaint, the court's clerk will notify the tenant that he or she has 5 business days to pay the rent into the court's registry.

- ▸ If the tenant fails to respond to the court's notice within the 5 business days, the landlord is entitled to an immediate default judgment for removal of the tenant without further notice or hearing.

- ▸ After the judgment has been issued in favor of the landlord, the clerk will issue a writ to the sheriff instructing the sheriff to post a 24-hour notice on the premises and then give possession of the unit to the landlord.

- ▸ After the sheriff signs the writ of possession, the landlord or the landlord's agent may remove the tenant's personal property remaining on the premises. The landlord may have the sheriff stand by to keep the peace while locks are changed and personal items are removed. The tenant may not hold the sheriff, the landlord, or the landlord's agent liable for any loss or damage to the property after it is removed.

If the eviction is a result of nonpayment of rent and the court finds in favor of the landlord, the court will enter a money judgment against the tenant that includes the amount of rent due and may include attorney's fees and costs. Until all money due is paid, the landlord will hold a lien against the all of the tenant's property, except beds, bedclothes, and wearing apparel (F.S. 83.09).

7 Fed./State Laws Pertaining to Real Estate
Snapshot Review

FAIR HOUSING AIMS
- enacted to create equal opportunity and access to housing and housing finance
- state laws generally reflect federal fair housing laws; federal laws do not pre-empt local zoning laws but prohibit them from discriminating

FEDERAL FAIR HOUSING AND OTHER LAWS

Civil Rights Act of 1866
- no discrimination in selling or leasing housing *based on race*; law is still in place
- Executive Order 11063: no race discrimination involving FHA- or VA-backed loans

Civil Rights Act of 1964
- prohibited segregation in schools
- prohibited discrimination on basis of race, color, religion, national origin in public accommodations
- prohibited state and local governments from denying access to public facilities

Civil Rights Act of 1968
- Title VIII (Fair Housing Act): no housing discrimination *based on race, color, religion, national origin, handicapped status and familial (addid in 1988)*
- certain exceptions permitted

Forms of illegal discrimination
- discriminatory misrepresentation, advertising, and financing; unequal services; steering; blockbusting; restricting access to market; redlining

Title VIII exemptions
- privately-owned single-family with no broker and no discriminatory advertising; 1-4 unit apartment building where owner is resident and no discriminatory advertising; private club facilities leased to members; religious organization-owned facilities for members and no discrimination

Jones v. Mayer
- no race discrimination, without exception

Equal Opportunity in Housing Poster
- must be displayed by brokers

Fair Housing Amendments Act of 1988
- no discrimination *based on sex or against the handicapped or families with children*

Discrimination by the client
- agent liable for complying with client's discriminatory acts

Violations and enforcement
- file HUD complaint, sue in court, or both; may obtain injunction, damages; violators subject to prosecution

Fair financing laws
- Equal Credit Opportunity Act: no discrimination in housing finance based on race, color, religion, sex, marital status, age; Home Mortgage Disclosure Act: no redlining

Americans with Disabilities Act of 1990
- no discrimination against those with disabilities; applies to employment, education, transportation, public facilities; equivalent access
- Titles I (employment) and III (public accommodation) most common for real estate agents

Interstate Land Sales Full Disclosure Act

- protects consumers when purchasing property sight unseen through interstate commerce
- requires subdivision of 100 or more lots to be registered and buyers to be given a property report; fewer than 25 lots are exempt

FLORIDA FAIR HOUSING AND LANDLORD-TENANT LAWS

Florida Fair Housing Act

- prohibits housing discrimination based on seven protected classes
- victims of discrimination may file complaint within 1 year or civil lawsuit within 2 years with fines imposed against violators

Florida Americans with Disabilities Accessibility Implementation Act

- incorporates federal accessibility standards into FL code with requirements for new residential buildings

Florida Residential Landlord and Tenant Act

- applies to residential rental units, not rent-to-own units or public lodging
- provides requirements for collecting and holding security deposits and advanced rent
- includes landlord's obligations to maintain the premises in good repair
- includes tenant's obligations to comply with applicable codes and keep unit clean
- designates when landlords may enter the premises for repairs and emergencies, etc.
- provides mandates for notices regarding the tenant vacating the unit and how to handle the security deposit and claims against it
- includes processes for termination of rental agreement by tenant or landlord
- provides procedures for collecting past due rent and evicting noncomplying tenants

SECTION SEVEN: Fed./State Laws Pertaining to Real Estate

Section Quiz

1. The principal theme of federal fair housing laws is to

   a. ensure all Americans a fair chance to own a home.
   b. prohibit discrimination in housing transactions.
   c. ensure that housing transactions are negotiated fairly.
   d. prohibit agents from dealing unfairly with clients and customers.

2. It is illegal to discriminate in selling a house based on race, color, religion, or national origin. This is provided for through

   a. the Civil Rights Act of 1866.
   b. Executive Order 11063.
   c. the Civil Rights Act of 1968.
   d. the Fair Housing Amendments Act of 1988.

3. Which of the following laws or rulings extended discrimination to include gender, handicapped status, and family status?

   a. Executive Order 11063
   b. the Civil Rights Act of 1968
   c. the Fair Housing Amendments Act of 1988
   d. Jones v Mayer

4. An agent informs numerous families in a neighborhood that several minority families are planning to move into the immediate area, and that the trend could have adverse effects on property values. This activity is

   a. blockbusting.
   b. legal but unprofessional redlining.
   c. discriminatory misrepresentation.
   d. negligent misrepresentation.

5. A minority family would like to buy a home in a certain price range. The agent shows the family all available properties in a neighborhood of families with similar backgrounds. The agent did not mention a number of homes in the family's price range in other neighborhoods. This agent could be liable for

   a. blockbusting.
   b. providing unequal services.
   c. steering.
   d. nothing; his services were legal and acceptable.

6. An agent does not like a particular minority buyer, and is very short with the person, refusing to engage in lengthy conversation or show him any properties. A second minority party visits the office the next day. The agent is very forthcoming, and shows the person five prospective properties. This agent could be liable for

   a. providing unequal services.
   b. steering.
   c. misrepresentation.
   d. nothing; both parties were minorities, and therefore no discrimination occurred.

7. Following the client's recommendation, an agent conceals the availability of a property from an employed but pregnant and unmarried minority woman. This agent could be liable for

   a. discriminatory misrepresentation.
   b. steering.
   c. violating fiduciary duty.
   d. nothing: an agent may show or not show any property at his or her discretion.

8. A condominium complex prohibits ownership of any unit by persons under 55 years of age. The association claims it has made the prohibition properly. Which of the following is true?

   a. They are violating the Civil Rights Act of 1866.
   b. They are violating the Fair Housing Amendments Act of 1988.
   c. They are guilty of age discrimination.
   d. The prohibition may be legal.

9. An owner suddenly pulls a property off the market after hearing from the agent on the phone that the agent had received a full-price offer from a minority party. The agent then informs the offeror that the home has been removed from the market and is unavailable. Which party or parties, if any, have violated fair housing laws?

   a. The agent only
   b. The owner only
   c. The agent and the owner
   d. Neither agent nor owner

10. The parts of the Americans with Disabilities Act that most concern real estate agents are those that deal with

    a. telecommunications and insurance.
    b. public accommodations and employment.
    c. state and local government.
    d. agency and public service.

11. The Interstate Land Sales Full Disclosure Act requires developers to provide land buyers with a property disclosure report. Once the buyer receives the report, he may cancel the purchase contract

    a. by end of business on the third day after receipt of the report.
    b. within 5 days of signing the contract.
    c. any time before midnight on the seventh day after signing the contract.
    d. by end of business on the fifth business day after receiving the report.

12. Which of the following acts is considered discriminatory?

    a. Licensee Lou shows a family with children a home in close proximity to a school.
    b. Joe owns an apartment building and has just interviewed a prospective tenant on the phone. When the tenant arrived to sign the lease, Joe realized the individual is Hispanic. Consequently, Joe refused to rent to this individual.
    c. A condominium association moves designated parking spaces for some residents to make room to designate handicapped parking for a disabled resident.
    d. Lou is showing a home to a Jewish family and points out the synagogue down the street.

13. Which of the following is not a requirement of the Florida Americans with Disabilities Accessibility Implementation Act?

    a. Allowing a service dog to live in a no-pet apartment building
    b. Installing a ramp at the entrance to an apartment building where a wheel-chair-bound tenant lives
    c. Widening the bathroom doorways to 29 inches in a new apartment building
    d. Providing handicapped parking in an apartment building's parking lot

14. If a lease agreement does not indicate where a security deposit is to be held, the landlord must provide that information to the tenant

    a. prior to signing the lease.
    b. within 15 business days of signing the lease.
    c. within 30 days of receiving the deposit.
    d. That information must be in the lease.

15. A landlord has _____ to notify a vacated tenant of a claim against the tenant's security deposit.

    a. 7 days
    b. 15 days
    c. 30 days
    d. 45 days

8 Property Rights: Estates & Tenancies; Condos, Coops, CDDs, HOAs, and Time-Sharing

Land, Real Estate, and Real Property
Real versus Personal Property
Basic Property Rights
Interests and Estates in Land
Freehold Estates
Ways of Holding Ownership
Leasehold Estates
Cooperatives
Condominiums
Time-sharing
Homeowners' Associations
Community Development Districts

Learning Objectives

- Define *real property* based on the definition in Chapter 475, FS.
- List and explain the physical components of real property
- Explain the four tests courts use to determine if an item is a fixture
- Distinguish between real and personal property
- Describe the bundle of rights associated with real property ownership
- List the principal types of estates (tenancies) and describe their characteristics
- Describe the features associated with the Florida homestead law
- Distinguish between cooperatives, condominiums and time-shares and describe the four main documents associated with condominiums

Key Terms

condominium	joint tenancy	remainderman
cooperative	land	right of survivorship
declaration	leasehold estate	separate property
estate for years	life estate	tenancy at sufferance
exempt property	personal property	tenancy at will
fee simple estate	proprietary lease	tenancy by entireties
fixture	Prospectus	tenancy in common
freehold estate	real estate	time-share
homestead	real property	

LAND, REAL ESTATE AND REAL PROPERTY

Real property definition
Real property components

Real property definition

A simple definition of real estate is that it is air, water, land, and everything affixed to the land. Real estate in the United States may be owned privately by individuals and private entities or publicly by government entities. Private ownership rights in this country are not absolute. The government can impose taxes and restrictions on private ownership rights, and it can take private property away altogether. In addition, other private parties can exert their rights and interests on one's real property. A bank, for example, can take a property if the owner fails to pay a mortgage. A neighbor can claim the right to walk across one's property whether the owner likes it or not, provided he or she has done so for a certain number of years.

In attempting to define real estate, it is essential to understand *what rights and interests parties have in a parcel of real estate*. And to understand real estate rights and interests, one must first recognize the distinctions between:

▶ land and real estate

▶ real estate and property

▶ real property and personal property

Real property components

Land. The legal concept of land encompasses

▶ the surface area of the earth

▶ everything beneath the surface of the earth extending downward to its center

▶ all *natural* things permanently attached to the earth

▶ the air above the surface of the earth extending outward to infinity.

Land, therefore, includes minerals beneath the earth's surface, water on or below the earth's surface, and the air above the surface. In addition, land includes all plants attached to the ground or in the ground, such as trees and grass. A **parcel**, or **tract**, of land is a portion of land delineated by boundaries.

Physical characteristics of land. Land has three unique physical characteristics: *immobility, indestructibility, and heterogeneity.*

Land is immobile, since a parcel of land cannot be moved from one site to another. In other words, the geographical location of a tract of land is fixed and cannot be changed. One can transport portions of the land such as mined coal, dirt, or cut plants. However, as soon as such elements are detached from the land, they are no longer considered land.

Land is indestructible in the sense that one would have to remove a segment of the planet all the way to the core in order to destroy it. Even then, the portion extending upward to infinity would remain. For the same reason, land is considered to be permanent.

Land is non-homogeneous, since no two parcels of land are exactly the same. Admittedly, two adjacent parcels may be very similar and have the same economic value. However, they are inherently different because each parcel has a unique location.

Real estate. The legal concept of real estate encompasses:

▸   land

▸   all *man-made structures* that are "permanently" attached to the land

Real estate therefore includes, in addition to land, such things as fences, streets, buildings, wells, sewers, sidewalks and piers. Such man-made structures attached to the land are called **improvements**. The phrase "permanently attached" refers primarily to one's intention in attaching the item. Obviously, very few if any manmade structures can be permanently attached to the land in the literal sense. But if a person constructs a house with the intention of creating a permanent dwelling, the house is considered real estate. By contrast, if a camper affixes a tent to the land with the intention of moving it to another camp in a week, the tent would not be considered real estate

The Legal Concept of Land and Real Estate

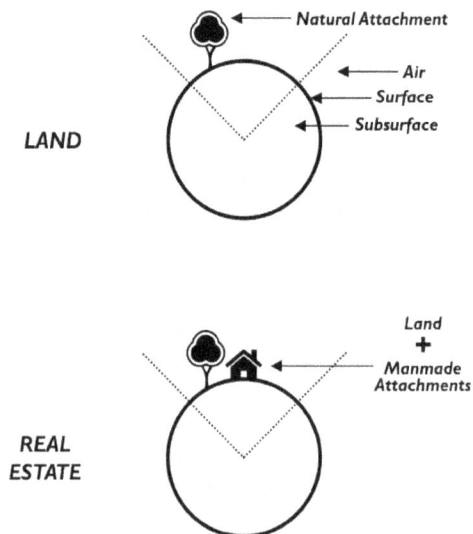

REAL VS. PERSONAL PROPERTY

Property essentials
Fixtures
Differentiation criteria
Trade fixtures
Emblements
Factory-built housing
Conversion

Property essentials

In common understanding, property is something that is owned by someone. A car is the property of Bill Brown if Bill Brown owns the car. If the item is not owned, it is not property. For example, if a car is abandoned and left to rust in the desert, the car is no longer property, since no one claims ownership. Similarly, the planet Jupiter is not property, since no one owns it.

From a more technical standpoint, property is not only the item that is owned but also a *set of rights to the item enjoyed by the owner*. These rights are commonly known as the "bundle of rights," explained further below.

In owning property, one has the right to possess and use it as the law allows. The owner has the right to transfer ownership of the item (sell, rent, donate, assign, or bequeath). The owner may also encumber the item by mortgaging it as collateral for debt. Finally, the owner has the right to exclude others from use of the item. In the example of the car, when Bill Brown bought the car, the car became his property: he owned the car itself. At the same time, he also acquired the legal rights to transfer, use, encumber, exclude, and possess the car.

Classifications of property. Our legal system recognizes two classifications of property: *real property* and *personal property*. **Real property** is ownership of real estate and the bundle of rights associated with owning the real estate. **Personal property** is ownership of anything which is not real estate, and the rights associated with owning the personal property item. Items of personal property are also called **chattels** or **personalty**.

Note: since all real estate in the United States is owned by some person, private organization, or government entity, all real estate in the country *is* real property. Given that fact, this text will follow the customary practice of using the two terms interchangeably and synonymously.

Tangible versus intangible property. Real and personal property may be further categorized as **tangible** or **intangible** property. Tangible property is physical, visible, and material. Intangible property is abstract, having no physical existence in itself, other than as evidence of one's ownership interest.

Tangible vs. Intangible Property

	Tangible	Intangible
Real Property	all types	
Personal Property	boat, car, jewelry	stock certificate, contract, patent

All real estate, by its physical nature, is tangible property. Personal property may be tangible or intangible. Boats, jewelry, coins, appliances, computers, and art work are examples of tangible personal property. Stocks, copyrights, bonds, trademarks, patents, franchises, and listing agreements are examples of intangible personal property.

Fixtures

In conveying real property, it is vitally important to recognize the distinctions between personal property and the real property that is to be conveyed. Confusion can arise because items of property *may be either personal property or real property, depending on circumstances.*

The primary criterion for distinguishing real from personal property is whether the item is permanently attached to the land or to structures attached to the land. For example, a tree growing in one's yard is an item of real property. However, when the owner cuts the tree down, it becomes personal property. Similarly, a swimming pool pump on a shelf in the owner's garage is personal property. When it is installed with the rest of the pool, it becomes real property.

While the "attachment" criterion is pivotal in distinguishing between real and personal property, there are other tests to be applied. In addition, the attachment rule is subject to exceptions.

A personal property item that has been converted to real property by attachment to real estate is called a fixture. Typical examples are chandeliers, toilets, water pumps, septic tanks, and window shutters.

The owner of real property inherently owns all fixtures belonging to the real property. When the owner sells the real property, the buyer acquires rights to all fixtures. Fixtures not included in the sale must be itemized and excluded in the sale contract.

Differentiation criteria

In the event that the attachment criterion is insufficient to determine whether an article of property is real or personal, a court may apply one or more of the following additional criteria.

Intention. One's original intention can override the test of movability in determining whether an item is a fixture or not. If someone attached an item to real property, yet intended to remove it after a period of time, the article may be deemed personal property. If a person intended an article to be a fixture, even though the item is easily removable, the article may be deemed a fixture.

For example, an apartment renter installs an alarm system, fully intending to remove the system upon lease expiration. Here, the alarm system would be considered personal property.

Adaptation. If an item is uniquely adapted to the property, or the property is custom-designed to accommodate the item, it may be deemed real property whether the item is easily removable or not. House keys, a garbage compactor, and a removable door screen are examples.

Functionality. If an item is vital to the operation of the building, it may be deemed a fixture, even though perhaps easily removable. Window-unit air conditioners and detachable solar panels are possible examples.

Relationship of parties. If a tenant installs a fixture in order to conduct business, the fixture may be considered a trade fixture, which is the tenant's personal property.

Sale or lease contract provisions. In a sale or lease transaction, the listing of an item in the contract as a personal property item or a fixture overrides all other considerations. Unless otherwise stated as exceptions, all fixtures are included in the sale. For example, if a sale contract stipulates that the carpeting is not included in the sale, it becomes a personal property item. If the carpeting is not mentioned, it goes with the property, since it is attached to the floor of the building.

Trade fixtures

Trade fixtures, or **chattel fixtures,** are items of a tenant's *personal property* that the tenant has temporarily affixed to a landlord's real property in order to conduct business. Trade fixtures may be detached and removed before or upon surrender of the leased premises. Should the tenant fail to remove a trade fixture, it may become the property of the landlord through *accession*. Thereafter, the fixture is considered real property.

Examples of trade fixtures include a grocer's food freezers, a merchant's clothes racks, a tavern owner's bar, a dairy's milking machines, and a printer's printing press.

Emblements

Growing plants, including agricultural crops, may be either real property or personal property. Plants and crops that grow naturally without requiring anyone's labor or machinery are considered real property.

Plants and crops requiring human intervention and labor are called **emblements**. Emblements, despite their attachment to land, are considered personal property. If an emblement is owned by a tenant farmer, the tenant has the right to the harvested crop whether the tenant's lease is active or expired. If the tenant grew the crop, it is his or her personal property, and the landlord cannot take it.

Factory-built housing

Factory-built housing consists of dwelling units constructed off-site and transported to and assembled on a building site. The category also includes readily moveable housing of the type that can be relocated from place to place, once known by the term **mobile home.** The National Manufactured Housing

Construction and Safety Standards Act of 1976 defined the types of factory-built housing and retired the mobile home designation. **Manufactured housing** is factory-built housing that conforms to HUD standards. Factory-built housing may be considered real property or personal property, depending on whether it is permanently affixed to ground that is owned or leased long-term by the housing owner, according to Florida law. Real estate practitioners should understand the local laws before selling any kind of factory-built housing.

Conversion

The classification of an item of property as real or personal is not necessarily fixed. The classification may be changed by the process of conversion. **Severance** is the conversion of real property to personal property by detaching it from the real estate, such as by cutting down a tree, detaching a door from a shed, or removing an antenna from a roof. **Affixing**, or attachment, is the act of converting personal property to real property by attaching it to the real estate, such as by assembling a pile of bricks into a barbecue pit, or constructing a boat dock from wood planks.

Real Property vs. Personal Property

Real Property	Personal Property
land fixtures attachments conversions by affixing	trade fixtures emblements conversions by severance

BASIC PROPERTY RIGHTS

Bundle of rights
Separable rights
Water rights

Bundle of rights

Real property rights consist of the bundle of rights associated with owning a parcel of real estate. Foremost of these rights is the *right of possession*.

The *right to use* a property refers to the right to use it in certain ways, such as mining, cultivating, landscaping, razing, and building on the property. The right is subject to the limitations of local zoning and the legality of the use. One's right to use may not infringe on the rights of others to use and enjoy their property. For example, an owner may be restricted from constructing a large pond on her property if in fact the pond would pose flooding and drainage hazards to the next door neighbor.

The *right to transfer* interests in the property includes the right to sell, bequeath, lease, donate, or assign ownership interests. An owner may transfer certain individual rights to the property without transferring total ownership. Also, one may transfer ownership while retaining individual interests. For example, a person may sell mineral rights without selling the right of possession. On the other hand, the owner may convey all rights to the property except the mineral rights.

While all rights are transferrable, the owner can only transfer what the owner in fact possesses. A property seller, for example, cannot sell water rights if there are no water rights attached to the property.

The *right to encumber* the property essentially means the right to mortgage the property as collateral for debt. There may be restrictions to this right, such as a spouse's right to limit the degree to which a homestead may be mortgaged.

The *right to exclude* gives the property owner the legal right to keep others off the property and to prosecute trespassers.

The Bundle of Rights

Separable rights   The bundle of real property rights also applies separately to the individual components of real estate: the air, the surface, and the subsurface. An owner can, for example, transfer subsurface rights without transferring air rights. Similarly, an owner can rent air space without encumbering surface or subsurface rights. This might occur in a city where adjoining building owners want to construct a walkway over a third owner's lot. Such owners would have to acquire the air rights for the walkway. If the city wants to construct a subway through the owner's subsurface, the city has to obtain the subsurface rights to do so.

An ordinary lease is a common example of the transfer of a portion of one's bundle of rights. The owner relinquishes the right to possess portions of the surface, perhaps a building, in return for rent. The tenant enjoys the rights to possess and use the building over the term of the lease, after which these rights revert to the landlord. During the lease term, the tenant has no rights to the property's subsurface or airspace other than what the building occupies. Further, the tenant does not enjoy any of the other rights in the bundle of rights: he cannot encumber the property or transfer it. To a limited degree, the tenant may exclude persons from the property, but he may not exclude the legal owner.

Surface rights. Surface rights apply to the real estate contained within the surface boundaries of the parcel. This includes the ground, all natural things affixed to the ground, and all improvements. Surface rights also include water rights.

Air rights. Air rights apply to the space above the surface boundaries of the parcel, as delineated by imaginary vertical lines extended to infinity. Since the advent of aviation, air rights have been curtailed to allow aircraft to fly over one's property, provided the overflights do not interfere with the owner's use and enjoyment of the property. The issue of violation of air rights for the benefit of air transportation is an ongoing battle between airlines, airports, and nearby property owners.

Subsurface rights. Subsurface rights apply to land beneath the surface of the real estate parcel extending from its surface boundaries downward to the center of the earth. Notable subsurface rights are the rights to extract mineral and gas deposits and subsurface water from the water table.

Water rights

Water rights basically concern the rights to own and use water found in lakes, streams, rivers, and the ocean. In addition, they determine where parcel boundaries can be fixed with respect to adjoining bodies of water. What water rights does an owner of a property that contains or adjoins a body of water enjoy? The answer depends on three variables:

- whether the state controls the water
- whether the water is moving
- whether the water is navigable

Doctrine of Prior Appropriation. Since water is a resource necessary for survival, some states -- particularly those where water is scarce -- have taken the legal position that the state owns and controls all bodies of water. Called the Doctrine of Prior Appropriation, this position requires that property owners obtain permits for use of water. Florida does not operate under this doctrine per se, but under the common law doctrines of *littoral rights* and *riparian rights*, as modified by the Prior Appropriation concept of "first in time, first in right" and codified in the Florida Water Resource Act.

Littoral rights. Littoral rights concern properties abutting bodies of water that are not moving, such as lakes and seas. Owners of properties abutting a navigable, non-moving body of water enjoy the littoral right of use, but do not own the water nor the land beneath the water. Ownership extends to the high-water mark of the body of water.

Littoral Rights

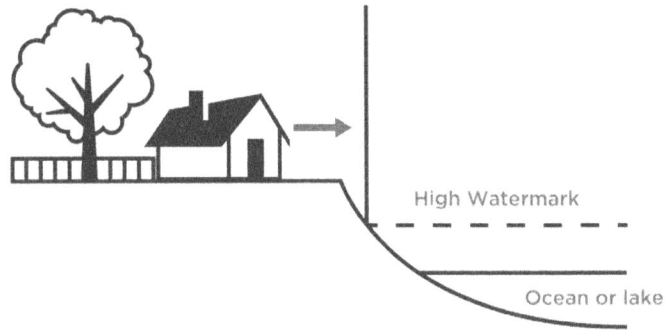

Oceans, Seas and Lakes

The legal premise underlying the definition of littoral rights is that a lake or sea is a *navigable body of water, therefore, public property* owned by the state. By contrast, a body of water entirely contained within the boundaries of an owner's property is not navigable. In such a case, the owner would own the water as well as unrestricted rights of usage.

Littoral rights attach to the property. When the property is sold, the littoral rights transfer with the property to the new owner.

Riparian rights. Riparian rights concern properties abutting moving water such as streams and rivers. If a property abuts a stream or river, the owner's riparian rights are determined by whether the water *is navigable or not navigable*. If the property abuts a non-navigable stream, the owner enjoys unrestricted use of the water and *owns the land beneath the stream to the stream's midpoint*. If the waterway in question is navigable, the waterway is considered to be a public easement. In such a case, the owner's property extends *to the water's edge* as opposed to the midpoint of the waterway. The state owns the land beneath the water.

Riparian Rights

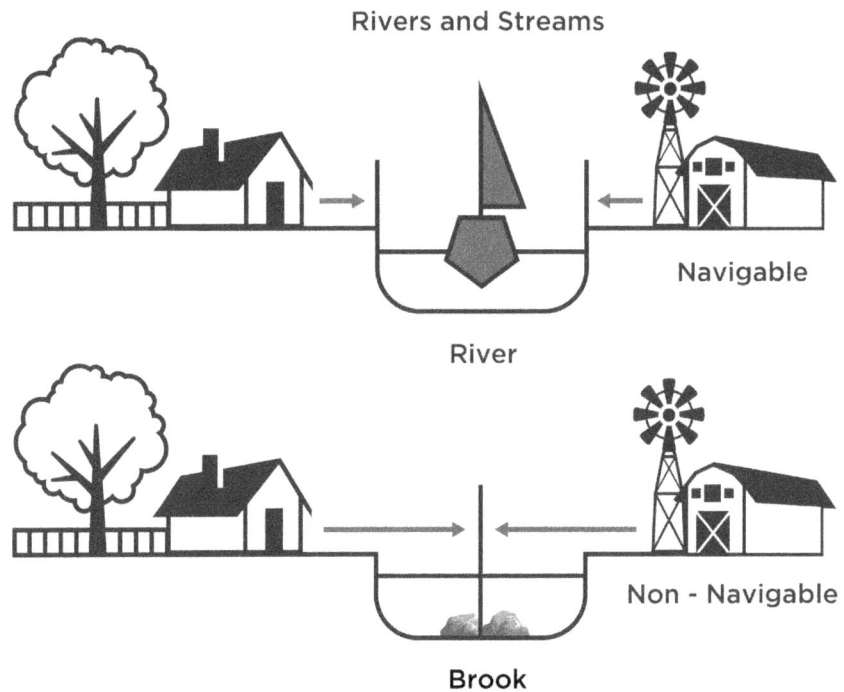

Rivers and Streams

River

Navigable

Brook

Non - Navigable

One's riparian rights to use flowing water are subject to the conditions that:

  ▸ the usage is reasonable and does not infringe on the riparian rights
    of other owners downstream
  ▸ the usage does not pollute the water
  ▸ the usage does not impede or alter the course of the water flow.

Like littoral rights, riparian rights attach to the property.

Processes that affect water rights and ownership. Through natural processes,
water moves and land grows and shrinks, possibly changing ownership rights.
Noteworthy among these processes are

  ▸ **accretion** – the process whereby land increases due to the
    accumulation of rock, soil, and sand carried by water

  ▸ **alluvion** – land that results from accretion, such as at the mouth of
    a river; the landowner owns the deposited material
  ▸ **erosion** – loss of land through the action of wind and water; the
    landowner may lose land
  ▸ **reliction** – the uncovering of underwater land by the receding of
    water; new land usually belongs to the owner of the previously
    covered area

INTERESTS AND ESTATES IN LAND

Interests
Estates in land

Interests

An interest in real estate is *ownership of any combination of the bundle of rights* to real property, including the rights to

- possess
- use
- transfer
- encumber
- exclude

Undivided interest. An undivided interest is an owner's interest in a property in which two or more parties share ownership. The terms "undivided" and "indivisible" signify that the owner's interest is in a fractional part of the entire estate, not in a physical portion of the real property itself. If two co-owners have an undivided equal interest, one owner may not lay claim to the northern half of the property for his or her exclusive use.

Examples of interests include:

- an owner who enjoys the complete bundle of rights
- a tenant who temporarily enjoys the right to use and exclude
- a lender who enjoys the right to encumber the property over the life of a mortgage loan
- a repairman who encumbers the property when the owner fails to pay for services
- a buyer who prevents an owner from selling the property to another party under the terms of the sale contract
- a mining company which temporarily owns the right to extract minerals from the property's subsurface
- a local municipality which has the right to control how an owner uses the property
- a utility company which claims access to the property in accordance with an easement

Interests differ according to

- how long a person may enjoy the interest
- what portion of the land, air, or subsurface the interest applies to
- whether the interest is public or private
- whether the interest includes legal ownership of the property

Interests in Real Estate

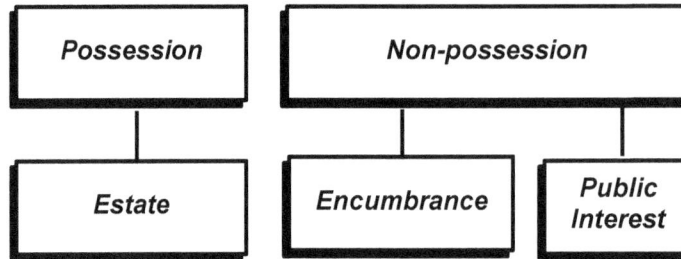

```
┌─────────────────┐     ┌─────────────────────┐
│   Possession    │     │   Non-possession    │
└────────┬────────┘     └──────────┬──────────┘
         │                  │              │
┌────────┴────────┐  ┌──────┴──────┐ ┌─────┴─────┐
│     Estate      │  │ Encumbrance │ │  Public   │
│                 │  │             │ │ Interest  │
└─────────────────┘  └─────────────┘ └───────────┘
```

Interests are principally distinguished by whether they include possession. If the interest-holder enjoys the right of possession, the party is considered to have an **estate in land**, or, familiarly an estate. If a private interest-holder does not have the right to possess, the interest is an **encumbrance.** If the interest-holder is not private, such as a government entity, and does not have the right to possess, the interest is some form of *public interest.*

An encumbrance enables a non-owning party to restrict the owner's bundle of rights. Tax liens, mortgages, easements, and encroachments are examples.

Public entities may own or lease real estate, in which case they enjoy an estate in land. However, government entities also have non-possessory interests in real estate which act to control land use for the public good within the entity's jurisdiction. The prime example of public interest is **police power**, or the right of the local or county government to **zone**. Another example of public interest is the right to acquire ownership through the power of eminent domain.

Estates in land

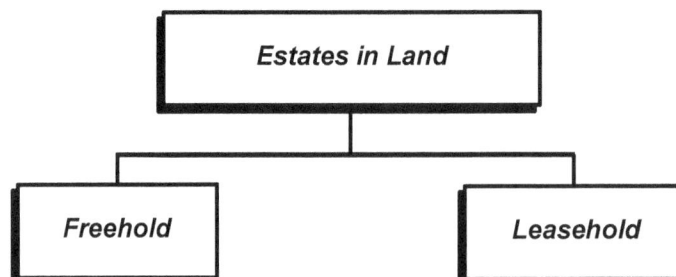

An estate in land is an interest that includes the right of possession. Depending on the length of time one may enjoy the right to possess the estate, the relationships of the parties owning the estate, and specific interests held in the estate, an estate is a freehold or a leasehold estate.

Estates in Land

```
              ┌─────────────────┐
              │  Estates in Land │
              └────────┬─────────┘
              ┌────────┴─────────┐
     ┌────────┴────────┐  ┌──────┴──────┐
     │    Freehold     │  │  Leasehold  │
     └─────────────────┘  └─────────────┘
```

In a **freehold estate**, the duration of the owner's rights cannot be determined: the rights may endure for a lifetime, for less than a lifetime, or for generations beyond the owner's lifetime.

A **leasehold estate** is distinguished by its specific duration, as represented by the lease term.

Ownership of a freehold estate is commonly equated with ownership of the property, whereas ownership of a leasehold estate is not so considered because the leaseholder's rights are temporary.

Both leasehold and freehold estates are referred to as **tenancies**. The owner of the freehold estate is the **freehold tenant**, and the renter, or lessee, is the **leasehold tenant**.

FREEHOLD ESTATES

Fee simple estate
Life estate
Conventional life estate
Legal life estate

Freehold estates differ primarily according to the duration of the estate and what happens to the estate when the owner dies. A freehold estate of potentially unlimited duration is a fee simple estate: an estate limited to the life of the owner is a life estate.

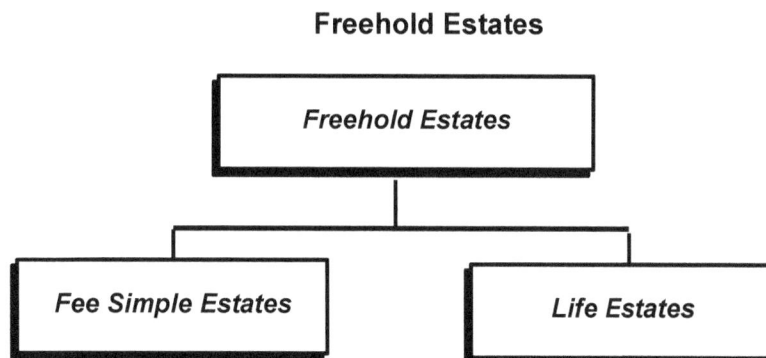

Freehold Estates

Freehold Estates → Fee Simple Estates | Life Estates

Fee simple estate

The **fee simple** freehold estate is the *highest form of ownership interest* one can acquire in real estate. It includes the complete bundle of rights, and the tenancy is unlimited, with certain exceptions indicated below. The fee simple interest is also called the "fee interest," or simply, the "fee." The owner of the fee simple interest is called the **fee tenant**.

Fee simple estates, like all estates, remain subject to government restrictions and private interests.

There are two forms of fee simple estate: **absolute** and **defeasible**.

Fee Simple Estates

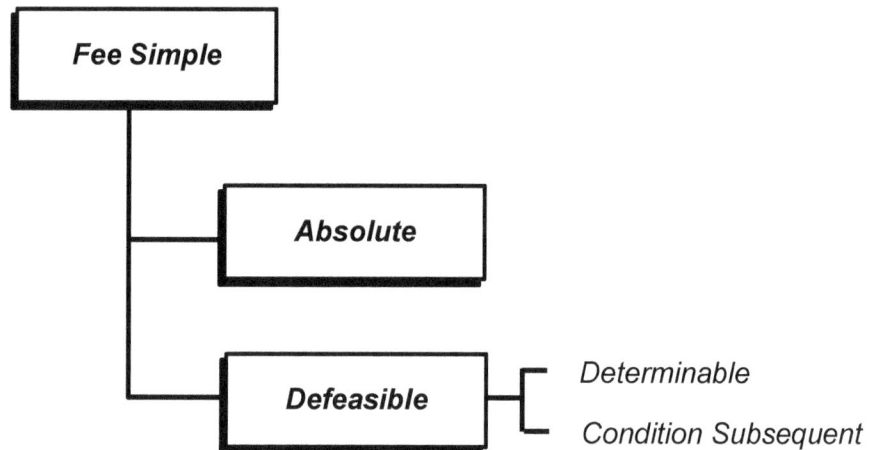

Fee Simple Absolute. The fee simple absolute estate is a perpetual estate that is *not conditioned by stipulated or restricted uses.* It may also be freely passed on to heirs. For these reasons, the fee simple absolute estate is the most desirable estate that can be obtained in residential real estate. It is also the most common.

Fee Simple Defeasible. The defeasible fee estate is perpetual, provided the usage *conforms to stated conditions.* Essential characteristics are:

> ▸ the property must be used for a certain purpose or under certain conditions
> ▸ if the use changes or if prohibited conditions are present, the estate reverts to the previous grantor of the estate.

The two types of fee simple defeasible are **determinable** and **condition subsequent**.

Determinable. The deed to the determinable estate states usage limitations. If the restrictions are violated, the estate automatically reverts to the grantor or heirs.

Condition subsequent. If any condition is violated, the previous owner may repossess the property. However, reversion of the estate is not automatic: the grantor must re-take physical possession within a certain time frame.

Life estate

A life estate is a freehold estate that is limited in duration to the life of the owner or other named person. Upon the death of the owner or other named individual, *the estate passes to the original owner or another named party.* The holder of a life estate is called the **life tenant**.

The distinguishing characteristics of the life estate are:

▶ the owner enjoys full ownership rights during the estate period

▶ holders of the future interest own either a reversionary or a remainder interest

▶ the estate may be created by agreement between private parties, or it may be created by law under prescribed circumstances.

Remainder. If a life estate names a third party to receive title to the property upon termination of the life estate, the party enjoys a future interest called a remainder interest or a remainder estate. The holder of a remainder interest is called a **remainderman**.

Reversion. If no remainder estate is established, the estate reverts to the original owner or the owner's heirs. In this situation, the original owner retains a reversionary interest or estate.

The two types of life estates are the **conventional** and the **legal** life estate.

Life Estates

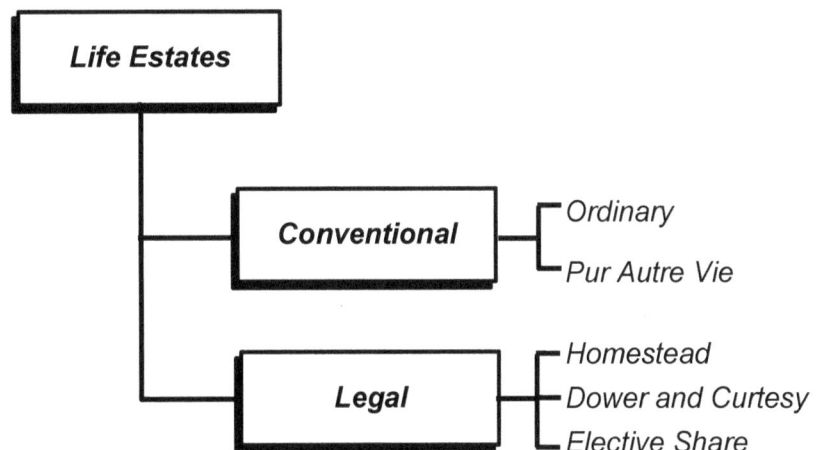

Conventional life estate

A conventional life estate is created by grant from a fee simple property owner to the grantee, the life tenant. Following the termination of the estate, rights pass to a remainderman or revert to the previous owner.

During the life estate period, the owner enjoys all ownership rights, provided he or she does not infringe on the rights of the remainder or reversion interest holders, such as by damaging the property or jeopardizing its value. Should such actions occur, holders of the future interest may take legal action against the property owners.

The two types of conventional life estate are the **ordinary** and the **pur autre vie** life estate.

Conventional Life Estates

	Ordinary Life Estate	Pur Autre Vie
With reversion	duration: owner's life reverts to grantor	duration: another's life reverts to grantor
With remainder	duration: owner's life reverts to another	duration: another's life reverts to another

Ordinary life estate. An ordinary life estate *ends with the death of the life estate owner* and may pass back to the original owners or their heirs (reversion) or to a named third party (remainder).

For example, John King grants a life estate in a property to Mary Brown, to endure over Mary's lifetime. John establishes that when Mary dies, the property will revert to himself.

Pur autre vie. A pur autre vie life estate endures over the lifetime of a third person, after which the property passes from the tenant holder to the original grantor (reversion) or a third party (remainderman).

For example, Yvonne grants a life estate to Ryan, to endure over the lifetime of Yvonne's husband Steve. Upon Steve's death, Yvonne establishes that her mother, Rose, will receive the property.

Legal life estate

A legal life estate is *created by law* as opposed to being created by a property owner's agreement. The focus of a legal life estate is defining and protecting the property rights of surviving family members upon the death of the husband or wife.

The major forms of legal life estate are the **homestead**, **dower and curtesy**, and **elective share**.

Homestead. A homestead is one's principal residence. Florida homestead laws protect family members against losing their homes to general creditors attempting to collect on debts.

Homestead laws provide that:

> ▸ all or portions of one's homestead *are exempt* from a forced sale executed for the collection of general debts (judgment liens). The various states place different limits on this exemption.

> ▸ tax debts, seller financing debt, debts for home improvement, and mortgage debt are *not exempt*

- the homestead interest cannot be conveyed by one spouse; both spouses must sign the deed conveying homestead property
- the homestead exemption and restrictions *endure over the life* of the head of the household, and pass on to children under legal age.
- homestead interests in a property *are extinguished* if the property is sold or abandoned

The homestead exemption from certain debts should not be confused with the *homestead tax* exemption, which exempts a portion of the property's value from taxation.

Dower and curtesy. Dower is a wife's life estate interest in the husband's property. When the husband dies, the wife can make a claim to portions of the decedent's property. Curtesy is the identical right enjoyed by the husband in a deceased wife's property. Property acquired under dower laws is owned by the surviving spouse for the duration of his or her lifetime.

To transfer property within dower and curtesy states, the husband (or wife) must obtain a release of the dower interest from the other spouse in order to convey clear title to another party. If both parties sign the conveyance, the dower right is automatically extinguished.

In Florida, elective share laws have supplanted dower and curtesy, and there is no recognition of community property.

Elective share. Elective share enables a surviving spouse to make a minimum claim to the deceased spouse's real and personal property in place of the provisions for such property in the decedent's will.

For example, if a husband's will excludes the wife from any property inheritance, the wife may, upon the husband's death make the elective share claim.

Florida's elective share law provides that:

- the surviving spouse is entitled to a percent of the deceased spouse's property, excepting homestead property and property the decedent owned exclusively
- the surviving spouse must file for the elective share within a limited time period
- if the spouse fails to file, the estate passes on according to the will or the state's laws of descent
- the elective share right pertains only to the surviving spouse and is not transferrable.

WAYS OF HOLDING OWNERSHIP

Tenancy in severalty
Co-ownership

Tenancy in severalty   If *a single party owns* the fee or life estate, the ownership is a **tenancy in severalty**. Synonyms are **sole ownership**, **ownership in severalty**, and **estate in severalty**.

The estate of a deceased tenant in severalty passes to heirs by probate

Co-ownership   If more than one person, or a legal entity such as a corporation, owns an estate in land, the estate is held in some form of co-ownership. Co-owners are also called **cotenants**.

Tenancy in common. The tenancy in common, also known as the **estate in common,** is the most common form of co-ownership when the owners are not married. The defining characteristics are:

> ▶   **two or more owners**
>
> Any number of people may be co-tenants in a single property.

> ▶   **identical rights**
>
> Co-tenants share an indivisible interest in the estate, i.e., all have equal rights to possess and use the property subject to the rights of the other cotenants. No co-tenant may claim to own any physical portion of the property exclusively. They share what is called undivided possession or unity of possession.

> ▶   **interests individually owned**
>
> All tenants in common have distinct and separable ownership of their respective interests. Co-tenants may sell, encumber, or transfer their interests without obstruction or consent from the other owners. (A co-tenant may not, however, encumber the entire property.)

> ▶   **electable ownership shares**
>
> Tenants in common determine among themselves what share of the estate each party will own. For example, three co-tenants may own 40%, 35%, and 25% interests in a property, respectively. In the absence of stated ownership shares, it is assumed that each has a share equal to that of the others.

▸ **no survivorship**

A deceased co-tenant's estate passes by probate to the decedent's heirs and devisees rather than to the other tenants in common. Any number of heirs can share in the ownership of the willed tenancy.

▸ **no unity of time**

It is not necessary for tenants in common to acquire their interests at the same time. A new co-tenant may enter into a pre-existing tenancy in common.

The following exhibit illustrates how tenants in common may transfer ownership interests to other parties by sale or will.

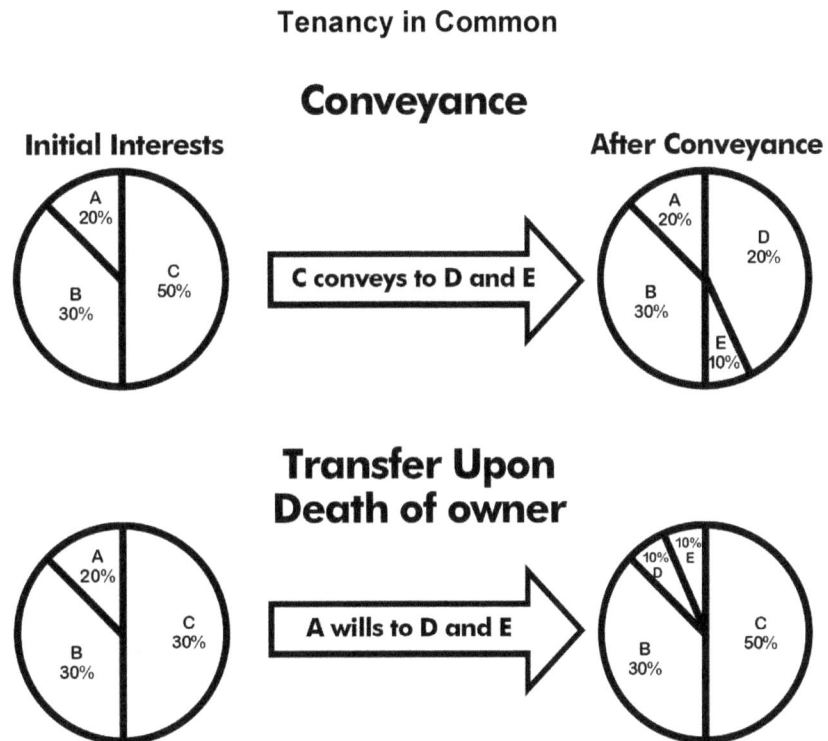

Tenancy in Common

Conveyance

Initial Interests

A 20%
B 30%
C 50%

C conveys to D and E →

After Conveyance

A 20%
D 20%
B 30%
E 10%

Transfer Upon Death of owner

A 20%
B 30%
C 30%

A wills to D and E →

10% D
10% E
B 30%
C 50%

The exhibit shows three owners of a property as tenants in common: A owns 20%, B owns 30%, and C owns 50%. C decides to sell 4/5 of his interest to D and 1/5 to E. D's interest in the estate will be 40% (4/5 times 50%), and E's will be 10% (1/5 times 50%). Both new tenants are tenants in common with A and B. Note that any owner may sell any portion of his or her interest to other owners or outside parties.

The second part of the exhibit shows how, when co-owner A dies, she might bequeath her 20% share of the ownership to heirs D and E equally. In such a case, the heirs would each acquire a 10% share of ownership as tenants in common with B and C.

Joint tenancy. In a joint tenancy, two or more persons collectively own a property as if they were a single person. Rights and interests are indivisible and equal: each has a shared interest in the whole property which cannot be divided up. Joint tenants may only convey their interests to outside parties as tenant-in-common interests. One cannot convey a joint tenant interest.

The defining characteristics and requirements of joint tenancy are:

> ▶ **unity of ownership**
>
> Whereas tenants in common hold separate title to their individual interests, joint tenants together hold a single title to the property.

> ▶ **equal ownership**
>
> Joint tenants own equal shares in the property, without exception. If there are four co-tenants, each owns 25% of the property. If there are ten co-tenants, each owns 10%.

> ▶ **transfer of interest**
>
> A joint tenant may transfer his or her interest in the property to an outside party, but only as a tenancy in common interest. Whoever acquires the interest co-owns the property as a tenant in common with the other joint tenants. The remaining joint tenants continue to own an undivided interest in the property, less the new cotenant's share.

> ▶ **survivorship**
>
> In a joint tenancy, joint tenants enjoy rights of survivorship: if a joint tenant dies, all interests and rights pass to the surviving joint tenants free from any claims of creditors or heirs. In Florida, survivorship must be expressly stated in the deed to be effected on transfer.
>
> When only one joint tenant survives, the survivor's interest becomes an estate in severalty, and the joint tenancy is terminated. The estate will be then probated upon the severalty owner's death.
>
> The survivorship feature of joint tenancy presents an advantage to tenancy in common, in that interests pass without probate proceedings. On the other hand, joint tenants relinquish any ability to will their interest to parties outside of the tenancy.

Joint Tenancy

Conveyance

Initial Interests

A 33 1/3 %
B 33 1/3 %
C 33 1/3 %

A and B are joint tenants

C sells to D

D is tenant in common with AB

After Conveyance

A 33 1/3 %
B 33 1/3 %
C 33 1/3 %

Transfer Upon Death of owner

A 33 1/3 %
B 33 1/3 %
C 33 1/3 %

C dies

A 50 %
B 50 %

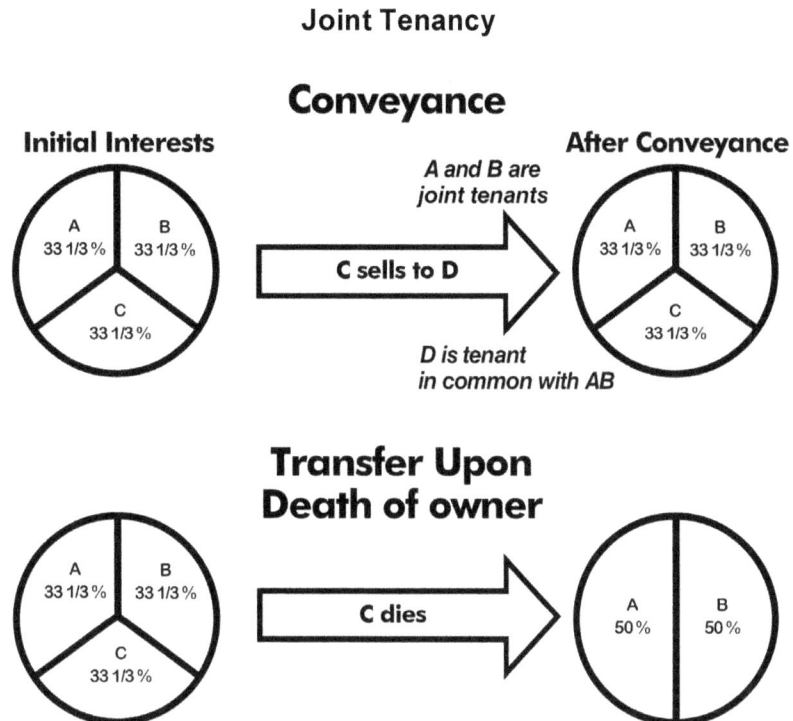

The exhibit shows three parties, A, B and C, who acquired a property as joint tenants. By definition, each owns a one-third share. If C sells to D, A and B automatically become joint tenants of two-thirds of the property. D becomes a tenant in common with A and B. D's interest will pass to her heirs upon her death.

If C dies, A and B receive equal shares of C's estate, making the remaining shares an equal 50%. If B then dies, A acquires the whole estate and becomes the sole owner. This event terminates the joint tenancy estate, and it becomes an estate in severalty.

Creation of joint tenancy. To create a joint tenancy, all owners must acquire the property at the same time, use the same deed, acquire equal interests, and share in equal rights of possession. These are referred to as the **four unities**.

> ▶ **unity of time**
>
> all parties must acquire the joint interest at the same time

> ▶ **unity of title**
>
> all parties must acquire the property in the same deed of conveyance

> ▶ **unity of interest**
>
> all parties must receive equal undivided interests

‣   **unity of possession**

all parties must receive the same rights of possession

In Florida, the conveyance must name the parties as joint tenants with rights of survivorship. Otherwise, and in the absence of clear intent of the parties, the estate will be considered a tenancy in common. In addition, a joint tenancy can only be created by agreement between parties, and not by operation of law.

Termination by partition suit. A partition suit can terminate a joint tenancy or a tenancy in common. Foreclosure and bankruptcy can also terminate these estates.

A partition suit is a legal avenue for an owner who wants to dispose of his or her interest against the wishes of other co-owners. The suit petitions the court to divide, or **partition**, the property physically, according to the owner's respective rights and interests. If this is not reasonably feasible, the court may order the property sold, whereupon the interests are liquidated and distributed proportionately.

Tenancy by the entireties. Tenancy by the entireties is a form of ownership traditionally reserved for **husband and wife,** though now available for legally married same-sex spouses in Florida. It features survivorship, equal interests, and limited exposure to foreclosure.

‣   **survivorship**

On the death of husband or wife, the decedent's interest passes automatically to the other spouse.

‣   **equal, undivided interest**

Each spouse owns the estate as if there were only one owner. Fractional interests cannot be transferred to outside parties. The entire interest may be conveyed, but only with the consent and signatures of both parties.

‣   **no foreclosure for individual debts**

The estate is subject to foreclosure only for jointly incurred debts.

‣   **termination**

The estate may be terminated by divorce, death, mutual agreement, and judgments for joint debt.

LEASEHOLD ESTATES

Estate for years
Estate from period-to-period
Estate at will
Estate at sufferance

A leasehold estate, or **leasehold**, arises from the execution of a lease by a fee owner- the **lessor,** or **landlord**-- to a **lessee**, or **tenant**. Since tenants do not own the fee interest, a leasehold estate is technically an item of personal property for the tenant.

Leasehold tenants are entitled to possess and use the leased premises during the lease term in the manner prescribed in the lease. They also have restricted rights to exclusion.

Estate for years

The estate for years is a leasehold estate for a definite period of time, with a beginning date and an ending date. The estate for years may endure for any length of term. At the end of the term, the estate automatically terminates, without any requirement of notice.

For example, a landlord grants a tenant a three-year lease. After the three years, the leasehold terminates, and the landlord may re-possess the premises, renew the lease, or lease to someone else.

Estate from period-to-period

In an estate from period-to-period, also called a **periodic tenancy**, the tenancy period automatically renews for an indefinite period of time, subject to timely payment of rent. At the end of a tenancy period, if the landlord accepts another regular payment of rent, the leasehold is considered to be renewed for another period.

For example, a two-year lease expires, and the landlord grants a six-month lease that is automatically renewable, provided the monthly rent is received on time. At the end of the six months, the tenant pays, and the landlord accepts another monthly rent payment. The acceptance of the rent automatically extends the leasehold for another six months.

The most common form of periodic tenancy is the month-to-month lease, which may exist without any written agreement.

Either party may terminate a periodic tenancy by giving proper notice to the other party. Proper notice is defined by state law.

Estate at will

The estate at will, also called a **tenancy at will**, has no definite expiration date and hence no "renewal" cycle. The landlord and tenant agree that the tenancy will have no specified termination date, provided rent is paid on time and other lease conditions are met.

For example, a son leases a house to his father and mother "forever," or until they want to move.

The estate at will is terminated by proper notice, or by the death of either party.

Estate at sufferance In an estate at sufferance, a tenant occupies the premises without consent of the landlord or other legal agreement with the landlord. Usually such an estate involves a tenant who fails to vacate at the expiration of the lease, continuing occupancy without any right to do so.

For example, a tenant violates the provisions of a lease and is evicted. The tenant protests and refuses to leave despite the eviction order.

COOPERATIVES

Interests, rights, and obligations
Organization and management
Cooperative disclosures

In a cooperative, or co-op, one owns **shares** in a non-profit corporation or cooperative association, which in turn acquires and owns an apartment building as its principal asset. Along with this stock, the shareholder acquires a **proprietary lease** to occupy one of the apartment units.

The number of shares purchased reflects the value of the apartment unit in relation to the property's total value. The ratio of the unit's value to total value also establishes what portions of the property's expenses the owner must pay.

The Cooperative

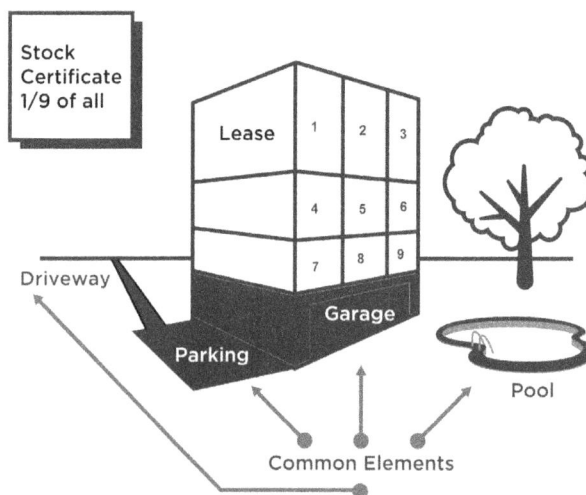

The exhibit shows a nine-unit apartment building. A cooperative corporation buys the building for $900,000. All nine units are of equal size, so the corporation decides that each apartment represents a value of $100,000, or 1/9 of the total. The co-op buyer pays the corporation $100,000 and receives 1/9 of the corporation's stock. The shareholder also receives a proprietary lease for apartment 1. The shareholder is now responsible for the apartment unit's pro rata share of the corporation's expenses, or 11.11%.

Interests, rights and obligations

Cooperative association's interest. The corporate entity of the cooperative association is the only party in the cooperative with a real property interest. The association's interest is an undivided interest in the entire property. There is no ownership interest in individual units, as with a condominium.

Shareholder's interest. In owning stock and a lease, a co-op unit owner's interest is *personal property* that is subject to control by the corporation. Unlike condominium ownership, the co-op owner owns neither a unit nor an undivided interest in the common elements.

Proprietary lease. The co-op lease is called a proprietary lease because the tenant is an owner (proprietor) of the corporation that owns the property. The lease has no stated or fixed rent. Instead, the proprietor-tenant is responsible for the unit's pro rata share of the corporation's expenses in supporting the cooperative. Unit owners pay monthly assessments. The proprietary lease has no stated term and remains in effect over the owner's period of ownership. When the unit is sold, the lease is assigned to the new owner.

Expense liability. The failure of individual shareholders to pay monthly expense assessments can destroy the investment of all the other co-op owners if the co-op cannot pay the bills by other means.

Since the corporation owns an undivided interest in the property, debts and financial obligations apply to the property as a whole, not to individual units. Should the corporation fail to meet its obligations, creditors and mortgagees may foreclose *on the entire property*. A completed foreclosure would terminate the shareholders' proprietary lease, and bankrupt the owning corporation. Compare this situation with that of a condominium, in which an individual's failure to pay endangers only that individual's unit, not the entire property.

Transfers. The co-op interest is transferred by assigning both the stock certificates and lease to the buyer.

Organization and management

A developer creates a cooperative by forming the cooperative association, which subsequently buys the cooperative property. The association's articles of incorporation, bylaws, and other legal documents establish operating policies, rules, and restrictions.

The shareholders elect a board of directors. The board assumes the responsibility for maintaining and operating the cooperative, much like a condominium board. Cooperative associations, however, also control the use and ownership of individual apartment units, since they are the legal owners. A shareholder's voting power is proportional to the number of shares owned.

Cooperative disclosures

The Cooperative Act. F.S. Chapter 719 (the Cooperative Act) requires developers to disclose to prospective cooperative buyers within the sale or lease contract the right to cancel the contract. The disclosure must be made in "conspicuous" type and include language providing the buyer the right to cancel the contract in writing within 15 days after the buyer signed the contract. The buyer may also cancel the contract within 15 days if the contract has been amended in such a way that the offering is materially altered or modified in an adverse way to the buyer. This right to cancel may not be waived. The disclosure must also include language that the budget provided to the buyer contains estimates which, if they do not match actual costs, do not constitute adverse changes to the offering.

The Act requires non-developers selling their shares in the association to disclose the buyer's right to cancel in writing within 3 business days of signing the contract. This disclosure also is to include language that the buyer has been provided current copies of the associations governing documents: the Articles of Incorporation, Bylaws, Rules of the Association, and a Question and Answer sheet prior to signing the contract.

If the cooperative parcels are being sold or leased prior to construction completion, the developer must disclose a copy of the plans and specifications for the completion of the unit and common areas. All contracts and disclosures must contain language that oral representations cannot be relied upon.

CONDOMINIUMS

Airspace and common elements
Interests and rights
Condominium creation
Organization and management
Owner responsibilities

A condominium is a hybrid form of ownership of multi-unit residential or commercial properties. It combines ownership of a fee simple interest in the **airspace** within a unit with ownership of an undivided share, as a tenant in common, of the entire property's **common elements,** such as lobbies, swimming pools, and hallways.

A condominium **unit** is one airspace unit together with the associated interest in the common elements.

Airspace and common elements

The unique aspect of the condominium is its fee simple interest in the airspace contained within the outer walls, floors, and ceiling of the building unit. This airspace may include internal walls which are not essential to the structural support of the building.

Common elements are all portions of the property that are necessary for the existence, operation, and maintenance of the condominium units. Common elements include:

> ▶ the land (if not leased)

> ▶ structural components of the building, such as exterior windows, roof, and foundation

> ▶ physical operating systems supporting all units, such as plumbing, power, communications installations, and central air conditioning

> ▶ recreational facilities

> ▶ building and ground areas used non-exclusively, such as stairways, elevators, hallways, and laundry rooms

The Condominium

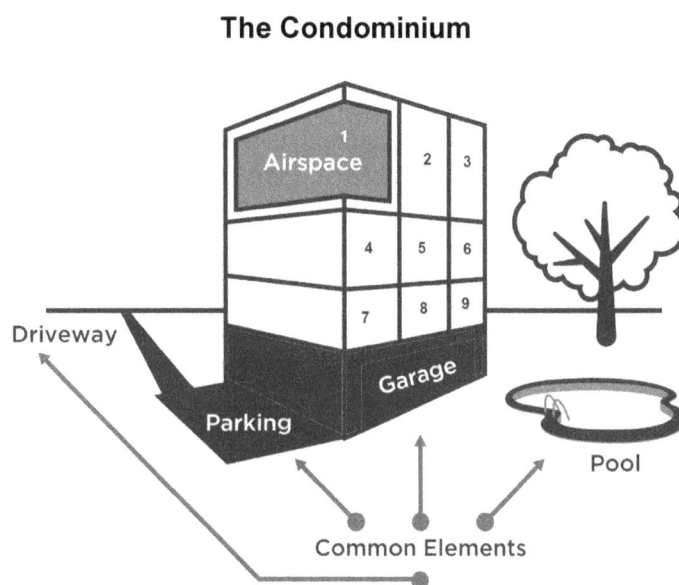

A buyer who purchases Unit #1 of the condominium illustrated obtains a fee simple interest in the airspace of apartment 1 and a tenancy in common interest in her pro rata share of the common elements. If all units in the building have the same ownership interest, the buyer would own an indivisible one-ninth interest in the common elements-- pool, parking lot, garage, pool, building structure, tree, etc.

Interests and rights

The condominium unit can be owned jointly, in severalty, in trust, or in any other manner allowed by state law. Unit owners hold an exclusive interest in their individual apartments, and co-own common elements with other unit owners as tenants in common.

Possession, use, and exclusion. Unit owners exclusively possess their apartment space, but must share common areas with other owners. The property's legal documents may create exceptions. For example, unit owners may be required to join and pay fees for use of a health club.

Unit owners as a group may exclude non-owners from portions of the common area, for instance, excluding uninvited parties from entering the building itself.

Transfer and encumbrance. Condominium units can be individually sold, mortgaged, or otherwise encumbered without interference from other unit owners. As a distinct entity, the condominium unit may also be foreclosed and liquidated. An owner may not sell interests in the apartment separately from the interest in the common elements.

Resale of a unit interest may entail limitations, such as the condominium association's prior approval of a buyer.

Condominium units are individually assessed and taxed. The assessment pertains to the value of the exclusive interest in the apartment as well as the unit's pro rata share of common elements.

Condominium creation

Condominium properties are created by executing and recording a condominium declaration and a **master deed**. The declaration must be legally correct in form and substance according to local laws. The party creating the declaration is referred to as the **developer**. The condominium may include ownership of the land or exclude it if the land is leased.

Declaration provisions. The condominium declaration may be required to include:

▶ a legal description and/or name of the property

▶ a survey of land, common elements, and all units

▶ plat maps of land and building, and floor plans with identifiers for all condominium units

▶ provisions for common area easements

▶ an identification of each unit's share of ownership in the overall property

▶ organization plans for creation of the condominium association, including its bylaws

▶ voting rights, membership status, and liability for expenses of individual owners

▶ covenants and restrictions regarding use and transfer of units

Organization and management

Organization. Condominium declarations typically provide for the creation of an **owner's association** to enforce the bylaws and manage the overall property. The association is often headed by a board of directors. The association board organizes how the property will be managed and by whom. It may appoint management agents, hire resident managers, and create supervisory committees. The board also oversees the property's finances and policy administration.

Management. Condominium properties have extensive management requirements, including maintenance, sales and leasing, accounting, owner services, sanitation, security, trash removal, etc. The association engages professional management companies, resident managers, sales and rental agents, specialized maintenance personnel, and outside service contractors to fulfill these functions.

Owner responsibilities

Individual units. Owner responsibilities relating to the apartment include:

▶ maintaining internal systems

▶ maintaining the property condition

▶ insuring contents of the unit

Common area assessments. Unit owners bear the costs of all other property expenses, such as maintenance, insurance, management fees, supplies, legal fees, and repairs. An annual operating budget totals these expenses and passes them through as **assessments** to unit owners, usually on a monthly basis.

Should an owner fail to pay periodic assessments, the condominium board can initiate court action to foreclose the property to pay the amounts owed.

The unit's pro rata share of the property's ownership as defined in the declaration determines the amount of a unit owner's assessment. For example, if a unit represents a 2% share of the property value, that unit owner's assessment will be 2% of the property's common area expenses.

Condominium disclosures

The Condominium Act. F.S. Chapter 718 (the Condominium Act) requires developers selling condominium units to provide the buyer with copies of the governing documents (Declaration, Articles of Incorporation, Bylaws, Rules of the Association, and Frequently Asked Questions sheet) and have the buyer sign a receipt for the documents. The developer must also include a disclosure with the sales contract that provides the buyer with 15 days after signing the contract and receiving the required materials to submit a written cancellation notice. The buyer may also cancel within 15 days of receiving a contract amendment that is adverse to the buyer. The disclosure must also include language that the budget provided to the buyer contains estimates which, if they do not match actual costs, do not constitute adverse changes to the offering.

The Act requires condominium unit owners who are reselling their units to provide the buyer with copies of the governing documents, current year-end financial report, Frequently Asked Questions sheet, and a governance form. The Division of Florida Condominiums, Timeshares, and Mobile Homes created the governance form as an informal educational overview of condominium governance. It includes such topics as the role and responsibilities of the board, owners' rights, remedies available to owners, and more. Sellers will want to have the buyer sign a receipt confirming he or she has received all of the required documents. The Act also requires the seller to include a disclosure with the sales contract that provides the buyer with the right to cancel in writing within 3 business days of signing the contract.

If the condominiums are being sold prior to construction completion, the developer must disclose a copy of the plans and specifications for the completion of the units and common areas. All contracts and disclosures must contain language that oral representations cannot be relied upon and that the right to cancel may not be waived.

TIME-SHARING

Time-share lease
Time-share freehold
Regulation
Time-share disclosures

Time-share ownership is a fee or leasehold interest in a property whose owners or tenants agree to use the property on a periodic, non-overlapping basis. This type of ownership commonly concerns vacation and resort properties. Time-share arrangements provide for equal sharing of the property's expenses among the owners.

Time-share lease

In a leasehold time-share, the tenant agrees to rent the property on a scheduled basis or under any pre-arranged system of reservation, according to the terms of the lease. Generally, the scheduled use is denominated in weeks or months over the duration of the lease, a specified number of years.

Time-share freehold

In a freehold time-share, or **interval ownership estate**, tenants in common own undivided interests in the property. Expense prorations and rules governing interval usage are established by separate agreement when the estate is acquired.

For instance, the Blackburns want a monthly vacation in Colorado once a year. They find a time-share condominium that needs a twelfth buyer. The available month is May, which suits the Blackburns. The total price of the condominium is $240,000, and annual expenses are estimated to be $9,600. The Blackburns buy a one-twelfth interest with the other tenants in common by paying their share of the price, $20,000. They are also obligated to pay one-twelfth of the expenses every year, or $800. They have use of the property for one-twelfth of the year, in the month of May.

Interval owners must usually waive the right of partition, which would enable an owner to force the sale of the entire property.

Regulation

The development and sale of time-share properties has come under increased regulation in recent years. Developers and brokers face stringent disclosure requirements regarding ownership costs and risks. Other laws provide for a cooling-off period after the signing of a time-share sales contract, and require registration of advertising.

In Florida, anyone selling time-share plans must hold a real estate license unless they are specifically exempted. Owners who occupy the timeshare for their own use are exempt from licensure. Owner/developers who sell timeshares may employ unlicensed individuals to sell the timeshares as long as those individuals are not paid commission on the sales and are not paid based on individual transactions.

If a timeshare plan is located in Florida but is being offered for sale outside of the state but within the United States, the offering or sale is not subject to the provisions of Florida time-share laws. If the timeshare plan is located in Florida but is being offered for sale outside of the United States, the offering is not subject to the provisions of Florida time-share laws as long as the developer files the timeshare plan with the Division of Florida Condominiums, Timeshares, and Mobile Homes for approval or the developer pays an exemption registration fee and files the required information to the Division for approval.

If a timeshare is located outside of Florida but is being offered for sale in Florida, the offering or sale is subject only to certain time-share laws, as specified in F.S. Chapter 721.03(1)(c).

Time-share disclosures

The Florida Vacation Plan and Timesharing Act and Rule 61J2-23.001, F.A.C. F.S. Chapter 721 (the Florida Vacation Plan and Timesharing Act) and Rule 61J2-23.001 0f the Florida Administrative Code require several disclosures to be included when timeshares are being sold.

Listing agreement disclosures. Listing agreements with brokers must be in writing and provided to the signing client at the time of signing. The agreement must include the following disclosures:

> ▸ *THERE IS NO GUARANTEE THAT YOUR TIME-SHARE PERIOD CAN BE SOLD AT ANY PARTICULAR PRICE OR WITHIN ANY PARTICULAR PERIOD OF TIME.*
>
> This disclosure must be included in conspicuous type and located directly above the signature line for the owner of the time-share period. The statement must also be included in any written advertising material used to solicit listing agreements.
>
> ▸ a complete and clear disclosure of fees, commissions, and other costs or compensation that will be paid to or received by the broker
>
> ▸ the term of the agreement with a statement regarding any party's ability to extend the agreement's term and a description of the conditions under which the agreement may be extended and at what cost
>
> ▸ a description of the services the broker will provide and the obligations of each party to the resale transaction, including costs and obligations in notifying the managing entity of the plan and any exchange company

- whether the broker has exclusive rights of obtaining a buyer during the agreement's term, to whom and when proceeds from the sale are to be disbursed, under what conditions any party may terminate the agreement, and the amount of commission or compensation owed to the broker at agreement termination prior to resale closing.

- whether the broker or anyone else may use the subject time-share period, a description of such use rights, and to whom rents or profits from the use will be paid

- the existence of any judgments or pending litigation against the broker due to or alleging a violation of Florida real estate statutes or consumer fraud

Resale contract disclosures. It is considered a violation of Florida real estate license laws if a licensee executes any contract or purchase agreement without complying with the required provisions. The contract or agreement must include the following disclosures, for which the broker may rely on written information provided by the managing entity:

- an explanation of the form of time-share ownership being purchased and a legally sufficient description of the time-share period being purchased

- the name and address of the plan's managing entity

- in conspicuous type and located directly above the signature line for the owner of the time-share period, the statement:

    THERE IS NO GUARANTEE THAT YOUR TIME-SHARE PERIOD CAN BE SOLD AT ANY PARTICULAR PRICE OR WITHIN ANY PARTICULAR PERIOD OF TIME.

- in at least 10-point type, all capitalized, and directly above the buyer's signature line, the statement:

    THE CURRENT YEAR'S ASSESSMENT FOR COMMON EXPENSES ALLOCABLE TO THE TIME-SHARE PERIOD YOU ARE PURCHASING IS ___ . THIS ASSESSMENT, WHICH MAY BE INCREASED FROM TIME TO TIME BY THE MANAGING ENTITY OF THE TIME-SHARE PLAN, IS PAYABLE IN FULL EACH YEAR ON OR BEFORE ___ . THIS ASSESSMENT (INCLUDES/DOES NOT INCLUDE) YEARLY AD VALOREM REAL ESTATE TAXES, WHICH (ARE/ARE NOT) BILLED AND COLLECTED SEPARATELY.

- if ad valorem real property taxes are not included in the current year's assessment for common expenses, the statement:

    THE MOST RECENT ANNUAL ASSESSMENT FOR AD VALOREM REAL ESTATE TAXES FOR THE TIME-SHARE PERIOD YOU ARE PURCHASING IS ___ .) EACH OWNER IS PERSONALLY LIABLE FOR THE PAYMENT OF HIS ASSESSMENTS FOR COMMON EXPENSES, AND FAILURE TO TIMELY PAY THESE ASSESSMENTS MAY RESULT IN

RESTRICTION OR LOSS OF YOUR USE AND/OR OWNERSHIP RIGHTS.

▶ if a time-share estate is being conveyed, in conspicuous type, the statement:

For the purpose of ad valorem assessment, taxation and special assessments, the managing entity will be considered the taxpayer as your agent pursuant to section 192.037, Florida Statutes.

▶ the terms and conditions of the purchase and closing, including the closing costs and title insurance obligations of the seller and/or the buyer

▶ the existence of any mandatory exchange program membership included in the plan

Disclosure for Florida timeshare being offered for sale outside of Florida. The following disclosure statement is required within the purchase contract in conspicuous type located directly above the buyer's signature line.

The offering of this timeshare plan outside the jurisdictional limits of the United States of America is exempt from regulation under Florida law, and any such purchase is not protected by the State of Florida. However, the management and operation of any accommodations or facilities located in Florida is subject to Florida law and may give rise to enforcement action regardless of the location of any offer.

Disclosure of right to cancel. All time-share purchase agreements must include a disclosure that buyers have the right to cancel without penalty or obligation within 10 calendar days after the date of contract signing or the date the buyer received all of the required documents, whichever is later. The buyer must notify the seller of the cancellation in writing. The transaction closing may not take place before the expiration of the 10-day cancellation period. This right to cancel may not be waived.

HOMEOWNERS' ASSOCIATIONS (HOA's)

Definition
Disclosures

Definition

F.S. Chapter 720, the Homeowners' Association Act, defines a homeowners' association as a Florida corporation responsible for the operation of a community or a mobile home subdivision in which the voting membership is made up of parcel owners or their agents, or a combination thereof, and in which membership is a mandatory condition of parcel ownership, and which is authorized to impose assessments that, if unpaid, may become a lien on the parcel. The term "homeowners' association" does not include a community development district or other similar special taxing district created pursuant to statute.

The association must be incorporated with the governing documents recorded in the local county's official records. The association includes officers and directors who have a fiduciary relationship to the members (owners). Owners of land parcels are required to become part of the community's membership and make up the voting membership. Any unpaid membership fee or assessment may result in a lien on the parcel.

Disclosures

Any developer or member who sells a parcel in a homeowner's association is required to provide the buyer with the following disclosure summary:

DISCLOSURE SUMMARY
FOR
(NAME OF COMMUNITY)

1. *As a purchaser of property in this community, you will be obligated to be a member of a homeowners' association.*
2. *There have been or will be recorded restrictive covenants governing the use and occupancy of properties in this community.*
3. *You will be obligated to pay assessments to the association. Assessments may be subject to periodic change. If applicable, the current amount is $___ per___. You will also be obligated to pay any special assessments imposed by the association. Such special assessments may be subject to change. If applicable, the current amount is $___ per___.*
4. *You may be obligated to pay special assessments to the respective municipality, county, or special district. All assessments are subject to periodic change.*
5. *Your failure to pay special assessments or assessments levied by a mandatory homeowners' association could result in a lien on your property.*
6. *There may be an obligation to pay rent or land use fees for recreational or other commonly used facilities as an obligation of membership in the homeowners' association. If applicable, the current amount is $___ per___.*
7. *The developer may have the right to amend the restrictive covenants without the approval of the association membership or the approval of the parcel owners.*
8. *The statements contained in this disclosure form are only summary in nature, and, as a prospective purchaser, you should refer to the covenants and the association governing documents before purchasing property.*
9. *These documents are either matters of public record and can be obtained from the record office in the county where the property is located, or are not recorded and can be obtained from the developer.*

DATE: *PURCHASER:*

The contract or agreement must also include in prominent language a statement that the buyer should not execute the contract until the disclosure summary has been received and read. The contract must also state that the buyer may cancel the contract with a written notice within 3 days after receiving the summary and prior to closing. This right applies when the disclosure summary was not provided prior to contract execution. This right to cancel may not be waived.

COMMUNITY DEVELOPMENT DISTRICTS (CDDs)

(See also CDDs under 'Disclosures' in Section 11)

Definition
Disclosures

Definition

F.S. Chapter 190 (the Community Development Districts Act of 1980) defines a Community Development District as a local unit of special-purpose government created to serve the long-term specific needs of its community. A CDD's purpose is the delivery of urban community development services.

CDDs have the authority to plan, finance, construct, operate, and maintain community-wide infrastructure and services specifically for the benefit of its residents. CDDs must comply with the Act in regard to the formation, powers, governing body, operation, duration, accountability, requirements for disclosure, and termination.

A CDD's responsibilities within a community may include such services as storm water management, potable and irrigation water supply, sewer and wastewater management, and street lights. Funding for these services is obtained through a CDD tax assessment on the homeowners used to refund bonds issued by the developer to finance construction of the infrastructure. The CDD tax assessments are separate to any city or county property taxes.

Disclosures

Contracts for the initial sale of a parcel of real property or a residential unit within the CDD must include the following disclosure:

THE *(Name of District)* COMMUNITY DEVELOPMENT DISTRICT MAY IMPOSE AND LEVY TAXES OR ASSESSMENTS, OR BOTH TAXES AND ASSESSMENTS, ON THIS PROPERTY. THESE TAXES AND ASSESSMENTS PAY THE CONSTRUCTION, OPERATION, AND MAINTENANCE COSTS OF CERTAIN PUBLIC FACILITIES AND SERVICES OF THE DISTRICT AND ARE SET ANNUALLY BY THE GOVERNING BOARD OF THE DISTRICT. THESE TAXES AND ASSESSMENTS ARE IN ADDITION TO COUNTY AND OTHER LOCAL GOVERNMENTAL TAXES AND ASSESSMENTS AND ALL OTHER TAXES AND ASSESSMENTS PROVIDED FOR BY LAW.

This disclosure must be printed in boldface and conspicuous type that is larger than the type for the remaining text within the contract.

8 Property Rights, Estates & Tenancies; Condos, Coops, CDDs, HOAs, Time-sharing

Snapshot Review

LAND, REAL ESTATE AND REAL PROPERTY

Real property definition
- air, water, land, and everything affixed to the land
- Constitution guarantees private ownership of real estate; ownership rights not absolute; others may exert claims against one's property

Real property components
- **land**: surface, all natural things attached to it, subsurface, and air above the surface; unique aspects: immobile, indestructible, heterogeneous
- **real estate**: land plus all permanently attached man-made structures, called improvements

REAL VS PERSONAL PROPERTY

Property definitions
- something that is owned by someone and the associated rights of ownership
- the bundle of rights: possession, use, transfer, exclusion, and encumbrance
- property is real or personal, tangible or intangible

Fixtures
- an item may be real or personal property depending on the "attachment" criterion and other circumstances
- real property converted from personal property by attachment to real estate

Differentiation criteria
- intention; adaptation; functionality; relationship of parties; contract provisions

Trade fixtures
- personal property items temporarily attached to real estate in order to conduct business; to be removed at some point

Emblements
- plants or crops considered personal property since human intervention is necessary for planting, harvesting

Factory-built housing
- housing pre-built off-site; includes mobile homes; real or personal depending on attachment to land

Conversion
- transforming real to personal property through severance, or personal to real property through affixing

BASIC PROPERTY RIGHTS

Bundle of rights
- the bundle of rights: possession, use, transfer, exclusion, and encumbrance

Separable rights
- any of the bundle of rights, applied to airspace (air rights), surface (surface rights), and subsurface (subsurface rights)

Water rights
- Doctrine of Prior Appropriation: state controls water usage; grants usage permits; Florida recognizes littoral and riparian rights
- littoral rights: abutting property owners own land to high water mark; may use, but state owns underlying land
- riparian rights: if navigable, abutting property owners own land to water's edge; may use, but state owns underlying land; if not navigable, owner owns land to midpoint of waterway
- rights can be affected by natural processes that change land: accretion, alluvion, erosion, reliction

INTERESTS AND ESTATES IN LAND

Interests
- any combination of bundle of rights
- estates, encumbrances, police powers

Estates in land	• include right of possession; also called tenancies
	• leaseholds: of limited duration
	• freeholds: duration is not necessarily limited

| **FREEHOLD ESTATES** | • implies "ownership" in contrast to leasehold |

Fee simple estate	• also "fee"; most common form of estate; not limited by one's lifetime
	• fee simple absolute: highest form of ownership interest
	• defeasible: can revert to previous owner for violation of conditions

Life estate	• fee estate passes to another upon death of a named party
	• remainder: interest of a named party to receive estate after holder's death
	• reversion: interest of previous owner to receive estate after holder's death

Conventional life estate	• full ownership interest, limited to lifetime of life tenant or another named party
	• created by agreements between parties
	• ordinary: on death of life tenant, passes to remainderman or previous owner
	• pur autre vie: on death of another; passes to remainderman or previous owner

Legal life estate	• automatic creation of estate through operation of law
	• designed to protect family survivors
	• homestead: rights to one's principal residence
	• laws protect homestead from certain creditors
	• dower and curtesy: a life estate interest of a widow(er) in the real property; supplanted by elective share
	• elective share: right to claim deceased spouse's property in lieu of will agreement

| **WAYS OF HOLDING OWNERSHIP** | |

| **Tenancy in severalty** | • sole ownership of a freehold estate |

Co-ownership	• ownership by two or more owners
	• **tenancy in common**: co-tenants enjoy an individually owned, undivided interest; any ownership share possible; no survivorship
	• **joint tenancy**: equal, undivided interest jointly owned, with survivorship; requires four unities to create-- time, title, interest, possession; survivorship must be stated in deed
	• **tenancy by the entireties**: equal, undivided interest jointly owned by husband and wife

| **LEASEHOLD ESTATES** | • non-ownership possessory estates of limited duration |

| **Estate for years** | • specific, stated duration, per lease |

| **Estate from period-to-period** | • lease term renews automatically upon acceptance of monthly or periodic rent |

| **Estate at will** | • tenancy for indefinite period subject to rent payment; cancelable with notice |

| **Estate at sufferance** | • tenancy against landlord's will and without an agreement |

| **COOPERATIVES** | |

| **Interests, rights and obligations** | • ownership of shares in owning corporation, plus proprietary lease in a unit; corporation has sole, undivided ownership |

| **Organization and management** | • developer forms association; buys property; incorporates; board of directors responsible for maintenance and operation |

| Cooperative disclosures | • | 15-day and 3-day right to cancel with no waiver allowed |
| | • | plans and specifications for completing unfinished parcels |

CONDOMINIUMS

Airspace and common elements	•	freehold ownership of a unit of airspace plus an undivided interest in the common elements as tenant in common with other owners
Interests and rights	•	may be sold, encumbered or foreclosed without affecting other unit owners
Condominium creation	•	creation: by developer's declaration
Organization and management	•	owners' association and board of directors determine management, hires managers
Owner responsibilities	•	maintain interior, insure contents, pay common area assessments
Condominium disclosures	•	15-day and 3-day right to cancel with no waiver allowed
	•	dollar amounts on budget are estimates
	•	plans and specifications for completing unfinished parcels
	•	oral representations cannot be relied upon
	•	provide required materials
TIME SHARES	•	a lease or ownership interest in a property for the purpose of periodic use by the owners or tenants on a scheduled basis
Time-share regulation	•	sellers of time-share plans must be real estate licensees unless exempted
	•	Some time-shares are not subject to Florida time-share laws
Time-share disclosures	•	listing agreement disclosures: no guaranteed sell price; broker compensation, services, and rights; term and extension; broker use rights; existing judgments
	•	resale disclosures: form of ownership; no guaranteed sell price; current year's assessments; ad valorem tax assessment; terms of closing; exchange program
	•	sale offered outside of Florida exempt from FL law
	•	10-day right to cancel with no waiver allowed
	•	sales in Florida require licensure; occupying owners exempt; developer employees exempt if not paid on per transaction basis
	•	Florida timeshares offered outside of state not subject to Florida time-share laws
	•	out-of-state timeshares offered in Florida are subject to Florida time-share laws
HOMEOWNER'S ASSOCIATIONS	•	corporation responsible for operation of community or mobile home park with owner membership
	•	disclosure summary required
	•	3-day right to cancel with no waiver allowed
COMMUNITY DEVELOPMENT DISTRICTS	•	special purpose government created to provide urban community development services
	•	tax and assessment disclosure

SECTION EIGHT: Property Rights, Estates and Tenancies

Section Quiz

1. The primary distinction between the legal concepts of real estate and real property is that

   a. real property includes ownership of a bundle of rights.
   b. real property includes improvements.
   c. real property is physical, not abstract.
   d. real estate can be owned.

2. Which of the following is included in the bundle of rights inherent in ownership?

   a. To inherit
   b. To tax
   c. To transfer
   d. To vote

3. Which of the following is an example of intangible property?

   a. Real estate
   b. Personal property
   c. Artwork
   d. Stock

4. The right to use real property is limited by

   a. the right of others to use and enjoy their property.
   b. the police.
   c. taxation and subordination.
   d. Title 12 of the U.S. Civil Code.

5. Surface rights, air rights and subsurface rights are

   a. inviolable.
   b. unrelated.
   c. separable.
   d. not transferrable.

6. Which of the following terms refers to the rights of a property that abuts a stream or river?

   a. Allodial
   b. Alluvial
   c. Littoral
   d. Riparian

7. What part of a non-navigable waterway does the owner of an abutting property own?

   a. To the low-water mark
   b. To the middle of the waterway
   c. To the high-water mark
   d. None

8. What is the "Doctrine of Prior Appropriation?"

   a. A pre-emptive zoning ordinance
   b. The right of government to confiscate land and improvements
   c. A doctrine that gives the state control of water use and the water supply
   d. A real estate tax applied to owners of water rights

9. Which of the following is considered real property?

   a. A tree growing on a parcel of land
   b. A tree that has been cut down and is lying on a parcel of land
   c. A tractor used to mow grass on a parcel of land
   d. A prefabricated shed not yet assembled on a parcel of land

10. The overriding test of whether an item is a fixture or personal property is

    a. how long it has been attached to the real property.
    b. its definition as one or the other in a sale or lease contract.
    c. how essential it is to the functioning of the property.
    d. how it was treated in previous transactions.

11. What is an emblement?

    a. A piece of equipment affixed to the earth
    b. A limited right to use personal property
    c. A sign indicating a property boundary
    d. A plant or crop that is considered personal property

12. An item can be converted from real to personal property and vice versa by means of which processes?

    a. Assemblage and plottage
    b. Application and dissolution
    c. Affixing and severance
    d. Personalty and severalty

13. A grocer temporarily installs special fruit and vegetable coolers in a leased grocery store in order to prevent spoilage. The coolers would be considered which of the following?

    a. Trade fixtures that are real property
    b. Trade fixtures that are personal property
    c. Permanent fixtures that are real property
    d. Permanent fixtures that are personal property

14. Under the doctrine of littoral rights, an owner claims ownership of all of the land underlying a lake where there are three other abutting property owners. Which of the following is true?

    a. The owner's claim is invalid, because the state owns the underlying land.
    b. The owner's claim is invalid, because the underlying land is shared equally with the other owners.
    c. The owner's claim is invalid, because he may only own underlying land to the middle of the lake.
    d. The owner's claim is valid, because the lake is navigable.

15. An interest in real estate is best defined as ownership of

    a. the full bundle of rights to real property.
    b. an estate.
    c. one or more of the bundle of rights to real property.
    d. the right to possession and use of real property.

16. Encumbrances and police powers are

    a. interests that do not include possession.
    b. limited forms of an estate.
    c. unrelated to interests.
    d. types of public interests.

17. What distinguishes a freehold estate from a leasehold estate?

    a. A freehold includes the right to dispose or use.
    b. A leasehold endures only for a specific period of time.
    c. A freehold cannot be defeasible.
    d. A leasehold is subject to government restrictions.

18. The highest form of ownership interest one can acquire in real estate is the

    a. dower and curtesy.
    b. conventional life estate.
    c. defeasible fee simple estate.
    d. absolute fee simple estate.

19. The distinguishing feature of a defeasible fee simple estate is that

    a. it can be passed on to heirs.
    b. it has no restrictions on use.
    c. the estate may revert to a grantor or heirs if the prescribed use changes.
    d. it is of unlimited duration.

20. Upon the death of the owner, a life estate passes to

    a. the original owner or other named person.
    b. the owner's heirs.
    c. the state.
    d. the owner's spouse.

21. How is a conventional life estate created?

    a. It happens automatically when title transfers unless a fee simple is specifically claimed.
    b. A fee simple owner grants the life estate to a life tenant.
    c. It is created by judicial action.
    d. It is created by a statutory period of adverse possession.

22. What distinguishes a pur autre vie life estate from an ordinary life estate?

    a. The pur autre vie estate endures only for the lifetime of the grantor.
    b. The pur autre vie estate endures only for the lifetime of the grantee.
    c. The pur autre vie estate endures only for the lifetime of a person other than the grantee.
    d. The pur autre vie estate cannot revert to the grantor.

23. Which of the following life estates is created by someone other than the owner?

    a. Conventional life estate
    b. Ordinary life estate
    c. Legal life estate
    d. Community property life estate.

24. Which of the following is true of a homestead?

    a. A homestead interest cannot be conveyed by one spouse.
    b. A homestead interest cannot be passed to the children of the head of household.
    c. A homestead interest is a form of conventional life estate.
    d. A homestead is a primary or secondary residence occupied by a family.

25. Dower refers to

    a. joint tenancy of husband and wife.
    b. a wife's life estate interest in her husband's property.
    c. a wife's homestead interest.
    d. a child's life estate interest in his or her parents' homestead.

26. Which of the following is an illustration of the legal concept of elective share?

    a. A surviving spouse places a lien on a debtor's property.
    b. A widow who was excluded from a will makes a claim to a portion of the couple's principal residence.
    c. A spouse who loses her home because of her husband's gambling debt sues in court for exemption from the debt.
    d. A widower whose spouse died without a will sues to change the provisions of the will.

27. A one-year lease on a house has expired, but the tenant continues sending monthly rent checks to the owner, and the owner accepts them. What kind of leasehold estate exists?

   a. Estate for years
   b. Estate from period to period
   c. Estate at will
   d. Estate at sufferance

28. When a single individual or entity owns a fee or life estate in a real property, the type of ownership is

   a. tenancy in severalty.
   b. tenancy by the entireties.
   c. absolute fee simple.
   d. legal fee simple.

29. Three people have identical rights but unequal shares in a property, share an indivisible interest, and may sell or transfer their interest without consent of the others. This type of ownership is

   a. joint tenancy.
   b. equal ownership.
   c. tenancy in common.
   d. estate in severalty.

30. The "four unities" required to create a joint tenancy include which of the following conditions?

   a. Parties must acquire respective interests at the same time.
   b. Parties must be legally married at the time of acquiring interest.
   c. Parties must be family members.
   d. Parties must have joint financial resources.

31. Unlike tenants in common, joint tenants

   a. own distinct portions of the physical property.
   b. cannot will their interest to a party outside the tenancy.
   c. may own unequal shares of the property.
   d. cannot sell their interest to outside parties.

32. The distinguishing features of a condominium estate are

   a. ownership of a share in an association that owns one's apartment.
   b. tenancy in common interest in airspace and common areas of the property.
   c. fee simple ownership of the airspace in a unit and an undivided share of the entire property's common areas.
   d. fee simple ownership of a pro rata share of the entire property.

33. Who owns the property in a time-share estate?

   a. Ownership is shared by the developer and the broker.
   b. The property is owned by tenants in common or by a freehold owner who leases on a time-share basis.
   c. A real estate investment trust holds a fee simple estate.
   d. A general partner holds a fee simple interest and interval estates are owned by limited partners.

34. Which of the following is true of a cooperative?

   a. A cooperative may hold an owner liable for the unpaid operating expenses of other owners.
   b. The owners have a fee simple interest in the airspace of their respective apartments.
   c. Owners may retain their apartments even if they sell their stock in the cooperative.
   d. The proprietary lease is guaranteed to have a fixed rate of rent over the life of the lease term.

35. One difference between a cooperative estate and a condominium estate is that

   a. a default by a coop owner may cause a foreclosure on the entire property instead of just a single unit, as with a condominium.
   b. the condominium owner must pay expenses as well as rent.
   c. the coop owner owns stock and a freehold real estate interest whereas the condominium owner simply owns real estate.
   d. the condominium owner owns the common elements and the airspace whereas the coop owner only owns the apartment.

36. Which disclosure requirement is consistent for condominiums, cooperatives, and HOAs?

   a. Budget estimates
   b. Right to cancel
   c. Exchange program membership
   d. No guaranteed selling price

37. Which type of sale allows a 10-day right to cancel?

   a. Homeowners' Association
   b. Condominium
   c. Cooperative
   d. Timeshare

38. Which sale requires a Governance Form to be provided to buyers?

   a. Condominium resales
   b. Timeshare sales
   c. Cooperative initial sales
   d. HOA unit sales

39. Which sale requires a disclosure summary?

    a. CDD
    b. HOA
    c. Timeshare
    d. Cooperative

9 Title, Deeds and Ownership Restrictions

The Concept of Title
Transfer by Voluntary Alienation
Transfer by Involuntary Alienation
Notice of Title
Protection of Title
Deeds
Government Ownership Limitations and Restrictions
Private Ownership Limitations and Restrictions

Learning Objectives

- Differentiate between voluntary and involuntary alienation
- Explain the various methods of acquiring title to real property and describe the conditions necessary to acquire real property by adverse possession
- Distinguish between actual notice and constructive notice
- Distinguish between an abstract of title and a chain of title
- Explain the different types of title insurance
- Describe the parts of a deed and the requirements of a valid deed
- List and describe the four types of statutory deeds and the legal requirements for deeds
- List and describe the various types of governmental and private restrictions on ownership of real property
- Distinguish among the various types of leases and liens

Key Terms

abstract of title	further assurance
acknowledgment	general warranty deed
actual notice	grantee
adverse possession	granting clause
alienation	grantor
assignment	gross lease
chain of title	ground lease
condemnation	habendum clause
construction lien	intestate
constructive notice	lien
deed	net lease
deed restriction	percentage lease
easement	police power
eminent domain	quiet enjoyment
encroachment	quitclaim deed
escheat	seisin

THE CONCEPT OF TITLE

Ownership in a bundle of rights
Legal and equitable title
Transferring title

Ownership in a bundle of rights

The bundle of rights is the set of legal privileges comprising the legal concept of ownership. These rights are conferred upon the buyer of a real property when the title of the property is transferred. The bundle includes everything the new owner can do with the property within the boundaries of applicable laws:

- ▸ **possession** – the fundamental right of property, allowing the owner to be on the property physically and to choose who else may or may not be on the property; this right may be lost if the mortgage loan, property taxes, or homeowners association dues are not paid
- ▸ **quiet enjoyment** – the owner's right to use the property for any legal activity without interference
- ▸ **control** – the owner's right to do what he or she wants with the property within local zoning codes and other laws or covenants; this right includes what is beneath and above the property
- ▸ **exclusion** – the owner's right to limit who may enter the property with some exceptions, such as easements and warrants.
- ▸ **disposition** – the right to transfer ownership (sell, lease, or gift) of all or a section of the property to someone else, temporarily or permanently; this right is fully realized only when the property is owned outright with no mortgage or liens

Legal and equitable title

Owning title to real property commonly connotes owning the complete bundle of rights that attach to the property, including the right to possession. More accurately, someone who possesses all ownership interests owns **legal title** to the property. Legal title is distinct from **equitable title**, which is the interest or *right to obtain legal title* to a property in accordance with a sale or mortgage contract between the legal owner and a buyer or creditor. During the contractual period of time when ownership of legal title is contingent upon the contract, the buyer or lender owns equitable title to the property.

For example, a buyer enters into a contract for deed to purchase a house. The seller lends the bulk of the purchase price to the buyer for a term of three years. The buyer takes possession of the property, and makes payments on the loan. During this period, the seller retains legal title, and the buyer owns equitable title. If the buyer fulfills the terms of the agreement over the three year period, the buyer has an enforceable contract to obtain legal title.

Another common example is a mortgage loan transaction that gives the lender the right to execute a strict foreclosure, which transfers legal title to the lender in the event of a default. With this contractual right, the lender has equitable title to the property.

In practice, the terms "title" and "legal title" are often used interchangeably.

Transferring title

Transfer of title to real estate, also called **alienation**, occurs both voluntarily and involuntarily. When the transfer uses a written instrument, the transfer is called a **conveyance.**

Transferring Title to Real Estate

Voluntary	Involuntary
public grant deed will	descent escheat foreclosure eminent domain adverse possession estoppel

Voluntary alienation. Voluntary alienation is an unforced transfer of title by sale or gift from an owner to another party. If the transferor is a government entity and the recipient is a private party, the conveyance is a **public grant.** If the transferor is a private party, the conveyance is a **private grant**.

A living owner makes a private grant by means of a **deed of conveyance**, or **deed**. A private grant that occurs when the owner dies is a **transfer by will**.

Involuntary alienation. Involuntary alienation is a transfer of title to real property without the owner's consent. Involuntary alienation occurs primarily by the processes of descent and distribution, escheat, foreclosure, eminent domain, adverse possession, and estoppel.

TRANSFER BY VOLUNTARY ALIENATION

Deeds
Wills

Deeds

Parties. A deed is a legal instrument used by an owner, the **grantor**, to transfer title to real estate voluntarily to another party, the **grantee**.

A deed is used when a title is voluntarily transferred by the sale or gift from the property owner to another party. The property owner must be alive for this transfer. For example, if the owner sells the property, the transfer takes place with a deed. If the owner donates the property to a charity, the transfer takes place with a deed.

Delivery and acceptance. Execution of a valid deed in itself does not convey title. It is necessary for the deed to be *delivered to and accepted by the grantee* for title to pass. To be legally valid, delivery of the deed requires that the grantor

- ▸ be *competent* at the time of delivery
- ▸ *intend to deliver* the deed, beyond the act of making physical delivery

Validity of the grantee's acceptance requires only that the grantee have physical possession of the deed or record the deed.

Once accepted, title passes to the grantee. The deed has fulfilled its legal purpose and it cannot be used again to transfer the property. If the grantee loses the deed, there is no effect on the grantee's title to the estate. The grantor, for example, cannot reclaim the estate on the grounds that the grantee has lost the deed after it was delivered and accepted. Nor can the grantee return the property by returning the deed. To do so, the grantee would need to execute a new deed.

Voluntary transfers in Florida. The general procedure for transferring title in Florida consists of the following steps. Deeds are discussed later in this section.

- ▸ locate the current deed that includes the property's legal description and the exact name of the current grantor
- ▸ prepare the new deed to include all required information
- ▸ sign and notarize the deed; the deed must be signed by the grantor, any spouse with homestead rights, and two witnesses; it must also be notarized
- ▸ file the deed with the county clerk in the county where the property is located; filing may include recording fees or documentary stamp taxes

Deeds are treated in greater detail later in this section.

Wills

Parties to a will. A will, or more properly, a **last will and testament**, is a legal instrument for the voluntary transfer of real and personal property after the owner's death. It describes how the maker of the will, called the **testator** or **devisor,** wants the property distributed. A beneficiary of a will is called an **heir** or **devisee**. The property transferred by the will is the **devise**. "Devise," "devisor," and "devisee" refer more specifically to real property transfers, while "bequest" and "beneficiary" are sometimes limited to transfers of personal property.

A will takes effect only after the testator's death. It is an **amendatory** instrument, meaning that it can be changed at any time during the maker's lifetime.

Commonly, the testator names an **executor**, or **personal representative**, to oversee the settlement of the estate. If a minor is involved, the testator may identify a **guardian** to handle legal affairs on behalf of the minor.

Types of will. A will generally takes one of the following forms:

> ▶ **witnessed**
>
> in writing and witnessed by two people

> ▶ **holographic**
>
> in the testator's handwriting, dated and signed

> ▶ **approved**
>
> on pre-printed forms meeting the requirements of state law

> ▶ **nuncupative**
>
> made orally, and written down by a witness; generally *not valid* for the transfer of real property

Validity. State law establishes requirements for a valid will. Florida law requires that:

> ▶ the testator be of legal age and mentally competent
> ▶ the will be signed
> ▶ the completion of the will be witnessed and signed by the witnesses
> ▶ the will be completed voluntarily, without duress or coercion

Probate. A court proceeding called **probate** generally settles a decedent's estate, whether the person has died **testate** (having left a valid will) or **intestate** (having failed to do so). Real property may be exempted from probate if it is held in a land trust. Probate of real property occurs *under jurisdiction of courts in the state where the property is located, regardless of where the deceased resided.*

The probate court's objectives are to:

> ▶ validate the will, if one exists
> ▶ identify and settle all claims and outstanding debts against the estate
> ▶ distribute the remainder of the estate to the rightful heirs If the will does not name an executor, the court will appoint an **administrator** to fulfill this role

Transfer of a Decedent's Estate by Probate

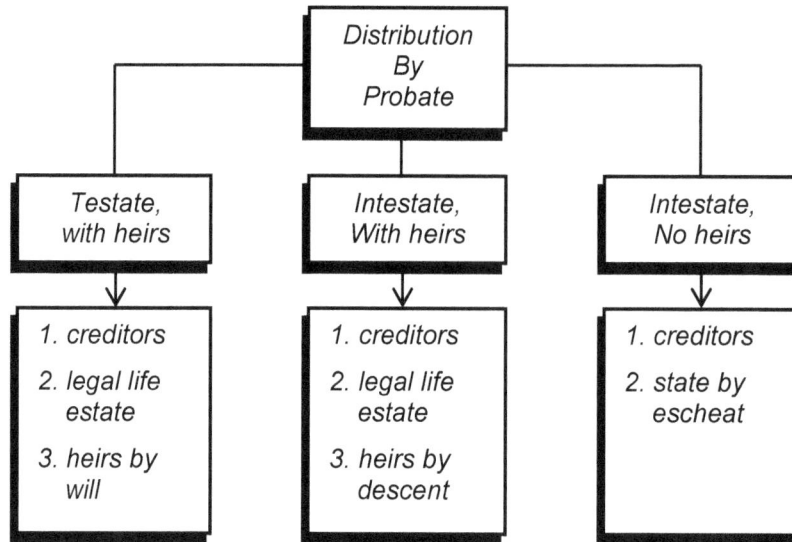

```
                    ┌──────────────┐
                    │ Distribution │
                    │      By      │
                    │    Probate   │
                    └──────────────┘
        ┌───────────────────┼───────────────────┐
        │                   │                   │
┌───────────────┐  ┌───────────────┐  ┌───────────────┐
│   Testate,    │  │   Intestate,  │  │   Intestate,  │
│  with heirs   │  │   With heirs  │  │    No heirs   │
└───────────────┘  └───────────────┘  └───────────────┘
        │                   │                   │
        ▼                   ▼                   ▼
┌───────────────┐  ┌───────────────┐  ┌───────────────┐
│ 1. creditors  │  │ 1. creditors  │  │ 1. creditors  │
│               │  │               │  │               │
│ 2. legal life │  │ 2. legal life │  │ 2. state by   │
│    estate     │  │    estate     │  │    escheat    │
│               │  │               │  │               │
│ 3. heirs by   │  │ 3. heirs by   │  │               │
│    will       │  │    descent    │  │               │
└───────────────┘  └───────────────┘  └───────────────┘
```

The exhibit shows three possible channels of probate deliberation, depending on whether there is a will and heirs.

Testate proceeding. If the decedent died with a valid will, the court hears the claims of lienors and creditors and determines their validity. First in line are the superior liens: those for real estate taxes, assessment taxes, federal estate taxes, and state inheritance taxes. If the estate's liquid assets are insufficient to pay all obligations, the court may order the sale of personal or real property to satisfy the obligations.

The court must also hear and satisfy legal life estate claims, including those for dower, curtesy, homestead, and elective share. These interests may prevail even if the will does not provide for them.

Once all claims have been satisfied, the balance of the estate's assets passes to the rightful heirs *free and clear of all liens and debts.*

Intestate proceeding with heirs. If the decedent died without a valid will, the estate passes to lawful heirs according to the state's laws of **descent and distribution**, or **succession**. Laws of descent stipulate who inherits and what share they receive, without regard to the desires of the heirs or the intentions of the deceased.

For example, John Astor dies intestate, leaving a wife and four children. Under Florida law, the surviving spouse receives the entire estate as long as all four children are descendants of both the decedent and the surviving spouse and there are no other children of either spouse.

Intestate proceeding with no heirs. If an intestate decedent has no heirs, the estate **escheats**, or reverts, to the state after all claims and debts have been validated and settled.

TRANSFER BY INVOLUNTARY ALIENATION

Laws of descent
Escheat
Foreclosure
Eminent domain
Adverse possession

Involuntary alienation occurs when a title-holder dies without a valid will. It also occurs under other special circumstances. State law regulates all forms of involuntary alienation, whether such transfer occurs by the laws of descent, abandonment, foreclosure, eminent domain, adverse possession, or estoppel.

Laws of descent

The state's statutes of descent and distribution identify heirs and the respective shares of the estate they will receive.

Escheat

In the absence of heirs, title transfers to the state by escheat. Property that has been abandoned for a statutory period may also escheat to the state.

Foreclosure

A property owner who fails to fulfill loan obligations or pay taxes may lose an estate through foreclosure.

Eminent domain

In many cases, public acquisition of property is a voluntary transaction between the government entity and the private owner. However, if the private party is unwilling to sell, the government may purchase the property anyway. The power to do this is called **eminent domain.**

Eminent domain allows a government entity to purchase a fee, leasehold, or easement interest in privately owned real property for the **public good** and for **public use**, regardless of the owner's desire to sell or otherwise transfer any interest. In exchange for the interest, the government must pay the owner "just compensation."

To acquire a property, the public entity initiates a condemnation suit. Transfer of title extinguishes all existing leases, liens, and other encumbrances on the property. Tenants affected by the condemnation sale may or may not receive compensation, depending on the terms of their agreement with the landlord.

Public entities that have the power of eminent domain include:

- ▸ all levels of government
- ▸ public districts (schools, etc.)
- ▸ public utilities

> ▸ public service corporations (power companies, etc.)
>
> ▸ public housing and redevelopment agencies
>
> ▸ other government agencies

To acquire a property, the public entity must first adopt a formal resolution to acquire the property, variously called a "resolution of necessity." The resolution must be adopted at a formal hearing where the owner may voice an opinion. Once adopted, the government agency may commence a condemnation suit in court. Subsequently, the property is purchased and the title is transferred in exchange for just compensation. Transfer of title extinguishes all existing leases, liens, and other encumbrances on the property. Tenants affected by the condemnation sale may or may not receive compensation, depending on the terms of their agreement with the landlord.

In order to proceed with condemnation, the government agency must demonstrate that the project is necessary, the property is necessary for the project, and that the location offers the greatest public benefit with the least detriment.

As an eminent domain proceeding is generally an involuntary acquisition, the condemnation proceeding must accord with due process of law to ensure that it does not violate individual property rights. Further, the public entity must justify its use of eminent domain in court by demonstrating the validity of the intended public use and the resulting "public good" or "public purpose" ultimately served.

The issue of eminent domain versus individual property rights has recently come under scrutiny in light of a 2005 Supreme Court ruling that affirmed the rights of state and local governments to use the power of eminent domain for urban re-development and revitalization. The ruling allowed that private parties could undertake a project for profit without any public guarantee that the project would be satisfactorily completed. The ruling brought the issue of "public use" into question, as the use of the re-development could well be private and even a private for-profit enterprise. The winning argument was that the "public purpose" is served when redevelopment creates much needed jobs in a depressed urban area. As a result of this decision, many see the power of eminent domain and the definition of public good as being in conflict with the constitutional rights of private property ownership. New and different interpretations of the public's right to pre-empt private property ownership by eminent domain may be expected.

Adverse possession   Florida laws allow a real property owner to lose legal title to an **adverse possessor**. An adverse possessor is someone who enters, occupies, and uses another's property without the knowledge or consent of the owner, or with the knowledge of an owner who fails to take any action over a statutory period of time.

To claim legal title, the adverse possessor must:

> ▸ be able to show a **claim of right** or **color of title** as reason for the possession

- ▶ have **notorious possession**, which is possession without concealment
- ▶ maintain a consistent claim of **hostile possession**, which is a claim to ownership and possession regardless of the owner's claims or consent
- ▶ occupy the property continuously for seven or more consecutive years without owner consent
- ▶ pay taxes

A **claim of right** is based on the adverse possessor's occupying and maintaining the property as if he or she were the legal owner. **Color of title** results when a grantee has obtained defective title, or received title by defective means, but occupies the property as if he or she were the legal owner. A court may hold that a claim of right or a claim of colored title is a valid reason for the possession.

Notorious possession and **hostile possession** give constructive notice to the public, including the legal owner, that a party other than the legal owner is occupying and claiming to own the property. It is possible for such notice to prevail over notice by recordation as the dominant evidence of legal ownership, provided the possessor has occupied the property continuously for the statutory period of time.

In Florida, the possessor must have paid taxes over the entire period of possession to obtain title. However, if the possessor has paid rent of any kind, the claim of ownership might be refuted.

Avoiding adverse possession. An owner can avert the danger of involuntary alienation by adverse possession by *periodically inspecting the property within statutory deadlines* and evicting any trespassers found. The owner may also sue to quiet title, which would eliminate the threat of the adverse possessor's claim to legal title.

NOTICE TO LEGAL TITLE

Actual notice
Constructive notice

In any legal system that permits private ownership of real property, there will always be disputes as to who truly owns a particular parcel of real estate. For example, an owner might "sell" his property to three unrelated parties. The first party buys the property at the earliest date, the second party pays the highest price, and the third party receives the best deed, a warranty deed. Who owns legal title to the property?

Ownership of legal title is a function of evidence. A court will generally rule that the person who has the preponderance of evidence of ownership is the owner of the property. In the example, if the first two buyers did not receive a deed while the third party did, the third party may have the best evidence and be ruled the legal title-holder. However, what if the first buyer had moved into the house and occupied it for six months before the original owner sold the property to the second and third buyers? And what if the second buyer, after searching title records, reports that the seller never really owned the property and therefore could not legally sell it to anyone! Now who owns the property?

The illustration underscores the difficulty of proving title to real estate: there is no absolute and irrefutable proof that a party holds legal title. Our legal system has developed two forms of title evidence-- actual notice and constructive notice-- to assist in the determination.

Actual notice

The term "notice" is synonymous with "knowledge." A person who has received *actual* notice has *actual knowledge* of something. Receiving actual notice means learning of something through direct experience or communication. In proving real estate ownership, a person provides actual notice by producing direct evidence, such as by showing a valid will. Another party receives actual notice by seeing direct evidence, such as by reviewing the deed, reading title records, or physically visiting the property to see who is in possession. Thus if Mary Pierce drives to a property and sees directly that John Doe is in possession of the home, Mary then has received actual notice of John Doe's claim of ownership. Her knowledge is obtained through direct experience.

Constructive notice

Constructive notice, or **legal notice**, is knowledge of a fact that a person *could have or should have obtained*. The foremost method of imparting constructive notice is by recordation of ownership documents in public records, specifically, *title records*. Since public records are open to everyone, the law generally presumes that when evidence of ownership is recorded, the public at large *has received constructive notice* of ownership. By the same token, the law presumes that the owner of record is in fact the legal owner. Thus, if John Doe records the deed of conveyance, he has imparted, and Mary Pierce has received, constructive notice of ownership. Possession of the property can also be construed as constructive notice, since a court may rule that Mary *should have visited the property* to ascertain whether it was occupied.

A combination of actual and constructive notice generally provides the most indisputable evidence of real property ownership.

PROTECTION OF TITLE

Title records
Title evidence
Title companies
Chain of title
Title abstract
Title opinion
Title insurance

Title records

Chapter 119.011 (12) identifies public records as "all documents, papers, letters, maps, books, tapes, photographs, films, sound recordings, data processing software, or other material, regardless of the physical form, characteristics, or means of transmission, made or received pursuant to law or ordinance or in connection with the transaction of official business by any agency."

State laws require the recording of all documents that affect rights and interests in real estate in the public real estate records of the county where the property is located. These public records, or **title records**, contain a history of every parcel of real estate in the county, including names of previous owners, liens, easements, and other encumbrances that have been recorded.

Deeds, mortgages, liens, easements, and sale contracts are among the documents that must be recorded. Other public records that affect real estate title are marriage, probate, and tax records.

Generally, a County Recorder's Office or other similarly named office maintains the title records.

Title records serve a number of purposes, not the least of which is to avoid ownership disputes. Other important purposes are:

> ▶ **public notice**
>
> Title records protect the public by giving all concerned parties **constructive notice** of the condition of a property's legal title: who owns the property, who maintains claims and encumbrances against the property.

> ▶ **buyer protection**
>
> Title records protect the buyer by revealing whether a property has **marketable title**, one free of undesirable encumbrances. The buyer is legally responsible for knowing the condition of title, since it is a matter of public record. Recording a transaction also protects a buyer by replacing the deed as evidence of ownership.

> **lienholder protection**
>
> Title records protect the lienholder by putting the public on notice that the lien exists, and that it may be the basis for a foreclosure action. Recording also establishes the lien's priority.

Title evidence

Marketable title. Since the value of a property is only as good as the marketability of its title, the evidence supporting the status of title is a significant issue. To demonstrate marketable title to a buyer, a seller must show that the title is free of

> - doubts about the identity of the current owner
> - defects, such as an erroneous legal description
> - claims that could affect value
> - undisclosed or unacceptable encumbrances

The four principal forms of evidence the owner can use to support these assurances are:

> - a Torrens certificate (not applicable to Florida)
> - a title insurance policy
> - an attorney's opinion of the title abstract
> - a title certificate

Title certificate. A title certificate is a summary of the condition of title as of the date of the certificate, based on a search of public records by an abstractor or title analyst. The certificate does not guarantee clear title against defects, unrecorded encumbrances or encroachments.

Title companies

A title company performs a **title search** to determine if the title to a particular property is legitimate. The company will examine property records to assure that the person claiming to own the property really does legally own it. The company looks for anyone else who could claim full or partial ownership of the property. It looks for unrecorded breaks in the chain of title. It also searches for outstanding mortgages, liens, judgments, unpaid taxes, restrictions, easements, leases, or any other issues that may affect the property's ownership. Sometimes, title companies require a property survey to be performed. The company may prepare a report on what it found, known as an abstract of title, and then provide a title opinion letter regarding the validity of the title.

Title companies may maintain an escrow account related to the property transfer, handle the transaction closing, and file the new title after closing. The title company may also issue title insurance policies but would complete the search before issuing a policy. If the search fails to discover any uninsurable defects, the company issues a **binder**, or commitment to insure. The binder recapitulates the property description, interest to be insured, names of insured parties, and exceptions to coverage.

Chain of title	Chain of title refers to the succession of property owners *of record* dating back to the original grant of title from the state to a private party. If there is a missing link in the chronology of owners, or if there was a defective conveyance, the chain is said to be broken, resulting in a **clouded title** to the property. To remove the cloud, an owner may need to initiate a **suit to quiet title**, which clears the title record of any unrecorded claims.
Title abstract	An abstract of title is a written, chronological summary of the property's title records and other public records affecting rights and interests in the property. It includes the property's chain of title and all current recorded liens and encumbrances, by date of filing. A title abstractor or title company analyst conducts the title search of public records needed to produce an abstract. Insurers and lenders generally require the search to identify title defects and ascertain the current status of encumbrances.
	A **title plant** is a duplicate set of records of a property copied from public records and maintained by a private company, such as a title company.
Title opinion	**Attorney's opinion of abstract.** An attorney's opinion of abstract states that the attorney has examined a title abstract, and gives the attorney's opinion of the condition and marketability of the title. Generally, an opinion is not a proof or guarantee of clear title. Further, it offers no protection in the event title turns out to be defective.
Title insurance	A title insurance policy is commonly accepted as the best evidence of marketable title. A title insurance policy indemnifies the policy holder against losses arising from defects in the insured title. Unlike other types of insurance that are based on problems that may happen in the future, title insurance is based on loss prevention by stopping title problems from happening.
	The common policy types are the lender's policy and the owner's policy, which protect the respective policy holders' interests in the property.
	Owner's policy. An owner's policy is issued for the property's initial or appreciated value and protects the buyer from unexpected or unknown defects with the title. It is paid in one premium payment. An owner's policy may have *standard coverage* or *extended coverage*. Standard coverage protects against title defects such as incompetent grantors, invalid deeds, fraudulent transaction documents, and defects in the chain of title. Extended coverage protects against liabilities that may not be of public record, including fraud, unrecorded ownership claims, unintentional recording errors, and unrecorded liens. Extended coverage may also protect against adverse possessors, boundary disputes, and prescriptive easements. Neither standard nor extended coverage insures against defects expressly excluded by the policy or defects that the owner might have been aware of but did not disclose. This policy is not transferrable.
	The American Land Title Association (ALTA) is the standardized title insurance policy used in Florida. Information on both types of policies as well

as a sample owner's policy, including conditions and exclusions, can be found at www.homeclosing101.org.

Lender's policy. A lender's policy is issued for the financed balance of the mortgage loan and protects the lender from title defects. If a property sells for $100,000, and the buyer pays $20,000 as a down payment, the balance of the purchase price, or $80,000, will be financed. Thus, a lender who holds an $80,000 mortgage on a property will obtain protection worth $80,000 against the possibility that the lender's lien cannot be enforced. The premium is a one-time payment, and the policy is transferrable to another lender if the loan is sold.

DEEDS

Deed essentials
Deed clauses
Types of statutory deed
Special purpose deeds

Deed essentials

Parties. A deed is a legal instrument used by an owner, the **grantor**, to transfer title to real estate voluntarily to another party, the **grantee**.

A deed is used when a title is voluntarily transferred from the grantor to the grantee by sale or gift. The property owner must be alive for this transfer. For example, if the owner sells the property, the transfer takes place with a deed. If the owner donates the property to a charity, the transfer takes place with a deed.

Components. Deeds consist of grantor, grantee, consideration, words of conveyance (granting clause), interest or estate being conveyed (habendum clause), deed restrictions, exceptions and reservations, appurtenances, legal description, voluntary delivery and acceptance, signatures of grantor and two witnesses.

Requirements for validity. Florida law requires a deed to meet the following for validity:

▸ be in writing

▸ be signed by the transferor

   The deed must be signed by the transferor (current owner) of the property or by the transferor's duly authorized agent or representative.

▸ be signed in the presence of two witnesses

   The deed must be signed in the presence of two witnesses who both must also sign the deed.

> ▸ include a space for the parcel identification number

The deed must include a space for the parcel identification number with the number filled in prior to filing. The law specifies the parcel identification number is not a legal description and may not be used as a substitute for the description. Further, an incorrect parcel identification number on the deed does not invalidate the deed.

Recording. Florida requires any conveyance or transfer of real property to be recorded according to the law. To legally record the deed, the following requirements must be met:

> ▸ The deed must include the name, address, and signature of the grantors and the name and address of the grantees.

> ▸ The deed must include the name, address, and signature of the natural person who prepared the deed.

> ▸ The deed must include the name and signature of each witness.

> ▸ The deed must be properly notarized.

> ▸ The deed must include a three-inch square white space at the top right-hand corner of the first page and a one-inch by three-inch square white space on the top right-hand corner of each subsequent page for use by the clerk of the court.

Deed clauses

Conveyance clauses and *covenant,* or *warrant, clauses* set forth all the necessary provisions of the conveyance.

Conveyance clauses. Conveyance clauses describe the details of the transfer. The principal conveyance clauses are:

> ▸ **granting clause, or premises clause --** *the only required clause*; contains the conveyance intentions; names the parties; describes the property; indicates nominal consideration

> ▸ **habendum clause --** describes the type of estate being conveyed (fee simple, life, etc.)

> ▸ **reddendum clause, or reserving clause --** recites restrictions and limitations to the estate being conveyed, e.g., deed restrictions, liens, easements, encroachments, etc.

> ▸ **tenendum clause --** identifies property being conveyed in addition to land

Covenant, or warrant, clauses. Covenant clauses present the grantor's assurances to the grantee. A deed of conveyance usually contains one or more of the following covenants, depending on the type of deed.

> ▶ **warrant of seisin** -- assures that the grantor owns the estate to be conveyed, and has the right to do so
>
> ▶ **warrant of quiet enjoyment** -- assures that the grantee will not be disturbed by third party title disputes
>
> ▶ **warrant of further assurance** -- assures that the grantor will assist in clearing any title problems discovered later
>
> ▶ **warranty forever; warranty of title** -- assures that the grantee will receive good title, and that grantor will assist in defending any claims to the contrary
>
> ▶ **warrant of encumbrances** -- assures that there are no encumbrances on the property except those expressly named
>
> ▶ **warranty against grantor's acts** -- states the assurance of a trustee, acting as grantor on behalf of the owner, that nothing has been done to impair title during the fiduciary period

Types of statutory deed

A deed of conveyance can make a variety of warranties and convey a range of interests. The most common deeds are statutory deeds, in which the covenants are defined in law and do not need to be fully stated in the deed. The prominent types are the following.

Bargain and sale deed. In a bargain and sale deed, the grantor covenants that the title is valid but may or may not warrant against encumbrances or promise to defend against claims by other parties. If there *is* a warrant of defense, the deed is a full warranty bargain and sale deed.

The overall bargain and sale covenant is: *"I own, but won't defend."*

General warranty deed. The general warranty deed, or **warranty deed** for short, is the most commonly used deed. It contains the fullest possible assurances of good title and protection for the grantee. The deed is technically a bargain and sale deed in which the grantor promises to defend against any and all claims to the title.

The overall general warranty covenant is: *"I own and will defend."*

Special warranty deed. In a special warranty deed, the grantor warrants only against title defects or encumbrances not noted on the deed that may have occurred during the grantor's period of ownership or trusteeship. The deed does not protect the grantee against claims that predate the owner's period of ownership. Special warranty deeds are often used by trustees and grantors who acquired the property through a tax sale.

The overall special warranty covenant is: *"I own and will defend against my acts only."*

Quitclaim deed. A quitclaim deed transfers real and potential interests in a property, whether an interest is known to exist or not. The grantor makes no claim to any interest in the property being conveyed and offers no warrants to protect the grantee.

The quitclaim is typically used to clear title rather than convey it. Where there is a possibility that prior errors in deeds or other recorded documents might **cloud** (encumber) the title, the relevant parties execute a quitclaim deed to convey "any and all" interest to the grantee.

If a party responsible for encumbering title refuses to quitclaim the interest, the owner may file a **quiet title suit.** This requires the lienor to prove the validity of an interest. If the defendant is unable to do so, the court removes the cloud by decree.

The overall quit claim covenant is: *"I may or may not own, and I won't defend."*

Special purpose deeds

A special purpose deed is one tailored to the requirements of specific parties, properties, and purposes. The principal types are:

- ▶ **personal representative's deed** -- used by an executor to convey a decedent's estate; also called an executor's deed

- ▶ **guardian's deed** -- used by a court-appointed guardian to transfer property of minors or mentally incompetent persons

- ▶ **committee's deed** – used by court order when grantor is mentally incompetent; court appoints a committed to handle the parties various affairs, including conveyancing. All committee members must sign the deed.

- ▶ **tax deed** -- used to convey property sold at a tax sale due to owner's failure to pay property taxes.

GOVERNMENT OWNERSHIP LIMITATIONS AND RESTRICTIONS

Police powers
Eminent domain
Taxation

Police powers

Through the U.S. and state constitutions, each state government has the right to regulate a person's behavior or property to protect the health, safety, welfare, and morals of the community. The government may apply restrictions necessary to regulate the use of real property.

Examples of such regulations include zoning, building codes, city planning, health standards, and rent controls.

County, city, and local governments may exercise police power as delegated by the state government.

Examples of the use of police power include inspections of certain construction work for building code violations, preserving historic structures to comply with zoning laws, and restricting land-use to comply with city planning regulations.

Unlike eminent domain, property owners are not typically compensated when the government takes possession of part or all of the owner's land. Police power is the broadest power of the government to limit property owners' rights.

Eminent domain

As mentioned previously, government entities have the power of eminent domain to purchase a fee, leasehold, or easement interest in privately owned real property for the public good and for public use, regardless of the owner's desire to sell or otherwise transfer any interest. In exchange for the interest, the government must pay the owner "just compensation."

Taxation

While there is no state income tax in Florida, homeowners are taxed when renting their property, when selling the property, and when they simply own the property. Owners with rental properties may be taxed on net profits from rental income and may be charged sales tax on short-term rentals. Owners who sell their property and realize a profit may be charged a capital gains tax on that profit. Additionally, local governments charge owners an annual property tax based on the value of the property. Property taxes help fund public schools and municipal infrastructure, including roads and emergency services. Owners may face foreclosure if they fail to pay their property taxes.

PRIVATE OWNERSHIP LIMITATIONS AND RESTRICTIONS

Encumbrances
Deed restrictions
Easements
Encroachments
Licenses
Leases
Liens

Encumbrances

An encumbrance is an interest in and right to real property that limits the legal owner's freehold interest. In effect, an encumbrance is another's right to use or take possession of a legal owner's property, or to prevent the legal owner from enjoying the full bundle of rights in the estate.

An encumbrance does not include the right of possession and is therefore a lesser interest than the owner's freehold interest. For that reason, encumbrances are not considered estates. However, an encumbrance can lead to the owner's loss of ownership of the property.

Easements and liens are the most common types of encumbrance. An easement, such as a utility easement, enables others to use the property, regardless of the owner's desires. A lien, such as a tax lien, can be placed on the property's title, thereby restricting the owner's ability to transfer clear title to another party.

The two general types of encumbrance are those that affect the property's use and those that affect legal ownership, value and transfer.

General Types of Encumbrance

Restrictions on Owner's Use by Others' Rights to Use	Restrictions on Ownership, Value and Transfer
easements encroachments licenses deed restrictions	liens deed conditions

Deed restrictions

A deed restriction is a limitation imposed on a buyer's use of a property by stipulation in the deed of conveyance or recorded subdivision plat.

A deed restriction may apply to a single property or to an entire subdivision. A developer may place restrictions on all properties within a recorded **subdivision plat**. Subsequent re-sales of properties within the subdivision are thereby subject to the plat's covenants and conditions.

A private party who wants to control the quality and standards of a property can establish a deed restriction. Deed restrictions take precedence over zoning ordinances if they are more restrictive.

Deed restrictions typically apply to:

- the land use
- the size and type of structures that may be placed on the property
- minimum costs of structures
- engineering, architectural, and aesthetic standards, such as setbacks or specific standards of construction

Deed restrictions in a subdivision, for example, might include a minimum size for the residential structure, setback requirements for the home, and prohibitions against secondary structures such as sheds or cottages.

Deed restrictions are either covenants or conditions. A **condition** can only be created within a transfer of ownership. If a condition is later violated, a suit can force the owner to forfeit ownership to the previous owner. A **covenant** can be created by mutual agreement. If a covenant is breached, an injunction can force compliance or payment of compensatory

Easements

An **easement** is an interest in real property that gives the holder the right to use portions of the legal owner's real property in a defined way. Easement rights may apply to a property's surface, subsurface, or airspace, but the affected area must be defined.

The receiver of the easement right is the **benefited party**; the giver of the easement right is the **burdened party**.

Essential characteristics of easements include the following:

- An easement must involve the owner of the land over which the easement runs, and another, non-owning party. *One cannot own an easement over one's own property.*

- an easement pertains to a specified physical area within the property boundaries

- an easement may be **affirmative**, allowing a use, such as a right-of-way, or **negative**, *prohibiting a use*, such as an airspace easement that prohibits one property owner from obstructing another's ocean view

The two basic types of easement are appurtenant and gross.

Easement appurtenant. An easement appurtenant gives a property owner a right of usage to portions of an *adjoining property* owned by another party. The property enjoying the usage right is called the **dominant tenement**, or **dominant estate**. The property containing the physical easement itself is the **servient tenement**, since it must serve the easement use.

The term appurtenant means "attaching to." An easement appurtenant attaches to the estate and transfers with it unless specifically stated otherwise in the transaction documents. More specifically, the easement attaches as a beneficial interest to the dominant estate, and as an encumbrance to the servient estate. The easement appurtenant then becomes part of the dominant estate's bundle of rights and the servient estate's obligation, or encumbrance.

Transfer. Easement appurtenant rights and obligations automatically transfer with the property upon transfer of either the dominant or servient estate, whether mentioned in the deed or not. For example, John grants Mary the right to share his driveway at any time over a five-year period, and the grant is duly recorded. If Mary sells her property in two years, the easement right transfers to the buyer as part of the estate.

Non-exclusive use. The servient tenement, as well as the dominant tenement, may use the easement area, provided the use does not unreasonably obstruct the dominant use.

Easements appurtenant

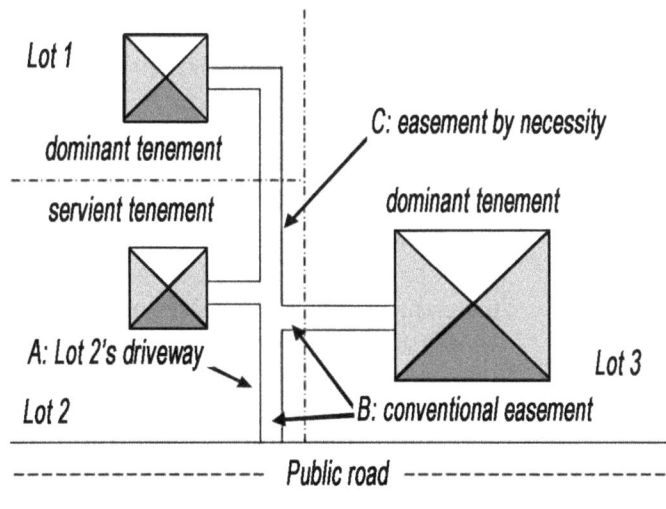

The exhibit shows a conventional easement appurtenant. The driveway marked A belongs to parcel #2. An easement appurtenant, marked B, allows parcel #3 to use #2's driveway. Parcel #3 is the dominant tenement, and #2 is the servient tenement.

Easement by necessity. An easement by necessity is an easement appurtenant granted by a court of law to a property owner because of a circumstance of necessity, most commonly the need for access to a property. Since property cannot be legally **landlocked**, or *without legal access to a public thoroughfare*, a court will grant an owner of a landlocked property an easement by necessity over an adjoining property that has access to a thoroughfare. The landlocked party becomes the dominant tenement, and the property containing the easement is the servient tenement.

In the exhibit, parcel #1, which is landlocked, owns an easement by necessity, marked C, across parcel #2.

Party wall easement. A party wall is a common wall shared by two separate structures along a property boundary.

Party wall agreements generally provide for severalty ownership of half of the wall by each owner, or at least some fraction of the width of the wall. In addition, the agreement grants a *negative* easement appurtenant to each owner in the other's wall. This is to prevent unlimited use of the wall, in particular a destructive use that would jeopardize the adjacent property owner's building. The agreement also establishes responsibilities and obligations for maintenance and repair of the wall.

For example, Helen and Troy are adjacent neighbors in an urban housing complex having party walls on property lines. They both agree that they separately own the portion of the party wall on their property. They also grant each other an easement appurtenant in their owned portion of the wall. The easement restricts any use of the wall that would impair its condition. They also agree to split any repairs or maintenance evenly.

Other structures that are subject to party agreements are common fences, driveways, and walkways.

Easement in gross. An easement in gross is a *personal right* that one party grants to another to use the grantor's real property. The right *does not attach* to the grantor's estate. It involves only one property, and, consequently, does not benefit any property owned by the easement owner. *There are no dominant or servient estates in an easement in gross.* An easement in gross may be personal or commercial.

Easements in Gross

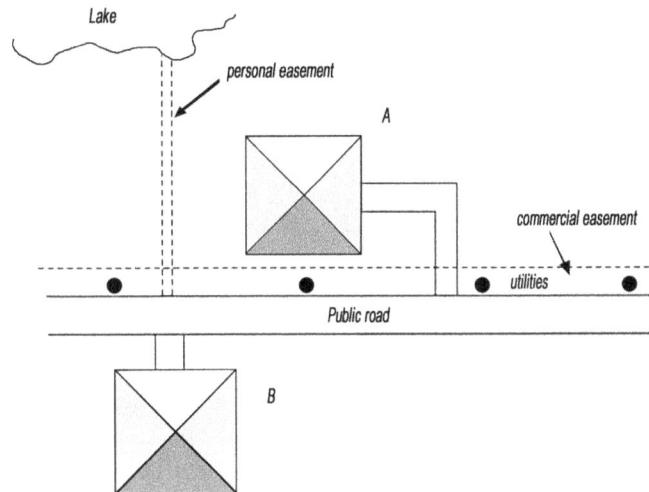

> ▸ **personal** -- A personal easement in gross is granted for the grantee's lifetime. The right is irrevocable during this period, but terminates on the grantee's death. It may not be sold, assigned, transferred, or willed. A personal gross easement differs from a license in that the grantor of a license may revoke the usage right.
>
> The exhibit shows that a beachfront property owner (A) has granted a neighbor (B) across the street the right to cross A's property to reach the beach.
>
> ▸ **commercial** -- a commercial easement in gross is granted to a business entity rather than a private party. The duration of the commercial easement is not tied to anyone's lifetime. The right may by assigned, transferred, or willed.
>
> Examples of commercial gross easements include:
>
> - a marina's right-of-way to a boat ramp
> - a utility company's right-of-way across a lot owners' property to install and maintain telephone lines (as illustrated in the exhibit)

Easement creation.   An easement may be created by *voluntary action, by necessary or prescriptive operation of law,* and *by government power of eminent domain.*

> ► **voluntary**-- a property owner may create a voluntary easement by express grant in a sale contract, or as a reserved right expressed in a deed

> ► **necessity -- s** court decree creates an easement by necessity to provide access to a landlocked property

Easement by prescription. If someone uses another's property as an easement without permission for a statutory period of time and under certain conditions, a court order may give the user the easement right by **prescription**, *regardless of the owner's desires.*

For a prescriptive easement order to be granted, the following circumstances must be true:

> ► **adverse and hostile use** -- the use has been occurring without permission or license

> ► **open and notorious use** -- the owner knows or is presumed to have known of the use

> ► **continuous use** -- the use has been generally uninterrupted over the statutory prescriptive period

For example, a subdivision owns an access road, which is also used by other neighborhoods to access a grocery store. One day, the subdivision blocks off the road, claiming it has never granted the neighbors permission to use the road. If the neighbors have been using the road for the prescribed period, they may sue for an easement by prescription, since the subdivision owners can be assumed to have known of the usage.

Eminent domain. Government entities can create easements through the exercise of eminent domain, wherein they condemn a portion of a property and cause it to be sold "for the greater good." A typical example is a town's condemnation of private land to create a new municipal sewer system.

Easement termination. Easements terminate by:

> ► *express release of the right* by the easement holder
> ► *merger*, as when a dominant tenement acquires the servient property, or vice versa
> ► *purposeful abandonment* by the dominant tenement
> ► *condemnation* through eminent domain
> ► *change or cessation of the purpose* for the easement
> ► *destruction* of an easement structure, such as a party fence
> ► *non-use* of an easement by prescription

Encroachments   An encroachment is the unauthorized, physical intrusion of one owner's real property into that of another.

Examples of encroachments are:

- a tree limb extending into the neighbor's property, violating his or her airspace
- a driveway extending beyond the lot line onto the neighbor's land
- a fence built beyond the property line

Encroachments cause infringements on the rights of the trespassed owner, and may diminish the property's value, particularly when the property is to be sold.

Encroachments often do not appear on a property's title records. A survey may be required to detect or demonstrate the existence of an encroachment.

An owner may sue for removal of an encroachment or for compensation for damages. If an encroached owner takes no remedial action over a prescribed number of years, the encroachment may become an easement by prescription.

Licenses

A license, much like a personal easement in gross, is a personal right that a property owner grants to another to use the property for a specific purpose. Licenses are not transferrable and do not attach to the land. They cease on the death of either party, or on the sale of the property.

Unlike a personal easement in gross, a license is revocable at any time. Licenses are often granted informally, as a verbal statement of permission.

A farmer granting a neighbor permission to cross his land to reach and fish in his pond is an example of a license.

Leases

Gross lease. A gross lease, or **full service** lease, requires the landlord to pay the property's operating expenses, including utilities, repairs, and maintenance, while the tenant pays only rent. Rent levels under a gross lease are higher than under a net lease, since the landlord recoups expense outlays in the form of added rent.

Gross leases are common for office and industrial properties. Residential leases are usually gross leases with the exception that the tenants often pay utilities expenses.

Net lease. A net lease requires a tenant to pay for utilities, internal repairs, and a proportionate share of taxes, insurance, and operating expenses in addition to rent. In effect, the landlord "passes through" actual property expenses to the tenant rather than charging a higher rent level. Net leases vary as to exactly what expenses the tenant is responsible for. The extreme form of net lease requires tenants to cover all expenses, including major repairs and property taxes.

Net leases are common for office and industrial properties. They are sometimes also used for single family dwellings.

In practice, the terms net and gross lease can be misleading: some gross leases still require tenants to pay some expenses such as utilities and repairs. Similarly, some net leases require the landlord to pay certain expenses. Prudent tenants and landlords look at all expense obligations in relation to the level of rent to be charged.

Percentage lease. A percentage lease allows the landlord to share in the income generated from the use of the property. A tenant pays **percentage rent**, or an amount of rent equal to a percentage of the tenant's periodic gross sales. The percentage rent may be:

- ▶ a fixed percent of gross revenue without a minimum rent
- ▶ a fixed minimum rent plus an additional percent of gross sales
- ▶ a percentage rent or minimum rent, whichever is greater

Percentage leases are used only for retail properties.

Variable/index. A variable lease is an agreement for the tenant to pay specified rent increases at set dates in the future. The increases may be based on a variable interest rate, a Consumer Price Index (CPI), a percentage of sales, or some other variable factor. The lease must state how the rent increases are to be calculated. An index lease agreement typically calculates the rent increases based on the CPI so that an increase in the CPI will result in a corresponding increase in the rent payment.

Residential lease. A residential lease may be a net lease or a gross lease. Usually, it is a form of gross lease in which the landlord pays all property expenses except the tenant's utilities and water. Since residential leases tend to be short in term, tenants cannot be expected to pay for major repairs and improvements. The landlord, rather, absorbs these expenses and recoups the outlays through higher rent.

Residential leases differ from commercial and other types of lease in that:

- ▶ lease terms are shorter, typically one or two years
- ▶ lease clauses are fairly standard from one property to the next, in order to reflect compliance with local landlord-tenant relations laws
- ▶ lease clauses are generally not negotiable, particularly in larger apartment complexes where owners want uniform leases for all residents

Commercial lease. A commercial lease may be a net, gross, or percentage lease, if the tenant is a retail business. As a rule, a commercial lease is a significant and complex business proposition. It may involve hundreds of thousands of dollars for improving the property to the tenant's specifications. Since the lease terms are often long, total rent liabilities for the tenant can easily be millions of dollars.

Some important features of commercial leases are:

- ▶ long term, ranging up to 25 years
- ▶ require tenant improvements to meet particular usage needs

- ▸ virtually all lease clauses are negotiable due to the financial magnitude of the transaction
- ▸ default can have serious financial consequences; therefore, lease clauses must express all points of agreement and be very precise

Ground lease . A ground lease, or **land lease**, concerns the land portion of a real property. The owner grants the tenant a leasehold interest in the land only, in exchange for rent.

Ground leases are primarily used in three circumstances:

- ▸ an owner wishes to lease raw land to an agricultural or mining interest
- ▸ unimproved property is to be developed and either the owner wants to retain ownership of the land, or the developer or future users of the property do not want to own the land
- ▸ the owner of an improved property wishes to sell an interest in the improvements while retaining ownership of the underlying land

In the latter two instances, a ground lease offers owners, developers, and users various financing, appreciation, and tax advantages. For example, a ground lease lessor can take advantage of the increase in value of the land due to the new improvements developed on it, without incurring the risks of developing and owning the improvements. Land leases executed for the purpose of development or to segregate ownership of land from ownership of improvements are inherently long term leases, often ranging from thirty to fifty years.

Proprietary lease. A proprietary lease conveys a leasehold interest to an owner of a cooperative. The proprietary lease does not stipulate rent, as the rent is equal to the owner's share of the periodic expenses of the entire cooperative. The term of the lease is likewise unspecified, as it coincides with the ownership period of the cooperative tenant: when an interest is sold, the proprietary lease for the seller's unit is assigned to the new buyer.

Leasing of rights. The practice of leasing property rights other than the rights to exclusive occupancy and possession occurs most commonly in the leasing of water rights, air rights, and mineral rights.

For example, an owner of land that has deposits of coal might lease the mineral rights to a mining company, giving the mining company the limited right to extract the coal. The rights lease may be very specific, stating how much of a mineral or other resource may be extracted, how the rights may be exercised, for what period of time, and on what portions of the property. The lessee's rights do not include common leasehold interests such as occupancy, exclusion, quiet enjoyment, or possession of the leased premises.

Another example of a rights lease is where a railroad wants to erect a bridge over a thoroughfare owned by a municipality. The railroad must obtain an air rights agreement of some kind, whether it be an easement, a purchase, or a lease, before it can construct the bridge.

Sale subject to lease. Sometimes when a property is being sold, the contract includes a "subject to" clause. If the property has been a rental property prior to the sale, the seller may want to assure the tenant is protected and allowed to continue leasing the property under the new owner. In such cases, the seller may include a "subject to lease" clause or statement on the contract. By signing the contract, the buyer has agreed to purchase the property with a lease remaining in effect as it stands prior to the sale.

Subletting and assignment. Subletting (subleasing) is the transfer by a tenant, the **sublessor**, of a *portion* of the leasehold interest to another party, the **sublessee**, through the execution of a **sublease**. The sublease spells out all of the rights and obligations of the sublessor and sublessee, including the payment of rent to the sublessor. The sublessor remains *primarily liable* for the original lease with the landlord. The subtenant is *liable* only to the sublessor.

For example, a sublessor subleases a portion of the occupied premises for a portion of the remaining term. The sublessee pays sublease rent to the sublessor, who in turn pays lease rent to the landlord.

An assignment of the lease is a transfer of the *entire leasehold interest* by a tenant, the **assignor**, to a third party, the **assignee**. There is no second lease, and the assignor retains no residual rights of occupancy or other leasehold rights unless expressly stated in the assignment agreement. The assignee becomes primarily liable for the lease and rent, and the assignor, the original tenant, remains secondarily liable. The assignee pays rent directly to the landlord.

All leases clarify the rights and restrictions of the tenant regarding subleasing and assigning the leasehold interest. Generally, the landlord cannot prohibit either act, but the tenant must obtain the landlord's written approval. The reason for this requirement is that the landlord has a financial stake in the creditworthiness of any prospective tenant.

Liens

Lien characteristics. A lien is a creditor's **claim** against personal or real property as security for a debt of the property owner. If the owner defaults, the lien gives the creditor the right to force the sale of the property to satisfy the debt.

For example, a homeowner borrows $5,000 to pay for a new roof. The lender funds the loan in exchange for the borrower's promissory note to repay the loan. At the same time, the lender places a lien on the property for $5,000 as security for the debt. If the borrower defaults, the lien allows the lender to force the sale of the house to satisfy the debt.

The example illustrates that a lien is an encumbrance that restricts free and clear ownership by securing the liened property as **collateral** for a debt. If the owner sells the property, the lienholder is entitled to that portion of the sales proceeds needed to pay off the debt. In addition, a defaulting owner may lose ownership altogether if the creditor forecloses.

In addition to restricting the owner's bundle of rights, a recorded lien effectively reduces the owner's equity in the property to the extent of the lien amount.

The creditor who places a lien on a property is called the **lienor**, and the debtor who owns the property is the **lienee**.

Liens have the following legal features:

> ▶ **a lien does not convey ownership, with one exception**
>
> A lienor generally has an equitable interest in the property, but not legal ownership. The exception is a **mortgage lien** on a property in a title-theory state (Florida is a lien-theory state). In title-theory states, the mortgage transaction conveys legal title to the lender, who holds it until the mortgage obligations are satisfied. During the mortgage loan period, the borrower has equitable title to the property.

> ▶ **a lien attaches to the property**
>
> If the property is transferred, the *new owner acquires the lien securing the payment of the debt.* In addition, the creditor may take foreclosure action against the new owner for satisfaction of the debt.

> ▶ **a property may be subject to multiple liens**
>
> There may be numerous liens against a particular property. The more liens there are recorded against property, the less secure the collateral is for a creditor, since the total value of all liens may approach or exceed the total value of the property.

> ▶ **A lien terminates on payment of the debt and recording of documents**
>
> Payment of the debt and recording of the appropriate satisfaction documents ordinarily terminate a lien. If a default occurs, a suit for judgment or foreclosure enforces the lien. These actions force the sale of the property.

Liens may be voluntary or involuntary, general or specific, and superior or inferior.

Voluntary or involuntary lien. A property owner may create a **voluntary** lien to borrow money or some other asset secured by a mortgage. An **involuntary** lien is one that a legal process places against a property regardless of the owner's desires.

If statutory law imposes an involuntary lien, the lien is a **statutory lien**. A real estate tax lien is a common example. If court action imposes an involuntary lien, the lien is an **equitable lien**. An example is a judgment lien placed on a property as security for a money judgment.

General or specific lien. A general lien is one *placed against any and all real and personal property* owned by a particular debtor. An example is an inheritance tax lien placed against all property owned by the heir. **A specific** lien *attaches to a single item* of real or personal property, and does not affect other property owned by the debtor. A conventional mortgage lien is an example, where the property is the only asset attached by the lien.

Lien priority. The category of superior, or **senior**, liens ranks above the category of inferior, or **junior**, liens, meaning that superior liens receive first payment from the proceeds of a foreclosure. The superior category includes liens for real estate tax, special assessments, and inheritance tax. Other liens, including income tax liens, are inferior.

Within the superior and inferior categories, a ranking of lien priority determines the order of the liens' claims on the security underlying the debt. The highest ranking lien is first to receive proceeds from the foreclosed and liquidated security. The lien with lowest priority is last in line. The owner receives any sale proceeds that remain after all lienors receive their due.

Lien priority is of paramount concern to the creditor, since it establishes the level of risk in recovering loaned assets in the event of default.

Two factors primarily determine lien priority:

- ▸   the lien's categorization as superior or junior
- ▸   the date of recordation of the lien

Priority of Real Estate Liens

Superior liens in rank order
1.   Real estate tax liens 2.   Special assessment liens 3.   Federal estate tax liens 4.   State inheritance tax liens

Junior liens: priority by date of recording
Federal income tax liens State corporate income tax liens State intangible tax liens Judgment liens Mortgage liens Vendor's liens Mechanic's liens (priority by date work was performed)

Superior liens. All superior liens take precedence over all junior liens regardless of recording date, since they are considered to be matters of public record not requiring further constructive notice. Thus, a real estate tax lien (senior) recorded on June 15 has priority over an income tax lien (junior) recorded on June 1.

Superior liens include real estate tax liens, special assessment liens, and federal and state inheritance liens.

▶ **real estate tax lien**

The local legal taxing authority annually places a real estate tax lien, also called an **ad valorem tax lien**, against properties as security for payment of the annual property tax. The amount of a particular lien is based on the taxed property's assessed value and the local tax rate.

▶ **special assessment lien**

Local government entities place assessment liens against certain properties to ensure payment for local improvement projects such as new roads, schools, sewers, or libraries. An assessment lien applies only to properties that are expected to benefit from the municipal improvement.

▸ **federal and state inheritance tax liens**

Inheritance tax liens arise from taxes owed by a decedent's estate. The lien amount is determined through probate and attaches to both real and personal property.

Junior liens. A junior lien is automatically inferior, or **subordinate**, to a superior lien. Among junior liens, date of recording determines priority. The rule is: *the earlier the recording date of the lien, the higher its priority.* For example, if a judgment lien is recorded against a property on Friday, and a mortgage lien is recorded on the following Tuesday, the judgment lien has priority and must be satisfied in a foreclosure ahead of the mortgage lien. The mechanic's lien (see further below) is an exception to the recording rule. Its priority dates from the point in time when the work commenced or materials were first delivered to the property, rather than from when it was recorded.

Junior liens include other tax liens, judgment liens, mortgage and trust deed liens, vendor's liens, municipal utility liens, and mechanic's liens.

▸ **other tax liens**

All tax liens other than those for ad valorem, assessment, and estate tax are junior liens. They include:

- **federal income tax lien** -- placed on a taxpayer's real and personal property for failure to pay income taxes

- **state corporate income tax lien** -- filed against corporate property for failure to pay taxes

- **state intangible tax lien** -- filed for non-payment of taxes on intangible property

- **state corporation franchise tax lien** -- filed to ensure collection of fees to do business within a state

▸ **judgment lien**

A judgment lien attaches to real and personal property as a result of a money judgment issued by a court in favor of a creditor. The creditor may obtain a **writ of execution** to force the sale of attached property and collect the debt. After paying the debt from the sale proceeds, the debtor may obtain a **satisfaction of judgment** to clear the title records on other real property that remains unsold.

During the course of a lawsuit, the plaintiff creditor may secure a **writ of attachment** to prevent the debtor from selling or concealing property. In such a case, there must be a clear likelihood that the debt is valid and that the defendant has made attempts to sell or hide property.

Certain properties are exempt from judgment liens, such as homestead property and joint tenancy estates.

▸ **mortgage and trust deed lien**

In lien-theory states (such as Florida), mortgages and trust deeds secure loans made on real property. In these states, the lender records a lien as soon as possible after disbursing the funds in order to establish lien priority.

▸ **vendor's lien**

A vendor's lien, also called a **seller's lien**, secures a purchase money mortgage, a seller's loan to a buyer to finance the sale of a property.

▸ **municipal utility lien**

A municipality may place a utility lien against a resident's real property for failure to pay utility bills.

▸ **mechanic's lien**

A mechanic's lien secures the costs of labor, materials, and supplies incurred in the repair or construction of real property improvements. If a property owner fails to pay for work performed or materials supplied, a worker or supplier can file a lien to force the sale of the property and collect the debt.

Any individual who performs approved work may place a mechanic's lien on the property to the extent of the direct costs incurred. Note that unpaid subcontractors may record mechanic's liens *whether the general contractor has been paid or not*. Thus it is possible for an owner to have to double-pay a bill in order to eliminate the mechanic's lien if the general contractor neglects to pay the subcontractors. The mechanic's lienor must enforce the lien within a certain time period, or the lien expires.

In contrast to other junior liens, the priority of a mechanic's lien *dates from the time when the work was begun or completed*. For example, a carpenter finishes a job on May 15. The owner refuses to pay the carpenter in spite of the carpenter's two-month collection effort. Finally, on August 1, the carpenter places a mechanic's lien on the property. The effective date of the lien for purposes of lien priority is May 15, not August 1.

The following example illustrates how lien priority works in paying off secured debts. A homeowner is foreclosed on a second mortgage taken out in 2018 for $25,000. The first mortgage, taken in 2016, has a balance of $150,000. Unpaid real estate taxes for the current year are $1,000. There is a $3,000 mechanic's lien on the property for work performed in 2017. The home sells for $183,000.

The proceeds are distributed in the following order:

1. $1,000 real estate taxes
2. $150,000 first mortgage
3. $3,000 mechanic's lien
4. $25,000 second mortgage
5. $4,000 balance to the homeowner

Note the risky position of the second mortgage holder: the property had to sell for at least $179,000 for the lender to recover the $25,000.

Subordination. A lienor can change the priority of a junior lien by voluntarily agreeing to subordinate, or lower, the lien's position in the hierarchy. This change is often necessary when working with a mortgage lender who will not originate a mortgage loan unless it is senior to all other junior liens on the property. The lender may require the borrower to obtain agreements from other lien holders to subordinate their liens to the new mortgage.

For example, interest rates fall from 8% to 6.5% on first mortgages for principal residences. A homeowner wants to refinance her mortgage, but she also has a separate home-equity loan on the house. Since the first-mortgage lender will not accept a lien priority inferior to a home equity loan, the homeowner must persuade the home equity lender to subordinate the home equity lien to the new first-mortgage lien.

9 Title, Deeds and Ownership Restrictions
Snapshot Review

CONCEPT OF TITLE

Ownership in a bundle of rights
- defined as the legal privileges given to a buyer upon purchase
- includes possession, quiet enjoyment, control, exclusion, disposition

Legal and equitable title
- legal title: ownership of the bundle of rights
- equitable title: a conditional right to legal title subject to an owner's agreements with buyers and creditors

Transferring title
- voluntary by grant, deed, or will
- involuntary by descent, escheat, eminent domain, foreclosure, adverse possession, estoppel

TRANSFER BY VOLUNTARY ALIENATION

Deeds
- instrument of voluntary conveyance by grantor to grantee
- legal title transfers upon competent grantor's intentional delivery and grantee's acceptance
- **in Florida:** locate current deed; prepare new deed; grantor, spouse, witnesses, notary signatures; file with county clerk

Wills
- last will and testament: voluntary transfer to heirs after death
- maker: devisor or testator; heir: devisee; estate: devise
- types: witnessed; holographic; approved; nuncupative
- validity: adult; competent; indicates "last will and testament"; signed; witnessed; voluntary
- probate: if testate, estate passes to heirs; if intestate, to successors by descent; if intestate with no heirs, estate escheats to state
- testate probate process: validate will; validate, settle claims and pay taxes; transfer balance of estate to heirs

TRANSFER BY INVOLUNTARY ALIENATION

Laws of descent
- state statutes determine heirs and shares

Escheat
- title transfers to state

Foreclosure
- title lost by forfeiture

Eminent domain
- title lost to public for the greater good

Adverse possession
- title taken by claim of right or color of title; continuous, notorious, hostile possession; must pay taxes

NOTICE OF TITLE
- how ownership is evidenced to the public

Actual notice	• actual notice: knowledge acquired or imparted directly through demonstrable evidence, e.g., presenting or inspecting a deed, visiting a party in possession
Constructive notice	• constructive notice: knowledge one could or should have obtained, as presumed by law; imparted by recording in public records "for all to see"

PROTECTION OF TITLE

Title records	• all instruments affecting title must be recorded
	• give public notice; protect owners; protect lienholders' claims
Title evidence	• needed to prove marketable title as well as who owns
	• forms of evidence: title insurance; attorney's opinion of abstract; title certificates
Title companies	• performs title search to determine title legitimacy
	• may require property survey; prepares abstract of title and title opinion letter
	• may maintain escrow account, handle transaction closing, and file new title; may issue title insurance
Chain of title	• successive property owners from original grant to present owner
	• abstract of title: chronology of recorded owners, transfers, encumbrances
Title abstract	• written chronological summary of title records; contains chain of title, documents that might cloud title
Title opinion	• written by an attorney; opinion of marketability of title
Title insurance	• best evidence of marketable title
	• **owner's policy** – covers property's appreciated value against title defects; standard or extended coverage; not transferrable
	• **lender's policy** – covers financed mortgage loan balance against title defects; is transferrable if loan is sold to another lender

DEEDS

Deed essentials	• parties: grantor, grantee
	• components: parties, consideration, granting clause, habendum clause, restrictions, inclusions, exceptions, reservations, appurtenances, description, delivery and acceptance, signatures, witnesses
	• Florida validity requirements: in writing, signed by transferor, two witnesses, space for parcel ID number
	• recording required in Florida; include grantor's info and signature; grantee's info; natural person who prepared the deed; witnesses; notarized; designated space for clerk's use
Deed clauses	• premises clause: granting
	• habendum clause: type of estate
	• reddendum clause: restrictions
	• tenendum clause: other property included
	• warrants: seizen; quiet enjoyment; further assurance; forever; encumbrances; grantor's acts
Types of statutory deed	• bargain and sale: "I own but won't defend"
	• general warranty: "I own and will defend"
	• special warranty: "I own and warrant myself only"
	• quitclaim: "I may or may not own, and won't defend"

| **Special purpose deeds** | • | used for different purposes, to convey certain interests, or by certain parties |
| | • | life estate deed to divide ownership between current grantor and future owners |

GOV'T OWNERSHIP LIMITATIONS/ RESTRICTIONS

Police powers	•	government's right to regulate use of property and to take possession of property; limits owners' rights
Eminent domain	•	power to take private property for public use; must compensate owner
Taxation	•	no Florida state income tax; taxed on net profits from rental property income and sales tax from short-term rentals; capital gains tax on profit from sale of property; annual property tax based on value of property

PRIVATE OWNERSHIP LIMITATIONS/ RESTRICTIONS

Encumbrances	•	non-possessory interests limiting the legal owner's rights; easements, encroachments, licenses, deed restrictions, liens, deed conditions
Deed restrictions	•	conditions and covenants imposed on a property by deed or subdivision plat
Easements	•	a right to use portions of another's property
	•	easement appurtenant: dominant tenement's right to use or restrict adjacent servient tenement; attaches to the real estate
	•	easement by necessity: granted by necessity, e.g. to landlocked owners
	•	party wall: negative easement in a shared structure
	•	easement in gross: a right to use property that does not attach to the real estate
	•	personal easement in gross: not revocable or transferrable; ends upon death of easement holder
	•	commercial easement in gross: granted to businesses; transferrable
	•	easement creation by voluntary grant, court decree by necessity or prescription, eminent domain
	•	easement creation by prescription: obtainable through continuous, open, adverse use over a period
	•	easement termination: release; merger; abandonment; condemnation; change of purpose; destruction; non-use
Encroachments	•	intrusions of real estate into adjoining property; can become easements
Licenses	•	personal rights to use a property; do not attach; non-transferrable; revocable
Leases	•	instrument of leasehold conveyance; contract of covenants and obligations
	•	landlord grants temporary, exclusive use in trade for rent and reversion
	•	lease type based on expense responsibility; how rent is paid; property type; rights leased
	•	gross lease: landlord pays expenses; tenant pays more rent
	•	net lease: tenant pays some or all expenses; rent is less
	•	percentage lease: landlord receives rent minimum plus percentage of retailer's sales
	•	variable/index lease: tenant pays specified rent with increases on set dates
	•	residential lease: gross lease hybrid; short term; uniform terms reflect landlord-tenant standards
	•	commercial lease: longer term; entails tenant improvements; complex, negotiable lease terms
	•	ground lease: landlord owns and leases ground but does not own improvements

- proprietary lease: for cooperative unit owners; indefinite term; assigned to new unit owner on sale
- leasing of rights: leasehold transfer of rights for limited use; examples: air, mineral, water rights
- sale subject to lease: property is sold with requirement to maintain current tenant lease
- subletting and assignment: transfer of a portion of leasehold to another (subletting); transfer of entire leasehold (assignment)

Liens

- claims attaching to real and personal property as security for debt
- lien types: voluntary and involuntary; general and specific; superior and junior
- lien priority: rank ordering of claims established by lien classification and date of recording; determines who gets paid first if lienee defaults
- superior liens: rank over junior liens; not ranked by recording date; real estate tax and assessment liens and inheritance taxes
- junior liens: rank by recording date: judgment; mortgage, vendor's, utility, mechanic's, other tax liens; mechanic's lien priority "dates back" to when work began

SECTION NINE: Title, Deeds and Ownership Restrictions

Section Quiz

1. Which of the following best describes the concept of "legal title" to real estate?"

   a. Ownership of the bundle of rights to real estate
   b. The right of a buyer or lender to obtain ownership under certain circumstances
   c. Possession of a deed
   d. Absolute proof of ownership of real estate

2. A person claims ownership of a parcel of real estate to a prospective buyer, stating that she has lived on the property for five years and nobody has ever bothered her. The claimant also shows the buyer a copy of the deed. The legal basis of this claim is referred to as

   a. prescriptive notice.
   b. constructive notice.
   c. hostile notice.
   d. actual notice.

3. Constructive notice of ownership of a parcel of real estate is primarily demonstrated through

   a. direct inspection to see who is in possession.
   b. title insurance.
   c. title records.
   d. a construction permit.

4. An owner transfers title to a property to a buyer in exchange for a consideration. This is an example of

   a. voluntary alienation.
   b. escheat.
   c. hypothecation.
   d. estoppel.

5. For a deed to convey title, it is necessary for the deed to be

   a. on a standard form.
   b. certified by the grantor.
   c. accepted by the grantee.
   d. signed by the grantee.

6. The only required clause in a deed of conveyance is one that

   a. states restrictions and limitations to the estate being conveyed.
   b. states the parties and the type of estate being conveyed.
   c. states that the grantor has done nothing to impair title to the property being conveyed.
   d. states the grantor's intention, names the parties, describes the property, and indicates a consideration.

7. The purpose of a covenant clause in a deed of conveyance is to

   a. state the grantor's assurance or warrant to the grantee that a certain condition or fact concerning the property is true.
   b. state the grantee's promise to use the property in a prescribed manner.
   c. warrant that the grantor has never encumbered title.
   d. describe the consideration that the grantee promises to give in return for title.

8. The type of statutory deed that contains the most complete protection for the grantee is a

   a. guardian's deed.
   b. special warranty deed.
   c. general warranty deed.
   d. quitclaim deed.

9. A person wishes to convey any and all interests in a property to another without making any assurances as to encumbrances, liens, or any other title defects on the property. This party would most likely use which of the following types of deed?

   a. A sheriff's deed
   b. A special warranty deed
   c. A partition deed
   d. A quitclaim deed

10. If a person dies with no legal heirs or relations and has left no valid will, what happens to real property owned by that person?

    a. It is taken by the state according to the process called escheat.
    b. It is reconveyed to the previous owner in the chain of title.
    c. It is taken by the title insurance company according to the process called involuntary alienation.
    d. It is conveyed to the highest bidder at a public auction.

11. Just prior to passing away, a person tells two witnesses that she would like her estate to pass to her husband. One witness records the statement and signs his name. This is an example of

    a. an enforceable holographic will.
    b. an unenforceable holographic will.
    c. an enforceable nuncupative will.
    d. an unenforceable nuncupative will.

12. If a person having several heirs dies intestate, the property will

    a. pass to heirs by the laws of descent and distribution.
    b. escheat to the state.
    c. pass to the surviving spouse through elective share.
    d. pass to the surviving heirs according to the provisions of the will.

13. A property owner can avert the danger of losing title by adverse possession by

    a. recording proof of ownership in county title records.
    b. inspecting the property and evicting any trespassers found.
    c. claiming hostile and notorious possession.
    d. filing a claim of right with the county recorder.

14. A hermit secretly lives in a cave on a 200-acre property. After twenty years, the person makes a claim of ownership to the property. This claim will likely be

    a. upheld through adverse possession.
    b. upheld because of the length of possession.
    c. declined through the doctrine of prior appropriation.
    d. declined because possession was secretive.

15. The fundamental purpose of recording instruments that affect real property is to

    a. prove ownership of the property.
    b. avoid adverse possession.
    c. give constructive notice of one's rights and interests in the property.
    d. assemble all relevant documents in a single place.

16. What is "chain of title?"

    a. The list of all parties who have ever owned real estate.
    b. The bundle of rights linked to the recorded title to a parcel.
    c. A chronology of successive owners of record of a parcel of real estate.
    d. Involuntary conveyance of title by statutory rules of descent.

17. To be marketable, title must be

    a. registered in Torrens.
    b. free of undisclosed defects and encumbrances.
    c. abstracted by an attorney.
    d. guaranteed by a title certificate.

18. Which of the following is commonly accepted as the best evidence of marketable?

    a. Signed deed.
    b. Title certificate.
    c. Title insurance.
    d. Attorney's opinion.

19. Easements and encroachments are types of

    a. lien.
    b. deed restriction.
    c. encumbrance.
    d. appurtenance.

20. An affirmative easement gives the benefited party

    a. the right to possess a defined portion of another's real property.
    b. the right to prevent the owner of a real property from using it in a defined way.
    c. the right to a defined use of a portion of another's real property.
    d. the right to receive a portion of any income generated by another's real property.

21. There are two adjoining properties. An easement allows property A to use the access road that belongs to property B. In this situation, property A is said to be which of the following in relation to property B?

    a. Subservient estate
    b. Servient estate
    c. Senior tenant
    d. Dominant tenement

22. Which of the following describes a situation in which an easement might be created against the wishes of the property owner?

    a. The property has been continuously used as an easement with the knowledge but without the permission of the owner for a period of time.
    b. The owner of an adjoining property asks the property owner for an easement, is refused, and then uses the property anyway without the knowledge of the owner.
    c. The owner of an adjoining property decides he needs to widen his driveway by sharing his neighbor's driveway and sues in court to create an easement by necessity.
    d. The owner of an adjoining property grants an easement to a third party that includes an easement on the first property.

23. What is the primary danger of allowing an encroachment?

    a. An encroachment automatically grants the benefiting party an easement.
    b. The encroached party may be liable for additional real estate taxes to cover the area being encroached upon by the neighboring property.
    c. Over time, the encroachment may become an easement by prescription that damages the property's market value.
    d. An encroachment creates a lien.

24. A property owner who is selling her land wants to control how it is used in the future. She might accomplish her aim by means of

    a. an injunction.
    b. a deed restriction.
    c. an easement.
    d. a land trust.

25. What distinguishes a lien from other types of encumbrance?

    a. It involves a monetary claim against the value of a property.
    b. It lowers the value of a property.
    c. It is created voluntarily by the property owner.
    d. It attaches to the property rather than to the owner of the property.

26. A certain property has the following liens recorded against it: a mortgage lien dating from three years ago; a mechanic's lien dating from two years ago; a real estate tax lien for the current year; and a second mortgage lien dating from the current year. In case of a foreclosure, which of these liens will be paid first?

    a. First mortgage lien
    b. Mechanic's lien
    c. Real estate tax lien
    d. Second mortgage lien

27. The lien priority of junior liens can be changed by a lienor's agreement to

    a. forgive portions of the debt.
    b. assign the note.
    c. foreclose on the note.
    d. subordinate.

28. Among junior liens, the order of priority is generally established according to

    a. the date of recordation.
    b. the amount.
    c. the order of disbursement.
    d. special agreement among lienees.

29. What is meant by a "lien-theory" state?

    a. A state in which liens are given priority over other encumbrances
    b. A state in which a mortgagor retains title to the property when a mortgage lien is created
    c. A state in which the holder of a mortgage lien receives title to the mortgaged property until the debt is satisfied
    d. A state in which liens exist in theory but not in practice

30. A homeowner has hired a contractor to build a room addition. The work has been completed and the contractor has been paid for all work and materials but fails to pay the lumber yard for a load of lumber. What potential problem may the home owner experience?

    a. The contractor may place a mechanic's lien for the amount of the lumber against the homeowner's real property.
    b. The lumber yard may place a vendor's lien against the contractor and the homeowner for the amount of the lumber.
    c. The lumber yard may place a mechanic's lien for the amount of the lumber against the homeowner's real property.
    d. The homeowner has no liability because the contractor was paid for the lumber.

31. A property survey reveals that a new driveway extends one foot onto a neighbor's property. This is an example of

    a. a easement appurtenant.
    b. an encroachment.
    c. an easement by prescription.
    d. a party wall easement.

32. A property owner has an easement appurtenant on her property. When the property is sold to another party, the easement

    a. terminates.
    b. transfers with the property.
    c. transfers with the owner to a new property.
    d. becomes a lien on the property.

33. A brick fence straddles the property line of two neighbors. The neighbors agree not to damage it in any way. This is an example of

    a. a party wall.
    b. an encroachment.
    c. a trade fixture.
    d. a deed restriction.

34. A property owner allows Betty Luanne to cross his property as a shortcut to her kindergarten school bus. One day the property owner dies. What right was Betty given, and what happens to it in the future?

a. A personal easement in gross, which continues after the owner's death
b. An easement by prescription, which continues after the owner's death
c. A license, which continues after the owner's death
d. A license, which terminates at the owner's death

35. A court renders a judgment which authorizes a lien to be placed against the defendant's house, car, and personal belongings. This is an example of a

a. specific judgment lien.
b. general judgment lien.
c. voluntary judgment lien.
d. superior judgment lien.

36. If a leased property is being sold, the seller can protect the renter and assure the buyer that the property can continue to be rented by

a. including a " sale subject to lease" clause in the contract.
b. appending a copy of the lease to the sale contract.
c. renewing the lease just before completing the sale.
d. obtaining a promissory note to that effect from the buyer.

37. What is one important difference between a sublease and a lease assignment?

a. In an assignment, responsibility for the original lease is transferred completely to the assignee.
b. In a sublease, the original tenant retains primary responsibility for performance of the original lease contract.
c. A sublease does not convey any of the leasehold interest.
d. A sublease conveys the entire leasehold interest.

38. Which of the following lease types conveys rights other than the rights to exclusive use and occupancy of the entire property?

a. A rights lease
b. A percentage lease
c. A gross lease
d. A net lease

39. An owner leases a property to a business in exchange for rent. The tenant is required to pay all operating expenses as well. This is an example of a

a. proprietary lease.
b. percentage lease.
c. gross lease.
d. net lease.

40. The percentage lease is most often used by

a. industrial landlords.
b. retail landlords.
c. residential landlords.
d. office landlords.

41. Which of the following summarizes the general terms of a ground lease?

a. The landlord sells the ground to another, then leases it back.
b. A tenant buys the landlord's ground, then leases the improvements.
c. The landlord leases the ground floor of the building to a commercial tenant.
d. The tenant leases the ground from the landlord and owns the improvements.

42. Which of the following statements is true?

a. Property transfers in Florida do not need to be recorded.
b. When a deed is being transferred, the grantee must sign the deed.
c. If a deed includes the legal description, no parcel identification number is necessary.
d. A deed can be valid with an incorrect parcel identification number on it.

10 Legal Descriptions

Purposes and Methods of Legal Descriptions
Metes and Bounds Method
Government (Rectangular) Survey System
Lot and Block (Recorded Parcel) Method
Describing Elevation
Assessor's Parcel Number
Preparation and Use of Surveys

Learning Objectives

- Describe the purpose for legal descriptions
- Understand the licensee's role and responsibilities as it pertains to legal descriptions
- Explain and distinguish among the three types of legal descriptions
- Describe the process of creating a legal description using the metes-and-bounds method
- Locate a township by township line and range
- Locate a particular section within a township
- Understand how to subdivide a section
- Calculate the number of acres in a parcel based on the legal description, and convert to square feet
- Explain the use of assessor's parcel numbers
- Apply the measurements associated with checks, townships and sections

Key Terms

base line	principal meridian
check	range
government survey system	section
legal description	survey
lot and block	tier
metes and bounds	township
monument	township line
point of beginning	

PURPOSES AND METHODS OF LEGAL DESCRIPTIONS

Definition and uses
Methods

Definition and uses   There are many common ways of describing properties: address (100 Main Street), name (Buckingham Palace), and general description ("the south forty acres"). Such informal descriptions are not acceptable for use in public recordation or, generally speaking, in a court of law because they lack both permanence and sufficient information for a surveyor to locate the property.

Even if a legal document or public record refers to an address, the reference is always supported by an accepted legal description.

A legal description of real property is one which *accurately locates and identifies the boundaries of the subject parcel to a degree acceptable by courts of law in the state where the property is located.*

The general criterion for a legal description is that it alone provides sufficient data for a surveyor to locate the parcel. A legal description identifies the property as unique and distinct from all other properties.

Legal description provides accuracy and consistency over time. Systems of legal description, in theory, facilitate transfers of ownership and prevent boundary disputes and problems with chain of title.

A legal description is required for:

> ▶ public recording
> ▶ creating a valid deed of conveyance or lease
> ▶ completing mortgage documents
> ▶ executing and recording other legal documents

In addition, a legal description provides a basis for court rulings on encroachments and easements.

Methods   The three accepted methods of legally describing parcels of real estate are:

> ▶ metes and bounds
> ▶ rectangular survey system, or government survey method
> ▶ recorded plat method, or lot and block method

Since the metes and bounds method preceded the inception of the rectangular survey system, the older East Coast states generally employ metes and bounds descriptions. States in the Midwest and West predominantly use the rectangular survey system. Some states, such as Florida, combine methods.

METES AND BOUNDS METHOD

A metes and bounds description identifies the boundaries of a parcel of real estate using reference points, distances, and angles. The description always identifies an *enclosed* area by starting at an origination point, called **point of beginning**, or POB, and returning to the POB at the end of the description. A metes and bounds description *must return to the POB in order to be valid.*

The term "metes" refers to distance and direction, and the term "bounds" refers to fixed reference points, or **monuments** and **landmarks**, which may be natural and artificial. Natural landmarks include trees, rocks, rivers, and lakes. Artificial landmarks are typically surveyor stakes.

Florida use metes and bounds description to describe properties within the rectangular survey system.

A metes and bounds description begins with an identification of the city, county, and state where the property is located. Next, it identifies the POB and describes the distance and direction from the POB to the first monument, and then to subsequent monuments that *define the property's enclosed perimeter.*

Metes and Bounds Description

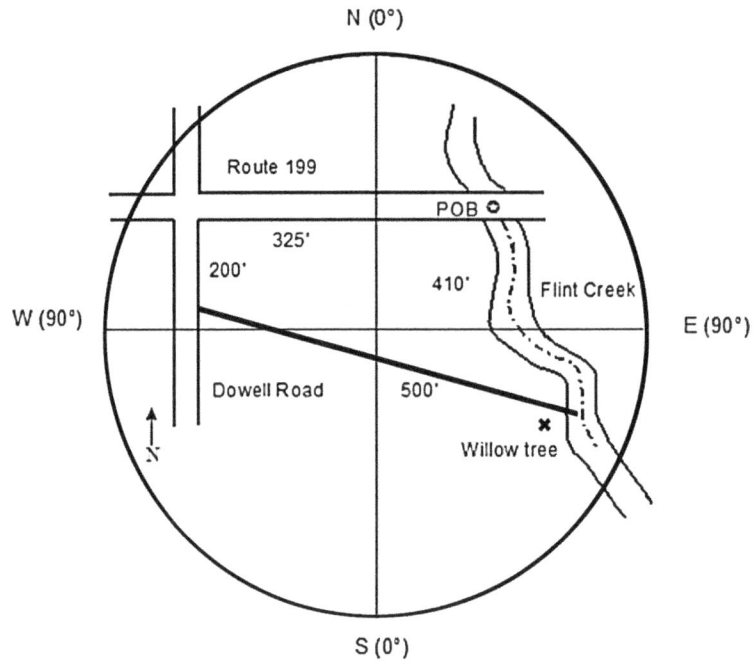

A parcel of land located in Bucks County, Pennsylvania, having the following description: commencing at the intersection of the south line of Route 199 and the middle of Flint Creek, thence southeasterly along the center thread of Flint Creek 410 feet, more or less, to the willow tree landmark, thence north 65 degrees west 500 feet, more or less to the east line of Dowell Road, thence north 2 degrees east 200 feet, more or less, along the east line of Dowell Road to the south line of Route 199, thence north 90 degrees east 325 feet, more or less, along the south line of Route 199 to the point of beginning.

GOVERNMENT (RECTANGULAR) SURVEY SYSTEM

The survey grid
Sections of township
Fractions of a section
Converting section fractions to acres

The federal government developed the **rectangular survey system**, or **government survey method**, to simplify and standardize property descriptions as a replacement for the cumbersome and often inaccurate metes and bounds method. The system was further modified to facilitate the transfer of large quantities of government-owned western lands to private parties.

To institute the system, all affected land was surveyed using latitude (east-west) and longitude (north-south) lines. The object was to create uniform grids of squares, called townships, which would have equal size and be given a numerical reference for identification.

The rectangular survey system works well for describing properties that are square or rectangular in shape, since these can be described as fractions of sections. However, for an irregular shape, such as a triangle, the rectangular system is inadequate as a method of legal description. The full description has to include a metes and bounds or lot and block description.

The survey grid   The following exhibit shows a portion of the rectangular survey system.

Sample Survey Grid: Florida

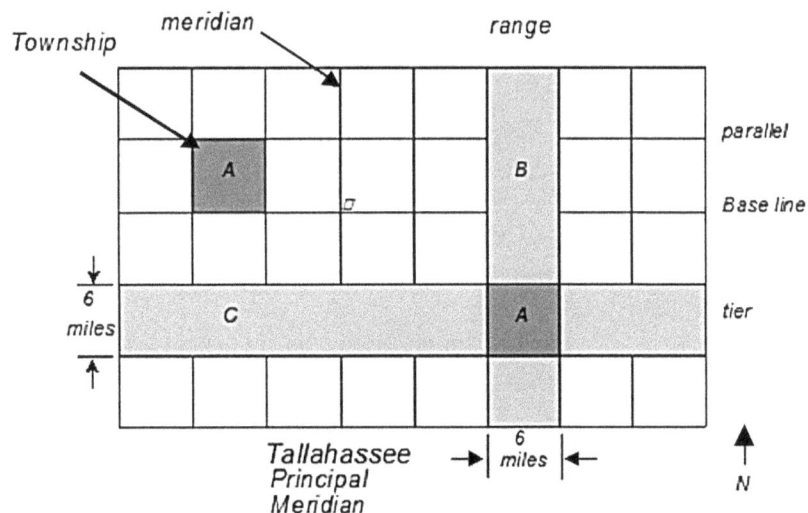

Meridian. The north-south, longitudinal lines on the survey grid are **meridians**. The **principal meridian** is the single designated meridian for identifying townships in the principal meridian's geographical "jurisdiction."

There are 37 principal meridians in the national survey. In the exhibit, the principal meridian is the Tallahassee Principal Meridian.

Parallel. The east-west, latitudinal lines are called **parallels.** The **base parallel** or **base line** is the designated line for identifying townships. There is a base parallel for each principal meridian

Correction lines. Because the earth is curved, meridians (including all range lines and north-south section lines) converge toward one common point at the north pole. Using meridians without correction would result in the north end of every township (and section) being narrower than its south end. To maintain a rectangular survey pattern on the earth's curvature, adjustments need to be made every 24 miles by a longitudinal shift of the standard parallels. The adjusted lines, called **correction lines** or standard parallel lines, restore the meridians to their original spacing, resulting in a slight eastward or westward shift between each row of quadrangles or every fourth township line.

Range. The north-south area between consecutive meridians is called a **range**. The area labeled "B" in the exhibit is a range. A range is identified by its relationship to the principal meridian. All ranges are six miles wide.

The principal meridian divides all ranges into east ranges and west ranges. A range to the west of the principal meridian is identified by an "R" for range, a number representing its ordinal position from the principal meridian, and a "W" representing that it is west of the principal meridian. For example, the third range west of the principal meridian would be denoted "R3W." A range east of the principal meridian is designated "E" instead of "W." Thus the fifth range east of the principal meridian would be identified as "R5E."

Tier. The east-west area between two parallels is called a **tier**, or a **township strip**. The area marked "C" in the exhibit is a tier. A tier is identified by its relationship to the base parallel. All tiers are six miles wide.

The principal base line in a survey area divides tiers into north tiers and south tiers. A tier is identified by a "T" for tier, a number representing its ordinal position from the base line, and an "N" or "S" for north or south, respectively, of the base line. Thus the eighth tier to the north of the base line would be identified as "T8N."

Township. A township is the area enclosed by the intersection of two consecutive meridians and two consecutive parallels, as the shaded square marked "A" in the exhibit illustrates. Since the parallels and meridians are six miles apart, a township is a square with six miles on each side. Its area is therefore 36 square miles.

Individual townships are identified by their *tier and range identification taken together, with the tier designation named first*. For example, a township two tiers south of the base line and three ranges east of the principal meridian would be denoted as "T2S, R3E."

Sections of a township

The rectangular survey system divides a township into thirty-six squares called **sections**. Each side of a section is one mile in length. Thus the area of a section is one square mile, or 640 acres. As the next exhibit illustrates, the sections in a township are numbered sequentially starting with Section 1 in the northeast corner, proceeding east to west across the top row, continuing from west to east across the next lower row, and so on, alternately, ending with Section 36 in the southeast corner.

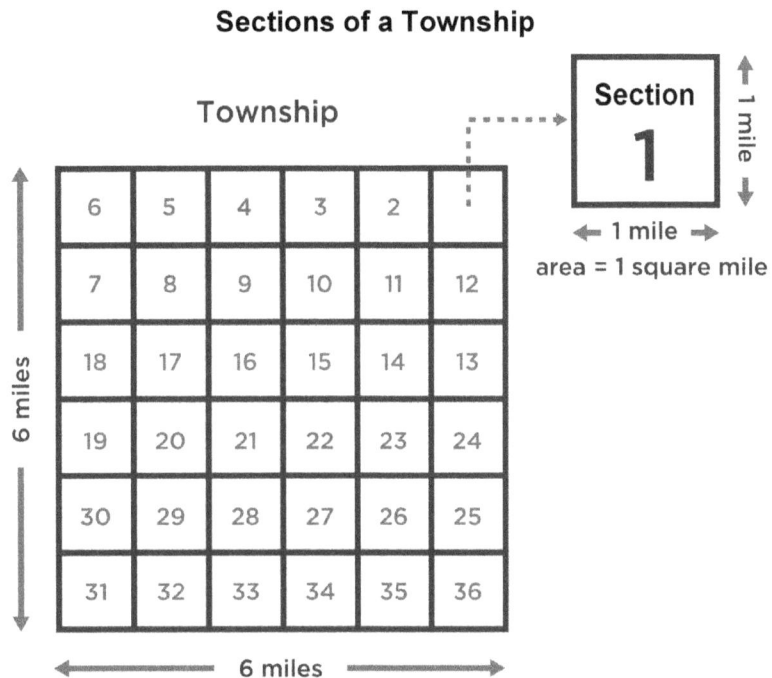

Sections of a Township

Township					
6	5	4	3	2	1
7	8	9	10	11	12
18	17	16	15	14	13
19	20	21	22	23	24
30	29	28	27	26	25
31	32	33	34	35	36

6 miles (vertical) — 6 miles (horizontal)

Section 1 — 1 mile × 1 mile, area = 1 square mile

Fractions of a section

A section of a township can be divided into fractions as the next exhibit shows.

Fractions of Sections and Acreage

1 section = 640 acres

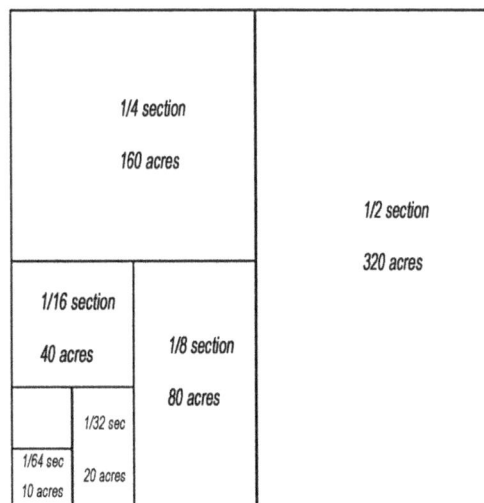

1/4 section — 160 acres

1/2 section — 320 acres

1/16 section — 40 acres

1/8 section — 80 acres

1/32 sec — 20 acres

1/64 sec — 10 acres

Describing a section fraction. A fraction of a section is legally described by indicating its size and location within successively larger quarters or halves of the section. In other words, the description proceeds from the smallest unit to the largest.

Describing Fractions of Sections

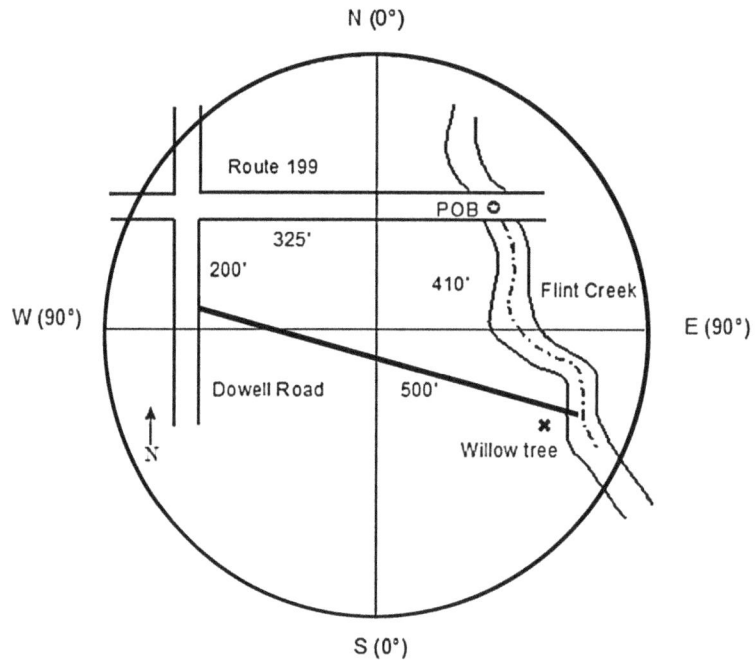

In the exhibit, the area marked "A" is one quarter of Section 8, located in the section's southeast corner. Its legal description first indicates its location (SE) in the next larger unit, in this case, the section. Second, the description states the fractional portion (1/4) of the next larger unit. Third, the description identifies the next larger unit, Section 8, and ends. Thus, the description is:

> The SE 1/4 of Section 8

The area marked "B" consists of the western half of the northwest quarter of the section. Its legal description is:

> The W 1/2 of the NW 1/4 of Section 8

Area C consists of the eastern half of the northeast quarter of the northeast quarter of the section. Its legal description is:

> The E 1/2 of the NE 1/4 of the NE 1/4 of Section 8

In sum, the method of describing a fraction of a section is:

> *(1)* Proceed *from* the smallest unit to the largest, ending with the section.

(2) First name the *location* of the unit within the next larger unit, then its fraction of the next larger unit.

(3) *Repeat* step (2) until you reach the section itself. Give the section number.

Converting section fractions to acres. The size in acres of a subsection of a township is a fraction of 640 acres, since there are 640 acres in a section.

For example, the SW 1/4 of a section is one quarter section. Thus, its acreage is one quarter of 640, or 160 acres. Going further, the E 1/2 of the SW 1/4 is one half of that one quarter, or 80 acres. The E 1/2 of the SW 1/4 of the SW ¼ is 20 acres.

A quick method of calculating the acreage of a parcel from its legal description is as follows:

(1) *Multiply the denominators* of the

$$\frac{640}{4} = 160 \; acres$$

(2) Divide 640 by the resulting numb

$$\frac{640}{(2x4)} = 80 \; acres$$

Applying this method to the foregoing descriptio

$$\frac{640}{(2x4x4)} = 20 \; acres$$

SW 1/4 of a section:

E 1/2 of the SW 1/4 of a section:

E 1/2 of the SW 1/4 of the SW 1/4 of a section:

LOT AND BLOCK (RECORDED PLAT) METHOD

Subdivision plat map
Description format

Subdivision plat map The recorded plat method, also called the **lot and block system**, is used to describe properties in residential, commercial, and industrial *subdivisions*.

Under this system, tracts of land are subdivided into lots. The entire group of lots comprises the subdivision. In a large subdivision, lots may be grouped together into **blocks** for ease of reference. The entire subdivision is surveyed to specify the size and location of each lot and block. The surveyor then incorporates the survey data into a **plat of survey**, or **subdivision plat map**, which must comply with local surveying standards and ordinances.

If local authorities accept it, the subdivision plat map is recorded in the county where the subdivision is located. The recorded lot and block numbers of a subdivision parcel, along with its section, township and meridian reference, become the property's legal description. The exhibit shows a sample subdivision plat map.

Subdivision Plat Map

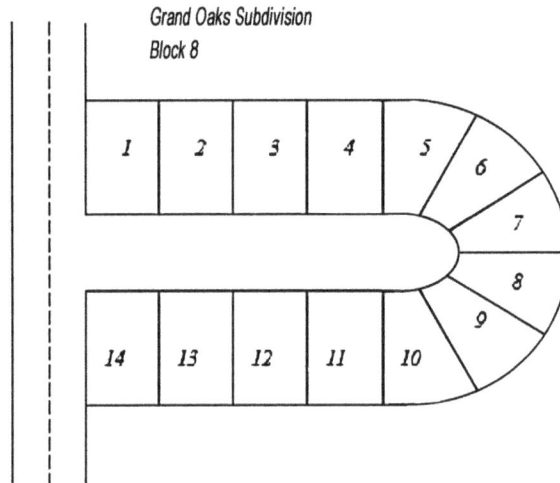

Grand Oaks Subdivision
Block 8

Description format   The description of a recorded plat property first presents the property's lot number or letter, then the block identifier and the subdivision name. Note that this is only a portion of the full legal description, which must describe the subdivision's location within a section, a township, a county, and a state. For example, if the subdivision in the exhibit is situated in the southeast quarter of Section 35 of Township T28S, R19E, of the Tallahassee Principal Meridian, the legal description of the lot marked "7" would be:

> "Lot 7, Block 8 of the Grand Oaks Subdivision of the SE 1/4 of Section 35, Township T28S, R19E of the Tallahassee Principal Meridian in Pinellas County, Florida."

DESCRIBING ELEVATION

To describe property located above or below the earth's surface, such as the air rights of a condominium, a surveyor must know the property's elevation. Standard elevation reference points, called **datums**, have been established throughout the country. The original datum was defined by the U.S. Geological Survey as mean sea level at New York harbor. A surveyor uses a datum as an official elevation point to describe the height or depth of a property. If, for example, the datum for an area is a point 100 feet above sea level, all surveys in the area will indicate elevation as a distance above or below 100 feet above sea level.

In many cases it is impractical for a surveyor to rely on a single datum for an entire surveying area. To simplify matters, surveyors have identified local elevation markers, called **benchmarks,** to provide reference elevations for nearby properties. Once a benchmark is registered, it provides a valid reference point for surveying other elevations in the immediate area.

ASSESSOR'S PARCEL NUMBER

Uses of the parcel number
Tax maps
Recorded plat maps
Assessment roll

Uses of the parcel number

County tax assessors in Florida assign an Assessor's Parcel Number (APN) to parcels of land in their counties. The number is used to identify property identification and track ownership for property tax purposes. Each county or jurisdiction has its own APN formatting codes, depending on the property location. The number may include such information as the type of property type and location within a plat map. The APN is also used in the preparation of tax maps. Property owners can find their APN on the annual tax bill, on property ownership documents, and at their local tax assessor's office.

Tax maps

A tax map is a special purpose map, drawn to scale and showing all of the land parcels within a city, town, or village. Tax maps are used to locate parcels and provide information needed for property assessment. The map for a parcel includes the parcel's size, shape, dimensions, and acreage. The assessor can use the tax map to record and analyze property transfers and to record features that impact the property's valuation, thereby using the map in the property assessment for tax collection and in the preparation of an assessment roll. The map is also used in the development of a Geographic Information System (GIS).

Recorded plat maps

Plat maps show property boundaries and include the property owner's name, mailing address, sales data, valuations, building information, and site address. Recorded plat maps contribute to the generating of the tax maps needed to create assessment rolls. Florida counties each elect a property appraiser to assess the property within the county for taxation.

Assessment roll

An assessment roll is a record of each parcel of land in a taxing jurisdiction. It is prepared by the tax assessor with the aid of the tax map and is certified to the tax collector. The roll is used in determining property taxes. It is updated annually and reviewed by the Florida Department of Revenue to ensure the established tax base is equitable, uniform, and in compliance with Florida law. The roll includes the following:

▶ a list of every land parcel in the county by parcel number

> ▶ the property owners' names and addresses of record
>
> ▶ the assessed value of the land and any structures

PREPARATION AND USE OF SURVEYS

Mechanics
Applications

Mechanics

Surveying is the technique and science of determining three-dimensional positions of points on the Earth's surface and the distances and angles between the points. Surveyors must comply with state-required reporting formats and individual elements. Florida statutes establish minimum standards for surveys, and professional surveyors find that American Land Title Association (ALTA) surveys not only meet those standards by showing correct boundary lines and all structures existing on the property, but do so in great detail.

To perform a survey, the surveyor visits the property and records all applicable information, such as improvements on the land. In addition to reviewing records and plats on file at the county recorder's office, the surveyor makes an independent determination about the land and its boundaries by using Global Positioning Systems (GPS),Computer Aided Drafting (CAD), Robotic Survey Systems (RSS), and Laser Scanning. The surveyor then prepares related reports, maps, and plots for clients and government agencies as needed.

Applications

Surveys provide data for engineering industries, construction projects, and map making. Among other uses, they are used to

> ▶ define legally recognized property boundaries and resolve property line disputes, as well as prepare for improvements that may be close to a neighboring property's boundary line
>
> ▶ verify the descriptions and locations of improvements on the land, such as buildings, fencing, and driveways, and the distance between improvements and boundary lines
>
> ▶ identify discrepancies between recorded instruments and the ground itself
>
> ▶ identify elevations on the land; Florida government agencies, including city building departments, often require a specific survey before granting building permits and allowing construction to begin
>
> ▶ verify that certain features, such as a creek or tree, are within the property's boundaries
>
> ▶ locate all utilities on the property, including underground drains, sewer systems, power cables, and above-ground utility poles and wiring; Florida has specific requirements for the placement of residential utilities because of the state's unique environmental characteristics.
>
> ▶ locate obvious and hidden easements and paths of access to the easements

- locate boundary line encroachments and rights of way
- identify setback requirements
- identify specific zoning, such as a flood zone

10 Legal Description Snapshot Review

PURPOSES AND METHODS OF LEGAL DESCRIPTION

Definition and uses
- legal description is sufficiently accurate, acceptable in court of law
- facilitates transfers; avoids disputes; used in legal contracts

Methods
- metes and bounds; rectangular survey system or government survey; recorded plat or lot and block

METES AND BOUNDS METHOD
- describes property perimeter by landmarks, monuments, distances, angles
- from point of beginning (POB), describes perimeter and returns to POB; usable within rectangular survey system

GOVERNMENT (RECTANGULAR) SURVEY SYSTEM

The survey grid
- meridians: north-south lines six miles apart
- parallels: east-west lines six miles apart
- correction lines – adjusted lines that restore guide meridians to original spacing to maintain a rectangular survey pattern on earth's curvature
- ranges: north-south strips of area between meridians; tiers: east-west strips of area between parallels; townships: the area representing the intersection of a range and a tier, consisting of six-mile by six-mile squares of land

Sections of a township
- 36 sections per township, each one-mile square (1 mile on each side)

Fractions of a section
- 1 section = 640 acres; fractions of sections described by size and location within progressively larger quarters of section
- converting section fractions to acres: multiply denominators of section fractions; divide product into 640

LOT AND BLOCK (RECORDED PLAT) METHOD
- or lot and block system; used in surveyed subdivisions

Subdivision plat map
- surveyed plat of subdivided tract; legal descriptor if approved and recorded

Description format
- lots within subdivision are identified by lot reference and block reference: "Lot 7 Block B of the Grand Oaks Subdivision"

DESCRIBING ELEVATION
- datum: a standard elevation reference point; benchmark: elevation marker officially surveyed and registered

ASSESSOR'S PARCEL NUMBER

Uses of the parcel number
- assigned to parcels of land to identify property and ownership for taxing and tax maps
- used to locate parcels and include parcel's size, shape, dimensions, and acreage

Tax maps
- used to assess property valuation for tax collection and assessment roll

Recorded plat maps	•	plat maps show boundaries and include owner's name, mailing address, sales date, valuations, building information, and site address
	•	used to generate tax maps to create assessment rolls
Assessment roll	•	record of each land parcel in a taxing jurisdiction to determine property taxes
	•	updated annually

PREPARATION & USE OF SURVEYS

Mechanics	•	surveyor to comply with state reporting format and required individual elements
	•	surveyor visits property and records necessary information; also reviews records and plats filed with the county recorder's office
Applications	•	construction projects, map making, and engineering industries
	•	define boundaries, locate improvements, identify discrepancies between recorded instruments and actual ground; identify elevations and features; locate utilities, easements, encroachments; identify setback requirements and flood zones

SECTION TEN: Legal Description

Section Quiz

1. What is the principal purpose underlying legal descriptions of real property?

   a. To create a consistent, unchanging standard for locating the property.
   b. To eliminate all possible boundary disputes.
   c. To comply with federal laws.
   d. To eliminate cumbersome metes and bounds descriptions.

2. Which of the following is a distinctive feature of metes and bounds descriptions?

   a. They use meridians and base lines.
   b. They identify an enclosed area, beginning and ending at the same point.
   c. They use lot and block numbers.as the street address.
   d. They incorporate elevation into the descriptions.

3. A certain legal description contains the phrase "...southeasterly along Happ Road to the stone landmark..." What kind of description is this?

   a. Plat survey plat of survey is
   b. Government grid
   c. Metes and bounds
   d. Rectangular survey

4. The abbreviation POB stands for

   a. perimeter of boundaries.
   b. point of beginning.
   c. point of bounds.
   d. plat of boundary.

5. What are the approximate dimensions of a township in the rectangular survey system?

   a. Thirty-six miles on a side
   b. Twenty-five square miles.
   c. Depends on the state.
   d. Six miles by six miles

6. The area running north and south between meridians is a

   a. range.
   b. township.
   c. strip.
   d. tier.

7. The area running east and west between base lines is a

   a. range.
   b. tier.
   c. parameter.
   d. parallel.

8. How many sections are there in a township?

   a. One
   b. Six
   c. Twelve
   d. Thirty-six

9. A section contains how many acres?

   a. 640
   b. 320
   c. 160
   d. 40

10. How many acres are there in the S 1/2 of the NW ¼ of Section 3?

   a. 20 acres
   b. 40 acres
   c. 80 acres
   d. 160 acres

11. If a parcel does not have a lot and block number and is too irregular to be described as a fraction of a section, the legal description

   a. is the street address.
   b. will include a metes and bounds description.
   c. will use an estimate of the sectional fraction.
   d. will create a special reference number.

12. The legal description of a parcel in a subdivision that has been recorded with lot and block numbers on a plat of survey is

   a. the lot and block number, with section, township and meridian references.
   b. the standard rectangular survey description.
   c. the subdivision plat map.
   d. the lot and block number.

13. A datum is a reference point used for legal descriptions of

   a. agricultural and ranch properties.
   b. properties that straddle state boundaries.
   c. properties located above or below the earth's surface.
   d. irregularly-shaped properties.

14. What is the purpose of correction lines in surveys?

    a. To fix errors that naturally occur during any survey
    b. To allow true meridians to converge to one common point
    c. To maintain a rectangle survey pattern on the earth's curvature
    d. To restore east-west section lines to their original spacing

15. An assessment roll includes

    a. special features on the property.
    b. the property's value.
    c. sales data.
    d. the property's site address.

16. Which of the following statements is false?

    a. When preparing for a survey, the surveyor must comply with the state reporting formats.
    b. Surveyors must comply with Florida minimum standards for surveys.
    c. Surveys are used in creating maps for tax purposes.
    d. Surveyors rely strictly on records and plats filed with the county recorder's office.

11 Real Estate Contracts

Contract Essentials
Classifications of Contracts
Contract Creation
Contract Termination
Employment (Listing) Agreements
Sales Contracts
Option Contracts
Installment Sales Contracts

Learning Objectives

- List and describe the essentials of a contract
- Distinguish among formal, parol, bilateral, unilateral, implied, express, executory and executed contracts
- Describe the various ways in which an offer is terminated
- Describe the various methods of terminating a contract
- Explain the remedies for breach of a contract
- Describe the effect of the Statute of Frauds and the Statute of Limitations
- Describe the elements of an option
- Differentiate among the various types of listings
- Explain and describe the various disclosures required in a real estate contract
- Recognize what constitutes fraud
- Recognize what constitutes culpable negligence

Key Terms

assignment
attorney-in-fact
bilateral contract
competent
contract
exclusive-agency listing
exclusive-right-of-sale listing
fraud
liquidated damages
meeting of the minds
net listing

novation
open listing
option contract
Statute of Frauds
Statute of Limitations
unenforceable
unilateral contract
valid contract
void contract
voidable contract

CONTRACT ESSENTIALS

Definition of a contract
Preparation of contracts
Legal status of contracts
Criteria for validity
Validity of a conveyance contract
Enforcement limitations
UETA & electronic contracting

Definition of a contract

A **contract** is an agreement between two or more parties who, in a "meeting of the minds," have pledged to perform or refrain from performing some act. A *valid* contract is one that is *legally enforceable* by virtue of meeting certain requirements of contract law. If a contract does not meet the requirements, it is not valid and the parties to it cannot resort to a court of law to enforce its provisions.

Note that a contract is not a legal form or a prescribed set of words in a document, but rather the intangible agreement that was made in "the meeting of the minds" of the parties to the contract.

Real estate contracts are the legal agreements that underlie the transfer and financing of real estate, as well as the real estate brokerage business. Sale and lease contracts and option agreements are used to transfer real estate interests from one party to another. Mortgage contracts and promissory agreements are part of financing real estate. Listing and representation contracts establish client relationships and provide for compensation.

In order to work with real estate contracts, it is imperative first to grasp basic concepts that apply to all contracts in general. These concepts provide a foundation for understanding the specifics of particular types of real estate contract.

Preparation of contracts

The preparation of contracts and other legal instruments is the practice of law and the exclusive business of attorneys. Real estate licensees, unless they are also attorneys, can lose their licenses for preparing such documents. The offense is known as the unauthorized practice of law.

The authority of real estate licensees to prepare contracts. Because real estate licensees must work with such contracts as listing agreements, buyer brokerage agreements, sale and purchase contracts, and option contracts as part of their normal course of business, they have received special dispensations to assist buyers and sellers with the drawing of these contracts to the extent that they may fill in the blanks on standardized forms prepared by attorneys.

Legal status of contracts

In terms of validity and enforceability, a court may construe the legal status of a contract in one of four ways:

- valid
- valid but unenforceable
- void
- voidable

Valid. A valid contract is one which meets the legal requirements for validity. These requirements are explained in the next section.

A valid contract that is in writing is enforceable within a statutory time period. A valid contract that is made orally is also generally enforceable within a statutory period, with the exceptions noted below.

Valid but unenforceable. State laws declare that some contracts are enforceable only if they are in writing. These laws apply in particular to the transfer of interests in real estate. Thus, while an oral contract may meet the tests for validity, if it falls under the laws requiring a written contract, the parties will not have legal recourse to enforce performance. An oral long-term lease and an oral real estate sales contract are examples of contracts that may be valid but not enforceable.

Note that such contracts, if valid, remain so even though not enforceable. This means that if the parties fully execute and perform the contract, the outcome may not be altered.

Void. A void contract is an agreement that does not meet the tests for validity, and therefore is no contract at all. If a contract is void, neither party can enforce it.

For example, a contract that does not include consideration is void. Likewise, a contract to extort money from a business is void. Void contracts and instruments are also described as "null and void."

Voidable. A voidable contract is one which initially appears to be valid, but is subject to rescission by a party to the contract who is deemed to have acted under some kind of disability. Only the party who claims the disability may rescind the legal effect of the contract.

For example, a party who was the victim of duress, coercion, or fraud in creation of a contract, and can prove it, may disaffirm the contract. However, the disaffirmation must occur within a legal time frame for the act of rescission to be valid. Similarly, if the party who has cause to disaffirm the contract elects instead to perform it, the contract is no longer voidable but valid.

A voidable contract differs from a void contract in that the latter does not require an act of disaffirmation to render it unenforceable.

Criteria for validity   A contract is valid only if it meets all of the following criteria.

Contract Validity Requirements

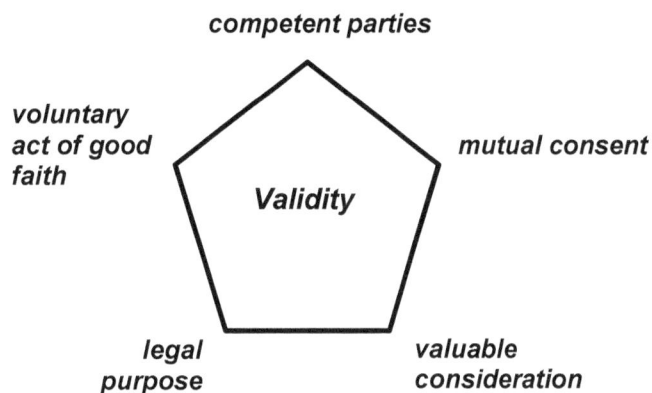

competent parties

voluntary
act of good
faith

Validity

mutual consent

legal
purpose

valuable
consideration

Competent parties. The parties to a contract must have the capacity to contract, and there must be at least two such parties. Thus, the owner of a tenancy for life cannot deed his interest to himself in the form of a fee simple, as this would involve only one party. Capacity to contract is determined by three factors:

> ▶   legal age
> ▶   mental competency
> ▶   legitimate authority

In Florida, a minor may contract, but the contract will be voidable and the minor can disaffirm the contract.

To be mentally competent, a party must have sufficient understanding of the import and consequences of a contract. Competency in this context is separate and distinct from sanity. Incompetent parties, or parties of "unsound mind," may not enter into enforceable contracts. The incompetency of a party may be ruled by a court of law or by other means. In some areas, convicted felons may be deemed incompetent, depending on the nature of the crime.

During the period of one's incompetency, a court may appoint a guardian who may act on the incompetent party's behalf with court approval.

If the contracting party is representing another person or business entity, the representative must have the *legal authority* to contract. If representing another person, the party must have a bona fide power of attorney. If the contracting party is representing a corporation, the person must have the appropriate power and approval to act, such as would be conferred in a duly executed resolution of the Board of Directors. If the contracting entity is a general partnership, any partner may validly contract for the partnership. In a limited partnership, only general partners may be parties to a contract.

Mutual consent. Mutual consent, also known as *offer and acceptance* and *meeting of the minds,* requires that a contract involve a clear and definite offer and an intentional, unqualified acceptance of the offer. In effect, the parties must agree to the terms without equivocation. A court may nullify a contract where the acceptance of terms by either party was partial, accidental, or vague.

Valuable consideration. A contract must contain a two-way exchange of valuable consideration as compensation for performance by the other party. The exchange of considerations must be two-way. The contract is not valid or enforceable if just one party provides consideration.

Valuable consideration can be something of tangible value, such as money or something a party promises to do or not do. For example, a home builder may promise to build a house for a party as consideration for receiving money from the home buyer. Or, a landowner may agree not to sell a property as consideration for a developer's option money. Also, valuable consideration can be something intangible that a party must give up, such as a homeowner's occupancy of the house in exchange for rent. In effect, consideration is the price one party must pay to obtain performance from the other party.

Valuable consideration may be contrasted with good consideration, or "love and affection," which does not qualify as consideration in a valid contract. Good consideration is something of questionable value, such as a child's love for her mother. Good consideration disqualifies a contract because, while one's love or affection is certainly valuable to the other party, it is not something that is specifically offered in exchange for something else. Good consideration can, however, serve as a nominal consideration in transferring a real property interest as a gift.

In some cases, what is promised as valuable consideration must also be deemed to be *sufficient* consideration. Grossly insufficient consideration, such as $50,000 for a $2 million property, may invalidate a contract on the grounds that the agreement is a gift rather than a contract. In other cases where there is an extreme imbalance in the considerations exchanged, a contract may be invalidated as a violation of good faith bargaining.

Consideration

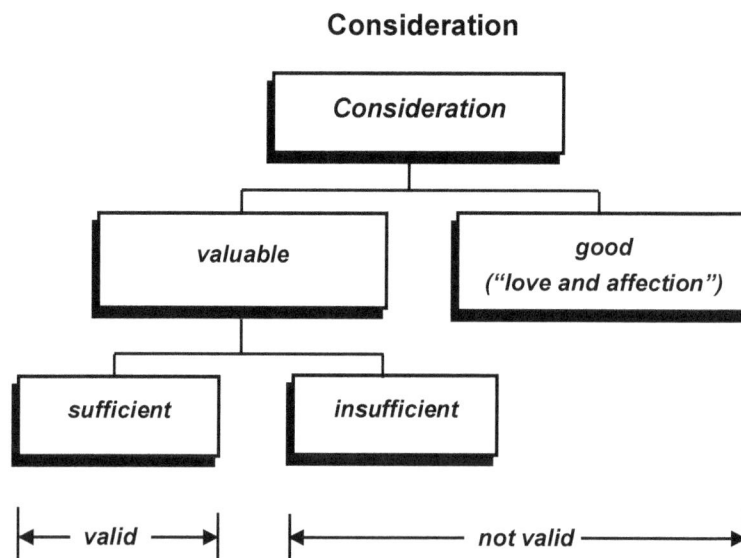

Legal purpose. The content, promise, or intent of a contract must be lawful. A contract that proposes an illegal act is void.

Voluntary, good faith act. The parties must create the contract in good faith as a free and voluntary act. A contract is thus voidable if one party acted under duress, coercion, fraud, or misrepresentation.

For example, if a property seller induces a buyer to purchase a house based on assurances that the roof is new, the buyer may rescind the agreement if the roof turns out to be twenty years old and leaky.

Validity of a conveyance contract

In addition to satisfying the foregoing requirements, a contract that conveys an interest in real estate must:

▶ be in writing
▶ contain a legal description of the property
▶ be signed by one or more of the parties

A lease contract that has a term of one year or less is an exception. Such leases do not have to be in writing to be enforceable.

Enforcement limitations

Certain contracts that fail to meet the validity requirements are voidable if a damaged party takes appropriate action. The enforcement of voidable contracts, however, is limited by **statutes of limitation.** Certain other contracts which are valid may not be enforceable due to the **statute of frauds**.

Statute of limitations. The statute of limitations restricts the time period for which an injured party in a contract has the right to rescind or disaffirm the contract. A party to a voidable contract must act within the statutory period.

Statute of frauds. The statute of frauds requires that certain contracts *must be in writing* to be enforceable. Real estate contracts that convey an interest in real property fall in this category, with the exception that a lease of one year's duration or less may be oral. All other contracts to buy, sell, exchange, or lease interests in real property must be in writing to be enforceable. In addition, *listing agreements* for a term longer than one year must be in writing.

The statute of frauds concerns the enforceability of a contract, not its validity. Once the parties to a valid oral contract have executed and performed it, even if the contract was unenforceable, a party cannot use the Statute of Frauds to rescind the contract.

For example, a broker and a seller have an oral agreement. Following the terms of the agreement, the broker finds a buyer, and the seller pays the commission. They have now executed the contract, and the seller cannot later force the broker to return the commission based on the statute of frauds.

UETA & electronic contracting

Contracting electronically through email and fax greatly facilitates the completion of transactions. Clients, lenders, title agents, inspectors, brokers, and other participants in a transaction can quickly share documentation and information. Electronic contracting is made possible by the Uniform Electronic Transactions Act (UETA) and the Electronic Signatures in Global and National Commerce Act (E-Sign), which are federal laws. UETA, which has been incorporated into Florida law, provides that electronic records and signatures are legal and must be accepted. E-Sign makes contracts, records, and signatures legally enforceable, regardless of medium, even where UETA is not accepted.

CLASSIFICATIONS OF CONTRACTS

Oral vs. written
Express vs. implied
Unilateral vs. bilateral
Executed vs. executory

Oral vs. written

A contract may be in writing or it may be an oral, or **parol**, contract. Certain oral contracts are valid and enforceable, others are not enforceable, even if valid. For example, Florida requires listing agreements of terms longer than one year, sales contracts, option contracts, deeds and mortgage instruments, and leases exceeding one year to be in writing to be enforceable.

Express vs. implied

An **express contract** is one in which all the terms and covenants of the agreement have been manifestly stated and agreed to by all parties, whether verbally or in writing.

An **implied contract** is an unstated or unintentional agreement that may be deemed to exist when the *actions of any of the parties* suggest the existence of an agreement.

A common example of an implied contract is an implied agency agreement. In implied agency, an agent who does not have a contract with a buyer performs acts on the buyer's behalf, such as negotiating a price that is less than the listing price. In so doing, the agent has possibly created an implied contract with the buyer, albeit unintended. If the buyer compensates the agent for the negotiating efforts, the existence of an implied agency agreement becomes even less disputable.

Bilateral vs. unilateral

A **bilateral contract** is one in which both parties promise to perform their respective parts of an agreement in exchange for performance by the other party.

An example of a bilateral contract is an exclusive listing: the broker promises to exercise due diligence in the efforts to sell a property, and the seller promises to compensate the broker when and if the property sells.

In a **unilateral contract**, only one party promises to do something, provided the other party does something. The latter party is not obligated to perform any act, but the promising party must fulfill the promise if the other party chooses to perform.

An option is an example of a unilateral contract: in an option-to-buy, the party offering the option (optionor) promises to sell a property if the optionee decides to exercise the option. While the potential buyer does not have to buy, the owner must sell if the option is exercised.

Executed vs. executory

An **executed contract** is one that has been fully performed and fulfilled: neither party bears any further obligation. A completed and expired lease contract is an executed contract: the landlord may re-possess the premises and the tenant has no further obligation to pay rent.

An **executory contract** is one in which performance is yet to be completed. A sales contract prior to closing is executory: while the parties have agreed to buy and sell, the buyer has yet to pay the seller and the seller has yet to deed the property to the buyer.

CONTRACT CREATION

Offer and acceptance
Counteroffer
Revocation of an offer
Termination of an offer
Assignment of a contract
Contract preparation

Offer and acceptance The mutual consent required for a valid contract is reached through the process of offer and acceptance: The **offeror** proposes contract terms in an **offer** to the **offeree**. If the offeree accepts all terms without amendment, the offer becomes a contract. The exact point at which the offer becomes a contract is when the offeree gives the offeror notice of the acceptance.

Offer, Counteroffer and Acceptance

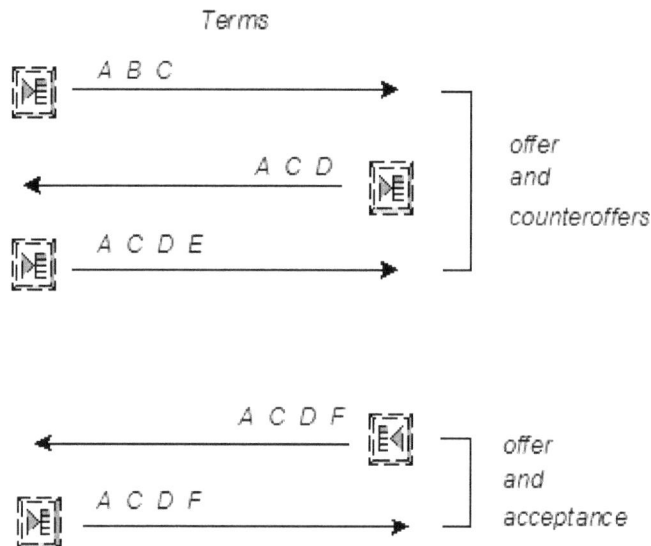

Terms

A B C →   ← A C D   A C D E →

offer
and
counteroffers

← A C D F   A C D F →

offer
and
acceptance

Offer. An offer expresses the offeror's intention to enter into a contract with an offeree to perform the terms of the agreement in exchange for the offeree's performance. In a real estate sale or lease contract, the offer must clearly contain all intended terms of the contract in writing and be communicated to the offeree.

If an offer contains an expiration date and the phrase "time is of the essence," the offer expires at exactly the time specified. In the absence of a stated time period, the offeree has a "reasonable" time to accept an offer.

Acceptance. An offer gives the offeree the power of accepting. For an acceptance to be valid, the offeree must manifestly and unequivocally accept all terms of the offer without change, and so indicate by signing the offer, preferably with a date of signing. The acceptance must then be communicated to the offeror. If the communication of acceptance is by mail, the offer is considered to be communicated as soon as it is placed in the mail.

Counteroffer

By changing any of the terms of an offer, the offeree creates a counteroffer, and the original offer is void. At this point, the offeree becomes the offeror, and the new offeree gains the right of acceptance. If accepted, the counteroffer becomes a valid contract provided all other requirements are met.

For example, a seller changes the expiration date of a buyer's offer by one day, signs the offer and returns it to the buyer. The single amendment extinguishes the buyer's offer, and the buyer is no longer bound by any agreement. The seller's amended offer is a counteroffer which now gives the buyer the right of acceptance. If the buyer accepts the counteroffer, the counteroffer becomes a binding contract.

Revocation of an offer

An offer may be revoked, or withdrawn, at any time before the offeree has communicated acceptance. The revocation extinguishes the offer and the offeree's right to accept it.

For example, a buyer has offered to purchase a house for the listed price. Three hours later, a family death radically changes the buyer's plans. She immediately calls the seller and revokes the offer, stating she is no longer interested in the house. Since the seller had not communicated acceptance of the offer to the buyer, the offer is legally cancelled.

If the offeree has paid consideration to the offeror to leave an offer open, and the offeror accepts, an option has been created which cancels the offeror's right to revoke the offer over the period of the option.

Termination of an offer

Any of the following actions or circumstances can terminate an offer:

- ▸ acceptance: the offeree accepts the offer, converting it to a contract
- ▸ rejection: the offeree rejects the offer
- ▸ revocation: the offeror withdraws the offer before acceptance
- ▸ lapse of time: the offer expires
- ▸ counteroffer: the offeree changes the offer
- ▸ death or insanity of either party

Assignment of a contract

A real estate contract that is not a personal contract for services can be assigned to another party unless the terms of the agreement specifically prohibit assignment.

Listing agreements, for example, are not assignable, since they are personal service agreements between agent and principal. Sales contracts, however, are assignable, because they involve the purchase of real property rather than a personal service.

Contract preparation

Remember, brokers and associates may not draft contracts, but they may use standard promulgated forms and complete the blanks in the form.

As a rule, a broker or associate who completes real estate contracts is engaging in the unauthorized practice of law unless the broker is a party to the agreement, such as a in a listing agreement or sales contract. Brokers and associates may not complete leases, mortgages, contracts for deed, or promissory notes to which they are not a party.

Licensees must be fully aware of what they are legally allowed to do and not do in preparing and interpreting contracts for clients. In addition to practicing law without a license, they expose themselves to lawsuits from clients who relied on a contract as being legally acceptable.

CONTRACT TERMINATION
Forms of contract termination
Breach of contract

Forms of contract termination

Termination of a contract, also called **cancellation** and **discharge**, may occur for any of the following causes.

Performance. A contract terminates when fully performed by the parties. It may also terminate for:

- partial performance, if the parties agree
- sufficient performance, if a court determines a party has sufficiently performed the contract, even though not to the full extent of every provision

Infeasibility. An otherwise valid contract can be canceled if it is not possible to perform. Certain personal services contracts, for example, depend on the unique capabilities of one person which cannot be substituted by someone else. If such a person dies or is sufficiently disabled, the contract is cancelable.

Mutual agreement. Parties to a contract can agree to terminate, or renounce, the contract. If the parties wish to create a new contract to replace the cancelled contract, they must comply with the validity requirements for the new contract. Such substitution is called **novation**.

Cooling-period rescission. Rescission is the act of nullifying a contract. In Florida, parties to certain contracts are allowed a statutory amount of time (usually three days) after entering into a contract, or "cooling period", to rescind the contract without cause. No reason need be stated for the cancellation, and the cancelling party incurs no liability for performance.

For example, consider the unsuspecting buyer of a lot in a new resort development. Such buyers are often the targets of hard-sell tactics which lead to a completed sales contract and a deposit. The statutory cooling period gives the buyer an opportunity to reconsider the investment in the absence of the persistent salesperson.

Revocation. Revocation is cancellation of the contract by one party without the consent of the other. For example, a seller may revoke a listing to take the property off the market. While all parties have the *power* to revoke, they may not have a defensible *right*. In the absence of justifiable grounds, a revocation may not relieve the revoking party of contract obligations.

For example, a seller who revokes a listing without grounds may be required to pay a commission if the broker found a buyer, or reimburse the broker's marketing expenses if no buyer was found.

Abandonment. Abandonment occurs when parties fail to perform contract obligations. This situation may allow the parties to cancel the contract.

Lapse of time. If a contract contains an expiration provision and date, the contract automatically expires on the deadline.

Invalidity of contract. If a contract is void, it terminates without the need for disaffirmation. A voidable contract can be cancelled by operation of law or by rescission.

Breach of contract

A breach of contract is a failure to perform according to the terms of the agreement. Also called **default**, a breach of contract gives the damaged party the right to take legal action.

The damaged party may elect the following legal remedies:

> ▸ rescission
> ▸ forfeiture
> ▸ suit for damages
> ▸ suit for specific performance

Rescission. A damaged party may rescind the contract. This cancels the contract and returns the parties to their pre-contract condition, including the refunding of any monies already transferred.

Forfeiture. A forfeiture requires the breaching party to give up something, according to the terms of the contract. For example, a buyer who defaults on a sales contract may have to forfeit the earnest money deposit.

Suit for damages. A damaged party may sue for money damages in civil court. The suit must be initiated within the time period allowed by the statute of limitations. When a contract states the total amount due to a damaged party in the event of a breach, the compensation is known as **liquidated damages**. If the contract does not specify the amount, the damaged party may sue in court for **unliquidated damages**.

Suit for specific performance. A suit for specific performance is an attempt to force the defaulting party to comply with the terms of the contract. Specific performance suits occur when it is difficult to identify damages because of the unique circumstances of the real property in question. The most common instance is a defaulted sale or lease contract where the buyer or seller wants the court to compel the defaulting party to go through with the transaction, even when the defaulter would prefer to pay a damage award.

EMPLOYMENT (LISTING) AGREEMENTS

Foundations in agency law
Types of listing agreements
Exclusive right to sell listing clauses
Exclusive buyer agency clauses

Foundations in agency law

A listing agreement, the document that puts an agent or broker in business, is a legally enforceable real estate agency agreement between a real estate broker and a client, authorizing the broker to perform a stated service for compensation. The unique characteristic of a listing agreement is that it is governed both by agency law and by contract law.

The cornerstones of agency law in the context of a listing agreement are:

▸ definition of the roles of parties involved
▸ fiduciary duties of the agent
▸ agent's scope of authority

Parties. The principal parties to the contract are the **listing broker** and the **client**. The client may be buyer, seller, landlord or tenant in the proposed transaction. Legally, the broker is the client's **agent**. The principal party on the other side of the transaction is a **customer** or a potential customer, called a **prospect**. A broker or associate who assists the listing broker in finding a customer is an **agent** of the listing broker and a **subagent** of the client. A broker who represents the party on the other side of the transaction is an agent of that party, and not an agent of the listing broker.

Fiduciary duties. A listing agreement establishes an agency relationship between agent and client that commits the agent to the full complement of fiduciary duties to the client in fulfilling the agreement.

Scope of authority. Customarily, a listing is a *special agency,* or *limited agency,* agreement. Special agency *limits* the scope of the broker's authority to specific activities, generally those which generate customers and catalyze the transaction. A special agency agreement usually *does not* authorize a broker to obligate the client to a contract as a principal party, unless the agreement expressly grants such authorization or the client has granted power of attorney to the broker. For example, a listing broker may not tell a buyer that the seller will accept an offer regardless of its terms. Telling the offeror that the offer *is* accepted would be an even more serious breach of the agreement.

Under agency law, a client is liable for actions the broker performs that are within the scope of authority granted by the listing agreement. A client is *not liable* for acts of the broker which go beyond the stated or implied scope of authority.

Thus, in the previous example, the seller would not be liable for the broker's statements that the offer would be accepted or was accepted, since the broker did not have the authority to make such statements. A broker who exceeds the scope of authority in the listing agreement risks forfeiting compensation and perhaps even greater liabilities.

Types of listing agreements

A broker may represent any principal party of a transaction: seller, landlord, buyer, tenant. An **owner listing** authorizes a broker to represent an owner or landlord. There are three main types of owner listing agreement: *exclusive right-to-sell (or lease)*; *exclusive agency*; and *open listing*. Another type of listing, rarely used today but legal in Florida, is a *net listing*. The first three forms differ in their statement of conditions under which the broker will be paid. The net listing is a variation on how much the broker will be paid. A listing contract in Florida may be written, oral, or implied. If the term is longer than one year, it must be written.

Exclusive-right-to-sell (or -lease). The exclusive right-to-sell, also called exclusive authorization-to-sell and, simply, the exclusive, is the most widely used owner agreement. Under the terms of this listing, a seller contracts exclusively with a single broker to procure a buyer or effect a sale transaction. If a buyer is procured during the listing period, the broker is entitled to a commission, *regardless of who is procuring cause*. Thus, if anyone-the owner, another broker-- sells the property, the owner must pay the listing broker the contracted commission.

The exclusive right-to-lease is a similar contract for a leasing transaction. Under the terms of this listing, the owner or landlord must pay the listing broker a commission if anyone procures a tenant for the named premises.

The exclusive listing gives the listing broker the greatest assurance of receiving compensation for marketing efforts.

An exclusive right-to-sell listing must have an expiration date if it is in writing.

Exclusive agency. An exclusive agency listing authorizes a single broker to sell the property and earn a commission, but *leaves the owner the right to sell the property without the broker's assistance*, in which case no commission is owed. Thus, if any party other than the owner is procuring cause in a completed sale of the property, including another broker, the contracted broker has earned the commission. This arrangement may also be used in a leasing transaction: if any party other than the owner procures the tenant, the owner must compensate the listing broker.

A written exclusive agency listing must have an expiration date.

Open listing. An open listing, or, simply, open, is a *non-exclusive* authorization to sell or lease a property. The owner may offer such agreements to any number of brokers in the marketplace. With an open listing, the broker who is the first to perform under the terms of the listing is the sole party entitled to a commission. Performance usually consists of being the procuring cause in the finding of a ready, willing, and able customer. If the transaction occurs without a procuring broker, no commissions are payable.

Open listings are rare in residential brokerage. Brokers generally shy away from them because they offer no assurance of compensation for marketing efforts. In addition, open listings cause commission disputes. To avoid such disputes, a broker has to register prospects with the owner to provide evidence of procuring cause in case a transaction results.

A **buyer agency** or **tenant representation agreement** authorizes a broker to represent a buyer or tenant. The most commonly used form is an *exclusive right-to-represent* agreement, the equivalent of an exclusive right-to-sell. However, exclusive agency and open types of agreement may be also used to secure a relationship on this side of a transaction.

Buyer and tenant agency agreements create a fiduciary relationship with the buyer or tenant just as seller listings create a fiduciary relationship with the seller. Generally, buyer and tenant representation agreements are subject to the same laws and regulations as those applying to owner listings. Thus:

▸ a representation agreement may be an exclusive, exclusive agency, or open listing. As with owner listings, the most widely used agreement is the exclusive. In this arrangement, the buyer agrees to only work with the buyer representative in procuring a property.

At the formation of the relationship, the buyer agent has the duty to explain how buyer or tenant agency relationships work. This is culminated by a signed agreement where the principal understands and accepts these circumstances. During the listing term, the buyer or tenant agent's principal duties are to diligently locate a property that meets the principal's requirements.

Net listing. A net listing is one in which an owner sets a minimum acceptable amount to be received from the transaction and allows the broker to have any amount received in excess as a commission, assuming the broker has earned a commission according to the other terms of the agreement. The owner's "net" may or may not account for closing costs.

For example, a seller requires $75,000 for a property. A broker sells the property for $83,000 and receives the difference, $8,000, as commission.

Net listings are generally regarded as unprofessional today. The argument against the net listing is that it creates a conflict of interest for the broker. It is in the broker's interest to encourage the owner to put the lowest possible acceptable price in the listing, regardless of market value. Thus, the agent violates fiduciary duty by failing to place the client's interests above those of the agent.

Net listings are legal in Florida as long as the broker does not misrepresent the value of the property to the seller to the broker's advantage. For example, if a property's likely market value is $300,000, it would be a violation for a broker to lead the seller to believe the value is $275,000 for the purpose of retaining any selling amount over $275,000 instead of any selling amount over $300,000. To prevent this misrepresentation, the seller and the broker work together to determine a listing price. Then the broker retains any selling amount above the agreed-upon listing price minus any costs.

Types of Listing

Exclusive Right	$ ➡ Broker	**IF customer is procured**
Exclusive Agency	$ ➡ Broker	**IF customer is procured and client does not procure**
Open	$ ➡ Broker	**IF broker procures customer**
Net	$ ➡ Broker	**IF customer is due commission, receives proceeds over seller's minimum**
"Multiple Listing"	$ ➡ Broker	**IF authority to enter listing in multiple listing service**

Transaction broker agreement. Recall from an earlier section that in a transaction broker relationship in Florida, the broker does not represent either party in a fiduciary capacity or as a single agent. Neither party has the right of the licensee's undivided loyalty. The transaction broker relationship is between the brokerage and the client. Florida law makes the presumption that all licensees are operating as transaction brokers unless the broker and the customer have entered into a written single agent or nonrepresentation agreement.

Multiple listing. A multiple listing is not a distinct listing contract but rather a provision in an exclusive listing authorizing the broker t o place the listing into a multiple listing service.

A **multiple listing service** (MLS) is an organization of member brokers who agree to cooperate in the sale of properties listed by other brokers in exchange for a share of the broker's resulting commission. Members of the service agree to enter all exclusive listings into the listing distribution network so that every member is promptly informed of new listings as they come on the market.

Most consumers expect brokers to make use of a multiple listing service in marketing and locating properties. Working with an MLS, however, requires that the listing or representation agreement contain the necessary provisions to allow the licensee to place the listing into a multiple listing service and to ensure that all parties understand and agree to the relevant policies and procedures.

The listing agreement used by members of a multiple listing service discloses relevant procedures and policies so that all principal parties to the agreement are aware of the pooling of the listing. A broker who works on a transaction listed in the MLS has all the duties and responsibilities inherent in the laws of agency as the client's fiduciary agent. The listing agreement sets forth specific duties.

Exclusive right to sell listing clauses

A written listing, particularly an exclusive, is a formal contract which contains the entirety of all agreements between the parties. If an agreement is left out, it is assumed not to exist. An agreement that is included is assumed to exist and is generally enforceable. If a written agreement contains mistakes, it is probably not valid or enforceable. For these reasons, it is extremely important for a listing agreement to be accurate, error-free, and complete.

Different agreement types may contain a variety of required clauses. Generally, a written listing agreement requires as a minimum:

- names of all owners
- address or legal description of the listed property
- listing price
- expiration date
- commission terms
- authority granted

The following clause descriptions are found in a typical exclusive right-to-sell listing agreement.

Parties and authorization. The agreement should name all legal owners of the property, or duly authorized representatives of the owners, as the client party. It must also name the broker.

An authorization clause sets forth the nature of what the broker is allowed to do, i.e., the type of listing. Note that the phrase "right-to-sell" is a misnomer. A broker cannot legally sell the property without proper power of attorney. The usual right is to effect a sale or find a buyer.

Real Property. A written listing agreement must include a property description. The real property description may include an address.

It is critical to identify both the real property and any personal property that are for sale and included in the listing price.

Fixtures. Typical agreements list what fixtures are included in the sale specifically, and "all other things attached or affixed to the property" generally. The seller must then enter which items are excluded from the sale.

Personal Property. The listing agreement should include all personal property that is to be included in the transaction and listing price.

Listing price. A clause usually sets forth the gross price for the property and possibly the financing terms the owner will accept, particularly if seller financing or assumption of the seller's loan is involved.

The listing price is the seller's asking price for the property. This may or may not be the price the seller ultimately accepts. The full listing price does not have to be obtained for the broker to earn a commission. The listing price clause may also state the seller's agreement to pay customary closing costs.

Listing term. In Florida, written listings must have a specific ending date. Failure to name a termination date in a written listing is grounds for revocation of the real estate license. Any provision for renewal of the listing term should be very specific. Automatic renewals are illegal.

To protect the broker, some listings contain a provision to extend the listing period in the event an expiration occurs during the period in which a sale contract is pending.

Agent's duties. This clause specifies the broker's responsibilities and authorization to carry out certain activities. These typically include marketing activities, multiple listing service activities, property access and showings, authority to allow other parties access, permission to inspect existing mortgage financing documents, and authority to accept deposits. Commonly, the clause specifically bars the broker from executing any contract on behalf of the owner.

Broker's compensation. A clause will identify the broker's fee and the necessary conditions for the fee to be earned. For instance, it may state that a commission is earned if a buyer is procured, a contract is executed, or the seller voluntarily transfers the property for any price during the listing period.

A fee clause usually provides for remedies in the event of default by the buyer or seller. In effect, if the seller breaches the listing without grounds after a buyer has been procured, the commission is payable. If the owner cannot sell the property for reasons beyond the owner's control, the owner is not liable for a commission. If the buyer breaches a sale contract, the seller typically claims the buyer's earnest money deposit as liquidated damages.

Procuring cause. Procuring cause is the compensation concept that identifies who has earned a commission or compensation as a result of his or her efforts in a given transaction. Specifically, procuring cause is attributable to the party who sets into motion a chain of events that leads uninterruptedly to a sale. Under the terms of certain listings, commissions are not generally payable unless the listing agent can claim to be the procuring cause.

Protection period. Many listings include a protection clause stating that, for a certain period after expiration, the owner is liable for the commission if the property sells to a party that the broker procured, unless the seller has since listed the property with another broker.

Multiple listing. This provision obtains the seller's consent to placing the listing in a multiple listing service and authorization to disseminate information about the listing to members.

Cooperation with other agents. This clause requires the seller to agree or refuse to cooperate with subagents or buyer agents in selling the property, under what terms, and whether the seller agrees to compensate these parties. Recent agreements stipulate that subagents and buyer agents must disclose their relationships to the buyer upon initial contact and subsequently in writing. There may also be a warning to the seller not to disclose confidential information to a buyer broker insofar as this agent is required to disclose all relevant information to the buyer.

Non-discrimination. Most exclusive listings contain an affirmation that the agent will conduct all affairs in compliance with state and federal fair housing and nondiscrimination laws.

Other disclosures by agent. In addition to agency, other disclosures might be included to cover any direct or indirect interest the broker has in the transaction and special compensation the broker might be receiving from other parties connected with the transaction.

Seller's representations and promises. In this clause, the owner represents that he or she in fact owns the property in the manner stated in the listing, and is legally capable of delivering fee simple, marketable title. The clause may further require the owner to warrant that he or she

- ▸ is not represented by another party and will not list the property elsewhere during the listing period
- ▸ will not lease the property during the listing period without approval
- ▸ agrees to provide necessary information
- ▸ will refer all prospects directly to the broker without prior direct negotiation
- ▸ has reviewed a sample "Offer to Purchase and Sell" contract
- ▸ will make the property presentable and available for showing at reasonable times upon notice by agent.

Seller's property condition disclosure. The listing form may require the seller to disclose the condition of the property to prospective buyers. Florida law may allow buyers to cancel a sale contract if they have not received the seller's property condition disclosure before closing or occupancy or other deadline. In addition, the listing may include among the seller's duties the requirement to complete and provide the agent with a Lead Paint Hazard addendum. A copy of the required notice to buyers may be attached to the listing agreement as part of the agreement.

Seller's title and deed. A provision usually requires the owner to promise to deliver good and marketable title, title insurance, and to convey the property using a general warranty deed to a buyer. Without this covenant, the broker has no assurance that a transaction will occur, and in turn that he or she will be paid for procuring a buyer.

Flood hazard insurance. This clause requires the seller to disclose whether he or she is required to or presently maintains flood insurance on the property.

Limitation of liability. There is often a clause requiring the owner to indemnify the broker against liability resulting from casualty, loss, and owner misrepresentation during the listing period. In practice, liability and indemnification clauses do not necessarily absolve a broker from liability.

Escrow authorization. The seller authorizes escrow officers to disburse earned commission funds to the broker upon the broker's instructions to do so.

IRS requirements; alien seller withholding. A clause may state that the seller will comply with IRS requirements for providing tax-related information. This ensures that a seller who is an alien understands that a buyer will be required to withhold a percentage of the sale price for the IRS.

Other listing provisions. An exclusive listing might also provide for:

> ▸ *mediation*: in the event of a dispute, the owner agrees to arbitrate differences before filing a lawsuit
> ▸ *attorney fees*: the losing party in a lawsuit must pay court costs and attorney fees
> ▸ *acknowledgment*: the owner acknowledges reading and understanding the agreement
> ▸ *entire agreement*: the listing cannot be changed without written agreement; the listing sets forth all agreements made
> ▸ *binding effect*: listing is binding and enforceable
> ▸ *saving clause*: if a portion of the agreement is invalid or unenforceable, the balance of the agreement remains valid as permitted by law

Notices to owner. Some listing agreements include notices to the seller concerning:

> ▸ *fee negotiability*: the broker's fee is the result of negotiations with the seller
> ▸ *fair housing laws*: the broker and seller must comply with discrimination laws
> ▸ *keyboxes; security*: the seller should take prudent measures to protect personal property and remove dangerous items that could cause injury
> ▸ *legal advice disclaimer*: the broker cannot give legal advice

Signatures. All owners and the broker must sign the listing and indicate the date of signing.

Exclusive buyer agency clauses

The exclusive buyer agency agreement is very similar to the exclusive right-to-sell agreement, the only significant differences being the agent's objectives and the fact that the principal is the buyer instead of the seller. The notable exception is how the agent is paid, as previously discussed.

The clauses which are virtually identical to the exclusive right-to-sell are:

> ▸ the identity of the principal and the agent's authorized activity
> ▸ the description of the property desired in terms of location, price, size, etc.
> ▸ the term of the agreement and its automatic termination
> ▸ the buyer's agreement to work exclusively through the agent
> ▸ the agent's duties to locate a suitable property according to the buyer's specifications
> ▸ the non-discrimination clause
> ▸ signatures of the parties

The following clauses distinguish the buyer agency agreement from the exclusive right-to sell agreement.

Buyer's representation of exclusivity. Here the buyer affirms that he or she is not represented by another agent. In addition the buyer acknowledges an understanding of the agency relationship.

Agent compensation. This clause sets forth how the agent is to be paid, whether by retainer or commission, who is to pay the commission, and what the buyer owes the agent in the event the seller does not participate in the agent's compensation. Second, the clause establishes the circumstances under which the agent has earned the commission. This includes finding a property during the agreement term or the buyer contracting to buy a property shown by the agent within a stipulated period of time following expiration. In addition, the clause provides that the agent will be paid in the event the buyer defaults on a sale contract.

Other buyers acknowledged. In this provision, the buyer acknowledges that the agent is working with other buyers who may be in competition for any property the buyer is shown by the agent.

SALE CONTRACTS

Legal characteristics
Contract creation
Earnest money escrow
Contract contingencies
Default
Contract provisions

A real estate sale contract is a binding and enforceable agreement wherein a buyer, the **vendee**, agrees to buy an identified parcel of real estate, and a seller, the **vendor**, agrees to sell it under certain terms and conditions. It is the document that is at the center of the transaction.

The conventional transfer of real estate ownership takes place in three stages. First, there is the negotiating period where buyers and sellers exchange offers in an effort to agree to all transfer terms that will appear in the sale contract. Second, when both parties have accepted all terms, the offer becomes a binding sale contract and the transaction enters the pre-closing stage, during which each party makes arrangements to complete the sale according to the sale contract's terms. Third is the closing of the transaction, when the seller deeds title to the buyer, the buyer pays the purchase price, and all necessary documents are completed. At this stage, the sale contract has served its purpose and terminates.

Other names for the sale contract are *agreement of sale, contract for purchase, contract of purchase and sale*, and *earnest money contract*.

Legal characteristics

Executory contract. A sale contract is *executory:* the signatories have yet to perform their respective obligations and promises. Upon closing, the sale contract is fully performed and no longer exists as a binding agreement.

Signatures. All owners of the property should sign the sale contract. If the sellers are married, both spouses should sign to ensure that both spouses release homestead, dower, and curtesy rights to the buyer at closing. Failure to do so does not invalidate the contract but can lead to encumbered title and legal disputes.

Enforceability criteria. To be enforceable, a sale contract must:

- be validly created (mutual consent, consideration, legal purpose, competent parties, voluntary act)
- be in writing
- identify the principal parties
- clearly identify the property, preferably by legal description
- contain a purchase price
- be signed by the principal parties

Written vs. oral form. A contract for the sale of real estate is enforceable only if it is in writing. A buyer or seller cannot sue to force the other to comply with an oral contract for sale, even if the contract is valid.

Assignment. Either party to a sale transaction can assign the sale contract to another party, subject to the provisions and conditions contained in the agreement.

Who may complete. A broker or agent may assist buyer and seller in completing an offer to purchase, provided the broker represents the client faithfully and does not charge a separate fee for the assistance. It is advisable for a broker to use a standard contract form promulgated by a state agency or real estate board, as such forms contain generally accepted language. This relieves the broker of the dangers of creating new contract language, which can be construed as a practice of law for which the broker is not licensed.

Contract creation

Offer and acceptance. A contract of sale is created by full and unequivocal acceptance of an offer. Offer and acceptance may come from either buyer or seller. The offeree must accept the offer without making any changes whatsoever. A change terminates the offer and creates a new offer, or counteroffer. An offeror may revoke an offer for any reason prior to communication of acceptance by the offeree.

Equitable title. A sale contract gives the buyer an interest in the property that is called equitable title, or *ownership in equity*. If the seller defaults and the buyer can show good faith performance, the buyer can sue for specific performance, that is, to compel the seller to transfer legal title upon payment of the contract price.

Earnest money escrow

The buyer's earnest money deposit fulfills the consideration requirements for a valid sale contract. In addition, it provides potential compensation for damages to the seller if the buyer fails to perform. The amount of the deposit varies according to local custom. It should be noted that the earnest money deposit is not the only form of consideration that satisfies the requirement.

The sale contract provides the *escrow instructions* for handling and disbursing escrow funds. The earnest money is placed in a third party trust account or escrow. A licensed escrow agent employed by a title company, financial institution, or brokerage company usually manages the escrow. An individual broker may also serve as the escrow agent.

The escrow holder acts as an impartial fiduciary for buyer and seller. If the buyer performs under the sale contract, the deposit is applied to the purchase price.

Strict rules govern the handling of earnest money deposits, particularly if a broker is the escrow agent. For example, Florida law directs the broker when to deposit the funds, how to account for them, and how to keep them separate from the broker's own funds.

Contract contingencies

A sale contract often contains contingencies. A contingency is a condition that must be met before the contract is enforceable.

The most common contingency concerns financing. A buyer makes an offer contingent upon securing financing for the property under certain terms on or before a certain date. If unable to secure the specified loan commitment by the deadline, the buyer may cancel the contract and recover the deposit. An appropriate and timely loan commitment eliminates the contingency, and the buyer must proceed with the purchase.

It is possible for both buyers and sellers to abuse contingencies in order to leave themselves a convenient way to cancel without defaulting. To avoid problems, the statement of a contingency should

- be explicit and clear
- have an expiration date
- expressly require diligence in the effort to fulfill the requirement

A contingency that is too broad, vague, or excessive in duration may invalidate the entire contract on the grounds of insufficiency of mutual agreement.

Default

A sale contract is bilateral, since both parties promise to perform. As a result, either party may default by failing to perform. Note that a party's failure to meet a contingency does not constitute default, but rather entitles the parties to cancel the contract.

Buyer default. If a buyer fails to perform under the terms of a sale contract, the breach entitles the seller to legal recourse for damages. In most cases, the contract itself stipulates the seller's remedies. The usual remedy is forfeiture of the buyer's deposit as **liquidated damages**, provided the deposit is not grossly in excess of the seller's actual damages. It is also customary to provide for the seller and broker to share the liquidated damages. The broker may not, however, receive liquidated damages in excess of what the commission would have been on the full listing price.

If the contract does not provide for liquidated damages, the seller may sue for damages, cancellation, or specific performance.

Seller default. If a seller defaults, the buyer may sue for specific performance, damages, or cancellation.

Contract provisions

Sale contracts can vary significantly in length and thoroughness. They also vary according to the type of sale transaction they describe. Some of the varieties are:

- Residential Contract of Sale
- Commercial Contract of Sale
- Foreclosure Contract of Sale
- Contract of Sale for New Construction
- Contract of Sale for Land
- Exchange Agreement

As the most common sale transaction is a residential sale, a Residential Contract of Sale is the type with which a licensee should first become familiar. A typical residential sale contract contains provisions of the following kind.

Parties, consideration, and property. One or more clauses will identify the parties, the property, and the basic consideration, which is the sale of the property in return for a purchase price.

There must be at least two parties to a sale contract: one cannot convey property to oneself. All parties must be identified, be of legal age, and have the capacity to contract.

The property clause also identifies fixtures and personal property included in the sale. Unless expressly excluded, items commonly construed as fixtures are *included* in the sale. Similarly, items commonly considered personal property are *not included* unless expressly included.

Legal description. A legal description must be sufficient for a competent surveyor to identify the property.

Price and terms. A clause states the final price and details how the purchase will occur. Of particular interest to the seller is the buyer's down payment, since the greater the buyer's equity, the more likely the buyer will be able to secure financing. In addition, a large deposit represents a buyer's commitment to complete the sale.

If seller financing is involved, the sale contract sets forth the terms of the arrangement: the amount and type of loan, the rate and term, and how the loan will be paid off.

It is important for all parties to verify that the buyer's earnest money deposit, down payment, loan proceeds, and other promised funds together equal the purchase price stated in the contract.

Loan approval. A financing contingency clause states under what conditions the buyer can cancel the contract without default and receive a refund of the earnest money. If the buyer cannot secure the stated financing by the deadline, the parties may agree to extend the contingency by signing next to the changed dates.

Earnest money deposit. A clause specifies how the buyer will pay the earnest money. It may allow the buyer to pay it in installments. Such an option enables a buyer to hold on to the property briefly while obtaining the additional deposit funds. For example, a buyer who wants to buy a house makes an initial deposit of $200, to be followed in twenty-four hours with an additional $2,000. The sale contract includes the seller's acknowledgment of receipt of the deposit.

Escrow. An escrow clause provides for the custody and disbursement of the earnest money deposit, and releases the escrow agent from certain liabilities in the performance of escrow duties.

Closing and possession dates. The contract states when title will transfer, as well as when the buyer will take physical possession. Customarily, possession occurs on the date when the deed is recorded, unless the buyer has agreed to other arrangements.

The closing clause generally describes what must take place at closing to avoid default. A seller must provide clear and marketable title. A buyer must produce purchase funds. Failure to complete any pre-closing requirements stated in the sale contract is default and grounds for the aggrieved party to seek recourse.

Conveyed interest; type of deed. One or more provisions will state what type of deed the seller will use to convey the property, and what conditions the deed will be subject to. Among common "subject to" conditions are easements, association memberships, encumbrances, mortgages, liens, and special assessments. Typically, the seller conveys a fee simple interest by means of a general warranty deed.

Title evidence. The seller covenants to produce the best possible evidence of property ownership. This is commonly in the form of title insurance.

Closing costs. The contract identifies which closing costs each party will pay. Customarily, the seller pays title and property-related costs, and the buyer pays financing-related costs. Annual costs such as taxes and insurance are prorated between the parties. Note that who pays any particular closing cost is an item for negotiation.

Damage and destruction. A clause stipulates the obligations of the parties in case the property is damaged or destroyed. The parties may negotiate alternatives, including seller's obligation to repair, buyer's obligation to buy if repairs are made, and the option for either party to cancel.

Default. A default clause identifies remedies for default. Generally, a buyer may sue for damages, specific performance, or cancellation. A seller may do likewise or claim the earnest money as liquidated damages.

Broker's representation and commission. The broker discloses the applicable agency relationships in the transaction and names the party who must pay the brokerage commission.

Seller's representations. The seller warrants that there will be no liens on the property that cannot be settled and extinguished at closing. In addition, the seller warrants that all representations are true, and if found otherwise, the buyer may cancel the contract and reclaim the deposit.

A sale contract may contain numerous additional clauses, depending on the complexity of the transaction. The following are some common additional provisions.

Inspections. The parties agree to inspections and remedial action based on findings.

Owner's association disclosure. The seller discloses existence of an association and the obligations it imposes.

Survey. The parties agree to a survey to satisfy financing requirements.

Environmental hazards. The seller notifies the buyer that there may be hazards that could affect the use and value of the property.

Compliance with laws. The seller warrants that there are no undisclosed building code or zoning violations.

Due-on-sale clause. The parties state their understanding that loans that survive the closing may be called due by the lender. Both parties agree to hold the other party harmless for the consequences of an acceleration.

Seller financing disclosure. The parties agree to comply with applicable state and local disclosure laws concerning seller financing.

Rental property; tenants' rights. The buyer acknowledges the rights of tenants following closing.

FHA or VA financing condition. A contingency allows the buyer to cancel the contract if the price exceeds FHA or VA estimates of the property's value.

Flood plain; flood insurance. Seller discloses that the property is in a flood plain and that it must carry flood insurance if the buyer uses certain lenders for financing.

Condominium assessments. Seller discloses assessments the owner must pay.

Foreign seller withholding. The seller acknowledges that the buyer must withhold 15% of the purchase price at closing if the seller is a foreign person or entity and forward the withheld amount to the Internal Revenue Service. Certain limitations and exemptions apply.

Tax deferred exchange. For income properties only, buyer and seller disclose their intentions to participate in an exchange and agree to cooperate in completing necessary procedures.

Merger of agreements. Buyer and seller state that there are no other agreements between the parties that are not expressed in the contract.

Notices. The parties agree on how they will give notice to each other and what they will consider to be delivery of notice.

Time is of the essence. The parties agree that they can amend dates and deadlines only if they both give written approval.

Fax transmission. The parties agree to accept facsimile transmission of the offer, provided receipt is acknowledged and original copies of the contract are subsequently delivered.

Survival. The parties continue to be liable for the truthfulness of representations and warranties after the closing.

Dispute resolution. The parties agree to resolve disputes through arbitration as opposed to court proceedings.

C.L.U.E. Report. CLUE (Comprehensive Loss Underwriting Exchange) is a claims history database used by insurance companies in underwriting or rating insurance policies. A CLUE Home Seller's Disclosure Report shows a five-year insurance loss history for a specific property. Among other things, it describes the types of any losses and the amounts paid. Many home buyers now require sellers to provide a CLUE Report (which only the property owner or an insurer can order) as a contingency appended to the purchase offer. A report showing a loss due to water damage and mold, for instance, might lead a buyer to decide against making an offer because of the potential difficulty of getting insurance. A report showing no insurance loss within the previous five years, on the other hand, is an indication that the availability and pricing of homeowner's insurance will not present an obstacle to the purchase transaction, and also that the property has not experienced significant damage or repair during that time period.

Addenda. Addenda to the sale contract become binding components of the overall agreement. The most common addendum is the seller's property condition disclosure. Examples of other addenda are:

agency disclosure	asbestos / hazardous materials
liquidated damages	radon disclosure
flood plain disclosure	tenant's lease

Required disclosures

To ensure that a seller complies with all Florida disclosure requirements when selling a property, Florida Realtors® provides the Sellers Real Property Disclosure form online at http://www.unlimitedmls.com/forms/Property-Disclosure-Form.pdf. The form gives the buyer an opportunity to evaluate the property in detail prior to signing a purchase contract. Following are disclosures required by Florida laws:

Radon. This is the easiest hazard to detect and mitigate. It is an odorless, colorless, tasteless, and radioactive gas that is created in the ground where uranium and radium exist. Prolonged exposure to radon can cause lung cancer. It can enter the home through any cracks, gaps, or cavities, including crawl spaces and openings around pipes. It can be easily detected by a radon test, so home inspections should include this test.

Florida statute requires real estate professionals to disclose the dangers of radon gas in writing and include the following required language:

RADON GAS: Radon is a naturally occurring radioactive gas that, when it has accumulated in a building in sufficient quantities, may present health risks to persons who are exposed to it over time. Levels of radon that exceed federal and state guidelines have been found in buildings in Florida. Additional information regarding radon and radon testing may be obtained from your county health department.

Energy efficiency disclosure. The Florida Building Energy-Efficiency Rating Act provides a statewide uniform energy efficiency rating system for new and existing residential, public, and commercial buildings. The Act requires sellers to provide an information brochure to the buyer either prior to or at the time of the buyer's execution of a purchase contract.

The brochure lets the buyer know there is an option for an energy-efficiency rating on the building and includes information about the class of the building as well as how to analyze the building's energy-efficiency rating, methods for improving the building's rating, and a notice to residential buyers that the rating may qualify them for an energy-efficient mortgage from a lender.

Lead-based paint. This hazard cannot be absorbed through the skin, but it becomes dangerous when it is ingested or inhaled. It can be found in most homes built before 1978 and can be present in the air, drinking water, food, contaminated soil, deteriorating paint, and dust from the paint. Children are particularly susceptible because young children are known to eat chips of the paint, allowing the lead to enter their bloodstreams. Homebuyers and renters are required to be given the EPA-HUD-US Consumer Product Safety Commission's booklet, "Protect Your Family from Lead in Your Home" and must be informed if lead-based paint is present in the home. Buyers may have a risk assessment performed prior to purchasing the home.

Homeowners' association. Florida law requires owners of real property subject to a homeowner's association to provide potential purchasers with a disclosure of the fact prior to contract execution. The form of the disclosure must be substantially in the form identified in the statute. The statute mandates disclosure of mandatory HOA membership and the associated assessments and fees. Failure to provide this disclosure can result in the sale being voided.

A typical HOA disclosure package also includes

- ▶ declarations
- ▶ articles of incorporation
- ▶ bylaws
- ▶ articles of organization
- ▶ operating agreements
- ▶ rules and regulations
- ▶ party wall agreements
- ▶ minutes of annual owners' meeting
- ▶ minutes of directors' or managers' meetings

> ► financial documents: balance sheet, income and expenditures, budget, reserve study, unpaid assessments, audit report, list of fees and charges
>
> ► list of insurance policies
>
> ► list of assessments by unit type

The seller is responsible for making the disclosures, but the buyer must exercise due diligence in the reading and understanding of them. The agent's responsibility is to make sure the disclosures are made.

Flood insurance. The Natural Hazards Disclosure law requires sellers to disclose if the property is located in a flood zone and whether flood insurance will be required. While there is no mandated language for the disclosure, it should notify the buyer that a mortgage lender may require flood insurance and that the National Flood Insurance Program provides flood insurance at premiums based on the risk of flooding where the property is located. It should also state that the buyer should not rely on the premium amounts paid by the seller as an indication of the premium the buyer will pay.

Property tax. Florida statute 689.261 requires inclusion of a property tax disclosure summary with the standard disclosure form, inserted in the contract or as a separate document. Statute mandates the language:

Buyers should not rely on the seller's current property taxes as the amount of property taxes that the buyer may be obligated to pay in the year subsequent to purchase. A change of ownership or property improvements triggers reassessments of the property that could result in higher property taxes. If you have any questions concerning valuation, contact the county property appraiser's office for information.

Building code violation. In Florida, if a property owner has been cited for a code violation and sells the property before the citation is settled in court, the owner must disclose the citation in writing to the buyer and provide the buyer a copy of all related materials, notify the new owner of the requirement to comply with the code, and notify the code enforcement official of the property transfer.

Known hazardous substances on the property. Florida requires the seller to disclose any known environmental contamination or hazards on the property, such as underground fuel or heating oil tank that is known to have leaked.

Transfer Disclosure Statement (TDS) – Florida law requires sellers to provide buyers a written statement disclosing items such as appliances, structural defects and modification, possible easements, neighborhood problems, and other material facts that may impact the buyer's decision to close the transaction.

Inundation zones. If the property is located near a dam, the seller should disclose that the property is subject to potential flooding in the event of a dam failure.

Very high fire hazard severity zones. A Florida seller must also disclose if the property is in an area where property owners may be obligated to undertake specific maintenance duties for fire prevention.

Wildland fire areas. The seller is to disclose if the property is in an area wherein the state has responsibility for fire suppression.

Coastal property. If the property is located near the coast, Florida statute requires disclosure of potential coastal erosion and that the property is subject to federal, state, and local construction limitations. An affidavit or survey must be provided indicating the location of the coastal construction control line.

Community Development District disclosure. Florida statute requires that each contract for the initial sale of a parcel of land or a residential unit within a community development district include the following disclosure immediately above the buyer's signature in a boldface type larger and more conspicuous than the rest of the contract text:

> *The   (name of district)   community development district may impose and levy taxes or assessments, or both taxes and assessments, on this property. These taxes and assessments pay the construction, operation, and maintenance costs of certain public facilities and services of the district and are set annually by the governing board of the district. These taxes and assessments are in addition to county and other local governmental taxes and assessments and all other taxes and assessments provided for by law.*

Megan's Law. Purchase contracts and leases are required to include notice that a sex offenders database is available for public review to learn about the proximity of registered sex offenders.

Material defects affecting residential property value

For many years, the rule utilized in property sales was caveat emptor, known as "let the buyer beware." The gist of this rule was that the seller had no obligation to let buyers know about any defects in the property that would affect its value, no matter how serious the defect might be. If the buyer asked, the seller could not lie; but if the buyer didn't ask, then the seller didn't tell.

Johnson v. Davis. This practice changed in 1985 because of the *Johnson v. Davis* case in which the Florida Supreme Court ruled that "where the seller of a home knows of facts materially affecting the value of the property [that] are not readily observable and are not known to the buyer, the seller is under duty to disclose them to the buyer." Sellers must now disclose the defect or provide the following statement:

> *"Seller knows of no facts materially affecting the value of the Real Property which are not readily observable and which have not been disclosed to Buyer."*

This disclosure is known as the *Johnson v. Davis* duty to disclose.

As a result of this case, buyers of residential property are not required to prove fraud or negligence when they are seeking relief for damages resulting from the seller's failure to disclose defects. Buyers need only prove that the seller knew of a latent, material defect and failed to disclose it, and thus, the buyer sustained damages. Latent defects are those that are not visible, obvious, or readily observable. Buyers are not obligated to search for latent defects. The *Johnson v. Davis* case concluded that "one should not be able to stand behind the impervious shield of caveat emptor and take advantage of another's ignorance."

"As is" provision. Standard purchase contracts include terms requiring sellers to make certain types of repairs to the property up to a specified dollar amount. However, "As Is" contracts allow the buyer to look at the property through an inspection with no repair obligations on the seller. During the 15-day inspection period, if the buyer does not agree with the seller's not repairing any discovered defects, the buyer can cancel the contract without penalty. A buyer who signs the "As is" contract is waiving any claims against the seller and the seller's agent for any defects that existed at closing but were not discovered until after closing.

However, the "As is" contract is not exempt from the *Johnson v. Davis* disclosure requirement. Not only must the seller disclose any known defect, but he or she must include additional language in the contract stating that other than the duty to disclose, the seller *"extends and intends no warranty and makes no representation of any type, either express or implied, as to the physical condition or history of the property."*

Licensee's duty to disclose. An agent has the duty to inform the client of all material facts, reports, and rumors that might affect the client's interests in the property transaction. A material fact is one that might affect the value or desirability of the property to a buyer if the buyer knew it. Material facts include

▸ the agent's opinion of the property's condition
▸ adverse facts about property condition, title defects, environmental hazards, and property defects

In recent years, the disclosure standard has been raised to require an agent to disclose items that a practicing agent *should know,* whether the agent actually had the knowledge or not, and regardless of whether the disclosure furthers or impedes the progress of the transaction.

Facts not considered to be material, and therefore not usually subject to required disclosure, include such items as property stigmatization (e.g., that a crime or death occurred on the property) and the presence of registered sex offenders in the neighborhood (in accordance with Megan's Law, federal legislation that requires convicted offenders to register with the state of residence; in Florida, agents must provide registry information to buyers).

The agent may be held liable for failing to disclose a material fact if a court rules that the typical agent in that area would detect and recognize the adverse condition. There is no obligation to obtain or disclose information that is immaterial to the transaction, such as property stigmas.

An agent who sees a "red flag" issue such as a potential structural or mechanical problem should advise the seller to seek expert advice. Red flags can seriously impact the value of the property and/or the cost of remediation. In addition to property condition per se, they may include such things as

- ▸ environmental concerns
- ▸ property anomalies, such as over-sized or peculiarly shaped lot
- ▸ neighborhood issues
- ▸ poor construction
- ▸ signs of flooding
- ▸ poor floorplan
- ▸ adjacent property features

OPTION CONTRACTS

Essential characteristics
Contract requirements
Common provisions
Legal aspects

Essential characteristics

An option-to-buy is an enforceable contract in which a potential seller, the **optionor**, grants a potential buyer, the **optionee**, the right to purchase a property before a stated time for a stated price and terms. In exchange for the right of option, the optionee pays the optionor valuable consideration.

For example, a buyer wants to purchase a property for $150,000, but needs to sell a boat to raise the down payment. The boat will take two or three months to sell. To accommodate the buyer, the seller offers the buyer an option to purchase the property at any time before midnight on the day that is ninety days from the date of signing the option. The buyer pays the seller $1,000 for the option. If buyer exercises the option, the seller will apply the $1,000 toward the earnest money deposit and subsequent down payment. If the optionee lets the option expire, the seller keeps the $1,000. Both parties agree to the arrangement by completing a sale contract as an addendum to the option, then executing the option agreement itself.

An option-to-buy places the optionee *under no obligation* to purchase the property. However, the seller must perform under the terms of the contract if the buyer exercises the option. An option is thus a *unilateral* agreement. Exercise of the option creates a bilateral sale contract where both parties are bound to perform. An unused option terminates at the expiration date.

An optionee can use an option to prevent the sale of a property to another party while seeking to raise funds for the purchase. A renter with a **lease option-to-buy** can accumulate down payment funds while paying rent to the landlord. For example, an owner may lease a condominium to a tenant with an option to buy. If the tenant takes the option, the landlord agrees to apply $100 of the monthly rent paid prior to the option date toward the purchase price. The tenant pays the landlord the nominal sum of $200 for the option.

Options can also facilitate commercial property acquisition. The option period gives a buyer time to investigate zoning, space planning, building permits, environmental impacts, and other feasibility issues prior to the purchase without losing the property to another party in the meantime.

Contract requirements

To be valid and enforceable, an option-to-buy must:

- include actual, non-refundable consideration

  The option must require the optionee to pay a specific consideration *that is separate from the purchase price.* The consideration cannot be refunded if the option is not exercised. If the option is exercised, the consideration may be applied to the purchase price. If the option is a lease option, portions of the rent may qualify as separate consideration.

- include price and terms of the sale

  The price and terms of the potential transaction must be clearly expressed and cannot change over the option period. It is customary practice for the parties to complete and attach a sale contract to the option as satisfaction of this requirement.

- have an expiration date

  The option must automatically expire at the end of a specific period.

- be in writing

  Since a potential transfer of real estate is involved, Florida's statute of frauds requires an option to be in writing.

- include a legal description

- meet general contract validity requirements

  The basics include competent parties, the optionor's promise to perform, and the optionor's signature. Note that it is not necessary for the optionee to sign the option.

Common provisions

Beyond the required elements, it is common for an option to include provisions covering:

- how to deliver notice of election

  A clause clarifies how to make the option election, exactly when the election must be completed, and any additional terms required such as an earnest money deposit.

- forfeiture terms

A clause provides that the optionor is entitled to the consideration if the option term expires.

  ▸ property and title condition warranties

The optionor warrants that the property will be maintained in a certain condition, and that title will be marketable and insurable.

  ▸ how option consideration will be credited

A clause states how the optionor will apply the option consideration toward the purchase price.

Legal aspects

Equitable interest. The optionee enjoys an equitable interest in the property because the option creates the right to obtain legal title. However, the option does not in itself convey an interest in real property, only a right to do something governed by contract law.

Recording. An option should be recorded, because the equitable interest it creates can affect the marketability of title.

Assignment. An option-to-buy is assignable unless the contract expressly prohibits assignment.

11 Real Estate Contracts
Snapshot Review

CONTRACT ESSENTIALS

Definition of a contract
- mutual promises based on "meeting of the minds" to do or refrain from doing something; potentially enforceable if created validly

Preparation of contracts
- only attorneys may legally prepare; real estate licensees may fill in standard forms for listing and buyer brokerage agreements, sale and option contracts

Legal status of contracts
- valid: meets criteria
- void: does not meet criteria
- voidable: invalid if disaffirmed
- valid yet unenforceable: certain oral contracts

Criteria for validity
- competent parties; mutual consent; valuable consideration; legal purpose; voluntary, good faith act

Validity of a conveyance contract
- must be in writing; contain a legal description; be signed by one or more parties

Enforcement limitations
- statute of frauds: must be written to be enforceable
- statute of limitations: must act within time frame

UETA & electronic contracting
- federal law: electronic records and signatures are legal and must be accepted; enforceable regardless of medium

CLASSIFICATIONS OF CONTRACTS
- oral or written; express or implied; unilateral or bilateral; executed or executory

CONTRACT CREATION

Offer and acceptance
- valid offer and valid acceptance creates contract
- offer becomes contract on communication of acceptance by offeree to offeror

Counteroffer
- any offer in response to an offer or any altered original offer; nullifies original offer

Revocation of an offer
- offeror may revoke offer prior to communication of acceptance by offeree

Termination of an offer
- acceptance; rejection; revocation; expiration; counteroffer; death or insanity

Assignment of a contract
- assignable unless expressly prohibited or a personal service

Contract preparation
- restricted unless licensed as attorney or a party to the contract

CONTRACT TERMINATION

Forms of contract termination
- performance; infeasibility; mutual agreement; cooling-period rescission; revocation; abandonment; lapse of time; invalidity of contract; breach of contract

Breach of contract
- default without cause
- legal remedies: rescission; forfeiture; suit for damages; specific performance

EMPLOYMENT AGREEMENTS

Foundations in agency law

- listing: broker's enforceable contract of employment with client establishing special agency relationship to procure a customer
- parties: listing broker and client; broker's subagents; customers and prospects
- fiduciary duties: loyalty; obedience; disclosure; care; diligence; accounting
- scope of authority: listings are special or limited agency, not general agency agreements; broker may not contract for client unless specifically authorized; clients liable only for broker's acts within scope of authority

Types of Listing agreements

- **owner listing**: authorization to sell or lease;
- **exclusive right-to-sell (or lease)**-- most prevalent; given to one broker; must usually be written; must expire; broker gets commission if property transfers during period
- **exclusive agency**-- exclusive excepting owner; oral or written; must expire; broker gets commission unless owner sells
- ▶ **buyer or tenant listing**: authorization to represent buyer or tenant; open or exclusive listings with buyers or tenants to represent their interests compensation in form stipulated by agreement; may be paid by seller or landlord at closing; payable if buyer defaults; agent has fiduciary and disclosure duties
- **open listing**-- non-exclusive; oral or written; no stated expiration; procuring cause gets commission; no commission if client procures customer
- **net listing**-- all sale proceeds above a seller's minimum price go to the broker; discouraged, if not illegal; legal in Florida
- **transaction broker agreements**-- non-agency; no fiduciary duties; agent does not work in the interests of or for the benefit of either party
- **multiple listing**-- placed in MLS; owners consent to rules and provisions of MLS

SALE CONTRACTS

Legal characteristics

- binding, bilateral contract for purchase and sale; enforceable; executory, or to be fulfilled; expires upon closing; must be in writing; contain valuable consideration; identify property; be signed by all; be a valid contract

Contract creation

- by unqualified acceptance of an offer; gives buyer equitable title, power to force specific performance

Earnest money escrow

- secures contract validity and buyer's equitable interest; varies in amount; deposit controlled by disinterested party who must act according to escrow instructions

Contract contingencies

- conditions that must be met for the contract to be enforceable

Default

- buyer may sue for cancellation and damages or for specific performance; seller may claim deposit as liquidated damages, or may sue for cancellation, other damages, or for specific performance

Contract provisions

- parties, consideration, legal description, price and terms, loan approval, earnest money, escrow, closing and possession dates, conveyed interest, type of deed, title evidence, property condition warranty, closing costs, damage and destruction, default, broker's representation, commission, seller's representations
- inspections, owner's association disclosure, survey, environmental hazards, compliance with laws, due-on-sale, seller financing disclosure, rental property tenant's rights, FHA or VA financing condition, flood plain and flood insurance, condominium assessments, foreign seller withholding, tax-deferred exchange,

merger of agreements, notices, time of the essence, fax transmission, survival, dispute resolution, addenda

Required disclosures
- Florida requires several disclosures – energy efficiency, known hazardous substances, transfer disclosure statement, flood insurance, inundation zones, high fire hazard zones, wildland fire areas, wildland fire, coastal property, HOA, condo and co-op, community development district, property tax, building code violation, Megan's law, radon

Material defects affecting residential property value
- as of 1985, caveat emptor no longer used; sellers required to disclose all known defects whether or not observable
- **Johnson vs. Davis:** all known defects are to be disclosed, even those not readily observed; buyers need not prove fraud or negligence, only failure to disclose
- as-is provision: buyers purchase with no seller's obligation to repair defects; sellers still required to disclose all known defects; buyers can cancel within 15-day inspection period
- licensee has duty to disclose all material facts; should advise seller of red flag issues detected; may include environmental concerns, property size and shape, neighborhood, construction quality, flooding, floorplan, adjacent property

OPTION CONTRACTS

Essential characteristics
- optionor gives option to optionee; unilateral contract: seller must perform; buyer need not; if option exercised, option becomes bilateral sale contract

Contract requirements
- must include: non-refundable consideration for the option right; price and terms of the sale; option period expiration date; legal description; must be in writing and meet contract validity requirements

Common provisions
- special provisions: how to exercise option; terms of option money forfeiture; how option money will be applied to purchase price

Legal aspects
- creates equitable interest; is assignable; should be recorded

SECTION ELEVEN: Real Estate Contracts

Section Quiz

1. An important legal feature of a contract is

   a. it represents a "meeting of the minds."
   b. it must use precise wording in a document.
   c. it is not voidable.
   d. it can be created only by an attorney.

2. According to contract law, every valid contract is also

   a. void.
   b. enforceable.
   c. enforceable or unenforceable.
   d. voidable.

3. The guardian for a mentally incompetent party enters into an oral contract with another party to buy a trade fixture. This contract

   a. does not meet validity requirements.
   b. is possibly valid and enforceable.
   c. must be in writing to be valid.
   d. is valid but unenforceable.

4. A prospective homebuyer submits a signed offer to buy a house with the condition that the seller pays financing points at closing. The seller disagrees, crosses out the points clause, then signs and returns the document to the buyer. At this point, assuming all other contract validity items are in order, the status of the offer is

   a. an accepted offer, therefore a valid contract.
   b. an invalid contract.
   c. a counteroffer.
   d. an invalid offer.

5. As part of a construction contract between a contractor and a buyer, the contractor promises to complete construction by November 20. This promise can be construed as

   a. competency on behalf of the contractor.
   b. mutual consent.
   c. good faith.
   d. valuable consideration.

6. An unscrupulous investor completes a contract with a buyer to sell a property the investor does not own. The sale contract for this transaction

   a. is voidable.
   b. must be in writing.
   c. is void.
   d. is illegal yet potentially enforceable.

7. A homeowner encourages an agent to aggressively persuade a buyer to purchase his house by overinflating historical appreciation rates. The agent and the seller agree that 25% annual appreciation would work, even though this figure is four times actual rates. The pitch succeeds, and the seller accepts the buyer's resulting offer. This contract is

   a. enforceable.
   b. voidable.
   c. void.
   d. valid.

8. The statute of limitations requires that parties to a contract who have been damaged or who question the contract's provisions

   a. must act within a statutory period.
   b. must select a specific, limited course of action for recouping their losses.
   c. must arbitrate prior to taking court action.
   d. must wait a statutory period before they may take legal action.

9. The purpose of the Statute of Frauds is to

   a. invalidate certain oral contracts.
   b. require certain conveyance-related contracts to be in writing.
   c. nullify oral leases and listing agreements.
   d. eliminate fraud in real estate contracts.

10. A seller immediately accepts a buyer's offer but waits eight days before returning the accepted document to the buyer. Meanwhile, the offer has expired. Which of the following is true?

    a. The buyer is bound to the contract since it was accepted immediately.
    b. The buyer has no obligations to the seller whatsoever.
    c. The buyer may not rescind the expired offer.
    d. The seller may sue for specific performance.

11. A buyer agrees to all terms of a seller's offer except price. The buyer lowers the price by $1,000, signs the form, and mails it back to the seller. At this point, the seller's offer

    a. is void.
    b. becomes an executory contract.
    c. becomes a counteroffer.
    d. has been accepted.

12. A buyer submits an offer to a seller. Two hours later, the buyer finds a better house, calls the first seller, and withdraws the offer. Which of the following is true?

    a. The buyer may not revoke the offer in such a short period of time.
    b. The first seller may sue the buyer for specific performance.
    c. If the seller accepted the offer, the buyer must perform.
    d. The original offer is legally extinguished.

13. Real estate contracts that are not personal service contracts

    a. may be assigned.
    b. are not assignable.
    c. must be in writing.
    d. are exempt from the statute of frauds.

14. Which of the following contracts must be in writing to be enforceable?

    a. A parol contract.
    b. A six-month lease.
    c. A two-year lease.
    d. An executory contract.

15. A good example of a unilateral contract is

    a. an option to purchase.
    b. a listing agreement.
    c. a personal services agreement.
    d. a sale contract.

16. A contract is discharged whenever

    a. there is a cooling period.
    b. both parties have signed it.
    c. it is performed.
    d. the parties agree to their respective promises.

17. A contract may be defensibly terminated without damages if

    a. it is abandoned by one party.
    b. it is impossible to perform.
    c. it is deemed to be valid.
    d. both parties breach its terms.

18. A landlord suddenly terminates a tenant's lease in violation of the lease terms. The tenant takes action to compel the landlord to comply with the violated terms. This is an example of a suit for

    a. rescission.
    b. specific performance.
    c. damages.
    d. forfeiture.

19. The type of listing that assures a broker of compensation for procuring a customer, regardless of the procuring party, is a(n)

    a. exclusive right-to sell agreement.
    b. exclusive agency agreement.
    c. open listing.
    d. net listing.

20. An owner agrees to pay a broker for procuring a tenant unless it is the owner who finds the tenant. This is an example of a(n)

    a. exclusive right-to sell agreement.
    b. exclusive agency agreement.
    c. open listing.
    d. net listing.

21. A landlord promises to compensate a broker for procuring a tenant, provided the broker is the procuring cause. This is an example of a(n)

    a. exclusive right-to sell agreement.
    b. exclusive agency agreement.
    c. open listing.
    d. net listing.

22. A property owner agrees to pay a broker a commission, provided the owner receives a minimum amount of proceeds from the sale at closing. This is an example of a(n)

    a. exclusive right-to sell agreement.
    b. exclusive agency agreement.
    c. open listing.
    d. net listing.

23. The most significant difference between an owner representation agreement and a buyer representation agreement is

    a. the client.
    b. the commission amount.
    c. agency law applications.
    d. contract law applications.

24. A multiple listing authorization gives a broker what authority?

    a. To list the owner's property in a multiple listing service
    b. To sell several properties for the owner at once
    c. To sell or lease the property
    d. To delegate the listing responsibilities to other agents

25. A "protection period" clause in an exclusive listing provides that

   a. the owner is protected from all liabilities arising from the agent's actions performed within the agent's scope of duties.
   b. the agent has a claim to a commission if the owner sells or leases to a party within a certain time following the listing's expiration.
   c. agents are entitled to extend a listing agreement's term if a transaction is imminent.
   d. an owner is not liable for a commission if a prospective customer delays in completing an acceptable offer.

26. Several buyers are competing for the last available home in a desirable new subdivision. One buyer calls the owner-developer directly on the phone and offers $10,000 over and above the listed price. The developer accepts the offer. At this point,

   a. the parties have a valid, enforceable sale contract on the home.
   b. the parties have completed a verbal, executory contract.
   c. the parties may not cancel their contract.
   d. the developer could not entertain other offers on the property.

27. An owner completes a contract to sell her property. Before closing, the seller runs into financial trouble and assigns the contract to her principal creditor. The buyer cries foul, fearing the property will be lost. Which of the following is true?

   a. The buyer can sue the assignee to disallow the illegal assignment.
   b. The buyer can take legal action against the assignor.
   c. The assignor has completed a legal action.
   d. The sale contract is nullified.

28. During the executory period of a sale contract, the buyer acquires an equitable title interest in the property. This means that

   a. the buyer can potentially force the seller to transfer ownership.
   b. both parties own the property equally.
   c. if contract contingencies are not met, the buyer takes legal title.
   d. the buyer owns equity in the subject property to the extent of the funds deposited in escrow.

29. The purpose of an escrow account is to

   a. entrust deposit monies to an impartial fiduciary.
   b. enable the principals to access the funds in escrow without interference from the other party.
   c. ensure that the broker receives her commission.
   d. prevent the buyer from withdrawing the offer.

30. A sale contract contains an open-ended financing contingency: if the buyer cannot obtain financing, the deal is off. Six months later, the buyer still cannot secure financing. Which of the following is true?

   a. The seller may cancel the contract, since it can be ruled invalid.
   b. The buyer can continue indefinitely to seek financing, and the seller's property must remain off the market.
   c. The seller must return the buyer's deposit.
   d. The seller can force a lender to commit to a loan under fair financing laws.

31. In the event of a buyer's default, a provision for liquidated damages in a sale contract enables a seller to

   a. sue the buyer for the anticipated down payment.
   b. force the buyer to quitclaim equitable title.
   c. sue the buyer for all liquid assets lost as a result of the default.
   d. claim the deposit as relief for the buyer's failure to perform.

32. A due-on-sale clause in a sale contract puts parties on notice that

   a. the full price of the property is due the seller at closing.
   b. any loans surviving closing become immediately payable.
   c. all of the seller's debts must be retired before or upon closing.
   d. third-party loans surviving closing may be accelerated by the lender.

33. A sale contract may specifically deal with tax withholding responsibility if the seller is a foreigner. What is this responsibility?

   a. The buyer must withhold 15% of the purchase price at closing for the seller's capital gain tax payment.
   b. The buyer must withhold 15% of the purchase price at closing for the buyer's capital gain tax payment.
   c. The seller must withhold 15% of the buyer's funds as a deposit on the buyer's capital gain tax.
   d. The seller must withhold 15% of the sale price to pay the seller's capital gain tax.

34. An important legal characteristic of an option-to-buy agreement is that

   a. the potential buyer, the optionee, is obligated to buy the property once the option agreement is completed.
   b. the optionor must perform if the optionee takes the option, but the optionee is under no obligation to do so.
   c. the contract can be executed at no cost to the optionee.
   d. it is a bilateral agreement.

35. A tenant has an option-to-purchase agreement with the landlord that expires on June 30. On July 1, the tenant frantically calls the landlord to exercise the option, offering the apology that she was busy with a death in the family. Which of the following is true?

   a. Since options contain grace periods, the landlord must sell.
   b. The tenant loses the right to buy, but can claim the money paid for the option from the landlord.
   c. The landlord does not have to sell, but must renew the option.
   d. The option is expired, and the tenant has no rightful claim to money paid for the option.

36. A tenant exercises an option to buy a condominium. The landlord agrees, but raises the agreed price by $3,000, claiming financial distress. The landlord does, however, offer the tenant two months of free rent before closing as an offset. Which of the following is true?

   a. The tenant can force the sale at the original terms.
   b. The landlord has taken a fully legal action which the tenant must abide by.
   c. The option is null, and the optionee may reclaim any option money paid.
   d. The landlord must offer sufficient free rent to equal the $3,000 price increase.

37. Which of the following is true regarding the legal nature of option contracts?

   a. They are not assignable.
   b. They are enforceable, whether written or oral.
   c. They give the optionee an equitable interest in the property.
   d. They must be recorded to be valid.

38. A landlord promises to compensate a broker for procuring a tenant, provided the broker is the procuring cause. This is an example of a(n)

   a. exclusive right-to sell agreement.
   b. exclusive agency agreement.
   c. open listing.
   d. net listing.

39. Which of the following is NOT a required disclosure when selling a property in Florida?

   a. Flood insurance disclosure
   b. Molly's Law disclosure
   c. Building code violation disclosure
   d. Property tax disclosure

40. What property sales practice changed as a result of *Johnson v. Davis*?

   a. As Is provision
   b. standardized contract provisions
   c. Caveat emptor
   d. Property tax disclosure

12 Residential Mortgages

Mortgage Concepts
Essential Legal Provisions of Mortgages
Common Mortgage Features
Purchasing Mortgaged Property
Default and Foreclosure

Learning Objectives

- Distinguish between title theory and lien theory
- Describe the essential elements of the mortgage instrument and the note
- Describe the various features of a mortgage including down payment, loan-to-value ratio, equity, interest, loan servicing, escrow account, PITI, discount points and loan origination fee
- Explain assignment of a mortgage and the purpose of an estoppel certificate
- Explain the foreclosure process and distinguish between judicial and nonjudicial foreclosure
- Describe the mortgagor's and mortgagee's rights in a foreclosure
- Calculate loan-to-value ratio
- Explain the use of discount points and calculate approximate yield on a loan
- Distinguish among the various methods of purchasing mortgaged property

Key Terms

acceleration clause
assumption
blanket mortgage
buydown
contract for deed (land contract)
defeasance clause
deed in lieu of foreclosure
discount points
due on sale clause
equity
equity of redemption
escrow
estoppel certificate
hypothecation
interest

lien theory
lis pendens
land development loans
loan origination fee
loan servicing
loan-to-value ratio
mortgage
mortgagee
mortgagor
note
novation agreement
partial release clause
PITI
prepayment clause
prepayment penalty

MORTGAGE CONCEPTS

Mortgage law
Loan instruments
Flow of mortgage transaction
Mortgage priority

Mortgage law

Hypothecation. It is common to use borrowed money to purchase real estate. When a borrower gives a note promising to repay the borrowed money and executes a mortgage on the real estate for which the money is being borrowed as security, the financing method is called mortgage financing. The term "mortgage financing" also applies to real estate loans secured by a deed of trust. The process of securing a loan by pledging a property without giving up ownership of the property is called **hypothecation**.

Lien theory vs. title theory. States differ in their interpretation of who owns mortgaged property. Those that regard the mortgage as a lien held by the mortgagee (lender) against the property owned by the mortgagor (borrower) are called **lien-theory** states. Those that regard the mortgage document as a conveyance of ownership from the mortgagor to the mortgagee are called **title-theory** states. Some states interpret ownership of mortgaged property from a point of view that combines aspects of both title and lien theory. Florida is considered a lien-theory state.

Loan instruments

A valid mortgage or trust deed financing arrangement requires

> ▸ a *note* as evidence of the debt
> ▸ the *mortgage or trust deed* as evidence of the collateral pledge

Promissory note. In addition to executing a mortgage or trust deed, the borrower signs a promissory note for the amount borrowed. The amount of the loan is typically the difference between the purchase price and the down payment. A promissory note creates a personal liability for the borrower to repay the loan.

A borrower who executes a promissory note is the **maker** or **payer** of the note. The lender is the **payee**. To be properly executed, all parties who have an interest in the property should sign the note. The note sets forth:

> ▸ the loan amount
> ▸ the term of the loan
> ▸ the method and timing of repayment
> ▸ the interest rate to be paid
> ▸ the borrower's promise to pay

The note may also state that it is payable to the bearer, if used with a deed of trust, or to the mortgagee, if used with a mortgage. Other items in the mortgage document or deed of trust may be repeated in the promissory note, especially:

> ▸ the right to prepay the loan balance

- charges for late payment
- conditions for default
- notifications and cures for default
- other charges

A promissory note is a **negotiable instrument**, which means the payee may *assign* it to a third party. The assignee would then have the right to receive the borrower's periodic payments.

Fannie Mae / Freddie Mac Uniform Florida Fixed-Rate Note. (See also "Fannie Mae," chapter 13 under 'Secondary Mortgage Market) This is a Florida-adapted standardized note form that was created and adopted through the joint efforts of the country's largest secondary mortgage market purchasers and traders. The Uniform Florida Fixed-rate Note contains all the necessary provisions for ready-acceptability as a marketable financial instrument. To view the form, see https://singlefamily.fanniemae.com/media/11241/display.

The essential characteristics and contents of this note are as follows:

- interest rate is fixed and remains constant over the life of the loan
- the debt amount (principal plus interest); (monthly) repayment method; loan term; default and late payment provisions to protect lender

Mortgage instrument. A mortgage is a legal document stating the pledge of the borrower to the lender. The mortgage document pledges the borrower's ownership interest in the real estate in question as collateral against performance of the debt obligation in a process referred to as **hypothecation**.

A borrower who executes a mortgage is a **mortgagor**. The lender named in the mortgage is the **mortgagee**. In a trust deed, the borrower is the **trustor** and the lender is **beneficiary**. The mortgage or trust document identifies the property being given as security, giving both its legal description and mailing address. The document contains much of the same information as the note, including:

- the debt amount
- the term of the loan
- method and timing of payments

The document does not usually provide details about the payment amount, interest rate, or charges.

Satisfaction of mortgage. The release clause, also known as a **defeasance** clause, may specify that the mortgagee will execute a **satisfaction of mortgage** (also known as **release of mortgage** and **mortgage discharge**) to the mortgagor. In the case of a deed of trust, the lender as beneficiary requests the trustee to execute a **release deed** or **deed of reconveyance** to the borrower as trustor. The release deed or satisfaction should be recorded as necessary in county records to show that the mortgagee/trustee has extinguished all liens against the property.

**Flow of a mortgage
transaction**

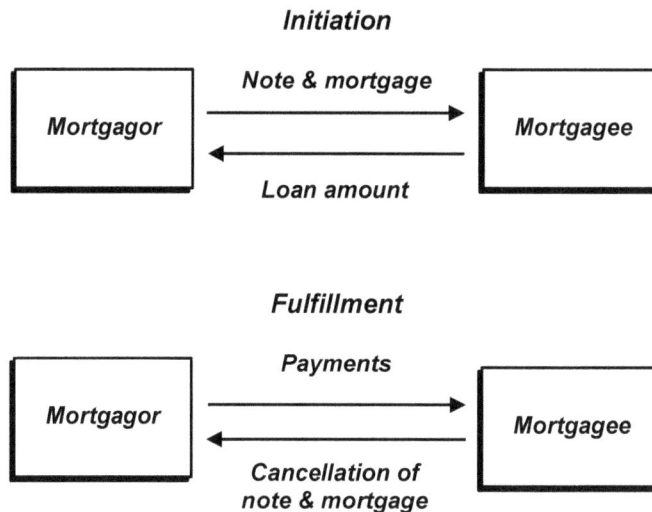

Flow of a Mortgage Transaction

Initiation

	Note & mortgage	
Mortgagor	→	*Mortgagee*
	←	
	Loan amount	

Fulfillment

	Payments	
Mortgagor	→	*Mortgagee*
	←	
	Cancellation of note & mortgage	

Mortgage priority   **First mortgages vs. junior mortgages.** As discussed in Section 9 under "Liens," lien priority determines the order of the liens' claims on the security underlying the debt. The highest ranking lien is first to receive proceeds from the foreclosed and liquidated security. The lien with lowest priority is last in line. The owner receives any sale proceeds that remain after all lienors receive their due.

Lien priority is of paramount concern to the creditor, since it establishes the level of risk in recovering loaned assets in the event of default. Date of recording determines priority. The rule is: *the earlier the recording date of the lien, the higher its priority.*

Subordination agreements. A lienor can change the priority of a lien by voluntarily agreeing to subordinate, or lower, the lien's position in the hierarchy. This change is often necessary when a mortgage lender will not originate a mortgage loan unless it is senior to all other junior liens on the property. The lender may require the borrower to obtain agreements from other lien holders to subordinate their liens to the new mortgage.

ESSENTIAL LEGAL PROVISIONS OF MORTGAGES

**Primary provisions
Other provisions**

Primary provisions   **Promise to repay.** The borrower must make timely payments according to the terms of the note.

Taxes and property insurance. Unless waived by the lender or prohibited by law, the borrower must make monthly payments to cover taxes and property, or hazard, insurance. If applicable, the borrower must also pay flood insurance and mortgage insurance installments.

Periodic payments of taxes and insurance are held in a reserve fund called the **escrow account**. The Real Estate Settlement Procedures Act (RESPA) limits the amount of funds that the lender can require and hold for this purpose.

The borrower's monthly payment to the lender for principal and interest is called the **P&I** payment (principal and interest). The amount which also includes the escrow payment is called **PITI** (principal, interest, taxes, insurance).

Maintenance and covenant of good repair (occupancy, preservation, maintenance and protection of the property). The borrower must take and maintain occupancy of the property as the borrower's principal residence according to the lender's requirements. The borrower must not use or neglect the property in such a way as to impair the lender's lien on the property. This could include using the property for illegal purposes, creating hazardous waste on the property, or destroying the improvements.

Other provisions

Prepayment. The borrower may pay off the loan, in whole or in a part, before loan maturity and without penalty. In Florida, this provision is assumed to be true unless a clause specifically states otherwise.

Acceleration. The requirement to repay the loan before the scheduled date is called **acceleration**.

Right to reinstate. If the lender holds the borrower in default under the terms of the mortgage and proceeds to enforce its rights under the document, such as by foreclosing, the borrower has the right to reinstate his or her interest by performing certain actions. This usually means paying overdue mortgage payments and any other expenses the lender may have incurred in protecting its rights. The clause, also known as a **redemption** clause, gives the borrower a period of time to satisfy obligations and prevent the lender from forcing a sale of the property.

Due on sale. If the borrower sells or transfers its interest in the property without the lender's approval, the lender may demand immediate and full repayment of the loan balance. This is an **alienation** clause, also known as a **due-on-sale** clause and a **call** clause. It allows the lender to prevent the assumption of the mortgage by a buyer if the borrower sells the property.

Release (defeasance). The lender agrees to release the mortgage or trust document to the borrower when the borrower has paid off the loan and all other sums secured by the document. The release deed or satisfaction should be recorded as necessary in county records to show that the mortgagee/trustee has extinguished all liens against the property.

Application of payments. The amount of each payment is applied to various items in order of priority. Unless local law provides otherwise, this order is: 1) prepayment charges; 2) escrow; 3) interest; 4) principal; 5) late charges.

Charges and Liens. The borrower is liable for paying any charges, liens, or other expenses that may have priority over the mortgage or trust instrument.

Hazard or Property Insurance. The borrower must keep the property insured as the lender requires. Insurance proceeds, in case of a claim, are applied first to restoring the property, or, if that is not feasible, to payment of the debt.

Protection of Lender's Rights in the Property. The lender may take actions it believes are necessary to protect its rights in the property if the borrower's actions threaten them. The costs of these actions would be charged to the borrower, and become part of the monthly payment.

Mortgage Insurance. The lender may require the borrower to obtain *private mortgage insurance, or PMI*. Mortgage insurance protects the lender against loss of a portion of the loan (typically 20-25%) in case of borrower default. Private mortgage insurance generally applies to loans that are not backed by the Federal Housing Administration (FHA) or Veterans Administration (VA) and that have a down payment of less than 20% of the property value.

Inspection. With proper notice, the lender may inspect the property if there is reasonable cause to fear damage to its lien.

Condemnation. If the property is condemned or taken by eminent domain, the lender declares a claim on any resulting proceeds.

Borrower Not Released; Forbearance by Lender Not a Waiver. The lender reserves the right to take future action against the borrower for default, even if the lender decides not to take immediate action. If the lender agrees to change the terms of the loan, it does not release the borrower from the original liability.

COMMON MORTGAGE FEATURES

Principal
Down payment
Loan-to-value ratio; equity
Interest
Servicing
Escrow account
Discount points
Origination fee
Take-out commitment
Term
Payment
Assignment of mortgages

Principal

The capital amount borrowed, on which interest payments are calculated, is the original loan **principal**. In an amortizing loan, part of the principal is repaid periodically along with interest, so that the principal balance decreases over the life of the loan. At any point during the life of a mortgage loan, the remaining unpaid principal is called the **loan balance**, or **remaining balance**.

Down payment

The difference between the purchase price of a property and the amount financed by a loan is the amount of cash the buyer must produce at the time of purchase. This amount is the down payment. The cash amount pledged and escrowed at the time of the offer is applied toward the down payment at closing.

Loan-to-value ratio & equity

Lenders usually lend only a portion of a property's value as a protection against loss. The relationship of the loan amount to the property value, expressed as a percentage, is called the **loan-to-value ratio, or LTV**. If the lender's loan to value ratio is 80%, the lender will lend only $80,000 per $100,000 of a home's appraised value. The difference between the property value and the borrower's indebtedness is referred to as the buyer's **equity**. If the LTV on a loan is 80%, then the equity is 100% - 80%, or 20%. At any given time following loan origination, the buyer's equity is the (current market value minus the loan balance.)

Interest

Interest is a charge for the use of the lender's money. Interest may be paid in *advance* at the beginning of the payment period, or in *arrears* at the end of the payment period, according to the terms of the note. Mortgage interest is most commonly paid in arrears. The **interest rate** is a percentage applied to the principal to determine the amount of interest due. The rate may be *fixed* for the term of the loan, or it may be *variable*, according to the terms of the note. A loan with a fixed interest rate is called a fixed-rate loan; a loan with a variable interest rate is commonly called an adjustable rate loan.

Because the interest rate on a mortgage loan does not reflect the full cost of the loan to the borrower, federal law requires a lender on a residential property to compute and disclose an **Annual Percentage Rate (APR)** that includes other finance charges in addition to the basic interest rate in the calculation.

Florida has laws against **usury**, which is the charging of excessive interest rates on loans. The laws prescribe maximum rates that can be charged on loans of varying amounts.

Servicing

Loan servicing involves the collecting and keeping records of loan payments and providing documentation of the loan to the borrower. The originating lender may provide the servicing and charge a percentage of the loan amount for the service, or it may pass the responsibility to another lender or financial services entity.

Escrow account

Mortgage lenders usually require borrowers to pay for property tax and hazard insurance in monthly instalments of 1/12 of the annual amount. These periodic payments are held in a reserve fund called the **escrow account** and paid out to the appropriate party as due . The Real Estate Settlement Procedures Act (RESPA) limits the amount of funds that the lender can require and hold for this purpose.

The borrower's monthly payment to the lender for principal and interest is called the **P&I** payment (principal and interest). The amount which also includes the escrow payment is called **PITI** (principal, interest, taxes, insurance).

Discount points

From the point of view of a lender or investor, the amount loaned in a mortgage loan is the lender's capital investment, and the interest paid by the borrower is the return earned by the invested capital. It is often the case that a lender needs to earn a greater return than the interest rate alone provides. For example, a lender may require additional yield on a low-interest VA loan which has an interest rate maximum. In such a case, the lender charges up-front **discount points** to make up the difference between the interest rate on the loan and the required return. This effectively raises the yield of the loan to the lender.

A discount point is *one percent of the loan amount*. Thus, one point on a $100,000 loan equals $1,000. The lender charges this as *pre-paid interest* at closing by funding only the face amount of the loan minus the discount points. The borrower, however, must repay the full loan amount, along with interest calculated on the full amount.

The value of one discount point to a lender is usually estimated to be equivalent to raising the interest rate on the loan by 1/8%. Thus, a lender has to charge eight points to raise the yield by 1%. If a lender needs to earn 7% on a loan offered at 6.5%, the number of points necessary would be figured as follows:

7.0% - 6.5% = .5%
.5% x 8 (points per 1%) = 4 points

On a loan of $100,000, the 4 points would cost the borrower:

100,000 x .04 = $4,000.

The borrower would effectively receive from the lender $96,000, and owe principal and interest based on $100,000. For tax reasons, it is usually advisable for the borrower to receive the full loan amount from the lender and pay the points in a check which is separate from that used for other closing costs. As pre-paid interest, points paid in this way may be deductible on the borrower's income tax return for the year of the purchase. The borrower should seek the advice of a tax consultant concerning this matter.

Origination fee

Lenders often charge borrowers a **loan origination fee** to cover costs of processing the loan application and obtaining supporting information such as credit reports. The fee is most often in the range of 1-2% of the loan amount.

Take-out commitment

A **take-out commitment** offers to make a loan that will "take out" another lender's loan, i.e., pay it off and replace it. The take-out loan is most often used to retire a construction loan. The take-out lender agrees to pay off the short-term construction loan by issuing a long-term permanent loan.

Term

The loan term is the period of time over which the loan must be repaid. A "30-year loan" is a loan whose balance must be fully paid off at the end of thirty years. A "five-year balloon loan" is a loan whose balance must be paid off at the end of five years, although its payments may be calculated on a term of another length, such as fifteen or thirty years. Such a loan is also sometimes described as a 30-year loan with a five-year "call."

Payments

The loan term, loan amount, and interest rate combine to determine the periodic payment amount. When these three quantities are known, it is possible to identify the periodic payment from a mortgage table or with a financial calculator. Mortgage payments are usually made on a monthly basis. On an amortizing loan, a portion of the payment goes to repay the loan balance in advance, and a portion goes to payment of interest in arrears.

For example, Mary and Jerry King borrow $400,000 to finance the purchase of a home. The loan has a term of thirty years at an interest rate of 5% and is amortizing. The monthly payment for this loan will be $2,147. For the first payment at the end of the month, the Kings owe interest on $400,000 for the monthly period. At 5%, this amounts to $1,666.67. Since their payment is $2,147 and the interest charge is $1,666.67, the difference, which is $480.33, is applied to an advance payment of principal. The following month, the Kings will pay interest on the new, smaller loan balance of $399,519.67 ($400,000.00 − 480.33).

If a borrower pays more than the scheduled payment amount, the excess is credited to repayment of the principal, which is reduced by the amount of the excess payment. The required minimum payment amount remains constant for the life of the loan, but the loan term can be reduced by this means, thereby also reducing the total amount of interest paid over the life of the loan.

Assignment of mortgages

The holder of rights and interests in a property can usually transfer them to another by contract. This right of assignment generally holds true of mortgages. The assignee takes on primary liability and the assignor remains secondarily liable for any contractual duties unless a novation agreement relieves the assignor of responsibility.

In the case of a mortgaged property, The mortgage instrument and the promissory note are transferred by means of an **assignment of mortgage**, but it is the assignment of the promissory note that actually conveys to the assignee the rights to the mortgaged property. The original mortgagor now must make loan payments to the assignee.

Estoppel. The assignor of the mortgage provides to the party who purchases the assigned mortgage a **certificate of estoppel** that states the loan balance, the rate of interest, and the most recent date of payment to ensure that no contrary claims about these factors can be made later.

PURCHASING MORTGAGED PROPERTY

Subject to the mortgage
Purchase money mortgage
Wraparounds
Assumptions
Contracts for deed

When a buyer pays cash for a property at closing, any existing mortgage on the property is paid off from the sale proceeds, and the seller's interests are transferred to the buyer. The cash may be the entirely buyer's, or some of it may be the proceeds of a new mortgage loan undertaken by the buyer. However, There are other ways for the buyer to purchase a mortgaged property, namely:

- ▸ subject to the existing mortgage
- ▸ with a wraparound mortgage
- ▸ by assumption of the existing mortgage
- ▸ by contract for deed

Subject to the mortgage

In buying a property subject to the existing mortgage, the buyer takes title and makes loan payments to the mortgagee (lender), while the seller (original mortgagor) remains personally responsible for the loan payments. In the event that the buyer defaults, the lender can force a foreclosure sale and sue the seller (not the buyer) for any deficiency if the sale proceeds do not satisfy the debt.

Purchase money mortgages

With a purchase money mortgage, the borrower gives a mortgage and note to the seller to finance some or all of the purchase price of the property. The seller in this case is said to "take back" a note, or to "carry paper," on the property. Purchase money mortgages may be either senior or junior liens.

Wraparounds

In a wraparound loan arrangement, the seller receives a junior mortgage from the buyer, and uses the buyer's payments to make the payments on the original first mortgage. A wraparound enables the buyer to obtain financing with a minimum cash investment. It also potentially enables the seller to profit from any difference between a lower interest rate on the senior loan and a higher rate on the wraparound loan. A wraparound is possible only if the senior mortgagee allows it.

Assumptions

With a mortgage assumption, the buyer acquires title to a mortgaged property and, signing a new promissory note with the lender, takes on personal responsibility for the terms and payments of the mortgage. The buyer is now primarily liable, but the original mortgagor remains secondarily liable under the original promissory note. Thus, if the buyer defaults, the lender can sue both the buyer and the seller for any deficiency in the proceeds of a foreclosure sale to satisfy the debt. A novation agreement, signed by seller, buyer, and lender, can relieve the seller of any further liability after the sale.

Contracts for deed

A contract for deed (land contract, installment sale contract, conditional sales contract, agreement for deed) allows the buyer of a property to defer payment of some or all of the purchase price over a specified period. During the period, the seller holds legal title while the buyer holds equitable title. The buyer takes possession of the property, makes payments of principal and interest to the seller, and maintains the property. At the end of the period, the buyer pays the seller the remainder of the full purchase price and the seller conveys legal title to the buyer.

A contract for deed serves several purposes for a seller. First, it facilitates a sale that might otherwise be impossible. Second, it may give the seller certain tax benefits. Since the seller is not liable for capital gains tax until the purchase price is received, the installment sale lowers the seller's tax liability in the year of the sale. There may also be a reduction in closing costs. Disadvantages for the seller include: the buyer might create encumbrances during the contract or cause disputes and litigation over the contract;

For the buyer, the contract for deed makes possible a purchase where adequate credit and funds for a down payment and loan qualification may be lacking.

Disadvantages for the buyer include: the seller may not be able to deliver marketable title at the end of the contract period, but the buyer must make payments nevertheless; or the seller may cloud the title with liens; or the seller may not have applied the buyer's payments to the seller's necessary loan payments.

Land development & construction loans

Land development loans overview. A land development loan is named for its purpose – to help finance the construction of infrastructure improvements to a tract of land. These would include streets, curbs, sewers, surveys, and landscaping.

Construction loans overview. Construction loans are used to help finance improvements on a specific site within a larger development. Such improvements would include the building, driveways, landscaping, etc. Here, increments of the total loan amount are disbursed as portions of the improvements are completed. Interest is charged on these portions of the loan as they are disbursed to the buyer. When improvements are complete, the borrower obtains permanent financing, and the construction loan is paid off.

Blanket loans. A blanket loan is one where the developer hypothecates other properties as collateral for additional financing. The blanket loan is retired when the hypothecated property – typically lots – is sold to buyers. In simpler terms, it is the developer's way to stair-stepping completion of a development – the developer uses completed lots as collateral for financing new, surveyed lots. The cycle is completed when a buyer purchases the collateralized lot with its completed infrastructure improvements – and the developer uses the funds to pay off the increments of the blanket loan and/or finance new lots.

Takeout commitment. The take-out commitment is a pledge to grant a longer-term, "permanent" loan on given portions of completed construction in the development – if not for the entire development itself. The prime example here is where a permanent lender pledges to give a homebuyer a long-term loan for a completed new home. The homebuyer gets the takeout loan and pays off all accumulated construction debt on the property. The takeout commitment facilitates obtaining the construction financing in the first place, since the construction lender knows he or she will be able to complete the development cycle.

Buydowns. Buydowns are a form of developer assistance to the buyer to help the buyer qualify for a given loan. In a buydown, the borrower prepays portions of the interest up front to the lender. This effectively lowers the interest rate for the borrower, who now achieves a more affordable financing situation for the loan underwriters. Now the qualifying ratios may be met since the payments are more affordable. The rate reduction is typically for the initial loan period.

DEFAULT AND FORECLOSURE

Enforcement
Foreclosure
Deed in lieu of foreclosure
Short sale

Enforcement

All liens can be enforced by the sale or other transfer of title of the secured property, whether by court action, operation of law, or through powers granted in the original loan agreement. The enforcement proceedings are referred to as foreclosure.

State law governs the foreclosure process. Broadly, a statutory or court-ordered sale enforces a general lien, including a judgment lien. A lawsuit or loan provision authorizing the sale or direct transfer of the attached property enforces a specific lien, such as a mortgage. Real estate tax liens are enforced through **tax foreclosure sales**, or **tax sales**.

The defaulting borrower may also offer the lender a **deed in lieu of foreclosure** to avoid the foreclosure process, but the lender does not have to accept it. Finally, there is the option of a **short sale**, which also avoids foreclosure but must be agreed to by the lender and borrower.

Foreclosure

Three types of foreclosure process enforce mortgage liens:

▶ judicial foreclosure
▶ non-judicial foreclosure
▶ strict foreclosure

Foreclosure Processes

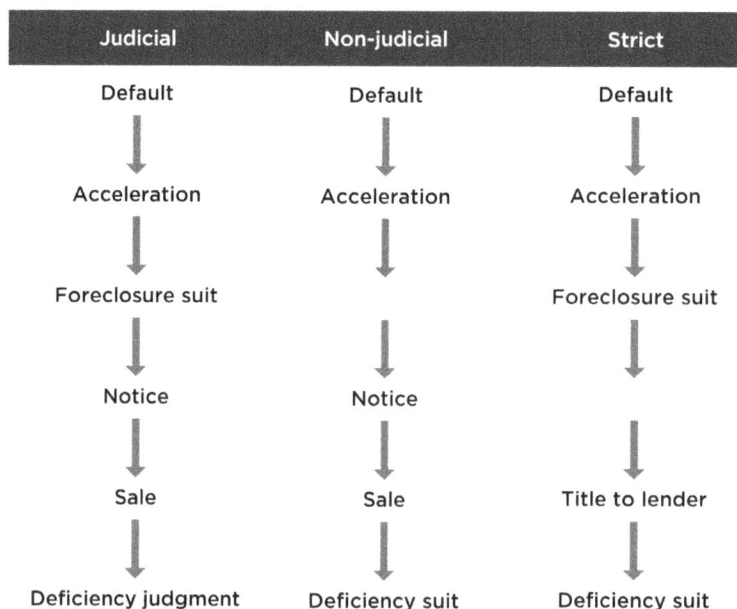

Judicial	Non-judicial	Strict
Default	Default	Default
↓	↓	↓
Acceleration	Acceleration	Acceleration
↓	↓	↓
Foreclosure suit		Foreclosure suit
↓	↓	↓
Notice	Notice	
↓	↓	↓
Sale	Sale	Title to lender
↓	↓	↓
Deficiency judgment	Deficiency suit	Deficiency suit

Judicial foreclosure. Judicial foreclosure occurs in states (such as Florida) that use a two-party mortgage document (borrower and lender) that does not contain a "power of sale" provision. Lacking this provision, a lender must file a **foreclosure suit** and undertake a court proceeding to enforce the lien.

▶ **acceleration and filing**

If a borrower has failed to meet loan obligations in spite of proper notice and applicable grace periods, the lender can **accelerate** the loan, or declare that the loan balance and all other sums due on the loan are payable immediately.

If the borrower does not pay off the loan in full, the lender then files a foreclosure suit, naming the borrower as defendant. The suit asks the court to:

- terminate the defendant's interests in the property
- order the property sold publicly to the highest bidder
- order the proceeds applied to the debt

▶ **lis pendens**

In the foreclosure suit, a **lis pendens** gives public notice that the mortgaged property may soon have a judgment issued against it. This notice enables other lienholders to join in the suit against the defendant.

▶ **writ of execution**

If the defendant fails to meet the demands of the suit during a prescribed period, the court orders the termination of interests of any and all parties in the property, and orders the property to be sold. The court's **writ of execution** authorizes an official, such as the county sheriff, to seize and sell the foreclosed property.

▶ **public sale and sale proceeds**

After public notice of the sale, the property is auctioned to the highest bidder. The new owner receives title free and clear of all previous liens, whether the lienholders have been paid or not. Proceeds of the sale are applied to payment of liens according to priority. After payment of real estate taxes, lienholders' claims and costs of the sale, any remaining funds go to the mortgagor (borrower).

▶ **deficiency judgment**

If the sale does not yield sufficient funds to cover the amounts owed, the mortgagee may ask the court for a deficiency judgment. This enables the lender to attach and foreclose a judgment lien on other real or personal property the borrower owns.

▸ **right of redemption**

The borrower's right of redemption, also called equity of redemption, is the right to *reclaim a property* that has been foreclosed by paying off amounts owed to creditors, including interest and costs. Redemption is possible within a **redemption period**. Florida allows redemption at any time until the foreclosure sale concludes.

Non-judicial foreclosure. When there is a "power of sale" provision in the mortgage or trust deed document, a non-judicial foreclosure can force the sale of the liened property *without a foreclosure suit*. The "power of sale" clause in effect enables the mortgagee to order a public sale without court decree.

▸ **foreclosure process**

On default, the foreclosing mortgagee records and delivers notice to the borrower and other lienholders. After the proper period, a "notice of sale" is published, the sale is conducted, and all liens are extinguished. The highest bidder then receives unencumbered title to the property.

▸ **deficiency suit**

The lender does not obtain a deficiency judgment or lien in a non-judicial foreclosure action. The lender instead must file a new deficiency suit against the borrower.

▸ **reinstatement and redemption**

During the notice of default and notice of sale periods, the borrower may pay the lender and terminate the proceedings. Reinstatement and redemption rights in Florida end with the conclusion of the foreclosure sale. There is no redemption right in non-judicial foreclosure.

Strict foreclosure. Strict foreclosure is a court proceeding that gives the lender title directly, by court order, instead of giving cash proceeds from a public sale.

On default, the lender gives the borrower official notice. After a prescribed period, the lender files suit in court, whereupon the court establishes a period within which the defaulting party must repay the amounts owed. If the defaulter does not repay the funds, the court orders transfer of full, legal title to the lender.

Deed in lieu of foreclosure

A defaulting borrower who faces foreclosure may avoid court actions and costs by voluntarily deeding the property to the mortgagee. This is accomplished with a deed in lieu of foreclosure which transfers legal title to the lienholder. The transfer, however, does not terminate any existing liens on the property.

Short sale

A **short sale** occurs when a property owner owes more than resale value and loan pay-off and agrees to let the lender sell it in exchange for release from the lien. The lender may or may not agree to accept the deficient price as satisfaction and may require the seller to pay the deficiency by way of a deficiency judgment. There may also be tax consequences for the seller. To avoid the deficiency, seller must make sure that the agreements include a full release of the underlying debt and a statement that it was fully satisfied.

After retaking property via foreclosure or short sale, the property becomes "bank owned." **Forbearance** or a **loan modification** allows the borrower to avoid legal action and keep the property under a new agreement with the lender.

The parties to a short sale are the buyer and seller. The lender is a third party contingency who must approve the sale. The process is generally as follows.

Short sale procedure

1. The borrower or borrower's agents contact the lender to discuss the short sale option.
2. If willing, the lender sets the required terms of the short sale.
3. The real estate agent provides the lender a Broker's Price Opinion (BPO).
4. The agent lists the property for sale at the price that will cover the mortgage.
5. The agent places a note in the Multiple Listing Service (MLS) stating that the lender will consider a short sale.
6. A buyer submits an offer.
7. The owner agrees to the contract
8. The lender approves the short sale.
9. The transaction closes.
10. Lender's action to recover deficiency may ensue.

Income property foreclosure

Salient characteristics. Just as with residential properties, loan instruments provide for default and recourse in the event the borrower fails to meet obligations – primarily the loan payments. One prime vehicle for effecting an income property foreclosure is the receivership clause.

Receivership clause. A receivership clause enables the lender to appoint a receiver to enforce recourse provisions upon the borrower's default. Specifically, the receiver is authorized to collect income proceeds directly from the property and apply such funds to payment of the delinquent loan funds.

12 Residential Mortgages Snapshot Review

MORTGAGE CONCEPTS

Mortgage law
- hypothecation: mortgage financing: using borrowed money secured by a mortgage to finance the purchase of real estate
- lien-theory—mortgagee holds a lien against the title; title theory—mortgage conveys title to mortgagee; Florida is a lien-theory state

Loan instruments
- promissory note: legal instrument executed by borrower stating debt amount, loan term, method and timing of repayment, interest rate, promise to pay; may repeat other provisions from mortgage document or deed of trust; negotiable instrument assignable to a third party
- mortgage instrument: pledges the property as collateral for the loan
- mortgage mechanics: borrower gives lender note and mortgage; lender gives borrower funds and records a lien
- **Fannie Mae / Freddie Mac Uniform Florida Fixed-Rate Note** – form used to standardize language for fixed-rate mortgage loans issued in Florida; see https://singlefamily.fanniemae.com/media/11241/display
- satisfaction of mortgage – lien release issued by lender upon borrowers fulfillment of loan obligations; used to verify clear title on title documents

Mortgage priority
- first mortgages are paid off before second or junior mortgages
- lienor can change priority by means of subordination agreement which changes priority of the lien

ESSENTIAL LEGAL PROVISONS OF MORTGAGES

Primary provisions
- promise to repay principal and interest, taxes and insurance, escrow, covenant of good repair

Other provisions
- may include, prepayment, acceleration, right to reinstate, due on sale, release, application of payments, charges and liens, insurance, lender's rights, private mortgage insurance, inspection, and other conditions of performance

COMMON MORTGAGE FEATURES

Principal
- original principal: capital amount borrowed on which interest payments are calculated

Down payment
- difference between purchase price and loan amount

Loan-to-value ratio
- loan amount divided by property value; percent of value a lender will finance

Interest
- charge for the use of money; rate fixed or variable
- Annual Percentage Rate (APR) includes interest and all other finance charges; lender must disclose on residential properties

Servicing
- collecting of payments; record-keeping; documentation; may be performed by original lender or passed to another entity

Escrow account
- reserve fund held in special account by lender for periodic payments of principal, interest, taxes and insurance

Discount points	• point = one percent of the loan amount, charged by lender at origination to obtain required return
Origination fee	• fee charged by lender to cover costs of processing loan application
Take-out commitment	• lender's offer to make a loan that retires another loan and replaces it
Term	• period of time for repayment of interest and principal
Payments	• scheduled periodic payments covering interest, principal, taxes and insurance
Assignment of mortgages	• original mortgagee transfers mortgage instrument and promissory note to another by means of assignment of mortgage; original mortgagor now makes payments to new mortgagee
	• estoppel: use of certificate of estoppel containing details of mortgage agreement to forestall contrary claims

PURCHASING MORTGAGED PROPERTY

Subject to the mortgage	• buyer takes title and makes loan payments to original mortgagee; original mortgagor (seller) remains responsible for loan
Purchase money mortgages	• seller acts as lender, takes mortgage and note from buyer, who makes payments to seller
Wraparounds	• seller receives junior mortgage from buyer, uses buyer's payments to continue payments to original lender
Assumptions	• buyer acquires title, makes new promissory note to lender, takes primary responsibility for loan; original mortgagor (seller) retains secondary responsibility unless novation note relieves seller
Contracts for deed	• seller holds legal title while buyer holds equitable title, takes possession, and makes payments to seller; legal title transferred when full sale price paid
Land development & construction loans	• loans used to finance new property development including land development loans; construction loans, blanket loans, buydowns and takeout loans

DEFAULT

Enforcement	• enforcement of mortgage lien by tax foreclosure sale, deed in lieu of foreclosure, or short sale
Foreclosure	• enforcement of liens through liquidation or transfer of encumbered property by judicial, non-judicial, or strict foreclosure
	• judicial: lawsuit and court-ordered public sale; deficiency judgments, redemption rights; used in Florida
	• non-judicial: "power of sale" granted to lender; no suit; no deficiency judgment; no redemption period after sale
	• strict: court orders legal transfer of title directly to lender without public sale
Deed in lieu of foreclosure	• defaulted borrower deeds property to lender to avoid foreclosure
Short sale	• borrower and lender agree to sell property for less than loan balance; lender may require seller to make up deficiency
Income property foreclosure	• remedy for defaulted income property where lender appoints a receiver to directly collect funds generated by the business. Called a receivership clause

SECTION TWELVE: Residential Mortgages

Section Quiz

1. A homeowner borrows money from a lender and gives the lender a mortgage on the property as collateral for the loan. The homeowner retains title to the property. This is an example of

   a. intermediation.
   b. forfeiture.
   c. hypothecation.
   d. subordination.

2. Which of the following best expresses the mechanics of a mortgage loan transaction?

   a. The borrower gives the lender a note and a mortgage in exchange for loan funds.
   b. The lender gives the borrower a mortgage and receives a note in exchange for loan funds.
   c. The borrower receives a note in exchange for a mortgage from the lender.
   d. The lender gives the borrower a note, loan funds and a mortgage.

3. A lender lends money to a homeowner and takes legal title to the property as collateral during the payoff period. They are in a

   a. title-theory state.
   b. lien-theory state.
   c. state allowing land trusts.
   d. state where hypothecation is illegal.

4. A lender who charges a rate of interest in excess of legal limits is guilty of

   a. redlining.
   b. usury.
   c. profit-taking.
   d. nothing; there are no legal limits to interest rates.

5. A lender is charging 3 points on a $500,000 loan. The borrower must therefore pay the lender an advance amount of

   a. $1,500.
   b. $3,000.
   c. $15,000.
   d. $30,000.

6. A distinctive feature of a promissory note is that

   a. it is not assignable.
   b. it must be accompanied by a mortgage.
   c. it is a negotiable instrument.
   d. it may not be prepaid.

7. When the terms of the mortgage loan are satisfied, the mortgagee

   a. may retain any overage in the escrow account.
   b. may inspect the property before returning legal title.
   c. may be entitled to charge the borrower a small fee to close the loan.
   d. may be required to execute a release of mortgage document.

8. The process of enforcing a lien by forcing sale of the lienee's property is called

   a. execution.
   b. attachment.
   c. foreclosure.
   d. subordination.

9. An important difference between a judicial foreclosure and a non-judicial foreclosure is

   a. there is no right to redeem the property in a non-judicial foreclosure.
   b. a judicial foreclosure forces a sale of the property.
   c. a non-judicial foreclosure ensures that all liens are paid in order of priority.
   d. the lienor receives title directly in a non-judicial foreclosure.

10. A defaulting borrower may avoid foreclosure by giving the mortgagee

    a. a promissory note.
    b. a deed in lieu of foreclosure.
    c. a redemption notice.
    d. a lis pendens.

11. The person who executes a mortgage is called the

    a. executor.
    b. trustor.
    c. mortgagor.
    d. mortgagee.

12. Why is mortgage priority important to a mortgage lender?

    a. It establishes the level of lender risk.
    b. It determines the importance of the loan in the lender's portfolio.
    c. It reassures the borrower that the lender will give full attention to servicing of the loan.
    d. It makes recording of the loan unnecessary, thereby saving the lender money.

13 Types of Mortgages and Sources of Financing

Qualifying for a Loan
Conventional Mortgages
Common Mortgage Types
Custom Mortgages
Government-insured FHA Program
VA Loan Guarantee Program
Primary Sources of Home Financing
Secondary Mortgage Market
Mortgage Fraud
Fair Credit and Lending Laws

Learning Objectives

- Describe the mechanics of an adjustable rate mortgage and the components of an ARM
- Describe the features of an amortized mortgage and amortize a level-payment plan mortgage when given the principal amount, the interest rate and the monthly payment amount
- Distinguish among the various types of mortgages
- Describe the characteristics of FHA mortgages and common FHA loan programs
- Identify the guarantee feature of VA mortgage loans and the characteristics of VA loan programs
- Explain the process of qualifying for a loan and how to calculate qualifying ratios
- Distinguish among the primary sources of home financing
- Describe the role of the secondary mortgage market and know the features of the major agencies active in the secondary market
- Describe the major provisions of the federal laws regarding fair credit and lending procedures
- Recognize and avoid mortgage fraud

Key Terms

adjustable rate mortgage (ARM)
amortized mortgage
balloon payment
biweekly mortgage
conforming loan
conventional mortgage loan
disintermediation
home equity conversion mortgage (HECM)
home equity loan
index
intermediation
level payment plan
lifetime cap
margin

mortgage insurance premium (MIP)
mortgage broker
mortgage fraud
mortgage loan originator (MLO)
negative amortization
nonconforming loan
nonconventional loan
package mortgage
partially amortized/balloon mortgage
payment cap
periodic cap
purchase money mortgage
reverse mortgage (HECM)
teaser rate

QUALIFYING FOR A LOAN

Equal Credit Opportunity Act
Loan application process
Loan underwriting
Qualifying the buyer
Loan commitment

To qualify for a mortgage loan, a borrower must meet the lender's qualifications in terms of *income, debt, cash, and net worth*. In addition, a borrower must demonstrate sufficient *creditworthiness* to be an acceptable risk.

Equal Credit Opportunity Act

The Equal Credit Opportunity Act (ECOA) requires a lender to evaluate a loan applicant on the basis of that applicant's own income and credit rating, unless the applicant requests the inclusion of another's income and credit rating in the application. In addition, ECOA has prohibited a number of practices in mortgage loan underwriting. Accordingly, a lender may not:

▶ discount or disregard income from part-time work, a spouse, child support, alimony, or separate maintenance. Further, the loan officer may not ask whether any of the applicant's income is derived from these sources.

▶ assume that income for a certain type of person will be reduced because of an employment interruption due to child-bearing or child-raising. The loan officer may not ask about the applicant's plans or behavior concerning child-bearing or birth control.

▶ refuse a loan solely on the basis that the security is located in a certain geographical area.

▶ ask applicants any question about their age, sex, religion, race or national origin, except as the law may require.

▶ require a spouse to sign any document unless the spouse's income is to be included in the qualifying income, or unless the spouse agrees to become contractually obligated, or the state requires the signature for some purpose such as clearing clouded title.

If a lender denies a request for a loan, or offers a loan under different terms than those requested by an applicant, the lender must give the applicant written notice providing specific reasons for the action.

Borrower requirements. The lender must rely on eight types of information to determine that the borrower has the ability to repay the loan:

1. current income or assets (excluding the value of the mortgaged property)
2. current employment status
3. credit history
4. monthly payment for the mortgage
5. monthly payments being made on other loans on the same property
6. monthly payments for other mortgage-related expenses
7. other debts
8. monthly debt payments compared to monthly income (debt-to-income ratio)

The lender cannot use a temporarily low rate (introductory or "teaser" rate) to determine qualification. For an adjustable rate mortgage (ARM), the highest rate the borrower might have to pay is generally to be used.

The "ability to repay" requirements are relaxed in certain circumstances where the borrower is attempting to refinance from a riskier loan (such as an interest-only loan) to a less risky one (such as a fixed-rate mortgage loan.

Qualified Mortgage. A Qualified Mortgage is one that meets the "ability-to-repay" requirements, has certain required features and is not allowed to have others. There are exceptions to these rules for certain kinds of small lenders. Issuing a Qualified Mortgage gives the lender certain legal protections in case the borrower fails to repay the loan.

Loan application process

The process of initiating a mortgage loan begins when a borrower completes a loan application and submits it to a lender for evaluation by the lender's underwriters.

Forms. Most lenders use some version of the "Uniform Residential Loan Application" promulgated by Fannie Mae. This form requests the borrower to provide information about the property and the borrower. The standard form includes the loan amount requested, based on an estimate of the purchase, refinance, or other underlying transaction.

Information required by the lender. The application must include supporting documentation for the information indicated in the following exhibit.

Property and Borrower Information

Property information	age & year built original cost	year acquired current loan balance
Borrower information	age employment history assets	education monthly income & expenses debts
Supporting documentation	appraisal report purchase contract	credit report income and employment verification

Completion. The application must be complete for the lender to consider it. The form must be signed and dated by the applicant(s) and delivered to the lending institution. The **initiation** of the application process occurs when the lender receives the completed application package from the applicant. Federal law requires the lender to accept all applications and to give applicants notice concerning the disposition of the application. If the lender denies the loan application because of fraudulent information on the application form, the borrower has no claim to a refund of the application fee.

Loan underwriting

Loan underwriting is the process of assessing the lender's risk in giving a loan. Mortgage underwriting includes:

> ▸ evaluating the borrower's ability to repay the loan
> ▸ appraising the value of the property offered as security
> ▸ determining the terms of the loan

Risk. A lender undertakes a number of risks in lending money. The principal risks are that the borrower will default on repayment of the loan, and that the borrower will damage the value of the property as security. In addition, the lender runs the risk that, in the event of a foreclosure, the sales proceeds from the property will be insufficient to cover the lender's loss.

Qualification. A lender assesses risks by examining, or *qualifying*, both borrower and property. In qualifying a borrower, an underwriter weighs the ability of the borrower to repay the loan. This requires an analysis of whether the borrower's income, cash resources, creditworthiness, net worth, and employment stability meet the lender's standards.

In qualifying a property, an underwriter assesses the ability of the property value to cover potential losses. In this evaluation, a lender requires that the appraised value of the property be more than adequate to cover the contemplated loan and costs. To protect further against loss, a lender will usually lend only a portion of the property's value. The relationship of the loan amount to the property value, expressed as a percentage, is called the **loan-to-value ratio, or LTV**. If the lender's loan to value ratio is 80%, the lender will lend only $320,000 on a home appraised at $400,000. The difference between what the lender will lend and what the borrower must pay for the property is the amount the borrower must provide in cash as a down payment.

Even if borrower and property qualify, a lender may, under certain circumstances, seek further protection against risk by requiring the borrower to obtain private mortgage insurance. This is frequently the case with loans requiring a relatively small down payment, leading to a high loan-to-value ratio.

Qualifying the buyer

Credit evaluation and credit scoring. A lender must obtain a written credit report on any applicant who submits a completed loan application. The credit report will contain the applicant's history regarding:

> ▸ outstanding debts
> ▸ payment behavior (timeliness, collection problems)
> ▸ legal information of public record (lawsuits, judgments,

bankruptcies, divorces, foreclosures, garnishments, repossessions, defaults)

Problems with payment behavior and legal actions are likely to cause a lender to deny the application, unless the applicant can provide an acceptable explanation of mitigating and temporary circumstances that caused the problem.

If a lender denies a loan on the basis of a credit report, the lender must disclose in writing that the applicant is entitled to a statement of reason from any creditor responsible for the negative report.

Since 1995, the Federal Home Loan Mortgage Corporation and the Federal National Mortgage Association have been encouraging lenders to use *credit scoring* to evaluate loan applicants. **Credit scoring** is a computer-based method of assigning a numerical value to an applicant's credit. The credit score is a statistical prediction of a borrower's likelihood of defaulting on a loan.

Qualifying ratios. Lenders want to be assured that the borrower has adequate means to make all necessary periodic payments on the loan in addition to other housing expenses and debts such as credit card payments and car payments. Most lenders use two ratios to estimate an applicant's ability to fulfill a loan obligation: an *income ratio,* or *housing expense ratio*, and a *debt ratio*, or *housing plus debt ratio or total obligations ratio*. They also consider the stability of an applicant's income. Please note that the income and debt ratios in the discussion below do not necessarily reflect the latest ratios used by FHA, VA, or other lenders. Check for updates on the websites of those agencies.

▸ **income ratio**

The income ratio, or housing expense ratio, establishes borrowing capacity by limiting the percent of gross income a borrower may spend on housing costs. Housing costs include principal, interest, taxes, and homeowner's insurance, and may include monthly assessments, mortgage insurance, and utilities. The income ratio formula is:

Income Ratio

$$\frac{monthly\ housing\ expense}{monthly\ GROSS\ income} = income\ ratio$$

To identify the maximum monthly housing expense an income ratio allows, modify the formula as follows:

monthly gross income x income ratio = monthly housing expense

Most conventional lenders require that this ratio be *no greater than 25-28%*. In other words, a borrower's total housing expenses cannot exceed 28% of gross income. For an FHA-backed loan, the ratio is 31%. VA-guaranteed loans do not use this qualifying ratio.

For example, if a couple has combined monthly gross income of $12,000, and a lender's maximum income ratio is 28%, the couple's monthly housing expense cannot exceed $3,360:

$$\$12,000 \times 28\% = \$3,360$$

▸ **debt ratio**

The debt ratio considers all of the monthly obligations of the income ratio *plus any additional monthly payments the applicant must make for other debts*. The lender will look specifically at minimum monthly payments due on revolving credit debts and other consumer loans. The debt ratio formula is:

Debt Ratio

$$\frac{monthly\ housing\ expense + monthly\ debt\ obligations}{monthly\ GROSS\ income} = debt\ ratio$$

To identify the housing expenses plus debt a debt ratio allows, modify the formula as follows:

monthly gross income x debt ratio =
monthly housing expense + monthly debt obligations

Most conventional lenders require that this debt ratio be *no greater than 36%*. For an FHA-backed loan, the debt ratio may not exceed 43%. The VA uses 41% and a variable "residual income" calculation. The FHA and VA include in the debt figure any obligation costing more than $100 per month and any debt with a remaining term exceeding six months.

Using the 36% debt ratio, the couple whose monthly income is $12,000 will be allowed to have monthly housing and debt obligations of $4,320:

$$\$12,000\ \text{gross income} \times 36\% = \$4,320\ \text{expenses and debt}$$

VA-guaranteed loans also require a borrower to meet certain qualifications based on net income after paying federal, state, and social security taxes, housing maintenance and utilities expenses. Such **residual income requirements** vary by family size, loan amount, and geographical region.

Income stability. A lender looks beyond income and debt ratios to assess an applicant's income stability. Important factors are:

▸ how long the applicant has been employed at the present job

▸ how frequently and for what reasons the applicant has changed jobs in the past

▸ how likely secondary income such as bonuses and overtime is to continue on a regular basis

> ▸ how educational level, training and skills, age, and type of occupation may affect the continuation of the present income level in the future.

Cash qualification. Since a lender lends only part of the purchase price of a property according to the lender's loan-to-value ratio, a lender will verify that a borrower has the cash resources to make the required down payment. If some of a borrower's cash for the down payment comes as a gift from a relative or friend, a lender may require a **gift letter** from the donor stating the amount of the gift and lack of any requirement to repay the gift. On the other hand, if someone is lending an applicant a portion of the down payment with a provision for repayment, a lender will consider this another debt obligation and adjust the debt ratio accordingly. This can lower the amount a lender is willing to lend.

Net worth. An applicant's **net worth** shows a lender the depth of the applicant's cash reserves, the value and liquidity of assets, and the extent to which assets exceed liabilities. These facts are important to a lender as an indication of the applicant's ability to sustain debt payment in the event of loss of employment.

Loan commitment

When a lender's underwriters have qualified an applicant and the lender has decided to offer the loan, the lender gives the applicant a written notice of the agreement to lend under specific terms. This written promise is the **loan commitment**. The commitment may take a number of common forms, including *a firm commitment, a lock-in commitment, a conditional commitment, and a take-out commitment.*

A **firm commitment** is a straight forward offer to make a specific loan at a specific interest rate for a specific term. This kind of commitment is the one most commonly offered to home buyers.

A **"lock-in" commitment** is an offer to lend a specific amount for a specific term at a specific interest rate, *but the interest rate is subject to an expiration date*, for instance, sixty days. This guarantees that the lender will not raise the interest rate during the application and closing periods. The borrower may have to pay points or some other charge for the lock-in.

A **conditional commitment** offers to make a loan if certain provisions are met. This kind of commitment generally applies to construction loans. A typical condition for funding the loan is completion of a development phase.

A **take-out commitment** offers to make a loan that will "take out" another lender's loan, i.e., pay it off and replace it. The take-out loan is most often used to retire a construction loan. The take-out lender agrees to pay off the short-term construction loan by issuing a long-term permanent loan.

CONVENTIONAL MORTGAGES

Down payment and LTV
PMI

A **conventional mortgage** loan is a permanent long-term loan that is not FHA-insured or VA-guaranteed. Market rates usually determine the interest rate on the loan.

Down payment and LTV

Because of the lack of insurance or guarantee by a government agency, the risk to a lender is greater for a conventional loan than for a non-conventional loan. This risk is usually reflected in higher interest rates and stricter requirements for the down payment and the borrower's income qualification.

The loan-to-value ratio (LTV) is often lower on conventional loans than on those with government backing, which means the down payment is higher. At the same time, conventional loans allow greater flexibility in fees, rates, and terms than do insured and guaranteed loans.

PMI

Because of the riskiness of conventional loans that have a down payment of less than 20% of the property value, lenders often require the borrower to obtain *private mortgage insurance, or PMI*. Mortgage insurance protects the lender against loss of a portion of the loan in case of borrower default. PMI can be paid as a lump sum annually or on a monthly basis. When the borrower has achieved 20 percent equity in the property (the loan balance falls to 80% of the home's original value), the lender or servicer must terminate the PMI requirement on the borrower's written request.

COMMON MORTGAGE TYPES

Amortized
Adjustable and fixed rate loans
Adjustable rate mortgages (ARM)

Variations in the structure of interest rate, term, payments, and principal payback produce a number of commonly recognized mortgage loan types. Among these are the following.

Amortized

Amortizing loan. Amortization provides for gradual repayment of principal and payment of interest over the term of the loan. The borrower's periodic payments to the lender include a portion for interest and a portion for principal. In a fully amortizing mortgage, the principal balance is zero at the end of the term. In a partially amortizing loan, the payments are not sufficient to retire the debt. At the end of the loan term, there is still a principal balance to be paid off.

Negatively amortized loan. Negative amortization causes the loan balance to increase over the term. This occurs if the borrower's periodic payment is insufficient to cover the interest owed for the period. The lender adds the amount of unpaid interest to the borrower's loan balance. Temporary negative amortization occurs on graduated payment loans, and may occur on an adjustable rate mortgage.

Adjustable and fixed rate loans

Loans may have fixed or variable rates of interest over the loan term. Adjustable rate mortgages (ARMs) allow the lender to change the interest rate at specified intervals and by a specified amount. Federal regulations place limits on incremental interest rate increases and on the total amount by which the rate may be increased over the loan term.

Adjustable rate mortgages (ARM)

Components and mechanics. There are numerous forms of adjustable rate loans, each with variations of the quantifications and limits on any or all of the following variables: the index, the margin, the adjustment interval, interest rate caps and whether the loan may amortize negatively.

▸ index – this is a financial indicator that determines whether the interest goes up or down, and how much.at the time of the loan's rate adjustment, the index has gone down, the loan's interest rate will go down

▸ margin – this is a number quantity indicating the spread to be maintained between the index and the loan's interest rate upon adjustment; if an index goes down a point, from 10 to 9 for example, then the rate would likewise go down a point, say from 5% to 4%

▸ adjustment interval – this is how often an interest rate is adjusted, which can be quarterly, annually, every 5 years, etc.

▸ interest rate caps- caps set upward or downward limit on how much an interest rate can increase or decrease; caps serve to minimize the potential damage or windfall that unlimited adjustments can create

▸ payment caps – this cap limits how much a payment can increase or decrease; some payment caps allow a borrower to actually pay less than what is owed at a given interest rate level; the lender then adds the unpaid amounts to the loan balance, which then begins to accrue more interest expense; here, the loan balance increases due to the deficient payment

▸ negative amortization – this is a loan with an increasing principal balance despite regular payments being made; usually there are caps as to how much balances can increase; this situation is remedied by requiring a balloon payment, or retiring the loan altogether

CUSTOM MORTGAGES

Partially amortized
Biweekly
Package
Home equity loans
Purchase money
Reverse annuity
Other loan types

Partially amortized

A loan that has a loan balance at the end of the loan term is a partially amortized, or balloon, loan. The monthly payments of principal and interest are not enough to fully repay the loan amount. A final payment (the balloon payment) is necessary to retire the loan. Florida requires a mortgage with such a loan to be clearly identified on the face of the mortgage, with the balloon payment amount specified.

Biweekly

If a loan is amortized in the way it would be for a regular amortized loan with twelve monthly payments per year, but payments are scheduled to be made twice per month (biweekly) instead of once, the result is that the equivalent of an extra monthly payment is made each year. This is because there are 52 weeks in a year, which means 26 biweekly payments, which equals 13 months. With this arrangement, the borrower pays off the loan more quickly and saves substantial interest.

Package

A package loan finances the purchase of real estate and personal property. For example, a package loan might finance a furnished condominium, complete with all fixtures and decor.

Home equity loans

The ostensible purpose of this type of loan is to obtain funds for home improvement. Structurally, the home equity loan is a junior mortgage secured by the homeowner's equity. For some lenders, the maximum home equity loan amount is based on the difference between the property's appraised value and the maximum loan-to-value ratio the lender allows on the property, inclusive of all existing mortgage loans. Thus if a home is appraised at $500,000 and the lender's maximum LTV is 80%, the lender will lend a total of $400,000. If the owner's existing mortgage balance is $325,000, the owner would qualify for a $75,000 home equity loan.

Purchase money

With a purchase money mortgage, the borrower gives a mortgage and note to the seller to finance some or all of the purchase price of the property. The seller in this case is said to "take back" a note, or to "carry paper," on the property. Purchase money mortgages may be either senior or junior liens.

Reverse annuity

In a reverse annuity mortgage, a homeowner pledges the equity in the home as security for a loan which is paid out in regular monthly amounts over the term of the loan. The homeowner, in effect, is able to convert the equity to cash without losing ownership and possession.

Other loan types

Senior and junior loans. When there are multiple loans on a single property, there is an order of priority in the liens which the mortgages create. The first, or senior, loan generally has priority over any subsequent loans. Second loans are riskier than first loans because the senior lender will be satisfied first in case of default. Therefore, interest rates on second mortgages are generally higher than on first mortgages.

Fixed and graduated payment loans. Loans may have variable payment amounts over the term of the loan, or a single fixed payment amount. With a graduated payment mortgage, the payments at the beginning of the loan term are not sufficient to amortize the loan fully, and unpaid interest is added to the principal balance. Payments are later adjusted to a level that will fully amortize the loan's increased balance over the remaining loan term.

Interest-only loan. In an interest-only loan, periodic payments over the loan term apply only to interest owed, not to principal. At the end of the term, the full balance must be paid off in a lump-sum, "balloon" payment. Since these loans have no periodic principal payback, their monthly payments are smaller than amortizing loans for the same amount at the same rate of interest.

Buydown loan. A buydown loan entails a prepayment of interest on a loan. The prepayment effectively lowers the interest rate and the periodic payments for the borrower. Buydowns typically occur in a circumstance where a builder wants to market a new development to a buyer who cannot quite qualify for the necessary loan at market rates. By "buying down" a borrower's mortgage, a builder enables the borrower to obtain the loan. The builder may then pass the costs of the buydown through to the buyer in the form of a higher purchase price.

Construction loan. A construction loan finances construction of improvements. This type of loan is paid out by the lender in installments linked to stages of the construction process. The loan is usually interest-only, and the borrower makes periodic payments based on the amount disbursed so far. As short-term, high-risk financing, the interest rates are usually higher than those for long-term financing. The borrower is expected to find permanent ("take out") financing elsewhere to pay off the temporary loan when construction is complete.

Bridge loan. A bridge, or gap, loan is used to cover a gap in financing between short-term construction financing and long-term permanent financing. For instance, a developer may have difficulty finding a long-term lender to take out the construction lender. However, as the construction loan is expensive and must be paid off as soon as possible, the developer may find an interim lender who will pay off the construction loan but not agree to a long-term loan.

Participation loan. In a participation loan, the lender participates in the income and/or equity of the property, in return for giving the borrower more favorable loan terms than would otherwise be justified. For instance, the borrower makes smaller periodic payments than the interest rate and loan amount require, and the lender makes up the difference by receiving some of the property's income. This type of loan usually involves an income property.

Permanent (take-out) loan. A permanent loan is a long-term loan that "takes out" a construction or short-term lender. The long-term lender pays off the balance on the construction loan when the project is completed, leaving the borrower with a long-term loan under more favorable terms than the construction loan offered.

Blanket. A blanket mortgage is secured by more than one property, such as multiple parcels of real estate in a development.

GOVERNMENT-INSURED FHA PROGRAM

Purpose
Characteristics of FHA loans

Purpose

The Federal Housing Administration (FHA) is an agency of the Department of Housing and Urban Development (HUD). It does not lend money, but *insures* permanent long-term loans made by others. The lender must be approved by the FHA, and the borrower must meet certain FHA qualifications. In addition, the property used to secure the loan must meet FHA standards. The FHA insures that the lender will not suffer significant loss in the case of borrower default. To provide this security, FHA provides insurance and charges the borrower an insurance premium. FHA loans typically have a higher loan-to-value ratio than conventional loans, enabling a borrower to make a smaller down payment.

Characteristics of FHA loans

The basic FHA-insured loan program is the **Title II, Section 203(b)** program for loans on one- to four-family residential properties. Among the features of this program are the following.

Qualifying ratios. FHA lenders use two ratios, the income ratio (also called the housing expense ratio, or HER) and the debt ratio (also called total obligations ratio or TOR) to assess a borrower's ability to repay a loan. These ratios are discussed in detail in a later section.

FHA mortgage insurance. The FHA determines how much mortgage insurance must be provided and charges the borrower an appropriate mortgage insurance premium (MIP). The initial premium is payable at closing (called an up-front mortgage insurance premium, UFMIP). Further annual premiums are charged monthly. The amount of the premium varies according to the loan term and the applicable loan-to-value ratio.

Lending source. The FHA does not make or process loans. It approves lenders, who then make loans according to FHA parameters.

Borrower default. The FHA reimburses the lender for losses due to default by the borrower, including costs of foreclosure.

Appraisal. The property must be appraised by an FHA-approved appraiser. The property must also meet the FHA's standards for type and quality of construction, neighborhood quality, and other features.

Maximum loan amount. The FHA has set maximum loan amounts for over 80 regions. Borrowers within a region are limited to the loan ceiling amount in effect for the region. In addition, the maximum loan amount is restricted by the loan-to-value ratios in effect. The maximum FHA-backed loan a borrower can obtain will be the lesser of the regional ceiling amount or the amount dictated by the loan-to-value standard. Calculations are based on the lesser of sale price or appraised value.

Down payment requirement. The minimum down payment for an FHA-backed loan is based on the lower of the appraised value or the sales price. The present requirement for single-family residential loans is 3.5%.

Maximum loan term. Thirty years is the maximum length of the repayment period.

Prepayment privilege. The borrower has the right to pay off the loan at any time without penalty, provided the lender is given prior notice. The lender may charge up to 30 days' interest if the borrower provides less than 30 days' notice.

Assumability. FHA-backed loans on owner-occupied properties are assumable if the buyer is qualified. Lenders and borrowers should check with FHA for current requirements.

Interest rate. The lender and borrower negotiate the interest rate on an FHA-backed loan without any involvement by FHA.

Points, fees and costs. The lender may charge discount points, a loan origination fee, and other such charges. These may be paid by buyer or seller. However, if the seller pays more than a specified percentage of the costs normally paid by a buyer, the FHA may regard these as sales concessions and lower the sales price on which the loan insurance amount is based.

In addition to Section 203(b) loan programs, FHA offers insurance coverage for other loan products. These include:

- ▶ home improvement loans
- ▶ subsidized loans for low- and middle-income families
- ▶ loans for condominiums
- ▶ loans for multi-family projects
- ▶ graduated-payment loans
- ▶ adjustable-rate loans

VA LOAN GUARANTEE PROGRAM

Guarantee feature
Characteristics of VA loans

Guarantee feature   The Veterans Administration (Department of Veterans Affairs) offers *loan guarantees to qualified veterans*. The VA, like the FHA, does not lend money except in certain areas where other financing is not generally available. Instead, the VA partially guarantees permanent long-term loans originated by VA-approved lenders on properties that meet VA standards. The VA's guarantee enables lenders to issue loans with higher loan-to-value ratios than would otherwise be possible. The interest rate on a VA-guaranteed loan is usually lower than one on a conventional loan. The borrower does not pay any premium for the loan guarantee, but does pay a VA funding fee at closing.

Characteristics of VA loans

Qualifications. VA –guaranteed loans are available veterans, their surviving spouse if not remarried, and persons on active duty.

Eligibility. Eligibility requirements vary depending on length of service and other circumstances. Prospective borrowers should consult the VA website https://www.va.gov/housing-assistance/home-loans/eligibility/ to learn how to acquire a Certificate of Eligibility to present to lenders.

Lending source. VA-approved lenders make most VA-guaranteed loans, although the VA can make direct loans where approved lenders are not available. The lender and the borrower negotiate interest rate, points, and closing costs.

Property eligibility. VA-guaranteed loans are issued for financing, refinancing, or construction of residential properties of one to four dwelling units provided the borrower resides in one of the units.

Qualifying ratios. The VA uses a debt ratio (total obligations ratio, or TOR) and calculations adjusted for regional incomes to qualify a borrower. This process is described further in a later section.

Borrower default. The VA reimburses the lender for losses up to the guaranteed amount if foreclosure sale proceeds fail to cover the loan balance.

Appraisal. The property must be appraised by a VA-approved appraiser. The VA issues a *Certificate of Reasonable Value* which creates a maximum value on which the VA-guaranteed portion of the loan will be based. The property must meet certain VA specifications.

Down payment requirement. The VA usually requires no down payment, although the lender may require one.

Maximum loan amount (entitlement). The VA does not cap the loan amount, but it does limit the liability it can assume, which usually influences the amount an institution will lend. The amount a qualified veteran with full entitlement can borrow without making a downpayment determines the practical loan limits. This amount varies by county. The basic entitlement available to each eligible veteran is $36,000. Lenders will generally lend a maximum of 4 times that amount without a down payment if the veteran is fully qualified and the property appraises for the asking price.

A veteran must apply for a *Certificate of Eligibility* to find out how much the VA will guarantee in a particular situation.

Maximum loan term. The maximum loan term for one- to four-family residences is 30 years. For loans secured by farms, the maximum loan term is 40 years.

Prepayment privilege. The loan may be paid off early without penalty.

Assumability. VA loans are assumable with lender approval. Usually, the person assuming the loan must have VA eligibility, and the assumption may have to be approved by the VA.

Interest rate. Lender and borrower negotiate the interest rate for all VA-insured loans.

Points, fees and costs. The lender may charge discount points, origination fees, and other reasonable costs. These may be paid by seller (with some limits) or buyer, but may not be financed. The VA funding fee, however, may be included in the loan amount. The funding fee is a percentage of the loan amount which varies based on the type of loan, military category, whether the loan is a first-time loan, and whether there is a down payment.

Other VA programs. In addition to insuring loans to veterans, the VA may insure loans for lenders who set up a special account with the VA. The VA may also actually lend money directly when an eligible veteran cannot find other mortgage money locally.

PRIMARY SOURCES OF HOME FINANCING

The mortgage market
Primary sources of home financing
Mortgage loan originators
Seller financing

The mortgage market Mortgage loans provide borrowers with funds to purchase real estate. Money for mortgages primarily comes from cash savings of individuals, government, and businesses. This money may become available through the process of **intermediation**, in which funds on deposit with financial institutions are loaned out to borrowers, or **disintermediation**, in which the owners of the savings invest their money directly by making loans or other investments. Government actions and investor activities affect the supply of money for mortgage loans and encourage or discourage the market for mortgage loans as an investment.

Supply and demand for money. Money is a limited commodity subject to the effects of supply and demand. The federal government's monetary policy *controls the supply of money* in order to achieve the country's economic goals. An excessive supply of money usually causes interest rates to fall and consumer prices to rise. Conversely, an excessive demand for money, such as for mortgage loans, causes interest rates to rise and prices to fall. Regulation of the money supply addresses these fluctuations with the aim to control and limit wide swings in the supply and demand cycle. These efforts, in turn, help to buffer the economy from severe inflationary or recessionary trends.

Regulating the money supply. The Federal Reserve System regulates the money supply by means of three methods:

> ▸ selling or re-purchasing government securities, primarily Treasury bills

- changing the reserve requirement for member banks. The reserve is a percentage of depositors' funds that banks and other regulated financial institutions may not lend out.

- changing the interest rate, or discount rate, the system charges member institutions for borrowing funds from the Federal Reserve System central banks

When the Federal Reserve sells Treasury bills, the money paid for the securities is removed from the economy's money supply. Conversely, when it repurchases Treasury bills, the cash paid out to investors puts money back into the economy.

The second control, regulating reserve requirements, effectively restricts how much money banks can put into the economy through the disbursement of loans. When the Federal Reserve *raises* reserve requirements, banks have less money to lend, decreasing the money supply. When the Fed *lowers* reserve requirements, banks have more money to lend, increasing the money supply.

The third control, and perhaps the most effective, is regulation of the discount rate which member banks must pay to borrow money. If the discount rate goes up, it becomes more cost-prohibitive to borrow. Therefore the money supply tightens. If the discount rate is lowered, banks have an incentive to borrow more money to lend to customers.

Primary sources of home financing

Primary mortgage market. The primary mortgage market consists of lenders who originate mortgage loans directly to borrowers. Primary mortgage market lenders include:

- savings and loans—residential mortgages and home equity loans; conventional, FHA, and VA loans

- commercial banks—construction loans; conventional, FHA, and VA loans

- mutual savings banks—residential and home improvement loans; conventional, FHA, and VA loans

- life insurance companies—commercial loans, especially for apartment, office, retail, industrial properties

- mortgage bankers—mortgage loan originations; FHA and VA loans

- credit unions—residential and home improvement loans; conventional, FHA, and VA loans

Mortgage brokers. Mortgage brokers are also part of the primary mortgage market, even though they do not lend to customers directly. Rather, they are instrumental in procuring borrowers for primary mortgage lenders.

The primary lender assumes the initial risk of the long-term investment in the mortgage loan. Primary lenders sometimes also **service** the loan until it is paid off. Servicing loans entails collecting the borrower's periodic payments, maintaining and disbursing funds in escrow accounts for taxes and insurance, supervising the borrower's performance, and releasing the mortgage on repayment. In many cases, primary lenders employ mortgage servicing companies, which service loans for a fee.

Portfolio lenders. A primary mortgage market lender may or may not sell its loans into the secondary market. Many lenders originate loans for the purpose of retaining the investments in their own loan *portfolio.* These loans are referred to as *portfolio loans*, and lenders originating loans for their own portfolio are called *portfolio lenders.* Portfolio lenders are less restricted by the standards and forms imposed on other lenders by secondary market organizations. In retaining their portfolio loans, portfolio lenders may vary underwriting criteria and hold independent standards for down payment requirements and the condition of the collateral.

Mortgage loan originators

Mortgage loan originators (MLOs) work for banks, credit unions, and savings and loan institutions, receiving and processing mortgage loan applications, negotiating loan terms and conditions, and selling existing mortgage loans to investors. An MLO license is necessary in Florida and requires a prescribed number of hours of education and passing of a test. The Secure and Fair Enforcement for Mortgage Licensing Act (SAFE Act) sets minimum standards for MLO licensing and registration. The Nationwide Mortgage Licensing System (NMLS) is the provider and registrar of MLO licenses.

Seller financing

The seller may provide some or all of the financing for the buyer's purchase. Some of the most common methods of seller financing are purchase money mortgages, including the wraparound, and the contract for deed.

Purchase money mortgage. With a purchase money mortgage, the borrower gives a mortgage and note to the seller to finance some or all of the purchase price of the property. The seller in this case is said to "take back" a note, or to "carry paper," on the property. Purchase money mortgages may be either senior or junior liens.

Wraparound. In a wraparound loan arrangement, the seller receives a junior mortgage from the buyer, and uses the buyer's payments to make the payments on the original first mortgage. A wraparound enables the buyer to obtain financing with a minimum cash investment. It also potentially enables the seller to profit from any difference between a lower interest rate on the senior loan and a higher rate on the wraparound loan. A wraparound is possible only if the senior mortgagee allows it.

Contract for deed. Under a contract for deed arrangement, the seller retains title and the buyer receives possession and equitable title while making payments under the terms of the contract. The seller conveys title when the contract has been fully performed.

SECONDARY MORTGAGE MARKET

Cycle of mortgage money flow
Fannie Mae
Government National Mortgage Association
Freddie Mac

Lenders, investors and government agencies that buy loans already originated by someone else, or originate loans indirectly through someone else, constitute the **secondary mortgage market**.

Secondary mortgage market organizations include:

▶ Federal National Mortgage Association (FNMA, or Fannie Mae)

▶ Federal Home Loan Mortgage Corporation (FHLMC, or Freddie Mac)

▶ Government National Mortgage Association (GNMA, or Ginnie Mae)

▶ investment firms that assemble loans into packages and sell securities based on the pooled mortgages

▶ life insurance companies

▶ pension funds

▶ primary market institutions who also invest as secondary lenders

Cycle of mortgage money flow

Secondary mortgage market organizations buy pools of mortgages from primary lenders and sell securities backed by these pooled mortgages to investors. By selling securities, the secondary market brings investor money into the mortgage market. By purchasing loans from primary lenders, the secondary market returns funds to the primary lenders, thereby enabling the primary lender to originate more mortgage loans.

The Mortgage Money Flow

Investors → Secondary Market → Primary Lenders → Borrowers

Primary lenders make a profit on the sale of loans to the secondary market. The secondary market acquires a profitable long-term investment without having to underwrite, originate, and service the loans. Secondary market organizations customarily hire primary lenders or loan servicing companies to service mortgage pools.

Secondary market loan requirements. The secondary market only buys loans that meet established requirements for quality of collateral, borrower and documentation. Since many primary lenders intend to sell their loans to the secondary market, the qualification standards of the secondary market limit and effectively regulate the kind of loans the primary lender will originate.

As major players in the secondary market, the Federal National Mortgage Association (FNMA, "Fannie Mae"), Government National Mortgage Association (GNMA, "Ginnie Mae), and Federal Home Loan Mortgage Corporation (FHLMC, "Freddie Mac") tend to set the standards for the primary market.

Fannie Mae

The Federal National Mortgage Association (FNMA, or Fannie Mae) is a government-sponsored enterprise, originally organized as a privately-owned corporation. As a secondary market player, it:

▸ buys conventional, FHA-backed and VA-backed loans

▸ gives banks mortgage-backed securities in exchange for blocks of mortgages

▸ offers lenders firm loan purchase commitments, provided they conform to Fannie Mae's lending standards

▸ sells bonds and mortgage-backed securities

▸ guarantees payment of interest and principal on mortgage-backed securities

Standardized note forms for Florida. The Fannie Mae / Freddie Mac Uniform Florida Fixed Rate Note for single-family properties can be reviewed via the following link: https://singlefamily.fammiemae.com/media/11241/display

Conforming and non-conforming loans. Loans that meet the guidelines of Fannie Mae are called conforming loans. Those that do not are, by the same token, called non-conforming loans.

Government National Mortgage Association

GNMA, or Ginnie Mae, is a division of the Department of Housing and Urban Development. Its purpose is to administer special assistance programs and to help Fannie Mae in its secondary market activities. Specifically, GNMA

▸ guarantees payment on FNMA high-risk, low-yield mortgages and absorbs the difference in yield between the mortgages and market rates

▸ guarantees privately generated securities backed by pools of VA-and FHA-guaranteed loans

Freddie Mac

The **Federal Home Loan Mortgage Corporation (FHLMC),** or Freddie Mac, is a government-sponsored enterprise, originally chartered as a corporation in 1970. As a secondary market player, FHLMC buys mortgages and pools them, selling bonds backed by the mortgages in the open market. Freddie Mac guarantees performance on FHLMC mortgages.

A federal conservator, the Federal Housing Finance Authority (FHFA), now operates Fannie Mae and Freddie Mac as conservator with the U.S. Treasury a majority owner of both organizations.

MORTGAGE FRAUD

Common types of mortgage fraud
Red flags

Mortgage fraud is a crime that involves an intentional misstatement, misrepresentation, or omission of information that a lender or underwriter relies on in making, buying, or insuring a mortgage loan secured by real property. Possible perpetrators include borrowers, loan officers, real estate agents, appraisers, attorneys, escrow and title officers, and others. Offenders may be prosecuted in both federal and state court.

Common types of mortgage fraud

Common examples of mortgage fraud include the following.

Applications. There many ways for a loan application to be fraudulent. For example, a borrower may attempt to obtain a loan on a property intended for investment at low interest rate by fraudulently stating that the borrower will occupy the property as a residence. In another context, the borrower may overstate income, understate liabilities, or make a false claim about employment to qualify for a loan.

Appraisals. An appraised value may be overstated or understated. Overstating may enable the borrower to obtain more money from the lender, possibly to share with the seller or an agent. Understating may allow a buyer to obtain a property at an artificially low price.

Multiple loans. A borrower may obtain more than one loan on the same property, creating unknown liabilities for lenders who have junior mortgages and requiring all the lenders to engage in litigation.

Lien stacking. Perpetrators may record multiple deeds of trust or assignment documents on the same property in a short period of time so that the liens won't be discovered in a title search. In this way, multiple lenders may be induced to make loans on the same property.

Identity theft. A person using a stolen identity may obtain a loan and abscond with the proceeds without making any payments to the lender. The person whose identity has been stolen may be left liable.

Straw borrowers. The credit information of an individual who is not the true buyer may be used to obtain a loan where the actual buyer would not qualify.

Loans. A buyer with poor credit may be qualified for a loan without being required to provide documentation of employment, income, assets, or indebtedness. When the borrower cannot repay the loan, the lender takes the collateral and profits from the fees and down payment.

Red flags

Inflated appraisals, inflated contract prices, missing or incomplete documentation, recently changed ownership, loan anomalies, and other such irregularities are red flags that may indicate that some sort of mortgage fraud is in progress. Associates should take note and report concerns to their brokers.

Mortgage fraud is a felony in Florida. The felony is one of the third degree if loan documents show a loan amount under $100,000, and second degree if it is greater. Florida's mortgage fraud statute can be viewed at http://www.leg.state.fl.us/statutes/index.cfm?App_mode=Display_Statute&URL =0800-0899/0817/Sections/0817.545.html.

FAIR CREDIT AND LENDING LAWS

Equal Credit Opportunity Act
Consumer Credit Protection Act
Truth-in-Lending and Regulation Z
Real Estate Settlement Procedures Act

Equal Credit Opportunity Act

ECOA prohibits discrimination in extending credit based on race, color, religion, national origin, sex, marital status, age, or dependency upon public assistance. A creditor may not make any statements to discourage an applicant on the basis of such discrimination or ask any questions of an applicant concerning these discriminatory items. A real estate licensee who assists a seller in qualifying a potential buyer may fall within the reach of this prohibition. A lender must also inform a rejected applicant in writing of reasons for denial within 30 days. A creditor who fails to comply is liable for punitive and actual damages. Other details of this act were discussed earlier.

Consumer Credit Protection Act

The Consumer Credit Protection Act (CCPA) is a comprehensive federal law composed of a number of specific acts relating to consumer credit and indebtedness. Among the specific acts that are most relevant to the real estate licensee are the Truth in Lending Act and Equal Credit Opportunity Act. These acts are discussed below.

Truth-in-Lending and Regulation Z

The Consumer Credit Protection Act, enacted in 1969 and since amended by the Truth-in-Lending Simplification and Reform Act, is implemented by the Federal Reserve's **Regulation Z**. Regulation Z applies to all loans secured by a residence. It does not apply to commercial loans or to agricultural loans over $25,000. Its provisions cover *the disclosure of costs, the right to rescind the credit transaction, advertising credit offers, and penalties for non-compliance with the act.*

The Dodd-Frank Wall Street Reform and Consumer Protection Act of 2010 (Dodd-Frank Act) established the Consumer Financial Protection Bureau (CFPB.) to protect consumers by carrying out federal consumer financial laws. The CFPB consolidates most Federal consumer financial protection authority in one place, including enforcement of RESPA, ECOA, and Truth in Lending.

Disclosure of costs. Under Regulation Z, a lender must disclose all finance charges as well as the true Annualized Percentage Rate (APR) in advance of closing. A lender does not have to show the total interest payable over the loan term or include in finance charges such settlement costs as fees for appraisal, title, credit report, survey, or legal work. Disclosure must be distinctly presented in writing.

Rescission. A borrower has a limited right to cancel the credit transaction, usually within three days of completion of the transaction. The right of rescission does not apply to "residential mortgage transactions," that is, to mortgage loans used to finance the purchase or construction of the borrower's primary residence.

Advertising. Any type of advertising to offer credit is subject to requirements of full disclosure if it includes:

- ▸ a down payment percentage or amount
- ▸ an installment payment amount
- ▸ a specific amount for a finance charge
- ▸ a specific number of payments
- ▸ a specific repayment period
- ▸ a statement that there is no charge for credit

If any of these items appears in the advertising, the lender must disclose the down payment amount or percentage, repayment terms, the APR, and whether the rate can be increased after consummation of the loan.

Noncompliance. Willful violation of Regulation Z is punishable by imprisonment of up to a year and/or a fine of up to $5,000. Other violations may be punished by requiring payment of court costs, attorneys' fees, damages, and a fine of up to $1,000.

Real Estate Settlement Procedures Act

RESPA (See also RESPA/TRID in next section) is a federal law which aims to *standardize settlement practices and ensure that buyers understand settlement costs*. RESPA applies to purchases of residential real estate (one- to four-family homes) to be financed by "federally related" first mortgage loans. Federally related loans include:

- ▸ VA- and FHA-backed loans
- ▸ other government-backed or -assisted loans
- ▸ loans that are intended to be sold to FNMA, FHLMC, GNMA, or other government-controlled secondary market institutions
- ▸ loans made by lenders who originate more than one million dollars per year in residential loans.

In addition to imposing settlement procedures, RESPA provisions prohibit lenders from paying kickbacks and unearned fees to parties who may have helped the lender obtain the borrower's business. This would include, for example, a fee paid to a real estate agent for referring a borrower to the lender.

To assist in informing and educating borrowers, RESPA requires that lenders provide a loan applicant with a **loan information booklet** and a **loan estimate**. The booklet, produced by the Consumer Financial Protection Bureau, explains RESPA provisions, general settlement costs, and the required **Closing Disclosure** form. The lender must provide the estimate of closing costs within three days following the borrower's application. RESPA is discussed further in the next section.

Disclosures. The Consumer Financial Protection Bureau (CFPB) requires lenders to use two specific forms to disclose settlement costs to the buyer. A lender must provide a Loan Estimate (H-24) within three days of receiving the loan application and allow the buyer to see the Closing Disclosure (H-25) three days before loan consummation. A lender must also provide a buyer with a copy of the information booklet, "Your Home Loan Toolkit," concerning mortgage loan, closing costs and closing procedures. The disclosures specify:

- ▸ settlement charges
- ▸ title charges
- ▸ recording and transfer fees
- ▸ reserve deposits required
- ▸ tax and insurance escrow deposits required
- ▸ any other fees or charges
- ▸ total closing costs

The disclosure forms vary, depending on loan type. The costs in the Closing Disclosure must match those in the Loan Estimate within certain standards.

13 Types of Mortgages and Sources of Financing Snapshot Review

QUALIFYING FOR A LOAN

Equal Credit Opportunity Act
- lender must evaluate applicant according to applicant's own income and credit information

Loan application process
- use required form; provide required information

Loan underwriting
- evaluate ability to repay; appraise property value; set loan terms; LTV: ratio of loan amount to property value

Qualifying the buyer
- income ratio and debt ratio qualify borrower's income; income ratio applied to gross income determines housing expense maximum; debt ratio takes revolving debt into account
- lender verifies applicant's sources of cash for down payment; extra cash enhances income qualification evaluation
- net worth: extent to which applicant's assets exceed liabilities as a further source of reserves
- credit evaluation: lender obtains credit reports to evaluate applicant's payment behavior

Loan commitment
- written pledge by lender to grant loan under specific terms; firm, lock-in, conditional, take-out

CONVENTIONAL MORTGAGES
- conventional mortgage loan: permanent, long-term loan not insured by FHA or guaranteed by VA

Down payment and LTV
- lack of government guarantee or insurance means higher down payment and lower loan-to-value ratio

PMI
- private mortgage insurance usually required if down payment less than 20% of value

COMMON MORTGAGE TYPES
- amortizing, negative amortizing, interest only, fixed rate, adjustable rate, senior, junior, fixed or graduated payment, balloon, buydown

Amortized
- principal and interest paid over loan term; if fully amortized, loan balance = 0 at end of term
- negatively amortized: loan balance increases over term; may occur on graduated and adjustable rate loans

Adjustable and fixed rate
- fixed-rate loans have unchanged interest rate over loan term; adjustable rate loans have changing rate, usually tied to a financial index

Adjustable rate mortgage components & mechanics
- key variables affect how rates and payments change; these are the index, the margin, the adjustment interval; interest rate and payment caps; negative amortization

CUSTOM MORTGAGES

Partially amortized
- monthly payments insufficient to pay down loan; balloon payment at end of term

Biweekly	• the loan is amortized for twelve months but half-payments are made twice a month, leading to an extra month's worth of repayment each year
Package	• the security for a mortgage loan incudes personal as well as real property
Home equity loans	• a junior mortgage secured by a home's equity
Purchase money	• borrower gives a mortgage and note to the seller; seller financing
Reverse annuity	• homeowner pledges home equity as security, receives periodic payments over loan term
Other loan types	• senior and junior, graduated payment, interest-only, buydown, construction, bridge, equity participation, take-out, blanket

GOVERNMENT-INSURED FHA PROGRAM

Purpose	• insure permanent long-term loans to protect lenders and enable buyers to make smaller down payment
Characteristics of FHA loans	• Section 203(b) program for 1-4 unit residential properties; income and debt ratios to qualify; mortgage insurance premiums; low down payment; points, fees, costs; assumable if qualified
	• insured loans granted by FHA-approved lenders to borrowers who meet FHA qualifications

VA LOAN GUARANTEE PROGRAM

Guarantee feature	• loans guaranteed for qualified veterans; enables lenders to lend more with lower down payment
Characteristics of VA loans	• borrower and property must be eligible; debt ratio with regional adjustments to qualify; no down payment required by VA; interest rate negotiable; points, fees, costs; loans granted by VA-approved lenders

PRIMARY SOURCES OF HOME FINANCING

The mortgage market	• originates mortgage loans directly to borrowers; savings and loans, commercial banks, mutual savings banks, life insurance companies, mortgage bankers, credit unions
	• relationship between money supply and demand affects interest rates, consumer prices, availability of mortgage money
	• Federal Reserve controls: T-bills; reserve requirement, discount rate
Mortgage lenders	• primary mortgage market: savings and loans, commercial banks, mutual savings banks, life insurance companies, mortgage bankers, credit unions; mortgage brokers find borrowers for lenders; portfolio lenders retain mortgage loans instead of selling to secondary market
Mortgage loan originators	• MLOs work for lenders; licensed and registered under SAFE Act
Seller financing	• purchase money mortgages: loans by the seller to the property buyer for all or part of the purchase price; contract for deed: installment sale where seller finances buyer and retains title until contract terms are met; wraparound: seller uses buyer's payments on second mortgage to make payments on first mortgage

SECONDARY MORTGAGE MARKET	• buys existing loans to provide liquidity to primary lenders; Fannie Mae, Ginnie Mae, Freddie Mac, investment firms, life insurance companies, pension funds
Cycle of mortgage money flow	• secondary market buys pooled mortgages from primary market, securitizes and sells to investors as securities; returns funds to primary lenders, maintains liquidity; secondary market sets lending standards
Fannie Mae	• FNMA buys conventional, FHA- and VA-backed loans and pooled mortgages; guarantees payment on mortgage-backed securities; sells mortgage-backed securities
Gov't Nat'l Mortgage Association	• GNMA guarantees payment on certain types of loans
Freddie Mac	• FHLMC buys and pools mortgages; sells mortgage-backed securities
MORTGAGE FRAUD	• intentional misstatement, misrepresentation, or omission of information in making, buying, or insuring a mortgage loan
Common types of mortgage fraud	• falsifying loan applications and appraisals; obtaining multiple loans, filing multiple liens; using stolen identity; using false credit information (straw buyer); issuing loans to unqualified buyers
Red flags	• signs of possible fraud: suspicious appraisals, contract prices, documentation, ownership, loan features
	• mortgage fraud a second or third degree felony in Florida
FAIR CREDIT AND LENDING LAWS	
Equal Credit Opportunity Act	• ECOA prohibits discrimination in lending
Consumer Credit Protection Act	• CCPA contains Truth-in-Lending Act and ECOA
Truth-in-lending and Reg Z	• Reg Z implements Truth-in-Lending Simplification and Reform Act and Consumer Credit Protection Act
	• provisions: lender must disclose finance charges and APR prior to closing; borrower has limited right of rescission; lender must follow disclosure requirements in advertising
Real Estate Settlement and Procedures Act	• RESPA standardizes settlement practices
	• provisions: lender must provide CFPB booklet explaining loans, settlement costs and procedures; lender must provide CFPB Loan Estimate of settlement costs within three days of application; lender must provide CFPB Closing Disclosure three days before loan consummation

SECTION THIRTEEN: Types of Mortgages and Sources of Financing

Section Quiz

1. Which laws or regulations require mortgage lenders to disclose financing costs and annual percentage rate to a borrower before funding a loan?

    a. The Equal Credit Opportunity Act
    b. Truth-in-Lending laws
    c. The Real Estate Settlement Procedures Act
    d. Federal Fair Housing Laws

2. Which laws or regulations prevent mortgage lenders from discriminating in extending credit to potential borrowers based on race, color, religion, national origin, sex, marital status, age, and dependency on public assistance?

    a. The Equal Credit Opportunity Act
    b. Truth-in-Lending laws
    c. The Real Estate Settlement Procedures Act
    d. Federal Fair Housing Laws

3. Which laws or regulations require mortgage lenders to provide an estimate of closing costs to a borrower and forbid them to pay kickbacks for referrals?

    a. the Equal Credit Opportunity Act.
    b. Truth-in-Lending laws.
    c. the Real Estate Settlement Procedures Act.
    d. Federal Fair Housing Laws.

4. The Federal Reserve System regulates the money supply in which of the following ways?

    a. Selling securities, printing money, and controlling lending underwriting requirements
    b. Buying securities, changing the discount rate, and controlling banking reserves
    c. Printing money, changing interest rates, and selling T-bills
    d. Controlling the prime rate, trading securities, and purchasing loans

5. One of the primary purposes for the secondary mortgage market is to

    a. cycle funds back to primary lenders so they can make more loans.
    b. issue second mortgages and sell them in the home equity market.
    c. lend funds to banks so they can make more loans.
    d. pay off defaulted loans made by primary mortgage lenders.

6. The major players in the secondary mortgage market are

    a. Fannie Mae, Freddie Mac, and Ginnie Mae.
    b. Fannie Mae, GMAC, and MGIC.
    c. Freddie Mac, FHA, and VA.
    d. Fannie Mae, Freddie Mac, and the Federal Reserve.

7. A principal role of FNMA is to

    a. guarantee FHA-backed and VA-backed loans.
    b. insure FHA-backed and VA-backed loans.
    c. purchase FHA-backed and VA-backed loans.
    d. originate FHA-backed and VA-backed loans.

8. The primary role of the Federal Housing Authority in the mortgage lending market is to

    a. guarantee loans made by approved lenders.
    b. insure loans made by approved lenders.
    c. purchase loans made by approved lenders.
    d. originate loans made by approved lenders.

9. The principal role of the Veteran's Administration in the mortgage lending market is to

    a. guarantee loans made by approved lenders.
    b. insure loans made by approved lenders.
    c. purchase loans made by approved lenders.
    d. originate loans made by approved lenders.

10. A graduated payment loan is a mortgage loan where

    a. loan funds are disbursed to the borrower on a graduated basis.
    b. the interest rate periodically increases in graduated phases.
    c. the loan payments gradually increase.
    d. the loan payments gradually increase and the loan term gradually decreases.

11. A buydown is a financing arrangement where

    a. the lender lowers the interest rate on a loan in exchange for a prepayment of principal.
    b. the borrower pays additional interest at the onset in order to obtain a lower interest rate.
    c. the lender requires the borrower to buy down the price of the property by increasing the down payment.
    d. the borrower pays the lender additional funds to buy down the term of the loan.

12. The key feature of an adjustable mortgage loan is that

    a. the interest rate may vary.
    b. the monthly payment increases over the life of the loan.
    c. the principal balance does not amortize.
    d. the loan term can be shortened or lengthened.

13. One feature of a wraparound mortgage loan is that

    a. the loan is a senior loan.
    b. the seller offering the buyer a wraparound can profit from a difference in interest rates.
    c. the underlying loan must be retired.
    d. the second mortgage borrower may make payments directly to the first mortgage lender.

14. A builder is required to secure a loan with mortgages on three properties. This is an example of

    a. a participation mortgage loan.
    b. a blanket mortgage loan.
    c. a permanent mortgage loan.
    d. a bridge loan.

15. Which of the following is true of a loan with negative amortization?

    a. The loan is an interest-only loan.
    b. Payments are not sufficient to retire the loan.
    c. The loan balance is diminishing, or going negative.
    d. Additional interest is being added to the monthly payment.

16. In addition to income, credit, and employment data, a mortgage lender requires additional documentation, usually including

    a. an appraisal report.
    b. a criminal record report.
    c. a subordination agreement.
    d. a default recourse waiver.

17. The three overriding considerations of a lender's mortgage loan decision are

    a. points, interest rate, and loan term.
    b. the location of the mortgaged property, the borrower's cash, and the amount of the borrower's equity.
    c. the ability to re-pay, the value of the collateral, and the profitability of the loan.
    d. the amount of the loan, the borrower's income, and the down payment.

18. The loan-to-value ratio is an important underwriting criterion, for the primary reason that

    a. borrowers with no equity will default and abandon the property.
    b. the lender wants to ensure the loan is fully collateralized.
    c. a borrower can only afford to borrow a portion of the entire purchase price.
    d. a fair amount of borrower equity demonstrates good faith.

19. The Equal Credit Opportunity Act (ECOA) requires lenders to

    a. extend equal credit to all prospective borrowers.
    b. consider the income of a spouse in evaluating a family's creditworthiness.
    c. discount the income of a person involved in child-rearing or child-bearing.
    d. specialize lending activity by geographical area for improved customer service.

20. The purpose of an income ratio in qualifying a borrower is to

    a. safeguard against over-indebtedness.
    b. compare one's earnings to one's short-term debt.
    c. identify the highest possible interest rate that the borrower can afford.
    d. quantify the borrower's assets to the fullest extent.

21. A borrower's debt ratio is derived by

    a. dividing one's total debt by one's debt payments.
    b. dividing one's gross income by one's assets.
    c. dividing one's gross income by one's debts.
    d. dividing one's debts by one's gross income.

22. A lender's commitment to lend funds to a borrower in order to retire another outstanding loan is called a

    a. conditional loan commitment.
    b. firm loan commitment.
    c. take-out loan commitment.
    d. lock-in loan commitment.

23. The difference between a balloon loan and an amortized loan is

    a. an amortized loan is paid off over the loan period.
    b. a balloon loan always has a shorter loan term.
    c. an amortized loan requires interest-payments.
    d. a balloon loan must be retired in five years.

14 Real Estate-Related Computations and Closing of Transactions

Basic Real Estate Computations
Preliminary Steps to Closing
The Closing Event
Real Estate Settlement Procedures Act
Financial Settlement of the Transaction
State Transfer Taxes
Other Charges
Rules of Thumb
Closing Disclosure Statement
Closing Cost Itemization: Case Illustration

Learning Objectives

- Compute the sales commission
- Calculate the percent of profit or loss, given the original cost of the investment, the sale price and the dollar amount of profit or loss
- Define settlement and title closing
- List the preliminary steps to a closing
- Prorate the buyer's and seller's expenses
- Calculate the dollar amount of transfer taxes on deeds, mortgages and notes
- Allocate taxes and fees to the proper parties and compute individual costs
- Explain the rules of thumb for Closing Disclosure entries
- Explain the major sections of the Closing Disclosure
- Demonstrate ability to read and check the Closing Disclosure for errors

Key Terms

arrears
credit
debit
preclosing inspection
profit
proration

BASIC REAL ESTATE COMPUTATIONS

Sales commissions
Calculating gain on sale

(See also Real Estate Math Section)

Sales commissions Sales commissions are negotiated between agent and client and are specified in the listing contract or buyer brokerage agreement. The seller is usually responsible for paying the commission in a listing agreement, and the seller or buyer may be responsible in a buyer brokerage agreement. Commissions are usually split between brokers and co-brokers and between brokers and their associates.

Co-brokerage commission

1. Formulas: sale price x commission rate = total commission

   total commission x split rate = co-brokerage commission

2. Example: A house sells for $600,000. The commission is 6%, and the co-brokerage split is 50-50.

   $600,000 x 6% = $36,000 total commission x 50% = $18,000 co-broker's commission

Associate's commission

1. Formula: broker's commission x sales associate's split rate = sales associate's commission

2. Example: Assume an $18,000 broker's commission and a 60% - 40% sales associate-broker split rate.

   $18,000 x .6 = $10,800 sales associate's commission

   ($7,200 to broker)

Calculating gain on sale Gain (or profit) is the amount one earns when selling an item over the amount one paid for the item. Thus, to calculate gain, it is necessary to know the total cost of the item and the amount realized from selling the item.

Total cost. In the sale of a residence, tax considerations aside, the total cost of the property is the original price paid plus other costs associated with the purchase and capital improvements made to the house.

> original price
> + <u>costs and capital improvements</u>
> total cost of property

Amount realized from sale. The amount realized from selling, also known as

net proceeds from sale, is the sale price received minus the costs of sale, such as commissions, fees, and other closing costs. Amount realized is expressed by the formula:

$$\begin{array}{r} \text{sale price} \\ - \quad \underline{\text{costs of sale}} \\ \text{amount realized on sale} \end{array}$$

Gain. Gain on sale is the difference between the amount realized on sale and the total cost of the property:

$$\begin{array}{r} \text{amount realized on sale} \\ - \quad \underline{\text{total cost of property}} \\ \text{gain on sale} \end{array}$$

Gain may now be expressed as a percentage of the total cost according to the formula:

$$\text{gain on sale} \div \text{total cost of property}$$

Thus, if a seller originally paid $300,000 for a house, including costs, spent another $50,000 putting on an addition, and sold it for $500,000 with $30,000 in selling costs, the percentage gain on sale is $120,000, or 34%, as follows:

$$\begin{array}{rl} \$300,000 & \text{original price} \\ + \quad \underline{\$50,000} & \text{costs and capital improvements} \\ \$350,000 & \text{total cost of property} \end{array}$$

$$\begin{array}{rl} \$500,000 & \text{sale price} \\ - \quad \underline{\$30,000} & \text{costs of sale} \\ \$470,000 & \text{amount realized on sale} \end{array}$$

$$\begin{array}{rl} \$470,000 & \text{amount realized on sale} \\ - \quad \underline{\$350,000} & \text{total cost of property} \\ \$120,000 & \text{gain on sale} \end{array}$$

$$\$120,000 \text{ gain} \div \$350,000 \text{ total cost} = 34\%$$

PRELIMINARY STEPS TO CLOSING

Contracting and escrow
The pre-closing period
Final preparations

Contracting and escrow

Fully executed purchase contract. Whether the contract is a standard form, such as the FAR/BAR "As Is" contract, or a custom agreement, it contains the terms and conditions governing the transaction. It sets forth the duties and obligations of each party, such as giving the buyer a certain timeframe to inspect the property. The contract should be reviewed and renegotiated until both parties are satisfied enough to sign it. The contract is enforceable only when it is fully executed.

Earnest money and other funds. After the execution of the contract (typically within three days), the buyer provides earnest money to the licensee as a good faith deposit. The licensee must turn the money over to his or her broker by the end of the next business day after receiving it. The broker must then deposit the earnest money into an escrow account within 3 business days from the date the licensee received the money.

The escrow account may be the broker's own escrow account or it may be with a title company or an attorney. The earnest money will remain in the escrow account until completion of the transaction (closing), at which time it will be transferred to the appropriate party. If the purchase contract calls for any additional funds from the buyer prior to closing, then those funds must be tracked and deposited into the escrow account as indicated in the contract.

The pre-closing period

Loan application and approval. A buyer who plans to finance the home purchase must obtain a mortgage loan prior to completing the purchase transaction. Buyers may obtain pre-approval for a loan before finding a home so they are aware of the maximum loan for which they qualify. Pre-approval also speeds up the closing process in that there is no additional wait time for loan approval. If the buyer has not been pre-approved, he or she must apply for and obtain loan approval. The buyer may also want to lock in the loan's interest rate in advance so there are no rate increases during the loan approval and transaction closing processes.

Most transactions allow for the contract to be contingent upon the buyer's obtaining conventional or FHA financing for the purchase. Since loan approval is typically a contingency within the purchase contract, the seller should be notified when the approval is obtained.

Contingencies. The purchase contract usually contains some contingencies to the purchase. Typical contingencies include the following:

- the buyer's obtaining financing
- the buyer's performing a home inspection and a pest inspection
- the seller's disclosing of all known material facts that can affect the home's value
- the seller's completing any agreed-upon repairs unless the contract is an "as is" agreement
- the buyer's right to cancel the contract based on the results of the inspections

The contract will include whether the contingencies are subject to active or passive approval. If they are to be actively approved, the contract must also include the dates by which the contingencies must be met and removed. If approval of the contingencies is to be passive, they will be considered approved if the buyer does not actively disapprove them.

Appraisal. The lender will order a property appraisal to ensure that the property's value is sufficient to cover the mortgage loan should the buyer ever default. The buyer will also be interested in the appraisal to determine if the selling price is in line with the property's actual value. The buyer has a right to receive a copy of the appraisal at least three business days before the scheduled closing.

Title search and insurance. A title search verifies the ownership of the property and uncovers any missing deeds and/or clouds on the title. The search is performed in the county where the property is located. Any issues found are the responsibility of the seller to correct. To protect against unknown title issues that appear down the road, both the lender and the buyer need separate title insurance policies.

Inspections. One of the most important steps in a real estate transaction is having the buyer inspect the property to ensure it is in saleable condition. This is especially important in a state as hot and humid as Florida, since the climate poses many risks to properties. The property inspection will check the structure and all systems on the property, such as plumbing, electric, HVAC, etc. Even with "As Is" contracts, property inspections are important to determine what issues, if any, the property has.

A pest inspection is separate from a property inspection and is especially critical in Florida where wood-destroying organisms (WDO), such as termites and carpenter ants, are a real threat. Inspectors issue a WDO report and provide copies to the buyer, lender, and title company. Contingencies in the contract should include actions to be taken if this inspection uncovers infestation or damage.

Required repairs. Unless the contract specifies the sale is "As Is," contingencies should include repairs, payment, or lowered sale price for any issues found in either inspection. Once the repairs are completed, the work should be inspected to assure it was completed and completed properly. Then this contingency can be removed.

Survey. Like inspections and title searches, a survey is crucial for confirming the suitability and representation of the property. Both title companies and lenders require surveys. Buyers should also require one, as a survey will confirm whether the property boundaries match what is stated in the publicly recorded legal description and whether there are any major encroachments on the property.

Buyer hazard insurance. Lenders require a property hazard insurance policy to be in place prior to closing. In Florida, insurance policies for flood and windstorms are also particularly important, and lenders will require them, depending on where the property is located (such as in a coastal and/or low-lying flood area). Property insurance rates are set by the company offering coverage, but standard flood coverage is a national program, so those rates are set by FEMA.

Final preparations

Final walkthrough. Before closing, the buyer and the buyer's agent should perform a walkthrough of the property to make sure the seller or tenant has vacated the property. They should also check for the removal of any furnishings and appliances that were not included in the sale and the completion of any previously agreed-upon repairs. This is the point to confirm that all related contingencies have been removed.

Review of closing documents. There are several vital closing documents that must be signed and executed before the closing is finalized. These include the warranty deed, bill of sale, closing disclosure, a closing statement, loan documents such as the note and mortgage, and title clearing documents. Some of these documents are prepared by the title company or attorney, and others are prepared by the lender.

Both the seller and the buyer need to review all of the documents they will be signing. While real estate licensees are not attorneys, they should be familiar with closing documents and be able to explain them to their clients and make any necessary changes or corrections they can legally make. They should go over the closing disclosure with their clients the day before closing is scheduled and plan to attend the actual closing.

Additional buyer funds. Prior to closing, the buyer may need to deposit additional funds into escrow. As the original earnest money is generally applied to the down payment, various additional payments may be required at different times before closing. For example, the lender may require the buyer to deposit money in the escrow account to pay for insurance and taxes for the property to protect the lender's collateral.

Just before escrow is closed, both the buyer and the seller receive a closing statement from the escrow officer which lists the purchase price and all the expenses associated with buying the property and how those expenses will be allocated between the buyer and the seller. Many of the fees listed on the closing statement will have already been paid. However, the final closing statement has the credits and debits, which are paid out of escrow on behalf of the party being debited. Both buyer and seller will want to inspect the closing statement to ensure that everything is in order. The seller will also want to be assured that the buyer has the money to close the transaction.

Earnest money transfer. In accordance with Florida license law, if the broker has held the earnest money in his or her own escrow account, the broker must account for and deliver all appropriate funds, deposits, payments, abstract of title, mortgage, conveyance, lease, and associated documents to the closing agent and/or other designated entitled individuals. When closing is imminent and the lender has approved the loan transaction closing, the closing agent will prepare to transfer the earnest money deposit, the additional buyer proceeds, and the mortgage loan funds to the seller.

THE CLOSING EVENT

The setting
The closing process
Transfer of title
Transfer of purchase funds
Escrow procedures
Lender closing requirements
Broker's role

The setting

The closing event is the culmination of the real estate transaction. During this event, the buyer pays the purchase price and receives title to the purchased real estate. At the same time, the buyer completes financing arrangements, and buyer and seller pay all required taxes, fees, and charges.

Customary practices. There are a number of customary procedures and practices for conducting real estate closings in Florida. For example, it is common for sellers to pay for the documentary stamp tax on the deed and for buyers to pay the documentary stamp tax on the note. See "Rules of thumb" later in this section for more examples.

Time. The sale contract sets the date of the closing, usually within sixty days of signing. The time period between signing and closing is expected to be sufficient for the removal of any contingencies, such as the buyer's obtaining of financing, the performance of inspections, and the correction of identified physical defects. Failure of either buyer or seller to perform pre-closing actions specified in the contract can delay or terminate the transaction. If the contract includes a statement that "time is of the essence," all parties agree to meet the time limitations exactly as stated. If both parties consent, however, they can re-schedule the closing date.

Location. Closings occur at various locations, such as the office of the title company, the lender, the escrow agent, one of the attorneys, the broker, or the county recorder. The sale contract specifies the location.

Parties at closing. The primary parties at the closing are normally buyer, seller, and a closing agent or escrow officer. Other parties who might be present include the title officer, attorneys, brokers or agents, and the lender's representative. It is not actually necessary for any of these parties to attend the meeting. The closing agent can complete the transaction, provided all documents have been duly executed in advance.

The closing process

The closing process consists of buyer and seller verifying that each has fulfilled the terms of the sale contract. If they have, then the mortgage loan, if any, is closed, all expenses are apportioned and paid, the consideration is exchanged for the title, final documents are signed, and arrangements are made to record the transaction according to local laws.

The Closing Process

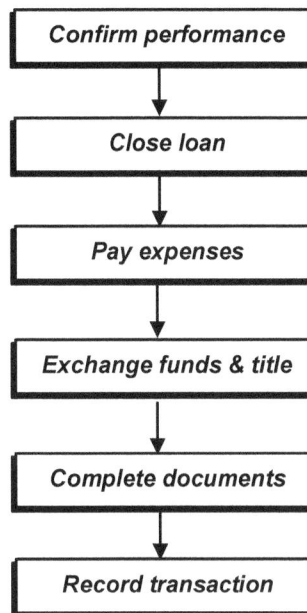

```
┌─────────────────────────┐
│  Confirm performance    │
└─────────────────────────┘
            │
            ▼
┌─────────────────────────┐
│      Close loan         │
└─────────────────────────┘
            │
            ▼
┌─────────────────────────┐
│     Pay expenses        │
└─────────────────────────┘
            │
            ▼
┌─────────────────────────┐
│  Exchange funds & title │
└─────────────────────────┘
            │
            ▼
┌─────────────────────────┐
│   Complete documents    │
└─────────────────────────┘
            │
            ▼
┌─────────────────────────┐
│   Record transaction    │
└─────────────────────────┘
```

Transfer of title

The seller must produce evidence of marketable title, such as a commitment for title insurance by a title insurer. Before making a title commitment, a title company performs a title search to discover any liens, encumbrances, restrictions, conditions, or easements attaching to the title.

If there are any encumbrances or liens that damage the title, the seller is expected to remove these prior to the date specified in the contract. The most common title cloud is an unpaid lien.

The seller may also be asked to execute an affidavit of title stating that, since the date of the original title search, the seller has incurred no new liens, judgments, unpaid bills for repairs or improvements, no unrecorded deeds or contracts, no bankruptcies or divorces that would affect title, or any other defects the seller is aware of.

The purchaser, purchaser's lender, or title company may require a survey to verify the location and size of the property. The survey also identifies any easements, encroachments, or flood plain hazard.

The buyer should inspect the property to make certain that the property is in the condition in which the seller states that it is, and that any repairs or other required actions have been performed. A final inspection, called a **buyer's walk-through**, should be conducted as close to the closing date as possible.

If the seller's mortgage lien(s) are to be satisfied at closing, the lender will provide a **payoff statement**, also called an **offset statement**, specifying the amount of unpaid principal and any interest due as of the closing date, plus fees that will be due the lender and any credits or penalties that may apply. The holder of a note secured by a trust deed will provide a similar statement, called a **beneficiary statement**, to show any unpaid balance. Even if the buyer is assuming the seller's mortgage loan, the buyer will want to know the exact amount of the unpaid balance as of the closing date.

Finally, the seller produces and/or deposits with the escrow agent the deed that conveys the property to the buyer.

Transfer of Purchase funds

The buyer usually produces and/or deposits with the escrow agent the following:

- earnest money
- loan funds and documents
- any other cash needed to complete the purchase

Escrow procedures

If the closing occurs "in escrow" rather than face-to-face, the principal parties deposit funds and documents with the appointed escrow agent, and the escrow agent disburses funds and releases documents to the appropriate parties when all the conditions of the escrow have been met. If for any reason the transaction cannot be completed, for instance if the buyer refuses the title as it is offered, or the buyer fails to produce the necessary cash, the escrow instructions usually provide a mechanism for reconveying title to the seller and funds to the buyer. In such a case, both parties return to their original status as if no sale had occurred.

Lender closing requirements

A lender is concerned about the quality of the collateral a borrower is providing in return for the mortgage loan. The collateral would be endangered by defects in the title, by liens that would take precedence over the mortgage lien, such as a tax lien, and by physical damage to the property which is not repaired. Consequently, the lender typically requires a survey; a property inspection; hazard insurance; a title insurance policy; a reserve account for taxes and insurance; and possibly, private mortgage insurance. In some cases the lender may also require a *certificate of occupancy* verifying that any new construction performed complies with local building codes.

Broker's role

A broker usually continues to provide service between the signing of the sale contract and the closing by helping to make arrangements for pre-closing activities such as inspections, surveys, appraisals and repairs and generally taking steps to ensure that the closing can proceed as scheduled.

A broker may conduct proceedings at the closing meeting, or may have no further role in the transaction after the sale contract is signed, depending on local practices and the transaction in question. In Florida, proceedings are conducted by a closing officer but the broker or associate is expected to be able to explain and verify entries on the closing documents and to attend the closing with the buyer and seller. The broker or associate is also responsible for delivering the escrow check to the closing.

Finally, if the seller of the property is a non-resident alien, U.S. law may require the broker to withhold and transmit to the Internal Revenue Service a portion of the sale proceeds to cover the alien seller's income tax liability. There are also special reporting requirements when the transaction involves a non-resident alien.

REAL ESTATE SETTLEMENT PROCEDURES ACT (RESPA)

**TRID
Information booklet
Loan Estimate
Mortgage servicing disclosure
Closing Disclosure
Disclosures after settlement
Limits on escrow accounts
Referral fees and kickbacks**

The **Real Estate Settlement Procedures Act** (RESPA) is a consumer protection statute enacted in 1974. Its purpose is to clarify settlement costs and to eliminate kickbacks and fees that increase settlement costs. RESPA specifies certain closing procedures when a purchase:

▶ involves a residential property, including one- to four-family residences, cooperatives and condominiums;

▶ involves a first or second mortgage lien; and

▶ is being financed by a "federally-related" mortgage loan, which includes loans made by a federally-insured lender; loans insured or guaranteed by the VA or FHA, loans administered by HUD, and loans intended to be sold to FNMA, FHLMC, or GNMA.

RESPA regulations do not apply to transactions being otherwise financed except in the case of an assumption in which the terms of the assumed loan are modified or the lender's charges for the assumption are greater than $50.

RESPA is directed at lenders and settlement companies, but licensees should be familiar with requirements and changes implemented as of January, 2014. The Dodd-Frank Act of 2010 granted rule-making authority under RESPA to the Consumer Financial Protection Bureau (CFPB) and generally granted the CFPB authority to supervise and enforce compliance with RESPA and its implementing regulations.

In 2013, the CFPB made substantive and technical changes to the existing regulations. Substantive changes included modifying the servicing transfer notice requirements and implementing new procedures and notice requirements related to borrowers' error resolution requests and information requests. The amendments also included new provisions related to escrow payments, force-placed insurance, general servicing policies, procedures, and requirements, early intervention, continuity of contact, loss mitigation and the relation of RESPA's servicing provisions to state law. These RESPA amendments went into effect on January 10, 2014.

TRID   Effective October 3, 2015, a TILA/RESPA Integrated Disclosure Rule (TRID) integrates the disclosure requirements of RESPA and Truth-in-Lending, replacing the old Good Faith Estimate form and HUD-1 Uniform Settlement Statement with a new Loan Estimate form and Closing Disclosure form, respectively.

Information booklet

A lender subject to RESPA must give loan applicants the CFPB booklet, "Your Home Loan Toolkit," within three days of receiving a loan application. This booklet describes loans, closing costs, and the Closing Disclosure form.

Loan Estimate

A lender must give the applicant, at the time of application or within three business days of application, a Loan Estimate (H-24) of likely settlement costs. This estimate is usually based on comparable transactions completed in the area. The terms stated in the Closing Disclosure must agree with those of the Loan Estimate within certain limits.

Mortgage servicing disclosure

The lender must disclose to the buyer whether the lender intends to service the loan or convey it to another lender for servicing. This disclosure must also be accompanied by information as to how the buyer can resolve complaints.

Closing Disclosure

Under CFPB rules, a lender must use the Closing Disclosure (H-25) to disclose settlement costs to the buyer. This form covers all costs that the buyer will have to pay at closing, whether to the lender or to other parties. Use of this form enforces RESPA's prohibitions against a lender's requiring a buyer to deposit an excessive amount in the tax and insurance escrow account or to use a particular title company for title insurance. The consumer must receive the completed form not later than three business days before closing and has the right to inspect a revised form one business day before closing. A description and example of this form are provided later in this section.

Disclosures after settlement

Loan servicers must provide borrowers with an annual escrow statement which summarizes all inflows and outflows in the prior 12-month period. The statement must also disclose shortfalls or overages in the account, and how the discrepancies will be resolved.

Limits on escrow accounts

Section 10 of RESPA limits the amounts lenders can require borrowers to place in escrow for purposes of paying taxes, hazard insurance, and other property-related expenses. The limitation applies to the initial deposits as well as deposits made over the course of the loan's term.

Referral fees and kickbacks

RESPA prohibits the payment of fees as part of a real estate settlement when no services are actually rendered. This prohibition includes referral fees for such services as title searches, title insurance, mortgage loans, appraisals, credit reports, inspections, surveys, and legal services.

Business relationships and affiliations among real estate firms, mortgage brokers, title insurance firms and other such companies that are involved in a transaction are permitted, provided the relationships are disclosed in writing to the consumer, the consumer is free to go elsewhere for the relevant service, and the companies do not exchange fees for referrals.

FINANCIAL SETTLEMENT OF THE TRANSACTION

Settlement process
Selling terms and closing costs
Debits and credits
Prorated items
Computing prorations

Settlement process   The process of settlement consists of five basic steps:

1. Identify selling terms and closing costs.
2. Determine non-prorated debits and credits.
3. Determine prorated debits and credits.
4. Complete the closing statement.
5. Disburse funds.

Selling terms and closing costs

Selling terms are the price of the property, the buyer's deposit and downpayment, and the terms and amounts of the buyer's financing arrangements. Closing costs are final expenses that buyer or seller must pay at closing to complete the transaction. The sale contract identifies all selling terms and who pays which costs. The apportionment of expenses is subject to negotiation, and in the absence of a specific agreement, is determined by custom. Closing costs include such items as brokerage fees, mortgage-related fees, title-related expenses, and real estate taxes.

Debits and credits   The closing statement accounts for the debits and credits of the buyer and seller to settle and complete the transaction. A debit is an amount that one party must pay at closing or has already paid prior to closing. A credit is an amount that a party must receive at closing or that has already been received prior to closing.

The excess of the buyer's debits over the buyer's credits is the amount the buyer must bring to the closing. The excess of the seller's credits over the seller's debits is the amount the seller will receive at closing.

An individual expense item that one party owes to a party unrelated to the transaction, such as an attorney or the state, is treated as *a debit to that party only*. An income or expense item that affects both parties is apportioned, or **prorated**, to each party to reflect the proper amount that each owes or should receive. A prorated item is treated as *a debit to one party and a credit to the other party for the same amount.*

Prorated items   **Non-prorated items.** Non-prorated items are costs *incurred by one party only.* Items not prorated include those listed in the next exhibit.

Non-Prorated Items

Buyer usually pays	Seller usually pays
Mortgage recording fees Documentary stamp tax Intangible tax on mortgage Mortgage-related fees: appraisal, credit, survey, loan Impound reserves: insurance, taxes Attorney fees	Stamp tax on deed Title insurance Brokerage fee Inspection fees Title-related expenses Attorney fees

Prorated items. Many of the items to be settled at the closing are partly the responsibility of the buyer and partly of the seller. Some are expense items that the seller has *paid in advance*, where the buyer owes the seller part of the expense. Some are income items that the seller received in advance, and the seller owes the buyer a part of the income. Others are items the buyer will have to pay *in arrears*, and the seller owes the buyer part of the expense. The method of dividing financial responsibility for such items is **proration**. With a prorated item, there is always a debit to one party and a corresponding credit for the same amount to the other party.

Items paid in advance. At the time of closing, the seller has paid some items in advance that cover a period of time that goes beyond the closing date. In effect, the seller has prepaid some of the buyer's expenses, and the buyer must reimburse the seller. Heating oil and natural gas are typical items. By the same token, the seller of a rental property may have received rent or rental deposits in advance, and must reimburse the buyer for the part that belongs to the buyer.
For an expense the seller paid in advance, *the buyer receives a debit and the seller receives a credit.*

For income the seller received in advance, *the buyer receives a credit and the seller receives a debit.*

Items paid in arrears. At the time of closing, the seller has incurred certain expenses that have not been billed or paid at the time of closing and that the buyer will have to pay later. A typical item is real estate taxes.

For an item the buyer will pay in arrears, *the buyer receives a credit and the seller receives a debit.*

Items Paid in Arrears and Advance

	arrears	advance
real estate taxes	x	
mortgage interest	x	
rents received by seller		x
utilities	x	

Computing prorations

The primary methods of calculating prorations are the 360/30-day method, which computes prorations on the basis of a 360-day year and 30-day month, and the 365-day method, which computes prorations on the basis of a 365-day year. The 360/30-day method is commonly used for prorating mortgage interest. Either method may be used for real estate taxes, depending on local practice.

It is customary in Florida that the seller owns the property up to midnight of the day before the closing date unless stated otherwise in the contract. Thus the closing day is apportioned to the buyer in computing prorations. The method of prorating, if not specified in the contract, will follow local custom.

12-month / 30-day method. The 12-month/30-day method determines an average daily rate of payment for an item to be prorated *based on a 30-day month and a 360-day year*. The method consists of the following steps for annual and monthly items.

Annual items

1. Identify the total amount to be prorated.
2. Divide this amount by 12 to obtain an average monthly rate.
3. Divide the monthly rate by 30 to obtain an average daily rate.
4. Multiply the monthly amount times the seller's number of months of ownership in the year of the sale up to the month of closing. For the month of closing, multiply the seller's number of days of ownership times the daily amount and add the result to the previous result. The final result is the seller's pro rata share of this item.
5. The buyer's pro rata share of an item is the total amount less the seller's pro rata share.

Monthly items

1. Identify the total amount to be prorated.
2. Divide this amount by 30 to obtain the average daily amount.
3. Multiply the daily amount times the seller's number of days of ownership. The result is the seller's pro rata share of this item.
4. The buyer's pro rata share of an item is the total amount less the seller's pro rata share.

Prorating Annual Item: Real Estate Tax
12-month/30-day Method

A sale transaction on a single-family house closes on March 2. County taxes for the previous year, to be paid in arrears, amount to $1,730. The seller owns the house through the day of closing. What are the seller's and buyer's prorated shares of this item?

Total amount due:		=	$	1,730.00
Monthly amount:	1,730 ÷ 12	=	$	144.17
Daily amount:	144.17 ÷ 30	=	$	4.81
Seller's share:	144.17 x 2 mo.	=	$	288.34
	4.81 x 2 days	=	$	9.62
	288.34 + 9.62	=	$	297.96
Buyer's share	1,730 - 297.96	=	$	1,432.04

Closing statement entries. The seller will be charged for the seller's share of the proration; an amount of $297.96 will be entered as a debit to the seller and a credit to the buyer because the buyer will have to pay the seller's share when the tax bill is received.

Prorating Monthly Item: Rent Received
12-month/30-day Method

The house in the previous example has been rented during the listing and selling period at a rate of $1800 per month. Rent for the month of March was paid to the seller on March 1. What is the buyer's prorated share of this rent? The day of closing, March 2, belongs to the seller.

Total received:		=	$	1,800.00
Daily amount:	1800 ÷ 30	=	$	60.00
Seller's share:	60.00 x 2 days	=	$	120.00
Buyer's share	1800.00 – 120.00	=	$	1,680.00

Closing statement entries. The seller will be charged for the buyer's share of the proration; an amount of $1,680.00 will be debited to the seller's account and credited to the buyer's account because the seller has received rent that belongs to the new owner after closing.

365-day method. The 365-day method uses the actual number of days in the calendar. The steps in the calculation are the same for annual and monthly prorations. The steps are:

1. Identify the total annual or monthly amount to be prorated.
2. For an annual proration, divide the total amount by 365 to obtain a daily amount (366 in a Leap Year). For a monthly proration, divide the total amount by the actual number of days in the month to obtain the daily amount.
3. Multiply the daily amount times the seller's number of days of ownership. The result is the seller's pro rata share of the item.
4. The buyer's pro rata share of an item is the total amount less the seller's pro rata share.

Prorating an Annual Tax Bill, 365-day Method

The seller in the previous example has a $1,730 tax bill, paid annually in arrears on December 31. Closing is on March 2, and the seller owns the day of closing. What is the seller's prorated share of this item?

Daily amount:	1730 ÷ 365	$ 4.74
Seller's share:	61 days x 4.75	$ 289.14
Buyer's share:	1730 - 289.14	$1,440.86

Closing statement entries. The seller will be charged for the seller's share of the proration; an amount of $289.14 will be debited to the seller's account and credited to the buyer's account because the buyer will have paid the seller's share of the tax bill in arrears.

STATE TRANSFER TAXES

State documentary stamp tax on deeds
State documentary stamp tax on notes
State intangible tax on mortgages

State documentary stamp tax on deeds

Transfer tax, or **documentary stamp tax** as it is referred to in Florida, is a tax imposed by states, counties, and cities on the transfer of the title of property from one person or entity to another within the jurisdiction. It is based on a percentage of the property's sale price, and it is due at closing or by the time the deed is recorded. Some jurisdictions in Florida mandate who is to pay the tax. The common practice is for the seller to pay the tax, but local market conditions influence who pays and allow for negotiations. For example, in a seller's market, the seller is in a position to negotiate for the buyer to pay; while a buyer's market puts the onus on the seller to pay.

Regardless of the market, sellers are mandated by law to deliver a recordable deed, which requires that the stamp tax has been paid. Consequently, if the seller is not able to convince the buyer to pay the tax, the seller will be responsible for paying it to be able to deliver the recordable deed. The party responsible for paying the tax would have been negotiated prior to closing, so the tax will show as a debit on that person's column on the closing statement.

Because the tax is a revenue source for local governments, tax rates are periodically raised when needed for the city or county's budgetary expenses. Currently, the rate is $0.70 (70 cents) per $100 of the sale price throughout Florida. However, in Miami-Dade County, the rate is $0.60 (60 cents) per $100 of the sale price for single family homes with an additional surtax of $0.45 (45 cents) per $100 for other residential dwellings such as townhouses.

To illustrate, if the sale price of a single-family home in Broward County is $300,000, or 3,000 of the $100 tax units, the procedure is: multiply the total tax units by the $0.70 tax rate. The documentary stamp tax on this sale would be $2,100.

In Miami-Dade County, the same home with the same sale price would still have 3,000 tax units. Multiply those units by the $0.60 Miami-Dade tax rate, and the documentary stamp tax on this single-family home sale would be $1,800.

On another note, if the $300,000 sales had concerned condominiums in each of the two counties, in Broward County (or any other Florida county except Miami-Dade), the tax units, rate, and documentary stamp tax would be the same as for the single-family home: $2,100.

In Miami-Dade County, the tax units, rate, and documentary stamp tax would also be the same as for the single-family home: $1,800. However, the 3,000 tax units would also be multiplied by the additional $0.45 surtax rate to equal $1,350. That amount would then be added to the $1,800 to result in $3,150 due for the stamp tax.

Exemptions. Florida property transfer tax exemptions include the following transfers:

- for no consideration (as a gift)
- between spouses with no consideration and no existing mortgage
- between ex-spouses within 1 year of the divorce
- through a will
- through a partition deed
- by the U.S. government or between government agencies
- by eminent domain
- from a nonprofit organization to a state agency

State documentary stamp tax on notes

Intangible tax is calculated on the amount of loan shown on the promissory note. The promissory note is the document that creates and explains the debt, shows the loan amount, and details how the loan will be repaid. Florida statute imposes a one-time nonrecurring tax of 2 mills ($0.002) on each dollar of a mortgage loan or other lien against the property. It may be easier to figure the tax as $0.20 (20 cents) per $100 or $2 per $1,000 of the total loan amount. The intangible tax is due at the closing of the loan and is shown as a debit to the buyer on the closing statement.

The intangible tax works as follows. These taxes are not based on the location of the property within the state, nor do they differentiate between single-family homes and other residential dwellings. They are determined by the amount of the loan and not the value of the property. So, let's go back to that $300,000 home sale.

Let's say the buyer placed an offer for the full $300,000 and paid a cash down payment of $50,000. He then financed the remaining $250,000, which equals 250 of the $1,000 tax units. Multiplying the 250 tax units by the $2 tax rate results in an intangible tax of $500.

State intangible tax on mortgages

In addition to the documentary stamp tax charged on the sale of property, Florida statute also imposes a documentary stamp tax on mortgages and liens against property within the state. The rate of the tax is $0.35 (35 cents) per $100 of the total owed in accordance with the promissory note. The tax is paid by the buyer/borrower and is due at closing.

To illustrate, let's go back to the home sale for $300,000. Again, location within Florida is irrelevant. Again, let's say the buyer paid the $50,000 down payment in cash and financed the remainder of the sale price. Divide the financed $250,000 by 100 to determine the 2,500 tax units. Then multiply the 2,500 tax units by the $0.35 tax rate. The tax owed on this note is $875 and will show as a debit for the buyer on the closing statement.

OTHER CHARGES

Document preparation
Recording
Broker's commission
Title insurance

Document preparation

It is customary for the person who has to sign a document to pay the cost of preparing it. Thus, the seller pays for preparing the deed, and the buyer pays for preparing the mortgage and note. Each item will appear as a debit to the paying party on the closing disclosure, with no corresponding credit to the other party.

Recording

The party who wants a document recorded customarily is the one who pays the fee for recording it. Thus the buyer pays for recording the deed, even though the seller paid for preparing it. Again, the fee will appear as a debit to the paying party on the closing disclosure.

Broker's commission The listing or representation agreement establishes who pays commissions, but it is common that the person who employs the broker is the one who pays. The commission is a debit to the paying party on the closing disclosure.

Title insurance There are fees and charges for title-related items such as providing a title abstract or an opinion of title. There are also costs associated with the purchase of a lender's title insurance policy and an owner's title insurance policy. The question of who pays these charges is open to negotiation.

RULES OF THUMB

Seller credits and debits
Buyer credits and debits

Rules of thumb concerning who pays what are customary practices, not legally prescribed.

Seller credits and debits

Credits. Sellers are customarily credited for

- ▶ prepaid items
- ▶ purchase price

Debits. The seller's debits customarily include

- ▶ prorated property tax
- ▶ documentary stamp tax on deed
- ▶ owner's title insurance policy
- ▶ deed preparation
- ▶ seller's attorney fees
- ▶ broker's commission (if hired by seller)
- ▶ mortgage loan payoff
- ▶ prorated prepaid rent
- ▶ tenant's security deposits

Buyer credits and debits

Credits. Buyers are customarily credited for

- ▶ prorated property tax
- ▶ earnest money deposit
- ▶ prorated prepaid rent
- ▶ tenant's security deposits
- ▶ new mortgage loan proceeds

Debits. The buyer's debits customarily include:

- ▶ purchase price
- ▶ documentary stamp tax on new note
- ▶ lender's title insurance policy
- ▶ intangible tax on new mortgage

- mortgage and note preparation
- buyer's attorney fees
- deed recording
- mortgage recording

CLOSING DISCLOSURE STATEMENT

Forms and procedures
Good faith
Types of charges
Applicable transactions
The H-25 Closing Disclosure form

Forms and procedures

As mentioned earlier, the TILA/RESPA Integrated Disclosures (TRID) rule mandates forms and procedures in the closing process. These are as follows.

- Lenders must give the consumer a copy of the **booklet**, "Your Home Loan Toolkit" **at the time** of loan application.

- Lenders must deliver or mail the **Loan Estimate** (Form H-24) to the consumer **no later than the third business day** after receiving a loan application. (A "business day" in this context is any day on which the lender's offices are open for business. An "application" exists when the consumer has given the lender or mortgage broker six pieces of information: name; income; Social Security number; property address; estimated value of property; loan amount sought).

- Lenders must provide the **Closing Disclosure** (Form H-25) to the consumer **at least three business days** before consummation of the loan. (A "business day" in this context is any calendar day except a Sunday or the day on which a legal public holiday is observed. "Consummation" refers to the day on which the borrower becomes indebted to the creditor; this may or may not correspond to the day of closing the transaction.)

Good faith

Creditors are responsible for ensuring that the figures stated in the Loan Estimate are made in good faith and consistent with the best information reasonably available to the creditor at the time they are disclosed.

Good faith is measured by calculating the difference between the estimated charges originally provided in the Loan Estimate and the actual charges paid by or imposed on the consumer in the Closing Disclosure.

Generally, if the charge paid by or imposed on the consumer exceeds the amount originally disclosed on the Loan Estimate it is not in good faith, regardless of whether the creditor later discovers a technical error, miscalculation, or underestimation of a charge, although there are exceptions.

Types of charges

For certain costs or terms, creditors are permitted to charge consumers more than the amount disclosed on the Loan Estimate without any tolerance limitation.

These charges are:

> ▸ prepaid interest; property insurance premiums; amounts placed into an escrow, impound, reserve or similar account

> ▸ charges for services required by the creditor if the creditor permits the consumer to shop and the consumer selects a third-party service provider not on the creditor's written list of service providers

> ▸ charges paid to third-party service providers for services not required by the creditor (may be paid to affiliates of the creditor)

However, creditors may only charge consumers more than the amount disclosed when the original estimated charge, or lack of an estimated charge for a particular service, was based on the best information reasonably available to the creditor at the time the disclosure was provided.

Charges for third-party services and recording fees paid by or imposed on the consumer are grouped together and subject to a 10% cumulative tolerance ("10% tolerance" charges). This means the creditor may charge the consumer more than the amount disclosed on the Loan Estimate for any of these charges so long as the total sum of the charges added together does not exceed the sum of all such charges disclosed on the Loan Estimate by more than 10%.

For all other charges ("zero tolerance" charges), creditors are not permitted to charge consumers more than the amount disclosed on the Loan Estimate under any circumstances other than changed circumstances that permit a revised Loan Estimate.

If the amounts paid by the consumer at closing exceed the amounts disclosed on the Loan Estimate beyond the applicable tolerance threshold, the creditor must refund the excess to the consumer no later than 60 calendar days after consummation.

Applicable transactions

The Integrated Disclosures rule applies to most closed-end consumer mortgages. It does not apply to:

> ▸ home equity lines of credit (HELOCs)
> ▸ reverse mortgages
> ▸ mortgages secured by a mobile home or by a dwelling that is not attached to real property (i.e., land)
> ▸ loans made by persons who are not considered "creditors" by virtue of the fact they make five or fewer mortgages in a year.

However, certain types of loans that used to be subject to TILA but not RESPA are now subject to the TILA-RESPA rule's integrated disclosure requirements, including:

- construction-only loans
- loans secured by vacant land or by 25 or more acres
- credit extended to certain trusts for tax or estate planning

Guides and detailed information about the current TILA-RESPA rule can be found on the Consumer Financial Protection Bureau (CFPB) website at https://www.consumerfinance.gov/policy-compliance/guidance/tila-respa-disclosure-rule/

The H-25 Closing Disclosure form

The H-25 Closing Disclosure form consists of five pages. Pages 1, 4, and 5 vary, depending on the loan type. To illustrate the form, we use a sample disclosure for a *30-year fixed rate* loan that is presented on the CFPB website.

Page 1 has four sections: general information, Loan Terms, Projected Payments, and Costs at Closing.

General information. This section has three columns:

- Closing information –issue date, closing date, disbursement date, settlement agent, file number, property address, and sale price
- Transaction information – names and addresses for borrower, seller and lender
- Loan information – loan term, loan purpose, product type, loan type and loan ID number

Loan Terms. This section states the loan amount, interest rate, and monthly principal and interest payment, and indicates whether any of those amounts can increase after closing. It also gives specifics of any prepayment penalty or balloon payment.

Projected Payment. This section displays the borrower's payment for principal and interest and mortgage insurance, an estimated escrow payment, and the total estimated monthly mortgage payment for years 1-7 and 8-30 of the loan term. It also provides an estimate of monthly tax, insurance, and assessment payments and indicates whether the payments will be held in escrow.

Costs at Closing. The last section of page 1 shows the borrowers' total closing costs (brought forward from page 2) and the total amount of cash the buyer needs to close (brought forward from page 3).

Page 2 details the closing costs. There are two sections divided into four columns:

- Description of the costs—loan costs and other costs
- Costs paid by the borrower – "at closing" or "before closing"
- Costs paid by the seller – "at closing" or "before closing"
- Costs paid by others (in the example, someone other than buyer or seller pays for the appraisal)

Loan Costs. The first section deals with the loan costs:

A.   Origination charges, such as points, application fee, and underwriting fee

B.   Charges for services the borrower did not shop for - items the lender requires, such as appraisals and credit reports

C.   Services the borrower did shop for - items the borrower orders on his own, such as pest inspections, survey fees, and title insurance

D.   The total of A, B, and C above

Other Costs. The second section deals with additional transaction-related costs:

E.   Taxes and other government fees, such as recording fees and transfer taxes

F.   Prepaid items, such as homeowner's insurance, mortgage insurance, prepaid interest, and property taxes to be paid before the first scheduled loan payment

G.   Initial escrow payment at closing – an amount the borrower will pay the lender each month to be held in escrow until due, typically for insurance premiums and tax instalments

H.   Other costs not covered elsewhere on the disclosure, such as items as association fees, home warranty fees, home inspection fees, real estate commission, and prorated items

I.   The total of the costs of E, F, G, and H above

J.   The total borrower-paid closing costs from D + I above. This total is carried to the bottom of page 1 as "Costs at Closing – Closing Costs."

Page 3 has two sections, one for calculating cash to close, the other for summarizing the transactions of borrower and seller.

Calculating Cash to Close. The first section compares the final costs of the loan with the lender's original Loan Estimate. This calculation considers costs paid before closing, down payment, deposits, seller credits, adjustments, and other credits. The last line of the calculation is "Cash to close," the amount the borrower needs to produce at closing.

When an amount has changed, the creditor must indicate where the consumer can find the amounts that have changed on the Loan Estimate. For example, if the Seller Credit amount changed, the creditor can indicate that the consumer should "See Seller Credits in Section L." When the increase in Total Closing Costs exceeds the legal limits, the creditor must disclose this fact and the dollar amount of the excess in the "Did this change?" column. A statement directing the consumer to the Lender Credit on page 2 must also be included if the creditor owes a credit to the consumer at closing for the excess amount.

Summaries of Transactions. The second section of page 3 is divided into two columns (or subsections), one to summarize the borrower's transaction and the other for the seller's transaction. The borrower's column includes:

K.   amounts due from the borrower at closing, including the sale price and adjustments for items paid by the seller in advance.

L.	amounts already paid by or on behalf of the borrower at closing, such as deposit, loan amount, loan assumptions, seller credits, other credits, and adjustments for items unpaid by the seller, such as taxes and assessments.

The calculation at the bottom of the left column subtracts the totals already paid by the borrower (line L) from the total due from the borrower (line K) to derive the Cash to Close due from the borrower at closing. This figure is the same as that at the bottom of page 1 under "Costs at Closing – Cash to Close."

The seller's column of the Summaries section includes:

M.	amounts due to the seller at closing, including the sale price of the property and adjustments for items paid by the seller in advance.

N.	amounts due from the seller at closing, such as closing costs the seller will pay, payoff of first or second mortgages, seller credit, and adjustments for items unpaid by the seller, such as taxes and assessments.

The calculation at the bottom of the right column subtracts the total due <u>from</u> the seller (line N) from the total due to the seller (line M) to derive the Cash to Seller, which is the amount the seller will receive at closing.

Page 4 provides additional Loan Disclosures:

▶ Assumption –whether the lender will allow a loan assumption on a future transfer

▶ Demand feature –whether the lender can require early repayment

▶ Late payment – the fee the lender will charge for a late payment

▶ Negative amortization –whether the loan is negatively amortized, which increases loan amount and diminishes the borrower's equity over the term

▶ Partial payments –whether the lender accepts partial payments and applies them to the loan

▶ Security interest –identifies the property securing the loan

▶ Escrow account – itemizes what is included in the escrow account and states the monthly escrow payment

Page 5 provides additional calculations, disclosures, and contact information:

▶ Loan Calculations –the total amount of all payments on the loan, the dollar amount of the finance charges over the life of the loan, the amount financed, the annual percentage rate (APR), and the total interest percentage (TIP)

▶ Other Disclosures –other important information for the borrower, including the right to a copy of the appraisal report and an indication of whether the borrower is protected against liability for the unpaid balance in the event of a foreclosure

- ▶ Contact Information –names, addresses, license numbers, contact names, email addresses, and phone numbers for persons involved in the transaction.
- ▶ Confirm Receipt –the borrowers' signatures confirming receipt of the Closing Disclosure document. **Signing the document does not indicate acceptance of the loan.**

Closing Disclosure

This form is a statement of final loan terms and closing costs. Compare this document with your Loan Estimate.

Closing Information

Date Issued	4/15/2013
Closing Date	4/15/2013
Disbursement Date	4/15/2013
Settlement Agent	Epsilon Title Co.
File #	12-3456
Property	456 Somewhere Ave
	Anytown, ST 12345
Sale Price	$180,000

Transaction Information

Borrower	Michael Jones and Mary Stone
	123 Anywhere Street
	Anytown, ST 12345
Seller	Steve Cole and Amy Doe
	321 Somewhere Drive
	Anytown, ST 12345
Lender	Ficus Bank

Loan Information

Loan Term	30 years
Purpose	Purchase
Product	Fixed Rate
Loan Type	☒ Conventional ☐ FHA ☐ VA ☐ _____
Loan ID #	123456789
MIC #	000654321

Loan Terms

		Can this amount increase after closing?
Loan Amount	$162,000	NO
Interest Rate	3.875%	NO
Monthly Principal & Interest *See Projected Payments below for your Estimated Total Monthly Payment*	$761.78	NO
		Does the loan have these features?
Prepayment Penalty	YES	• As high as $3,240 if you pay off the loan during the first 2 years
Balloon Payment	NO	

Projected Payments

Payment Calculation	Years 1-7	Years 8-30
Principal & Interest	$761.78	$761.78
Mortgage Insurance	+ 82.35	+ —
Estimated Escrow *Amount can increase over time*	+ 206.13	+ 206.13
Estimated Total Monthly Payment	**$1,050.26**	**$967.91**

Estimated Taxes, Insurance & Assessments *Amount can increase over time* *See page 4 for details*	$356.13 a month	This estimate includes ☒ Property Taxes ☒ Homeowner's Insurance ☒ Other: Homeowner's Association Dues *See Escrow Account on page 4 for details. You must pay for other property costs separately.*	In escrow? YES YES NO

Costs at Closing

Closing Costs	$9,712.10	Includes $4,694.05 in Loan Costs + $5,018.05 in Other Costs – $0 in Lender Credits. *See page 2 for details.*
Cash to Close	$14,147.26	Includes Closing Costs. *See Calculating Cash to Close on page 3 for details.*

Sample H-25 Closing Disclosure, Page 2

Closing Cost Details

Loan Costs		Borrower-Paid At Closing	Borrower-Paid Before Closing	Seller-Paid At Closing	Seller-Paid Before Closing	Paid by Others
A. Origination Charges		**$1,802.00**				
01 0.25 % of Loan Amount (Points)		$405.00				
02 Application Fee		$300.00				
03 Underwriting Fee		$1,097.00				
04						
05						
06						
07						
08						
B. Services Borrower Did Not Shop For		**$236.55**				
01 Appraisal Fee	to John Smith Appraisers Inc.					$405.00
02 Credit Report Fee	to Information Inc.		$29.80			
03 Flood Determination Fee	to Info Co.	$20.00				
04 Flood Monitoring Fee	to Info Co.	$31.75				
05 Tax Monitoring Fee	to Info Co.	$75.00				
06 Tax Status Research Fee	to Info Co.	$80.00				
07						
08						
09						
10						
C. Services Borrower Did Shop For		**$2,655.50**				
01 Pest Inspection Fee	to Pests Co.	$120.50				
02 Survey Fee	to Surveys Co.	$85.00				
03 Title – Insurance Binder	to Epsilon Title Co.	$650.00				
04 Title – Lender's Title Insurance	to Epsilon Title Co.	$500.00				
05 Title – Settlement Agent Fee	to Epsilon Title Co.	$500.00				
06 Title – Title Search	to Epsilon Title Co.	$800.00				
07						
08						
D. TOTAL LOAN COSTS (Borrower-Paid)		**$4,694.05**				
Loan Costs Subtotals (A + B + C)		$4,664.25	$29.80			

Other Costs		Borrower-Paid At Closing	Borrower-Paid Before Closing	Seller-Paid At Closing	Seller-Paid Before Closing	Paid by Others
E. Taxes and Other Government Fees		**$85.00**				
01 Recording Fees	Deed: $40.00 Mortgage: $45.00	$85.00				
02 Transfer Tax	to Any State			$950.00		
F. Prepaids		**$2,120.80**				
01 Homeowner's Insurance Premium (12 mo.) to Insurance Co.		$1,209.96				
02 Mortgage Insurance Premium (mo.)						
03 Prepaid Interest ($17.44 per day from 4/15/13 to 5/1/13)		$279.04				
04 Property Taxes (6 mo.) to Any County USA		$631.80				
05						
G. Initial Escrow Payment at Closing		**$412.25**				
01 Homeowner's Insurance $100.83 per month for 2 mo.		$201.66				
02 Mortgage Insurance per month for mo.						
03 Property Taxes $105.30 per month for 2 mo.		$210.60				
04						
05						
06						
07						
08 Aggregate Adjustment		– 0.01				
H. Other		**$2,400.00**				
01 HOA Capital Contribution	to HOA Acre Inc.	$500.00				
02 HOA Processing Fee	to HOA Acre Inc.	$150.00				
03 Home Inspection Fee	to Engineers Inc.	$750.00			$750.00	
04 Home Warranty Fee	to XYZ Warranty Inc.			$450.00		
05 Real Estate Commission	to Alpha Real Estate Broker			$5,700.00		
06 Real Estate Commission	to Omega Real Estate Broker			$5,700.00		
07 Title – Owner's Title Insurance (optional) to Epsilon Title Co.		$1,000.00				
08						
I. TOTAL OTHER COSTS (Borrower-Paid)		**$5,018.05**				
Other Costs Subtotals (E + F + G + H)		$5,018.05				

J. TOTAL CLOSING COSTS (Borrower-Paid)		$9,712.10				
Closing Costs Subtotals (D + I)		$9,682.30	$29.80	$12,800.00	$750.00	$405.00
Lender Credits						

CLOSING DISCLOSURE

PAGE 2 OF 5 • LOAN ID # 123456789

Sample H-25 Closing Disclosure, Page 3

Calculating Cash to Close

Use this table to see what has changed from your Loan Estimate.

	Loan Estimate	Final	Did this change?
Total Closing Costs (J)	$8,054.00	$9,712.10	YES • See Total Loan Costs (D) and Total Other Costs (I)
Closing Costs Paid Before Closing	$0	– $29.80	YES • You paid these Closing Costs before closing
Closing Costs Financed (Paid from your Loan Amount)	$0	$0	NO
Down Payment/Funds from Borrower	$18,000.00	$18,000.00	NO
Deposit	– $10,000.00	– $10,000.00	NO
Funds for Borrower	$0	$0	NO
Seller Credits	$0	– $2,500.00	YES • See Seller Credits in Section L
Adjustments and Other Credits	$0	– $1,035.04	YES • See details in Sections K and L
Cash to Close	$16,054.00	$14,147.26	

Summaries of Transactions

Use this table to see a summary of your transaction.

BORROWER'S TRANSACTION

K. Due from Borrower at Closing	$189,762.30
01 Sale Price of Property	$180,000.00
02 Sale Price of Any Personal Property Included in Sale	
03 Closing Costs Paid at Closing (J)	$9,682.30
04	
Adjustments	
05	
06	
07	
Adjustments for Items Paid by Seller in Advance	
08 City/Town Taxes to	
09 County Taxes to	
10 Assessments to	
11 HOA Dues 4/15/13 to 4/30/13	$80.00
12	
13	
14	
15	

L. Paid Already by or on Behalf of Borrower at Closing	$175,615.04
01 Deposit	$10,000.00
02 Loan Amount	$162,000.00
03 Existing Loan(s) Assumed or Taken Subject to	
04	
05 Seller Credit	$2,500.00
Other Credits	
06 Rebate from Epsilon Title Co.	$750.00
07	
Adjustments	
08	
09	
10	
11	
Adjustments for Items Unpaid by Seller	
12 City/Town Taxes 1/1/13 to 4/14/13	$365.04
13 County Taxes to	
14 Assessments to	
15	
16	
17	

SELLER'S TRANSACTION

M. Due to Seller at Closing	$180,080.00
01 Sale Price of Property	$180,000.00
02 Sale Price of Any Personal Property Included in Sale	
03	
04	
05	
06	
07	
08	
Adjustments for Items Paid by Seller in Advance	
09 City/Town Taxes to	
10 County Taxes to	
11 Assessments to	
12 HOA Dues 4/15/13 to 4/30/13	$80.00
13	
14	
15	
16	

N. Due from Seller at Closing	$115,665.04
01 Excess Deposit	
02 Closing Costs Paid at Closing (J)	$12,800.00
03 Existing Loan(s) Assumed or Taken Subject to	
04 Payoff of First Mortgage Loan	$100,000.00
05 Payoff of Second Mortgage Loan	
06	
07	
08 Seller Credit	$2,500.00
09	
10	
11	
12	
13	
Adjustments for Items Unpaid by Seller	
14 City/Town Taxes 1/1/13 to 4/14/13	$365.04
15 County Taxes to	
16 Assessments to	
17	
18	
19	

CALCULATION

Total Due from Borrower at Closing (K)	$189,762.30
Total Paid Already by or on Behalf of Borrower at Closing (L)	– $175,615.04
Cash to Close ☒ From ☐ To Borrower	**$14,147.26**

CALCULATION

Total Due to Seller at Closing (M)	$180,080.00
Total Due from Seller at Closing (N)	– $115,665.04
Cash ☐ From ☒ To Seller	**$64,414.96**

CLOSING DISCLOSURE

Sample H-25 Closing Disclosure, Page 4

Additional Information About This Loan

Loan Disclosures

Assumption
If you sell or transfer this property to another person, your lender
☐ will allow, under certain conditions, this person to assume this loan on the original terms.
☒ will not allow assumption of this loan on the original terms.

Demand Feature
Your loan
☐ has a demand feature, which permits your lender to require early repayment of the loan. You should review your note for details.
☒ does not have a demand feature.

Late Payment
If your payment is more than 15 days late, your lender will charge a late fee of 5% of the monthly principal and interest payment.

Negative Amortization (Increase in Loan Amount)
Under your loan terms, you
☐ are scheduled to make monthly payments that do not pay all of the interest due that month. As a result, your loan amount will increase (negatively amortize), and your loan amount will likely become larger than your original loan amount. Increases in your loan amount lower the equity you have in this property.
☐ may have monthly payments that do not pay all of the interest due that month. If you do, your loan amount will increase (negatively amortize), and, as a result, your loan amount may become larger than your original loan amount. Increases in your loan amount lower the equity you have in this property.
☒ do not have a negative amortization feature.

Partial Payments
Your lender
☒ may accept payments that are less than the full amount due (partial payments) and apply them to your loan.
☐ may hold them in a separate account until you pay the rest of the payment, and then apply the full payment to your loan.
☐ does not accept any partial payments.
If this loan is sold, your new lender may have a different policy.

Security Interest
You are granting a security interest in
456 Somewhere Ave., Anytown, ST 12345

You may lose this property if you do not make your payments or satisfy other obligations for this loan.

Escrow Account
For now, your loan
☒ will have an escrow account (also called an "impound" or "trust" account) to pay the property costs listed below. Without an escrow account, you would pay them directly, possibly in one or two large payments a year. Your lender may be liable for penalties and interest for failing to make a payment.

Escrow		
Escrowed Property Costs over Year 1	$2,473.56	Estimated total amount over year 1 for your escrowed property costs: Homeowner's Insurance Property Taxes
Non-Escrowed Property Costs over Year 1	$1,800.00	Estimated total amount over year 1 for your non-escrowed property costs: Homeowner's Association Dues You may have other property costs.
Initial Escrow Payment	$412.25	A cushion for the escrow account you pay at closing. See Section G on page 2.
Monthly Escrow Payment	$206.13	The amount included in your total monthly payment.

☐ will not have an escrow account because ☐ you declined it ☐ your lender does not offer one. You must directly pay your property costs, such as taxes and homeowner's insurance. Contact your lender to ask if your loan can have an escrow account.

No Escrow		
Estimated Property Costs over Year 1		Estimated total amount over year 1. You must pay these costs directly, possibly in one or two large payments a year.
Escrow Waiver Fee		

In the future,
Your property costs may change and, as a result, your escrow payment may change. You may be able to cancel your escrow account, but if you do, you must pay your property costs directly. If you fail to pay your property taxes, your state or local government may (1) impose fines and penalties or (2) place a tax lien on this property. If you fail to pay any of your property costs, your lender may (1) add the amounts to your loan balance, (2) add an escrow account to your loan, or (3) require you to pay for property insurance that the lender buys on your behalf, which likely would cost more and provide fewer benefits than what you could buy on your own.

Sample H-25 Closing Disclosure, Page 5

Loan Calculations

Total of Payments. Total you will have paid after you make all payments of principal, interest, mortgage insurance, and loan costs, as scheduled.	$285,803.36
Finance Charge. The dollar amount the loan will cost you.	$118,830.27
Amount Financed. The loan amount available after paying your upfront finance charge.	$162,000.00
Annual Percentage Rate (APR). Your costs over the loan term expressed as a rate. This is not your interest rate.	4.174%
Total Interest Percentage (TIP). The total amount of interest that you will pay over the loan term as a percentage of your loan amount.	69.46%

Questions? If you have questions about the loan terms or costs on this form, use the contact information below. To get more information or make a complaint, contact the Consumer Financial Protection Bureau at **www.consumerfinance.gov/mortgage-closing**

Other Disclosures

Appraisal
If the property was appraised for your loan, your lender is required to give you a copy at no additional cost at least 3 days before closing. If you have not yet received it, please contact your lender at the information listed below.

Contract Details
See your note and security instrument for information about
- what happens if you fail to make your payments,
- what is a default on the loan,
- situations in which your lender can require early repayment of the loan, and
- the rules for making payments before they are due.

Liability after Foreclosure
If your lender forecloses on this property and the foreclosure does not cover the amount of unpaid balance on this loan,

☒ state law may protect you from liability for the unpaid balance. If you refinance or take on any additional debt on this property, you may lose this protection and have to pay any debt remaining even after foreclosure. You may want to consult a lawyer for more information.

☐ state law does not protect you from liability for the unpaid balance.

Refinance
Refinancing this loan will depend on your future financial situation, the property value, and market conditions. You may not be able to refinance this loan.

Tax Deductions
If you borrow more than this property is worth, the interest on the loan amount above this property's fair market value is not deductible from your federal income taxes. You should consult a tax advisor for more information.

Contact Information

	Lender	Mortgage Broker	Real Estate Broker (B)	Real Estate Broker (S)	Settlement Agent
Name	Ficus Bank		Omega Real Estate Broker Inc.	Alpha Real Estate Broker Co.	Epsilon Title Co.
Address	4321 Random Blvd. Somecity, ST 12340		789 Local Lane Sometown, ST 12345	987 Suburb Ct. Someplace, ST 12340	123 Commerce Pl. Somecity, ST 12344
NMLS ID					
ST License ID			Z765416	Z61456	Z61616
Contact	Joe Smith		Samuel Green	Joseph Cain	Sarah Arnold
Contact NMLS ID	12345				
Contact ST License ID			P16415	P51461	PT1234
Email	joesmith@ ficusbank.com		sam@omegare.biz	joe@alphare.biz	sarah@ epsilontitle.com
Phone	123-456-7890		123-555-1717	321-555-7171	987-555-4321

Confirm Receipt

By signing, you are only confirming that you have received this form. You do not have to accept this loan because you have signed or received this form.

_____   _____   _____   _____
Applicant Signature   Date   Co-Applicant Signature   Date

CLOSING DISCLOSURE

CLOSING COST ITEMIZATION: CASE ILLUSTRATION

Selling terms and closing costs
Prorations and charges

The Closing Disclosure summarizes the financial settlement of a transaction. At closing, the closing agent also generally provides a statement to the buyer and/or seller detailing receipts and disbursements from relevant escrow accounts to which the buyer and seller have contributed funds as part of the transaction. The following illustration shows how some of these cost components are calculated and allocated in a sample transaction.

Selling terms and closing costs

Lawrence and Sandy Binder have accepted an offer on their house located at 928 Elm Street, Littleburg. The buyers, Bill and Dillis Waite, offered $450,000, with earnest money of $70,000 and the remaining $380,000 of the purchase price to come from a new conventional loan from Scepter Mortgage Company. The loan is for 30 years at 5.5% interest, with a monthly principal plus interest payment of $2,158. The lender is charging 1.5 points and a 1% origination fee. Closing is set to occur at Alta Title Company at 4 p.m. on May 10 of the current (non-leap) year.

The Binders have an agreement to pay a broker's commission of 6% to Littleburg Realty. Their unpaid mortgage loan balance as of May 1 will be $184,000. Their monthly interest payments are $613.00. The annual interest rate is 4%. The previous year's county taxes, amounting to $2,572, have been paid by the seller in arrears. The current year's taxes, not yet billed or paid, are assumed to be the same as the previous year's. The parties agree to prorate using the 365-day method, and that the day of closing belongs to the seller. The relevant facts and costs, and who pays them according to the terms of the sale contract, are summarized below.

Selling terms

Sale price:	$450,000
Deposit/downpayment	$70,000
Loan amount	$380,000

Seller-paid Costs

Commissions:	6% of sale price (.06)
Real estate taxes:	$2,572, to be prorated
Title insurance:	$900 owner's coverage
Seller's attorney:	$1,500
Record Release Deed:	$25
Survey:	$550
Transfer stamps	
state:	$162
county:	$162
Seller's loan payoff:	$184,000 + 10 days' prorated May interest @ $613/month

Buyer- paid Costs

Sale price:	$450,000 ($70,000 earnest money already deposited by buyer)
Appraisal fee:	$400 already paid by buyer
Credit report:	$50 already paid by buyer
Closing fee:	$350
Recording fees:	$55
Title insurance:	$250 for lender's coverage
Buyer's attorney:	$1200
Pest inspection:	$100
Buyer's loan:	$380,000; 30-year fixed @ 5.5% (.055) points: 1.5% of loan amount (.015) origination fee: 1.0% of loan amount (.01)
Hazard insurance:	$2,400/year
Real estate taxes:	$2,572.00, to be prorated
Tax and insurance escrow:	8 months' taxes, 4 months' insurance
Prepaid interest:	from day after closing to end of month

Prorations and charges

According to the summarized sale contract, the only cost to be prorated and shared between seller and buyer is the real estate tax. Other costs to be computed are the broker's commission, the seller's unpaid mortgage interest, the buyer's loan fees and points, the buyer's tax and insurance escrows, and the buyer's prepaid mortgage interest.

Commission. The commission paid by the seller is:

$450,000 x 6%   = $27,000.00

At closing this amount will be charged, or debited, to the seller.

Real estate taxes. Using the 365-day method, the daily amount is $2,572 ÷ 365, or $7.05 (rounded). The total number of days is the number of days in January, February, March and April, plus 10 days in May, or (31+28+31+30+10), or 130 days. At closing, the seller's share of $916.50 is charged to the seller and the buyer is credited with the same amount.

Total amount due:		=	$	2,572.00
Daily amount:	2,572 ÷ 365	=	$	7.05
Seller's share	7.051 x 130	=	$	916.50
Buyer's share:	2,572 – 916.50	=	$	1,655.50

Seller's unpaid mortgage interest. Since mortgage interest is paid in arrears, the seller owes the lender for interest not yet charged for the ten days of the month of closing. This amount is therefore debited to the seller.

Daily amount:	613 ÷ 31 days	=	$	19.77
Seller's charge:	19.77 x 10 days	=	$	197.70

Buyer's loan origination and points. The buyer's debits for loan fees and points are:

Fee:	380,000 x 1%	=	$	3,800
Points:	380,000 x 1.5%	=	$	5,700

Buyer's escrow. The lender requires the buyer to establish an escrow account to cover eight months of real estate taxes and four months of hazard insurance. The debits charged to the buyer are therefore:

Taxes:

Annual amount:		=	$	2,572.00
Monthly amount:	2,572 ÷ 12	=	$	214.33
Amount due:	214.33 x 8 mo.	=	$	1,714.64

Insurance:

Annual amount:		=	$	2400.00
Monthly amount:	2400 ÷ 12	=	$	200.00
Amount due:	200 x 4 mo.	=	$	800.00

Prepaid interest. The lender requires the buyer (borrower) to pay, in advance, the interest on the loan amount disbursed at closing to cover the 21 days of the closing month that would be due in arrears later. Note that the lender is not charging the borrower for interest for the day of closing. The buyer's first mortgage payment, which will cover the month of June, will not be due until July 1. Charged to buyer:

Monthly amount:	380K x 5.5% ÷ 12	=	$	1741.67
Daily amount:	1,741.67 ÷ 31	=	$	56.18
Total prepaid interest	56.18 x 21 days	=	$	1179.78

14 Real Estate-Related Computations and Closing of Transactions

BASIC REAL ESTATE COMPUTATIONS

Sales commissions
- negotiated between agent and client; specified in contract; split between brokers and co-brokers and between brokers and associates

Calculating gain on sale
- original price + costs/improvements = total cost; sale price – sale costs = amount realized; amount realized – total cost = gain on sale

PRELIMINARY STEPS TO CLOSING

Contracting and escrow
- fully executed purchase contract: contains terms and conditions of the transaction; sets duties of each party; enforceable only when fully executed
- earnest money and other funds: good faith deposit from buyer; broker to deposit into broker, title company, or attorney's escrow account within 3 business days of receipt; funds remain in account until closing; additional funds to be deposited and tracked

The pre-closing period
- loan application and approval: buyer to apply for loan to finance purchase; may get pre-approved; should lock in interest rate
- contingencies: typical include buyer financing, inspections, disclosures, repairs, buyer right to cancel; contingencies subject to active or passive approval
- appraisal: lender orders to confirm property value to support mortgage loan; to confirm appropriate selling price
- title search and insurance: search verifies ownership and finds clouds on title; seller responsible for corrections; lender and buyer need insurance for unknown issues in the future
- inspections: property inspection for structural and system issues; pest inspection for WDOs
- repairs: unless "As Is" contract, property repairs should be contingency
- survey: required by lender and title company; confirms boundaries and encroachments
- hazard insurance: hazard and flood separate policies; both may be required by lender

Final preparations
- final walkthrough: before closing to assure repairs made, property vacated, contingencies removed
- closing documents: buyer and seller should review closing documents prior to closing
- additional buyer funds: additional payments may be required for both buyer and seller; included on closing statement
- earnest money transfer: broker is responsible for funds belonging to third party; transfer happens after lender approves closing

THE CLOSING EVENT

The setting
- sale contract sets date, location, and who participates

The closing process
- verify contract fulfillment; exchange consideration and title; pay expenses; sign final documents; arrange for recording the transaction

Transfer of title
- seller gives evidence of marketability-- title abstract or title insurance commitment; may also need affidavit stating no new encumbrances incurred; seller must remove encumbrances or liens prior to the specified date; if seller is paying off mortgage lien, lender provides a payoff statement

Transfer of purchase funds	• buyer produces funds and documents needed to complete the transaction
Escrow procedures	• if closing "in escrow," escrow agent holds and disburses funds and releases documents when escrow conditions have been met
Lender closing requirements	• common: survey, inspections, hazard insurance, title insurance, certificate of occupancy, reserves for taxes and insurance, private mortgage insurance
Broker's role	• broker's role ranges from nil to conducting the proceedings to reporting the transaction
RESPA	• for residential property, first or second mortgage, federally-related mortgage, assumption modifying loan terms, lender charging over $50 for assumption
TRID	• TILA/RESPA Integrated Disclosure Rule requires use of Loan Estimate and Closing Disclosure forms
Information booklet	• lender must provide borrower with CFPB booklet, "Your Home Loan Toolkit"
Loan Estimate	• lender must provide CFPB's H-24 Loan Estimate of settlement costs
Mortgage servicing disclosure	• lender must disclose who will be servicing loan
Closing Disclosure	• lender must use CFPB's H-25 Closing disclosure
Disclosures after settlement	• loan servicers must provide annual escrow statements to borrowers
Limits on escrow accounts	• places ceiling on amounts lenders may compel borrowers to place in escrow
Referral fees and kickbacks	• RESPA prohibits payment of referral fees and kickbacks; business relationships between firms involved in the transaction must be disclosed

FINANCIAL SETTLEMENT OF THE TRANSACTION

Settlement process	• identify closing costs; determine who pays what; do prorations; assign debits and credits; complete closing statement; disburse funds
Selling terms and closing costs	• price, deposits, downpayment, financing, final expenses to be paid at closing; apportionment of expenses determined by sale contract or custom
Debits and credits	• excess of buyer's debits over credits is amount buyer must produce at closing; excess of seller's credits over debits is amount seller must receive
Prorated expenses	• non-prorated items : incurred by one party only; not shared
	• prorated items: incurred by buyer or seller in advance or arrears; shared by buyer and seller; typical: real estate taxes, insurance premiums, mortgage interest, rents
Computing prorations	• sale contract or local custom establishes methods of proration to be used for particular items
	• 12-month/30-day method: determines average daily amount based on 12-month year and 30-day month
	• 365-day method: determines an amount using the actual number of calendar days

STATE TRANSFER TAXES

State documentary stamp tax on deeds

- based on percentage of property's sale price; usually paid by seller but is negotiable
- current rate of 70 cents per $100 of sale price in all of Florida except Miami-Dade where it is 60 cents per $100 of sale price on single-family homes and a surtax of 45 cents per $100 of sales price on other residential dwellings
- exemptions include gifts, one spouse to the other, one ex-spouse to the other, inheritance, partition deed, U.S. government or between government agencies, eminent domain, nonprofit to state agency

State intangible tax on mortgages

- based on loan amount; $2 per $1,000 of loan amount; due at closing

State documentary stamp tax on notes

- based on mortgage and lien amounts; 35 cents per $100 of promissory note total due at closing

OTHER CHARGES

Document preparation

- person who has to sign usually pays for preparation

Recording

- party who wants to record usually pays for recording

Broker's commission

- person who employs usually pays commission; set in contract

Title insurance

- fees and charges negotiable as to who pays

RULES OF THUMB

Seller credits and debits

- customary seller credits: prepaid items, purchase price
- customary seller debits: property tax (prorated), stamp tax on deed, owner's title policy, deed preparation, seller's attorney, broker's commission (if hired), loan payoff, prepaid rent (prorated), security deposits

Buyer credits and debits

- customary buyer credits: property tax (prorated), earnest money deposit, prepaid rent (prorated), security deposits, loan proceeds
- customary buyer debits: purchase price, stamp tax on note, lenders title policy, intangible tax on mortgage, mortgage and note preparation, buyer's attorney, deed recording, mortgage recording

CLOSING DISCLOSURE

Forms and procedures

- mandatory: Your Home Loan Toolkit booklet at loan application; Loan Estimate form 3 business days after loan application; Closing disclosure 3 business days before consummation

Good faith

- lender must ensure good faith: Loan Estimate costs based an best information available; Closing Disclosure costs must equal estimate costs within certain tolerances

Types of charges

- specific charges may exceed estimate; most cannot

Applicable transactions

- most closed-end consumer mortgages, including construction loans, loans secured by vacant land, loans to trusts
- not covered: home equity loans, reverse mortgages, loans on mobile homes, loans by small lenders (no more than 5 loans per year)

The H-25 Closing Disclosure form

- form varies depending on loan type; describes terms, payments, costs

SECTION FOURTEEN: Real Estate-Related Computations and Closing of Transactions

Section Quiz

1. The purpose of the closing event is to

    a. confirm that the buyer has fulfilled all contract requirements prior to title transfer immediately after closing.
    b. ensure that the seller has marketable title before monies are transferred.
    c. conclude the process for loan approval.
    d. exchange legal title for the sale price.

2. A buyer's financing arrangements are often concluded at closing, because

    a. lenders do not fund loans unless title is being transferred.
    b. the lender wants to ensure proper handling of the collateral for the loan.
    c. the loan term must coincide with title transfer.
    d. the deed will be held as collateral for the loan.

3. The Real Estate Settlement Procedures Act prescribes closing procedures that must be followed whenever

    a. a first, second, or third mortgage lien is involved.
    b. the loan is to be sold to the FNMA.
    c. the buyer pays all cash for the property.
    d. the property is a residential complex in excess of four units.

4. A sale contract stipulates that a buyer is to pay the seller's title insurance expenses. This practice is not customary in the area. In this case,

    a. the buyer and seller must amend the contract before closing.
    b. the contract is voidable, since the seller must pay the expense.
    c. the buyer may pay or not pay the expense, at his or her option.
    d. the buyer must pay the expense.

5. A prorated expense on the settlement statement is

    a. a debit to the buyer and seller
    b. a credit to the buyer and seller
    c. a debit and credit to the buyer and seller
    d. a debit to one party and a credit to the other.

6. The amount a buyer owes at closing is equal to

    a. the excess of the buyer's debits over the buyer's credits.
    b. the excess of the buyer's credits over the buyer's debits.
    c. the excess of the seller's debits over the seller's credits
    d. the excess of the seller's credits over the seller's debits.

7. Which of the following are examples of closing items not prorated between buyer and seller?

    a. Taxes and rents
    b. Inspection fees
    c. Utilities and hazard insurance
    d. Condominium assessments and special assessment payments

8. Which of the following items are paid in arrears?

    a. Taxes and insurance
    b. Rents and interest
    c. Taxes and interest
    d. Rents and insurance

9. Which of the following items are paid in advance?

    a. Taxes and insurance
    b. Rents and interest
    c. Insurance and interest
    d. Rents and insurance

10. If a sale contract indicates that the day of closing is "the seller's day," this means that

    a. the seller must pay prorated expenses inclusive of the day of closing.
    b. the seller does not own the property on the day of closing.
    c. the seller may elect the proration method on the day of closing.
    d. the seller must pay the buyer's portion of prorated expenses instead of the seller's portion.

11. Assume a seller at closing must pay transfer taxes at the rate of $1.00 for every $500 of purchase price, or fraction thereof. If the sale price is $345,600, how much tax must the seller pay?

    a. $69.12
    b. $70.00
    c. $691
    d. $692

12. If a seller paid $488 for transfer taxes at closing, and the rate was $1.00 for every $400 or fraction thereof of the sale price, what was the sale price?

    a. $195,500
    b. $1,950,000
    c. $195,200
    d. $1,952,000

13. When a licensee receives earnest money from a buyer, the licensee must turn the money over to his or her broker

    a. by the end of the next business day.
    b. by transaction closing.
    c. within 3 business days of receiving the money.
    d. within 3 days of receiving the money.

14. Who should perform the final walkthrough of the property prior to closing?

    a. The property inspector
    b. The property appraiser
    c. The property seller
    d. The property buyer

15. Florida's documentary stamp tax rate for deeds in Pinellas County is

    a. 60 cents on the dollar.
    b. 70 cents on each $100 of the sale price.
    c. 60 cents on each $1,000 of the sale price.
    d. 45 cents on each $100 of the sale price.

16. Florida's intangible tax on a $200,000 mortgage loan would be

    a. $70.
    b. $900.
    c. $400.
    d. $4,000

15 Real Estate Markets and Analysis

Physical Characteristics of Real Estate
Economic Characteristics of Real Estate

Learning Objectives

- Describe the physical characteristics of real estate
- Describe the economic characteristics of real estate
- Identify the factors that influence demand
- Identify the factors that influence supply
- Distinguish among different ways of interpreting market conditions
- Demonstrate understanding of the different market indicators

Key Terms

buyer's market
demand
household
seller's market
situs
supply
vacancy rate

PHYSICAL CHARACTERISTICS OF REAL ESTATE

Legal concepts of land and real estate
Unique physical features of land

Legal concepts of land and real estate

Land. As discussed in an earlier section, the legal concept of land encompasses

▶ the surface area of the earth

▶ everything beneath the surface of the earth extending downward to its center

▶ all *natural* things permanently attached to the earth

▶ the air above the surface of the earth extending outward to infinity.

Land, therefore, includes minerals beneath the earth's surface, water on or below the earth's surface, and the air above the surface. In addition, land includes all plants attached to the ground or in the ground, such as trees and grass.

Real estate. The concept of real estate, in addition to land, encompasses *man-made structures,* known as improvements, that are "permanently" attached to the land. "Permanently attached," as mentioned earlier, is a question of intention; if a person constructs a house with the intention of creating a permanent dwelling, the house is considered real estate. If a camper affixes a tent to the land with the intention of moving it to another camp in a week, the tent is not considered real estate.

Unique physical features of land

The unique physical characteristics of land, also mentioned earlier, are: *immobility, indestructibility, and heterogeneity.*

Immobility and location. Land is immobile, since a parcel of land cannot be moved from one site to another. In other words, the geographical location of a tract of land is fixed and cannot be changed. One can transport portions of the land such as mined coal, dirt, or cut plants. However, as soon as such elements are detached from the land, they are no longer considered land.

As the upcoming appraisal section will demonstrate, the economics of land reflect the effects of immobility and location in the following ways:

- ▸ valuation of land and real estate is heavily influenced by conditions and changes in the surrounding area
- ▸ highest and best use, a valuation concept, is fundamentally determined by the locational and environmental value of a site to different potential users intending different uses

    The use and user that yield the greatest value for the site constitute the highest and best use. A decline in this value, relative to other uses, often leads to a change in highest and best use and a change in actual land use for the site.

Indestructibility. Land is indestructible in the sense that one would have to remove a segment of the planet all the way to the core in order to destroy it. Even then, the portion extending upward to infinity would remain. For the same reason, land is considered to be permanent.

The indestructibility of land is reflected in real estate investment, tax accounting, and insurance, in that

- ▸ real estate investors tend to regard real estate as a long-term investment, meaning they hold onto their investments for a long time
- ▸ land does not depreciate (while improvements do)
- ▸ improvements, but not land, are covered by property insurance

Heterogeneity. Land is non-homogeneous, since no two parcels of land are exactly the same. Admittedly, two adjacent parcels may be very similar and have the same economic value. However, they are inherently different because each parcel has a unique location.

ECONOMIC CHARACTERISTICS OF REAL ESTATE

Real estate as an economic product
Relationship between supply, demand, and price
Supply factors
Demand factors
Market influences on supply and demand
Interpreting market indicators

Real estate as an economic product

As an economic commodity, real estate is bought, sold, traded, and leased as a product within a real estate market. Like other products and services, real estate is:

- ▶ subject to the laws of supply and demand
- ▶ governed in the market by the price mechanism
- ▶ influenced by the producer's costs to bring the product to market
- ▶ influenced by the determinants of value: utility, scarcity, desire, and purchasing power

Distinguishing features. In comparison with other economic products and services, real estate has certain unique traits. These include:

- ▶ **inherent product value**

  Land is a scarce resource as well as a required factor of production. Like gold and silver, it has both inherent value and utility value.

- ▶ **unique appeal of product**

  Since no two parcels of real estate can be alike (each has a different location), every parcel of real property has its own appeal. Likewise, no two parcels of real estate can have exactly the same value, except by coincidence.

- ▶ **demand must come to the supply**

  Since real property cannot be moved, real property investors and users must come to the supply. This creates risk, because if demand drops, the supply cannot be transported to a higher demand market.

- ▶ **illiquid**

  Real estate is a relatively illiquid economic product, meaning it cannot always be readily sold for cash. Since it is a large, long-term investment that has no exact duplicate, buyers must go through a complex process to evaluate and purchase the right parcel of real estate.

> ▶ **slow to respond to changes**
>
> Real estate is relatively slow to respond to market imbalances. Because new construction is a large-scale, time-consuming process, the market is slow to respond to increases in demand. The market is similarly slow to respond to sharp declines in demand, since the product cannot be moved and sold elsewhere. Instead, owners must wait out slow periods and simply hope for the best.

> ▶ **decentralized, local market**
>
> A real property cannot be shipped to a large, central real estate marketplace. Real estate markets are thus local in nature and highly susceptible to swings in the local economy.

Relationship between supply, demand, and price

In a market economy, the primary interactions between supply, demand and price are:

> ▶ if supply increases relative to demand, price decreases
> ▶ if supply decreases relative to demand, price increases
> ▶ if demand increases relative to supply, price increases
> ▶ if demand decreases relative to supply, price decreases

These relationships reflect simple common sense: if a valued product becomes increasingly scarce, its value and price go up as consumers compete for the limited supply. If there is an overabundance of a product, the price falls, as demand is largely met. On the other side, if demand for a product or service increases in relation to supply, prices will go up as consumers compete for the popular item. If demand diminishes, the price drops with it.

The inverse of these principles also applies. By tracking a price trend, one can draw conclusions about supply and demand trends:

> ▶ if price decreases, demand is declining in relation to supply
> ▶ if price increases, demand is increasing in relation to supply

To assess price movements, the supply and demand of a product or service must always be considered together. It is always possible for demand and supply to rise and fall together at the same rate, with no detectable price change resulting.

For example, if demand for bicycles jumps a million units, and manufacturers easily produce the necessary new supply, there may be no increase in price. The price may even go down as manufacturers obtain better prices on the larger quantities of raw materials they now use.

Supply factors

Supply. In real estate, supply is the *amount of property available* for sale or lease at any given time. Note that supply is generally not the number of properties available, except in the case of residential real estate. The units of supply used to quantify the amount of property available differ for different categories of property. These supply units, by property type, are:

- residential: dwelling units
- commercial and industrial: square feet
- agricultural: acreage

Factors influencing supply. In addition to the influences of demand and the underlying determinants of value, real estate supply responds to

- development costs, particularly labor
- availability of financing
- investment returns
- a community's master plan
- government police powers and regulation

Demand factors

Demand. Real estate demand is the amount of property buyers and tenants wish to acquire by purchase, lease or trade at any given time. Units of demand, by property classification, are:

- residential: households
- commercial and industrial: square feet
- agricultural: acreage

The unit of residential demand is the household, which is an individual or family who would occupy a dwelling unit. Residential demand can be further broken down into demand to lease versus buy, and demand for single family homes versus apartments.

Residential demand can be very difficult to quantify. One measure is the number of buyers employing agents to locate property. Another measure is the net population change in an area, plus families that attempted to move in but could not.

The unit of commercial (retail and office) and industrial real estate demand is the square foot, further broken down into demand for leased space versus purchased space. In most instances, the area demanded refers to the improved area rather than the total lot area.

Demand for office and industrial real estate is calculated by identifying employment growth or shrinkage in a market, then multiplying the employment change times the average area of floor space a typical employee uses. For example, consider an office property market where employment in the community increases by 500 employees. If each employee uses an average of 120 square feet, the increased demand for space is 60,000 square feet.

Factors affecting demand. The demand for particular types of real estate relates to the specific concerns of users. These concerns revolve around the components of value: desire, utility, scarcity, and purchasing power.

Residential users are concerned with:

- employment
- quality of life
- neighborhood quality
- convenience and access to services and other facilities
- dwelling amenities in relation to household size, lifestyle, and costs

Retail users are concerned with:

- sufficient trade area population and income
- the level of trade area competition
- sales volume per square foot of rented area
- consumer spending patterns
- growth patterns in the trade area

Office users are concerned with:

- costs of occupancy to the business
- efficiency of the building and the suite in accommodating the business's functions
- accessibility by employees and suppliers
- matching building quality to the image and function of the business

Industrial users are concerned with:

- functionality
- the availability and proximity of the labor pool
- compliance with environmental regulations
- permissible zoning
- health and safety of the workers
- access to suppliers and distribution channels

Base employment and total employment. The engine that drives demand for real estate of all types in a market is employment-- *base* employment and *total* employment.

Basis of Real Estate Demand

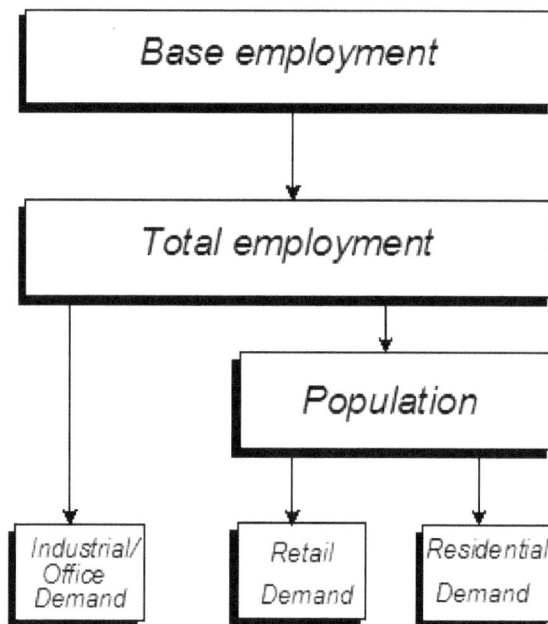

Base employment is the number of persons employed in the businesses that represent the economic foundation of the area. For example, the auto industry has traditionally been the primary base employer of the Detroit metropolitan area.

Base industries lead to the rise of supporting and secondary industries in the market. If the auto industry is the base, auto parts manufacturers and assembly industries will develop to support the auto manufacturing plants. In addition, service businesses emerge to support the many needs of the local population engaged in primary and secondary employment.

Thus, base employment feeds total employment. Total employment in a market includes base, secondary, and support industries. Total employment creates a demand for a labor force. From total employment derives demand for industrial and office space on the one hand; on the other hand, as employment grows, so grows the population, leading to the demand for housing and for retail support. In addition to creating demand for real estate, employment creates the purchasing power necessary for households to acquire dwellings and retail products.

Without employment, a real estate market evaporates, as there is no demand for commercial or industrial facilities, nor is there demand for retail services or housing. The best example of this phenomenon is a gold rush boom town: as soon as the gold runs out, there is no more mining. Without mining employment, everyone moves away and the town becomes a ghost town.

Market influences on supply and demand

Numerous factors in a market influence the real estate cycle to speed up or slow down. These influences can be local or national, and from the public or private economic sector.

Local market influences. Since the real estate market is local by definition, local factors weigh heavily in local real estate market conditions. Among these are:

- cost of financing
- availability of developable land
- construction costs
- capacity of the municipality's infrastructure to handle growth
- governmental regulation and police powers
- changes in the economic base
- in- and out-migrations of major employers

National trends. Regional and national economic forces influence the local real estate market in the form of:

- changes in money supply
- inflation
- national economic cycles

In recent years international economic trends have increasingly influenced local real estate markets, particularly in border states, large metropolitan areas, and in markets where the economic base is tied to foreign trade. In these instances, currency fluctuations have significant impact on the local economy.

Governmental influences. Governments at every level exert significant influence over local real estate markets. The primary forms of government influence are:

- local zoning power
- local control and permitting of new development
- local taxing power
- federal influence on interest rates
- environmental legislation and regulations

A good example of government influence over the local real estate market is a city government's power to declare a moratorium on new construction, regardless of demand. Such officially declared stoppages may occur because of water or power shortages, insufficiency of thoroughfares, or incompatibility with the master plan.

Interpreting market indicators

Real estate supply and demand, like supply and demand for other economic products, interact in the marketplace to produce *price movements.*

Exhibit 15.2
Real Estate Supply-Demand Cycle

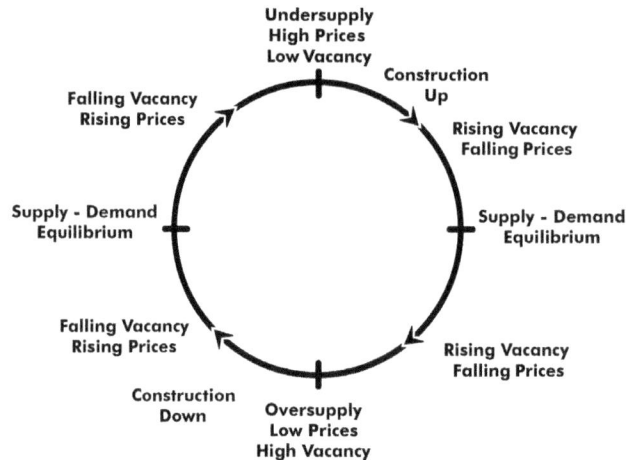

As the exhibit illustrates, prices, construction, and vacancy move up and down in the cycle. Construction represents the addition of new supply. **Vacancy** is the amount of total real estate inventory of a certain type that is unoccupied at a given time. **Absorption** is the amount of available property that becomes occupied over a period of time.

Taking the point of undersupply, or high demand, as a starting point in the cycle, vacancy is low and prices are high. This situation stimulates suppliers to construct additional housing or commercial space. New construction, by adding supply, causes vacancy to rise and prices to fall until supply-demand equilibrium results. As more new space is added, supply begins to outstrip demand, vacancy continues to rise, and prices continue to fall. At the bottom of the cycle, prices and vacancy are at unacceptable levels, and construction ceases. The market "dies" until excess supply can be absorbed. The absorption process continues through the equilibrium point until price and vacancy conditions are sufficiently attractive to encourage renewed construction. Then the cycle repeats.

Thus, by considering indicators such as vacancy rates, construction numbers, building permits, supply and demand factors, sales volume, and price levels over time, one can identify where a market is in the supply-demand cycle and gain some insight into what is coming next—whether prices will rise or fall, tending to favor buyers (buyers' market) or sellers (sellers' market); and by comparing submarkets within a market, one can identify trends in area preferences: which local areas are now or soon likely will be most sought out, which ones are falling into disfavor, and so on.

15 Real Estate Markets and Analysis
Snapshot Review

PHYSICAL CHARACTERISTICS OF REAL ESTATE

Legal concepts of land and real estate

- land: surface, all natural things attached to it, subsurface, and air above the surface; unique aspects: immobile, indestructible, heterogeneous
- real estate: land plus all permanently attached man-made structures, called improvements

Unique physical features of land

- immobility and location: location is fixed is a major factor in use and valuation
- indestructibility: considered permanent, therefore long-term as investment; does not depreciate
- heterogeneity: no two parcels alike

ECONOMIC CHARACTERISTICS OF REAL ESTATE

Real estate as an economic product

- governed by supply, demand, price, costs, value components, government influence
- inherent value; unique appeal; immovable supply; illiquid; slow response to cycles; decentralized market

Relationship between supply, demand, price

- if supply increases relative to demand, price decreases; if demand increases relative to supply, price increases

Supply factors

- supply: property available for sale or lease; measured in dwelling units, square feet, acres; influenced by costs, finance, returns, government regulation

Demand factors

- demand: property buyers and tenants wish to acquire; measured in households, square feet, acres; influences: residential—employment, quality, amenities, price convenience; retail-trade area, sales, competition, site access, visibility; growth patterns; office-efficiency, costs, functionality; industrial-- functionality, labor, regulatory compliance, access to labor, supplies, distribution channels
- base employment, total employment, population determine overall demand
- if employment and population increase, demand and prices increase; if they decrease, the opposite occurs

Market influences on supply and demand

- local economic factors; national economic trends in money supply, inflation; government regulation at all levels

Interpreting market Indicators

- supply-demand indicators are price, vacancy, and absorption; vacancy is existing, unoccupied supply; absorption is the "filling up" of vacancy
- real estate supply-demand cycle: undersupply > accelerated construction adds supply > equilibrium > construction adds more supply > oversupply > construction stops > equilibrium > demand absorbs supply

SECTION FIFTEEN: Real Estate Markets and Analysis

Section Quiz

1. Which of the following is the best definition of real estate?

   a. Land and personal property
   b. Unimproved land
   c. Land and everything permanently attached to it
   d. An ownership interest in land and improvements

2. Which of the following is included in the legal concept of land?

   a. The surface of the earth and all natural things permanently attached to the earth
   b. Only the surface of the earth that is delineated by boundaries
   c. The surface of the earth except for lakes and streams
   d. Everything above, on and below the surface of the earth

3. What are the three unique physical characteristics of land?

   a. Fixed, unchangeable, homogeneous
   b. Immobile, indestructible, heterogeneous
   c. Three-dimensional, buildable, marketable
   d. Natural, measurable, inorganic

4. The primary distinction between the legal concepts of land and real estate is that

   a. real estate includes air above the surface and minerals below the surface.
   b. real estate is indestructible.
   c. land has no defined boundaries.
   d. land does not include man-made structures.

5. Price is best described as

   a. what suppliers charge for goods and services.
   b. the amount of money consumers are willing to pay for a product or service.
   c. the amount of money a buyer and seller agree to exchange to complete a transaction.
   d. a control placed on prices by the federal government.

6. Four principal determinants of value underlying the price for a product are

   a. durability, quality, scarcity, and materials.
   b. desire, utility, scarcity, and purchasing power.
   c. popularity, utility, quality, and discount.
   d. desire, costs, convenience, and time.

7. A town has a rapidly growing population, but there are no longer any vacant lots around the lake to build more houses. In this case, it is likely that the price of existing homes on the lake

   a. will stabilize, since the population must stabilize.
   b. will increase.
   c. will decline, since no further building can take place.
   d. will not show any predictable movement.

8. If there is a significant undersupply of homes in a market, construction will tend to increase. This is an example of

   a. supply outstripping demand.
   b. overpricing products.
   c. the price mechanism.
   d. the market tending toward equilibrium.

9. If commercial real estate rental prices are falling in a market, it is likely that

   a. demand has outstripped supply of space.
   b. the market is in equilibrium.
   c. the market is over-supplied.
   d. employment is increasing.

10. Which of the following is an important economic characteristic of real estate?

    a. The demand must literally come to the supply.
    b. Real estate is a highly liquid product.
    c. The product is quick to adapt to market changes.
    d. The market is centralized.

11. The foremost factor contributing to commercial and residential demand in a market is

   a. marketing.
   b. base employment.
   c. existing supply of properties.
   d. household income.

12. A construction boom in a market is an indication that prices

   a. have been increasing.
   b. have been declining.
   c. have been in equilibrium.
   d. have exceeded supply.

13. A local government could stimulate the real estate market by

   a. increasing labor costs and curbing the money supply.
   b. increasing taxes and interest rates.
   c. declaring a moratorium on construction.
   d. expanding the sewer system.

14. Two important concerns of retail property users are

   a. trade area population and spending patterns.
   b. quality of life and dwelling amenities.
   c. costs of occupancy and building efficiency.
   d. environmental regulations and access by suppliers.

15. Two important concerns of office property users are

   a. trade area population and visibility.
   b. convenience and neighborhood make-up.
   c. costs of occupancy and building efficiency.
   d. environmental regulations and zoning.

16 Real Estate Appraisal

Regulation of Appraisal
Concepts of Value
The Sales Comparison Approach
The Cost Approach
The Income Capitalization Approach
Preparing a Comparative Market Analysis

Learning Objectives

- Describe federal and state regulations pertaining to appraising
- Identify the appraisers fiduciary relationship
- Identify the economic and physical characteristics of real estate that affect market value
- Explain what the Uniform Standards of Professional Appraisal Practice (USPAP) is and how it affects the appraisal process of real property
- Distinguish among the various types of value
- Define market value and describe its underlying assumptions
- Distinguish among value, price and cost
- Describe the four characteristics of value
- Distinguish among the principles of value
- Differentiate among the three approaches to estimating the value of real property
- Estimate value of subject property using Comparable Sales Approach
- Estimate value of subject property using Cost Approach
- Estimate value of subject property using Income Approach
- Reconcile three approaches to establish final value estimate
- Calculate value using gross multiplier analysis
- Explain how to prepare a Comparative Market Analysis (CMA), comparing and contrasting with sales comparison approach

Key Terms

appraisal
assemblage
automated valuation models
comparative market analysis (CMA)
cost-depreciation approach
curable
depreciation
economic life
federally related transaction
gross income multiplier (GIM)
gross rent multiplier (GRM)
highest and best use
income approach
incurable
market value

over-improvement
plottage
principle of substitution
progression
reconciliation
regression
replacement cost
reproduction cost
sales comparison approach
situs
subject property
Uniform Standards of Professional Appraisal Practice (USPAP)
valuation

REGULATION OF APPRAISAL

FIRREA
The Appraisal Foundation
USPAP
State licensed and certified appraisers
Appraisal service of real estate

FIRREA

In 1989, Congress passed the Financial Institutions Reform, Recovery and Enforcement Act (FIRREA) in response to the savings and loan crisis. This act included provisions to regulate appraisal.

Title XI of FIRREA requires that competent individuals whose professional conduct is properly supervised perform all appraisals used in federally-related transactions. Such federally-related appraisals must be performed only by state-certified appraisers. A state-certified appraiser is one who has passed the necessary examinations and competency standards as established by each state in conformance with the federal standards stated in FIRREA and USPAP (Uniform Standards of Professional Appraisal Practice). The criteria for certification as a minimum must follow those established by the Appraiser Qualifications Board of the Appraisal Foundation.

The Appraisal Foundation

The Appraisal Foundation and USPAP. In the 1980s, a team of professional appraisal organizations agreed on a set of appraisal standards, known as the Uniform Standards of Professional Appraisal Standards (USPAP), and in 1987 established The Appraisal Foundation (TAF) as a not-for-profit organization to administer those standards and generally to advance the profession of appraisal.

TAF provides consulting, citation development, standards of practice procedures, implementation guidelines and other appraisal-related services. To support its mission, TAF established the

> ▸ Appraiser Qualification Board (AQB)
> ▸ Appraisal Standards Board (ASB)
> ▸ Appraisal Practices Board (APB) (as of July 1, 2010)
> ▸ Board of Trustees (BOT)
> ▸ Appraisal Subcommittee

Appraisal Qualifications Board. The Appraiser Qualifications Board (AQB) is the education and licensing arm of USPAP. This board creates and maintains the National Appraisal Examination, administers the National USPAP courses, and certifies national USPAP instructors.

Appraisal Standards Board. The Appraisal Standards Board (ASB) is the primary source for the content and substance of USPAP standards. It establishes the standards, issues advisory opinions, and works with the AQB to develop courses and certify instructors.

Appraisal Subcommittee. The ASC oversees TAF and the state licensing agencies. It also maintains a registry of all state-certified and licensed appraisers who are qualified to perform appraisals of properties that are the subject of federally-related transactions.

USPAP

USPAP standards. The Uniform Standards of Professional Appraisal Practice (USPAP) is a set of standards, guidelines and provisions for the appraisal industry. It resulted from the cooperation of nine national appraisal organizations in 1985.

The "competence" provision requires appraisers to assess whether they have the necessary knowledge and competence to perform a specific assignment. If they do not, they must disclose this fact.

The "departure" provision permits appraisers to perform an appraisal that does not meet all the USPAP guidelines provided they have informed the client of the limitations of the incomplete appraisal and if the partial appraisal will not be misleading.

The "standards" concern:

> ▶ recognized appraisal methods
> ▶ definition of due diligence
> ▶ how appraisal results are reported
> ▶ disclosures and assumptions
> ▶ appraisal review
> ▶ real estate analysis
> ▶ mass appraisals
> ▶ personal property appraisals
> ▶ business appraisals
> ▶ compliance with USPAP
> ▶ compliance with the Code of Professional Ethics and Standards of Professional Practice

Florida appraiser licensing and certification requires at least 15 hours of prelicensure education in USPAP and additional post-licensure coursework in USPAP.

State licensed and certified appraisers

Florida statute mandates that a person may not use the titles "certified real estate appraiser," " licensed real estate appraiser," or "registered trainee real estate appraiser," or any words or titles similar to these, nor may a person issue an appraisal report unless the person is certified, licensed, or registered under the requirements of F.S. 475.612. However, someone who is not certified, licensed, or registered may perform the work necessary to complete an appraisal report if that person is supervised, the work approved, and the report signed by a certified or licensed appraiser. Only the certified or licensed appraiser may receive direct compensation for providing valuation services for the report.

Certified appraisers include *certified residential appraisers,* who issue appraisal reports for residential properties consisting of one to four units, and *certified general appraisers,* who issue appraisal reports for any type of property.

However, Florida licensed real estate brokers, sales associates, and broker associates may provide valuation services for compensation as long as they do not represent themselves as certified or licensed appraisers or registered appraiser trainees. Real estate licensees may also prepare comparative market analyses, price opinions, and opinions of the value of real estate as long as they do not represent any of these as an appraisal.

Requirements for federally-related transactions. Federal banking law defines a federally-related transaction as "any real estate-related financial transaction which a federal financial institutions regulatory agency or the Resolution Trust Corporation engages in, contracts for, or regulates, and which requires the services of a state-licensed or state-certified appraiser." The financial transaction must require the services of a certified appraiser to be considered a federally-related transaction. This definition is reiterated in Florida statute.

Federal banking law expands the definition to include a real-estate-related financial transaction as "Any transaction involving:

(A) the sale, lease, purchase, investment in or exchange of real property, including interests in property, or the financing thereof;

(B) the refinancing of real property or interests in real property; and

(C) the use of real property or interests in property as security for a loan or investment, including mortgage-backed securities."

To be determined a federally-related transaction, the transaction must satisfy the following requirements:

> ▸ meet the definition of a real-estate-related financial transaction
> ▸ be engaged in, contracted for, or regulated by any of the five federal financial institutions regulatory agencies: the Board of Governors of the Federal Reserve System, the Federal Deposit Insurance Corporation, the Office of the Comptroller of the Currency, the Office of Thrift Supervision, or the National Credit Union Administration

▶ require the services of an appraiser

In accordance with FIRREA, all financial transactions involving Freddie Mac, Fannie Mae, FHA, and VA require certified appraisals.

Out-of-state appraiser licenses and certifications are recognized in Florida on a temporary basis if the nonresident appraiser is appraising property for a federally-related transaction.

Certified appraisal reports. A certified appraisal involves information that needs to be recorded, photographed, measured, checked, and verified for accuracy. This information is to be included in a certified appraisal report as a legal document that will hold up in court.

Florida statute defines an appraisal report as "any communication, written or oral, of an appraisal, appraisal review, appraisal consulting service, analysis, opinion, or conclusion relating to the nature, quality, value, or utility of a specified interest in, or aspect of, identified real property, and includes any report communicating an appraisal analysis, opinion, or conclusion of value, regardless of title." The report is certified when it is signed by the authorized appraiser who, by signing the report, is attesting to its facts and procedures being true and correct.

To be recognized in a federally-related transaction, an appraisal report must be in writing and conform to USPAP.

Appraisal service of real estate

Part I, Chapter 475. Florida real estate brokers, broker associates, and sales associates are licensed and regulated by F.S. Chapter 475, Part I. Within this chapter, brokers and sales associates are defined as individuals who perform certain services for other people with the intention of being compensated for those services, the sales associate being required to work under a broker. The services listed in the definition are many but include selling, buying, renting, exchanging, and appraising.

As licensed real estate professionals, brokers and sales associates are not required to be licensed or certified appraisers to perform appraisals. However, they may not appraise federally-related transactions or represent themselves as certified or licensed appraisers. They also may not perform appraisals which require a state-licensed or -certified appraiser or those appraisals which may be performed by a registered trainee appraiser. When performing an appraisal, real estate licensees should obtain a written statement from the client that no federally-related transaction is involved and that a certified appraiser is not required for the appraisal.

Appraisal reports must conform to USPAP. To perform appraisals and prepare appraisal reports, real estate licensees must be familiar with and comply with USPAP standards.

Individuals who apply for registration or certification as an appraiser are required to sign a pledge to comply with USPAP. In complying with the standards of practice, appraisers are required to set aside their personal interests and use impartiality, objectivity, and independence when performing appraisals. Ethical practices under the standards prohibit appraisers from accepting or charging compensation that is based on the value of the property. Failure to comply with USPAP may result in the appraiser or real estate licensee facing discipline.

Comparative Market Analysis (CMA). Real estate licensees routinely prepare comparative market analyses in the course of their business practice. Although licensees are required to comply with USPAP when they prepare actual appraisals, they are exempt from the standards when they perform comparative market analyses as long as these services are not referred to as appraisals.

Broker Price Opinion (BPO). Real estate licensees also routinely prepare broker price opinions. Again, while they are required to comply with USPAP for appraisal services, they are exempt from the standards when they perform broker price opinions or opinions of real estate value as long as these services are not referred to as appraisals.

CONCEPTS OF VALUE

Market cost/price/value
Real estate value types
Fundamental value characteristics
Valuation principles

Market cost/price/ value

What is a market? A market is a place where supply and demand encounter one another: suppliers sell or trade their goods and services to demanders, who are consumers and buyers. It is a *transaction arena* where the price mechanism is constantly defining and quantifying the value produced by the relative elements of supply and demand.

Supply and demand. The goal of an economic system is to produce and distribute a *supply* of goods and services to satisfy the *demand* of its constituents. Economic activity therefore centers on the production, distribution and sale of goods and services to meet consumer demand. Consumers demand goods and services; suppliers and sellers produce and distribute the goods and services for a negotiated price.

Cost, price, and value. To produce a good or service, a supplier incurs **costs**, or those expenses necessary to generate and deliver the item to the market. The essential production costs are the costs of capital, materials, and supplies; labor; management; and overhead.

Costs play an important role in the dynamics of supply, demand, and value. Since a producer has limited resources, it is imperative to maximize the efficiency of the production process and minimize its costs. Moreover, since consumers will pay the lowest possible price for comparable goods and services, the producer must be price-competitive to stay in business. A competitor who can produce an item of similar quality for less will eventually force higher-priced items out of the market. At that point, the elements of value-- desire, utility, scarcity, and purchasing power-- do not matter: if the consumer wants the item at all, he or she must cover the producer's costs and profit.

In addition to supply and demand, the other critical component of an economic system is the price mechanism, or simply, price. A **price** is the amount of money or other asset that a buyer has agreed to pay and a seller has agreed to accept to complete the exchange of a good or service. It is a quantification of the value of an item traded.

Price in this context means the final trading price; it is not the preliminary asking price of the seller nor the initial bidding price of the purchaser. Asking and bidding prices are pricing positions in a negotiation between the parties prior to the exchange. The true price of an item or service is the final number the parties agree to.

Real estate value types

The purpose of an appraisal influences an estimate of the value of a parcel of real estate. This is because there are different types of value related to different appraisal purposes. Some of the possibilities are listed below.

Types of Real Estate Value

market	condemned
reproduction	depreciated
replacement	appraised
going concern	rental
salvage	leasehold
plottage	insured
assessed	book

Market value. Market value is an estimate of the price at which a property will sell at a particular time. This type of value is the one generally sought in appraisals and used in brokers' estimates of value. It is an opinion of the price that a willing seller and willing buyer would probably agree on for a property at a given time if:

- the transaction is a cash transaction
- the property is exposed on the open market for a reasonable period
- buyer and seller have full information about market conditions and about potential uses
- there is no abnormal pressure on either party to complete the transaction
- buyer and seller are not related (it is an "arm's length" transaction)
- title is marketable and conveyable by the seller
- the price is a "normal consideration," that is, it does not include hidden influences such as special financing deals, concessions, terms, services, fees, credits, costs, or other types of consideration.

Reproduction value. Reproduction value is the value based on the cost of constructing a precise duplicate of the subject property's improvements, assuming current construction costs.

Replacement value. Replacement value is the value based on the cost of constructing a functional equivalent of the subject property's improvements, assuming current construction costs.

Going concern value. The value of a property plus the operating business located on it as determined by a commercial appraisal

Salvage value. Salvage value refers to the nominal value of a property that has reached the end of its economic life. Salvage value is also an estimate of the price at which a structure will sell if it is dismantled and moved.

Plottage value. Plottage value is an estimate of the value that the process of assemblage adds to the combined values of the assembled properties.

Assessed value. Assessed value is the value of a property as estimated by a taxing authority as the basis for ad valorem taxation.

Condemned value. Condemned value is the value set by a county or municipal authority for a property which may be taken by eminent domain.

Depreciated value. Depreciated value is a value established by subtracting accumulated depreciation from the purchase price of a property.

Appraised value. Appraised value is an appraiser's opinion of a property's value.

Rental value. Rental value is an estimate of the rental rate a property can command for a specific period of time.

Leasehold value. Leasehold value is an estimate of the market value of a lessee's interest in a property.

Insured value. Insured value is the face amount a casualty or hazard insurance policy will pay in case a property is rendered unusable.

Book value. Book value is the value of the property as carried on the accounts of the owner. The value is generally equal to the acquisition price plus capital improvements minus accumulated depreciation.

Liquidated value. The value of the property when converted to cash.

Fundamental value characteristics

Value characteristics. Price is not something of value in itself. It is only a number that *quantifies value*. The economic issue underlying the interplay of supply and demand is, how do trading parties arrive at the value of a good or service as indicated by the price?

Consider consumer demand for air conditioners. Why do air conditioners have value? How do they command the price they do?

The value of something is based on the answers to four questions:

- How much do I desire it?
- How useful is it?
- How scarce is it?
- Am I able to pay for it?

Demand / desire. One determinant of value is how dear the item is to the purchaser. Returning to the air conditioner example, the question becomes "how much do I desire to be cool, dry, and comfortable?" To a person who lives in the tropics, it is safe to say that air conditioning is *more valuable* than a heating system. It is also safe to say the opposite is true for residents of northern Alaska.

Utility. The second determinant of value is the product's *ability to do the job*. Can the air conditioner satisfy my need to stay cool? How cool does it make my house? Does it even work properly? Of course, I won't pay as much if it is old or ineffectual.

Scarcity. The third critical element of value is a product's *availability in relation to demand*. The air conditioner is quite valuable if there are only five units in the entire city and everyone is hot. On the other hand, the value of an air conditioner goes down if there are ten thousand units for sale in a 500-person market.

Purchasing power. A fourth component of value is the *consumer's ability to pay* for the item. If one cannot afford to buy the air conditioner, the value of the air conditioner is diminished, since it is financially out of reach. If all air conditioners are too expensive, consumers are forced to consider alternatives such as ceiling fans.

In the marketplace, the relative presence or absence of the four elements of value is constantly changing due to innumerable factors. Since price is a reflection of the total of all value factors at any time, changes in the underlying factors of value trigger changes in price.

Valuation principles   A number of economic forces interact in the marketplace to contribute to real estate value. Appraisers must consider these forces in estimating the value of a property. Among the most recognized of these principles are those listed below.

Substitution. According to the principle of substitution, a buyer will *pay no more for a property than the buyer would have to pay for an equally desirable and available substitute property*. For example, if three houses for sale are essentially similar in size, quality and location, a potential buyer is unlikely to choose the one that is priced significantly higher than the other two

Highest and best use. This principle holds that there is, theoretically, a single use for a property that produces the greatest income and return. A property achieves its maximum value when it is put to this use. If the actual use is not the highest and best use, the value of the property is correspondingly less than optimal. Technically, highest and best use must be legally permissible, physically possible, financially feasible, and maximally productive.

For example, a property with an old house on it may not be in its highest and best use if it is surrounded by retail properties. If zoning permits the property to be converted to a retail use, its highest and best use may well be retail rather than residential.

Conformity. This principle holds that a property's maximal value is attained when its form and use are in tune with surrounding properties and uses. For example, a two-bedroom, one-bathroom house surrounded by four-bedroom, three-bathroom homes may derive maximal value from a room addition.

Supply and demand. The availability of certain properties interacts with the strength of the demand for those properties to establish prices. When demand for properties exceeds supply, a condition of scarcity exists, and real estate values rise. When supply exceeds demand, a condition of surplus exists, and real estate values decline. When supply and demand are generally equivalent, the market is considered to be in balance, and real estate values stabilize.

Utility. The fact that a property has a use in a certain marketplace contributes to the demand for it. Use is not the same as function. For instance, a swampy area may have an ecological function as a wetland, but it may have no economic utility if it cannot be put to some use that people in the marketplace are willing to pay for.

Anticipation. The benefits a buyer *expects to derive from a property over a holding period* influence what the buyer is willing to pay for it. For example, if an investor anticipates an annual rental income from a leased property to be one million dollars, this expected sum has a direct bearing on what the investor will pay for the property.

Contribution. The principal of contribution focuses on the degree to which a particular improvement affects market value of the overall property. In essence, the contribution of the improvement is *equal to the change in market value that the addition of the improvement causes*. For example, adding a bathroom to a house may contribute an additional $15,000 to the appraised value. Thus the contribution of the bathroom is $15,000. Note that an improvement's contribution to value has little to do with the improvement's cost. The foregoing bathroom may have cost $5,000 or $20,000. Contribution is what the market recognizes as the change in value, not what an item cost. If continuous improvements are added to a property, it is possible that, at some point, the cost of adding improvements to a property no longer contributes a corresponding increase in the value of the property. When this occurs, the property suffers from *diminishing marginal return,* where the costs to improve exceed contribution.

Progression and regression. The value of a property influences, and is influenced by, the values of neighboring properties. If a property is surrounded by properties with higher values, its value will tend to rise (progression); if it is surrounded by properties with lower values, its value will tend to fall (regression).

Assemblage and plottage. Assemblage, or the conjoining of adjacent properties, sometimes creates a combined value that is greater than the values of the unassembled properties. The excess value created by assemblage is called **plottage value.**

Subdivision. The division of a single property into smaller properties can also result in a higher total value. For instance, a one-acre suburban site appraised at $50,000 may be subdivided into four quarter-acre lots worth $30,000 each. This principle contributes significantly to the financial feasibility of subdivision development.

THE SALES COMPARISON APPROACH

Steps in the approach
Identifying comparables
Adjusting comparables
Weighting comparables
Broker's comparative market analysis

The sales comparison approach, also known as the *market data approach*, is used for almost all properties. It also serves as the basis for a broker's opinion of value. It is based on the principle of substitution-- that a buyer will pay no more for the subject property than would be sufficient to purchase a comparable property-- and contribution-- that specific characteristics add value to a property.

The sales comparison approach is widely used because it takes into account the subject property's specific amenities in relation to competing properties. In addition, because of the currency of its data, the approach incorporates present market realities.

The sales comparison approach is limited in that every property is unique. As a result, it is difficult to find good comparables, especially for special-purpose properties. In addition, the market must be active; otherwise, sale prices lack currency and reliability.

Steps in the approach

The sales comparison approach consists of comparing sale prices of recently sold properties that are comparable with the subject, and making dollar adjustments to the price of each comparable to account for competitive differences with the subject. After identifying the adjusted value of each comparable, the appraiser weights the reliability of each comparable and the factors underlying how the adjustments were made. The weighting yields a final value range based on the most reliable factors in the analysis.

Steps in the Sales Comparison Approach

> 1. Identify comparable sales.
> 2. Compare comparables to the subject and make adjustments to comparables.
> 3. Weight values indicated by adjusted comparables for the final value estimate of the subject.

Identifying comparables

To qualify as a comparable, a property must:

▸ resemble the subject in size, shape, design, utility and location
▸ have sold recently, generally within six months of the appraisal
▸ have sold in an arm's-length transaction

An appraiser considers three to six comparables, and usually includes at least three in the appraisal report.

Appraisers have specific guidelines within the foregoing criteria for selecting comparables, many of which are set by secondary market organizations such as FNMA. For example, to qualify as a comparable for a mortgage loan appraisal, a property might have to be located within one mile of the subject. Or perhaps the size of the comparable must be within a certain percentage of improved area in relation to the subject.

The time-of-sale criterion is important because transactions that occurred too far in the past will not reflect appreciation or recent changes in market conditions.

An arm's length sale involves objective, disinterested parties who are presumed to have negotiated a market price for the property. If the sale of a house occurred between a father and a daughter, for example, one might assume that the transaction did not reflect market value.

Principal sources of data for generating the sales comparison are tax records, title records, and the local multiple listing service.

Adjusting comparables

The appraiser adjusts the sale prices of the comparables to account for competitive differences with the subject property. Note that the sale prices of the comparables are known, while the value and price of the subject are not. Therefore, adjustments can be made *only to the comparables' prices, not to the subject's*. Adjustments are made to the comparables in the form of a value deduction or a value addition.

Adding or deducting value. If the comparable is *better* than the subject in some characteristic, an amount is *deducted* from the sale price of the comparable. This neutralizes the comparable's competitive advantage in an adjustment category.

For example, a comparable has a swimming pool and the subject does not. To equalize the difference, the appraiser deducts an amount, say $6,000, from the sale price of the comparable. Note that the adjustment reflects the contribution of the swimming pool to market value. The adjustment amount is not the cost of the pool or its depreciated value.

If the comparable is *inferior* to the subject in some characteristic, an amount is *added* to the price of the comparable. This adjustment equalizes the subject's competitive advantage in this area.

Adjustment criteria. The principal factors for comparison and adjustment are *time of sale, location, physical characteristics, and transaction characteristics.*

> ▸ **time of sale**
>
> An adjustment may be made if market conditions, market prices, or financing availability have changed significantly since the date of the comparable's sale. Most often, this adjustment is to account for appreciation.
>
> ▸ **location**
>
> An adjustment may be made if there are differences between the comparable's location and the subject's, including neighborhood desirability and appearance, zoning restrictions, and general price levels.
>
> ▸ **physical characteristics**
>
> Adjustments may be made for marketable differences between the comparable's and subject's lot size, square feet of livable area (or other appropriate measure for the property type), number of rooms, layout, age, condition, construction type and quality, landscaping, and special amenities.
>
> ▸ **transaction characteristics**
>
> An adjustment may be made for such differences as mortgage loan terms, mortgage assumability, and owner financing.

Weighting comparables

Adding and subtracting the appropriate adjustments to the sale price of each comparable results in an adjusted price for the comparables that indicates the value of the subject. The last step in the approach is to perform a weighted analysis of the indicated values of each comparable. The appraiser, in other words, must identify which comparable values are more indicative of the subject and which are less indicative.

An appraiser primarily relies on experience and judgment to weight comparables. There is no formula for selecting a value from within the range of all comparables analyzed. However, there are three quantitative guidelines: the total number of adjustments; the amount of a single adjustment; and the net value change of all adjustments.

As a rule, *the fewer the total number of adjustments, the smaller the adjustment amounts, and the less the total adjustment amount, the more reliable the comparable.*

Number of adjustments. In terms of total adjustments, the comparable with the fewest adjustments tends to be most similar to the subject, hence the best indicator of value. If a comparable requires excessive adjustments, it is increasingly less reliable as an indicator of value. The underlying rationale is that there is a margin of error involved in making any adjustment. Whenever a number of adjustments must be made, the margin of error compounds. By the time six or seven adjustments are made, the margin becomes significant, and the reliability of the final value estimate is greatly reduced.

Single adjustment amounts. The dollar amount of an adjustment represents the variance between the subject and the comparable for a given item. If a large adjustment is called for, the comparable becomes less of an indicator of value. The smaller the adjustment, the better the comparable is as an indicator of value. If an appraisal is performed for mortgage qualification, the appraiser may be restricted from making adjustments in excess of a certain amount, for example, anything in excess of 10-15% of the sale price of the comparable. If such an adjustment would be necessary, the property is no longer considered comparable.

Total net adjustment amount. The third reliability factor in weighting comparables is the total net value change of all adjustments added together. If a comparable's total adjustments alter the indicated value only slightly, the comparable is a good indicator of value. If total adjustments create a large dollar amount between the sale price and the adjusted value, the comparable is a poorer indicator of value. Fannie Mae, for instance, will not accept the use of a comparable where total net adjustments are in excess of 15% of the sale price.

For example, an appraiser is considering a property that sold for $100,000 as a comparable. After all adjustments are made, the indicated value of the comparable is $121,000, a 21% difference in the comparable's sale price. This property, if allowed at all, would be a weak indicator of value.

Broker's comparative market analysis

A broker or associate who is attempting to establish a listing price or range of prices for a property uses a scaled-down version of the appraiser's sales comparison approach called a comparative market analysis, or CMA (also called a competitive market analysis). While the CMA serves a useful purpose in setting general price ranges, brokers and agents need to exercise caution in presenting a CMA as an appraisal, which it is not. Two important distinctions between the two are objectivity and comprehensiveness.

First, the broker is not unbiased: he or she is motivated by the desire to obtain a listing, which can lead one to distort the estimated price. Secondly, the broker's CMA is not comprehensive: the broker does not usually consider the full range of data about market conditions and comparable sales that the appraiser must consider and document. Therefore, the broker's opinion will be less reliable than the appraiser's.

The following exhibit illustrates the sales comparison approach. An appraiser is estimating market value for a certain house. Four comparables are adjusted to find an indicated value for the subject. The grid which follows the property and market data shows the appraiser's adjustments for the differences between the four comparables and the subject.

Sales Comparison Approach Illustration

Data

Subject property:	8 rooms-- 3 bedrooms, two baths, kitchen, living room, family room; 2,000 square feet of gross living area; 2-car attached garage; landscaping is good. Construction is frame with aluminum siding.
Comparable A:	Sold for 1,000,000 within previous month; conventional financing at current rates; located in subject's neighborhood with similar locational advantages; house approximately same age as subject; lot size smaller than subject; view similar to subject; design less appealing than subject's; construction similar to subject; condition similar to subject; 7 rooms-- two bedrooms, one bath; 1,900 square feet of gross living area; 2-car attached garage; landscaping similar to subject.
Comparable B:	Sold for 1,200,000 within previous month; conventional financing at current rates; located in subject's neighborhood with similar locational advantages; house six years newer than subject; lot size smaller than subject; view is better than the subject's; design is more appealing than subject's; construction (brick and frame) better than subject's; better condition than subject; 10 rooms-four bedrooms, three baths; 2,300 square feet of gross living area; 2-car attached garage; landscaping similar to subject.
Comparable C:	Sold for 1,150,000 within previous month; conventional financing at current rates; located in subject's neighborhood with similar locational advantages; house five years older than subject; lot size larger than subject; view similar to subject; design and appeal similar to subject's; construction similar to subject; condition similar to subject; 8 rooms-- three bedrooms, two baths; 2,000 square feet of gross living area; 2-car attached garage; landscaping similar to subject.
Comparable D:	Sold for 1,090,000 within previous month; conventional financing at current rates; located in a neighborhood close to subject's, but more desirable than subject's; house approximately same age as subject; lot size same as subject; view similar to subject; design less appealing than subject's; construction (frame) poorer than subject's; poorer condition than subject; 7 rooms-- two bedrooms, one and one half baths; 1,900 square feet of gross living area; 2-car attached garage; landscaping similar to subject.

Sales Comparison Approach Illustration, cont.

Adjustments

	Subject	A	B	C	D
Sale price		1,000,000	1,200,000	1,150,000	1,090,000
Financing terms		standard	standard	standard	standard
Sale date	NOW	equal	equal	equal	equal
Location		equal	equal	equal	-20,000
Age		equal	-12,000	+10,000	equal
Lot size		+10,000	+10,000	-10,000	equal
Site/view		equal	-10,000	equal	equal
Design/appeal		+10,000	-12,000	equal	+5,000
Construction quality	good	equal	-30,000	equal	+10,000
Condition	good	equal	-50,000	equal	+20,000
No. of rooms	8				
No. of bedrooms	3	+5,000	-5,000	equal	+5,000
No. of baths	2	+10,000	-15,000	equal	+5,000
Gross living area	2,000	+10,000	-20,000	equal	+10,000
Other space					
Garage	2 car/attd.	equal	equal	equal	equal
Other improvements					
Landscaping	good	equal	equal	equal	equal
Net adjustments		+45,000	-144,000	0	+35,000
Indicated value	1,120,000	1,045,000	1,056,000	1,150,000	1,125,000

For comparable A, the appraiser has made additions to the lot value, design, number of bedrooms and baths, and for gross living area. This accounts for the comparable's *deficiencies* in these areas relative to the subject. A total of five adjustments amount to $45,000, or 4.5% of the purchase price.

For comparable B, the appraiser has deducted values for age, site, design, construction quality, condition, bedrooms, baths, and living area. This accounts for the comparable's superior qualities relative to the subject. The only addition is the lot size, since the subject's is larger. A total of nine adjustments amount to $144,000, or 12% of the sale price.

For comparable C, the appraiser has added value for the age and deducted value for the lot size. The two adjustments offset one another for a net adjustment of zero.

For comparable D, one deduction has been made for the comparable's superior location. This is offset by six additions reflecting the various areas where the comparable is inferior to the subject. A total of seven adjustments amount to $35,000, or 3.2% of the sale price.

In view of all adjusted comparables, the appraiser developed a final indication of value of $1,120,000 for the subject. Underlying this conclusion is the fact that Comparable C, since it only has two minor adjustments which offset each other, it is by far the best indicator of value. Comparable D might be the second best indicator, since the net adjustments are very close to the sale price. Comparable A might be the third best indicator, since it has the second fewest number of total adjustments. Comparable B is the least reliable indicator, since there are numerous adjustments, three of which are of a significant amount. In addition, Comparable B is questionable altogether as a comparable, since total adjustments alter the sale price by 12%.

THE COST APPROACH

Types of cost appraised
Depreciation
Steps in the approach

The cost approach is most often used for recently built properties where the actual costs of development and construction are known. It is also used for special-purpose buildings which cannot be valued by the other methods because of lack of comparable sales or income data.

The strengths of the cost approach are that it:

▶ provides an upper limit for the subject's value based on the undepreciated cost of reproducing the improvements

▶ is very accurate for a property with new improvements which are the highest and best use of the property.

The limitations of the cost approach are that:

▶ the cost to create improvements is not necessarily the same as market value

▶ depreciation is difficult to measure, especially for older buildings

Types of cost appraised

The cost approach generally aims to estimate either the *reproduction cost* or the *replacement cost* of the subject property.

Reproduction cost is the cost of constructing, at current prices, a *precise duplicate* of the subject improvements. **Replacement cost** is the cost of constructing, at current prices and using current materials and methods, a *functional equivalent* of the subject improvements.

Replacement cost is used primarily for appraising older structures, since it is impractical to consider reproducing outmoded features and materials. However, reproduction cost is preferable whenever possible because it facilitates the calculation of depreciation on a structure.

Depreciation

A cornerstone of the cost approach is the concept of depreciation. Depreciation is the *loss of value in an improvement over time*. Since land is assumed to retain its value indefinitely, depreciation only applies to the improved portion of real property. The loss of an improvement's value can come from any cause, such as deterioration, obsolescence, or changes in the neighborhood. The sum of depreciation from all causes is accrued depreciation.

An appraiser considers depreciation as having three causes: physical deterioration, functional obsolescence, and economic obsolescence.

Physical deterioration. Physical deterioration is wear and tear from use, decay, and structural deterioration. Such deterioration may be either *curable or incurable*.

Curable deterioration occurs when the costs of repair of the item are less than or equal to the resulting increase in the property's value. For example, if a paint job costs $6,000, and the resulting value increase is $8,000, the deterioration is considered curable. Incurable deterioration is the opposite: the repair will cost more than can be recovered by its contribution to the value of the building. For example, if the foregoing paint job cost $10,000, the deterioration would be considered incurable.

Functional obsolescence. Functional obsolescence occurs when a property has outmoded physical or design features which are no longer desirable to current users. If the obsolescence is curable, the cost of replacing or redesigning the outmoded feature would be offset by the contribution to overall value, for example, a lack of central air conditioning. If the functional obsolescence is incurable, the cost of the cure would exceed the contribution to overall value, for example, a floor layout with a bad traffic pattern that would cost three times as much as the ending contribution to value.

Economic obsolescence. Economic (or **external**) obsolescence is the loss of value due to adverse changes in the surroundings of the subject property that make the subject less desirable. Since such changes are usually beyond the control of the property owner, economic obsolescence is considered *an incurable value loss*. Examples of economic obsolescence include a deteriorating neighborhood, a rezoning of adjacent properties, or the bankruptcy of a large employer.

Steps in the approach   The cost approach consists of estimating the value of the land "as if vacant;" estimating the cost of improvements; estimating and deducting accrued depreciation; and adding the estimated land value to the estimated depreciated cost of the improvements.

Steps in the Cost Approach

1. Estimate land value.
2. Estimate reproduction or replacement cost of improvements.
3. Estimate accrued depreciation.
4. Subtract accrued depreciation from reproduction or replacement cost.
5. Add land value to depreciated reproduction or replacement cost.

Estimate land value. To estimate land value, the appraiser uses the sales comparison method: find properties which are comparable to the subject property in terms of land and adjust the sale prices of the comparables to account for competitive differences with the subject property. Common adjustments concern location, physical characteristics, and time of sale. The indicated values of the comparable properties are used to estimate the land value of the subject. The implicit assumption is that the subject land is vacant (unimproved) and available for the highest and best use.

Estimate reproduction or replacement cost of improvements. There are several methods for estimating the reproduction or replacement cost of improvements. These are as follows.

▶ **Unit comparison method (square-foot method)**

The appraiser examines one or more new structures that are similar to the subject's improvements, determines a cost per unit for the benchmark structures, and multiplies this cost per unit times the number of units in the subject. The unit of measurement is most commonly denominated in square feet.

▶ **Unit-in-place method**

The appraiser uses materials cost manuals and estimates of labor costs, overhead, and builder's profit to estimate the cost of constructing separate components of the subject. The overall cost estimate is the sum of the estimated costs of individual components.

▶ **Quantity survey method**

The appraiser considers in detail all materials, labor, supplies, overhead and profit to get an accurate estimate of the actual cost to build the improvement. More thorough than the unit-in-place method, this method is used less by appraisers than it is by engineers and architects.

▶ **Cost indexing method**

The original cost of constructing the improvement is updated by applying a percentage increase factor to account for increases in nominal costs over time.

Estimate accrued depreciation. Accrued depreciation is often estimated by the **straight-line** method, also called the **economic age-life method**. This method assumes that depreciation occurs at a steady rate over the economic life of the structure. Therefore, a property suffers the same incremental loss of value each year.

The **economic life** is the period during which the structure is expected to remain useful in its original use. The cost of the structure is divided by the number of years of economic life to determine an annual amount for depreciation. The straight-line method is primarily relevant to depreciation from physical deterioration.

Subtract accrued depreciation from reproduction or replacement cost. The sum of accrued depreciation from all sources is subtracted from the estimated cost of reproducing or replacing the structure. This produces an estimate of the current value of the improvements.

Add land value to depreciated reproduction or replacement cost. To complete the cost approach, the estimated value of the land "as if vacant" is added to the estimated value of the depreciated reproduction or replacement cost of the improvements. This yields the final value estimate for the property by the cost approach.

Cost Approach Illustration

I. LAND VALUE

Land value, by direct sales comparison	80,000

II. IMPROVEMENTS COST

Main building (by one or more of the four methods)	260,000
Plus: other structures	16,000
Total cost new	276,000

III. ACCRUED DEPRECIATION

Physical depreciation	
Curable	10,000
Incurable	14,000
Functional obsolescence	6,000
External obsolescence	
Total depreciation	30,000

IV. IMPROVEMENTS COST MINUS DEPRECIATION

Total cost new	276,000
Less: total depreciation	30,000
Depreciated value of improvements	246,000

V. OVERALL ESTIMATED VALUE

Total land value	80,000
Depreciated value of improvements	246,000
Indicated value by cost approach	326,000

THE INCOME CAPITALIZATION APPROACH

Steps in the approach
Gross rent and gross income multiplier approach

The income capitalization approach, or income approach, is used for income properties and sometimes for other properties in a rental market where the appraiser can find rental data. The approach is based on the principle of anticipation: the expected future income stream of a property underlies what an investor will pay for the property. It is also based on the principle of substitution: that an investor will pay no more for a subject property with a certain income stream than the investor would have to pay for another property with a similar income stream.

The strength of the income approach is that it is used by investors themselves to determine how much they should pay for a property. Thus, in the right circumstances, it provides a good basis for estimating market value.

The income capitalization approach is limited in two ways. First, it is difficult to determine an appropriate capitalization rate. This is often a matter of judgment and experience on the part of the appraiser. Secondly, the income approach relies on market information about income and expenses, and it can be difficult to find such information.

Steps in the approach

The income capitalization method consists of estimating annual net operating income from the subject property, then applying a capitalization rate to the income. This produces a principal amount that the investor would pay for the property.

Steps in the Income Capitalization Approach

1. Estimate potential gross income.
2. Estimate effective gross income.
3. Estimate net operating income.
4. Select a capitalization rate.
5. Apply the capitalization rate.

Estimate potential gross income. Potential gross income is the scheduled rent of the subject plus income from miscellaneous sources such as vending machines and telephones. Scheduled rent is the total rent a property will produce if fully leased at the established rental rates.

Scheduled rent
+ Other income
Potential gross income

An appraiser may estimate potential gross rental income using current market rental rates (market rent), the rent specified by leases in effect on the property (contract rent), or a combination of both. Market rent is determined by market studies in a process similar to the sales comparison method. Contract rent is used primarily if the existing leases are not due to expire in the short term and the tenants are unlikely to fail or leave the lease.

Estimate effective gross income. Effective gross income is potential gross income minus an allowance for vacancy and credit losses.

Potential gross income
- Vacancy & credit losses
Effective gross income

Vacancy loss refers to an amount of potential income lost because of unrented space. Credit loss refers to an amount lost because of tenants' failure to pay rent for any reason. Both are estimated on the basis of the subject property's history, comparable properties in the market, and assuming typical management quality. The allowance for vacancy and credit loss is usually estimated as a percentage of potential gross income.

Estimate net operating income. Net operating income is effective gross income minus total operating expenses.

$$
\begin{array}{l}
\text{Effective gross income} \\
- \text{Total operating expenses} \\
\hline
\text{Net operating income}
\end{array}
$$

Operating expenses include fixed expenses and variable expenses. Fixed expenses are those that are incurred whether the property is occupied or vacant, for example, real estate taxes and hazard insurance. Variable expenses are those that relate to actual operation of the building, for example, utilities, janitorial service, management, and repairs.

Operating expenses typically include an annual reserve fund for replacement of equipment and other items that wear out periodically, such as carpets and heating systems. Operating expenses do not include debt service, expenditures for capital improvements, or expenses not related to operation of the property.

Select a capitalization rate. The capitalization rate is an estimate of the *rate of return* an investor will demand on the investment of capital in a property such as the subject. The judgment and market knowledge of the appraiser play an essential role in the selection of an appropriate rate for the subject property. In most cases, the appraiser will research capitalization rates used on similar properties in the market.

Apply the capitalization rate. An appraiser now obtains an indication of value from the income capitalization method by dividing the estimated net operating income for the subject by the selected capitalization rate

$$\frac{NOI}{capitalization\ rate} = value$$

Using traditional symbols for income (I), rate (R) and value (V), the formula for value is

$$\frac{I}{R} = V$$

Income Capitalization Method Illustration

I. ESTIMATE POTENTIAL GROSS INCOME

Potential gross rental income	192,000
Plus: other income	2,000
Potential gross income	194,000

II. ESTIMATE EFFECTIVE GROSS INCOME

Less: vacancy and collection losses	9,600
Effective gross income	184,400

III. ESTIMATE NET OPERATING INCOME

Operating expenses	
Real estate taxes	32,000
Insurance	4,400
Utilities	12,000
Repairs	4,000
Maintenance	16,000
Management	12,000
Reserves	1,600
Legal and accounting	2,000
Total expenses	84,000
Effective gross income	184,400
Less: total expenses	84,000
Net operating income	100,400

IV. SELECT CAPITALIZATION RATE

Capitalization rate: 7%

V. APPLY CAPITALIZATION RATE

$$\frac{I}{R} = V = \frac{100,400}{.07} = 1,434,300 \text{ (rounded)}$$

Indicated value by income approach: 1,434,300

Gross rent and gross income multiplier approach

The gross rent multiplier (GRM) and gross income multiplier (GIM) approaches are simplified income-based methods used primarily for properties that produce or might produce income but are not primarily income properties. Examples are single-family homes and duplexes.

The methods consist of applying a multiplier to the estimated gross income or gross rent of the subject. The multiplier is derived from market data on sale prices and gross income or gross rent.

The advantage of the income multiplier is that it offers a relatively quick indication of value using an informal methodology. However, the approach leaves many variables out of consideration such as vacancies, credit losses, and operating expenses. In addition, the appraiser must have market rental data to establish multipliers.

Steps in the gross rent multiplier approach. There are two steps in the gross rent multiplier approach.

First, select a gross rent multiplier by examining the sale prices and monthly rents of comparable properties which have sold recently. The appraiser's judgment and market knowledge are critical in determining an appropriate gross rent multiplier for the subject. The gross rent multiplier for a property is:

$$\frac{Price}{Monthly\ rent} = GRM$$

Second, estimate the value of the subject by multiplying the selected GRM by the subject's monthly income.

GRM x Subject monthly rent = estimated value

Gross Rent Multiplier Illustration

Property	Sale price	Monthly rent	GRM
Comparable A	500,000	1660	151
Comparable B	248,000	1500	165
Comparable C	324,000	2,200	147
Comparable D	304,000	1,800	169
Subject	320,000	2,000	160

In the illustration, the indicated GRM for the subject is 160, based on the appraiser's research and judgment. Applying the GRM to a rental rate of $2,000, the indicated value for the subject is $320,000.

Steps in the gross income multiplier approach. The GIM approach is identical to the GRM approach, except that a different denominator is used in the formula. Step one is to select a gross income multiplier by examining the sale prices and gross annual incomes of comparable properties which have sold recently. The gross income multiplier for a property is:

$$\frac{Price}{Gross\ annual\ income} = GIM$$

Step two is to estimate the value of the subject by multiplying the selected GIM by the subject's gross annual income:

GIM x Subject gross annual income = estimated value

Gross Income Multiplier Illustration

Property	Sale price	Gross income	GIM
Comparable A	250,000	19,920	12.55
Comparable B	248,000	18,000	13.78
Comparable C	324,000	26,400	12.27
Comparable D	304,000	21,600	14.07
Subject	324,000	24,000	13.50

In the illustration, the indicated GIM for the subject is 13.5 , based on the appraiser's research and judgment. Applying the GIM to the property's gross annual income gives an indicated value for the subject of $324,000.

PREPARING A COMPARATIVE MARKET ANALYSIS (CMA)

Gathering data
Selecting comparables
Adjusting comparables
Computer-generated CMAs
Automated valuation models (AVM)

Gathering data

Real estate licensees prepare comparative market analyses (CMAs) in the normal course of business to assist sellers in determining the value of their property and establishing an appropriate listing price. To prepare a CMA, a licensee first has to gather the appropriate information on the subject property. This includes the location of the property, features of the neighborhood, square footage of the home, acreage, year of construction and renovations, number of bedrooms and bathrooms, and any additional features or amenities such as a swimming pool.

Appraisals, surveys, and property deeds can provide much of this information on the subject property.

Selecting comparables

After gathering the appropriate information on the property, the licensee will want to find and select similar properties for comparison.

Current property listings are a good source of information on the pricing of similar properties. Comparing the common elements of similar properties and their listing prices provides a basis for a competitive listing price for the subject property. MLS listings are a good source for detailed information.

Recently sold properties and those with pending contracts indicate market values for similar properties, what buyers are willing to pay, and how long the properties were listed before selling.

Properties whose listings have expired without a sale provide valuable information about appropriate pricing. Listings often expire without a sale because the listing price is too high. A number of recently expired listings is a good indicator that the market trend is changing and market values are decreasing.

Adjusting comparables

In searching for similar properties, the licensee should use the information gathered on the subject at the beginning of the CMA preparation-- location, size, number of rooms, age, and additional features-- and look for other properties with attributes as similar as possible to those of the subject property. Any differences can be adjusted when determining value in the same manner as with the sales comparison approach discussed earlier.

Computer-generated CMAs

CMA software allows licensees to create CMAs and listing presentations quickly and easily. Although a few online programs are available for homeowners themselves to fill out a form to gather data on the home, those programs may not be as accurate as the more robust programs available to licensees through REALTOR® associations. These programs still require the licensee's knowledge in thoroughly gathering the appropriate data, entering the data into the program, and letting the program organize the data into the CMA presentation.

Automated valuation models (AVM)

An automated valuation model (AVM) is a service that combines mathematical modeling with databases of existing properties and transactions to calculate property values. Most AVMs compare the values of similar properties at the same point in time and work best in areas where the homes are alike rather than in areas where the homes are more customized and dissimilar. The service is available to real estate licensees, mortgage lenders, and major financial institutions.

AVM reports can be obtained in seconds by lenders and licensees to generate a price estimate and typically include the tax assessor's value, the property's sales history, and comparables' sales history. They are quicker than appraisals, cost less, and remove subjectivity from the valuation process. What they do not include is the property's condition when determining its value, nor do they include measurements, photographs, and other information included in an appraisal. Consequently, they do not qualify as appraisals and do not comply with USPAP standards. AVM services are available online.

16 Real Estate Appraisal
Snapshot Review

REGULATION OF APPRAISAL

FIRREA
- requires state-licensed or -certified appraisers for federally-related appraisals

The Appraisal Foundation
- established 1987 to administer USPAP; Appraiser Qualification Board for education and licensing; Appraisal Standards Board for setting standards; Appraisal Subcommittee oversees the Foundation and state licensing; maintains list of qualified appraisers

USPAP
- USPAP states appraisal standards, guidelines and provisions
- Florida requires 15 hours of prelicense education in USPAP plus post license education

State licensed and certified appraisers
- must be certified, licensed, or registered trainee to be called appraiser or issue appraisal report; others can perform appraisal under supervision of certified or licensed appraiser; must be certified or licensed to receive direct compensation
- FL real estate licensees may appraise for compensation but cannot represent themselves as certified or licensed appraisers
- federally related transactions – real estate financial transaction that federal financial institution regulatory agency engages in, contracts for, or regulates that requires licensed or certified appraiser; must meet specific requirements
- certified appraisal reports – legal document that holds up in court; certified when signed by certified appraiser; in writing and USPAP compliant for federally related transaction

Appraisal service of real estate
- Part I, Chapter 475 – allows real estate licensees to appraise properties that do not require certified appraisals; may not appraise federally related transactions
- Appraisal reports conform to USPAP – appraisal applicants to sign pledge to comply with USPAP; prohibited from accepting compensation based on property value
- CMA – no USPAP compliance required for CMA preparation
- BPO – no USPAP compliance required for BPO preparation

CONCEPTS OF VALUE

Market cost/price/value
- supply: goods or services available for sale, lease, or trade
- demand: goods or services desired for purchase, lease, or trade
- price mechanism: quantified value of an exchange

Real estate value types
- market, reproduction, replacement, going concern, salvage, plottage, assessed, condemned, depreciated, appraised, rental, leasehold, insured, book

Fundamental value characteristics
- value components: desire; utility; scarcity; purchasing power

Valuation principles
- substitution; highest and best use; conformity; supply and demand; utility; anticipation; contribution; progression and regression; assemblage and plottage; subdivision

SALES COMPARISON APPROACH
- most commonly used; relies on principles of substitution and contribution

Steps in the approach
- compare sale prices, adjust comparables to account for differences with subject

Identifying comparables	• must be physically similar, in subject's vicinity, recently sold in arm's length sale
Adjusting comparables	• deduct from comp if better than subject; add to comp if worse than subject
Weighting comparables	• best indicator has fewest and smallest adjustments, least net adjustment from the sale price
Broker's comparative market analysis	• abridged sales comparison approach by brokers and agents to find a price range
COST APPROACH	• most often used for recently built properties and special-purpose buildings
Types of cost appraised	• reproduction: precise duplicate; replacement: functional equivalent
Depreciation	• loss of value from deterioration, or functional or economic obsolescence
Steps in the approach	• land value plus depreciated reproduction or replacement cost of improvements
INCOME APPROACH	• used for income properties and in a rental market with available rental data
Steps in the approach	• value = NOI divided by the capitalization rate
GRM and GIM approach	• GRM: price divided by monthly rent; value: GRM times monthly rent; GIM: price divided by gross annual income; value: GIM times annual income
PREPARING A CMA	
Gathering data	• property location and neighborhood, square footage and acreage, age, renovations, number of rooms, amenities; gathered from appraisals, surveys, deeds
Selecting comparables	• current listings as basis for competitive pricing
	• recently sold show market, purchase prices, and length of time listed
	• expired listings indicate too-high listing price and market trend changes
Adjusting comparables	• location, size, number of rooms, age, amenities compared between properties with adjustments made for differences
Computer-generated CMAs	• software for creating CMAs and listing presentations
AVMs	• online service that calculates property values; not an appraisal

SECTION SIXTEEN: Real Estate Appraisal

Section Quiz

1. As a component of real estate value, the principle of substitution suggests that

   a. if two similar properties are for sale, a buyer will purchase the cheaper of the two.
   b. if one of two adjacent homes is more valuable, the price of the other home will tend to rise.
   c. if too many properties are built in a market, the prices will tend to go down.
   d. people will readily move to another home if it is of equal value.

2. Highest and best use of a property is that use which

   a. is physically and financially feasible, legal, and the most productive.
   b. is legal, feasible, and deemed the most appropriate by zoning authorities.
   c. entails the largest building that zoning ordinances will allow developers to erect.
   d. conforms to other properties in the area.

3. The concept of market value is best described as

   a. the price a buyer will pay for a property, assuming other similar properties are within the same price range.
   b. the price an informed, unhurried seller will charge for a property assuming a reasonable period of exposure with other competing properties.
   c. the price a buyer and seller agree upon for a property assuming stable interest rates, appreciation rates, and prices of other similar properties.
   d. the price that a willing, informed, and unpressured seller and buyer agree upon for a property assuming a cash price and the property's reasonable exposure to the market.

4. A significant difference between an appraisal and a broker's opinion of value is

   a. the appraiser tends to use only one or two of the approaches to value.
   b. the broker may not be a disinterested party.
   c. the broker is subject to government regulation in generating the opinion.
   d. the appraiser uses less current market data.

5. A notable weakness of the sales comparison approach to value is that

   a. there may be no recent sale price data in the market.
   b. the approach is not based on the principle of substitution.
   c. the approach is only accurate with unique, special purpose properties.
   d. sale prices cannot be compared, since all real estate is different.

6. The steps in the market data approach are

   a. choose nearby comparables, adjust the subject for differences, estimate the value.
   b. gather relevant price data, apply the data to the subject, estimate the value.
   c. select comparable properties, adjust the comparables, estimate the value.
   d. identify previous price paid, apply an appreciation rate, estimate the value.

7. In the sales comparison approach, an adjustment is warranted if

   a. the buyer obtains conventional financing for the property.
   b. the seller offers below-market seller financing.

   c. a comparable is located in another, albeit similar neighborhood
   d. one property has a hip roof and the other has a gabled roof.

8. To complete the sales comparison approach, the appraiser

   a. averages the adjustments.
   b. weights the comparables.
   c. discards all comparables having a lower value.
   d. identifies the subject's value as that of the nearest comparable.

9. One weakness of the cost approach for appraising market value is that

   a. builders may not pay market value for materials or labor.
   b. market value is not always the same as what the property cost.
   c. comparables used may not have similar quality of construction.
   d. new properties have inestimable costs and rates of depreciation.

10. The cost of constructing a functional equivalent of a subject property is known as

    a. reproduction cost.
    b. replacement cost.
    c. restitution cost.
    d. reconstruction cost.

11. An office building lacks sufficient cooling capability to accommodate modern computer equipment. This is an example of

    a. physical deterioration.
    b. economic obsolescence.
    c. incurable depreciation.
    d. functional obsolescence.

12. A home is located in a neighborhood where homeowners on the block have failed to maintain their properties. This is an example of

    a. curable external obsolescence.
    b. incurable economic obsolescence.
    c. functional obsolescence.
    d. physical deterioration.

13. In appraisal, loss of value in a property from any cause is referred to as

    a. deterioration.
    b. obsolescence.
    c. depreciation.
    d. deflation.

14. The first two steps in the cost approach are to estimate the value of the land and the cost of the improvements. The remaining steps are

    a. estimate depreciation, subtract depreciation from cost, and add back the land value.
    b. subtract deterioration from cost, estimate land depreciation, and total the two values.
    c. estimate depreciation of land and improvements, subtract from original cost.
    d. estimate obsolescence, subtract from the cost of land and improvements.

15. The roof of a property cost $10,000. The economic life of the roof is 20 years. Assuming the straight-line method of depreciation, what is the depreciated value of the roof after 3 years?

    a. $10,000
    b. $8,500
    c. $7,000
    d. $1,500

16. The income capitalization approach to appraising value is most applicable for which of the following property types?

    a. Single family homes
    b. Apartment buildings
    c. Undeveloped land
    d. Churches

17. The steps in the income capitalization approach are:

    a. estimate gross income, multiply times the gross income multiplier.
    b. estimate effective income, subtract tax, apply a capitalization rate.
    c. estimate net income, and apply a capitalization rate to it.
    d. estimate potential income, apply a capitalization rate to it.

18. Net operating income is equal to

    a. gross income minus potential income minus expenses.
    b. effective gross income minus debt service.
    c. potential gross income minus vacancy and credit loss minus expenses.
    d. effective gross income minus vacancy and credit loss.

19. If net income on a property is $20,000 and the cap rate is 5%, the value of the property using the income capitalization method is

    a. $100,000.
    b. $400,000.
    c. $1,000,000.
    d. $4,000,000.

20. The principal shortcoming of the gross rent multiplier approach to estimating value is that

    a. numerous expenses are not taken into account.
    b. the multiplier does not relate to the market.
    c. the method is too complex and cumbersome.
    d. the method only applies to residential properties.

21. If the monthly rent of a property is $3,000, and the gross rent multiplier (GRM) is 80, what is the value of the property?

    a. $45,000
    b. $240,000
    c. $267,000
    d. $288,000

22. Under what circumstances may an out-of-state appraiser appraise property in Florida?

    a. When the property is nonresidential
    b. Under the supervision of a Florida resident appraiser
    c. For federally related transaction appraisals
    d. Never

23. Florida statute prohibits real estate licensees from performing which property appraisals?

    a. Residential properties with less than four units
    b. Commercial properties
    c. Federally related transactions
    d. All properties

24. Which of the following statements is true?

   a. If prepared properly, CMAs meet the qualifications of an appraisal.
   b. Appraisals can be used in preparing CMAs.
   c. Automated valuation models meet the standards of appraisals.
   d. No value adjustments should be necessary between comparable properties and the subject property.

17 Real Estate Investments & Business Opportunity Brokerage

Investment Fundamentals
Real Estate as an Investment
Taxation of Real Estate Investments
Investment Analysis of a Residence
Investment Analysis of an Income Property
Business Brokerage

Learning Objectives

- *Distinguish* among the different types of real estate investments
- Identify the advantages and disadvantages of investing in real estate
- Distinguish among the various types of risk
- Explain the importance of investment analysis
- Describe the similarities and differences between real estate brokerage and business brokerage
- Describe the types of expertise required in business brokerage
- Distinguish among the methods of appraising businesses
- Describe the steps in the sale of a business

Key Terms

appreciation	goodwill
asset	leverage
basis	liquidation analysis
capital gain (loss)	liquidity
cash flow	Real estate investment trust (REIT)
equity	risk
going concern value	tax shelter

INVESTMENT FUNDAMENTALS

Investment characteristics
Rewards
Risks
Types of investments

Investment characteristics

The idea of investment is simple: take something of value and put it to work in some way to increase its value over time. With any investment, one wants the original investment to grow, without losing it. This idea is called **conservation of capital**. Unfortunately, no investment is truly secure. External conditions change, and the investment itself can change. Even if you do nothing with it, its value does not remain constant.

Risk versus return. The general rule in investments is that the safer the investment, the more slowly it gains in value. The more you want it to gain, and the more quickly, the more you must risk losing it. How much do you want to earn, and how much are you willing to risk to earn it? Reward in investing corresponds directly to the degree of risk.

Management. Another aspect of investment is the amount of attention you must pay to it to make it work. You can deposit cash in a passbook account and forget about it. You can use your cash to buy a business and then run the business yourself to make your asset grow and earn. How much do you want to be involved in managing your investment?

Liquidity. The issue of exchangeability is an important one in investment. How easy is it to recover your invested resource, without loss, and exchange it for another one that you want? If there is a **market** for the type of resource you have-- other people want to buy and sell it for themselves-- your investment is **liquid**.

Rewards

The basic aim of financial investment is to increase one's wealth, to add value to what you have. This can occur in several ways.

Income. An investment can generate income in some way on a periodic basis. You may consume this cash, spending it for goods and services that, when used up, have no further value. Or, you may use the cash to put into another investment.

Appreciation. Your invested asset itself may gain value over time because of an increase in market demand for it. When you sell or exchange it for something else you prefer to have, you get more than you originally put into the investment.

Leverage. You may pledge the value of your resource to borrow funds in order to make an investment that is larger than your own resource permits you to do directly. The small resource is used as a lever to make a larger investment, and thus increases your opportunity to benefit from income, appreciation, and the other rewards of investment.

Tax benefits. Some investments receive treatment under tax laws that enables the investor to reduce or defer the amount of tax owed. Tax dollars you don't have to pay are dollars you have available for some other use, such as consuming or further investing.

Risks

Investment risks come from a variety of general sources, including the market, business operations, the value of money, and changes in the interest rate.

Market risk. Changes in the demand for your invested resource may cause your investment to lose value and to become illiquid.

Business risk. Changes in the operation of a business with which your investment is connected may reduce or eliminate the income- and appreciation-earning capacity of your investment.

Purchasing power risk. Changes in the value of money as an exchange medium, such as through inflation, may decrease the practical value of your invested resource.

Financial risk. Changes in financial markets, particularly in interest rates, may reduce the value of your investment by making it less desirable to others and by making it more expensive for you to maintain.

Types of investments

Four of the most important types of investment are investments in money, equity, debt, and real estate.

Money investments. A money investment is one in which the basic form of the investment remains money. Examples are: deposit accounts, certificates of deposit, money funds, and annuities. The basic reward from a money investment comes in the form of interest. Money investments are relatively safe, with correspondingly conservative rates of return.

Debt investments. A debt investment is one in which an investor buys a debt instrument. Examples are bonds, notes, mortgages, and bond mutual funds. The basic reward comes in the form of interest. Debt investments are usually riskier than money investments and less risky than stocks or real estate.

Equity investments. An equity investment is one in which an investor buys an ownership interest in a business concern. Examples are stocks and stock mutual funds. The basic rewards come in the form of dividends and appreciation of share value. Equity investments are generally riskier than money and debt investments.

Real estate investments. A real estate investment is one in which an investor *buys real estate for its investment benefits rather than primarily for its utility*. It may have the features of both an equity and debt investment, depending on the type of real estate involved and numerous other factors, such as the type of interest one owns. A real estate investor may invest in an income-producing property or a non-income producing property.

▶ **non-income property**

a residential property used as the investor's primary residence. The basic reward, beyond the enjoyment of use, comes in the form of appreciation. There may also be tax benefits, depending on how the purchase is financed.

> ▸ **income property**

a property owned specifically for the investment rewards it offers. Examples are multi-family residential properties, retail stores, industrial properties, and office buildings. Rewards come in any or all of the forms mentioned earlier: income, appreciation, leverage and tax advantages.

REAL ESTATE AS AN INVESTMENT

Risk and reward
Illiquidity
Management requirements

Real estate investments participate in the general risks and rewards of all investments. However, real estate investments are often complex. They are also distinguished by their lack of liquidity and by the amount of management they require. In addition, each investor has specific aims and circumstances that affect the viability of any particular real estate investment for that individual. Licensees who lack expertise in the area of real estate investment analysis should refer potential investors to a competent advisor. Nevertheless, a licensee should be familiar with the basics of real estate as an investment.

Risk and reward

Capital put into real estate is always subject to the full range of risk factors: market changes, income shortfalls, negative leverage, tax law changes, and poor overall return.

Market demand for a specific type of property can decline. For example, a business district's retailers may vacate stores in an area in order to obtain better space in a new shopping center. Market downturns leave the income property investor with an unmarketable property or one which can only be re-leased at a loss of some portion of the original investment. Thus the expected reward from income or appreciation may never be obtained.

Another risk of the investment property is the cost of development or operation. If start-up costs or ongoing operating costs exceed rental income, the owner must dip into additional capital resources to maintain the investment until its income increases. If income does not rise, or if costs do not decline, the investor can simply run out of money.

Leverage is a constant risk in real estate investment. If the property fails to generate sufficient revenue, the costs of borrowed money can bankrupt the owner, just as development and operating costs can. Investors often overlook the fact that leverage only works when the yield on the investment exceeds the costs of borrowed funds.

Tax law is an ongoing risk in long-term real estate investment. If the investor's tax circumstances change, or if the tax laws do, the investor may end up paying more capital gains and income taxes than planned, undermining the return on the investment. An investor needs to consider carefully the value of such potential tax benefits as deductions for mortgage interest, tax losses, deferred gains, exemptions, and tax credits for certain types of real estate investment.

Another consideration is *opportunity cost*. Opportunity cost is the return that an investor could earn on capital invested with minimal risk. If the real estate investment, with all its attendant risk, cannot yield a greater return than an investment elsewhere involving less risk, then the opportunity cost is too high for the real estate investment. Despite all the risks, real estate remains a popular investment, because, historically, the rewards have outweighed the risks. Real estate has proven to be relatively resistant to adverse inflationary trends that have hurt money, debt, and stock investments. In addition, real estate has proven to be a viable investment in view of the economy's continued expansion over the last fifty years.

Illiquidity

Compared with other classes of investment, real estate is relatively illiquid. Even in the case of liquidating a single-family residence, one can expect a marketing period of at least several months in most markets. In addition, it takes time for the buyer to obtain financing and to complete all the other phases of closing the transaction. Commercial and investment properties can take much longer, depending on market conditions, leases, construction, permitting, and a host of other factors. The investor who is in a hurry to dispose of such an investment can expect to receive a lower sales price than may be ideal. Compare this with the ease of drawing money out of a bank account or selling a stock.

Management requirements

Real estate tends to require a high degree of investor involvement in management of the investment. Even raw land requires some degree of maintenance to preserve its value: drainage, fencing, payment of taxes, and periodic inspection, to name a few tasks. Improved properties often require extensive management, including repairs, maintenance, onsite leasing, tenant relations, security, and fiscal management.

TAXATION OF REAL ESTATE INVESTMENTS

Taxable income
Cost recovery
Gain on sale
Interest

Real estate investments are taxed on the income they produce and on the increase in value, or gain, when the investment is sold. These forms of taxation are distinct from the ad valorem taxation of real estate.

Taxable Income

Taxable income from investment real estate is *the gross income received minus any expenses, deductions or exclusions that current tax law allows.* Taxable income from real estate is added to the investor's other income and taxed at the investor's marginal tax rate. The "Investment Analysis of an Income Property" section below gives details.

Cost recovery

Cost recovery, or **depreciation**, allows the owner of income property to deduct a portion of the property's value from gross income each year over the life of the asset. The "life of the asset" and the deductible portion are defined by law. In theory, the owner recovers the full cost of the investment if it is held to the end of the asset's economic life as defined by the Internal Revenue Service. At the time of selling the asset, the accumulated cost recovery is subtracted from the investment's original value as part of determining the taxable capital gain.

Cost recovery is allowed only for income properties and that portion of a non-income property which is used to produce income. It applies only to improvements. Land cannot be depreciated. The part of a property which can be depreciated is called the **depreciable basis**.

Depreciation schedules. Residential rental properties are depreciated over a period of 27.5 years. The basic annual deduction for such property is 3.636%, with adjustments for the month of the taxable year in which the property was placed in service. Non-residential income properties placed in service after 1994 are depreciated over a period of 39 years (basic annual percentage is 2.564%). The proper method of depreciation should be determined in consultation with a qualified tax advisor.

Gain on sale

When real estate, whether non-income or income, is sold, a *taxable event* occurs. If the sale proceeds *exceed* the original cost of the investment, subject to some adjustments, there is a **capital gain** that is subject to tax. If the sales proceeds are less than the original cost with adjustments, there is a **capital loss**.

An investor can sometimes defer the reporting of gain or loss, and, hence, taxation of gain, by participating in an exchange of like-kind assets. The legislation that deals with like-kind exchanges is contained in Section 1031 of the IRS code. These tax-deferred exchanges are sometimes called **Section 1031 exchanges** and **Starker exchanges**, named for an investor who won a case against the IRS.

To qualify under Section 1031, there must have been a legitimate exchange of the assets involved. The property being transferred must have been held for productive use in a trade or business or held as an investment and must be exchanged for property that will also be used in a trade or business or be held as an investment. Tax on gain is deferred until the investment or business property is sold and not exchanged.

Interest

Mortgage interest incurred by loans to buy, build, or materially improve a primary or secondary residence is deductible from gross income. The interest on a home equity loan may be deducted only if the loan is used to "buy, build or substantially improve" the home that secures the loan. Principal payments on a loan are *not* deductible.

For income properties that are held as investments, interest on debts incurred to finance the investment is deductible as **investment interest** up to the amount of net income received from the property.

INVESTMENT ANALYSIS OF A RESIDENCE

Appreciation
Deductibles
Tax liability
Gains tax exclusion

Investment analysis examines the economic performance of an investment. The analysis includes costs, income, taxation, appreciation, and return.

A property acquired and used as a primary residence is an example of a non-income property. If a portion of a residence is used for business (i.e., a home office), this portion only may be treated as an income property for tax purposes. Since, by definition, a non-income property does not generate income, its value as an investment must come from one or more of the other sources: appreciation, leverage, or tax benefits.

Appreciation

Appreciation is the increase in value of an asset over time. A simple way to estimate appreciation on a primary residence is to subtract the price originally paid from the estimated current market value:

$$Current\ value - original\ price = total\ appreciation$$

For example, if a house was bought for $300,000 and its estimated market value now is $400,000, it has appreciated by $100,000.

Original price:	$300,000
Current market value:	$400,000
Total appreciation:	$100,000

Total appreciation can be stated as a percentage increase over the original price by dividing the estimated total appreciation by the original price.

The house in the last example has appreciated by 33%:

$$\frac{(Total\ appreciation)}{Original\ price} = \%\ appreciated$$

$$\frac{100,000}{300,000} = 33\%$$

To estimate the percentage of *annual appreciation*, divide the percent appreciated by the number of years the house has been owned:

$$\frac{\%\ total\ appreciation}{years\ owned} = \%\ appreciation\ per\ year$$

If the house in the previous example has been owned for three years, the annual appreciation has been 11%.

$$\frac{33\%}{3\ years} = 11\%\ appreciation\ per\ year$$

Deductibles

The primary tax benefit available to the owner of a non-income property is the *annual deduction for mortgage interest*. The portion of annual mortgage payments that goes to repay principal must be subtracted to determine the amount paid for interest. Principal repayment is not deductible. Furthermore, depreciation is not allowed for non-income properties.

Tax liability

The seller of a principal residence may owe tax on capital gain that results from the sale. The IRS defines gain on the sale of a home as **amount realized** from the sale minus the **adjusted basis** of the home sold.

Amount realized. The amount realized, also known as **net proceeds from sale**, is expressed by the formula:

sale price
- costs of sale

amount realized

The sale price is the total amount the seller receives for the home. This includes money, notes, mortgages or other debts the buyer assumes as part of the sale.

Costs of sale include brokerage commissions, relevant advertising, legal fees, seller-paid points and other closing costs. Certain *fixing-up expenses*, as discussed further below, can be deducted from the amount realized to derive an **adjusted sale price** for the purpose of postponing taxation on gain.

For example, Larry and Mary sold their home for $350,000. Their selling costs, including the commission they paid Broker Betty and amounts paid to inspectors, a surveyor, and the title company, amounted to ten percent of the selling price, or $35,000. The amount they realized from the sale was therefore $315,000.

Adjusted basis. Basis is a measurement of how much is invested in the property for tax purposes. Assuming that the property was acquired through purchase, the **beginning basis** is the cost of acquiring the property. Cost includes cash and debt obligations, and such other settlement costs as legal and recording fees, abstract fees, surveys, charges for installing utilities, transfer taxes, title insurance, and any other amounts the buyer pays for the seller.

The beginning basis is increased or decreased by certain types of expenditures made while the property is owned. Basis is increased by the cost of **capital improvements** made to the property. Assessments for local improvements such as roads and sidewalks also increase the basis. Examples of capital improvements are: putting on an addition, paving a driveway, replacing a roof, adding central air conditioning, and rewiring the home.

Basis is decreased by any amounts the owner received for such things as easements.

The basic formula for **adjusted basis** is:

Beginning basis
+   capital improvements
-   <u>exclusions, credits or other amounts received</u>

adjusted basis

For example, Mary and Larry originally paid $200,000 for their home. They spent an additional $10,000 on a new central heating and cooling unit. Their adjusted basis at the time of selling it is therefore $210,000.

Gain on sale. The gain on sale of a primary residence is represented by the basic formula:

amount realized (net sales proceeds)
-   <u>adjusted basis</u>

gain on sale

Gain on sale, if it does not qualify for an exclusion under current tax law, is taxable.

Gain on Sale

	Selling price of old home	$350,000
-	Selling costs	35,000
=	Amount realized	315,000
	Beginning basis of old home	200,000
+	Capital improvements	10,000
=	Adjusted basis of old home	210,000
	Amount realized	315,000
-	Adjusted basis	210,000
=	Gain on sale	105,000

In the case of Mary and Larry, their capital gain was $315,000 - $210,000, or $105,000. They will owe tax on this amount in the year of the sale unless they qualify for the exclusion described below.

Gains tax exclusion   Tax law provides an exclusion of $250,000 for an individual taxpayer and $500,000 for married taxpayers filing jointly. The exclusion of gain from sale of a residence can be claimed *every two years*, provided the taxpayer

1.   <u>owned</u> the property for at least two years during the five years preceding the date of sale;

2.   <u>used</u> the property as principal residence for a total of two years during that five-year period;

3. <u>has waited</u> two years since the last use of the exclusion for any sale.

Losses are not deductible, and there is no carry-over of any unused portion of the exclusion. Postponed gains from a previous home sale under the earlier rollover rules reduce the basis of the current home if that home was a qualifying replacement home under the old rule.

INVESTMENT ANALYSIS OF AN INCOME PROPERTY

Pre-tax cash flow
Tax liability
After-tax cash flow
Investment performance

Income properties are those which are held primarily for the generation of income. In addition to commercial and investment properties such as office buildings, this category includes residential rental properties. An important difference between income and non-income properties is that deductions for depreciation are allowed on income properties. Income properties, like non-income properties, generate a gain (or loss) on sale, and they also create an annual income stream. The annual income streams are determined on both a pre-tax and after-tax basis in order to determine the productivity of the investment.

Pre-tax cash flow

Cash flow is the difference between the amount of actual cash flowing into the investment as revenue and out of the investment for expenses, debt service, and all other items. Cash flow concerns cash items only, and therefore excludes depreciation, which is not a cash expense **Pre-tax cash flow**, or cash flow before taxation, is calculated as follows:

	potential rental income
-	vacancy and collection loss
=	effective rental income
+	other income
=	gross operating income (GOI)
-	operating expenses
-	reserves
=	net operating income (NOI)
-	debt service
=	pre-tax cash flow

Potential rental income is the annual amount that would be realized if the property is fully leased or rented at the scheduled rate. **Vacancy and collection loss** is rental income lost because of vacancies or tenants' failure to pay rent. **Effective rental income** is the potential income adjusted for these losses. To that is added any **other income** the property generates, such as from laundry or parking charges, to obtain **gross operating income**. **Operating expenses** paid by the landlord include such items as utilities and maintenance. These are deducted from gross operating income. Some owners also set aside a cash **reserve** each year to build up a fund for capital replacements in the future, for example, to replace a roof or a furnace. Cash reserves are <u>not</u> deductible for tax purposes until spent as deductible repairs or maintenance. The remainder is **net operating income (NOI)**. When the annual amount paid for **debt service**, including principal and interest, is subtracted, the remainder is the **pre-tax cash flow**.

For instance, a small office building of 3,500 square feet rents at $20 per square foot. If fully rented, the annual rental income would be $70,000. Historically, the property averages $4,200 in vacancy and collection losses. Equipment rental will provide an additional $2,000 per year in income. The owner will have to pay operating expenses amounting to ten dollars per square foot, or $35,000 per year. The owner sets aside one dollar per square foot, or $3,500 per year, for reserves. The owner financed the purchase of the building with a loan that requires annual debt service in the amount of $20,000. The pre-tax cash flow for the building is illustrated in the following exhibit.

Pre-tax Cash Flow

	potential rental income	$70,000
-	vacancy and collection loss	4,200
=	effective rental income	65,800
+	other income	2,000
=	gross operating income (GOI)	67,800
-	operating expenses	35,000
-	reserves	3,500
=	net operating income (NOI)	29,300
-	debt service	20,000
=	pre-tax cash flow	9,300

Tax liability

The owner's tax liability on taxable income from the property is based on *taxable income* rather than cash flow. Taxable income and tax liability are calculated as follows:

	net operating income (NOI)
+	reserves
-	interest expense
-	cost recovery expense
=	taxable income
x	tax rate
=	tax liability

Taxable income is net operating income minus all allowable deductions. Cost recovery expense is allowed as a deduction, while allowances for reserves and payments on loan principal payback are not allowed. Thus, since reserves were deducted from gross operating income to determine NOI, this amount must be added back in. As only the interest portion of debt service is deductible, the principal amount must be removed from the debt service payments and the *interest expense* deducted from NOI. Taxable income, multiplied by the owner's marginal tax bracket, gives the **tax liability**.

Note on tax rate: when a rental property is owned as an individual or by way of a pass-through entity (partnership, LLC treated as a partnership for tax purposes, or S corporation), its net income is taxed at the individual's personal marginal income tax rate. The next exhibit shows the tax liability for the previous example using an individual rate of 24%.

Tax Liability

	net operating income (NOI)	29,300
+	reserves	3,500
-	interest expense	10,000
-	cost recovery expense	22,000
=	taxable income	800
x	tax rate (24%)	
=	tax liability	192

After-tax cash flow

After-tax cash flow is the amount of income from the property that actually goes into the owner's pocket *after income tax is paid*. It is figured as:

	pre-tax cash flow
-	tax liability
=	after-tax cash flow

The after-tax cash flow for the sample property is illustrated in the following exhibit.

After-tax Cash Flow

	pre-tax cash flow	9,300
-	tax liability	192
=	after-tax cash flow	9,108

Investment performance

Investors measure the investment performance of an income property in many different ways, depending on their needs. A few of the common measures are:

$$\frac{Net\ operating\ income}{price} = return\ on\ investment\ (ROI)$$

$$\frac{cash\ flow}{cash\ invested} = cash\text{-}on\text{-}cash\ return\ (C\ on\ C)$$

$$\frac{cash\ flow}{equity} = return\ on\ equity\ (ROE)$$

BUSINESS BROKERAGE

Business brokerage vs. real property brokerage
Transaction knowledge
Accounting
Determining a price
Business brokerage regulation
Steps in the sale of a business

Business brokerage is *effecting a sale or exchange of an existing business.* In most cases, the sale of a business entails the simultaneous transfer of an estate in land, whether a leasehold or a fee. Thus to sell businesses, a broker must generally hold a real estate license.

Business brokerage may be classified into *opportunity brokerage* and *enterprise brokerage* in accordance with the size of the business being sold, although Florida does not make this distinction. **Opportunity brokerage** concerns a small business, usually a proprietorship or partnership, where the transaction consists of a sale of assets and an assignment of a lease. **Enterprise brokerage** concerns a larger company, usually a corporation, where the transaction involves the sale of stock and multiple real estate parcels leased or owned by the seller.

The process of business brokerage is similar to real estate brokerage: a broker secures a listing, procures a purchaser, and facilitates the closing. Once a ready, willing, and able buyer is found, the broker earns a commission.

Business brokerage vs real property brokerage

The critical difference between selling a business and selling real estate is that selling a business includes the transfer of *business income, personal property assets, goodwill,* and, possibly, *liabilities,* in addition to real property.

Goodwill is an intangible asset that is tied to the reputation of the business and that adds value to the business opportunity. Goodwill is discussed further below. Franchises, copyrights, and patents are examples of other intangible assets that add value.

Another non-real-estate value transferred with a business is the going-concern value, or the monetary value that is expected from ongoing business operations and profits as opposed to the value of just the physical assets.

Among the similarities of selling a business and selling real estate are the facts that both usually involve real property or a long-term lease and both require the broker to be licensed in accordance with Florida Statute Chapter 475, Part I., wherein the definition of a broker and the licensure requirements of a broker include "...the sale, exchange, purchase, or rental of business enterprises or business opportunities or any real property ..."

To be competent in this brokerage specialty, a business broker must have specialized skills concerning transactions, accounting, and pricing. A business broker must also rely on a professional team to complete the transaction.

Members of this team would include the client's legal counsel, accountant, and, preferably, a professional appraiser.

Transaction knowledge

Types of sale. There are generally two types of business sale transaction for a business broker to be aware of: the *asset sale* and the *stock sale*. In an **asset sale**, the purchaser takes possession of some or all of the assets of the business, as well as the real estate, in exchange for the sale price. The purchase usually does not include acquiring the existing business entity or its liabilities. An asset sale is preferred by buyers who want to buy only portions of a business, or to avoid liabilities inherent in a stock purchase.

In a **stock sale**, a purchaser acquires complete ownership of a business, including the legal corporate entity, all assets, all financial liabilities, and any current or future legal liabilities arising from incidents that have occurred prior to the sale. A purchaser may prefer a stock sale to avoid creating a new business entity or to benefit from a possible tax advantage. In addition, a stock sale keeps a business identity intact, which can be very valuable.

Transaction documents. The most common transaction documents in business brokerage are a *sale contract,* an *assignment* or *real estate sale contract,* a *no-compete agreement,* and a *consulting agreement.*

A **sale contract** sets forth all terms and conditions of the agreement, including exactly what is being sold. An **assignment** or **real estate sale agreement** is an agreement for transferring any and all real property involved in the transaction. A **no-compete agreement** is a seller's covenant, for compensation, not to compete with the buyer under prescribed conditions and time periods. A **consulting agreement** is an employment agreement that hires the seller to assist the buyer in taking over business operations.

For the most part, transaction documents in business brokerage are not fully standardized. For that reason, a business broker must exercise caution in dealing with document language so as to avoid the unauthorized practice of law.

Accounting

A broker or agent who wants to undertake business brokerage needs basic proficiency in accounting. In particular, one must know how to read and interpret:

▸ income, expenses, and profit on an income statement
▸ assets, liabilities, and net worth on a balance sheet

Income, expenses, and profit. A business's profit is the revenue remaining from gross income after all expenses have been paid. A business broker must evaluate an owner's income and expenses in order to determine what the business may be worth to a buyer. This often involves interpreting which income and expense items will change after the business is sold. For example, a seller owns a grocery store and uses family members to perform clerical work without pay. If a buyer is a bachelor without children, much of the clerical work will have to be hired out. The additional payroll suddenly changes the store's profitability significantly. Neglecting to consider how income and expenses might change is likely to lead to serious problems in working with buyers.

Business assets. The assets of a business include **tangible** assets and **intangible** assets. Tangible assets include:

- cash and marketable securities
- inventory
- trade fixtures and equipment
- real property
- accounts receivable

Intangible assets include:

- the company name
- trademarks
- copyrights
- patents
- licenses
- contracts for future sales of goods or services
- goodwill
- going concern

In valuing a business, both tangible and intangible assets must be taken into account, even though intangible assets may be very difficult to appraise.

Business liabilities. Business liabilities acquired in a corporate stock sale include short-term debt, such as accounts payable, and long-term liabilities, such as mortgages and leases.

Goodwill. Goodwill, mentioned earlier, is a business brokerage term with two meanings. In one sense, goodwill is an intangible asset consisting of any factor that an owner values in the business, apart from any other specific asset. For example, goodwill might include reputation, a long history of success in a market, name recognition, a dominant market share, and an excellent business location. In the second sense, which is more familiar to accountants, goodwill is the difference in value between an owner's price and the value of all other business assets. For example, if an owner wants $400,000 for a business, and the totality of tangible and intangible assets is valued at $320,000, the goodwill is an $80,000 asset.

Determining a price

The most difficult task for a business broker is often finding the proper price range for a business. An owner of a smaller business has probably built the business from scratch and tends to overvalue it. Moreover, such an owner may have incomplete and disorganized accounting records, making the valuation of assets quite difficult. Finally, a business's true income may be different for one owner than it would be for another because of variations in management style and ability.

In any case, the value of the business is a function of the following:

- past, present, and future net profits, and capitalized value of these
- amount of risk and certainty associated with realizing future profits
- value of all assets as reflected in the books of account

> ▸ impact of goodwill on the value of the business
> ▸ prices paid for similar businesses
> ▸ all other risks associated with the business

Business brokerage regulation

Licensing. A business broker generally must have an active real estate license. In addition, the broker may need to have a valid securities license since a transaction may entail the sale of securities.

Uniform Commercial Code (UCC). The Uniform Commercial Code regulates the sale of personal property on a state-by-state basis, and forms the basis for standardized sale documents. Standard documents include promissory notes, security agreements, and bills of sale.

Bulk Sales Act. The Bulk Sales Act protects creditors against loss of collateral in an indebted business through the undisclosed sale of the business's inventory. If a business sells over half of its inventory to a buyer, the act declares that the sale is a bulk sale, and, as such, is potentially an asset sale. Since a creditor could lose security in such a sale, the seller must disclose the names of creditors to the buyer in a Bulk Sales Affidavit. The buyer must notify the creditors of the sale, who may then take appropriate action to secure their loans.

Steps in the sale of a business

The sale of a business commonly involves the following steps:

> ▸ signing a broker
>
> The assists in valuing the business, lists the business for sale, finds qualified buyers, negotiates the deal, and manages the overall process.

> ▸ valuing the business
>
> Valuation of the business requires determining discretionary earnings, identifying the business assets, and subtracting liabilities. Liabilities may include stocks, which are valued by dividing the net value of the business by the number of common shares of stock outstanding.

> ▸ preparing the business financials and related documentation
>
> Items to be provided to buyers include tax returns, profit and loss statements, business licenses, contracts, accounts payable and receivable, inventory lists, etc.

> ▸ hiring an attorney and an accountant
>
> These professionals assist with financials and legal compliance.

> ▸ marketing the business

Marketing and sales activities are necessary to procure buyers.

▸ securing a buyer

Negotiating the deal and ensuring that the buyer signs a nondisclosure agreement before releasing confidential business information are key actions in securing a buyer.

▸ executing the purchase agreement

The agreement should allow the buyer a designated period of time to perform due diligence before closing the transaction.

▸ preparing for closing

It is essential to confirm that contracted contingencies are met, to research and assign leases or property title, and to schedule the closing date.

▸ closing the transaction

All parties must sign the agreement and prior to transferring funds and ownership.

17 Real Estate Investments & Business Opportunity Brokerage
Snapshot Review

INVESTMENT FUNDAMENTALS

Investment characteristics
- the greater the risk, the higher the expected return
- some investments require more investor involvement than others
- some investments are more liquid (convertible to cash) than others

Rewards
- investors seek to increase wealth through income, appreciation, leverage and tax benefits

Risks
- risks: changes in supply and demand for the investment (market risk), changes in businesses with which the investment is connected (business risk), changes in the value of money (purchasing power risk), and changes in interest rates (financial risk)

Types of investments
- among the investor's choices are investments in money (e.g., certificates of deposit), equity (e.g., stocks), debt (e.g., bonds and mortgages), and real estate (income and non-income properties)

REAL ESTATE AS AN INVESTMENT

Risk and reward
- the real estate investor must weigh the potential risks and returns inherent in market variability, expected vs. real income, use of borrowing leverage, changes in tax treatment of capital gains and income, and the cost of capital

Illiquidity
- real estate is generally less liquid than other investment types: it takes time to market a property

Management requirements
- real estate tends to require more investor involvement than other investments do: maintenance, management, operation

TAXATION OF REAL ESTATE INVESTMENTS

Taxable income
- gross income received minus allowable expenses, deductions and exclusions

Cost recovery
- deduction of a portion of a property's value from gross income each year over the

Gain on sale
- an excess of proceeds from sale of a property over the original cost of the property, subject to adjustments

Interest
- mortgage interest is deductible from annual gross income from a property, subject to limitations

INVESTMENT ANALYSIS OF A RESIDENTIAL PROPERTY

Appreciation
- increase in the value of an asset over time; may be stated as a difference between the original price and current market value, or as a percentage increase over the original price; not a true measure of investment return

Deductibles
- for non-income properties, primary tax benefit is annual deduction for mortgage

Tax liability
- the seller of a principle residence owes tax on any capital gain that results from the sale unless excluded; capital gain is defined as the amount realized minus the adjusted basis

Gains tax exclusion	• up to $250,000 for a single seller and $500,000 for a married couple can be excluded from gains tax every two years

INVESTMENT ANALYSIS OF AN INCOME PROPERTY

Pre-tax cash flow	• annual pre-tax cash flow is net operating income minus debt service
Tax liability	• tax liability on income from a property is based on taxable income: net operating income minus interest expense and cost recovery
After-tax cash flow	• annual after-tax cash flow is pre-tax cash flow minus tax liability
Investment performance	• a few common measures of investment performance are: - return on investment (net operating income divided by price) - cash-on-cash return (cash flow divided by cash invested) - return on equity (cash flow divided by equity) - discounted cash flow analysis - internal rate of return

BUSINESS BROKERAGE

BUSINESS BROKERAGE	• sale of existing business and its real estate; opportunity and enterprise brokerage
Business brokerage vs real property brokerage	• differences – selling business includes transfer of business income, personal property assets, goodwill, and liabilities; intangible assets include franchises, copyrights, patents, going concern value (monetary value from ongoing business operations) • similarities – real property or lease; broker licensure per FL statute
Transaction knowledge	• types of sale: asset sale and stock sale • documents: sale contract; real estate sale contract or assignment; no-compete agreement; consulting agreement
Accounting	• income, expenses, and profit • balance sheet: assets, liabilities, net worth • assets: tangible and intangible • goodwill: intangible asset--difference between price & other assets
Determining a price	• reconciliation of income, cost, and market data approaches; influenced by risk and stability of future income
Business brokerage regulation	• may need securities license; must comply with Bulk Sales law
Steps in the sale of a business	• signing broker; determining business valuation; preparing business; documentation; hiring attorney and accountant; marketing the business; securing buyer; executing purchase contract ; preparing for closing; closing transaction

SECTION SEVENTEEN:
Real Estate Investments & Business Opportunity Brokerage

Section Quiz

1. All investors desire their investments to increase in value. However,

    a. the degree of return is inversely related to the degree of risk.
    b. the more the investor stands to gain, the greater the risk that the investor may lose.
    c. investments requiring intense management have lesser returns.
    d. the more liquid an investment is, the greater the chances are that the investment will not appreciate.

2. Two of the rewards that investments offer are

    a. income and tax benefits.
    b. negative leverage and appreciation.
    c. appreciation and taxation.
    d. positive leverage and prestige.

3. An investor invests in fifteen diversified bond funds. This is an example of an investment in

    a. money.
    b. equity.
    c. debt.
    d. real estate.

4. A real estate investment can take a long period of time to sell. For the investor, this means that real estate is

    a. management intensive.
    b. insensitive to marketing.
    c. vulnerable to seller's markets.
    d. relatively illiquid.

5. Compared to a stock portfolio, a real estate investment would be considered

    a. a riskier investment.
    b. a more management-intensive investment.
    c. a shorter-term investment.
    d. a more leveraged investment.

6. Taxable income produced by an income property is

    a. gross income minus expenses plus land and building depreciation.
    b. gross income minus expenses minus land and building depreciation.
    c. gross income minus building depreciation plus land depreciation.
    d. gross income minus expenses minus building depreciation.

7. As a general rule, in deriving taxable income on an investment property, it is legal to

    a. deduct principal and interest payments from income.
    b. deduct principal payments from income.
    c. deduct interest payments from income.
    d. deduct principal and interest payments from income and capital gain.

8. Which of the following is true of the tax treatment of a principal residence?

    a. The owner may deduct the property's interest and principal from ordinary income.
    b. The owner may depreciate the property and deduct depreciation expenses.
    c. The owner can deduct any capital gain when the property is sold.
    d. The owner may be able to exclude capital gain from taxable income when the property is sold.

9. An investment property seller pays $14,000 in closing costs. These costs

    a. may be deducted from personal income.
    b. may be deducted from the property's income.
    c. may be deducted from the sale price for gains tax purposes.
    d. may be deducted from the adjusted basis for gains tax purposes.

10. Capital gain tax is figured by multiplying one's tax bracket times

    a. the sum of the beginning basis plus gain.
    b. the difference between net sale proceeds and adjusted basis.
    c. the sum of net sale proceeds and capital gain.
    d. the difference between net sale proceeds and capital gain.

11. Cash flow is a measure of how much pre-tax or after-tax cash an investment property generates. To derive cash flow it is therefore necessary to exclude

    a. cost recovery expense.
    b. interest expense.
    c. loan principal payments.
    d. net operating income.

12. One way investors measure the yield of an investment is by

    a. dividing net operating income by cash flow.
    b. multiplying the investor's required yield times after-tax cash flow.
    c. dividing cash flow by the investor's equity.
    d. multiplying cash flow times the price paid for the property.

13. A corporation would like an agent to sell its country grocery store. Included in the sale are the inventory, equipment, and real property. The agent locates a full-price buyer who does not want to acquire any of the business's actual or potential liabilities. To do this transaction, the corporation would most likely

    a. propose an asset sale.
    b. undertake a stock sale.
    c. propose an exchange.
    d. enter into a sale-leaseback transaction.

14. A broker is reviewing the balance sheet of her new listing to sell a business. Three of the entries on the books are licenses, trademarks, and goodwill. These would be examples of

    a. tangible assets.
    b. intangible assets.
    c. short-term liabilities.
    d. long-term liabilities.

15. In business brokerage, the notion of goodwill is best defined as

    a. the commitment by the agent to expend maximum effort on the listing.
    b. establishing pricing levels that will generate the good will of prospective customers.
    c. the value or price of the business over and above the value of its other assets.
    d. the portion of the sale price that is depreciable.

16. Which of the following is a similarity between selling real estate and selling a business?

    a. Real property
    b. Intangible assets
    c. Liabilities
    d. Personal property assets

17. Once a business seller and buyer enter into a purchase agreement, the buyer is given time to

    a. sign a nondisclosure agreement.
    b. negotiate the contract.
    c. perform due diligence.
    d. transfer related funds.

18 Taxes Affecting Real Estate

Real Property Taxation
Special Assessments
Tax Lien Enforcement
Federal Income Taxes

Learning Objectives

- Distinguish among immune, exempt and partially exempt property
- Describe the various personal exemptions available to qualified owners of homestead property
- Compute the property tax on a specific parcel, given the current tax rate, assessed value, eligible exemptions and transfer of assessment limitation difference (save our homes portability) if applicable
- List the steps involved in the tax appeal procedure
- Describe the purpose of Florida's Green Belt Law
- Calculate the cost of a special assessment, given the conditions and amounts involved
- Describe the tax advantages of home ownership
- Explain how to determine taxable income of investment real estate
- Distinguish between installment sales and like-kind exchange

Key Terms

ad valorem
assessment limitation (save our homes benefit)
assessed value
capital gains
community development districts
debt service
exempt properties
installment sale

immune properties
just value
like-kind exchange
mill
special assessment
tax rate
taxable income
taxable value

REAL PROPERTY TAXATION

Taxing entities
Ad valorem taxation
Exemptions from property taxes
Homestead exemption
Florida Greenbelt Law
Special assessments

Taxing entities

Real estate taxation refers to the taxation of real estate as property. Real estate property taxes are imposed by "taxing entities" or "taxing districts" at county and local levels of government.

There are *no federal taxes on real property*. The Constitution of the United States specifically prohibits such taxes. The federal government does, however, tax income derived from real property and gains realized on the sale of real property. The federal government can impose a tax lien against property for failure to pay any tax due the Internal Revenue Service.

State government. States may legally levy taxes on real property, but most delegate this power to counties, cities, townships and local taxing districts. Florida is one such state that passes property taxing on to local governments and tax districts. The state does not use any of the revenue derived from property taxes. Some states place limits on how local governments may levy such taxes. The State of Florida limits millage rates to 10 mills. States may impose a tax lien against property for failure to pay any real property taxes which the state has levied or delegated to local taxing bodies.

County and local government. Counties, cities and municipalities, townships and special tax districts levy taxes on real property to raise funds for providing local services. It is common for the county to collect all real property taxes and distribute it among the other taxing bodies.

Tax districts. County and local governments establish **tax districts** to collect funds for providing specific services. The boundaries of such districts typically do not coincide with municipal boundaries. The major tax district in most areas is the school district. Other important tax districts are those for fire protection, community colleges, and parks.

A property tax bill might include tax levies from such districts as the following.

- bridge and highway	- health services
- nursing home	- historical museum
- storm water management	- sanitorium
- township	- forest preserve/land management
- fire district	- public library district
- school district	- park district
- retirement fund	- community college district

In addition to generally established tax districts, a local government authority may establish a **special tax district** to pay for the cost of a specific improvement or service that benefits that area. For instance, a special tax district might be created to fund extension of municipal water service to a newly incorporated area. Unlike a permanent tax district such as the school district, a special tax district is temporary, ceasing to exist once the costs of the specific project have been paid for.

Ad valorem taxation   General property taxes are levied on an ad valorem basis, meaning that they are based on the **assessed value** of the property. Assessed value is determined according to state law, usually by a county or township assessor or appraiser. The actual tax, though based on assessed value, may be derived as a legislated percentage of the assessed value. Land and improvements may be assessed separately.

Florida tax schedule. Ad valorem taxes are paid annually. The tax schedule is from January 1 to December 31. In August, the local appraiser sends a Truth in Millage (TRIM) tax notice to homeowners, which includes proposed tax rates and the estimated property taxes for that year. The actual tax bill is sent out in late October.

Property owners can pay the taxes in one payment due on November 1, or they can make installment payments. The following January 1, unpaid taxes become a lien on the property which is superior to any other lien, and any payments made after March 1 must be for the full unpaid balance. On April 1, unpaid taxes for the previous year become delinquent.

Tax base totalling.   The **tax base** of an area is the total of the appraised or assessed values of all real property within the area's boundaries, excluding partially or totally exempt properties:

tax base = assessed values - exemptions

Taxing entities generate the annual revenues they require by levying taxes on the tax base. The **tax rate**, or **millage rate**, determines how much of a tax levy the tax base will receive. The tax rate for each taxing entity is calculated by dividing the amount of revenue required by the tax base. This rate is then applied to the taxable value of each individual real property to determine its tax levy.

Value assessment in Florida. Every county in Florida has an elected property appraiser who is responsible for annual appraisals to value the real property within their jurisdiction for purposes of levying taxes. This valuation process results in an **assessed value**.

In Florida, state statutes require that property be assessed at **just value** (market value), using the property's cash value, location, size, improvements, use, replacement cost, and condition.

The role of the assessor in the taxing process is limited to physically or electronically (using imaging technology) inspecting the property every 5 years, making the valuation, and notifying the owner of the assessed value; other tax officials determine the tax rate and the tax levy.

Protesting assessed value. Property owners may object to the assessed value of their property, but not to the tax rate. An owner has 25 days to protest or appeal after the TRIM notice is mailed. According to local law, a property owner must present evidence that the assessor made an error to a review board or appeal board.

A Florida owner who wishes to protest the assessed value may initiate an appeal or protest by following these three steps:

> ▸ Step 1 – the homeowner may contact the property appraiser to seek an adjustment to the assessed value.
>
> ▸ Step 2 – if the appraiser rejects the adjustment request, the owner may file an appeal with the Value Adjustment Board.
>
> ▸ Step 3 – if the Value Adjustment Board rejects the adjustment request, the property owner may pay the taxes under protest and initiate litigation in the courts against the appraiser and the tax collector.

Tax district budgeting. The derivation of a tax rate, or millage rate, begins with the taxing body determining its funding requirements to provide services for the year. This requirement is formalized in the annual budget. Then the county or district looks at its sources of revenue, such as sales taxes, business taxes, income taxes, state and federal grants, fees, and so forth. The part of the budgeted expenditures that cannot be funded from other income sources *must come from real property taxes.* This budgetary shortfall becomes the ad valorem **tax levy.** The tax levy is derived every year, since budget requirements and revenue tallies are performed on an annual cycle.

Calculating taxable value. After the county or district develops its annual budget and determines the ad valorem tax levy, it must then consider the total assessed value, known as the tax base, of all taxable property in the county or district. Looking at each property's assessed value, the next step is to subtract all applicable exemptions from the assessed value, applying the SOH limitations, to determine the taxable value of the property. If no exemptions apply, the taxable value and the assessed value are the same.

Tax rate. Each individual taxing body has its own tax rate. The tax rate is determined by dividing the taxing body's budgeted amount to be collected from real estate taxes by the tax base:

$$\frac{\text{tax requirement}}{\text{tax base}} = \text{tax rate (millage rate)}$$

If, for example, a taxing body needs $500,000 from property taxes, and the tax base for the district is $15,000,000, the tax rate for this body is:

$$\frac{500,000}{15,000,000} = .03$$

This tax rate of .03 or 3% may be expressed in a number of ways, depending on local practice: as **mills**, as dollars per $100 of assessed value, or as dollars per $1,000 of assessed value. A mill is one one-thousandth of a dollar ($.001). A tax rate of one mill means that the owner pays one dollar for every thousand dollars of assessed value. Thus the rate of .03 above could be expressed as:

> 30 mills
> $3 per $100
> $30 per $1,000
> 3 percent

In Florida, property taxes are collected on a county level, and each county has its own method of assessing and collecting taxes. As a result, no single property tax rate applies uniformly to all properties in Florida.

Calculating property taxes. To determine the actual tax, the taxable value is multiplied by the county's tax rate. Just as the county's financial needs and operating budget may change every year, consequently, so may the tax rate.

Tax rate limitations. Some states, counties or other taxing districts place limitations or **caps** on the absolute millage rate or the annual increase in millage for property taxes. Florida limits millage rates to 10 mills. With a tax cap, taxing bodies are *forced to limit their budget requirements*, unless there has been a sufficient increase in tax base to produce the required funds without raising the millage rate.

Exemptions from property taxes

Immune property. In Florida, property owned by federal government, state, county, or city governments is 100% immune from ad valorem taxation as long as the property is being used by the government for governmental purposes. For example, federally owned military bases, state municipal buildings, county and city police headquarters, fire stations, and public schools are immune from property taxes. However, when government-owned property is used by a nongovernment entity or person for a nonexempt use, the property is no longer immune from taxes.

Exempt or partially exempt property. Properties in Florida that are owned by churches, church schools, and nonprofit organizations are 100% exempt from property taxation. Properties owned and occupied as homestead properties are partially exempt from taxation through the application of homestead tax exemptions which are deducted from the assessed value of the property before the taxable value is determined.

Homestead exemption

A homestead is a parcel of real property that is owned and occupied as a family home. Some states exempt a portion of the value of the homestead from judgments to protect families against eviction by creditors. States and counties may *exempt a portion of the assessed value of the principal residence from property taxation*.

Qualified Florida residents may receive a homestead exemption up to $50,000, which is divided into two parts: first is $25,000 for property taxes to include school district taxes, and second is $25,000 dependent on the property's assessed value between $50,000 and $75,000, not to include school district taxes.

A property owner generally qualifies for a homestead exemption by meeting the following criteria:

- holds title to the homestead
- resides on the property for the entire year starting on January 1
- uses the home as the permanent residence
- apply for the exemption by March 1 to qualify for the same year

Secondary homes do not qualify for the exemption. The homeowner must apply by March 1 for the exemption to apply to that year's taxes.

Florida does not restrict the exemption to the head of the family as some states do. Instead, Florida allows a single person to claim the homestead exemption as well.

In Florida, once a homeowner has applied and qualified for an exemption, the exemption is automatically applied every year going forward. The homeowner simply needs to notify the county if his or her homestead has changed so that the exemption is no longer valid.

Assessment limitation (Save Our Homes benefit). The SOH amendment to the Florida constitution keeps property taxes from rising out of control by limiting the increase in the annual assessed value of a homestead to 3% of the previous year's assessed property value or the percentage of change in the Consumer Price Index for the previous year, whichever is less.

The SOH assessment limitation requires that all property be assessed for tax purposes at its just value. With the limitation, the assessed value cannot exceed the just value of a property. SOH is defined in Florida statute as "the accumulated difference between the assessed value and the just (market) value." Homeowners must apply for a homestead exemption to receive the SOH benefit.

Surviving spouse exemption. Surviving spouses who have not remarried receive an additional $500 exemption applied to the assessed value of their homestead. The surviving spouse of a first responder within Florida who died in the line of duty is exempt from property taxation.

Disability exemption. Individuals who are quadriplegic or totally and permanently disabled or must use a wheel chair are exempt from all property taxation as long as the gross household income is less than the current gross income limit. Disabled individuals must submit certification of the disability from two Florida doctors or from U.S. Veterans Affairs.

Blind persons exemption. Individuals who are legally blind are also exempt from paying property taxes on their homestead. They too must submit certification of their blindness from either two Florida doctors or one Florida doctor and one Florida optometrist.

Cumulative homestead tax exemption. Homestead taxpayers may qualify for multiple exemptions, known as cumulative exemptions, that are added together and then subtracted from the homestead's assessed value.

Military service-connected total and permanent disability tax exemption. Veterans who are Florida residents and were honorably discharged with a service-connected total and permanent disability may qualify for a total property tax exemption on their homestead. This exemption is also available to a military member's surviving spouse if the member died while on active duty.

Florida Greenbelt Law

Nature. Under Florida's Greenbelt Law, property assessments for taxation are based on the actual use of the property and not the highest and best use, such as urban growth and development. The result is a lower property assessment and lower taxes for the farmer.

Purpose. Florida's Green Belt Law was created to protect farmers from having property taxes raised to the point where it no longer would be economically feasible for that farmer to continue the agricultural use.

Provisions. To qualify for the classification and resulting exemption, the farmer must apply before March 1 of the tax year. The land must be used primarily for bona fide agricultural purposes or good faith commercial agricultural use. Further, while Florida does not have a minimum size requirement to qualify, the land must be large enough to support a commercial agricultural operation. Hobby farms and livestock or produce for personal use do not qualify for the exemption. To maintain the agricultural classification and discourage land purchases by speculators and investors, the land is required to be classified every year and reassessed at least every 3 years.

The Greenbelt Law does not require the property owner to reside on the property or be the person who actually performs the work on the property. The owner is allowed to lease the property to other individuals who will maintain the agricultural use and operation. Leased properties still qualify for the exemption as long as the lessee is using the property for the required use.

SPECIAL ASSESSMENTS

A special assessment is a tax levied against specific properties that will benefit from a public improvement. Common examples are assessments for sidewalks, water service and sewers. Special assessments are based on the cost of the improvement and apportioned on a pro rata basis among benefiting properties according to the value that each parcel will receive from the improvement.

For example, a dredging project is approved to deepen the canals for a canal-front subdivision. The project cost is $200,000. Although there are 100 properties in the subdivision, only the 50 that are directly on the canal stand to benefit. Therefore, assuming each canal-front lot receives equal benefit, the 50 properties are each assessed $4,000 as a special assessment tax. Note that once the work is completed and paid, the assessment is discontinued.

If a taxing entity initiates an assessment, the assessment creates an **involuntary tax lien**. If property owners initiate the assessment by requesting the local government to provide the improvement, the assessment creates a **voluntary tax lien.** Special assessment liens are secondary to property tax liens.

Special assessments are usually paid in installments over a number of years. However, taxpayers generally have the option of paying the tax in one lump sum or otherwise accelerating payment.

TAX LIEN ENFORCEMENT

Sale of tax certificates
Tax deed
Tax sale

Remember that property taxes are due on November 1 of the tax year but may be paid in installments through March 1, when they must be paid in full or be deemed delinquent on April 1. As of January 1 following the tax year, unpaid taxes become a superior lien on the property. If the taxes are paid in full before April 1, the lien is lifted. If they are not paid, the tax collector may enforce the lien and issue a *tax certificate* for the delinquent property.

Sale of tax certificates

The tax certificate is a claim against the property for the amount of unpaid property tax and non-ad valorem assessments, including a 3% penalty, a 5% tax collector's commission, and advertising costs.

Florida statutes require the tax collector to conduct a sale or auction of the tax certificates on or before June 1 for delinquent taxes from the previous year. The sale may be conducted online. However, prior to selling the tax certificate, the tax collector must advertise the delinquent property for three consecutive weeks in a local newspaper with general circulation. The ads must include the time, date, and location of the auction.

The buyer of a tax certificate, typically an investor, agrees to pay the taxes due. At the auction, the prospective purchasers are bidding on the interest rate they are willing to accept, not on an amount to purchase the property itself. The interest rate starts at 18% and is bid down. The investor who bids the lowest rate is issued the tax certificate and pays the certificate amount to the county. The tax certificate remains in force for 7 years from the date of purchase, at which time it expires.

The certificate holder earns simple interest on the certificate each month at the rate of the winning bid. If and when the tax certificate is redeemed by the property owner, the certificate holder receives the certificate face value plus all of the accrued interest up to the redemption date. If the property owner fails to pay the overdue taxes and accrued interest within 2 years after the certificate was sold, the holder of the tax certificate may then apply for a **tax deed**.

Tax deed

A tax deed is a legal instrument for conveying title when a property is sold for non-payment of taxes. The certificate holder may be required to pay additional taxes and fees to the county on top of the redemption amount owed. The application for a tax deed causes the taxing agency to institute a **tax sale** or **tax foreclosure**.

Tax sale

A tax sale is frequently some type of auction. If the tax has not already been paid through the tax certificate process, the buyer of the property must pay the taxes due. If the taxpayer can redeem the property by paying the delinquent taxes and any other charges before the tax sale occurs, this right is known as an **equitable right of redemption**. In Florida, there is a 2-year **redemption period** during which the defaulted taxpayer has the equitable right to buy back the property and reclaim title.

If the taxpayer can redeem the property after the tax sale, this right is known as a **statutory right of redemption**. In this case, the taxpayer must pay the amount paid by the winning bidder at the tax sale, plus any charges, additional taxes, or interest that may have accumulated.

If the defaulted taxpayer does not redeem the property within the allotted time, the state issues the tax deed to convey title to the highest bidder at the tax sale auction. If the highest bidder is someone other than the certificate holder, the bidder must pay the holder all amounts paid by the holder plus all accrued interest.

Tax Lien Enforcement

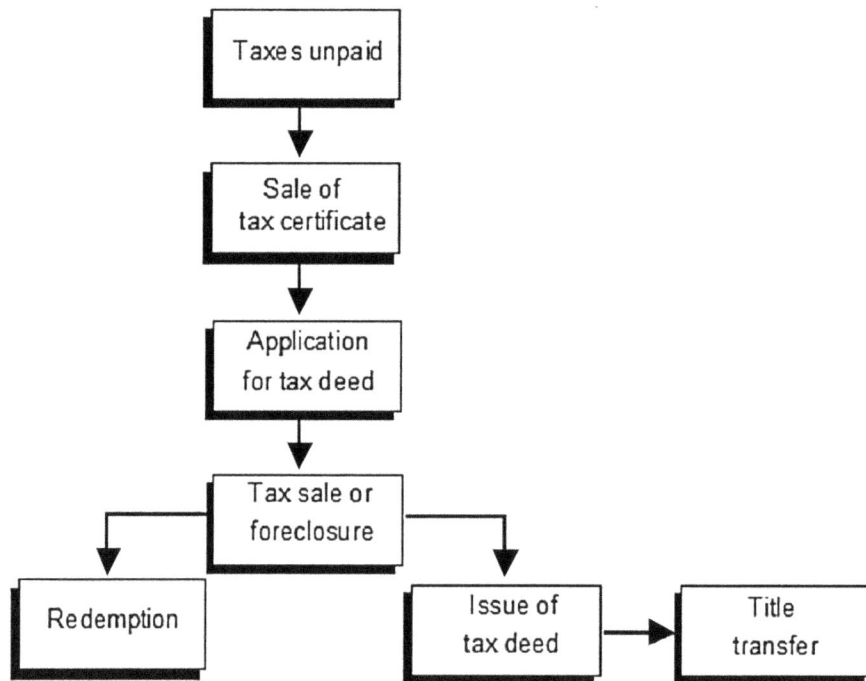

```
                    ┌──────────────┐
                    │ Taxes unpaid │
                    └──────┬───────┘
                           │
                           ▼
                    ┌──────────────┐
                    │   Sale of    │
                    │ tax certificate │
                    └──────┬───────┘
                           │
                           ▼
                    ┌──────────────┐
                    │ Application  │
                    │ for tax deed │
                    └──────┬───────┘
                           │
                           ▼
                    ┌──────────────┐
          ┌─────────┤ Tax sale or  ├─────────┐
          │         │ foreclosure  │         │
          │         └──────────────┘         │
          ▼                                  ▼
   ┌──────────────┐                   ┌──────────────┐      ┌──────────────┐
   │  Redemption  │                   │   Issue of   │─────▶│    Title     │
   └──────────────┘                   │   tax deed   │      │   transfer   │
                                      └──────────────┘      └──────────────┘
```

FEDERAL INCOME TAXES

Sale of real property
Principal residence
Investment real estate

Sale of real property   **Capital gain.** When real estate is sold, a *taxable event* occurs. If the sale proceeds *exceed* the original cost of the investment, subject to some adjustments, there is a capital gain that is subject to tax. If the sales proceeds are less than the original cost with adjustments, there is a capital loss. As discussed in the section on real estate investments, gain on sale is the amount realized from the sale, net of selling costs, minus the adjusted basis of the property, which is the beginning cost plus capital improvements minus exclusions and credits.

Tax law provides an exclusion of gain on a residential sale of $250,000 for an individual taxpayer and $500,000 for married taxpayers filing jointly. The exclusion of gain from sale of a residence can be claimed every two years, provided the taxpayer meets ownership and use requirements. Losses are not deductible, and there is no carry-over of any unused portion of the exclusion.

Foreign sellers. The sale of real property by foreign sellers is regulated by the Foreign Investment Real Property Tax Act (FIRPTA), which requires buyers of such properties to withhold up to 15% of the gross proceeds from sale against the potential gains tax liability. In addition to individual sellers and buyers, the withholding obligation applies to foreign and domestic corporations, qualified investment entities, and fiduciaries of certain trusts and estates. The transaction must be reported to the Internal Revenue Service and the withheld funds transmitted with the proper form. Instructions and the form may be found at https://www.irs.gov/forms-pubs/about-form-8288.

Principal residence

Tax advantages. In addition to the exclusion on gains discussed above, ownership of residential real estate offers tax advantages in the form of deductions and exclusions from taxable income. Under current tax law, some of these advantages are reduced by an increase in the standard deduction and by limits on certain deductions. Owners should consult a tax professional for advice on these matters. Potential deductions and exclusions include:

▸ mortgage interest

   With limitations, mortgage loan interest paid for a principal and second home is deductible.

▸ property tax

   With limitations, property taxes paid for a principal and second home are deductible.

▸ home equity loan interest

   If a home equity loan is used to improve the home, interest payments on the loan are deductible.

▸ points and fees

   If a mortgage loan is used to purchase or build a principal residence, origination fees and points are deductible. Points are amortized on a refinance loan and deducted over the loan term on a loan to finance a second home.

▸ gain on sale exclusions

   As discussed above.

▸ IRA withdrawals

   First-time homebuyers may make withdrawals without penalty from tax-deferred IRA accounts for use as a down payment.

Investment real estate

Taxable income. The taxation of income from investment real estate involves the application of the investor's tax rate to the income generated by the property after deductions and other adjustments are subtracted.

Depreciation. Cost recovery expense, or depreciation, was discussed in the section on appraisal. To review, depreciation is the estimated loss of value in an improvement over time. This loss pertains only to the improved portion of real property, not to land.

In the straight-line method of estimating depreciation, it is assumed that loss occurs equally and incrementally across a period of time called the economic life of the improvement. The economic life is currently established by the IRS as 27.5

years for residential income property and 39 years for non-residential income property. The annual cost recovery expense is the total cost of the improvement (depreciable basis) divided by the economic life period. For a simple example, if the total cost to acquire a residential income property was $1,000,000, and the land is valued at $200,000, the value of the improvement may be said to be $800,000. The annual cost recovery expense is then $800,000, divided by 27.5, or $29,091.

Installment sales. An installment sale, land contract, or contract for deed, as discussed in the section on real estate contracts, allows the seller to defer receipt of some or all of the purchase price of a property over a specified period of time. At the end of the period, the buyer pays the vendor the full purchase price and the vendor deeds legal title to the vendee. Since the seller is not liable for capital gains tax until the purchase price is received, the installment sale lowers the seller's tax liability in the year of the sale.

Like-kind exchanges. Also as discussed in the section on real estate investment, an investor can sometimes defer the reporting of gain or loss, and, hence, taxation of gain, by participating in an exchange of like-kind assets. The legislation that deals with like-kind exchanges is contained in Section 1031 of the IRS code. These tax-deferred exchanges are sometimes called **Section 1031 exchanges** and **Starker exchanges**, named for an investor who won a case against the IRS.

18 Taxes Affecting Real Estate
Snapshot Review

REAL PROPERTY TAXATION

Taxing entities
- no federal ad valorem taxes, only federal tax on income and gain; federal government can impose a tax lien against real property
- FL passes property taxation to local governments and tax districts
- FL requires property to be assessed at just value for taxing purpose
- annual tax schedule from January 1 to December 31 with taxes due before March 1 of following year
- counties, cities, municipalities, townships and special tax districts levy taxes on real property
- tax districts are established to collect funds for providing specific services, e.g., schools, fire protection, parks, community colleges, libraries, road maintenance

Ad valorem taxation
- property tax levied annually on the taxable value of a property in order to help fund government and public services
- tax base equals the total of assessed values of all real property within the area, excluding exemptions
- each FL county has its own elected property appraiser to assess property
- FL requires properties to be assessed at just value (market value)
- Amendment I provides homestead exemptions, portability of SOH limits, assessment cap for non-homestead properties
- protest procedure: contact property appraiser for adjustment; file appeal with Value Adjustment Board; initiate litigation against appraiser and tax collector with writ of certiorari
- property's assessed value – exemptions and SOH = taxable value
- taxable value: assessed value minus exemptions and adjustments; if no exemptions, assessed value and taxable value are the same
- taxing entity determines what budget requirements must be met by ad valorem tax; tax rate = tax requirement divided by the tax base
- tax rate stated as mills ($.001), or dollars per $100 of assessed value, or dollars per $1,000 of assessed value, or as a percentage of assessed value
- taxable value X tax rate = property tax; tax rate may change every year; FL millage rates limited to 10 mills

Exemptions from property taxes
- Immune property: government owned and used properties are 100% immune from property taxation
- nonprofit properties are 100% exempt; homestead properties are partially exempt if qualified

Homestead exemption
- qualified for exemption if title holder, property resident for 1 year, permanent address, apply for exemption by March 1 for same year
- exemption automatically applied each year
- Save Our Homes amendment limits assessed value increases to 3% annually or percentage of consumer price index; assessed value not to exceed just value
- exemptions for surviving spouses, disabled, blind, military disabled; cumulative exemptions

Florida

Greenbelt Law	• assessed based on actual use of property and not highest and best use; created to protect farmers from high taxes; farmer must apply by March 1 and use land for commercial agriculture; owner may lease property to tenant who will maintain agriculture operation
SPECIAL ASSESSMENTS	• tax levied against specific properties that will benefit from a public improvement; amount is based on a pro rata share of the cost of the improvement and the value each parcel will receive from the improvement
TAX LIEN ENFORCEMENT	• unpaid property tax lien is superior to all other liens
Sale of tax certificates	• the buyer of a tax certificate agrees to pay the taxes due and after a period of time may apply for a tax deed on the property
	• claim against property for unpaid property tax; FL requires sale of certificates annually for delinquent taxes; buyers bid on interest rate, not property; lowest bidder wins; certificate valid for 7 years with interest earned each month; property owner has 2 years to pay taxes and interest to redeem property
Tax deed	• conveys title in the tax sale
	• certificate holder may apply for tax deed if owner does not redeem property; initiates tax sale
Tax sale	• the buyer must pay the taxes due, if still unpaid; the defaulted taxpayer may be able to redeem the property and reclaim title; if not redeemed, the state issues the tax deed to convey title to the buyer
	• for properties unredeemed within 2 years; property goes to highest bidder who pays certificate holder certificate face value plus accrued interest
FEDERAL INCOME TAXES	
Sale of real property	• gain on sale may be taxable; in residential sales, a portion of gain is excluded from taxable gain
	• foreign sellers subject to withholding of tax on gain by buyers
Principal residence	• tax advantages may include: deductions and exclusions for mortgage interest, property tax, home equity loan interest, points and fees, gain on sale , IRA withdrawals
Investment real estate	• investment income is taxable; tax rate is applied to taxable income derived from net operating income; depreciation or cost recovery expense is not included in taxable income
	• installment sales: purchase price is paid over time in installments; seller retains title; buyer takes possession; at end of period, buyer pays balance of price, gets legal title; gain not taxed until full purchase price received
	• like-kind Section 1031 exchanges: tax on gain deferrable until property finally sold and not exchanged

SECTION EIGHTEEN: Taxes Affecting Real Estate

Section Quiz

1. Which of the following is true with respect to real property taxation by the federal government?

   a. It may impose ad valorem property taxes and capital gain tax.
   b. It may not impose property taxes nor tax liens.
   c. There are no federal ad valorem taxes on real property.
   d. It may impose ad valorem tax, but not capital gain tax.

2. According to law, states

   a. may not levy real estate taxes.
   b. may not impose tax liens.
   c. may delegate taxing authority to county governments.
   d. may prevent federal taxation of real estate within their respective jurisdictions, if properly legislated.

3. The role of local tax districts is to

   a. levy income, sales, and property taxes to meet their budget requirements.
   b. manage their budgeted portion of real estate tax revenues levied and distributed by the state.
   c. impose property taxes for specific municipal services.
   d. place tax liens on its facilities.

4. A special tax district might be created to

   a. construct and manage a park district.
   b. create a two-mile extension of county sewer facilities.
   c. establish and maintain a public library.
   d. create a fire department.

5. Ad valorem taxes are based on

   a. the replacement value of property.
   b. the assessed value of property.
   c. the millage value of property.
   d. the broker's estimate of value.

6. The ad valorem tax base of a municipal jurisdiction is equal to

   a. the jurisdiction's annual budget times the tax rate.
   b. the total of all assessed values of properties minus exemptions.
   c. the total amount of ad valorem taxes required by the budget.
   d. the municipality's budget multiplied times the millage rate.

7. As part of the assessment process, many taxing entities utilize equalization boards in order to

   a. adjust millage rates within the district to ensure fairness.
   b. modify the tax rate from one neighborhood to the next.
   c. ensure that property owners have nearly equal tax bills.
   d. smooth out wide discrepancies of assessed values within the district.

8. A homeowner receives a tax bill that she feels is outrageous. This taxpayer may

   a. appeal to adjust the millage rate.
   b. appeal to adjust the district's budget.
   c. appeal to adjust the assessed valuation.
   d. not appeal.

9. The purpose of a homestead tax exemption is

   a. to exempt qualified property owners from ad valorem taxation.
   b. to offer an amount of tax relief on an owner's principal residence.
   c. to encourage multiple property investment.
   d. to exempt owners of principal residences who rent their properties.

10. A millage rate is derived by

    a. dividing the tax requirement by the tax base.
    b. multiplying the tax base times the tax requirement.
    c. adding an inflation factor to the prior year's tax rate.
    d. dividing the tax base by the tax requirement.

11. A homeowner's total tax bill is derived by

    a. dividing the tax requirement by the tax base.
    b. multiplying each district's tax rate times the assessed value of the property.
    c. multiplying each district's tax rate times the taxable value of the property.
    d. averaging the tax rate for each tax district, and multiplying the average tax rate times the assessed value.

12. A unique characteristic of a special assessment tax is that

    a. it only applies to properties which will benefit from the public improvement.
    b. the equalization board discounts levies for properties not affected by the public improvement.
    c. more valuable properties which stand to benefit will pay proportionately more taxes.
    d. it creates an involuntary junior lien on the property.

13. A tax certificate

    a. certifies to tax collectors that a property owner has paid all ad valorem taxes on the property for the calendar year.
    b. entitles its holder to apply for a tax deed after a certain period.
    c. exempts its holder from paying taxes on the particular property referenced by the certificate.
    d. waives a property owner's rights of redemption in a foreclosure.

14. An equitable right of redemption

    a. allows a holder of a tax certificate to redeem it for a tax deed.
    b. gives a delinquent taxpayer a grace period prior to the tax sale to pay property taxes.
    c. gives a holder of a tax deed the right to acquire the property named in the tax certificate.
    d. gives a delinquent taxpayer a grace period after the tax sale to pay property taxes.

15. In Florida, millage rates are limited to

    a. 2 mills.
    b. 5 mills.
    c. 7 mills.
    d. 10 mills.

16. Just value is another term for the

    a. assessed value.
    b. market value.
    c. taxable value.
    d. appraised value.

17. When a homeowner wants to protest a property assessed amount, what is the final step he may make?

    a. File an appeal with the adjuster
    b. Request a judicial review
    c. Initiate litigation
    d. Appeal to a higher court

18. Which is not required to qualify for a homestead exemption on property taxes?

    a. Head of the family
    b. Homestead title holder
    c. Homestead resident for 1 year starting on January 1
    d. Permanent residence

19. Taxable value of a property is calculated by

    a. multiplying the assessed value by the tax rate.
    b. subtracting the appraised value from the just value.
    c. subtracting exemptions from the assessed value.
    d. adding the assessed value to the just value.

19 Planning, Zoning, and Environmental Hazards

Planning and Zoning
Florida's Growth Policy and Community Planning Act (CPA)
Public Land Use Control
Flood Zones
Environmental Controls

Learning Objectives

- Describe the composition and authority of the local planning agency
- Explain the purpose of land-use controls and the role of zoning ordinances
- Identify the provisions of Florida's comprehensive plan and the Growth Management Act
- Distinguish among the five general zoning classifications
- Distinguish among zoning ordinances, building codes and health ordinances
- Explain the purpose of a variance, special exception and a nonconforming use
- Calculate the number of lots available for development, given the total number of acres contained in a parcel, the percentage of land reserved for streets and other facilities and the minimum number of square feet per lot
- Describe the characteristics of a planned unit development
- Understand the basic provisions of the national flood insurance program
- Describe the impact Comprehensive Environmental Response Compensation and Liability Act (CERCLA)
- Explain the various environmental hazards associated with real estate

Key Terms

asbestos
buffer zone
building code
building inspection
building permit
certificate of occupancy
concurrency
environmental impact statement

health ordinance
nonconforming use
planned unit development
special exception
special flood hazard area
special purpose property
variance
zoning ordinance

PLANNING AND ZONING

Goals of land use control
The master plan
Planning objectives
Plan development
Planning management

While the Constitution guarantees the right of individual ownership of real estate, it does not guarantee the uncontrolled sale, use, and development of real estate. As American history demonstrates, unregulated use of real estate has significant potential for eventual damage to property values as well as to the environment. Moreover, with the explosive urban growth in this century, it has become clear that regulation of land use is necessary to preserve the interests, safety, and welfare of the community.

Without a central authority to exert control, land use tends to be chaotic. For example, rapid growth can outpace the support capabilities of basic municipal services such as sewers, power, water, schools, roads and communications. On an aesthetic level, communities need controls to keep certain commercial and industrial land uses away from residential areas to avoid the undermining of property values by pollution, noise, and traffic congestion.

Goals of land use control

Over time, public and private control of land use has come to focus on certain core purposes. These are:

- preservation of property values
- promotion of the highest and best use of property
- balance between individual property rights and the public good, i.e., its health, safety and welfare
- control of growth to remain within infrastructure capabilities
- incorporation of community consensus into regulatory and planning activities

The optimum management of real property usage must take into account both the interests of the individual and the interests of the surrounding community. While maintaining the value of an individual estate is important, the owner of an estate must realize that unregulated use and development can jeopardize the value not only of the owner's estate but of neighboring properties. Similarly, the community must keep in mind the effect of government actions on individual property values, since local government is largely supported by taxes based on the value of property.

Public Land Use Control

A community achieves its land usage goals through a three-phase process, as the exhibit illustrates:

- *development of a master plan* for the jurisdiction
- *administration of the plan* by a municipal, county, or regional planning commission
- *implementation of the plan* through public control of zoning, building codes, permits, and other measures

Municipal, county, and regional authorities develop comprehensive land use plans for a particular community with the input of property owners. A planning commission manages the master plan and enforces it by exercising its power to establish zones, control building permits, and create building codes.

In addition to public land use planning and control, some private entities, such as subdivision associations, can impose additional standards of land use on owners within the private entity's legal jurisdiction. Private controls are primarily implemented by deed restrictions.

The master plan

Public land use planning incorporates long-term usage strategies and growth policies in a **land use plan**, or **master plan**. In Florida, the process of land use planning begins when the state legislature enacts laws *requiring all counties and municipalities to adopt a land use plan*. The land use plan must not only reflect the needs of the local area, but also conform to state and federal environmental laws and the plans of regional and state planning agencies. The state enforces its planning mandates by giving state agencies the power to approve county and local plans.

The master plan therefore fuses state and regional land use laws with local land use objectives that correspond to the municipality's social and economic conditions. The completed plan becomes the overall guideline for creating and enforcing zones, building codes, and development requirements.

Planning objectives

The primary objectives of a master plan are generally to control and accommodate social and economic growth.

Amount of growth. A master plan *sets specific guidelines on how much growth the jurisdiction will allow*. While all communities desire a certain degree of growth, too much growth can overwhelm services and infrastructure.

To formulate a growth strategy, a plan initially forecasts growth trends, then estimates how well the municipality can keep pace with the growth forecast. The outcome is a policy position that limits building permits and development projects to desired growth parameters. A growth plan considers:

- nature, location and extent of permitted uses
- availability of sanitation facilities
- adequacy of drainage, waste collection, and potable water systems
- adequacy of utilities companies
- adequacy and patterns of thoroughfares
- housing availability
- conservation of natural resources
- adequacy of recreational facilities
- ability and willingness of the community to absorb new taxes, bond issues, and assessments

Growth patterns. In addition to the quantity of growth, a master plan also *defines what type of growth will occur, and where*. Major considerations are:

- the type of enterprises and developments to allow
- residential density and commercial intensity
- effects of industrial and commercial land uses on residential and public sectors, i.e., where to allow such uses
- effect of new developments on traffic patterns and thoroughfares
- effects on the environment and environmental quality (air, water, soil, noise, visual aspects)
- effect on natural resources that support the community
- code specifications for specific construction projects

Accommodating demand. As the master plan sets forth guidelines for how much growth will be allowed, it must also *make plans for accommodating expanding or contracting demand for services and infrastructure*. The plan must identify:

- facilities requirements for local government
- new construction requirements for streets, schools, and social services facilities such as libraries, civic centers, etc.
- new construction required to provide power, water and sewer services

Plan development

In response to land use objectives, community attitudes, and conclusions drawn from research, the planning personnel formulate their plan. In the course of planning, they analyze

- population and demographic trends
- economic trends
- existing land use

	▸ existing support facilities
	▸ traffic patterns

Planning management

Public land use management takes place within county and municipal **planning departments**. These departments are responsible for:

- ▸ long-term implementation of the master plan
- ▸ creating rules and restrictions that support plans and policies
- ▸ enforcing and administering land use regulation on an everyday basis

The planning commission. In most jurisdictions, a planning commission or board comprised of officials appointed by the government's legislative entity handles the planning function.

The commission oversees the operations of the department's professional planning staff and support personnel. In addition, the commission makes recommendations to elected officials concerning land use policy and policy administration.

Commission authority and duties. The planning commission is responsible for:

- ▸ approving site plans and subdivision plans
- ▸ approving building permits
- ▸ ruling on zoning issues
- ▸ controlling signage

Commission support staff. After the planning commission proposes policies and sets goals and standards, the Commission's support staff carries out the collection and analysis of land use information necessary to develop the comprehensive plan.

FLORIDA'S GROWTH POLICY AND COMMUNITY PLANNING ACT (CPA)

Chapter 163 F. S. growth policy
Department of Economic Opportunity
Required elements
Land development regulation
Required elements

Chapter 163 F.S. growth policy

Florida's Growth Policy and Community Planning Act recognizes and promotes the beneficial impact that strong urban centers have on local and state economies and resources and, thus, urges respective governments to revitalize urban centers by providing adequate infrastructure, human services, safe neighborhoods, educational facilities, and economic development.

The Act refers to this effort as infill development and redevelopment, wherein public services such as water, transportation, schools, etc., are already in place prior to capital improvements in areas that suffer from pervasive poverty and unemployment with substandard properties.

Florida's Community Planning Act was established to strengthen the power of local governments in establishing comprehensive planning programs for future development; in encouraging appropriate use of land, water, and resources in the interest of the public; and in overcoming current and future problems caused by land use and development.

The intent of the Act was to have local governments concentrate on community land use and growth for the protection of public health, safety, and general welfare while the state government concentrates on protecting state resources and facilities.

The Act protects the traditional economic base of Florida, i.e., agriculture, tourism, and military presence, and encourages economic diversification, workforce development, and community planning. The Act also protects private property and the rights of private property owners.

Department of Economic Opportunity

The Department of Community Affairs (DCA), which monitored housing and commercial development in Florida, was abolished in 2011. The DCA was originally established to prevent sprawl and congestion. In its stead, the **Department of Economic Opportunity (DEO)** was created and the power to make development decisions was relegated to local governments, thereby diminishing state oversight. The DEO supervises funds used to incentivize businesses to come to Florida.

Required elements

A comprehensive plan must be implemented by adopting sufficient land use control ordinances and capital improvement programs. The plan must contain the following required elements.

Future land use. The plan must designate proposed future distribution and location of residential, commercial, industrial, agricultural, recreational, conservation, education, public facilities, and other categories of land use. The plan must also include the standards for control and distribution of population densities and building intensities.

Traffic circulation. The plan must include a transportation element to plan for a multimodal transportation system with emphasis on public transportation systems. The transportation element must address traffic circulation to include the types, locations, and extent of existing and proposed major thoroughfares and transportation routes and maps showing the existing and proposed system features. An airport plan may be incorporated into the master plan.

Conservation of natural resources. A conservation element must be included in the plan for the conservation, use, and protection of air, water, water recharge areas, wetlands, water wells, marshes, soils, beaches, shores, flood plains, rivers, lakes, forests, wildlife, marine habitat, minerals, and other resources.

Recreation. The plan is also to include an element for a comprehensive system of public and private sites for recreation to include natural reservations, parks and playgrounds, parkways, beaches, open spaces, waterways, and other recreation facilities.

Housing. A mandated housing element must include principles, guidelines, standards, and strategies for providing housing for all current and future residents, the elimination of substandard dwelling conditions, the improvement of existing housing, sites for future housing, relocation housing, and affordable housing.

Coastal zone protection where relevant. Another element of the plan is for coastal management to maintain and restore the quality of the coastal zone environment, preserve populations of wildlife and marine life, protect coastal zone resources, and manage coastal zone development.

Intergovernmental coordination. An intergovernmental coordination element must be included that shows the relationships and states principles and guidelines to be used in coordinating the comprehensive plan with 1) plans from local government units that do not have regulatory authority over land use, 2) comprehensive plans of adjacent municipalities and areas, and 3) the state comprehensive plan. The comprehensive plan must show consideration for plans of these other entities.

Utilities. An element for sanitary sewer, solid waste, drainage, potable water, and natural groundwater aquifer recharge must also be included in the plan to indicate means for providing protection for these facilities in the area.

Concurrency. Concurrency is a set of land use regulations that local governments within Florida adopt to assure that new development does not exceed the local government's ability to handle it. The local government needs to have enough infrastructure capacity to support any proposed development.

Regulations require the governments to meet concurrency requirements for sanitary sewer, solid waste, drainage, and potable water by the time a certificate of occupancy is issued for the development. Parks and recreation, schools, and transportation facilities no longer fall under the state's concurrency requirements. They and other non-mandatory public facilities may, however, fall under a local government's concurrency requirements if the local government's plan provides the principles, guidelines, standards, and strategies for applying the concurrency to the facility.

Optional elements may include historical, scenic preservation, economic, and public buildings.

PUBLIC LAND USE CONTROL

Zoning
Zoning administration
Subdivision regulation
Building codes

At the state level, the legislature enacts laws that control and restrict land use, particularly from the environmental perspective. At the local level, county and city governments control land use through the authority known as **police power**. The most common expressions of police power are county and municipal **zoning**. Other examples of public land use control are:

> ▶ subdivision regulations
> ▶ building codes
> ▶ eminent domain
> ▶ environmental restrictions
> ▶ development requirements

Governments also have the right to **own** real property for public use and welfare. In exercising its ownership rights, a municipality may **annex** property adjacent to its existing property or purchase other tracts of land through conventional transfers. Where necessary, it may force property owners to sell their property through the power of **eminent domain**.

Zoning

Zoning is the primary tool by which cities and counties regulate land use and implement their respective master plans. The Constitution grants the states the legal authority to regulate, and the states delegate the authority to counties and municipalities through legislation called **enabling acts**.

The zoning ordinance. The vehicle for zoning a city or county is the **zoning ordinance**, a regulation enacted by the local government. The intent of zoning ordinances is to specify land usage for every parcel within the jurisdiction. In some areas, state laws permit zoning ordinances to apply to areas immediately beyond the legal boundaries of the city or county.

Zoning ordinances implement the master plan by regulating **density**, **land use intensity**, **aesthetics**, and **highest and best use**. Ordinances typically address:

> ▶ the nature of land use-- office, commercial, residential, etc.
> ▶ size and configuration of a building site, including setbacks, sidewalk requirements, parking requirements, and access
> ▶ site development procedures
> ▶ construction and design methods and materials, including height restrictions, building-to-site area ratios, and architectural styles
> ▶ use of space within the building
> ▶ signage

Ordinance validity. Local planners do not have unlimited authority to do whatever they want. Their zoning ordinances must be clear in import, apply to all parties equally, and promote health, safety, and welfare of the community in a reasonable manner.

Building permits. Local governments enforce zoning ordinances by issuing building permits to those who want to improve, repair, or refurbish a property. To receive a permit, the project must comply with all relevant ordinances and codes. Further zoning enforcement is achieved through periodic inspections.

Types of zones. One of the primary applications of zoning power is the separation of residential properties from commercial and industrial uses. Proper design of land use in this manner preserves the aesthetics and value of neighborhoods and promotes the success of commercial enterprises through intelligently located zones.

Six common types of zones and their respective priorities are as follows.

- **residential**
- **commercial**
- **industrial**
- **agricultural**
- **public**
- **planned unit development (PUD)**

Residential. Residential zoning restricts land use to private, non-commercial dwellings. Sub-zones in this category further stipulate the types of residences allowed, whether single-family, multi-unit complexes, condominiums, publicly subsidized housing, or other form of housing.

Residential zoning regulates:

- *density,* by limiting the number and size of dwelling units and lots in an area
- values and aesthetics, by limiting the type of residences allowed. Some areas adopt **buffer zones** to separate residential areas from commercial and industrial zones.

Commercial. Commercial zoning regulates the location of office and retail land usage. Some commercial zones allow combinations of office and retail uses on a single site. Sub-zones in this category may limit the type of retail or office activity permitted, for example, a department store versus a strip center.

Commercial zoning regulates:

- intensity of usage, by limiting the area of store or office per site area. Intensity regulation is further achieved by minimum parking requirements, setbacks, and building height restrictions.

Industrial. Industrial zoning regulates:

- intensity of usage
- type of industrial activity
- environmental consequences

A municipality may not allow some industrial zones, such as heavy industrial, at all. The industrial park is a relatively recent concept in industrial zoning.

Agricultural. Agricultural zoning restricts land use to farming, ranching, and other agricultural enterprises.

Public. Public zoning restricts land use to public services and recreation. Parks, post offices, government buildings, schools, and libraries are examples of uses allowed in a public zone.

Planned Unit Development (PUD). planned unit development zoning restricts use to development of whole tracts that are designed to use space efficiently and maximize open space. A PUD zone may be for residential, commercial, or industrial uses, or combinations thereof.

Zoning administration

Zoning Board of Adjustment. A county or local board, usually called the zoning board of adjustment or zoning appeals board, administers zoning ordinances. The board rules on interpretations of zoning ordinances as they apply to specific land use cases presented by property owners in the jurisdiction. In effect, the zoning board is a court of appeals for owners and developers who desire to use land in a manner that is not entirely consistent with existing ordinances.

The board conducts hearings of specific cases and renders official decisions regarding the land use based on evidence presented.

A zoning board generally deals with such issues and appeals as:

- nonconforming use
- variance
- special exception or conditional use permit
- zoning amendment

If the board rejects an appeal, the party may appeal the ruling further in a court of law.

Nonconforming use. A nonconforming use is one *that clearly differs from current zoning*. Usually, nonconforming uses result when a zoning change leaves existing properties in violation of the new ordinance. This type of nonconforming use is a **legal** nonconforming use. A board usually treats this kind of situation by allowing it to continue either

- indefinitely
- until the structures are torn down
- only while the same use continues, or

‣ until the property is sold

For instance, a motel is situated in a residential area that no longer allows commercial activity. The zoning board rules that the motel may continue to operate until it is sold, destroyed or used for any other commercial purpose.

An **illegal nonconforming use** is one that conflicts with ordinances that were in place before the use commenced. For instance, if the motel in the previous example is sold, and the new owner continues to operate the property as a motel, the motel is now an illegal, nonconforming use.

Variance. A zoning variance allows a use that differs from the applicable ordinance for a variety of *justifiable* reasons, including that:

‣ compliance will cause unreasonable hardship
‣ the use will not change the essential character of the area
‣ the use does not conflict with the general intent of the ordinance

For example, an owner mistakenly violates a setback requirement by two feet. His house is already constructed, and complying with the full setback now would be extremely expensive, if not impossible. The zoning board grants a variance on the grounds that compliance would cause an unreasonable hardship.

A grant of a zoning variance may be unconditional, or it may require conditions to be fulfilled, such as removing the violation after a certain time.

Special exception. A special exception grant authorizes a use that is not consistent with the zoning ordinance in a literal sense, yet is clearly *beneficial or essential to the public welfare* and does not materially impair other uses in the zone.

A possible example is an old house in a residential zone adjacent to a retail zone. The zoning board might grant a special exception to a local group that proposes to renovate the house and convert it to a local museum, which is a retail use, since the community stands to benefit from the museum.

Amendment. A current or potential property owner may petition the zoning board for an outright change in the zoning of a particular property. For example, a property zoned for agricultural use has been idle for years. A major employer desires to develop the property for a local distribution facility, which would create numerous jobs, and petitions for an amendment. The board changes the zoning from agricultural to light industrial to permit the development. Since a change in zoning can have significant economic and social impact, an appeal for an amendment is a difficult process that often involves public hearings.

Subdivision regulation

In addition to complying with zoning ordinances, a developer of multiple properties in a subdivision must meet requirements for subdivisions.

Subdivision plat approval. The developer submits a plat of subdivision containing surveyed plat maps and comprehensive building specifications. The plat, as a minimum, shows that the plan complies with local zoning and building ordinances. The project can commence only after the relevant authority has approved the plat.

Subdivision requirements typically regulate:

- ▶ location, grading, alignment, surfacing, street width, highways
- ▶ sewers and water mains
- ▶ lot and block dimensions
- ▶ building and setback lines
- ▶ public use dedications
- ▶ utility easements
- ▶ ground percolation
- ▶ environmental impact report
- ▶ zoned density

Concurrency. Florida has adopted policies that require developers, especially of subdivisions, to take responsibility for the impact of their projects on the local infrastructure by taking corrective action. Concurrency is a policy that requires the developer to make accommodations *concurrently* with the development of the project itself, not afterwards. For example, if a project will create a traffic overload in an area, the developer may have to widen the road while constructing the project.

FHA requirements. In addition to local regulation, subdivisions must meet FHA (Federal Housing Authority) requirements to qualify for FHA financing insurance. The FHA sets standards similar to local ordinances to ensure an adequate level of construction quality, aesthetics, and infrastructure services.

Building codes

Building codes allow the county and municipality to protect the public against the hazards of unregulated construction. Building codes establish standards for virtually every aspect of a construction project, including offsite improvements such as streets, curbs, gutters, drainage systems, and onsite improvements such as the building itself.

The Florida Building Commission developed the *Florida Building Code* after Hurricane Andrew uncovered the need for more robust codes throughout the state. The statewide Code governs the design, construction, erection, alteration, modification, repair, and demolition of public and private buildings, structures, and facilities in the state. Separate books are available for plumbing, residential, energy conservation, hurricane zone test protocols, building, accessibility, existing building, fuel gas, and mechanical codes. The Code is updated every 3 years and often amended annually.

The Code now includes risk categories for building types based on three wind speed maps. Because Florida coastal areas encounter higher wind speed storms, those areas must meet the higher wind load requirements. The Code defines those areas and provides options for meeting the building code requirements through initial construction and upgrades to existing structures.

Building permits. Florida statute mandates that anyone who plans to construct, enlarge, alter, repair, move, demolish, or change the occupancy of a building or structure or perform any work that is regulated by the Florida Building Code must first obtain the required permit. Depending on the work to be done, one project may require multiple permits. For example, renovating a structure may require a general building permit but may also require an electrical and/or plumbing permit.

Florida permits usually require drawn plans of the work to be done and proof of the property's ownership. Again, depending on the work to be done, the permit may also require proof of insurance and/or proof of current licenses for any contractors or other professionals performing the work. New construction will also require a Florida energy code compliance certificate. Submission of the work plans will allow the city or county building department to also determine if the work will comply with wind load requirements.

Building inspections. During building construction or renovation, work completed will need to be inspected for code compliance and correctness. When an inspection is required for a particular phase of construction, work may not continue or resume until the inspector signs off on that phase. Inspections typically are required several times during a build or renovation. When the project is completed, a final inspection is required so that a *certificate of occupancy* can be issued and the property can be approved for occupancy and use.

R-value. An R-value is a measurement of the effectiveness of insulation and its resistance to heat flow. The higher the R-value, the higher the resistance, or the better the energy efficiency. City and county building and energy codes specify the minimum R-value required for the building envelope which is defined as the parts of the structure that separate the outdoor environment from the interior environment, or the roof, walls, and floors.

FLOOD ZONES

National Flood Insurance Program (NFIP)
Residential structures requirements
Nonresidential structures requirements
Proportion of NFIP purchasers in Florida

The National Flood Insurance Act of 1968 created the Federal Insurance Administration and made flood insurance available for the first time. The Act also led to the creation of the National Flood Insurance Program, whose goals were to provide flood insurance for structures and their contents that are located in communities with minimal floodplain management standards and to establish insurance rates for structures located in identified flood hazard areas.

The Flood Disaster Protection Act of 1973 amended the NFIP by making the purchase of flood insurance mandatory for the protection of property located in Special Flood Hazard Areas.

**National Flood
Insurance Program
(NFIP)**

Qualifying for NFIP. The Federal Emergency Management Agency (FEMA) administers the NFIP and has established requirements communities must meet to participate in the program. The communities must agree to adopt and enforce regulations that reduce flood risks. Homeowners, renters, and business owners may obtain flood loss insurance through insurance agencies if the subject property is located in a community that participates in the program.

NFIP criteria for "Special Flood Hazard Areas" (SFHA). FEMA has identified flood zones throughout the U.S. and shows those areas on their Flood Insurance Rate Maps (FIRM), including the categories of flood risk for each area: low-risk, moderate-risk, and high-risk.

Any high-risk area is also identified as a special flood hazard area, which is defined as an area with a 1% chance of flooding in any year. That does not mean the area will flood every year; rather, it means there is a 1% statistical possibility of flooding every year. The 1% annual chance flood is also referred to as the base flood or 100-year flood. This is of special interest to mortgage lenders because that means there is a 1 in 4 chance of flooding during a 30-year mortgage. Thus, mortgage lenders holding loans on property located in a SFHA typically require the homeowner to carry flood insurance on the property.

SFHAs are identified as either A zones (SFHA floodplain areas) or V zones (SFHA coastal land area).

Development within SFHAs restrictions. Before beginning development within a SFHA, a developer must obtain a permit to ensure the project will meet the NFIP requirements and local community ordinances. Requirements vary based on the actual zone where the property is located and the type of structure being built.

Because V zones have higher flood risks, structures in those areas must be anchored to withstand the force of waves, high winds, and erosion and to prevent collapse and/or movement. Development sites are to be graded to prevent waterflow from entering into ground floor structures. Structures built on slopes must have drainage paths to guide waterflow away from the structures.

Development within SFHAs must not obstruct the natural flow of flood waters. For example, removing sand from beaches removes the natural barrier built up over years and exposes inland areas to increased flood risks. These standards protect residents and property from flooding, and they preserve floodplains as a natural means of flood control.

Residential structures requirements

Residential structures in the SFHA's V zone must have the lowest floor above the "Base Flood Elevation" or have an open foundation (often referred to as pilings or stilts) to allow water flooding the area to flow under the structure without causing damage.

Nonresidential structures requirements

Nonresidential structures in the SFHA's V zone must have the lowest floor above the Base Flood Elevation, be water-tight below the Base Flood Elevation, or have an open foundation.

It has been estimated that approximately 15% of American homeowners have flood insurance policies. However, due to hurricane-related flooding in recent years, approximately 35–40% of those policyholders are Floridians. Even Texas, South Carolina, and Louisiana, who are also flood prone, do not come close to that number of policyholders.

ENVIRONMENTAL CONTROLS

**Areas of concern
Major legislation
Responsibilities and liabilities**

In recent years, federal and state legislatures have enacted laws to conserve and protect the environment against the hazards of growth and development, particularly in terms of air, water, and soil quality.

Regional, county, and local planners must integrate environmental laws into their respective land use plans and regulations. Private property owners are responsible for complying with these laws.

Areas of concern

Air. Air quality, both indoor and outdoor, has been a matter of concern since the 1960's. With today's construction methods creating airtight, energy-efficient structures, attention to sources of indoor air pollution is more important than ever. Off-gassing from synthetic materials and lack of ventilation can lead to such consequences as Sick Building Syndrome (SBS) and Building-Related Illness (BRI) as well as other health problems. Among the significant threats are:

▶ *asbestos*, a powdery mineral once commonly used as a fireproof insulating material around pipes, in floor tiles and linoleum, in siding and roofing, in wallboard, joint compound, and many other applications.

When airborne, it is a health hazard. Its use today is highly restricted, and removal can be expensive and dangerous. Inspection by a certified asbestos inspector is the best way to determine whether a building needs treatment.

▶ *carbon monoxide*, a colorless, odorless, poisonous gas that may result from faulty heating equipment. Home and commercial detection devices are available.

▶ *formaldehyde,* a chemical used in building materials and in other items such as fabrics and carpeting. As it ages, formaldehyde gives off a colorless, pungent gas.

Its use in urea-formaldehyde foam insulation (UFFI) was banned 1982 (ban later reduced to a warning) but the material is still present in many structures. *Other substances known in general as volatile organic compounds (VOCs) and* used in construction materials such as adhesives emit toxic fumes. Professional testing can identify levels and, in some cases, sources of formaldehyde gas and other VOCs.

- *lead,* a heavy metal once widely used in paints and plumbing materials. It has been banned in paint since 1978 and in new plumbing since 1988.

  It continues to be a health threat, particularly to children, as it occurs in airborne paint particles, paint chips, and soil and groundwater polluted by various external sources of emission. Inspection should be performed by licensed lead inspectors.

- *mold,* a fungus that grows in the presence of moisture and oxygen on virtually any kind of organic surface.

  It often destroys the material it grows on and emits toxic irritants into the air. Tightly sealed structures with inadequate ventilation are most susceptible. Roof leaks, improper venting of appliances, runoff from gutters and downspouts, and flood damage are common contributors. In recent years, mold- and mildew-related lawsuits and claims have become substantial.

- *radon*, a colorless, odorless, radioactive gas that occurs naturally in the soil throughout the United States.

  It enters buildings through foundation and floor cracks, wall seams, sump pits, and windows, among other ways. At accumulations above certain levels, it is suspected of contributing to cancer. Excessive radon can be removed by special ventilation systems. Professional and home inspections are available.

Structural damage. *Wood-destroying organisms (WDO)* are such an issue in Florida that WDO inspections are often required real estate transactions. Termites, certain beetles, and wood-decaying fungi fall under the category of wood-destroying organisms. Carpenter ants are not reportable as WDOs on the Florida report form.

Building inspections do not include WDOs. Instead, the property is inspected by a pest control company inspector who is licensed by the Florida Department of Agriculture and Consumer Services. The inspection must be completed in compliance with appropriate standards and must inspect for all forms of wood-destroying organisms.

If an inspection is performed for a real estate transaction, the report must be completed on a specific form required by Florida law, found online with instructions for its completion at https://www.fdacs.gov/content/download/3136/file/Instructions_for_13645.pdf .

The report is limited to the day and time of the inspection and does not include any anticipation of future WDO infestations. It includes the date of the inspection, the inspector's business name and business license number, the types and number of structures inspected, the inspection findings, any obstructions or inaccessible areas, evidence of past treatment, whether or not the structure was treated at the time of inspection and all related details, and the following statement:

> *"Neither the licensee nor the inspector has any financial interest in the structure(s) inspected or is associated in any way in the transaction with any party other than for inspection purposes."*

The report should also state that the inspector has no association with the structures or parties to the transaction except for inspection purposes. One copy of the report goes to the person requesting the inspection. A second copy is to be posted in an easily visible access point to the property. A third copy is to be maintained by the inspection company for at least 3 years.

Soil and water. Soil, groundwater, and drinking water supplies are vulnerable to pollution from leaking landfills; improper waste disposal; agricultural runoff; industrial dumping in waterways; highway and rail spills; industrial emissions; internal combustion emissions; and underground tanks leaking fuels and chemicals, to mention but a few sources. Some of the problems subject to controls are:

- dioxins, a family of compounds produced as a byproduct of manufacturing and incinerating materials that contain chlorine
- lead and *mercury*
- MTBE, Methyl Tertiary Butyl Ether, a gasoline additive
- PCB, Polychlorinated Biphenyl, a substance formerly widely used as an electrical insulation
- *Underground Storage Tanks* (USTs), regulated since 1984
- *Wetlands,* considered part of the natural water filtering system as well as special habitats, subject to restrictions on development and use.

Other ambient and natural conditions. Other regulated and controlled environmental conditions include:

- *Electromagnetic Fields* (EMFs) created by powerlines
- *noise* created by airports, air, rail and highway traffic
- *earthquake and flood hazards* that affect hazard insurance, lending practices, and construction requirements for buildings in designated flood and earthquake zones.

Environmental Concerns

	Indoors	Outdoors
Air	asbestos, BRI, carbon monoxide, formaldehyde, lead-based paint, mold, radon, SBS, VOCs	airborne lead, carbon dioxide, mercury, sulfur, dioxins
Soil		dioxins, lead, PCBs, waste, hazardous materials
Water	dioxins, lead plumbing, lead-paint, mercury, MTBE, PCBs	dioxins, lead, mercury, MTBE, PCBs, USTs, waste, hazardous materials
Ambience		EMFs, noise
Structure		flood, earthquake

BRI: Building-Related Illness SBS: Sick Building Syndrome VOC: Volatile Organic Compound MTBE: Methyl Tertiary Butyl Ether

PCB: Polychlorinated Biphenyl
UST: Underground Storage Tank
EMF: Electromagnetic Field
UFFI: Urea-Formaldehyde Foam Insulation

Major legislation

National Environmental Policy Act (1969). This act created the Environmental Protection Agency (EPA) and the Council for Environmental Quality, giving them a mandate to establish environmental standards for land use planning. The act also required environmental impact surveys on large development projects.

Clean Air Amendment (1970). This act authorized the EPA to establish air quality standards for industrial land uses as well as for automobile and airplane emissions.

Water Quality Improvement Act (1970), the Water Pollution Control Act amendment (1972), the Clean Water Act Amendment (1977). These acts addressed standards to control water pollution and industrial wastes from the standpoints of future prevention as well as remediation of existing pollution.

Resource Recovery Act (1970), the Resource Conservation and Recovery Act (1976), the Comprehensive Environmental Response, Compensation and Liability Act (Superfund) (1980), the Superfund Amendment and Reauthorization Act (1986). These acts addressed disposal of solid and toxic wastes and measures for managing waste. In addition, the Superfund act provided money for hazardous waste disposal and the authority to charge cleanup costs to responsible parties.

Lead-based paint ban (1978) and Residential Lead-based Paint Hazard Reduction Act (1992, 1996). These regulations banned lead in the manufacture of paint and established disclosure requirements and guidelines for testing and remediation.

CERCLA/Superfund. Under the Comprehensive Environmental Response, Compensation, and Liability Act of 1980 (CERCLA) and the Superfund Amendment of 1986, current landowners as well as previous owners of a property may be held liable for environmental violations, even if "innocent" of a violation. Sellers often carry the greatest exposure, and real estate licensees may be held liable for improper disclosure.

A real property owner can be held liable for the entire cost of remediating soil, groundwater, or indoor air contamination. A tenant can be held liable for cleanup costs as an "operator" if tenant operations are linked to contamination

Responsibilities & liabilities

Licensees are expected to be aware of environmental issues and to know where to look for professional help. They are not expected to have expert knowledge of environmental law nor of physical conditions in a property. Rather, they must treat potential environmental hazards in the same way that they treat other material facts about a property: disclosure.

In sum, for their own protection, licensees should be careful to:

> ▶ be aware of potential hazards
> ▶ disclose known material facts
> ▶ distribute the HUD booklet (below)
> ▶ know where to seek professional help.

Lead. The Lead-based Paint Act of 1992 requires a seller or seller's agent to disclose known lead problems in properties built before 1978. The licensee must give the buyer or lessee a copy of the EPA-HUD-US Consumer Product Safety Commission booklet, "Protect Your Family from Lead in your home."

Further, the 1996 lead-based paint regulation requires sellers or lessors of almost all residential properties built before 1978 to disclose known lead-based paint hazards and provide any relevant records available. The seller is not required to test for lead but must allow the buyer a ten-day period for lead inspection. Only a licensed lead professional is permitted to deal with testing, removal or encapsulation. It is the real estate practitioner's responsibility to ensure compliance.

Sale of a contaminated property. Selling a property with an environmental problem does not avoid liability for the seller, although seller and buyer may agree to share or transfer some liability. As mentioned above, sellers often carry the greatest exposure for environmental violations under CERCLA, and real estate licensees may be held liable for improper disclosure.

If there is a concern, a Phase I audit or Environmental Site Assessment (ESA) should be conducted before proceeding with the transaction. A Phase I audit identifies

> ▶ prior uses
> ▶ presence of hazardous materials

The Phase I ESA reviews environmental documents; conducts a title search for environmental liens and restrictions; and includes a visual inspection of the site and surrounding properties. There is no sampling or testing. Fannie Mae, Freddie Mac, and HUD require special Phase I ESAs on certain properties.

A Phase II audit (ESA) is conducted if a site is considered contaminated. This is a more detailed investigation using chemical analysis to uncover hazardous substances and/or petroleum hydrocarbons in samples of soil, groundwater or building materials.

A Phase III audit (ESA) involves remediation. Intensive testing, sampling, monitoring, and modeling are applied to design plans for remediation, cleanup, and follow-up monitoring. Remediation may use a variety of techniques and technologies, such as excavation and removal, dredging, chemical treatment, pumping, and solidification. Major remediation efforts usually require extensive consultation with the surrounding community. Federal funding may be available.

Landmarks in Environmental Control Legislation

Legislation	Date	Regulated
Solid Waste Disposal Act (later part of RCRA)	1965 (1976, 1999, 2002)	landfills
Air Quality Act, Clean Air Act	1967 (1970)	air quality standards
National Environmental Policy Act (NEPA)	1969 (1970)	created EPA
Flood Control Act	amended 1969	building in flood zones; flood insurance
Resource Recovery Act	1970	solid waste disposal
Water Quality Improvement Act	1970	dumping in navigable waters; wetlands
Water Pollution Control Act amendment	1972	dumping in navigable waters; wetlands
Marine Protection Research and Sanctuaries Act	1972	offshore waste dumping
Noise control legislation	1972	airport- and transportation-related noise
Coastal Zone Management Act	1972	beaches, marine habitats
Clean Water Act	1972 (1977)	dumping in navigable waters; wetlands
Safe Drinking Water Act	1974	public water supply, lead
Resource Conservation and Recovery Act (RCRA)	1976	hazardous waste, solid waste
Toxic Substances Control Act	1976	industrial chemicals
Lead-based paint ban (US Consumer Product Safety Commission rule)	1978	lead-based paint in residences
PCB ban (EPA rule)	1979	polychlorinated biphenyls
RCRA amendment	1984	underground storage tanks
Comprehensive Environmental Response, Compensation and Liability Act (CERCLA)	1980	hazardous waste disposal
UFFI ban	1982	formaldehyde in insulation materials
Superfund Amendment and Reauthorization Act	1986	hazardous waste cleanup costs
Asbestos ban (EPA rule)	1989	asbestos in building materials
Residential Lead-based Paint Hazard Reduction Act (EPA and HUD rule)	1992 (1996)	lead-based paint disclosure and treatment
Flood Insurance Reform Act	1994	flood insurance in flood zones
Brownfields legislation	2002	industrial site cleanup

19 Planning, Zoning, and Environmental Hazards Snapshot Review

PLANNING AND ZONING

Goals of land use control
- preserve property values; promote highest and best use; safeguard public health, safety and welfare; control growth; incorporate community consensus
- process: develop plan; create administration; authorize controls

The master plan
- long term growth and usage strategies; often required by state law
- local plans fuse municipal goals and needs with state and regional laws

Planning objectives
- control growth rates: how much growth will occur and at what rate
- control growth patterns: type of growth desired, where it should be located
- accommodate demand for services and infrastructure

Plan development
- research trends and conditions; blend local and state objectives into master plan

Planning management
- commission makes rules, approves permits, codes, and development plans

FLORIDA'S GROWTH POLICY & COMPREHENSIVE PLAN

Chap. 163 growth policy
- promotes strong urban centers wherein public services are in place prior to capital improvements
- for local governments to establish planning programs for future development, encourage appropriate land, water, and resource use, overcome problems caused by land use and development; protects private property rights

Department of Economic Opportunity (DEO)
- DEO relegates power to local governments to make development decisions; diminishes state oversight; supervises funds used to incentivize businesses to come to Florida

Required elements
- comprehensive plans to include future land use, traffic circulation, conservation of natural resources, recreation, housing, coastal zone protection, intergovernmental coordination, utilities, and concurrency

PUBLIC LAND USE CONTROL
- state laws; local regulations, zones, codes; public ownership; private restrictions

Zoning
- "police power" granted by state-level enabling acts; zoning ordinance: creates zones, usage restrictions, regulations, requirements
- types of zones: residential, commercial, industrial, agricultural, public, PUD

Zoning administration
- Zoning Board of Adjustment oversees rule administration and appeals
- nonconforming use: legal if use prior to zone creation; variance: exception based on hardship; special exception: based on public interest; amendment: change of zones; rezoning

Subdivision regulation
- plat of subdivision and relevant requirements must be met and approved; must meet FHA requirements for insured financing

Building codes
- comprehensive onsite and offsite construction and materials standards; must be met to receive certificate of occupancy

- Florida Building Code governs design, construction, erection, alteration, modification, repair, and demolition of public and private structures; includes wind speed risk categories; defines coastal high wind load areas
- building permits: any work regulated by the Florida Building Code must obtain required permit(s) with requirements based on work to be done; must submit work plans to prove compliance with wind load requirements; new construction requires Florida energy code compliance certificate
- building inspections: code compliance inspections required as project progresses; work to stop until inspection completed; final inspection required for certificate of occupancy
- R-value: measurement of insulation's effectiveness and resistance to heat flow; minimum R-value is specified by building and energy codes

FLOOD ZONES

National Flood Insurance Program (NFIP)

- created to provide flood insurance for structures located in flood hazard areas
- FEMA requires communities to adopt and enforce regulations to reduce flood risks to qualify for NFIP
- SFHAs identified by FEMA and shown on FIRM as low-, moderate-, or high-risk; high-risk is a special flood hazard area with 1% statistical possibility of flooding each year
- special permit required for development within SFHAs with requirements based on A or V zone; restrictions include no obstruction of flood waters' natural flow

Residential structures requirements

- lowest floor above base flood elevation or open foundation to allow water to flow under the structure

Nonresidential structures requirements

- lowest floor above base flood elecation or water tight below base flood elevation or open foundation

Proportion of NFIP purchasers in Florida

- 35-40% of all flood policy holders are in Florida

ENVIRONMENTAL CONTROLS

Areas of concern

- air, soil, water quality; ambient health hazards; natural hazards
- **wood-destroying organisms** – real estate transactions require inspections for WDOs; must use state mandated form for inspection report; inspectors licensed by FL Department of Agriculture and Consumer Services; report based on the day and time of inspection with no predictions of future WDO infestations; report requires specified information and statements; copies go to inspection requestor, property itself, and inspection company

Major legislation

- limits damage to environment; standards for air, land, water, materials use

Responsibilities & liabilities

- disclosure and information for practitioners; remediation for owners; lead disclosure; CERCLA/Superfund exposure; Phase I, II, III Environmental Site Assessments to detect and mitigate contamination

SECTION NINETEEN: Planning, Zoning, and Environmental Hazards

Section Quiz

1. A central goal of public land use planning is to

    a. balance individual property rights with the community's welfare.
    b. develop an accord between property owners and tenants.
    c. impede development by for-profit developers and construction contractors.
    d. subordinate private interests to the public good.

2. The best definition of a master plan is

    a. an annual review of all land use permits and zones.
    b. a comprehensive analysis of existing land use patterns in a market.
    c. a state or regional land use law requiring compliance on a county-by-county basis.
    d. a fusion of land use laws and local land use objectives and strategies.

3. The principal mechanism for implementing a master plan is

    a. zoning.
    b. referendum.
    c. public elections.
    d. property management.

4. Zoning, building codes, and environmental restrictions are forms of local land use control known as

    a. force majeure.
    b. pre-emption.
    c. police power.
    d. concurrency.

5. A municipality may use its power of eminent domain to require a property owner to

    a. pay higher property taxes.
    b. cede an easement without receiving any compensation.
    c. clean up the property.
    d. sell the property to the municipality.

6. In most jurisdictions, the master plan is managed by

    a. the mayor or county superintendent.
    b. the Board of Equalization.
    c. the planning commission.
    d. the zoning board of adjustment.

7. Counties and municipalities have the legal right to control land use due to

    a. the doctrine of appropriation.
    b. delegation of authority by state-level enabling acts.
    c. custom and tradition.
    d. consensus of the local community through referendum.

8. To be valid, a local zoning ordinance must

    a. reasonably promote community health, safety and welfare.
    b. comply with federal zoning laws.
    c. apply only to unique properties.
    d. be published periodically in the local newspaper.

9. What is the fundamental purpose of a building permit?

    a. To restrict the number of new development projects
    b. To establish the basis for an inspection
    c. To promote certificates of occupancy
    d. To ensure that improvements comply with codes

10. A primary objective of residential zoning is to

    a. control the value ranges of homes in a neighborhood.
    b. regulate density.
    c. ensure that only a limited amount of commercial and industrial activity is permitted in a particular residential zone.
    d. maximize intensity of usage.

11. A non-profit organization wants to erect a much-needed daycare center in a residential zone. Given other favorable circumstances, the local authorities grant permission by allowing

    a. a special exception.
    b. an illegal nonconforming use.
    c. a variance.
    d. a license.

12. A property that conformed with zoning ordinances when it was developed but does not conform to new ordinances is said to be

    a. a special exception.
    b. a variance.
    c. a legal nonconforming use.
    d. an anomaly.

13. One situation in which a zoning board might permit a variance is when

    a. it would cause the property owner unreasonable hardship to bring the property into compliance with zoning ordinances.
    b. the property owner is the one who brings the variance to the attention of the zoning board.
    c. the variance was caused by a contractor rather than by the property owner.
    d. the property is in conflict with no more than one zoning ordinance.

14. The approval process for development of multiple properties in an area includes submission of

    a. a covenant of restriction.
    b. a plat of subdivision.
    c. a court order.
    d. a developer's pro forma.

15. A county or municipal authority usually grants a certificate of occupancy for new construction only after

    a. all contractors have been paid for services.
    b. all work has been completed for at least thirty days.
    c. the construction complies with building codes.
    d. the tax assessor has valued the improvement.

16. Which of the following promotes strong urban centers in local and state communities?

    a. Florida's Growth Policy Act
    b. Florida's Community Planning Act
    c. Florida's Department of Community Affairs
    d. Florida Building Commission

17. Which of a comprehensive plan's elements must include standards for control of population densities?

    a. Traffic circulation
    b. Conservation of natural resources
    c. Intergovernmental coordination
    d. Future land use

18. The Florida Building Code

    a. is developed and updated at the local government level.
    b. includes risk categories based on wind speed.
    c. is updated every 5 years.
    d. was developed after Hurricane Katrina showed the need for more robust codes throughout the state.

19. R-value

    a. refers to the risk factor of wind speed storms in coastal areas.
    b. refers to insulation's resistance to heat flow.
    c. refers to requirements for building inspections.
    d. refers to the rate of population growth within special flood hazard areas.

20. In real estate transactions, inspections for wood-destroying organisms must be performed by

    a. a licensed building inspector.
    b. a licensed or certified building appraiser.
    c. a licensed pest control company inspector.
    d. any of the above.

Real Estate Mathematics

Basic Formulas and Functions
Real Estate Applications

Answer Key is on page <ins>506</ins>

BASIC FORMULAS AND FUNCTIONS

Adding and multiplying fractions
Converting decimals and percentages
Converting fractions and percentages
Multiplying percentages
Calculating area

Adding and multiplying fractions

Adding

1. Formulas:

   Same denominator:

   $$\frac{a}{c} + \frac{b}{c} = \frac{a+b}{c}$$

   Different denominator:

   $$\frac{a}{c} + \frac{b}{d} = \frac{ad+bc}{cd}$$

2. Examples:

   $$\frac{2}{5} + \frac{6}{5} = \frac{8}{5}$$

   $$\frac{3}{4} + \frac{4}{7} = \frac{(3 \times 7) + (4 \times 4)}{(4 \times 7)} = \frac{37}{28}$$

   Problem 1:

   $$\frac{3}{19} + \frac{2}{7} = ?$$

Multiplying

1. Formula:
$$\frac{a}{c} \times \frac{b}{d} = \frac{ab}{cd}$$

2. Example:
$$\frac{4}{9} \times \frac{2}{3} = \frac{8}{27}$$

Problem 2:
$$\frac{4}{14} \times \frac{3}{8} = ?$$

Converting decimals and percentages

Converting a decimal to a percent

1. Formula: (decimal number) x 100 = percent number

2. Examples:
.473 x 100   = 47.3%
3.456 x 100   = 345.6%
.0042 x 100   = .42%

Problem 3: Convert the following decimals to percentages:

2.65 =   %
0.294 =   %
0.005 =   %

Converting a percent to a decimal

1. Formula:
$$\frac{percent\ number}{100} = decimal\ number$$

2. Examples:
$$\frac{47.3\%}{100} = .473$$

$$\frac{345.6\%}{100} = 3.456$$

Problem 4: Convert the following percentages to decimals:

72.1% =
90.2% =
5.79% =

Converting fractions and percentages

Converting a fraction to a percent

1. Formulas:

    (1) $\dfrac{a}{b}$ = a divided by b = decimal number

    (2)   decimal number x 100 = percent number

2. Examples: $\dfrac{4}{5}$ = 4 divided by 5 = 0.8 = 80%

    $\dfrac{9}{3}$ = 9 divided by 3 = 3.0 = 300%

    Problem 5:   Convert the following fractions to percentages:

    $\dfrac{8}{9}$ =   %

    $\dfrac{3}{6}$ =   %

    $\dfrac{14}{42}$ =   %

Converting a percent to a fraction and reducing it

1. Formula: $X\% = \dfrac{X}{100}$

    $\dfrac{X \div a}{100 \div a}$ = reduced fraction

    where "a" is the largest number that divides *evenly* into numerator and denominator. If unknown, try 2, 3, 5, or 7.

2. Example $45\% = \dfrac{45}{100} = \dfrac{45 \div 5}{100 \div 5} = \dfrac{9}{20}$

    Problem 6:   Convert and reduce the following percentages:

    40%   =

    16%   =

Multiplying Percentages

1. Formulas:

    (1)   convert percent to decimal by dividing by 100

    (2)   whole amount x decimal = partial amount

2. Example: 33% of 400

    (1)   33% divided by 100 = .33

    (2)   400 x .33 = 132

    Problem **7:**   What is 75% of 280?

Calculating area

To find the area of an irregular shape, try dividing it into triangles, rectangles, squares or trapezoids and calculate the areas of those parts; the area of the whole shape is then the sum of the areas of all of its subparts.

Base and height

1. Formulas for area of three- and four-sided shapes use a product of base and height. In the formulas, *a* represents area, *b* represents base, *h* represents height, *SF* represents square feet.

2. The base of a triangle, square, or rectangle may be any side; a trapezoid has two bases, its two parallel sides.

3. The height of a triangle is the length of a perpendicular line from the base to the triangle's opposite point. Height in a square, rectangle or trapezoid is the length of a line which is perpendicular to the base line(s).

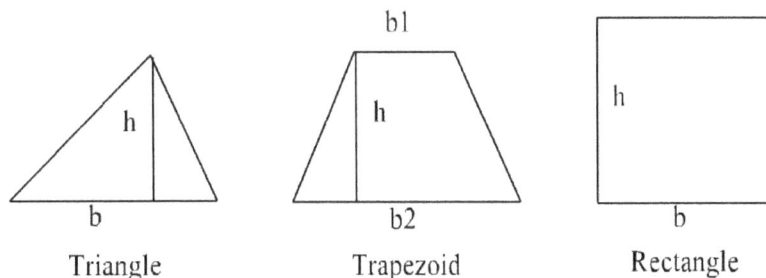

Triangle   Trapezoid   Rectangle

Area of a square or rectangle

1. Formula: area (a) = base (b) x height (h) $a = bxh$

2. Example: A square measures 3 feet on each side.

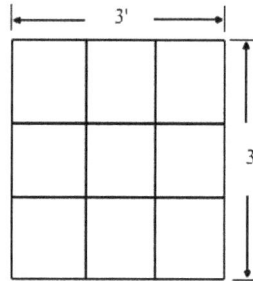

Its area is: 3 x 3 = 9 SF

Area of a triangle

1. Formula: $a = \dfrac{b \; x \; h}{2}$

2. Example: A triangle has a 20' base and a 4' height.

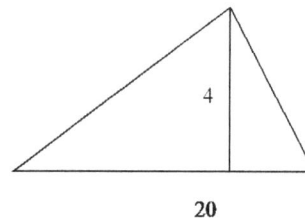

Its area is: $a = \dfrac{20 \; x \; 4}{2} = 40 \; SF$

Area of a trapezoid

1. Formula: $a = \dfrac{a \; (b1 + b2)}{2}$

2. Example: A trapezoid's two bases are 10' and 15', and its height is 7'.

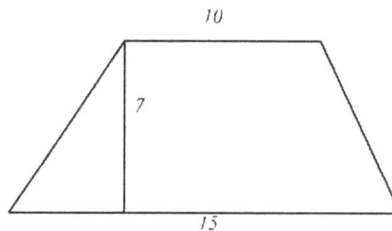

Its area is: $a = \dfrac{7 \; (10 + 15)}{2} = 87.5 \; SF$

Problem 8:   Calculate the areas of the following shapes:

a rectangle with height of 4' and base of 36'

   a =

a square with a side of 16'

   a =

a trapezoid with height of 5' and bases of 6' and 8'

   a =

REAL ESTATE APPLICATIONS

Legal descriptions
Listing agreements
Brokerage business
Sales contracts
Appraisal
Finance
Investments
Taxation
Closings

Legal descriptions

Linear measures

(cm = centimeter; m = meter; km = kilometer)

1 inch	=	1/12 foot	=	1/36 yard
1 foot	=	12 inches	=	1/3 yard
1 yard	=	36 inches	=	3 feet
1 rod	=	16.5 feet	=	1/320 mile
1 mile	=	5280 feet	=	1760 yards = 320 rods

1 centimeter	=	1/100th m		
1 meter	=	100 cm	=	1/1000th km
1 kilometer	=	1,000 m		

Area measures

1 square inch	=	1/144th square foot
1 square foot	=	1/9th square yard
1 square yard	=	9 square feet

1 acre	=	1/640 sq. mi	=	43,560 SF	=	208.71 ft x 208.71 ft
1 square mile	=	640 acres	=	1 section	=	1/36 township
1 section	=	mile x 1 mile	=	640 acres	=	1/36 township
1 township	=	6 mi x 6 mi	=	36 sq. mi.	=	36 sections

Metric conversions

(cm = centimeter; m = meter; km = kilometer)

1 inch	=	2.54 cm					
1 foot	=	30.48 cm	=	.3048 m			
1 yard	=	91.44 cm	=	.9144 m			
1 mile	=	1609.3 m	=	1.60 km			
1 centimeter	=	.3937 inch					
1 meter	=	39.37 inches	=	3.28 feet	=	1.094 yards	
1 kilometer	=	3,281.5 feet	=	.621 mile			

Fractions of sections, acres, and linear dimensions

Fraction	# Acres	Feet X Feet
1 section	640 acres	5280 X 5280
1/2 section	320 acres	5280 X 2640
1/4 section	160 acres	2640 X 2640
1/8 section	80 acres	2640 X 1320
1/16 section	40 acres	1320 X 1320
1/32 section	20 acres	660 X 1320
1/64 section	10 acres	660 X 660

Calculating area from the legal description

   1.   Formula:

      (1)   First multiply all the denominators of the fractions in the legal description together

      (2)   Then divide 640 by the resulting product.

   2.   Examples:

      N 1/2 of the SW 1/4 of Section 6:

$$\frac{640}{(2 \times 4)} = \frac{640}{8} = 80 \; acres$$

      W 1/2 of the NW 1/4 of the NE 1/4 of Section 8

$$\frac{640}{(2 \times 4 \times 4)} = \frac{640}{32} = 20 \; acres$$

      Problem 9:   Calculate the acreage of the following:

          SW 1/4 of the N 1/2 of the E 1/2 of Section 14

          SE 1/4 of the NW 1/4 of the SE 1/4 of Section 20

Listing agreements

Co-brokerage commission

1. Formulas: sale price x commission rate = total commission

    total commission x split rate = co-brokerage commission

2. Example: A house sells for $600,000. The commission is 6%, and the co-brokerage split is 50-50.

    $600,000 x 6% = $36,000 total commission x 50% = $18,000 co-broker's commission

Agent's commission

1. Formula: broker's commission x agent's split rate = agent's commission

2. Example: Assume an $18,000 broker's commission and a 60% - 40% agent-broker split rate.

    $18,000 x .6 = $10,800 agent's commission ($7,200 to broker)

Problem 10:   A property is co-brokered by listing broker Schroeder and selling broker Hobson for $425,000. The co-brokerage split is 50-50. Schroeder's agent, Joachim, is on a 65% split schedule. Hobson's selling agent, Wallace, splits 50-50 with her broker. If the total commission rate is 7%, what are the participants' commissions?

Broker Schroeder: $
Broker Hobson: $
Schroeder's agent, Joachim: $
Hobson's agent, Wallace: $

Brokerage business

Goodwill calculation

1. Formula: Goodwill = Price - Value of assets

2. Example: A seller wants $1 million for a business. Assets in the business, including inventory, furniture, equipment, leasehold improvements, and working capital, have a total value of $750,000. The goodwill is:

$1,000,000 - 750,000 = $250,000 goodwill

Problem 11: A prospective purchaser complained to a seller that the selling price had far too much goodwill: $200,000. After all, the assets only totaled $352,000. What was the price?

Sales contracts

"Percentage of listing price" calculation

1. Formula: Percentage of listing price = offer divided by listing price

2. Example: A property listed for $400,000 receives an offer for $360,000. The percentage of listing price is:

$360,000 divided by 400,000 = 90%

Problem 12: A seller receives an offer of $674,000 on a property listed at $749,000. How much is the offer as a percent of the listing price?

Earnest money deposit calculation

1. Formula: Deposit = Listing price x required percentage

2. Example: A seller requires a 2% deposit on a property listed for $320,000. The required deposit is:

$320,000 x 2% = $6,400

Problem 13: A seller requires a 1.5% deposit on all offers. A buyer wants to offer $312,000 for the property. What must the deposit be?

Rent escalations

1. Formula: New rent = current rent x (100% + escalation rate)

2. Example: An apartment's rent is scheduled to increase by 6%. If the current rent is $1800, the new rent is:

$1800 x (100% + 6%) = $1,800 x 106% = $1,908

Problem 14:   A tenant's rent is currently $650 per month. This rent is scheduled to increase 5% per year. What will the tenant's rent be at the beginning of the **third** year from now?

FIRPTA withholding

1. Formula: FIRPTA withholding = gross proceeds from sale x 15%

2. Example: Gross proceeds on a FIRPTA-regulated property sale are $340,000. The required withholding amount is:

$340,000 x 15% = $51,000

Appraisal

Adjusting comparables

1. Rules:
   a. NEVER adjust the subject!

   b. If the comparable is better than the subject, subtract value from the comparable

   c. If the comparable is **worse** than the subject, **add** value to the comparable

2. Examples:
   a. A comparable has a pool and the subject does not. The appraiser estimates the value contribution to be $25,000. Adjust the comparable by entering -25,000 in the CMA.

   b. A comparable has 3 bedrooms and the subject as 4. The appraiser estimates the value contribution of a bedroom to be $15,000. Adjust the comparable by entering +15,000 in the CMA.

Problem **15:** Identify the proper adjustments for the following:

   (a) The subject has a two-car garage, while the comparable does not. Value of garage is $33,000.

   Adjustment:

   (b) A comparable has a fireplace, and the subject does not. Value of fireplace is $8,000.

   Adjustment:

   (c) The subject has 1,500 square feet. The comparable has 1,600 square feet. The value of extra square feet is $200/SF.

   Adjustment:

Income capitalization

Gross rent multiplier (GRM)

   1. Formula: gross rent x multiplier = value

   2. Example: $20,000 x 9 = $1,800,000

Net income capitalization

   1. Formula: net income (NOI) ÷ capitalization rate = value

$$\frac{net\ income\ (\ NOI\ )}{capitalization\ \ rate} = value$$

   2. Example: $50,000 ÷ 10\% = 50,000 ÷ .10 = $500,000

   Problem 16: A property grosses $450,000, nets 350,000, and has a capitalization rate of 9%. Prevailing GRMs are 8.

   (a) What is the property value using the GRM?

   (b) What is the property value using net income capitalization?

Finance

Interest only loans

1. Formulas: interest payment (I) = principal (P) x interest rate (R)

    annual interest payment $\div$ 12 = monthly interest payment

    monthly interest payment x 12 = annual interest payment

    $$I = P \times R$$
    $$R = \frac{I}{P}$$
    $$P = \frac{I}{R}$$

2. Examples: A $300,000 interest-only loan @ 10% has annual payments of $30,000 and monthly payments of $2,500.

    Annual interest = $300,000 x 10% = $30,000
    Monthly interest = $30,000 $\div$ 12 = $2,500

    The loan amount of an interest-only loan that has an annual interest rate of 8% and a monthly interest payment of $700 is $105,000.

    Annual interest = $700 x 12 = $8,400
    Loan amount = $8,400 $\div$ .08 = $105,000

    Problem 17:

    (a) A $250,000 loan carries a 7% rate. What is the monthly interest payment?

    (b) A $300,000 loan has monthly payments of $2,000. What is its annual interest rate?

    (c) A 12% loan has annual payments of $15,000. What is the loan amount?

Loan-to-value (LTV) ratio

1. Formulas: loan amount = market value x LTV

    LTV = loan amount ÷ market value

2. Example: A 75% LTV will allow a lender to make a loan of
    $375,000 on a $500,000 property.

    loan amount = $500,000 x 75% = $375,000

    LTV = $375,000 ÷ $500,000 = 75%

Problem 18:

(a) A lender requires $90,000 down on a $400,000
property. Calculate the lender's required LTV.

(b) A property is valued at $600,000. The lender will
allow a maximum LTV of 75%. How much can the
buyer borrow on the property?

Income underwriting ratio calculation

1. Formulas: Conventional:

    monthly PITI = (25-28%) x monthly gross income

    FHA:

    monthly PITI = 31% x monthly gross income

2. Examples: A borrower has monthly gross income of $2,000.
    Conventional lenders are using a ratio of 28%. The
    borrower can afford the following monthly PITI
    payments:

    Conventional:

    PITI = 28% x $2,000 = $560

    FHA:

    PITI = 31% x $2,000 = $620

Problem 19: A borrower earns $4,000/month and pays $600/month in debt repayments. A conventional lender requires a 26% income ratio, and an FHA lender requires 31%. What monthly PITI can this person afford based on the income ratio?

Conventional: $

FHA: $

Debt underwriting ratio calculation

1. Formulas: Conventional:

Expense = (36% x gross income) – monthly debt

FHA:

Expense = (43% x gross income) - monthly debt

2. Example: An individual has a monthly gross income of $6,000, and has monthly debt payments of $900. The borrower can afford the following monthly housing expense:

Conventional:

Expense = (36% x $6,000) - 900 = $1,260

FHA:

Expense = (43% x $6,000) – 900 = $1,680

Problem 20: A borrower earns $4,000/month and makes monthly debt payments of $600. What monthly payment for housing can this person afford based on the debt ratio?

Conventional: $

FHA: $

Points

1. Formula: 1 point = 1% (.01) of loan amount

2. Example: A lender charges 3 points (3%) on a $350,000 loan. The points charges are:

                    3 points = 3%
                    .03 x $350,000 = $10,500

Problem 21:   A lender is charging 2.75 points on a $240,000 loan. How much must the borrower pay for points?

Investments

Appreciation

1. Formulas: total appreciation = current value – original price

                    Error! Bookmark not defined.total appreciation rate = total appreciation / original price

                    one-year appreciation rate = one-year appreciation / prior-year value

2. Example: A house bought for $500,000 appreciates $50,000 each Year for 3 years.

                    total appreciation = $650,000 - 500,000 = $150,000

                    total appreciation rate = $150,000 ÷ $500,000 = 30%

                    first- year rate = $50,000 ÷ $500,000 = 10%

Problem 22:   A property is purchased for $360,000. A year later it is Sold for $410,000. What is the amount of appreciation, and what is the appreciation rate?

Equity

1. Formula: equity = current value – current loan amount

2. Example: A buyer bought a property for $600,000 with a loan of $450,000. The house has appreciated $60,000 and the buyer has reduced the original loan by $30,000. The buyer's current equity is:

    Equity = ($600,000 + 60,000) - ($450,000 - 30,000) = $240,000

> **Problem 23:** A property is purchased for $450,000 with a $75,000 downpayment. Five years later the property is worth $540,000, and the loan balance has dropped $12,500. What is the owner's new equity?

Pre-tax cash flow

1. Formula
    and example:

potential rental income	$50,000
- vacancy and collection loss	3,000
= effective rental income	47,000
+ other income	2,000
= gross operating income (GOI)	49,000
- operating expenses	20,000
- reserves	3,000
= net operating income (NOI)	26,000
- debt service	15,000
= pre-tax cash flow	11,000

> **Problem 24:** An apartment building has a potential income of $300,000 and vacancy of $12,000. Its bills total $128,000, and $12,000 has been reserved for repairs. Payments on the loan total $88,000. What is the property's pre-tax cash flow?

Tax liability

1. Formula
    and example:

net operating income (NOI)	26,000
+ reserves	3,000
- interest expense	15,000
- cost recovery expense	5,000
= taxable income	9,000
x tax rate (28%)	
= tax liability	2,520

> **Problem 25:** The property from the previous problem has annual cost recovery of $28,000. Out of the annual debt service, $8,000 is non-interest principal payback. The property owner's tax rate is 28%. What is the property's annual tax?

Annual depreciation (cost recovery) expense

1. Calculation:
    a. identify improvements-to-land ratio

    b. identify value of improvements: ratio x property price

    c. divide value of improvements by total depreciation term

2. Example:
    A property was bought for $400,000. 75% of the value is allocated to the improvement. The property falls in the 39-year depreciation category.

    (1) improvements-to-land ratio = 3:1, or 75%

    (2) improvement value = $400,000 x 75% = $300,000

    (3) annual depreciation = $300,000 ÷ 39 = $7,692

> Problem 26: A property is purchased for $400,000. Improvements account for 80% of the value. Given a 39-year depreciation term, what is the annual depreciation expense?

Capital gain

1. Formula
   and example: (residential property)

	Selling price of property	$300,000
-	Selling costs	24,000
=	Amount realized (ending basis)	$276,000
	Beginning basis (price) of property	$250,000
+	Capital improvements	10,000
-	Total depreciation expense	0
=	Adjusted basis of property	260,000
	Amount realized (ending basis)	$276,000
-	Adjusted basis of property	260,000
=	Capital gain	$ 16,000

Problem 27: A principal residence is bought for $360,000. A new tile roof is added, costing $15,000. Five years later the home sells for $440,000, and the closing costs $35,000. What is the homeowner's capital gain?

Return, rate of return, and investment amount

1. Formulas:

$$\frac{net\ operating\ income}{price} = return\ on\ investment\ (ROI)$$

$$\frac{cash\ flow}{cash\ invested} = cash\text{-}on\text{-}cash\ return\ (C\ on\ C)$$

$$\frac{cash\ flow}{equity} = return\ on\ equity\ (ROE)$$

2. Example: A property is bought for $200,000 with a $50,000 down payment and a $150,000 interest-only loan. The property has a net income of $20,000 and a cash flow of $8,000. In addition, the property has appreciated $30,000.

ROI	=	$20,000 ÷ $200,000 = 10%
C on C	=	$8,000 ÷ $50,000 = 16%
ROE	=	$8,000 ÷ $80,000 = 10%

Problem 28: A multi-unit rental property was bought four years ago for $1,200,000 with a $200,000 down payment. The property now rents for $8,500 per month. Expenses and debt service are $1,000/month and $6,500/month respectively. An appraiser estimates the property's current value at $1,450,000. The investor pays off her principal balance at a rate of $5,000 per year. Compute the following investment returns for the investor:

ROI   =
C on C =
ROE   =

Taxation

Tax rate calculation

1. Formula: $$\text{tax rate (millage rate)} = \frac{\text{tax requirement}}{\text{tax base}}$$

2. Example: A municipality has a revenue requirement of $10,000,000 after accounting for its revenues from sale of utilities. This requirement has to be covered by property tax. The real estate tax base, after homestead exemptions, is $300,000,000. The tax rate will be:

$$\frac{10,000,000}{300,000,000} = .0333 \quad 33.33 \text{ mills}$$

Problem 29: Barrington has an annual budget of $25,000,000 to be paid by property taxes. Assessed valuations are $300,000,000, and exemptions total $25,000,000. What must the tax rate be to finance the budget?

Homestead exemption calculation

1. Formula and example

	assessed value	$360,000
-	homestead exemption	50,000
	taxable value	$310,000

Taxing the property

1. Formulas: taxable value of property x tax rate (mill rate) for each taxing authority in jurisdiction

   total tax = sum of all taxes by taxing authority

2. Example: The taxable value of a property after exemptions is 400,000 and tax rates are as shown. The property's tax bill will be:

School tax:	$400,000 x 10 mills	= $4,000
City tax:	$400,000 x 4 mills	= 1600
County tax:	$400,000 x 3 mills	= 1200
Total tax:		$6,800

Problem 30: A homeowner's assessed valuation is $225,000. The homestead exemption is $25,000. Tax rates for the property are 8 mills for schools; 3 mills for the city; 2.5 mills for the county; and .5 mills for the local community college. What is the homeowner's tax bill?

Special assessments calculation

1. Formula: a. Identify total costs to be assessed

   b. Calculate prorated share for each property impacted

   c. Multiply cost x prorated share

2. Example: A canal will be dredged at a cost of $200,000. The improvement affects 30 properties with a total canal frontage of 4,000 feet. One property has 200' of frontage. Its assessment bill will be:

   (1) 200' ÷ 4,000' = 5% share

   (2) $200,000 x 5% = $10,000 assessment

Problem 31: A street beautification project is to cost $25,000. The project affects 20 properties having a total of 2,000 front feet. One owner's lot has 75 front feet. What will this owner's special assessment be?

Closings

Prorations

1. Formulas
    and rules:

Accounting for common items paid (or received) in advance vs arrears

	arrears	advance	debit	credit
real estate taxes	x		seller	buyer
rents received by seller		x	seller	buyer
utilities	x		seller	buyer

Whose share is charged to whom?

- if buyer pays taxes in arrears: charge seller, credit buyer for seller's portion

- if seller received rents in advance: charge seller, credit buyer for buyer's portion

- if seller pays utilities in advance: credit seller, charge buyer for seller's portion

Calculating the proration: 360-day method and 365-day method

1. **Calculate the daily proration amount**

    a. 360-day method: divide the annual amount by 360 or monthly amount by 30

    b. 365-day method: divide the annual proration amount by 365, or monthly amount by # days in that month

2. **Calculate # of seller's days**

    a. 360-day method: use 30 days for each month; actual number of seller days within the month, counting (or not counting) the day of closing

    b. 365-day method: use actual number of days for each month and partial month

3. **Calculate the seller's share**

    Multiply the daily amount times the number of seller's days – both methods

4. **Calculate buyer's share (both methods)**

    Subtract seller's share (from #3) from total share

2. Example: A rental property closes on January 25 and the closing day is the seller's. The 365-day method will be used for the prorations. Monthly rent already received by seller is $2,400. Annual real estate taxes to be paid in arrears by buyer are $4,000. Round to the nearest cent.

1. **Rent proration**: (monthly; 365-day method)

    Daily amount: $2,400 monthly rent ÷ 31 days in January = $77.42
    # Seller's days: 25
    Seller's share: $77.42 x 25 = $1,935.50
    Buyer's share: $2,400 – 1,935.50 = $464.50

    Credit buyer and debit seller for buyer's share of $464.50

2. **Tax proration**: (annual; 365-day method)

    Daily amount: $4,000 ÷ 365 = $10.96
    # Seller's days: 25
    Seller's share: $10.96 x 25 = $274
    Buyer's share: $4,000 – 274 = $3,726

    Credit buyer and debit seller for seller's share of $274

Problem 32:   A rental property closes on March 15th. Proratable income and expenses are: rental income of $1,800/month, received in advance by seller, March 1; annual taxes of $4,800/year, to be paid in arrears by buyer, January 1 of the year after sale. The day of closing is the seller's. February has 28 days. Prorate the items using the 365-day method, and assign debits and credits.

rent:	seller's share	$
	buyer's share	$
	debit seller/credit buyer	$
	debit buyer/credit seller	$
taxes:	seller's share	$
	buyer's share	$
	debit seller/credit buyer	$
	debit buyer/credit seller	$

Real Estate Mathematics: Answer Key

Problem 1: $\dfrac{3}{19} + \dfrac{2}{7} = \dfrac{21+38}{133} = \dfrac{59}{133}$

Problem 2: $\dfrac{4}{14} \times \dfrac{3}{8} = \dfrac{12}{112}$

Problem 3: 2.65 = 265%
0.294 = 29.4%
0.005 = .5%

Problem 4: 72.1% = .721
90.2% = .902
5.79% = .0579

Problem 5: 8/9 = 88.8%
3/6 = 50%
14/42 = 33.3%

Problem 6: 40% = 40/100 = 2/5
16% = 16/100 = 4/25

Problem 7: 210

Problem 8: 144 SF
256 SF
35 SF

Problem 9: 40 acres
10 acres

Problem 10: Schroeder: $5,206.25
Hobson: $7,437.50
Joachim $9,668.75
Wallace: $7,437.50

Problem 11: $552,000

Problem 12: 90%

Problem 13: $4,680

Problem 14: $716.63 keep or change?

Problem 15: (a) +33,000 to comparable
     - 8,000 to comparable
     - 20,000 to comparable

Problem 16: (a) $3,600,000
(b) $3,888,888

Problem 17: (a) $1,458
     8%
     $125,000

Problem 18: (a) 77.5%
(b) $450,000

Problem 19: Conventional: $1,040/month
FHA & VA: $1,240/month

Problem 20: Conventional: $840
FHA: $1,120

Problem 21: $6,600

Problem 22: $50,000; 13.89%

Problem 23: **$177,500**

Problem 24: $60,000

Problem 25: $14,560

Problem 26: $8,205

Problem 27: $30,000

Problem 28: (a) ROI   = 7.5%
(b) C on C = 6.0%
(c) R O E = 2.5 5%

Problem 29: 90.9 mills, or 9.09%

Problem 30: $2,800

Problem 31: $937.50

Problem 32:

rent:	seller's share	$870.96
	buyer's share	$929.04
	debit seller/credit buyer	$929.04
taxes:	seller's share	$973.16
	buyer's share	3,826.84
	debit seller/credit buyer	$973.16

Section Tests Answer Key

SECTION ONE: COURSE OVERVIEW: THE REAL ESTATE BUSINESS
1. a. absentee ownership (13)
2. b. developers. (8)
3. b. retail, office and industrial properties. (10)
4. a. Brokers and agents (12)
5. b. By geography (12)
6. c. It is an opinion of a property's value. (13)
7. b. state government. (16)

SECTION TWO: REAL ESTATE LICENSE LAW AND QUALIFICATIONS FOR LICENSURE
1. c. The Florida Legislature passed F. S. Chapter 475 as the first real estate license law. (22)
2. c. if the defect materially affects the value of the property. (23)
3. a. Chapter 120 (24)
4. b. Must disclose any criminal history (25)
5. d. Initial licensing fee (27)
6. c. An applicant's fingerprints are sent to the FBI for a criminal background check. (27)
7. a. 90 (28)
8. d. If a student misses more than 8 hours due to illness (29)
9. c. are exempt from prelicense education but must take the state exam. (30)
10. c. pass the state license exam with a score of 75% or higher. (31)
11. a. Applicants who fail the state license exam may retake it only once within a year of failing it. (32)
12. d. 2-year experience requirement (33)
13. a. the fundamentals of real estate appraising. (33)
14. c. has resided in Florida continuously for 4 or more months within the previous year. (34)
15. b. active duty military personnel who are licensed in another state. (36)
16. d. Every licensed person or entity (36)
17. a. 60 (37)
18. b. During the first license period prior to license expiration (37)
19. c. 8 hours (39)
20. c. Having a hardship (39)

SECTION THREE: REAL ESTATE LICENSE LAW AND COMMISSION RULES
1. c. F.S. Chapter 120. (48)
2. d. protect the public from unregulated business practices. (49)
3. c. Division of Professions (48)
4. a. for 2 years. (50)
5. b. support the Florida Real Estate Commission. (50)
6. c. must include one current member of the FREC. (51)
7. a. five members who hold real estate licenses. (51)
8. c. Members of the FREC must not serve more than two consecutive terms. (51)
9. d. decrease the amount of appropriate fees to be collected. (52)
10. a. report the violation to the State Attorney. (48)
11. b. on March 31 or September 30. (53)
12. c. September 30, 2020 (53)
13. d. Sally's license will become null and void. (56)

14. d. Sally is exempt from renewal requirements. (54)
15. c. The license becomes involuntarily inactive. (55)
16. c. must report the violation to the State Attorney. (53)

SECTION FOUR: AUTHORIZED RELATIONSHIPS, DUTIES, AND DISCLOSURE
1. d. trust, confidence, and good faith. (63)
2. c. provide sufficient information for the agent to complete the agent's tasks. (69)
3. b. general agency. (64)
4. b. special agency. (64)
5. c. a party creates an agency relationship outside of an express agreement. (64)
6. a. Death or incapacity of the agent (65)
7. a. The agent has violated the duty of confidentiality. (66)
8. b. the agent has not violated fiduciary duty. (66)
9. d. inform the seller. (67)
10. a. fairness, care, and honesty. (68)
11. b. has an exposure to a charge of negligent misrepresentation. (68)
12. d. practicing law without a license. (68)
13. c. a subagent. (71)
14. b. Bob and Sue are acting as transaction brokers. (72)
15. a. may not represent any party's interests to the detriment of the other party in the transaction. (72)
16. c. Whenever the licensee and principal agree to do so. (73)
17. a. A sales associate designated by a broker to represent one party in a transaction while another associate of the broker is designated to represent the other party (75)
18. c. Five years (76)
19. b. at the time of signing a listing or representation agreement or before showing a property . (71)
20. a. None (70)
21. c. Dual agency (71)
22. a. Disclosing facts that materially affect the property's value (70)
23. b. the nonresidential buyer and seller have assets of $1 million or more. (74)
24. c. Transaction brokers have no duty of undivided loyalty. (72)
25. c. for 5 years. (76)

SECTION FIVE: REAL ESTATE BROKERAGE ACTIVITIES AND PROCEDURES
1. d. a joint venture. (103)
2. c. the advertising must not be misleading. (85)
3. b. price fixing. (97)
4. b. Separate enclosed offices for each broker and associate (83)
5. d. The registration for a closed branch office may not be transferred to a new branch office. (84)
6. c. considered blind advertising. (85)
7. c. Turn the check over to the employing broker by end of the next business day. (90)
8. b. No later than the end of the third business day following receipt of the funds (90)
9. a. obtain written agreement from all involved parties. (91)
10. a. within 15 business days of the last demand. (92)

11. c. interpleader action. (93)
12. c. Release the escrow funds to the buyer without notifying the FREC (94)
13. d. This is legal. (107)
14. b. When the licensee obtains the opinion of title from an attorney and passes the information on to the client (95)
15. d. third-degree felony. (96)
16. b. Sue Stan for not paying Sarah her share of the commission. (97)
17. c. within 10 days after the change. (99)
18. d. Limited partnership (101)
19. a. Sales associates are not permitted to use a trade name. (104)
20. b. is a legally binding relationship among its members. (104)
21. c. participating members must have joint control. (103)
22. b. limited liability company. (102)
23. d. Not for profit corporation (101)
24. c. Ostensible partnership (101)
25. a. Cooperative association (103)
26. a. still owes the duty of confidentiality to the former broker and principals. (99)
27. d. removing records from the previous broker's office. (99)

SECTION SIX: VIOLATIONS OF LICENSE LAW, PENALTIES, AND PROCEDURES
1. d. within 5 years (116)
2. c. If the offense is a criminal act (116)
3. a. When the complaint is for a first-time minor violation (116)
4. c. When the DBPR believes the licensee poses an immediate danger to the public (116)
5. c. 20 days. (117)
6. b. 1 (117)
7. d. 30 (117)
8. b. When no probable cause is determined (117)
9. c. A formal complaint will be filed against the offender. (118)
10. d. Do not dispute the allegations and waive the right to a hearing (118)
11. a. FREC. (118)
12. d. None (119)
13. a. the license may be revoked without prejudice. (126)
14. b. 2 years (126)
15. c. punitive (127)
16. b. appropriating client or customer deposits for use in the agency's business. (115)
17. d. mixing escrow funds with the broker's operating funds. (115)

SECTION SEVEN: FEDERAL AND STATE LAWS PERTAINING TO REAL ESTATE
1. b. prohibit discrimination in housing transactions. (132)
2. c. the Civil Rights Act of 1968. (134)
3. c. the Fair Housing Amendments Act of 1988 (135)
4. a. blockbusting. (134)
5. c. steering. (134)
6. a. providing unequal services. (134)
7. a. discriminatory misrepresentation. (134)
8. d. The prohibition may be legal. (135)
9. c. The agent and the owner (136)

10. b. public accommodations and employment. (138)
11. c. any time before midnight on the seventh day after signing the contract. (139)
12. b. Joe owns an apartment building... (140)
13. a. Allowing a service dog to live in a no-pet apartment building (141)
14. c. within 30 days of receiving the deposit. (142)
15. c. 30 days (143)

SECTION EIGHT: PROPERTY RIGHTS, ESTATES & TENANCIES
1. a. real property includes ownership of a bundle of rights. (153)
2. c. To transfer (153)
3. d. Stock (154)
4. a. the right of others to use and enjoy their property. (156)
5. c. separable. (157)
6. d. Riparian (159)
7. b. To the middle of the waterway (159)
8. c. A doctrine that gives the state control of water use and the water supply (158)
9. a. A tree growing on a parcel of land (154)
10. b. its definition as one or the other in a sale or lease contract. (155)
11. d. A plant or crop that is considered personal property (155)
12. c. Affixing and severance (156)
13. b. Trade fixtures that are personal property (155)
14. a. The owner's claim is invalid, because the state owns the underlying land (158)
15. c. one or more of the bundle of rights to real property. (161)
16. a. interests that do not include possession. (162)
17. b. A leasehold endures only for a specific period of time. (163)
18. d. absolute fee simple estate. (163)
19. c. the estate may revert to a grantor or heirs if the prescribed use changes. (164)
20. a. the original owner or other named person. (164)
21. b. A fee simple owner grants the life estate to a life tenant. (165)
22. c. The pur autre vie estate endures only for the lifetime of a person other than the grantee. (166)
23. c. Legal life estate (166)
24. a. A homestead interest cannot be conveyed by one spouse. (167)
25. b. a wife's life estate interest in her husband's property. (167)
26. b. A widow who was excluded from a will makes a claim to a portion of the couple's principal residence. (167)
27. b. Estate from period to period (173)
28. a. tenancy in severalty. (168)
29. c. tenancy in common. (168)
30. a. Parties must acquire respective interests at the same time. (171)
31. b. cannot will their interest to a party outside the tenancy. (170)
32. c. fee simple ownership of the airspace in a unit and an undivided share of the entire property's common areas. (176)
33. b. The property is owned by tenants in common or by a freehold owner who leases on a time-share basis. (180)
34. a. A cooperative may hold an owner liable for the unpaid operating expenses of other owners. (175)
35. a. a default by a coop owner may cause a foreclosure on the entire property instead of just a single unit, as with a condominium. (175)

36. b. Right to cancel (184)
37. d. Timeshare (183)
38. a. Condominium resales (179)
39. b. HOA (184)

SECTION NINE: TITLE, DEEDS AND OWNERSHIP RESTRICTIONS

1. a. Ownership of the bundle of rights to real estate (194)
2. d. actual notice. (202)
3. c. title records. (202)
4. a. voluntary alienation. (195)
5. c. accepted by the grantee. (196)
6. d. states the grantor's intention, names the parties, describes the property, and indicates a consideration. (207)
7. a. state the grantor's assurance or warrant to the grantee that a certain condition or fact concerning the property is true. (208)
8. c. general warranty deed. (208)
9. d. A quitclaim deed (209)
10. a. It is taken by the state according to the process called escheat. (199)
11. d. an unenforceable nuncupative will. (197)
12. a. pass to heirs by the laws of descent and distribution. (198)
13. b. inspecting the property and evicting any trespassers found. (201)
14. d. declined because possession was secretive. (200)
15. c. give constructive notice of one's rights and interests in the property. (203)
16. c. A chronology of successive owners of record of a parcel of real estate. (205)
17. b. free of undisclosed defects and encumbrances. (204)
18. c. Title insurance (205)
19. c. encumbrance. (211)
20. c. the right to a defined use of a portion of another's real property. (212)
21. d. Dominant tenement (213)
22. a. The property has been continuously used as an easement with the knowledge but without the permission of the owner for a period of time. (216)
23. c. Over time, the encroachment may become an easement by prescription that damages the property's market value. (217)
24. b. a deed restriction. (212)
25. a. It involves a monetary claim against the value of a property. (220)
26. c. Real estate tax lien (223)
27. d. subordinate. (226)
28. a. the date of recordation. (224)
29. b. A state in which a mortgagor retains title to the property when a mortgage lien is created (225)
30. c. The lumber yard may place a mechanic's lien for the amount of the lumber against the homeowner's real property. (225)
31. b. an encroachment. (217)
32. b. transfers with the property. (213)
33. a. a party wall. (214)
34. d. A license, which terminates at the owner's death (217)
35. b. general judgment lien. (222)
36. a. including a " sale subject to lease" clause in the contract. (220)
37. b. In a sublease, the original tenant retains primary responsibility for performance of the original lease contract. (135)
38. a. A rights lease (219)

39. d. net lease. (217)
40. b. retail landlords.(218)
41. d. The tenant leases the ground from the landlord and owns the improvements. (219)
42. d. A deed can be valid with an incorrect parcel identification number on it. (207)

SECTION TEN: LEGAL DESCRIPTIONS

1. a. To create a consistent, unchanging standard for locating the property. (236)
2. b. They identify an enclosed area, beginning and ending at the same point. (237)
3. c. Metes and bounds (237)
4. b. point of beginning. (237)
5. d. Six miles by six miles. (240)
6. a. range. (207)
7. b. tier. (208)
8. d. Thirty-six (241)
9. a. 640 (241)
10. c. 80 acres (243)
11. b. will include a metes and bounds description. (239)
12. a. the lot and block number, with section, township and meridian references. (244)
13. c. properties located above or below the earth's surface. (244)
14. c. To maintain a rectangle survey pattern on the earth's curvature (240)
15. b. the property's value. (245)
16. d. Surveyors rely strictly on records and plats filed with the county recorder's office. (246)

SECTION ELEVEN: REAL ESTATE CONTRACTS

1. a. it represents a "meeting of the minds." (253)
2. c. enforceable or unenforceable. (254)
3. b. is possibly valid and enforceable. (255)
4. c. a counteroffer. (260)
5. d. valuable consideration. (256)
6. c. is void. (257)
7. b. voidable. (254)
8. a. must act within a statutory period. (257)
9. b. require certain conveyance-related contracts to be in writing. (257)
10. b. The buyer has no obligations to the seller whatsoever. (261)
11. a. is void. (259)
12. d. The original offer is legally extinguished. (260)
13. a. may be assigned. (261)
14. c. A two-year lease. (258)
15. a. an option to purchase. (259)
16. c. it is performed. (261)
17. b. it is impossible to perform. (262)
18. b. specific performance. (263)
19. a. exclusive right-to sell agreement. (265)
20. b. exclusive agency agreement. (264)
21. c. open listing. (265)
22. d. net listing. (266
23. a. the client. (264)
24. a. To list the owner's property in a multiple listing service. (267)
25. b. the agent has a claim to a commission if the owner sells or leases to a party within a certain time following the listing's expiration. (269)
26. b. the parties have completed a verbal, executory contract. (273)
27. c. The assignor has completed a legal action. (273)
28. a. the buyer can potentially force the seller to transfer ownership. (273)

29. a. entrust deposit monies to an impartial fiduciary. (274)
30. a. The seller may cancel the contract, since it can be ruled invalid. (274)
31. d. claim the deposit as relief for the buyer's failure to perform. (274)
32. d. third-party loans surviving closing may be accelerated by the lender. (277)
33. a. The buyer must withhold 15% of the purchase price at closing for the seller's capital gain tax payment. (277)
34. b. the optionor must perform if the optionee takes the option, but the optionee is under no obligation to do so. (283)
35. d. The option is expired, and the tenant has no rightful claim to money paid for the option. (283)
36. a. The tenant can force the sale at the original terms. (283)
37. c. They give the optionee an equitable interest in the property. (285)
38. c. open listing. (265)
39. b. Molly's Law disclosure (278)
40. c. Caveat emptor (281)

SECTION TWELVE: RESIDENTIAL MORTGAGES
1. c. hypothecation. (294)
2. a. The borrower gives the lender a note and a mortgage in exchange for loan funds. (294)
3. a. title-theory state. (294)
4. b. usury. (299)
5. c. $15,000. (300)
6. c. it is a negotiable instrument. (295)
7. d. may be required to execute a release of mortgage document. (297)
8. c. foreclosure. (107)
9. a. there is no right to redeem the property in a non-judicial foreclosure. (306)
10. b. a deed in lieu of foreclosure. (306)
11. c. mortgagor. (295)
12. a. It establishes the level of lender risk. (296)

SECTION THIRTEEN: TYPES OF MORTGAGES AND SOURCES OF FINANCING
1. b. Truth-in-Lending laws (331)
2. a. The Equal Credit Opportunity Act (331)
3. c. the Real Estate Settlement Procedures Act. (332)
4. b. Buying securities, changing the discount rate, and controlling banking reserves (325)
5. a. cycle funds back to primary lenders so they can make more loans. (328)
6. a. Fannie Mae, Freddie Mac, and Ginnie Mae. (329)
7. c. purchase FHA-backed and VA-backed loans. (322)
8. b. insure loans made by approved lenders. (322)
9. a. guarantee loans made by approved lenders. (323)
10. c. the loan payments gradually increase. (321)
11. b. the borrower pays additional interest at the onset in order to obtain a lower interest rate. (321)
12. a. the interest rate may vary. (319)
13. b. the seller offering the buyer a wraparound can profit from a difference in interest rates. (327)
14. b. a blanket mortgage loan. (322)
15. b. Payments are not sufficient to retire the loan. (319)
16. a. an appraisal report. (313)
17. c. the ability to re-pay, the value of the collateral, and the profitability of the loan. (314)
18. b. the lender wants to ensure the loan is fully collateralized. (314)
19. b. consider the income of a spouse in evaluating a family's creditworthiness. (312)

20. a. safeguard against over-indebtedness. (315)
21. d. dividing one's debts by one's gross income. (316)
22. c. take-out loan commitment. (317)
23. a. an amortized loan is paid off over the loan period. (320)

SECTION FOURTEEN: REAL ESTATE-RELATED COMPUTATIONS AND CLOSING OF TRANSACTIONS
1. d. exchange legal title for the sale price. (346)
2. b. the lender wants to ensure proper handling of the collateral for the loan. (348)
3. b. the loan is to be sold to the FNMA. (349)
4. d. the buyer must pay the expense. (351
5. d. a debit to one party and a credit to the other. (352)
6. a. the excess of the buyer's debits over the buyer's credits. (351)
7. b. Inspection fees (352)
8. c. Taxes and interest (352)
9. d. Rents and insurance (352)
10. a. the seller must pay prorated expenses inclusive of the day of closing. (353)
11. d. $692 (356)
12. c. $195,200 (356)
13. a. by the end of the next business day. (343)
14. d. The property buyer (345)
15. b. 70 cents on each $100 of the sale price. (356)
16. c. $400. (357)

SECTION FIFTEEN: REAL ESTATE MARKETS AND ANALYSIS
1. c. Land and everything permanently attached to it (379)
2. a. The surface of the earth and all natural things permanently attached to the earth (378)
3. b. Immobile, indestructible, heterogeneous (379)
4. d. land does not include man-made structures. (378)
5. c. the amount of money a buyer and seller agree to exchange to complete a transaction. (396)
6. b. desire, utility, scarcity, and purchasing power. (398)
7. b. will increase. (398)
8. d. the market tending toward equilibrium. (386)
9. c. the market is over-supplied. (386)
10. a. The demand must literally come to the supply. (380)
11. b. base employment. (383)
12. a. have been increasing. (386)
13. d. expanding the sewer system. (385)
14. a. trade area population and spending patterns. (383)
15. c. costs of occupancy and building efficiency. (383)

SECTION SIXTEEN: REAL ESTATE APPRAISAL
1. a. if two similar properties are for sale, a buyer will purchase the cheaper of the two. (399)
2. a. is physically and financially feasible, legal, and the most productive. (398)
3. d. the price that a willing, informed, and unpressured seller and buyer agree upon for a property assuming a cash price and the property's reasonable exposure to the market. (396)
4. b. the broker may not be a disinterested party. (403)
5. a. there may be no recent sale price data in the market. (400)
6. c. select comparable properties, adjust the comparables, estimate the value. (400
7. b. the seller offers below-market seller financing. (402)
8. b. weights the comparables. (402)
9. b. market value is not always the same as what the property cost. (406)

10. b. replacement cost. (407)
11. d. functional obsolescence. (407)
12. b. incurable economic obsolescence. (407)
13. c. depreciation (407)
14. a. estimate depreciation, subtract depreciation from cost, and add back the land value. (408)
15. b. $8,500 (409)
16. b. Apartment buildings (410)
17. c. estimate net income, and apply a capitalization rate to it. (411)
18. c. potential gross income minus vacancy and credit loss minus expenses. (412)
19. b. $400,000 (412)
20. a. numerous expenses are not taken into account. (414)
21. b. $240,000 (414)
22. c. For federally related transaction appraisals (394)
23. c. Federally related transactions (394)
24. b. Appraisals can be used in preparing CMAs. (415)

SECTION SEVENTEEN: REAL ESTATE INVESTMENTS & BUSINESS OPPORTUNITY BROKERAGE

1. b. the more the investor stands to gain, the greater the risk that the investor may lose. (423)
2. a. income and tax benefits. (423)
3. c. debt. (424)
4. d. relatively illiquid. (426)
5. b. a more management-intensive investment. (426)
6. d. gross income minus expenses minus building depreciation. (426)
7. c. deduct interest payments from income. (429)
8. d. The owner may be able to exclude capital gain from taxable income when the property is sold. (430)
9. c. may be deducted from the sale price for gains tax purposes. (429)
10. b. the difference between net sale proceeds and adjusted basis. (430)
11. a. cost recovery expense. (431)
12. c. dividing cash flow by the investor's equity. (433)
13. a. propose an asset sale. (435)
14. b. intangible assets. (436)
15. c. the value or price of the business over and above the value of its other assets. (436)
16. a. Real property (434)
17. c. perform due diligence. (438)

SECTION EIGHTEEN: TAXES AFFECTING REAL ESTATE

1. c. There are no federal ad valorem taxes. (444)
2. c. may delegate taxing authority to county governments. (444)
3. c. impose property taxes for specific municipal services. (444)
4. b. create a two-mile extension of county sewer facilities. (445)
5. b. the assessed value of property. (445)
6. b. the total of all assessed values of properties minus exemptions. (445)
7. d. smooth out wide discrepancies of assessed values within the district. (446)
8. c. appeal to adjust the assessed valuation. (446)
9. b. to offer an amount of tax relief on an owner's principal residence. (447)
10. a. dividing the tax requirement by the tax base. (446)
11. c. multiplying each district's tax rate times the taxable value of the property. (447)

12. a. it only applies to properties which will benefit from the public improvement. (449)
13. b. entitles its holder to apply for a tax deed after a certain period. (450)
14. b. gives a delinquent taxpayer a grace period prior to the tax sale to pay property taxes. (451)
15. d. 10 mills. (444)
16. b. market value. (445)
17. d. Appeal to a higher court (446)
18. a. Head of the family (448)
19. c. subtracting exemptions from the assessed value. (446)

SECTION NINETEEN: PLANNING, ZONING, AND ENVIRONMENTAL HAZARDS

1. a. balance individual property rights with the community's welfare. (460)
2. d. a fusion of land use laws and local land use objectives and strategies. (461)
3. a. zoning. (461)
4. c. police power. (466)
5. d. sell the property to the municipality. (466)
6. c. the planning commission. (463)
7. b. delegation of authority by state-level enabling acts. (466)
8. a. reasonably promote community health, safety and welfare. (467)
9. d. To ensure that improvements comply with codes (467)
10. b. regulate density. (467)
11. a. a special exception. (469)
12. c. a legal nonconforming use. (468)
13. a. it would cause the property owner unreasonable hardship to bring the property into compliance with zoning ordinances. (469)
14. b. a plat of subdivision. (470)
15. c. the construction complies with building codes. (471)
16. a. Florida's Growth Policy Act (463)
17. d. Future land use (464)
18. b. includes risk categories based on wind speed. (470)
19. b. refers to insulation's resistance to heat flow. (471)
20. c. a licensed pest control company inspector. (474)

Practice Exam

Answer key is on p. 520

1. Which of the following professionals involved in the real estate business are most concerned about managing real estate for clients?

   a. Brokers and agents
   b. Property managers
   c. Corporate real estate managers
   d. Appraisers

2. Real estate can be defined as

   a. land and all property contained therein.
   b. unimproved land.
   c. land and everything permanently attached to it.
   d. air, surface, and subsurface rights.

3. Which of the following is included in the bundle of rights inherent in ownership?

   a. To tax
   b. To encroach
   c. To possess
   d. To inherit

4. The overriding test of whether an item is a fixture or personal property is

   a. whether the owner owns the property the item is affixed to.
   b. how it is described in a sale or lease contract.
   c. what the title records on the property indicate.
   d. how the buyer defines the item.

5. An owner of a lakefront property tells a fisherman that he cannot fish in a boat within fifty feet of the owner's shoreline. The fisherman protests that the owner cannot prevent him. Which of the following is true?

   a. The fisherman is correct because the water and the land underlying it are public property.
   b. The owner's prohibition is valid, since the underlying land belongs to abutting properties to the middle of the lake.
   c. The owner can prevent the fisherman from fishing within ten feet, but not beyond.
   d. The owner's prohibition is valid if all lakefront property owners have agreed to it.

6. The distinguishing feature of a defeasible fee simple estate is that

   a. it only endures for the lifetime of the defeasee.
   b. it has no restrictions or conditions on use.
   c. it may revert to a grantor if the prescribed use changes.
   d. it is of limited duration.

7. Dower can best be defined as

   a. a grant of foreclosure immunity extended to a homestead claimant.
   b. a wife's life estate interest in her husband's property.
   c. a husband's homestead exemption.
   d. a grantor who endows property to heirs.

8. A distinct feature of a joint tenancy is that joint tenants

   a. may elect to have any percent of ownership in the property.
   b. cannot will their interest to a party outside the tenancy.
   c. own separate physical portions of the land.
   d. cannot lease the property.

9. Interests in a condominium differ from those in a cooperative, in that

   a. a default by a condominium owner may cause a foreclosure on the entire property instead of just a single unit, as with a cooperative.
   b. the condominium owner owns the common elements and the airspace, whereas the coop owner owns only the apartment.
   c. the coop owner owns stock in the cooperative association, whereas the condominium owner simply owns real estate.
   d. the cooperative owner must pay a pro rata share of the cooperative's expenses as well as rent.

10. There are two adjoining properties. An easement allows property A to use the access road that belongs to property B. In this situation, property B is said to be which of the following in relation to property A?

    a. Dominant tenement
    b. Subordinate tenant
    c. Servient estate
    d. Conditional life tenant

11. Title records of a property reveal several recorded liens: a one-year old judgment lien; a mechanic's lien dating from two years ago; a special assessment tax lien recorded last month; and a first mortgage lien recorded five years ago. In case of a foreclosure, which of these liens will be paid first?

    a. First mortgage lien
    b. Special assessment tax lien
    c. Mechanic's lien
    d. Judgment lien

12. A lender may terminate foreclosure proceedings if the defaulting borrower executes

    a. a wraparound mortgage.
    b. a lis pendens.
    c. a waiver of redemption.
    d. a deed in lieu of foreclosure.

13. A person has occupied a property for seven years, and no one has ever attempted to evict her or co-occupy the parcel. In this case, the person might base a claim of legal ownership on

    a. her prescriptive easement.
    b. title records.
    c. constructive notice of possession.
    d. tenancy in severalty.

14. A person wishes to convey any and all interests in a property to another with full assurances against encumbrances, liens, or any other title defects on the property. This party would most likely use which of the following types of deed?

    a. A quitclaim deed
    b. A general warranty deed
    c. A deed in lieu of warrant
    d. A guardian's deed

15. The chain of title to a property refers to which of the following?

    a. An abstract of the condition and marketability of title
    b. The genealogy of successive heirs to a property
    c. The list of all current encumbrances and clouds "chained" to title
    d. A chronology of successive owners of record

16. A government entity takes title to a leased property by way of eminent domain. What happens to the lease?

    a. It is extinguished.
    b. It remains in effect.
    c. It automatically renews at closing for its original term.
    d. It moves with the owner to a new property, if purchased within one year.

17. The Florida Residential Landlord and Tenant Act fundamentally attempts to

    a. promote the rights of tenants, particularly in lease defaults.
    b. standardize rental rates.
    c. prevent the use of unfair lease provisions.
    d. minimize rent escalations in economically depressed zones.

18. A primary objective of residential zoning is

    a. regulate rates of appreciation and depreciation of residences.
    b. promote the value and planned land use of a neighborhood.
    c. eliminate nonconforming uses, variances, and special exceptions.
    d. disperse intensity of usage.

19. A shop was originally built in a commercial zone. The zone has since been changed to a residential zone. Zoning authorities permit the use, most likely as

    a. a variance.
    b. a special exception.
    c. an illegal nonconforming use.
    d. a legal nonconforming use.

20. Authorities conduct comprehensive land use planning in order to

    a. balance public interests with individual property rights.
    b. prevent the public from exercising police powers.
    c. ensure positive market conditions for development projects.
    d. limit growth.

21. The purpose of a formal legal description of a property is to

    a. eliminate encroachments.
    b. locate and identify the property reliably.
    c. eliminate the possibility of surveyor error.
    d. qualify for title recordation.

22. A parcel is described as the SW 1/4 of the N 1/2 of the E 1/2 of Section 14. What is its acreage?

    a. 160 acres   b. 80 acres
    c. 40 acres   d. 20 acres

23. A suburb has a growing need for single-family housing, but the land available for new construction is running low. In this case, it is likely that the price of existing homes

    a. will decline.
    b. will increase.
    c. will stabilize.
    d. will not show any predictable movement.

24. The demand for homes in a market is best expressed in terms of

    a. square feet of housing required.
    b. number of contracts signed with developers.
    c. number of houses listed in the multiple listing service.
    d. number of households seeking housing.

25. What is the significance of base employment in a real estate market?

    a. It gives the basic number of people who will need housing.
    b. It indicates the number of people at the low end of the buying power spectrum.
    c. It drives total employment and population growth, which lead to demand for real estate.
    d. It indicates the number of people who want to move into the market.

26. The concept known as substitution states that

    a. buyers will not substitute the quality of one home for the price of another.
    b. the replacement cost of an item cannot be substituted for the item's original value.
    c. a new improvement will only increase market value to the extent of the cost of a similar improvement.
    d. buyers will not pay more for a certain house than they would for another, similar house.

27. The "price that a willing, informed, and unpressured seller and buyer agree upon for a property, assuming a cash price and reasonable exposure of the property to the market" describes which of the following concepts of value?

    a. Highest and best value
    b. Substitution value
    c. Desirability
    d. Market value

28. A warehouse building lacks sufficient ceiling height for the operation of modern forklifts. This is an example of

    a. non-conforming use.
    b. functional obsolescence.
    c. overimprovement.
    d. economic obsolescence.

29. To derive value using the income capitalization approach, one must

    a. divide the capitalization rate by net income.
    b. multiply net income times the capitalization rate.
    c. divide the capitalization rate into net income.
    d. multiply cash flow by the capitalization rate.

30. An office building rents for $600,000, has expenses of $400,000, and a cash flow of $100,000. The prevailing gross rent multiplier is 8. Using the GRM, what is the value of the building?

    a. $800,000   b. $1,600,000
    c. $3,200,000   d. $4,800,000

31. An owner obtains a loan and gives the mortgagee a mortgage on the property as collateral. The mortgagor/owner retains title to the property, and the mortgagee records a lien. This is an example of

    a. intermediation.
    b. contracting for deed.
    c. subordination.
    d. hypothecation.

32. An important characteristic of a promissory note is that

    a. it is assignable.
    b. it must be secured by collateral.
    c. it is not a negotiable instrument.
    d. it must be recorded to be enforceable.

33. Disclosure of estimated closing costs is required of a lender in order to comply with

    a. the Equal Credit Opportunity Act.
    b. Truth-in-Lending laws.
    c. Federal Fair Housing Laws.
    d. the Real Estate Settlement Procedures Act.

34. The secondary mortgage market organizations do all of the following EXCEPT

    a. guarantee performance on mortgages.
    b. buy pools of mortgages from primary lenders.
    c. sell securities based on pooled mortgages.
    d. directly originate loans.

35. Negative amortization of a loan occurs whenever

    a. monthly payments are interest-only.
    b. a payment does not pay the full amount of interest owed.
    c. the principal loan balance is diminishing.
    d. the interest rate increases on an adjustable rate loan.

36. A borrower earns $3,000/month and makes credit card and car note payments of $500. A conventional lender requires a 27% income ratio. What monthly amount for housing expenses (principal, interest, taxes, insurance) will the lender allow this person to have in order to qualify for a conventional mortgage loan?

    a. $810   b. $675
    c. $972   d. $1,040

37. A $250,000 interest-only loan carries a 7% rate. Monthly payments are

    a. $1,750.
    b. $1,458.
    c. $17,500.
    d. Cannot be determined without loan term data.

38. A lender is charging 2.75 points on a $240,000 loan. How much must the borrower pay for points?

    a. $550.   b. $5,500.
    c. $6,600.   d. $660.

39. Which of the following is generally true of a real estate investment?

    a. The lower the price, the lower the liquidity
    b. The greater the return, the greater the risk
    c. The more management, the less return
    d. The more liquidity, the greater the return

40. The capital gain on sale of an investment is computed as

    a. beginning basis plus gain.
    b. sale price minus beginning basis.
    c. net sales proceeds minus beginning basis.
    d. net sales proceeds minus adjusted basis.

41. The formula for return on equity is

    a. cash flow divided by equity.
    b. required yield times gross income.
    c. net operating income divided by equity.
    d. cash flow times the capitalization rate.

42. Mary Bright bought a home for $80,000, paying $10,000 down and taking a mortgage loan of $70,000. The following year she had a new roof put on, at a cost of $2,000. What is Mary's adjusted basis in the house if she now sells the house for $300,000?

    a. $12,000   b. $218,000
    c. $230,000   d. $82,000

43. An office building has a potential income of $500,000 and vacancy of 10%. Its cash-paid bills total $300,000, and annual depreciation is $5,000. Payments on the loan total $100,000. What is the property's pre-tax cash flow?

a. $45,000
b. $50,000
c. $150,000
d. $155,000

44. A property is purchased for $200,000. Improvements account for 75% of the value. Given a 39-year depreciation term, what is the annual depreciation expense?

a. $3,846
b. $5,128
c. $6,410
d. $8,294

45. An income property is bought for $500,000. Gross income is $100,000, and net operating income is $60,000. Cash flow is $10,000. What is the return on investment (ROI)?

a. 2.00%
b. 12%
c. 10.00%
d. 60.00%

46. Which of the following is the formula for deriving the tax base of a jurisdiction?

a. The total tax required divided by assessed values
b. The total of all assessed values minus exemptions
c. The annual budget times the tax rate
d. The annual budget divided by the millage rate

47. The purpose of a homestead tax exemption is

a. to exempt owners from ad valorem taxation.
b. to offer tax abatement on a principal residence.
c. to encourage owners to finance their principle residences.
d. to exempt owners of principal residences who rent their properties.

48. A homeowner's tax bill for a taxing district is derived by

a. dividing the tax base by the district's needed revenues.
b. multiplying the tax rate times the assessed value of the property.
c. multiplying the tax rate times the taxable value of the property.
d. multiplying the millage rate times the equalization factor.

49. The village of Parrish has an annual budget requirement of $20,000,000 to be funded by property taxes. Assessed valuations are $400,000,000, and exemptions total $25,000,000. What must the tax rate be to finance the budget?

a. 4.70%
b. 5.33%
c. 5.00%
d. 11.25%

50. A canal dredging project is to cost $100,000. There are 40 properties along the canal, and 40 others across the street from the canal. The total canal footage to be dredged is 2,500 feet. How much will the assessment be for a 150-foot property on the canal?

a. $1,250
b. $2,500
c. $3,000
d. $6,000

51. A prospective homebuyer offers to buy a house if the seller agrees to pay financing points at closing. The seller gets the offer, signs it, and gives it to his agent to deliver. At this point the status of the offer is

a. a valid contract.
b. an invalid contract.
c. still an offer.
d. an invalid offer.

52. One aim of the statute of frauds is to

a. set time limits for disputing contract provisions.
b. require certain conveyances to be in writing.
c. prevent fraudulent assignments of listing agreements.
d. make all oral agreements unenforceable.

53. A buyer agrees to all terms of a seller's offer and sends notice of acceptance back to the seller. The seller now tells the buyer the deal is off because he has learned that the home was underpriced. Which of the following is true?

a. The buyer must offer the new price to get the property.
b. The seller may counteroffer.
c. The contract is cancelled.
d. The buyer has a binding contract.

54. A principal discloses to the listing agent that she must sell a property within two months to avoid a financial problem. Nearly seven weeks later, a buyer's agent hears of the seller's difficulty from the listing agent and advises his buyer to submit an offer for 80% of the listed price. The buyer complies, and the seller accepts the offer. Which of the following is true?

a. The buyer's agent has violated fiduciary duties owed the customer.
b. The listing agent has violated fiduciary duties owed the customer.
c. The buyer's agent has violated fiduciary duties owed the client.
d. The listing agent has violated fiduciary duties owed the client.

55. An owner's agent is showing a buyer an apartment building. The buyer questions the agent as to whether some cracking paint contains lead. The agent's best course of action is to

a. contract to re-paint the cracked area.
b. assure the buyer the paint is lead-free.
c. suggest the buyer make a lower-price offer to cover the possible problem.
d. inform the seller of the inquiry and test the paint.

56. A type of agency relationship that is illegal in Florida is

a. single agency.
b. dual agency.
c. buyer agency.
d. nonrepresentation.

57. When must a transaction broker disclose his or her agency relationship to the transaction principals?

    a. Before receipt of any offer
    b. Upon completion of the listing agreement
    c. Disclosure not required
    d. Upon initial contact of any kind with either principal

58. An agent obtains a listing which ensures compensation for procuring a customer, provided the agent is the procuring cause. This agent has entered into a(n)

    a. exclusive right-to sell agreement.
    b. exclusive agency agreement.
    c. open listing.
    d. net listing.

59. A landlord promises to compensate a broker for procuring a tenant, provided the landlord's brother decides not to rent the property within a month. This would be an example of a(n)

    a. exclusive right-to-lease agreement.
    b. exclusive agency agreement.
    c. open listing.
    d. net listing.

60. The amount of a real estate brokerage commission is determined by

    a. state license law guidelines.
    b. negotiation with the client.
    c. the Board of Realtors.
    d. agreement among competing brokers.

61. The Brokerage Relationship Disclosure Act applies to transactions involving all the following property types EXCEPT

    a. commercial properties.
    b. agricultural properties of ten acres or less.
    c. residential properties with four or fewer dwelling units.
    d. unimproved properties zoned for four or fewer residential units.

62. A Florida licensee representing an owner as a single agent must be careful to

    a. avoid an overpriced offer that will cause buyer's remorse or lawsuits.
    b. present any offer a buyer might decide to make.
    c. disclose what price the owner will accept.
    d. avoid completing an offer that contains contingencies.

63. An example of conversion is

    a. depositing escrow funds in a business operating account.
    b. spending a customer deposit on a surety bond for the agency.
    c. spending operating income from an apartment on roof repairs.
    d. depositing a commission into an escrow account.

64. Three leading agencies charge identical commission rates for brokering office properties in Phoenix. Which of the following is true?

    a. This is a perfectly legitimate business practice.
    b. The brokers have engaged in legal collusion.
    c. The brokers have allocated the Phoenix market.
    d. The brokers have illegally fixed prices.

65. A business owner insists on a price for his enterprise that exceeds the value of the tangible assets, claiming that it is a well-known family business with a loyal clientele. The excess value is known as

    a. the buyer's premium.
    b. goodwill.
    c. the risk factor.
    d. the profit margin.

66. An agent informs owners in an area that a decline in property values over the past five years is due to an influx of minority families. He suggests that the trend will continue, and advises them to sell before it is too late. This agent is probably guilty of

    a. blockbusting.
    b. redlining.
    c. discriminatory misrepresentation.
    d. negligent misrepresentation.

67. An agent spends two hours with a minority buyer, then shows the buyer five available properties all over town. Later, a similarly qualified minority couple enter the office. The agent spends twenty minutes with the couple, gives them the MLS book to review, and encourages them to drive by the listings on their way home. If they like anything, they should come back the next day to discuss terms. This agent could be liable for

    a. misrepresentation.
    b. steering.
    c. providing unequal services.
    d. nothing.

68. An owner suddenly pulls a property off the market after hearing from the agent that a minority party has made a full-price offer. The agent then goes back to the minority party and reports that the seller has decided to wait until next year to sell the home. Who, if anyone, has violated fair housing laws?

    a. Both owner and agent.
    b. The owner.
    c. The agent.
    d. No one.

69. An owner completes a contract to sell her property. Before closing, she runs into financial trouble and assigns the contract to her mortgagor. Which of the following is true?

    a. The owner has defaulted.
    b. The buyer can sue to nullify the mortgage.
    c. The assignment can take effect only after the closing.
    d. The sale contract remains valid.

70. Buyers and sellers rely on escrow accounts in order to

 a. allow a third party fiduciary to handle the funds.
 b. have access to the funds without interference from the broker.
 c. prevent the broker from receiving a commission until after closing.
 d. earn equal interest on their funds.

71. An option-to-purchase expires. The landlord agrees to extend it in exchange for a higher price. The optionee claims he can exercise the option within the redemption period. Which is true?

 a. The landlord must honor the option and sell immediately.
 b. The landlord can extend the option term, but cannot raise the price.
 c. The landlord must extend the option but is allowed to raise the price.
 d. The landlord is under no obligation, since options do not have a redemption period.

72. RESPA requires specific closing procedures whenever

 a. the loan is to be guaranteed.
 b. the loan is to be sold to the FNMA.
 c. the commercial property is to be bought by FHLMC.
 d. a borrower does not fully understand closing costs.

73. When an item is prorated between buyer and seller on a settlement statement, the closing officer must

 a. debit the buyer and seller.
 b. credit the buyer and seller.
 c. debit and credit both buyer and seller.
 d. debit one party and credit the other.

74. Which of the following items are paid in arrears?

 a. Taxes and insurance
 b. Rents and interest
 c. Taxes and interest
 d. Rents and insurance

75. A sale transaction on rental property closes on December 16. The landlord received the December rent of $713 on December 1. Assuming the closing day is the seller's, and that the 365-day method is used for prorating, which of the following entries would appear on the settlement statement?

 a. Debit seller $345.00
 b. Credit seller $713.00
 c. Debit buyer $345.00
 d. Credit buyer $368.00

76. Which of the following persons selling a time-share must hold a real estate license?

 a. An owner selling a time-share she occupies
 b. Any person being paid a commission to sell the time-share
 c. A salaried individual selling time-shares for a developer
 d. A developer's assistant selling the time-share as a favor to the developer for no compensation

77. Listing agreements are governed by two bodies of laws. These are agency laws and

 a. contract laws.
 b. common laws.
 c. statutory laws.
 d. case laws.

78. In the contracting process, a licensee must be careful to avoid

 a. giving the principal any advice about the transaction.
 b. describing the normal requirements of a contract to a client.
 c. drafting a contract illegally.
 d. pointing out to the principals the importance of meeting contingency deadlines.

79. If a license is issued by a mistake of the Commission, the Commission can justifiably

 a. charge the licensee a punitive fee.
 b. file a civil suit to retrieve the license.
 c. refer the case for mediation.
 d. revoke the license without prejudice.

80. A broker responsible for handling a trust account is violating the law by

 a. depositing an earnest money check in a personal account.
 b. following the seller's instructions to hold an earnest money check uncashed.
 c. removing an earned commission from a trust account without permission of the depository institution.
 d. opening an account that names the licensee as the trustee of the account.

81. The sending of unsolicited commercial email to cell phones is banned by the

 a. Florida Telephonic Junk Prevention law.
 b. CAN-SPAM Act.
 c. FREC rules.
 d. Florida licensing law.

82. Which of the following actions by a Florida real estate licensee would violate a federal or Florida telemarketing law?

 a. Calling a potential client at 9:00 a.m.
 b. Calling someone on another licensee's client list.
 c. Calling a potential seller to solicit a listing.
 d. Calling a potential client while blocking caller ID.

83. A landlord refuses to rent to a single pregnant woman. The woman feels there has been illegal discrimination. How long do she have to file a complaint with the Florida commission on Human Relations?

 a. There is no time limit.
 b. She must file immediately after the alleged violation.
 c. She has one year from the date of the alleged discrimination.
 d. This is not a violation of Florida law.

84. When do Florida counties send out property tax bills to homeowners?

   a. On January first of each year
   b. In late October of each year
   c. On November first and April first of each year
   d. On November first of every even-numbered year

85. What is likely to happen if a homeowner fails to pay an authorized assessment to a homeowner's association?

   a. The unpaid assessment may become a lien against the property.
   b. The association may impose a tax sale on the property.
   c. The association may have the sheriff evict the homeowner.
   d. The property may be dropped from association membership.

86. An unlicensed applicant may be denied licensure if he presented himself as a licensee prior to applying for a license

   a. during the previous 5 years.
   b. within 1 year.
   c. within 2 years.
   d. at any time.

87. Some fees may be waived for certain individuals. The _____ is not one of those fees.

   a. examination fee
   b. initial unlicensed activity fee
   c. initial licensing fee
   d. initial application fee

88. When is a sales associate's license issued?

   a. When the application is approved
   b. When the prelicense course is completed
   c. When the applicant passes the state license exam
   d. When the applicant registers with an employing broker

89. A real estate license ceases to be in force when

   a. the licensee fails to complete post-license education.
   b. the licensed broker changes business address.
   c. a licensed sales associate applies for a broker license.
   d. the licensee fails to renew the license by the expiration date.

90. If a licensee fails to renew the license within 2 years of becoming involuntarily inactive,

   a. the licensee must complete 12 hours of continuing education for each year the license was inactive.
   b. the license will be revoked.
   c. the license becomes null and void.
   d. the license is deemed delinquent.

91. Florida disclosure requirements apply to

   a. unimproved residential property to be used for four or fewer units.
   b. all improved residential property with five or more units.
   c. agricultural property of 15 or fewer acres.
   d. industrial property of 10 or fewer acres.

92. When offering a representation of value, the broker may not

   a. perform a comparative market analysis.
   b. perform a broker price opinion.
   c. represent his own opinion as an appraisal.
   d. use only a property survey.

93. Under which of the following conditions might a kickback be legal?

   a. When the broker has an affiliated business arrangement with a service provider
   b. When all involved parties are fully informed of the kickback
   c. When the kickback is something other than cash
   d. Never

94. A sales associate or broker associate must notify the FREC of a change of employing broker within ____ of the change.

   a. three days
   b. one week
   c. 10 days
   d. 30 days

95. Which of the following entities may not register as a brokerage?

   a. Not for profit corporation
   b. Joint venture
   c. Limited partnership
   d. Sole proprietorship

96. If a licensee does not agree with a final hearing order, the licensee may file an appeal within _____ days of receiving the order.

   a. 10
   b. 20
   c. 30
   d. 60

97. Which of the following entities is authorized to impose criminal penalties?

   a. FREC
   b. Administrative judges
   c. Criminal courts
   d. DRE

98. Tenants who have been given a notice to vacate the rental unit for nonpayment of rent have _____ to vacate.

   a. 24 hours
   b. 3 days
   c. 7 days
   d. 30 days

99. In which type of community is there a governing body responsible for providing community development services?

   a. CDD
   b. HOA
   c. Cooperative
   d. Condominium

100. Which of the following best describes the person who is the "procuring cause" of a transaction sale?

   a. The person who met the buyer first.
   b. The broker who employs the agent who made the sale
   c. The person who started a series of events that led to a sale
   d. The buyer

101. An Assessor Parcel Number's primary use is

   a. for tax purposes.
   b. to create plot maps.
   c. to identify a property's boundaries.
   d. to track property transfers.

102. Which of the following statements is true?

   a. Disclosure of Megan's Law requires sellers to tell buyers exactly where nearby sex offenders are located.
   b. The property tax disclosure requires sellers to inform buyers what the property taxes will be going forward.
   c. The Florida coastal property disclosure requires documentation indicating the location of the coastal construction control line.
   d. The energy efficiency disclosure requires sellers to provide energy efficient appliances when selling their property.

103. Florida places an intangible tax on

   a. deeds.
   b. mortgage loans.
   c. deeds and liens.
   d. mortgages and deeds.

104. In Florida, an unlicensed personal assistant

   a. Must be compensated as an employee
   b. May be compensated by a commission
   c. Cannot be a licensed party
   d. May perform administrative duties such as negotiating contracts

105. In the sale of a business, liabilities are considered when

   a. determining the business valuation.
   b. preparing the business documents.
   c. preparing for closing.
   d. closing the transaction.

106. Which is true regarding the Florida Greenbelt Law?

   a. Farmers must meet Florida's minimum land size requirement.
   b. Property assessment is based on the highest and best use of the property.
   c. The land must be classified every year.
   d. Homeowners must reside on the land.

107. When is a superior lien placed on a property for unpaid property taxes?

   a. April 1 following the tax year
   b. January 1 following the tax year
   c. November 1 of the tax year
   d. March 1 of the tax year

108. In Florida, when a tax certificate is purchased at a tax certificate sale, the certificate is valid for

   a. 1 year.
   b. 2 years.
   c. 7 years.
   d. 10 years.

109. Which of the following is an NFIP requirement specific to nonresidential structures in a special flood hazard area?

   a. An elevated open foundation
   b. Lowest floor above the base flood elevation
   c. Water tight below the base flood elevation
   d. There are no requirements specific to nonresidential structures.

110. Which flood zone has the highest flood risk?

   a. A zone
   b. R zone
   c. V zone
   d. Z zone

Practice Examination Answer Key

1. b. Property managers (8)
2. c. land and everything permanently attached to it. (151)
3. c. To possess (153)
4. b. how it is described in a sale or lease contract. (155)
5. a. The fisherman is correct because the water and the land underlying it are public property. (158)
6. c. it may revert to a grantor if the prescribed use changes. (164)
7. b. a wife's life estate interest in her husband's property. (167)
8. b. cannot will their interest to a party outside the tenancy. (170)
9. c. the coop owner owns stock in the cooperative association, whereas the condominium owner simply owns real estate. (174)
10. c. Servient estate (213)
11. b. Special assessment tax lien (223)
12. d. a deed in lieu of foreclosure. (306)
13. c. constructive notice of possession. (202)
14. b. A general warranty deed (208)
15. d. A chronology of successive owners of record (205)
16. a. It is extinguished. (200)
17. c. prevent the use of unfair lease provisions. (141)
18. b. promote the value and planned land use of a neighborhood. (467)
19. d. a legal nonconforming use. (468)
20. a. balance public interests with individual property rights. (460)
21. b. locate and identify the property reliably. (236)
22. c. 40 acres (243)
23. b. will increase. (381)
24. d. number of households seeking housing. (382)
25. c. It drives total employment and population growth, which lead to demand for real estate. (383)
26. d. buyers will not pay more for a certain house than they would for another, similar house. (399)
27. d. Market value (396)
28. b. functional obsolescence. (407)
29. c. divide the capitalization rate into net income. (412)
30. d. $4,800,000 (414)
31. d. hypothecation. (294)
32. a. it is assignable. (295)
33. d. the Real Estate Settlement Procedures Act. (333)
34. d. directly originate loans. (328)
35. b. a payment does not pay the full amount of interest owed. (319)
36. a. $810 (316)
37. b. $1,458. (300)
38. c. $6,600. (300)
39. b. The greater the return, the greater the risk (423)
40. d. net sales proceeds minus adjusted basis. (430)
41. a. cash flow divided by equity. (433)
42. d. $82,000 (430)
43. b. $50,000 (431)
44. a. $3,846 (427)
45. b. 12% (433)
46. b. The total of all assessed values minus exemptions (445)
47. b. to offer tax abatement on a principal residence. (447)
48. c. multiplying the tax rate times the taxable value of the property. (447)
49. b. 5.33% (446)
50. d. $6,000 (449)
51. c. still an offer. (259)
52. b. require certain conveyances to be in writing. (257)
53. d. The buyer has a binding contract. (259)
54. d. The listing agent has violated fiduciary duties owed the client. (66)
55. d. inform the seller of the inquiry and test the paint. (67)
56. b. dual agency. (71)
57. c. Disclosure not required (72)
58. c. open listing. (265)
59. b. exclusive agency agreement. (265)
60. b. negotiation with the client. (341)
61. a. commercial properties. (69)
62. b. present any offer a buyer might decide to make. (71)
63. b. spending a customer deposit on a surety bond for the agency. (115)
64. a. This is a perfectly legitimate business practice. (97)
65. b. goodwill. (436)
66. a. blockbusting. (134)
67. c. providing unequal services. (134)
68. a. Both owner and agent. (136)
69. d. The sale contract remains valid. (273)
70. a. allow a third party fiduciary to handle the funds. (274)
71. d. The landlord is under no obligation, since options do not have a redemption period. (283)
72. b. the loan is to be sold to the FNMA. (349)
73. d. debit one party and credit the other. (351)
74. c. Taxes and interest (352)
75. a. Debit seller $345.00 (355)
76. b. Any person being paid a commission to sell the time-share (181)
77. a. contract laws. (63)
78. c. drafting a contract illegally. (96)
79. d. revoke the license without prejudice. (122)
80. a. depositing an earnest money check in a personal account. (520)
81. b. CAN-SPAM Act. (88)
82. d. Calling a potential client while blocking caller ID (88)
83. c. She has one year from the date of the alleged discrimination. (140)
84. b. In late October of each year (445)
85. a. The unpaid assessment may become a lien against the property. (183)
86. b within 1 year. (26)
87 a examination fee (27)
88. c When the applicant passes the state license exam (32)
89. b the licensed broker changes business address. (56)
90. c the license becomes null and void. (56)
91. a unimproved residential property to be used for four or fewer units. (69)
92. c represent his own opinion as an appraisal. (393)
93. b When all involved parties are fully informed of the kickback (98)
94. c 10 days (99)
95. b Joint venture (103)
96. c 30 (120)
97. c Criminal courts (125)

98. b   3 days (144)
99. a   CDD (185)
100. c   The person who started a series of events that led to a sale (13)
101. a   for tax purposes. (245)
102. c   The Florida coastal property disclosure requires documentation indicating the location of the coastal construction control line. (281)
103. b   mortgage loans. (356)
104. a   Must be compensated as an employee (106)
105. a   determining the business valuation. (437)
106. c   The land must be classified every year. (449)
107. b   January 1 following the tax year (450)
108. c   7 years. (450)
109. c   Water tight below the base flood elevation (472)
110. c   V zone (472)

GLOSSARY OF GENERAL REAL ESTATE TERMS

absentee owner A property owner who does not occupy the home. A primary reason for increases in property management practitioners.

absorption The consumption of available vacant property in a building or market.

abstract of title A written, chronological record of the title records affecting rights and interests in a parcel of real property.

acceleration A right granted through a loan clause enabling the lender to call all sums immediately due and payable on a loan should the borrower violate certain provisions of the loan agreement.

accretion An increase in land caused by natural phenomena, for example a deposit of sand on a beachfront property due to a tropical storm.

acknowledgement A formal declaration made before a duly authorized officer, usually a notary public. Also known as notarization.

active license A licensee who is approved by the state to provide the services of real estate.

actual notice Knowledge given or received directly through demonstrable evidence. Actual notice of ownership: reading a bill of sale, inspecting a deed, searching title records. See also *constructive notice*.

adjudication withheld The final decision in a disputed case; a form of deferred judgment which may allow someone to avoid jail time and keep their public record clear.

adjustable-rate mortgage A mortgage loan having an interest rate that can be periodically raised or lowered in accordance with the movement of a financial index.

adjusted basis The beginning basis, or cost, of a property plus the costs of capital improvements, minus all depreciation expense.

administrative complaint The original complaint issued by a member of the public that leads to investigation of a licensee.

ad valorem tax A real property's annual tax levied by taxing entities according to the property's assessed value.

adverse possession The entry, occupation, and use of another's property without the consent of the owner or where the owner took no action to evict the adverse possessor. May lead to loss of legal title if the adverse possessor fulfills certain requirements.

agency A fiduciary relationship between an agent and a principal where respective rights and duties are prescribed by laws of agency and by the agency agreement executed by the two parties. See *universal agency*, *limited agency*, and *fiduciary*.

agent The party in an agency relationship who is hired by the principal to perform certain duties. In so doing, the agent must also uphold fiduciary duties owed the principal.

air rights Rights in real property as they apply to the property's airspace, or all space above the surface within the parcel's legal boundaries.

air space The air portion of real property. In a condominium unit, the freehold space enclosed by the unit's outer walls, floor, and ceiling.

alienation A transfer of title to real property by voluntary or involuntary means.

allocation of markets An act of collusion where two or more competitors agree to limit competitive activity in portions of the market in exchange for reciprocal restrictions from the others.

amortization A partial or complete reduction of a loan's principal balance over the loan term, achieved by periodic payments which include principal as well as interest. See *negative amortization*.

annual percentage rate (APR) The total cost of credit to a borrower inclusive of finance charges and the stated interest rate, expressed as an annual rate of interest.

antitrust laws Legislation aimed at preventing unfair trade practices and monopoly, including collusion, price fixing, and allocation of markets.

appraisal An opinion of value of a property developed by a professional and disinterested third party and supported by data and evidence.

appraiser A duly trained and licensed professional authorized to perform appraisals for other parties.

appreciation An increase in the value of a property generally owing to economic forces beyond the control of the owner.

appurtenance A right, interest, or improvement that attaches to and transfers with a parcel of real property, such as an easement or a riparian right.

arbitration A dispute-settlement protocol where a selected third-party hears a case presented by both sides of a disagreement and makes an opinion on who wins the case. Often both sides sign an agreement that they will abide by the decision of the arbitrator. Also known as binding arbitration.

arrears Payment that occurs at the end of a payment term rather than at the beginning. Examples of items paid in arrears include taxes and interest.

asbestos A fire resistant material used in a vary of building products. Asbestos is known to be carcinogenic. Contractors must have special training to remove building materials containing asbestos.

assemblage A combining of contiguous parcels of real estate into a single tract, performed with the expectation that increased value will result.

assessed value The value of a property as established by assessors for the purpose of ad valorem taxation.

assessment A periodic charge payable by condominium owners for the maintenance of the property's common elements.

asset A tangible or intangible item of value.

asset sale A sale of a business involving the transfer of assets as opposed to the liabilities or stock.

assignment A transfer of one's entire interest in an item of real or personal property. The assignor transfers the interest to the assignee.

assumption In a sale of real property, the transfer of the seller's mortgage loan obligations to the buyer. Requires, in most cases, the approval of the lender.

attorney-at-fact A third party who is authorized by another person to act in his place. Usually done by means of a power of attorney.

automated valuation model A software-based tool using statistics and math used in residential and commercial real estate to determine property value.

balloon mortgage See *partial amortized mortgage*.

balloon payment A lump sum payment on any loan which retires the remaining loan balance in full.

base line An imaginary latitude line within the rectangular survey system that is designated in relation to a principal meridian for purposes of identifying townships.

beginning basis The original cost or market value of an acquired asset.

benchmark A registered marker denoting an official elevation above sea level; used by surveyors to identify other elevations in the area.

beneficiary A party named to benefit from the yield or disposition of an asset identified in a trust, insurance policy, or will.

bilateral contract A contract where both parties promise to perform in exchange for performance by the other party. See *unilateral contract*.

binder A temporary agreement to buy a property evidenced by a valuable deposit. Receipt of the deposit binds a seller to a good-faith agreement to sell a property, provided a complete sale contract is executed within a certain period.

biweekly mortgage A mortgage where payments are made once every two weeks. This results in one extra payment per month causing the mortgage to be paid off early and saving thousands in interest.

blanket mortgage A mortgage use by developers to cover an entire building project. Usually contains a partial release clause allowing one piece of property to be released as a specific sum of money is paid to the bank.

blind ad An advertisement that does not contain the identity of the advertiser.

blockbusting Inducing property owners to sell or rent their holdings due to an impending downturn in their property ,values, often owing to a change in the area's ethnic or social composition.

breach of trust A failure of the agent to properly render the duties owed to the principal.

broker A direct agent of the principal who is hired for compensation to perform a stated service such as procuring a customer.

broker's opinion of value An estimate of a property's value rendered by a party who is not necessarily licensed, objective, or qualified. The estimate may not be a complete appraisal.

brokerage The business of procuring customers on behalf of clients for the purpose of completing a real estate transaction.

buffer zone A strip of land separating one land use from another land use.

business brokerage The brokerage of a business enterprise in addition to any real property it may own or lease.

Building code A specific standard of construction or maintenance of any aspect of an improved property established by local government officials.

bundle of rights A set of rights associated with ownership of property, including the rights to possess, use, transfer, encumber and exclude.

business broker A person who is a licensed real estate agent who brokers business concerns for other parties.

business trust See *syndication*.

buydown A loan arrangement where the borrower pays extra interest in advance for the future benefit of a lower interest rate over the loan term.

buyer representation agreement A broker's listing with a buyer to locate a suitable property for purchase or lease.

buyer's market A market characterized by an excess of sellers over buyers.

capital gain (or loss) The difference between the net sales proceeds of an asset and its adjusted basis.

capital improvement An upgrading of improved property having sufficient magnitude to constitute an addition to the property's basis. Contrasts with repair and maintenance.

capitalization rate The rate of return on capital an investor will demand from the investment property, or the rate of return that the property will actually produce.

cash flow The remaining positive or negative amount of income an investment produces after subtracting all operating expenses and debt service from gross income.

caveat emptor Latin for 'let the buyer beware'. FREC was created to do change this mindset among licensees in residential real estate transactions. Effected primarily by requiring certain disclosures of defects.

ceases to be enforced A licensee cannot perform real estate when his or her license ceases to be enforced. Usually happens when a broker moves the office and does not notify DBPR of the new address.

certificate of occupancy A document confirming that a newly constructed or renovated property has fully complied with all building codes and is ready for occupancy and use.

certificate of title A document expressing the opinion of a title officer or attorney that a property seller is in fact the owner of good title based on a review of title records.

chain of title Successive property owners of record dating back to the original grant of title from the state to a private party.

chattel An item of personal property.

check A 24 x 24 mile set of lines used in appraisals to allow for the curvature of the earth.

citation A punishment given by FREC for violation of a rule. Usually contains a monetary amount that must be paid.

closing A meeting of principal parties where a seller transfers title and a buyer pays monies owed the seller and lender.

closing statement A financial summary and settlement of a property transaction indicating sums due and payable by the buyer and seller.

cloud An encumbrance or claim on title to property impeding or diminishing its marketability.

co-brokerage A brokerage practice where agents and brokers outside of the listing broker's agency assist as subagents in procuring a customer in exchange for portions of the commission.

collateral Property liened by a lender as security for a loan.

collusion An unlawful agreement between competitors to monopolize a market, disadvantage other competitors, or otherwise undertake activities in violation of fair trade laws.

color of title A defective title transfer or the transfer of a defective title where the new owner is originally unaware of the defect. Color of title may be used as a grounds for adverse possession, which, if successful, would nullify the original defect.

commingling An unlawful practice of mixing escrow funds with the agency's operating funds.

common elements 1. Portions of a condominium property that are owned by all unit owners, for example the grounds, parking facilities, lobby, and elevators. 2. Portions of a commercial property used by all occupants as well as the public, for which the tenants may have to share in the repair and maintenance costs.

common law A body of law developed by court judgments, decrees, and case decisions.

Community Association Manager (CAM) A specialty-licensed individual who manages a Homeowner's or Condominium Association with more than 10 units or a budget of $100,000 or more.

community development districts A managed development area whose management entity takes out loans to develop the infrastructure of such an area, or community. The community is then charged non-ad valorum taxes to repay the loan.

community property A system of property ownership established by law which generally defines rights of property ownership of spouses; community property is co-owned by spouses, and separate property is owned by a single spouse. Generally, property acquired during the marriage with jointly held funds is community property.

comparable A property having similar characteristics to a subject property in an appraisal. The value or sale price of the comparable is used to estimate the value of the subject.

comparable sales approach See *sales comparison approach*.

comparative market analysis (CMA) A method used by brokers and salespeople for estimating the current value of a property using sale price data from similar properties. Not to be confused with a bona fide appraisal performed by a licensed appraiser.

compensation Payment for services rendered by licensees. May be money or anything of value.

competent party A person who has the legal capacity to enter into a contract.

complaint A formal document that outlines the grievances one person has against another person or company.

concealment The act of intentionally or unintentionally not revealing information that should be disclosed

concurrency A local, county, or regional planning policy that requires developers to correct foreseen negative impacts of a development during the construction period of the project itself rather than afterwards; for example, widening a road during construction to accommodate a future increase in traffic.

condemnation 1. A decree by a court or municipal authority that a parcel of private property is to be taken for public use under the power of eminent domain. 2. A government order that a particular property is no longer fit for use and must be demolished.

condominium estate An estate distinguished by fee simple ownership of the airspace of a unit plus an undivided interest with the other unit owners in the overall property's common elements.

conflicting demands When both the buyer and seller are requesting the earnest money deposits after a sales contract falls through.

conforming loan

consent to transition

consideration An item of tangible or intangible value, or one's promise to do or not do some act which is used as an inducement to another party to enter into a contract.

constructive notice Knowledge one could or should have, according to the presumption of law; a demonstration to the public of property ownership through title recordation, "for all to see." See *actual notice*.

contingency A condition that must be satisfied for a contract to be binding and enforceable.

contract A potentially enforceable agreement between two or more parties who agree to perform or not perform some act. If valid, the contract is enforceable, with limited exceptions.

contract for deed A financial contract where a seller retains legal title to a property and gives the buyer equitable title and possession over a period of time. During the contract period, the seller finances all or part of the purchase price. If the buyer makes timely payments and abides by all contract provisions, the seller conveys legal title at the end of the contract period.

contribution The increment of market value added to a property through the addition of a component or improvement to the property. Not to be confused with the cost of the component.

conventional loan A permanent long-term loan that is not FHA-insured or VA-guaranteed.

conversion 1. Changing real property to personal property, and vice versa. 2. An illegal act of appropriating escrow funds for payment of an agency's operating expenses.

conveyance A voluntary transfer of real property interests.

cooperative estate Ownership of shares in a cooperative association which acquires a multi-unit dwelling as its primary asset. Shareholders also receive a proprietary lease on a unit for the duration of their share ownership.

corporation A legal entity created under state law. It must register as a brokerage. All officers or directors performing the services of real estate must be registered as active brokers.

cost approach A method for determining value that takes into account the cost of the land and the replacement or reproduction cost of the improvements net of estimated depreciation.

cost recovery See *depreciation*.

counteroffer Any new offer or amended offer made in response to an offer. See *offer*.

covenant A written warrant or promise set forth in a contract or other legal document by one or both of the parties to the contract.

credit 1. An accounting entry on a closing statement indicating an amount a party has paid or is to receive. 2. Loan funds advanced to a borrower.

credit evaluation A lender's opinion of a borrower's ability to repay a loan in view of financial capabilities and past repayment patterns.

culpable negligence Failing to do something which a reasonably careful person would do, or the lack of the usual ordinary care and caution in the performance of an act usually and ordinarily exercised by a person under similar circumstances and conditions.

curable In correcting the deficiency of a given property improvement, if the cost to remedy the deficiency is equal to or less than the anticipated increase in the value of the property, the deficiency is considered to be curable – as opposed to incurable.

curtesy A widower's life estate claim to portions of his deceased spouse's real property. See also *dower*.

customer In agency law, a party outside of the fiduciary relationship of client and agent. If an agent treats a customer as a client, an implied agency may result.

datum A standard elevation reference point used by surveyors to measure elevations of property in an area.

debit An accounting entry on a closing statement indicating an amount a party must pay.

debt coverage ratio An underwriting equation reflecting how much debt service an investment property can reasonably afford to pay out of its net operating income; used to identify how large a loan the property can afford given an interest rate and loan term.

debt ratio An underwriting equation that is used to determine how much debt an individual can reasonably afford in view of the party's or household's income.

debt service Periodic payments of interest and/or principal on a mortgage loan.

declaration A legal document that a developer must file with the state to create a condominium. A copy must be given to potential buyers.

dedication Land given back to the local government to maintain as part of a plat map.

deed A written instrument that conveys real property from one party to another.

deed in lieu of foreclosure An instrument used to convey mortgaged property back to the lender rather than have the lender foreclose on the property.

deed in trust An instrument used to convey real property to the trustee of a land trust. The trustor is also the beneficiary. See *land trust*.

deed of trust An instrument used by a borrower to convey title to mortgaged property to a trustee to be held as security for the lender, who is the beneficiary of the trust.

deed restriction A provision in a deed that limits or places rules on how the deeded property may be used or improved.

defeasance clause Found in mortgages, a clause that states that, once the buyer has paid the entire amount due in the mortgage, the lender's hold on the property is defeated.

defeasible fee A fee estate where ownership is perpetual, provided that usage restrictions or other conditions stated in the deed are upheld. If not, the fee reverts to the grantor either automatically (determinable fee) or by the grantor's actions (condition subsequent).

deficiency judgment A court order enabling a damaged lender to attach a lien on the defaulted borrower's property for an amount equal to the difference between the debt and the proceeds of a foreclosure sale.

demand A quantity of a product or service that is desired for purchase, lease, or trade at any given time.

density A measure of the degree of residential land use within a given area for purposes of residential zoning and land use control.

deposit Valuable consideration accompanying an offer to purchase real estate that signifies the offeror's good faith intention to complete a sale or lease contract.

depreciable basis The portion of a property's total basis that may be depreciated, generally the basis of the improvements, since land cannot be depreciated.

depreciation 1. A non-cash expense taken against the income of investment property that allows the owner to recover the cost of the investment through tax savings. 2. A loss of value to improved property.

descent and distribution, laws of A body of state-level laws that stipulates how an estate will be passed on to heirs in the absence of a valid will.

designated sales associate A type of real estate relationship that is created in a nonresidential transaction where one agent is assigned to the buyer and one agent is assigned to the seller as single agent. Both parties must have assets of at least $1 million.

determinable fee A defeasible fee estate where title automatically reverts to the grantor if usage conditions stated in the deed are violated.

devise A transfer of real or personal property from the devisor to the devisee(s) by means of a will.

disability A physical or mental impairment that substantially impacts one or more of the major life functions such as walking, seeing, learning or working.

discount point A fee charged by the lender that increases the lenders yield on a given loan. Currently, each point increases the bank's yield by 1/8%.

discounting A financial practice of reducing the value of dollars received in the future by an amount that reflects the interest that would have been earned if the dollars had been received today. Performed to measure the present value of an investment's future income.

discounted cash flow analysis A financial analysis to identify the discounted value of the cash flow of an investment over a given number of years. See *discounting* and *cash flow*.

discrimination in housing A failure to provide equal opportunity for persons to acquire or finance housing based on race, color, religion, national origin, sex, handicapped status, marital status, or family status.

disintermediation Direct investment without the intermediation of a bank or other depository institution to make loans and other investments.

documentary stamp A tax stamp affixed to a property document or record as evidence that the owner has paid taxes related to the financing or transfer of real property.

dominant tenement The property that benefits from the existence of an easement appurtenant. The holder of the easement is the dominant tenant. See *servient tenement*.

dower A widow's life estate interest in portions of her deceased spouse's real property.

dual agency Representing both principal parties to a transaction.

due on sale A loan provision defining the lender's right to accelerate a note upon the transfer of collateralized property.

earnest money escrow An impound account used for the safekeeping of a buyer's earnest money deposit; accompanied by specific instructions to the escrow agent for holding and disbursing the funds.

easement An interest in real property giving the interest holder the right to use defined portions of another's property. May or may not attach to the estate.

economic life The period during which an improvement is expected to remain useful in its original use. Establishes the improvement's annual depreciation amounts in appraisal. Depreciation in tax accounting is determined by a property's cost recovery class, which is related to economic life.

economic obsolescence A loss of value in a property because of external factors generally beyond the control of the owner, for example, a municipality's lack of funds to improve deteriorated roadways. Also called external obsolescence.

effective gross income The actual income of an investment property before expenses, expressed as total potential income minus vacancy and collection losses.

elective share A right of a surviving spouse to claim a prescribed portion of the decedent's real and personal property in place of the provisions of the decedent's will.

emblements Plants and crops considered personal property, since human labor is required for planting, growing and harvesting.

emergency summary suspension See *summary suspension.*

eminent domain A power of a government entity to force the sale of private property for subsequent public use.

encroachment An unauthorized physical intrusion of one's real property into the real property of another.

encumbrance An interest, right or intrusion that limits the freehold interest of an owner of real property or otherwise adversely effects the marketability of title.

enforceability Legal status of a valid contract or other document that a court of law will force to be performed.

environmental impact statement A report required by the EPA whenever a given development project will significantly impact a piece of land and its surrounding area.

equalization An averaging of assessed valuations in an area to compensate for ad valorem tax inequities.

equilibrium A theoretical market state in which the forces of supply and demand are in balance.

equitable title An interest that gives a lienholder or buyer the right to acquire legal title to a property if certain contractual conditions occur.

equity That portion of a property's value owned by the legal owner, expressed as the difference between the property's market value and all loan balances outstanding on the property.

equity of redemption A mortgagor's right to pay off a defaulted mortgage and reclaim the property, provided the redemption occurs before the completion of the foreclosure sale.

escalator clause A lease clause providing for an increase in rent.

escheat A reversionary transfer of real property to the state or county when the legal owner dies without a will and without heirs.

escrow 1. A trust or impound account used for the proper handling of funds and documents in the closing of a real property transaction. 2. An account that a lender requires a borrower to establish to ensure that adequate funds will be available for payment of taxes and insurance on a mortgaged property.

escrow account A disinterested third party who holds funds in trust for another party until the terms of the sales contract are fulfilled.

escrow disbursement order (EDO) A FREC-originated order issued to an agent who has conflicting escrow account demands by a buyer and seller sends all pertinent information to FREC for a decision on how to disburse the disputed funds.

estate 1. A set of rights to real property that includes the right of possession. 2. The totality of one's personal and real property ownership.

estate for years An estate where one party leases property for a specific period of time.

estate in land An estate.

estoppel A legal restraint to prevent a person from claiming a right or interest that is inconsistent with the person's previous statements or acts. An estoppel certificate documents the party's initial position or act, which cannot be contradicted later.

ethics Standards governing proper and professional business practices.

eviction Removal of a tenant from a property because of a lease default.

evidence of title Actual or constructive notice of real property ownership, including opinion of title, certificate of title, and title insurance.

exclusion One of the bundle of legal rights to real property enabling the owner to prevent others from entry or use.

exclusive agency A listing agreement which pays the listing broker a commission if anyone other than the property owner procures a customer.

exclusive right to sell A listing agreement which pays the listing broker a commission if anyone at all procures a customer.

executory contract A completed agreement which enjoins one or both principal parties to perform certain actions in order for the contract to become fully executed.

exempt property Property that does not have to pay property taxes due to its IRS status, for example, a 501(c)3 charity.

expungement A type of lawsuit in which a first-time offender of a prior criminal conviction seeks to seal or eliminate the official records of such a conviction.

facilitator A transaction broker who assists principal parties in completing a transaction without acting as a fiduciary agent of either party.

failure to account and deliver Situation where one party in a transaction does not meet their obligation to either pay for or deliver an asset

fair financing laws Anti-discrimination legislation designed to ensure that all parties have equal access to mortgage financing.

fair housing laws Anti-discrimination legislation designed to ensure equal opportunity in housing to all home buyers.

familial status A protected class that involves households with one or more individuals under the age of 18 or a person expecting a child.

farm area A geographical area wherein a real estate agent practices brokerage and over time becomes the market expert of such area

Federal Deposit Insurance Corporation A quasi-governmental agency that insures deposits of depository institutions and otherwise develops regulations for the banking industry.

Federal Home Loan Mortgage Corporation (Freddie Mac) A major secondary mortgage market organization which buys conventional, FHA, and VA loans and sells mortgage-backed securities.

Federal Housing Administration An agency of the Department of Housing and Urban Development which insures permanent long-term loans that meet certain qualifications.

Federal National Mortgage Association (Fannie Mae) A government-sponsored agency in the secondary mortgage market which buys conventional, FHA, and VA loans, sells mortgage-backed securities, and guarantees payment of principal and interest on the securities.

Federal Reserve System The principal regulator of the money supply as well as of the American banking system.

federally-related transaction Any sales transaction which involves, at some point in the transaction, a federal agency. The agency is commonly a primary or secondary mortgage market lender.

fee simple An estate representing the highest form of legal ownership of real property, particularly the fee simple absolute estate.

fiduciary The agent in an agency relationship; receives the trust and confidence of the principal and owes fiduciary duties to the principal.

fiduciary duties Duties of an agent to the principal in an agency relationship, including skill, care, diligence, loyalty, obedience, confidentiality, disclosure, and accounting.

fixture An item permanently attached to land so as to be defined as real property.

Florida resident A person who resides in Florida for 4 or more months within one year.

foreclosure A procedure for forcing sale of a secured property to satisfy a lienholder's claim.

formal complaint A written complaint filed against a licensee.

fraud An intentional deception to secure unfair or unlawful gain, or to deprive a victim of a legal right.

freehold estate An ownership estate of indeterminable duration; contrasts with a leasehold estate.

full-service lease A lease requiring the landlord to pay all of a property's operating expenses, including those that pertain to an individual tenant.

functional obsolescence A loss of value in an improved property because of design flaws or failure of the property to meet current standards. May be curable or incurable.

further assurance A promise that the grantor will do whatever is necessary to remove a defect associated with title, such as an encumbrance, if it arises, and if the problem is not fixed, damages will be awarded

general agency A fiduciary relationship which authorizes the agent to conduct a broad range of activities for the principal in a particular business enterprise. May or may not include authority to enter into contracts.

general lien A lien against any and all property owned by a lienee.

general partnership A for-profit business where two or more co-owners agree to share management responsibilities and profits. Does not involve silent partners, as in a limited partnership.

general warranty deed A bargain and sale deed containing the assurance that the grantor will defend against any and all claims to the title.

going concern value The value of an on-going business which takes into account the tangible and intangible assets of the business.

good faith doubt When the broker has doubt as to who should receive a given escrow deposit.

goodwill An intangible business asset valued at the difference between the sale price and the value of all other assets of the business.

Government National Mortgage Association (Ginnie Mae) A division of HUD which guarantees FNMA mortgages and securities backed by pools of VA-guaranteed and FHA-insured mortgages.

government survey system See *rectangular survey system.*

grantee A party who receives a right, interest, or title to real property from another.

granting clause Phraseology in a deed that indicates the grantor's intent to transfer an interest in property.

grantor A party who transfers a right, interest, or title to real property to another.

gross easement A personal right to use another's property, granted by the owner; does not attach to the estate, and there are no dominant or servient tenements.

gross income multiplier A shortcut method for estimating the value of an income property. The procedure involves multiplying the property's gross annual income times a multiplier that reflects the ratio between gross annual income and sale price that is typical for similar properties in the area.

gross rent multiplier A shortcut method for estimating the value of an income property. The procedure involves multiplying the property's gross monthly rent times a multiplier that reflects the ratio between gross monthly rent and sale price that is typical for similar properties in the area.

gross lease See *full-service lease.*

ground lease A lease of the land-only portion of a parcel of real property

group license A license issued to a Sales Associate or Broker's Associate who works for an owner/developer who owns multiple entities.

habendum clause The clause in the deed describing the quality and duration of ownership.

handicap status See *disability.*

hazard insurance Insurance against loss or damage to real property improvements; required by most mortgage lenders to protect the collateral.

health ordinance Laws set out to protect the health and welfare of the people.

highest and best use A theoretical use of a property that is legally permissible, physically possible, financially feasible, and maximally productive, usually in terms of net income generation.

holographic will A will prepared entirely in the testator's handwriting, complete with date and signature.

Home equity conversion mortgage (HECM) A mortgage where the equity in the home is taken out by an owner, older than 62 years old. The funds do not need to be paid back until after the owner's death. Also known as a *reverse mortgage.*

home equity loan A junior mortgage loan on a residence, secured by portions of the owner's equity in the home.

homestead laws Laws that protect a homeowner against loss of the homeowner's principle residence to a sale forced by creditors to collect debts. Homestead laws also protect the interests of individual spouses by requiring both spouses to sign any conveyance of the homestead property.

homestead tax exemption An exemption of a portion of the assessed value of a homeowner's principal residence from ad valorem taxation.

household A family or group of people living within a single residence.

hypothecation Use of real property as collateral for a mortgage loan.

immune property Government-owned property that is not required to pay property taxes.

implied agency An agency relationship that arises by implication from the actions and representations of either agent or principal.

implied contract An unstated or unintentional agreement that may be deemed to exist by implication because of acts or statements by any of the parties to the agreement.

implied listing See *implied agency.*

improvement Any manmade structure or item affixed to land.

inactive license A license that is not active, thus the licensee can't perform the services of real estate.

income capitalization A method of appraising the value of a property by applying a rate of return to the property's net income.

income ratio An underwriting ratio that relates a borrower's gross or net income and the debt service of a loan; used to determine how large a loan a borrower can reasonably afford.

Incurable A term used in appraising, when the cost of an improvement is greater than the value it adds to the property.

independent contractor A sales agent who works for a broker but is not legally an employee. The employer exerts only limited control over the contractor's actions, does not provide employee benefits, and does not withhold taxes from the contractor's pay.

index The component of an adjustable-rate mortgage that, as a changing financial indicator, determines the upward or downward movement of the loan's interest rate

inferior lien A lien whose priority is subordinate to that of a superior lien. Priority among inferior liens is established according to the time of recordation, with the exception of the mechanic's lien. Also called junior lien.

installment contract See *contract for deed.*

interest 1. A right to real property. 2. A lender's charge for the use of the principal amount of a loan.

interest rate The percentage of a loan amount that a borrower must pay a lender annually as interest on a loan amount.

intermediation Investment by a depository institution on behalf of depositors.

internal rate of return The rate at which inflows from an income property investment must be discounted in order for the total inflows over time to equal the initial outlay, expressed as a percent; may include projected proceeds from the future sale of the property as an inflow.

interval ownership See *time-share.*

intestate Legal condition of a person who dies without leaving a will.

investment Expenditure to purchase an asset with the expectation of deriving a future profit or benefit from the asset.

involuntary alienation A transfer of title to real property without the consent or against the will of the owner, for example, eminent domain, foreclosure, and adverse possession.

involuntary inactive A license status that is triggered whenever a license is not renewed in a timely manner. It may stay in this status for 24 months. After 24 months the license becomes null and void,

involuntary lien A lien imposed by legal process irrespective of the owner's wishes or consent.

joint tenancy A form of real property ownership in which co-owners share all rights and interests equally and indivisibly; entails right of survivorship. Parties must establish tenancy at the same time and with a single deed.

joint venture A partnership created for a specific, pre-determined business endeavor, after which the joint venture is usually dissolved.

judgment A court decision resulting from a lawsuit. If a creditor sues to collect a debt, a favorable ruling is followed by a judgment lien against the defaulting borrower's property.

judicial foreclosure A court proceeding triggered by a foreclosure suit. Involves notice, debt acceleration, the termination of the owner's interests in the property, and a public sale where proceeds are applied to the debt.

junior lien See *inferior lien*.

just value The fair market value of a piece of property as assessed for the purpose of establishing its property taxes.

kickback A payment made to someone who has facilitated a transaction or appointment. Can be legal or illicit.

land The surface area of the earth, all natural things permanently attached to the earth, and everything beneath the surface to the earth's center and above the surface extending upward to infinity.

land contract See *contract for deed*.

land development loans Loans used specifically to build homes or infrastructure. Usually given to contractors or developers.

land trust A trust in which a trustor conveys a fee estate to a trustee and names himself or herself as beneficiary. The beneficiary in turn controls the property and the actions of the trustee.

land use control Regulation of how individual owners use property in a municipality or planning district. Control patterns are generally in accordance with a master plan.

landlocked A parcel of property lacking legal access to a public thoroughfare; requires a court-ordered easement by necessity to relieve the condition.

law of agency A body of law defining roles, duties and responsibilities of an agent and a principal. Laws also set forth standards of conduct agent and principal owe to a customer.

lease A legal contract and instrument of conveyance which transfers to the tenant, or lessee, a leasehold fee for a certain duration. The lease contract sets forth all tenant and landlord covenants, financial terms, and grounds for default. The landlord is referred to as the lessor.

legal life estate A life estate established by operation of law rather than by the actions or wishes of the property owners. Examples are homestead law, dower, curtesy, and elective share.

legal title Full legal ownership of property and the bundle of rights as they apply to it. Contrasts with equitable title.

leasehold estate An estate that entails temporary rights of use, possession, and to an extent, exclusion, but not legal ownership. Compare *freehold estate*.

legal description A description of a parcel of property which accurately locates and identifies the boundaries of the subject parcel to a degree acceptable by local courts of law.

leverage The relationship between the yield rate of an investment and the interest rate of funds borrowed to finance the investment. If the yield rate is greater than the loan rate, positive leverage results. If the yield rate is less than the loan rate, negative leverage results.

liability 1. An accounting entry representing a claim against the assets of a business by a creditor. 2. A condition of vulnerability to lawsuits seeking redress for potentially wrongful acts or statements.

license 1. Legal authorization to conduct business. 2. An individual's personal right to use the property of another for a specific purpose. Revocable at any time at the owner's discretion. Does not attach to the property and terminates upon the death of either party.

licensure Granted once a person has met all of the legal requirements to obtain a real estate license. These include registration, Commission approval, education, and passing the examination.

lien A creditor's claim against real or personal property as security for a property owner's debt. A lien enables a creditor to force the sale of the property and collect proceeds as payment toward the debt.

lien priority The order in which liens against a property are satisfied; the highest priority lien receives sale proceeds from a foreclosure before any other lien.

lien theory state A state whose laws give a lender on a mortgaged property equitable title rather than legal title. The mortgagor in a lien theory state retains legal title. See *title theory state*.

life estate A freehold estate that is limited in duration to the life of the owner or other named person. On the death of this person, legal title passes to the grantor or other named party.

lifetime cap The maximum amount the interest rate on an adjustable rate mortgage may increase over the life of the loan.

like-kind exchange A tax-deferred transaction that allows for the disposal of an asset and the acquisition of another similar asset without generating a capital gains tax liability from the sale of the first asset. Also known at a 1031 Exchange.

limited agency An agency relationship which restricts the agent's authorizations to a specific set of duties. The relationship usually terminates on performance of these duties, as in a real estate broker's listing agreement. Also called special agency.

Limited liability company (LLC) A state-approved business entity that conjoins a sole proprietorship with the limited personal protections afforded by a corporation.

Limited liability partnership (LLP) A state-approved partnership entity that melds a partnership with the limited personal protections of a corporation.

limited partnership A business enterprise consisting of general and limited partners where the general partners manage the affairs of the business while the limited partners are silent investors.

Limited representation In the law of agency, a transaction broker's set of responsibilities to the customer. These include avoiding discussions of the price, terms or motivation of the transaction with either side.

liquidated damages In a contract, a clause that expressly provides for compensation a defaulting party owes the damaged party. In the absence of such a clause, a damaged party may sue for unliquidated damages.

liquidity The degree to which an investment is readily marketable, or convertible to another form of asset. If immediately salable, an investment is liquid; the longer it takes to sell, the more illiquid the investment. Real property is relatively illiquid in comparison with other types of investment.

lis pendens A public notice in a foreclosure proceeding that the mortgaged property may soon have a judgment issued against it. Enables other investors to join in the proceeding if they wish to collect their debts.

listing A legal contract that establishes and controls the dynamics of the agency relationship between principal and agent. The principal to the listing may be buyer, seller, landlord, or tenant.

Litigation The process of resolving disputes by filing or answering a complaint through the public court system.

littoral rights A set of water rights defined by state law relating to properties abutting navigable bodies of water such as lakes and bays. Generally, a property owner enjoys usage rights but owns land only to the high-water mark. See *riparian rights* and *prior appropriation*.

living trust A trust established during one's lifetime in which the trustor conveys legal title to property to a trustee and names another party as beneficiary. The trustee discharges management duties and the beneficiary receives all profit and gain net of the trustee's fees.

loan commitment A lender's written pledge to lend funds under specific terms. May contain deadlines and conditions.

loan origination fee A fee charged by the lender to process the initial paperwork of the mortgage. Usually based on a percentage of the loan.

loan servicing Managing the fulfillment of a mortgage loan's primary obligations such as making timely payments.

loan-to-value ratio (LTV) An underwriting ratio that relates the size of a loan to the market value of the collateral. The closer the loan value is to market value, the riskier the loan is for the lender, since the lender is less likely to recover the debt fully from the proceeds of a foreclosure sale.

lot and block system A method for legally describing property in a subdivision where lots are identified by block and number. A recorded metes and bounds or rectangular survey description of the subdivision underlies the lot and block system.

margin The number of percentage points added to an adjustable rate loan's index after the initial rate period has ended. Thus, (index amount + margin) = interest rate)

market 1. Buyers and sellers exchanging goods and services through the price mechanism. 2. The totality of interactions between supply and demand for a specific set of products or services in a particular geographic area.

market equilibrium See *equilibrium*.

market value An opinion of the price at which a willing seller and buyer would trade a property at a given time, assuming a cash sale, reasonable exposure to the market, informed parties, marketable title, and no abnormal pressure to transact.

marketable title A condition of title to a property where there are no claims, liens, or encumbrances clouding title or impeding the property's transferability.

marketing plan An agent's design for procuring a customer for a client, including selling and promotional activities.

master deed A deed used to convey land to a condominium developer.

master plan An amalgamated land use plan for a municipality, county, or region which incorporates community opinion, the results of intensive research, and the various land use guidelines and regulations of the state. Acts as a blueprint for subsequent zoning ordinances and rulings.

materialman's lien See *mechanic's lien*

mechanic's lien A junior lien enabling property builders, suppliers, and contractors to secure debt arising from labor and materials expended on a property. Distinguished by its order or priority, which is based on when the work was performed rather than when the lien was recorded.

mediation A process where an independent third party helps to solve a dispute between parties through negotiation.

meeting of the minds The culmination of the negotiating process where both parties to an agreement agree to all of the terms of the contract.

meridian A north-south line used in the rectangular survey system of legal descriptions.

metes and bounds A method of legally describing property which utilizes physical boundary markers and compass directions for describing the perimeter boundaries of a parcel.

millage rate The ad valorem tax rate of a taxing district, derived by dividing revenues required from taxpayers by the district's tax base. If the millage rate is 30, the tax rate

is 3%, or $3.00 per $100 of assessed valuation (net of exemptions).

mill One one-thousandth of a dollar ($.001). Used to quantify the ad valorem tax rate in dollars.

mineral rights Separable subsurface rights to mineral deposits; transferrable by sale or lease to other parties.

misrepresentation A statement or act, or failure to make a statement or act, that misleads a party in a transaction. May be intentional or unintentional. May warrant legal recourse or license revocation.

monument A fixed, artificial or natural landmark used as a reference point in a metes and bounds legal description.

moral turpitude A phrase that describes unethical, immoral, or deviant behavior constituting an inordinate and/or illegal departure from ordinary social standards such that it seriously taints an individual's professional reputation.

mortgage A legal document wherein a mortgagor pledges ownership interests in a property to a lender, or mortgagee, as collateral against performance of the mortgage debt obligation.

mortgage broker A third party intermediary who brokers mortgage loans on behalf of individuals or businesses.

mortgage financing Financing that uses mortgaged real property as security for borrowed funds.

Mortgage insurance premium (MIP) An insurance premium paid by homeowners who take out loans backed by the Federal Housing Administration (FHA). Usually paid on loans with less than 20% equity.

mortgage loan originator A third party who initiates new mortgage loans.

mortgagee The lender.

mortgagor The party who gives the mortgage, i.e., the borrower.

multiple licenses A broker who oversees multiple brokerages must have a license for each separate company and must apply for this authorization through DBPR.

multiple listing service An organization of brokers who agree to cooperate in marketing the pooled listings of all members.

mutual consent Consent by all principals to a contract to all provisions of the contract. A requirement for validity.

mutual recognition agreement An agreement with another state which has similar licensing laws and educational requirements. License applicants in these jurisdictions are required to pass a Florida-specific exam prior to getting a Florida license.

negative amortization A situation in which the loan balance of an amortizing loan increases because periodic payments are insufficient to pay all interest owed for the period. Unpaid interest is added to the principal balance.

negotiable instrument A legal instrument that can be sold, traded, assigned, or otherwise transferred to another party, such as a promissory note.

net lease A lease which requires a tenant to pay rent as well as a share of the property's operating expenses to the extent provided for in the lease contract.

net listing A listing which states a minimum sale or lease price the owner will accept, with any excess going to the broker as a commission. Professionally discouraged, if not illegal.

net operating income The amount of pre-tax revenue generated from an income property after accounting for operating expenses and before accounting for any debt service.

nolo contendere A plea where a defendant does not plead guilty or innocent. They simply ask the court to determine the sentence. Also known as a "no contest" plea.

non-conforming use A land use that is not consistent with the current zoning ordinance. May be legal or illegal.

non-conventional loan A loan with some form of Federal government backing or involvement.

non-judicial foreclosure A forced sale of mortgaged property without a formal foreclosure suit or court proceeding. Authorized through a "power of sale" clause in a mortgage or trust deed document.

non-prorated expense An expense incurred by buyer or seller in closing a real estate transaction that is not shared with the other party. Examples include attorney fees, documentary tax stamps, and lender fees.

note An agreement to repay a loan of an indicated amount under certain terms.

notice of noncompliance A letter given to a licensee which outlines a first-time minor violation. It also gives instructions on how to remedy the violation and a time frame in which to complete it.

notice of title Actual or recorded public evidence of real property ownership. See *actual notice* and *constructive notice*.

novation Substitution of an obligation to one party from another party with the original party being released from the obligation.

null and void Without legal force or effect. See *void*.

obsolescence A loss of property value because of functional or economic (external) factors. See *functional obsolescence* and *economic obsolescence*.

offer A proposal to enter into a binding contract under certain terms, submitted by an offeror to an offeree. If accepted without amendment, an offer becomes a contract.

offer and acceptance A process that creates a contract. Acceptance is the offeree's unequivocal, manifest agreement to the terms of an offer. The offer becomes a contract when the acceptance has been communicated to the offeror.

open listing A non-exclusive listing which pays an agent a commission only if the agent is procuring cause of a ready, willing, and able customer.

operating expense A recurring or periodic expense necessary for the operation of an income property. Examples include utilities, management, and ad valorem tax expenses. Excluded are debt service and the property's income tax liability.

opinion of title An attorney's or title officer's opinion of the condition and marketability of title to a parcel of property based on a recent search of title records by a competent party.

opinion of value See *broker's opinion of value*.

option A unilateral contract in which an owner, or optionor, grants a buyer or tenant, the optionee, a future right to be exercised before a deadline, in exchange for valuable consideration. The terms of the right, such as a right to purchase or lease, must be clearly stated and cannot be changed during the option period.

origination fee A lender's charge for funding a loan.

ostensible partnership Causing a party to believe that a business relationship exists when in fact there is no such relationship.

over-improvement Where the cost of an improvement is greater than the increment of property value that accompanies such improvement.

owner/developer A person or company who owns the property being sold or developed.

package mortgage A mortgage that collateralizes both real property and personal property as security for the loan.

parallel See *base line*.

parol contract An oral agreement. Potentially enforceable if validly created.

partial release clause See *blanket mortgage*.

partially amortized An amortized mortgage where there is a remaining principal balance. Such a loan if paid to its full term would require a large final payment at the end of the term. Also known as a *balloon mortgage*.

partition suit A lawsuit requesting the court to alter or cancel the interests of a co-owner in a parcel of real property. Initiated when co-owners do not agree to make the change voluntarily.

party wall easement An easement appurtenant where owners of two adjacent properties share an improvement along the property boundary. The parties agree not to perform acts that would adversely affect the other party's interest in the shared improvement.

payment cap In an adjustable rate loan, a maximum amount that a periodic payment can be upon its adjustment.

percentage lease A retail property lease which requires a tenant to pay a minimum amount of rent plus an additional increment that reflects the sales achieved by the tenant.

performance Fulfillment of the terms of a contract.

periodic cap In an adjustable rate mortgage, the maximum amount the interest rate may increase over a specific period of time.

periodic tenancy A leasehold interest for a lease term where, in the absence of default, the term automatically renews itself until proper notice of termination is provided by either party.

personal assistant A person hired as an employee or contractor to a licensee. The duties assistants may perform will depend on whether or not they are licensed.

personal property All property that is not considered real property; all property that is not land or permanently attached to land, excepting trade fixtures and emblements.

physical deterioration A loss of value to property because of decay or natural wear and tear. Exacerbated by deferred maintenance, or the failure to repair or maintain property on a regular basis.

PITI Stands for principal, interest, property tax, and hazard insurance. Together, they comprise the monthly mortgage payment for non-assessment properties. The borrower's property tax and hazard insurance payments are escrowed and paid when due by the mortgage servicer.

planned unit development (PUD) A multi-use development project requiring special zoning and involving deed restrictions.

plat A map of one or more properties indicating each parcel's lot and block number, boundaries, and dimensions.

plottage An increment of value added by the assemblage of contiguous properties.

point One-percent of a loan amount, a lender's finance charge.

point of beginning (POB) The origination and termination point in a metes and bounds legal description.

police power A state's or local government's legal authority to create, regulate, tax, and condemn real property in the interest of the public's health, safety, and welfare.

potential gross income The maximum amount of revenue a property could generate before accounting for vacancy, collection loss, and expenses. Consists of total rent with full occupancy at established rent rates, plus other income from any source.

power of attorney An authorization granting a fiduciary the power to perform specified acts on the principal's behalf. Used to establish a universal agency relationship.

pre-closing inspections An inspection done prior to closing to ensure there is no damage to the property when the seller was moving out. Inspections additionally ensure that all of the personal property and fixtures to be conveyed are present after the seller has vacated.

prepayment clause A clause in the mortgage that allows the mortgagor to make early payments and payoff the mortgage in advance of loan maturity.

prepayment penalty A clause in the mortgage that does not allow the mortgagor to make extra payments to pay off the mortgage early. It specifies the penalty and timeframe for when the penalty is valid.

present value The discounted value of an amount of money to be received in the future that accounts for the interest that would have been earned if the money had been received in the present.

price fixing An act of collusion where competitors agree to establish prices at certain levels to the detriment of customers or other competitors.

price mechanism An interaction of supply and demand that determines a price a buyer and seller agree is the value of a good or service to be exchanged. A quantification of value in a transaction.

prima facie evidence A fact which is presumed to be true or legally sufficient to establish that fact unless it is rebutted or disproved by evidence to the contrary.

primary mortgage market Lenders and mortgage brokers who originate mortgage loans directly to borrowers.

principal 1. The employer in an agency relationship, to whom the agent owes fiduciary duties. 2. The loan balance to which interest charges are applied.

principal meridian A designated meridian in the rectangular survey system that is used in conjunction with a base line to identify ranges, tiers, and townships.

prior appropriation A legal doctrine granting a state the power to control and regulate the use of water resources within state boundaries.

priority See *lien priority*.

private grant A voluntary conveyance of property by a private party.

private mortgage insurance (PMI) An insurance policy, purchased by a borrower, that protects a lender against loss of that portion of a mortgage loan which exceeds the acceptable loan-to-value ratio.

probable cause panel A panel of two FREC members empowered to look at a complaint and its evidence to determine whether to move forward with formal charges against the licensee.

probate A court proceeding to validate and distribute a decedent's estate to creditors, tax authorities, and heirs.

probation A penalty issued in administrative and criminal cases in which the licensee is watched for a period of time to ensure they do not break the law for a specific period of time.

procuring cause A party who was first to obtain a ready, willing, and able customer, or a party who expended the effort to induce the customer to complete the transaction.

professional association (PA) A legal sanction for a business that provides professional services. The designation allows for some protection of the individual owner's assets.

profit Income less expenses.

progression A valuation concept where the location of a property causes a value increase due to its proximity to another property with a higher value.

promissory note See *note*.

promulgates To publish or print.

property An item that has a legal owner, along with the attendant rights to legal ownership.

property management The business of managing the physical and financial condition of an investment property for an owner.

property report Under ILSA, a developer is required to provide a report that covers important information to the buyer on the property.

proprietary lease A cooperative owner's lease on a unit in the cooperative building. The lease runs concurrently with the owner's ownership interest in the cooperative.

proration Apportionment of expense and income items at closing. Examples of items prorated between buyer and seller include interest, insurance, taxes, and rent.

prospectus A document builders must give to the buyer of a condominium. The prospectus provides information regarding the rules of the condo association, fees, and other pertinent information.

public grant A voluntary conveyance of property by a government entity to a private party.

pur autre vie A life estate where the grantee's interest endures over the lifetime of another party named by the grantor.

purchase money mortgage A mortgage loan where a seller lends a buyer some or all of the purchase price of a property.

qualification 1. A mortgage underwriting procedure to determine the financial capabilities and credit history of a prospective borrower. 2. A listing and marketing procedure to determine the needs and urgency of a client or customer.

quiet enjoyment A right of an owner or tenant to use a property without interference from others.

quiet title suit A court proceeding to clear a property's title of defects, claims, and encumbrances.

quit claim deed A deed which conveys one's possible ownership interests to another party. The grantor does not claim to own any interest and makes no warrants.

range A north-south area bounded by consecutive meridians.

real estate Land and all manmade structures permanently attached to it.

real estate investment trust (REIT) An investment in which owners purchase shares in a trust which owns or acquires real property. Investors receive income and gain on a per-share basis.

real estate services The eight services that a person must have a real estate license to perform when done for compensation and for another person. These are: advertising, buying, appraising, renting, selling, auctioning, leasing, or exchanging.

real property Real estate and the bundle of rights associated with ownership of real estate.

reciprocity The mutual exchange of privileges between two states for the benefit of licensees.

recommended order A report sent to FREC from the Administrative Law Judge on the guilt or innocence of a licensee, and the Judge's recommendation as to the penalty to be imposed.

reconciliation An appraiser's weighted blending of the results of different approaches to value into a final value estimate.

recording An act of entering into public title records any document or transaction affecting title to real estate. Recording gives constructive notice of one's rights and interests in a property and establishes the priority of inferior liens.

rectangular survey system A method of legally describing real property which uses longitude and latitude lines to identify ranges, tiers, and townships. Also called government survey system.

redemption period A statutory period after a foreclosure sale during which the foreclosed owner may buy back the property by paying all sums due the lender. See also *equity of redemption*.

redlining The illegal lending practice of restricting loans by geographical area.

refinancing Obtaining a new loan to replace an existing loan, usually to take advantage of lower interest rates, to obtain a longer-term loan, or to liquidate equity.

registration The process of reporting to DPBR important information on the licensee and individuals involved in the management of a brokerage.

regression An appraisal concept where the location of a piece of property can decrease the value of the property due to its proximity to a piece of property of lower value.

Regulation Z A fair financing law applying to residential loans; lenders must disclose financing costs and relevant terms of the loan to the borrower.

remainder A future freehold interest in a life estate held by a third party remainderman named by the grantor. When the life tenant dies, the estate passes to the remainderman. See also *reversion.*

replacement cost The cost of constructing a functional equivalent of a property at current labor and materials costs using current construction methods.

reproduction cost The cost of constructing a precise duplicate of a property, at current labor and materials prices.

reserve allowance An amount of money allocated from a property's income to cover future repair and maintenance costs.

residential sale The sale of a piece of property with four or fewer units; vacant land intended for four or fewer units; or, ten acres of agricultural land.

restriction A limitation on the use of a property imposed by deed, zoning, state statute, or public regulation.

reverse mortgage See *home equity conversion mortgage.*

reversion 1. A transfer of title from a life estate tenant back to the grantor. 2. Proceeds from the sale of a property at the end of a holding period in a cash flow analysis.

revocation 1. Cancellation of a contract. 2. Cancellation of a real estate license.

right of redemption See *equity of redemption.*

right to reinstate A delinquent borrower's right to pay off delinquent amounts in their mortgage payments, along with any attorney fees and court costs. This action returns the mortgage to good standing.

riparian rights Water rights of a property that abuts a watercourse (stream, river).

risk The possibility of loss of money or property.

sale contract A contract for the purchase and sale of real property containing all terms and provisions of the sale and describing the responsibilities of the parties.

sale leaseback A sale of a property executed simultaneously with a lease on the property from the buyer back to the seller as tenant.

sales comparison approach A method of appraising property that relies on the principle that a property is generally worth what other, similar properties are worth. See *substitution.*

sales associate A licensed employee or independent contractor hired by a broker to perform authorized activities on behalf of the broker's client.

satisfaction of mortgage A document that must be given within 90 days of the final mortgage payment. evidencing that the mortgage has been paid off. Usually recorded in public records.

scarcity The degree of unavailability of a product or service in relation to demand for the product or service. A critical element of value.

sealed A court-ordered action where the criminal record of a person is closed.

second mortgage A mortgage loan whose lien priority is subordinate to a senior, or first, mortgage.

secondary mortgage market Lenders, investors, and government agencies who buy, sell, insure, or guarantee existing mortgages, mortgage pools, and mortgage-backed securities.

section An area defined by the rectangular survey system and consisting of 1/36th of a township, or one square mile.

securities license An authorization to broker securities. The Series 39 and 22 securities licenses authorize licensees to broker real estate securities.

security 1. Collateral for a loan. 2. A type of personal property investment, for example, bonds, stocks, and mutual funds.

seisin A clause in a deed which states that the seller has the right to convey the property to the buyer.

seller financing Any financing arrangement where a seller takes a note and mortgage from the buyer for all or part of the purchase price of the property.

seller's market A market condition characterized by an excess of buyers over sellers.

senior lien See *superior lien.*

separate property Florida is a separate property state. Here, when a married couple obtains a divorce, they retain any assets they had before the marriage. They also receive inheritance or gifts they acquired during the marriage.

servient tenement A property containing an easement that must "serve" the easement use belonging to a dominant tenement.

severalty See *tenancy in severalty.*

severance A conversion of real property to personal property through detachment of the item from the land.

short sale The sale of a property where the proceeds would normally be insufficient to retire the loans owed on the mortgage. Clear title is achieved by the lender agreeing to alternative arrangements.

single agent An agency relationship between the principal and agent. Both parties owe fiduciary duties to each other.

situs The legal, jurisdictional location of a property. Also, a property's unique characteristics that contribute or detract from its value or desirability.

sole proprietorship A business entity with an individual as sole owner. The death of the owner terminates the business.

special agency See *limited agency.*

special assessment lien A lien against property to secure a tax levy for a specific public improvement, such as a new road or sewer. Only properties benefitting from the improvement are taxed and liened.

special exception A land use in conflict with current zoning that is nevertheless authorized because of its perceived benefit to the public welfare.

special purpose property A combination of land and improvements with a unique design and use, such as a church, hospital, or school.

specific lien A lien placed against a specific item of property rather than against all of an owner's property.

specific performance Forced performance of one's obligations in an agreement, to the letter of the agreement. A legal remedy for a damaged party to take against a defaulting party.

statute of frauds A law requiring certain contracts to be in writing in order to be enforceable. Examples are real property conveyances, listing agreements, and longterm leases.

statute of limitations A law which restricts the period during which a damaged party may seek to rescind or disaffirm a contract or take other legal actions.

stay of enforcement Common in eviction cases. It allows the tenant time to get out before the sheriff initiates eviction.

steering The prohibited practice of channeling prospective buyers and tenants toward or away from a particular area.

stipulation An agreement as to the penalty reached between the attorneys for the DRE and the licensee or licensee's attorney. Similar to a plea bargain.

stock sale A conveyance of an incorporated business through the purchase of the stock. Entails the purchase of all liabilities as well assets. See also *asset sale*.

straight-line cost recovery An accounting method for deducting depreciation expense from income. Periodic cost-recovery charges are made in equal amounts over a depreciation period. For example, the straight-line cost recovery of a $5,000 item over 5 years would be $1,000 per year.

strict foreclosure A court proceeding which gives a creditor legal title to a liened property rather than cash proceeds from a court-ordered sale.

subagency An agency relationship between the client of a listing broker and other brokers and associates who have agreed to assist the broker in procuring a customer for the client. The assisting brokers are agents of the listing broker and subagents of the listing broker's client.

subdivided land Land that has been divided into lots.

subdivision plat map A map that shows the location and boundaries of individual pieces of property.

subject property The piece of property that is being evaluated for its market value.

subject to The seller remains responsible any mortgages on the property while the buyer takes possession of the property.

sublease A transfer by a tenant of portions of the rights and obligations of a lease to another party, the sublessee. The original tenant, who is sublessor in the sublease, is still lessee in the original lease and remains primarily liable to the landlord for fulfilling lease obligations.

subordination A voluntary or involuntary placing of a lien's priority below that of another. A mortgage lien, for example automatically subordinates to a real estate tax lien.

subpoena A legal process ordering a someone to comply with court orders or appear before the court.

substantive contact Contact between an agent and others that is deemed relevant to a transaction; used as a benchmark to define when an agent should disclose agency status to a prospective client or customer . If a contact is substantive, the agent must disclose agency status at the time of the contact.

substitution An appraisal principle that holds that a buyer will pay no more for a property than the buyer would pay for an equally desirable and available substitute property. Forms the foundation for the sales comparison approach to value.

subsurface rights Rights and interests to whatever is beneath the surface of one's parcel of real property.

suit for possession A landlord's formal legal avenue for evicting a tenant.

Summary suspension Also known as *emergency suspension.*

superior lien 1. One of a class of liens that by law have a higher priority than any junior lien; all are tax liens. 2. A junior lien whose priority is higher than that of another lien.

supply The quantity of a product or service available for sale, lease, or trade at any given time.

surface rights Rights to the surface area of a parcel of real estate.

survey A formal measurement of the boundaries, dimensions, and elevations of a parcel of real estate performed by a professional surveyor. Required by lenders to identify possible encroachments, easements, and flood hazards.

survivorship, right of A surviving joint tenant's right to receive all rights and interests in the property enjoyed by another joint tenant in the event of the latter's death.

syndication A real estate investment structure in which investors provide capital and organizers provide management expertise to develop or acquire and manage investment real estate for profit.

take-out commitment A written pledge given by a lender to a developer or owner to provide permanent financing which replaces a short-term loan. The commitment contains a date when the loan is to be issued.

target marketing A selling or marketing strategy that is profiled to be compatible with or attractive to a given customer.

tax base The total of the assessed valuations of real properties within a taxing jurisdiction, less the total of exemptions.

tax certificate An instrument that gives the holder the right to apply for a tax deed after paying taxes on a property and after a statutory period.

tax deed A deed used to convey title to property sold in a tax foreclosure.

tax district A local government entity authorized by state, county, or municipality to levy taxes for a particular purpose.

tax rate See *millage rate*.

tax sale A court-ordered sale of a property to satisfy unpaid real estate taxes.

tax shelter An investment that produces depreciation or other non-cash losses that a taxpayer can deduct from other income to reduce tax liability.

taxable gain Capital gain subject to taxation. See *capital gain*.

taxable income Annual income from an investment property that is subject to taxation, generally equal to net operating income plus reserves minus depreciation and interest expense.

taxable value The assessed value of a property net of all exemptions.

teaser rate An adjustable rate mortgage in which the initial interest rate is lower that the market rate.

tenancy A freehold or leasehold estate held by a tenant.

tenancy in common An estate where each co-owner owns an electable share of the property and can transfer this share to any other party. Does not include right of survivorship; interests of deceased owners pass to heirs.

tenancy in severalty An estate in real property owned by a single party.

tenancy at sufferance Occurs when the renter's lease expires and the tenant continues to occupy the premises without paying rent and without permission from the owner.

tenancy at will Occurs when the renter's lease expires and the tenants continue to occupy the rental unit and pay rent with the consent and permission of the landlord.

testate The legal condition of a person who dies leaving a valid will.

tier An area between consecutive parallels, as defined in the *rectangular survey system*. Also, known as a *township line.*

time share A fee or leasehold interest in a property that is shared by owners who have use of the property at different times.

title Ownership of real property as well as evidence of such ownership; legal title.

title insurance A policy that protects the holder against loss arising from defects in title or documents conveying title.

title plant A duplicate set of title records copied from public records and maintained by a title company

title records Public records of real property documenting the history of ownership, claims, ownership, conveyances, legal descriptions, and surveys.

title theory state A state whose laws give legal title of a mortgaged property to the mortgagee until the mortgagor satisfies the terms and obligations of the loan. See *lien theory state*.

Torrens System A title recording system that registers title to property, as well as liens and encumbrances, on a title certificate. The certificate is the title and reflects everything there is to be known about the condition of the title.

township An area six miles square, bounded by two consecutive parallels and two consecutive meridians in the rectangular survey system. Contains 36 sections.

trade fixture A fixture necessary for the conduct of a business. Although affixed to the land, it is personal property.

trade name An assumed name used to identify the business or activities of an individual or organization. Sometimes a trade name is referred to as a "doing business as", "DBA", or "assumed" name.

trust A fiduciary relationship between a trustor and trustee. The trustor conveys legal title to property to the trustee, who holds and manages the estate for the benefit of another party, the beneficiary (in a land trust, trustor and beneficiary are the same person).

transaction brokerage An agency relationship in which there is no fiduciary responsibility owed any of the parties. It is presumed in Florida that real estate agents are acting in this manner unless expressed otherwise in writing.

underwriting 1. A process of investigating the financial capabilities and creditworthiness of a prospective borrower and granting credit to a qualified borrower. 2. The act of insuring or financing a party, business venture, or investment.

unequal services Services that differ in nature or quality from those normally rendered, with the alteration based on race, color, sex, national origin, or religion.

Unenforceable A contract that can't be upheld in a court. Usually because it is missing some aspect of a legal contract.

Uniform Standards of Professional Appraisal Practices (USPAP) A set of rules appraisers and real estate agents are required to follow when they perform an appraisal.

unilateral contract An agreement in which only one party promises to perform, contingent on the other party's performance of an optional action.

universal agency A fiduciary relationship which empowers an agent to perform any and all actions for a principal that may be legally delegated.

usury Excessive or illegal interest charged on a loan.

utility A determinant of the value of an item reflecting the item's ability to perform a desired function.

vacancy A measure of the unoccupied supply of exiting space in a building or market at any point in time. A vacancy rate is the amount of vacant space divided by the total amount of existing space.

validity Legal status of a contract that meets requirements of: competence of parties, mutual consent, valuable consideration, legal purpose, and voluntary good faith. A prerequisite for enforceability.

value In general, the worth of an item as determined by its utility, desirability, scarcity, affordability, and other components and quantified as price.

valuation Estimating the value of real or personal property asset.

variance A land use that conflicts with current zoning but is authorized for certain reasons, including undue hardship to comply and minimal negative impact to leave it alone.

void Without legal force or effect; unenforceable and null, such as an illegal contract.

void contract An agreement that is null and cannot be enforced.

voidable contract An agreement that is subject to being nullified because a party to the agreement acted under some legal disability. Only the disadvantaged party can take action to void the contract.

voluntarily inactive A license status where the real estate agent wishes to keep the license, without performing any of the services of real estate or working under a broker.

voluntary relinquishment for permanent revocation When an agent gives up his or her license permanently. Here, the licensee sacrifices ever returning to the real estate profession.

water rights Rights of a property that abuts a body of water to own or use the water. See *littoral rights*, *riparian rights*, and *prior appropriation*.

will Last and testament; a written or verbal statement by a testator instructing how to distribute the testator's estate to heirs.

writ of execution A court order requiring the seizure and sale of a piece of property to settle a debt.

writ of supersedeas "You shall desist." A stay of the enforcement of a judgment pending appeal; suspends a creditor's power to levy execution.

yield Investment return expressed as a dollar amount or a percent of the original investment amount

zoning ordinance A municipal land use regulation

Appendix: Testable Dates to Remember

Legal circumstance	Timeframe / Deadline
Eligibility period for taking state exam after passing prelicense course	2 years
DBPR to approve or deny license application	90 days of receipt
Upon application, broker applicants must have maintained an active license	2 of past 5 years
To be licensed as a Florida resident, must have continuously resided in FL (or presently with intent to reside) for	4 months
License expiration periods	every 2 years
14 hours of CE or initial postlicense course must be completed by	March 31 or September 30
Florida Real Estate Commissioners serve terms of	4 years
Deadline after which license becomes null and void via voluntary non-renewal, non-completion of postlicense course, or failure to activate an inactive license	2 years
Must notify FREC of mailing address change within	10 days
Florida resident licensee becoming a nonresident must notify FREC within	60 days
Brokers must retain records for	5 years
Deadline for sales associates to convey trust funds to broker	End of following business day
Broker must deposit trust funds received	Immediately or end of 3rd business day following receipt
If there is an escrow account disbursement dispute, broker must notify FREC within	15 days
Deadline to notify FREC of employer change	10 days following change
Complaints against licensees must be filed within	5 years of violation
Fair housing complaints must be made to the FL Commission on Human Relations or HUD within	1 year (2 years if suing)
FREC can suspend a license for up to	10 years
Landlord must return tenant deposit in	15 days if full; 30 days claiming a portion
Upon default, a lease termination by the landlord or tenant requires	7-day written notice

The rescission period for condominium and cooperative units is	15 days if new; 3 days if resale
The rescission period for timeshares is	10 days
Recission period for a purchased property with a homeowner's association	3 days after receipt of HOA disclosure summary
Period of continuous occupation to claim adverse possession	7 years
Easement by prescription period	7 years
Lender must provide Loan Estimate (H-24) within _____ of receiving the loan application and allow the buyer to see the Closing Disclosure (H-25) _____ before loan consummation	3 days 3 days
Buyer's right to receive copy of appraisal	3 or more business days before closing
Loan applicants must receive the CFPB booklet "Your Home Loan Toolkit" within _____ of receiving a loan application.	3 days
Homeowners can protest the assessed value of their house after the TRIM notice is mailed within	25 days
Property taxes due dates	November 1st ; delinquent on April 1st
Right of redemption period in foreclosure	Up until foreclosure sale completed
Right of redemption period in tax certificate sale	Two years from date of sale
"As-in" inspection period following sale contract execution	15 days
Copies of legal documents to principals	Upon execution

INDEX

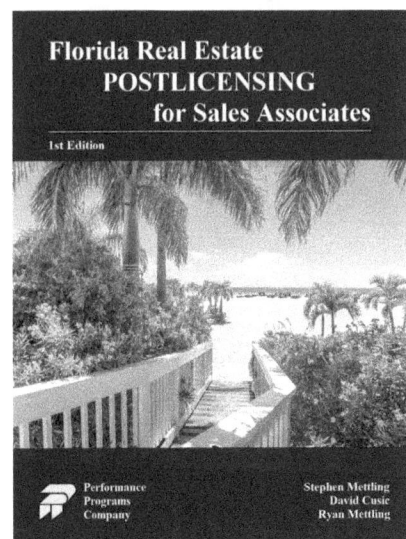